DIGITAL SYSTEM
DESIGN

DIGITAL SYSTEM DESIGN

Barry Wilkinson

Department of Electrical and Electronic Engineering,
Brighton Polytechnic, England

Prentice/Hall International

Englewood Cliffs, NJ   London , Mexico   New Delhi   Rio de Janeiro
Singapore   Sydney   Tokyo   Toronto

Library of Congress Cataloging in Publication Data

Wilkinson, Barry.
   Digital system design.

   Bibliography: p.
   Includes index.
   1. Digital electronics.   I. Title.
TK7868.D5W46   1987   621.391'6   86–15141
ISBN 0-13-214289 9

British Library Cataloguing in Publication Data

Wilkinson, Barry, *1947–*
   Digital system design.
   1. Digital electronics
   I. Title
   621.3815'3   TK7868.D5

   ISBN 0-13-214289-9
   ISBN 0-13-214271-6 Pbk

Prentice-Hall Inc., Englewood Cliffs, New Jersey
Prentice-Hall International (UK) Ltd, London
Prentice-Hall of Australia Pty Ltd, Sydney
Prentice-Hall Canada Inc., Toronto
Prentice-Hall Hispanoamericana S.A., Mexico
Prentice-Hall of India Private Ltd, New Delhi
Prentice-Hall of Japan Inc., Tokyo
Prentice-Hall of Southeast Asia Pte Ltd, Singapore
Editora Prentice-Hall do Brasil Ltda, Rio de Janeiro

Printed and bound in Great Britain for Prentice-Hall
International (UK) Ltd, 66 Wood Lane End, Hemel Hempstead,
Hertfordshire, HP2 4RG, at the University Press, Cambridge.

1 2 3 4 5 90 89 88 87 86

ISBN 0-13-214289-9
ISBN 0-13-214271-6 PBK

To my wife, Wendy
and to my daughter, Johanna

Contents

3 COMBINATIONAL CIRCUIT DESIGN   52

4 SEQUENTIAL CIRCUIT DESIGN   100

5   LOGIC CIRCUIT IMPLEMENTATION   146

PART 2   MICROPROCESSOR SYSTEM DESIGN

6   COMPUTER AND MICROPROCESSOR SYSTEMS   183

9 SEMICONDUCTOR PRIMARY MEMORY DEVICES   281

10 INPUT/OUTPUT CIRCUITS AND OPERATION   308

11 MAGNETIC SECONDARY MEMORY   339

PART 3 FURTHER ASPECTS OF DIGITAL SYSTEM DESIGN

12 FORMAL SEQUENTIAL CIRCUIT DESIGN   365

13 PROCESSOR DESIGN   399

17 RELIABILITY   512

Preface

This book introduces the fundamental topics in digital system design, and is divided into three parts. Part 1 is devoted to logic design, and Part 2 is devoted to the components of a microprocessor system. Part 3 contains further aspects of digital system design and extends topics introduced in Part 1 and Part 2. Overall, the purpose of the book is to provide a broad but comprehensive coverage in concise chapters (seventeen in all).

Part 1 consists of Chaps. 1 to 5. Chapter 1 considers the basic topic of binary numbers and codes which are used in digital systems. Chapter 2 introduces Boolean variables, expressions and simplification methods including both the Karnaugh map method and Quine–McCluskey method. Chapter 3 describes the function of fundamental logic devices in which outputs depend upon present input values irrespective of any past values (i.e. combinational logic circuits). Logic devices in the TTL family are quoted as examples. Chapter 4 analyzes sequential logic circuits (whose outputs may depend upon past input values). The concept of a state diagram is introduced early in this chapter firstly to derive flip-flop logic circuits and subsequently for counters. Electronic circuit details of logic devices are separated into Chap. 5. This chapter could be omitted if electronic details are not required, though any essential electronic concepts are briefly explained where necessary.

Part 2 consists of Chaps. 6 to 11. Chapter 6 outlines the basic stored program concept embodied in computer and microprocessor systems. Various possible instruction formats are described. The general architecture of a microprocessor and a microprocessor system is then given. Assembly language programming aspects are outlined. It is normal practice to select a particular microprocessor for study, often an 8-bit microprocessor. Since the Z–80 microprocessor is perhaps the most widely used microprocessor, the Z–80 is selected in Chap. 7 for detailed study. The system configuration is presented including the components of a simple Z–80 system. Then, the instructions are described mostly by presenting a requirement first, rather than simply listing the instructions which can be found in the manufacturer's manual. However, a complete set of Z–80 instruction tables are given, showing valid source and destination operands as these tables are extremely useful. Chapter 8 outlines the 16-bit 68000 microprocessor, chosen because it is a popular 16-bit microprocessor and incorporates important techniques. Some differences in the assembly language notation are exposed. Valid source and destination operands of all 68000 instructions are given. Chapter 9 is devoted to semiconductor memory devices, as used in microprocessor systems and in computer systems generally. Chapter 10 deals with input/output circuits and operation, including interrupt and DMA operation. Chapter 11 is devoted to magnetic secondary memory (backing store) found in microprocessor systems. All the major magnetic recording codes are described.

Part 3 begins with Chap. 12, a continuation of Chap. 4 on sequential circuit design, and includes both synchronous and asynchronous sequential circuit designs. This chapter could be studied immediately after Chap. 4, or could be omitted if the extra detail is not required. A particularly relevant section for microprocessor system design and other computer system design is on synchronizing asynchronous signals (section 12.2.4). Chapter 13 considers the design of a central processor. The concept of a register transfer notation is introduced and applied to a model of the Z–80 microprocessor. Microprogramming is explained, using the Am2901A and Am2910A devices in an example of a bit-slice microprogrammed system. Finally overlap and pipelining are described. Chapter 14 considers the system schemes that can be employed to manage the memory hierarchy in a computer system, including a microprocessor system. The chapter contains both primary–secondary memory management schemes and the use of cache memory between the processor and the primary memory. Chapter 15 describes multiprocessor system architectures, particularly the time-shared bus architecture as applied to microprocessor systems. In a final section, the dataflow architecture is presented in detail, as one alternative to traditional von-Neumann computers. Chapter 16 is a continuation of Chap. 5 and considers engineering aspects of creating a working system. Assessments of transmission line reflections, cross-talk and noise are presented. In Chap. 17, the reliability of a digital system is calculated. Tables giving the reliability of devices are included to enable the reliability of typical systems to be computed. Methods to increase the reliability are discussed.

Problems are set at the end of chapters (except Chap. 6). A Teacher's Manual containing solutions to the problems is available from the publishers.

I am particularly grateful to have been able to undertake much of the work on the manuscript of this book at the College at New Paltz, State University of New York. I should also like to thank Mr. Glen Murray, Acquisitions Editor of Prentice-Hall International, for the support received throughout the preparation of this book.

Barry Wilkinson
Brighton, England

About the Author

Barry Wilkinson gained a BSc degree (first class hons.) in Electrical Engineering from Salford University in 1969, and MSc and PhD degrees from Manchester University (Department of Computer Science) in 1971 and 1974 respectively. From 1969 to 1970, he worked on process control computer systems at Ferranti Ltd. In 1973, he was appointed a Lecturer in the Computer Centre at Aston University and moved to the Department of Electrical and Electronic Engineering at University College, Cardiff in 1976. He was appointed an Associate Professor at the College at New Paltz, State University of New York in 1983 and joined the Department of Electrical and Electronic Engineering, Brighton Polytechnic as Principal Lecturer in 1984. He is a senior member of the IEEE, a member of the IEE, a member of the BCS, and the co-author of *Computer Peripherals* (1980).

PART 1

LOGIC DESIGN

1

Binary Numbers

1.1 NUMBER SYSTEMS

When a number such as:

259

is written, it is generally taken to mean:

$$2 \times 10^2 + 5 \times 10^1 + 9 \times 10^0$$

i.e. two hundreds plus five tens plus nine units. In this number system, the *decimal* number system, there are ten different characters or digits 0, 1, 2, 3, 4, 5, 6, 7, 8 and 9 and the position of each digit indicates the power of ten to multiply the value represented by the digit. Formally, the number is defined as:

$$(a_n, a_{n-1}, \cdots a_1, a_0)_b = a_n b^n + a_{n-1} b^{n-1} + \cdots a_1 b^1 + a_0 b^0$$

where a_n is the digit in position n and b is the base, ten in this case. Fractions are simply an extension of the above, i.e.

$$(0.145)_{10} = 1 \times 10^{-1} + 4 \times 10^{-2} + 5 \times 10^{-3}$$

Formally a number including a fractional part is defined as:

$$(a_n, \cdots a_1, a_0.a_{-1}, \cdots a_{-m})_b = a_n b^n + \cdots a_1 b^1 + a_0 b^0 + a_{-1} b^{-1} + \cdots a_{-m} b^{-m}$$

The subscript 10 is introduced to indicate that the base is 10, i.e. a decimal number. Using the base ten is only one possibility of this form of number representation. Whatever value we choose for b, there needs to be the same number of different symbols for the digits. For example, if $b = 8$, there need to be eight different digit symbols. The number system using the base 8 is known as the *octal* number system. The eight symbols used are 0, 1, 2, 3, 4, 5, 6 and 7. In the octal number system, the number:

$$(257)_8$$

would equal

$$2 \times 8^2 + 5 \times 8^1 + 7 \times 8^0$$

or

$$2 \times 64 + 5 \times 8 + 7 \times 1 = (175)_{10}$$

3

Notice even here we are using the decimal number system to represent the numbers in the calculation because we are familiar with decimal numbers. We use the decimal number system because we have ten fingers to count with. If the human race had been given eight fingers, perhaps the octal number system would be used.

If the base is 2, there are only two digit symbols, 0 and 1. This system is known as the *binary* number system. Each binary digit is known as a *bit*. The following are examples of the binary number system:

$$(101)_2 = 1 \times 2^2 + 0 \times 2^1 + 1 \times 2^0$$
$$(1.11)_2 = 1 \times 2^0 + 1 \times 2^{-1} + 1 \times 2^{-2}$$

The binary number system is always used within digital computers because of having only two symbols to represent. Each of the digits can be represented within the computer by one of two voltages, say $0\,V$ to represent a binary 0 and $5\,V$ to represent a binary 1. (In practice, a range of voltages would represent each digit, say $0\,V$ to $0.8\,V$ to represent a 0, and $2\,V$ to $5\,V$ to represent a 1.) For permanent storage purposes, magnetized surfaces can be used and the two states of magnetization can directly or indirectly represent the binary digits. In the past, punched holes in paper tape or cards have been used for storage purposes. The presence of a hole in the tape or card represents a 1 and the absence of a hole represents a 0.

The number system using the base 16 is known as the *hexadecimal* number system, abbreviated to 'hex'. As we will see, this number system is sometimes used to represent binary numbers. In the hexadecimal number system, there are 16 different digit symbols, the numerals 0 to 9 and the first six letters of the alphabet, A,B,C,D,E and F. The letters are used to represent 10 to 15. For example:

$$
\begin{aligned}
(1AE)_{16} &= 1 \times 16^2 + A \times 16^1 + E \times 16^0 \\
&= 1 \times 16^2 + 10 \times 16^1 + 14 \times 16^0 \\
&= 1 \times 256 + 10 \times 16 + 14 \times 1 \\
&= (430)_{10}
\end{aligned}
$$

Table 1.1 lists the numbers from 0 to 20 in decimal and the equivalent binary, octal and hexadecimal numbers.

1.2   CONVERSION FROM ONE NUMBER SYSTEM TO ANOTHER NUMBER SYSTEM

1.2.1 Conversion between binary and octal or hexadecimal numbers

Conversion between binary and octal or hexadecimal numbers is particularly easy because the octal and hexadecimal bases, 8 and 16, are powers of the binary base, 2 (third and fourth powers respectively). This leads to a direct

Table 1.1 Decimal, binary, octal and hexadecimal numbers

Decimal	Binary	Octal	Hexadecimal
0	00000	0	0
1	00001	1	1
2	00010	2	2
3	00011	3	3
4	00100	4	4
5	00101	5	5
6	00110	6	6
7	00111	7	7
8	01000	10	8
9	01001	11	9
10	01010	12	A
11	01011	13	B
12	01100	14	C
13	01101	15	D
14	01110	16	E
15	01111	17	F
16	10000	20	10
17	10001	21	11
18	10010	22	12
19	10011	23	13
20	10100	24	14

relationship between groups of digits in octal or hexadecimal numbers and binary numbers.

For octal, groups of three digits of the binary number are equivalent to one digit of the octal number. For example:

(i) Conversion of $(1100101)_2$ into octal. Dividing the binary number into groups of three:

    1 100 101

Encoding each group into one octal digit:

    1 4 5

Therefore

    $(1100101)_2 = (145)_8$

(ii) Conversion of $(011110111)_2$ into octal. Dividing the binary number into groups of three:

    011 110 111

Encoding each group into one octal digit:

    3 6 7

Therefore
    $(011110111)_2 = (367)_8$.
Clearly the reverse process can be performed.

The hexadecimal base, 16, is the fourth power of the binary number and groups of four digits of the binary number become equivalent to one hexadecimal digit. For example:

(i) Conversion of $(1011101)_2$ into hexadecimal. Dividing the binary number into groups of four digits:

(0)101 1101

Encoding each group into one hexadecimal digit:

5 D

Therefore

$$(1011101)_2 = (5D)_{16}$$

(ii) Conversion of $(11110111)_2$ into hexadecimal. Dividing the binary number into groups of four digits:

1111 0111

Encoding each group into one hexadecimal digit:

F 7

Therefore

$$(11110111)_2 = (F7)_{16}$$

Fractional numbers can be converted using the same method, by taking groups of three or four as appropriate working away from the 'point'. For example:

(i) $(111101.101111)_2 = (75.57)_8$

(ii) $(111101.101111)_2 = (3D.BC)_{16}$

Unless the same number of digits can represent a number in each base, the larger the base, the smaller the number of digits required to represent a particular number; for example

$$(1011001101010001010)_2 = (1315212)_8 = (59A8A)_{16}$$

This fact, together with the simple conversion, has led to octal and hexadecimal numbers being used to represent the binary numbers held within computers, especially for a close examination of stored numbers. It was convenient with computers using 24-bit numbers to represent each 24-bit number in documentation by eight octal digits. The symbol * has been used preceding the octal number for recognition purposes, i.e.

$$(10111101)_2 = *275$$

More recently, 8-bit, 16-bit and 32-bit microprocessor systems have been developed and in these cases, the hexadecimal number system is convenient, as two, four and eight hexadecimal digits can represent 8-bit, 16-bit and 32-bit numbers respectively. The letter H is sometimes used to indicate hexadecimal numbers, i.e.:

$$(10101111)_2 = \text{AFH}$$

The letter H is not a valid hexadecimal digit and thus does not cause confusion with the valid hexadecimal digits preceding it. Eight bits are called a *byte*.

Generally though, we would prefer to use decimal numbers in our documentation. Let us consider methods of converting numbers from one base to another base where one base is decimal. We shall consider integer numbers and fractional numbers separately. When a number consists of both an integer part and a fractional part, each part is converted separately using the appropriate method on each part.

1.2.2 Conversion from decimal to binary/octal/hexadecimal/other

(a) Integer conversion algorithm

By rearranging the formal representation of an integer, we obtain:

$$a_0 + b(a_1 + b(a_2 + b(a_3 + b(a_4 + \cdots b(a_n)\cdots))$$

Dividing by the base, b, we get:

$$a_1 + b(a_2 + b(a_3 + b(a_4 + \cdots b(a_n)\cdots)) \text{ plus a remainder } a_0$$

By successive division of the resultant quotient by the base, the digits of the number can be extracted as the remainder digits and hence all the digits of the number can be found. This leads to a formal integer conversion algorithm, where b is the base of the converted number and the divisions are done using arithmetic of the original number system. It can be applied to any number system but unless the original number system is decimal, the arithmetic is not familiar.

For the conversion of a decimal number into a number of a new base the steps would be:

     Step 1   Divide the decimal number, N, by the new base, b, giving the result as a quotient, Q_0 and a remainder, r_0

     Step 2   Divide Q_0 by b, giving Q_1 and a remainder r_1

     Step 3   Continue the process until Q_n is zero.

The remainders are the digits of the required binary number where r_0 is the least significant digit (rightmost digit). For example, to convert the decimal number 47 into binary we perform the following division processes:

$$47 \div 2 = 23 \text{ remainder 1; least significant bit}$$
$$23 \div 2 = 11 \text{ remainder 1}$$
$$11 \div 2 = 5 \text{ remainder 1}$$
$$5 \div 2 = 2 \text{ remainder 1}$$
$$2 \div 2 = 1 \text{ remainder 0}$$
$$1 \div 2 = 0 \text{ remainder 1; most significant bit (leftmost digit)}$$

Therefore $(47)_{10} = (101111)_2$. Generally, the number of digits in a binary number is about three times that of the equivalent decimal number.

Let us take another example, decimal 862 into hexadecimal:

decimal   *hexadecimal*

		decimal	*hexadecimal*	
$862 \div 16 = 53$ remainder	14	E	;least significant bit
$53 \div 16 = 3$ remainder	5	5	
$3 \div 16 = 0$ remainder	3	3	;most significant bit

Therefore

$$(862)_{10} = (35E)_{16}$$

(b) Fraction conversion algorithm

Starting from the formal definition of a fractional number:

$$(.a_{-1}, \cdots a_{-m})_b = a_{-1}b^{-1} + \cdots a_{-m}b^{-m}$$

we get the number equal to:

$$(1/b)(a_{-1} + (1/b)(a_{-2} + (1/b)(a_{-3} + \cdots (1/b)a_{-m}) \cdots)$$

by rearrangement. Hence by multiplying by the base, b, we get:

$$a_{-1} + (1/b)(a_{-2} + (1/b)(a_{-3} + \cdots (1/b)a_{-m}) \cdots)$$

This number consists of an integer part (a_{-1}) which is the first digit of the required number, and a fractional part. By repeated multiplications of the fractional part by the base, the required digits of the number are extracted. A comparison can be made with the integer method which uses division operations rather than multiplication operations. Again the method could be applied to any number system conversion but the arithmetic must be done in the original number system. Therefore it is particularly suitable for conversions from decimal numbers to other number systems. Describing the conversion as a series of steps we get:

Step 1 Multiply the decimal number, N, by the new base, b, giving a product consisting of an integer part I_0 and a fractional part F_0.

Step 2 Multiply F_0 by b, giving a product, $I_1.F_1$.

Step 3 Continue the process until a fractional part, F_n is zero.

The integer parts, I_n to I_0 are the digits of the required number, where I_0 is the most significant digit.

Consider for example, the conversion of the decimal number $(0.485)_{10}$ into binary:

Fractional parts		*Integer parts*
0.485	$\times 2 = 0.97$	0
0.97	$\times 2 = 1.94$	1

$$
\begin{array}{lll}
0.94 & \times 2 = 1.88 & 1 \\
0.88 & \times 2 = 1.76 & 1 \\
0.76 & \times 2 = 1.52 & 1 \\
0.52 & \times 2 = 1.04 & 1 \\
0.04 & \times 2 = 0.08 & 0 \\
\end{array}
$$

Therefore

$$(0.485)_{10} = (0.0111110 \cdots)_2.$$

A finite fraction in one number system will not necessarily convert into a finite fraction in another system. Normally the process is terminated when a given number of digits is obtained. Consider another example, the conversion of $(0.347)_{10}$ into hexadecimal:

Fractional parts			*Integer parts*	
			Decimal	*Hexadecimal*
0.347	$\times 16 =$	5.552	5	5
0.552	$\times 16 =$	8.832	8	8
0.832	$\times 16 =$	13.312	13	D
0.312	$\times 16 =$	4.992	4	4
0.992	$\times 16 =$	15.872	15	F

Therefore

$$(0.347)_{10} = (0.58D4F \cdots)_{16}.$$

The conversion of a large decimal number into binary can be shortened by first converting into octal and then to binary by inspection, because the number of divisions (or multiplications) of eight to convert into octal is less than the number of divisions (or multiplications) of two to convert into binary.

1.2.3 Conversion from binary/octal/hexadecimal/other to decimal

We could use the same methods as above using arithmetic of the original base for conversions to decimal (or between any base). However it is rather inconvenient to use any base other than decimal for arithmetic. (The reader may care to perform the reverse conversions above using the general method.) Alternative algorithms exist using arithmetic of the new base.

(a) Integer conversion algorithm

The required number can be obtained directly from the formal representation given in section 1.1 by the summation of products of each digit multiplied by the base raised to the corresponding power. The calculation can be achieved from the rearrangement used in section 1.2.2, leading to a process of successive multiplications. We can describe this method by the following series of steps using the arithmetic of the new base:

Step 1   Multiply the most significant digit by the old base, b.
Step 2   Add the result to the next most significant digit.
Step 3   Multiply the result by b.
Step 4   Repeat steps 2 and 3 in succession until the least significant digit is reached.

The final sum is the required decimal number, for example $(11010)_2$ into decimal:

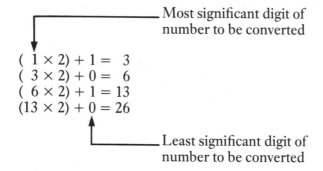

Most significant digit of number to be converted

$$(\ 1 \times 2) + 1 = \ \ 3$$
$$(\ 3 \times 2) + 0 = \ \ 6$$
$$(\ 6 \times 2) + 1 = 13$$
$$(13 \times 2) + 0 = 26$$

Least significant digit of number to be converted

Therefore

$$(11010)_2 = (26)_{10}.$$

Another example, $(9CE)_{16}$ into decimal:

$$(9 \times 16) \quad\ \ + C = \ \ 144 + 12 = \ \ 156$$
$$(156 \times 16) \ \ + E = 2496 + 14 = 2510$$

Therefore

$$(9CE)_{16} = (2510)_{10}.$$

(b) Fraction conversion algorithm

For fractions we have a process of repeated division beginning at the least significant digit (again using the arithmetic of the new base):

Step 1   Divide the least significant digit by the base, b.
Step 2   Add the result to the next least significant digit.
Step 3   Divide the result by b.
Step 4   Repeat steps 2 and 3 in succession until the most significant digit is reached. Include the final division.

The result is the required decimal number, for example $(0.1101)_2$ into decimal:

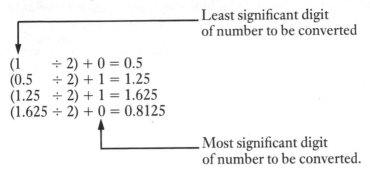

$$(1 \div 2) + 0 = 0.5$$
$$(0.5 \div 2) + 1 = 1.25$$
$$(1.25 \div 2) + 1 = 1.625$$
$$(1.625 \div 2) + 0 = 0.8125$$

Therefore

$(0.1101)_2 = (0.8125)_{10}$.

Another example, $(0.4562)_8$ into decimal:

$$(2 \div 8) + 6 = 6.25$$
$$(6.25 \div 8) + 5 = 5.78125$$
$$(5.78125 \div 8) + 4 = 4.72265625$$
$$(4.72265625 \div 8) + 0 = 0.59033203125$$

Therefore

$(0.4562)_8 = (0.59033203125)_{10}$.

1.3 BINARY ARITHMETIC

1.3.1 Binary addition

In decimal arithmetic, we add two numbers as shown below:

$$
\begin{array}{ll}
A & 1\ 7\ 4\ 3 \\
+B & {}_1\ 9_1 8\ 4 \\
\hline
\text{Sum} & 2\ 7\ 2\ 7
\end{array}
$$

Carry digits are generated as shown when the sum of the A and B digits (including any carry from the lower significant digit addition) is greater than nine. Similarly, carry digits may be generated in binary addition of two binary digits (including any carry from the previous digit addition) is greater than one, as shown in the addition of two numbers in binary shown below:

$$
\begin{array}{llll}
\text{Augend}, A & 0\ 0\ 1\ 1\ 1\ 1\ 0\ 0 & (60)_{10} \\
\text{Addend}, B & 0\ 0_1\ 1_1\ 0_1\ 1_1\ 1\ 1\ 0 & (46)_{10} \\
\\
\text{Sum} & 0\ 1\ 1\ 0\ 1\ 0\ 1\ 0 & (106)_{10}
\end{array}
$$

Leading 0's are introduced to form (positive) binary words of a defined length, in this case eight bits. Addition of binary numbers follow a similar procedure to decimal addition. First the digits in the furthest right-hand column are added together, in this case $0 + 0 = 0$. Only in one instance could the sum be greater than one digit, i.e. $1 + 1 = 10$. This would have caused a carry of 1 to be passed over to the next stage. (Compare with decimal arithmetic. When the sum is greater then 9, a carry is generated and there are many instances of this.) Other columns of digits are added working from right to left. When a binary carry is generated three digits need to be added in the next column, the A and B digits of the column and the carry digits from the previous column.

We can recognize two types of addition processes in the above. First there is the addition of two binary digits in the first column where there is no previous carry. Second there are the other additions when a carry from the previous addition requires three digits to be added together, the A digit, the B digit and the carry (in) digit. Both these forms of addition produce a two-digit result consisting of a sum digit and a carry (out) digit.

Two binary digits, A and B, can each take on one of two values, 0 or 1. Therefore there are four possible combinations of A and B. When $A = B = 0$, both the sum digit and the carry digit are a 0. When $A = 0$, $B = 1$ or $A = 1$, $B = 0$, the sum digit is a 1 and carry digits is a 0. Finally, when both A and B are a 1, the sum digit is a 0 and the carry digit is a 1. This can be given in tabular form:

A	B	Sum	Carry (out)
0	0	0	0
0	1	1	0
1	0	1	0
1	1	0	1

There are eight combinations of three binary digits, A, B and carry in. The sum digit alone is a 1 whenever only one of the three inputs is a 1 (including the carry in digit). The carry out digit is a 1 whenever two of the three input digits are a 1. Only when all three input digits are a 1 are both sum and carry out digits a 1 (i.e. $1+1+1 = 11$). In tabular form, we have:

A	B	Carry in	Sum	Carry out
0	0	0	0	0
0	0	1	1	0
0	1	0	1	0
0	1	1	0	1
1	0	0	1	0
1	0	1	0	1
1	1	0	0	1
1	1	1	1	1

Tables such as the above giving input values and corresponding output values are known as *truth tables*. Circuits to add together two binary digits A and B are known as *half adders*. Circuits to add together two binary digits and a carry (in) are known as *full adders*. These circuits will be considered in detail in Chap. 3.

1.3.2 Binary subtraction and negative numbers

Rules can be devised to achieve binary subtraction in a similar fashion to the rules of binary addition. For example to subtract $(46)_{10}$ from $(60)_{10}$ we have:

Minuend	0	0	1	1	^{1}1	^{1}1	^{1}0	0
Subtrahend	0	0	1	0_1	1_1	1_1	1	0
Difference	0	0	0	1	0	0	1	0

In cases where the subtrahend digit is greater than the minuend digit a borrow digit is required to complete the subtraction of one digit from another. However, we have the problem of dealing with negative numbers, as we do if negative numbers are to be manipulated generally. One way to incorporate negative numbers in the number representation is to assign one bit as a 'sign' bit set to a 0 if the number is positive and set to a 1 if the number is negative. The absolute value of the number is represented in pure binary separately. This representation is known as the *sign plus magnitude* representation. Though this representation is used for particular applications (for example floating point numbers, section 1.4), it is inconvenient for the central representation of numbers within a computer as it requires the sign bits to be examined before any arithmetic operation is performed.

It is very convenient if the process of subtraction can be considered as the addition of one number to the negative of the other number, i.e.:

$$A - B = A + [-B]$$

Where $[-B]$ is the negative of $+B$. Then circuits used to perform addition can also be used to perform subtraction, by presenting the negative of B to the addition unit.

One approach is to represent the negative number $[-B]$ by the result of subtracting B from a number one larger than the maximum number that can be represented by the digits provided. The largest number that can be represented by an n-digit number is $2^n - 1$. Therefore $[-B]$ would be represented in this system by:

$$[-B] \equiv 2^n - B$$

This is known as the *2's complement system*. For example, if $n = 4$ and $B = 0101$ (5_{10}), then:

$$[-B] \equiv 2^4 - 0101 = 10000 - 0101 = 1011$$

In the 2's complement system, all positive numbers must begin with a 0. In consequence, all negative numbers will begin with a 1. Zero is regarded as positive. Clearly if we use this representation, addition of numbers must lead to the correct answer according to the representation.

Consider both A and B positive and A greater than B. If we now subtract B from A by using the equivalent for $-B$ and adding, we get:

$$A - B = A + [-B] = A + (2^n - B)$$
$$= 2^n + (A - B) \qquad (A \text{ greater than } B)$$

Truncating the result to n digits removes the 2^n to give $A - B$, the required answer. ($2^n = 100\cdots0$, i.e. 1 followed by n 0's. Adding this to an n-digit number does not affect the first n digits. The $(n+1)$th digit simply becomes a 1.) If $A - B$ happens to be negative (i.e. B greater than A), the result is the appropriate equivalent negative number:

$$A - B = A + [-B] = A + (2^n - B)$$
$$= 2^n - (B - A) \qquad (A \text{ less than } B)$$

The reader may care to verify that all combinations of positive and negative numbers compute correctly (Problem 1.5). An example producing a positive result is $7 - 5$ (decimal):

$$7 - 5 = 0111 - 0101 = 0111 + 1011 = 10010$$
truncating gives $0010 \equiv 2$ in decimal

An example producing a negative result is $5 - 7$:

$$5 - 7 = 0101 - 0111 = 0101 + 1001 = 1110 \ (-2 \text{ in decimal})$$

Table 1.2 (third column) gives the number representation in the 2's complement system for 4-bit numbers, which gives a range from -8 to $+7$. If a greater number of bits were used, leading 0's are repeated in the positive numbers, e.g. $+5 = 0101 = 00000101$ for 8-bit numbers. For negative numbers, leading 1's are repeated, e.g. $-5 = 1011 = 11111011$. A quick method of obtaining the negative representation of a number is to invert all the digits of the positive number, i.e. change all occurrences of 1's to 0's and all

Table 1.2   4-bit binary, 2's complement and 1's complement numbers

Decimal	Binary	2's complement binary	1's complement binary
+7	0111	0111	0111
+6	0110	0110	0110
+5	0101	0101	0101
+4	0100	0100	0100
+3	0011	0011	0011
+2	0010	0010	0010
+1	0001	0001	0001
0	0000	0000	0000 or 1111
−1	-----	1111	1110
−2	-----	1110	1101
−3	-----	1101	1100
−4	-----	1100	1011
−5	-----	1011	1010
−6	-----	1010	1001
−7	-----	1001	1000
−8	-----	1000	----

occurrences of 0's to 1's, and then add 1 to the result. For example, -5 can be obtained as follows:

$$+5 \quad 0101$$

Inverting we get   1010
Adding 1 we get $1011 = -5$ in the 2's complement system

This is because $2^n - 1$ is always $11 \cdots 11$ irrespective of the value of n, and subtracting any number from $11 \cdots 11$ inverts each digit. Adding 1 produces the same result as subtracting the number from 2^n.

An alternative representation, known as the *1's complement system*, represents negative numbers by:

$$[-B] \equiv (2^n - 1) - B$$

Generating the negative representation is particularly simple; all the digits are inverted. Using this representation to subtract B from A, we have:

$$A + (2^n - 1 - B) = 2^n - 1 + (A - B) \qquad (A \text{ greater than } B)$$

To obtain the correct result, $A - B$, 1 must be added. However, if A is less than B, we obtain the correct result:

$$A + (2^n - 1 - B) = 2^n - 1 - (B - A) \qquad (A \text{ less than } B)$$

It is found that whenever a final carry is generated during the addition process, a 1 must be added to the result (Problem 1.6). This process is known as *end-around-carry*. Table 1.2 (column 4) lists 1's complement numbers. There are two representations of zero, 0000 and 1111, and the range of 4-bit 1's complement numbers is from -7 to $+7$. Most computers employ the 2's complement representation.

Complement schemes can be applied to decimal numbers. The decimal 10's complement system is equivalent to the binary 2's complement system using 10^n rather than 2^n and the decimal 9's complement system is equivalent to the binary 1's complement using $10^n - 1$ rather than $2^n - 1$.

1.3.3 Range of binary numbers

The range of numbers that can be represented by a fixed number of bits is zero to $2^n - 1$ where n is the numbers of bits, if only positive numbers are represented (i.e. *pure* binary numbers). The largest number is $11 \cdots 111$. Using the 2's complement system, the range of numbers is from -2^{n-1} through zero to $+2^{n-1} - 1$. The most positive number is $011 \cdots 11$ and the most negative number is $100 \cdots 00$. When two binary numbers are added together, there may be a final carry generated from the most significant column, for example:

A		1	0	0	1	0	1	0	1
$+B$	1	0_1	1_1	1_1	1	0_1	1	1 $\cdot$	0
Sum		0	0	0	0	1	0	1	1

This leads to a result with one extra digit, i.e. nine bits in our example, when the final carry is brought into the result. Usually a fixed number of bits are allowed to represent numbers in computers, and the final carry, if generated, is separated. If a carry is generated during an addition process with two pure binary numbers, the result without the final carry is of course incorrect. If we employ the 2's complement system, we discard any 2^n term appearing is the final result. This term appears as a final carry, which is not considered in the result. However, the final result without the final carry may still be incorrect if the desired result is outside the range permitted with a given number of bits. In the above example, it is correct using the 2's complement system. A is negative (-107_{10}) and B is positive $(+118_{10})$ leading to the correct positive number $(+11_{10})$. An incorrect result is obtained if we add two positive numbers which apparently give a negative result or we add two negative numbers which apparently give a positive result (without considering the final carry). A correct result is always obtained if we add a positive number and negative number together. In a computer, an incorrect result due to insufficient number of digits (or other reason, for example in a division operation when an attempt is made to divide by zero) is indicated by an *overflow* bit or flag being set to 1.

1.4   FLOATING POINT NUMBERS

We have highlighted above that there is a fixed number of binary digits provided in digital computers to represent an individual number. Microprocessors, for example, have commonly employed 8-bit and 16-bit numbers. The 2's complement number system is used almost universally which would allow any integer value from -128 to $+127$ for 8-bit numbers and any integer value from $-32,768$ to $+32,767$ for 16-bit numbers. A 32-bit number would give a range of $-2,147,483,648$ to $+2,147,483,647$. Fractions or numbers including a fractional part can be accommodated by including the notation of a binary point. The binary point has no effect on the internal arithmetic of the computer. All these types of number are known as *fixed point numbers*.

If we wish to represent a large or small number in decimal, such as two millions, it can conveniently be written as 2×10^6 rather than 2,000,000. This type of representation can be carried over to binary for numbers outside the range permitted by the fixed point representation. The representation is known as *floating point* representation and is composed of two parts, a *mantissa* and an *exponent*. The relationship between these parts and the actual number is:

$$\text{Number} = \text{mantissa} \times \text{base}^{\text{exponent}}$$

The base for binary is 2 or a power of 2, for example 8 or 16. The binary word representing the number contains two *fields*, one for the mantissa and one for the exponent. The number of bits assigned to each field depends upon the resolution required for the number and its range. Standards have been laid down to enable interchangeability of program data.

Both the mantissa and the exponent can be either positive or negative fixed point numbers. A negative mantissa enables negative numbers to be represented and a negative exponent enables very small numbers to be represented. The mantissa usually employs the sign plus magnitude convention where the first bit indicates the sign and the rest of the mantissa bits indicate the magnitude, usually a fractional number.

To utilize the maximum resolution, floating point numbers are *normalized*. In a normalization procedure, the number is arranged so that the first bit of the magnitude is always a non-zero digit. The exponent is then adjusted accordingly. We can compare the normalization process to the normalization of a decimal number such as 0.0000345×10^9. Leading zeros are removed to produce a non-zero first digit, i.e. 0.3450000×10^5. Hence we have more digits available to represent magnitude of the number. Similarly in binary, the number 0.0010101×2^{-7} normalized would be 0.10100×2^{-9}. If the base is, for example, 16, the normalization process would lead to a non-zero hexadecimal digit, though not necessarily a 1 in the first place, since we would only be able to adjust the number in powers of 16. For example, the floating point number 0.06E (i.e. 0.000001101110) $\times 16^{45}$ normalized would be 0.6E (i.e. 0.01101110000) $\times 16^{44}$. With the base 2, it is not necessary to store the most significant bit of the magnitude of a normalized number as it is always a 1. However, a larger base enables a larger range of numbers to be stored, at the expense of the precision of the mantissa, given a fixed number of bits for the sum of mantissa and exponent bits.

The exponent usually employs a *biased integer* notation. In this notation, a bias number is added to the exponent before it is stored, to make the stored exponent always positive. Therefore the number is represented by:

$$\text{Number} = \text{mantissa} \times 2^{\text{stored exponent} - \text{bias}}$$

For example, a bias of 2^{n-1} would be suitable with a 2's complement exponent (where n is the number of digits in the number). A bias of $2^{n-1} - 1$ is also used. Having only positive stored exponents simplifies comparison of exponents which is necessary during floating point addition and subtraction. Normally, zero has a special representation, for example, with all bits of the mantissa and exponent set to 0. Numbers smaller or larger than can be represented lead to underflow and overflow conditions respectively.

EXAMPLE

A 32-bit floating point format is given as follows:

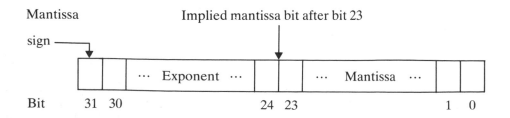

The first byte (8 bits) stores the sign of the number and a 7-bit biased exponent using the base 2. The three subsequent bytes store the mantissa excluding the sign. The bias is $2^{n-1}-1$ (63) and the (stored) exponent is a positive binary number. The mantissa is represented as a fraction in the sign-magnitude convention. Numbers are stored in normalized form. There is an assumed 1 after bit 23 and an assumed binary point after this 1. Hence the mantissa is in effect a 25-bit fraction.

Assuming that all values of mantissa and exponent are allowed with the bits provided, the range of numbers that can be represented is computed as follows:

(i)   Negative mantissa range is $-0.11\cdots11$ (25 1's) to $-0.10\cdots00$
(ii) Positive mantissa range is $+0.10\cdots00$ to $+0.11\cdots11$ (25 1's)
(iii) Exponent range is from -63 (stored exponent $= 0$) through zero (stored exponent $= 63$) to $+64$ (stored exponent $= 127$).

Hence we can represent normalized positive numbers from $+0.10\cdots00 \times 2^{-63}$ to $+0.11\cdots11 \times 2^{+64}$ (or 2^{-64} to approximately 2^{+64}) and normalized negative numbers from $-0.10\cdots00 \times 2^{-63}$ to $-0.11\cdots11 \times 2^{+64}$ (or -2^{-64} to approximately -2^{+64}) where in all cases there are 24 bits following the binary point. The approximate ranges in decimal are $+5.4 \times 10^{-20}$ to $+1.8 \times 10^{+19}$ and from -5.4×10^{-20} to $+1.8 \times 10^{+19}$. Normalized numbers cannot be represented outside these ranges. It is left to the reader to compute the ranges assuming that a stored exponent of zero is reserved for the floating point number zero. A 25-bit mantissa gives the equivalent of eight significant decimal digits.

1.5   BINARY CODED DECIMAL NUMBERS

In some applications (e.g. calculators and check-out tills), decimal numbers are continually displayed or entered. Clearly, the decimal numbers can be converted to binary and vice versa as we have seen, and this can be done by computer. However, the decimal nature of the numbers can be retained within the computer using the *binary coded decimal* (BCD) number system. In BCD, each decimal digit is converted into a four-bit binary equivalent and each four-bit word is joined together to form the coding of the number. For example, the number $(259)_{10}$ in BCD is the 12-bit number:

    0010 0101 1001

In the BCD coding system, the digits are not 'weighted' in the normal ascending power of the base as in binary or decimal numbers or in any other normal positional number system. The weighting in BCD is:

$$\cdots,100 \times 2^4 \ 100 \times 2^2 \ 100 \times 2^1 \ 100 \times 2^0, \ 10 \times 2^4 \ 10 \times 2^2 \ 10 \times 2^1 \ 10 \times 2^0, \ 1 \times 2^4$$
$$1 \times 2^2 \ 1 \times 2^1 \ 1 \times 2^0$$

Within each group, the binary combinations from decimal 10 to 15, i.e. 1010, 1011, 1100, 1101, 1110 and 1111 are not used and would be invalid if they occurred. Hence more digits are used to represent the number than strictly necessary.

Two BCD digits can be held in one 8-bit word, four BCD digits can be held in one 16-bit word, and eight BCD digits can be held in one 32-bit word. BCD numbers with more than one BCD digit contained in a binary word are called *packed BCD* numbers. Microprocessors in particular, because of being suited for applications such as check-out tills and calculators and similar BCD applications, can manipulate and perform arithmetic operations on packed BCD numbers. For example, two 8-bit words, each holding two BCD digits, can be added together with the result as a packed 8-bit BCD word. Similarly, BCD numbers can be subtracted.

The addition process can be performed firstly without regard to the special nature of the BCD numbers and subsequently a correction process is performed when necessary to produce the correct BCD result. Firstly an example in which no correction is necessary the addition of 25_{BCD} and 44_{BCD} shown below:

Binary coded decimal	*Binary*
$(2\ 5)_{\text{BCD}}$	0010 0101
$(4\ 4)_{\text{BCD}}$	0100 0100
$(6\ 9)_{\text{BCD}}$	0110 1001

We can see here that simply adding two binary words representing the BCD digits results in the binary pattern representing the correct BCD result. However, if a BCD digit in the result should be greater than 9, we will not obtain the correct result. Table 1.3 shows the results of adding two numbers each in the range 0 to 9 inclusive, which produces a number up to 18. The second

Table 1.3   Correction in BCD addition

Decimal	*Binary*	*Binary coded decimal*	
0	00000	0000 0000	
1	00001	0000 0001	
2	00010	0000 0010	
3	00011	0000 0011	
4	00100	0000 0100	No correction
5	00101	0000 0101	
6	00110	0000 0110	
7	00111	0000 0111	
8	01000	0000 1000	
9	01001	0000 1001	
10	01010	0001 0000	
11	01011	0001 0001	
12	01100	0001 0010	
13	01101	0001 0011	Correction (add 6)
14	01110	0001 0100	
15	01111	0001 0101	
16	10000	0001 0110	
17	10001	0001 0111	
18	10010	0001 1000	

column in the table gives the result in pure binary, and the third column the required BCD representation. In all cases above 9, the correct representation can be obtained by adding six to the binary result. This leads to a BCD carry digit being passed on to the next stage, which must be included in the subsequent digit addition. We can identify two groups of incorrect results.

Firstly, one of the unused binary patterns from 10_{10} to 15_{10} would appear if we add together two BCD digits resulting in a sum between 10 and 15 inclusive. This is corrected in the following example:

Binary coded decimal	*Binary*
$(2 \quad 5)_{BCD}$	0010 0101
$(4 \quad 8)_{BCD}$	0100 1000
6 13	0110 1101
+ 6	0110
$(7 \quad 3)_{BCD}$	0111 0011

A carry digit is passed to the second stage after the correction process. For the results 16 to 18 inclusive, a carry from the fourth stage will already have occurred in the binary addition as in:

Binary coded decimal	*Binary*
$(5 \ 9)_{BCD}$	0101 1001
$(2 \ 8)_{BCD}$	0010 1000
8 1	1000 0001
+ 6	0110
$(8 \ 7)_{BCD}$	1000 0111

One way to view the correction process is that of bypassing unused codes. Each of the six unused codes in each 4-bit group is bypassed by the addition of a +6 correction factor at each level of significance. Whether correction is necessary can be detected by recognizing an invalid pattern (10_{10} to 15_{10} inclusive in Table 1.3) or a carry being generated (16_{10} to 18_{10} inclusive in Table 1.3). BCD subtraction can be done, for example, by using a decimal complement representation.

1.6   ALPHANUMERIC CODES

People need to communicate with a computer through the medium of letters of their spoken and written language, in our case English. Therefore it is clear that some coding method of representing the letters of the alphabet needs to be provided within the computer. It would also be helpful if the same method were used for all computers to assist in information transfer between computers and between computers and their peripheral devices. One coding method that has emerged to gain widespread acceptance is called the *American Standard Code for Information Interchange* (ASCII). This is a 7-bit code capable of representing up to 94 printed characters and provides a representation for all of the upper-case (capital) letters and lower-case letters of the alphabet, the numerals 0 to 9 and various punctuation symbols. In addition, 32 special control codes are provided for the control of data transmission and peripheral devices. The complete ASCII specification is given in Table 1.4. Referring to the table, the bits are numbered b_7, b_6, b_5, b_4, b_3, b_2, and b_1. Bits b_7, b_6 and b_5 define a column in the table and b_4, b_3, b_2 and b_1 define a row. The first two columns define control codes which are described in the table with two- or three-letter mnemonics.

Table 1.4   ASCII code

b4	b3	b2	b1	Row	0	1	2	3	4	5	6	7
0	0	0	0	0	NUL	DLE	SP	0	@	P	'	p
0	0	0	1	1	SOH	DC1	!	1	A	Q	a	q
0	0	1	0	2	STX	DC2	"	2	B	R	b	r
0	0	1	1	3	ETX	DC3	#	3	C	S	c	s
0	1	0	0	4	EOT	DC4	$	4	D	T	d	t
0	1	0	1	5	ENQ	NAK	%	5	E	U	e	u
0	1	1	0	6	ACK	SYN	&	6	F	V	f	v
0	1	1	1	7	BEL	ETB	'	7	G	W	g	w
1	0	0	0	8	BS	CAN	(	8	H	X	h	x
1	0	0	1	9	HT	EM	)	9	I	Y	i	y
1	0	1	0	10	LF	SUB	*	:	J	Z	j	z
1	0	1	1	11	VT	ESC	+	;	K	[	k	{
1	1	0	0	12	FF	FS	,	<	L	\	l	¦
1	1	0	1	13	CR	GS	−	=	M	]	m	}
1	1	1	0	14	SO	RS	.	>	N	∧	n	~
1	1	1	1	15	SI	US	/	?	O	—	o	DEL

Bits: b_7 b_6 b_5 columns (Column) — 000=0, 001=1, 010=2, 011=3, 100=4, 101=5, 110=6, 111=7

Control codes

Abbreviations:

NUL	Null	FF	Form feed	CAN	Cancel
SOH	Start of heading	CR	Carriage return	EM	End of medium
STX	Start of text	SO	Shift out	SUB	Substitute
ETX	End of text	SI	Shift in	ESC	Escape
EOT	End of transmission	DLE	Data link escape	FS	File separator
ENQ	Enquiry	DC1	Device control 1	GS	Group separator
ACK	Acknowledge	DC2	Device control 2	RS	Record separator
BEL	Bell	DC3	Device control 3	US	Unit separator
BS	Backspace	DC4	Device control 4	SP	Space
HT	Horizontal tabulation	NAK	Negative acknowledge	DEL	Delete
LF	Line feed	ETB	End of transmission block		
VT	Vertical tabulation	SYN	Synchronous idle		

1.7 ERROR DETECTION

It is often necessary to be able to check whether any errors have been introduced during transmission to and from a computer and sometimes within a computer. Since a binary digit can only be either a 1 or 0, simple methods of detecting the presence of errors can be devised. Consider as an example, the transmission of an ASCII-coded character represented by seven binary digits. If one bit becomes corrupted and changes from a 0 to a 1 or from a 1 to a 0, the number of 1's in the whole word will change. If the total number of 1's in the correct number were odd it would become even and conversely an even number of 1's would become odd. Therefore if the transmitted word was always arranged to have say an even number of 1's, all single bit errors could be detected by checking whether there was an even or odd number of 1's in the received word. Always having an even number of 1's at the source of transmission can be achieved by appending an extra bit to the code, in the case of ASCII making an eight-bit code and setting this eighth bit to a 1 or 0 so as to make the total number of 1's even. An odd number of 1's in the received word would indicate an error. The scheme of appending an extra bit to make the total number of 1's even is known as the *even parity* scheme. An alternative, known as the *odd parity* scheme, appends a bit with a value such that the total number of 1's is odd. Any subsequent single bit error would result in an even number of 1's and this can be detected in the similar fashion as previously. Both odd and even parity methods are used. Odd and even parity methods will also detect multiple odd numbers of errors.

Some codes have an inbuilt error detection mechanism. For example, the now rather little used *2-out-of-5* code encodes the numerals 0 to 9 with five digits such that the total number of 1's in all codes is two. Consequently, any single bit error would corrupt this characteristic. Methods of detecting multiple errors and methods of automatically correcting errors are described in Chap. 17, section 17.4.2.

1.8 GRAY CODE

A variety of codes have been devised for particular reasons. One code of some importance is *Gray* code. Gray code has the property that only one bit changes from one number to the next number in the sequence, as shown in Table 1.5 for four bits. Gray code reduces the likelihood of unwanted transient changes occurring when changing from one code to the next code. A particular application is the encoding of the position of a continuously revolving shaft. The shaft is marked at various angular positions. Figure 1.1 shows markings in 4-bit Gray code. As the shaft revolves, markings are sensed which enable the position of the shaft to be determined. If binary code is used, a totally incorrect code might occur due to mechanical misalignment of the sensors or delays in the

Table 1.5 Gray code

Decimal	Binary	Gray
0	0000	0000
1	0001	0001
2	0010	0011
3	0011	0010
4	0100	0110
5	0101	0111
6	0110	0101
7	0111	0100
8	1000	1100
9	1001	1101
10	1010	1111
11	1011	1110
12	1100	1010
13	1101	1011
14	1110	1001
15	1111	1000

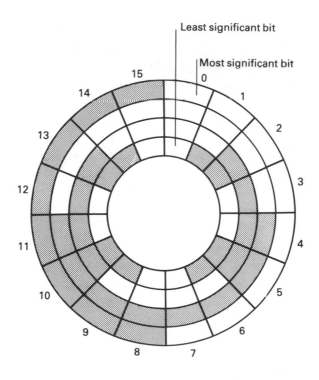

Figure 1.1   Shaft with 4-bit Gray code markings

circuits when several changes are necessary such as from 0111 to 1000, where all four bits must change. With Gray code, only single changes are necessary between adjacent codes, which limits errors to one position. We shall use Gray code in asynchronous sequential circuit design (Chap. 12) to reduce the likelihood of unwanted transients occurring in logic systems designs. Gray code also occurs in the labeling of Karnaugh maps (Chap. 3).

PROBLEMS

1.1   Convert the following binary numbers into octal and hexadecimal:

(a)   101010101010
(b)   10000.000001

1.2   Convert the following hexadecimal numbers into octal:

(a)   FE45
(b)   0.567
(c)   F.FF

1.3   Convert the following decimal numbers into binary:

(a)   48729
(b)   666
(c)   0.7239
(d)   6.8941

1.4   Convert the following binary numbers into decimal:

(a)   11000
(b)   01010
(c)   0.00111
(d)   11.11

1.5   Verify mathematically that when two numbers in the 2's complement system are added, all combinations of positive and negative numbers, and combinations of relative magnitudes, compute correctly.

1.6   Verify mathematically that when two numbers in the 1's complement system are added, all combinations of positive and negative numbers, and combinations of relative magnitudes, compute correctly using the end-around carry mechanism (i.e. a 1 is added to the result if a carry is generated from the most significant stage).

1.7   Convert the following decimal numbers into binary and perform the operation shown using 2's complement arithmetic where appropriate:

(a) $67 - 5$
(b) $123 + 998 - 754$
(c) $45 - 124$
(d) $-78 - 23$

Confirm that the results are correct by converting them back into decimal.

1.8   Represent the following numbers in normalized floating point form, with a fractional sign plus magnitude mantissa and 7-bit unsigned biased exponent using the base of 2 and a bias of 64:

(a)   123567
(b)   −45.89
(c)   0.00567

1.9   In a computer system, one floating point number employs two adjacent 24-bit words. The bits of these words are numbered B_0 through to B_{47}. B_0 is the least significant bit. B_{47} is the mantissa sign bit, B_8 to B_{46} is the mantissa considered as a binary fraction. B_0 to B_7 is an unsigned biased exponent using the base of 2 and a bias of 127. The floating point numbers are normalized and there is an assumed leading 1 in the mantissa. Deduce the approximate range of numbers that can be stored. What is the smallest number that can be stored? Give your answer in decimal assuming that 2^{10} is equal to 10^3.

1.10   Convert the following BCD numbers into binary and perform the operation shown, applying any correction process necessary to obtain the correct BCD result:

(a)   44 + 33
(b)   29 + 99
(c)   55 + 78

1.11   Deduce the value of an even parity bit added to the ASCII code for the character N. Repeat for the ASCII control operation NUL.

Boolean Algebra and Minimization

2.1 BOOLEAN VARIABLES

We presented a study of number systems in Chap. 1 as this is fundamental to the design of digital systems. The binary number system is chosen for the number representation as this number system has only two types of digit, 0 and 1, which can be represented by two voltages. Having made this decision, we now need some mathematical methods to manipulate these binary quantities with a view to designing digital systems. Fortunately, such methods had been developed well before the advent of digital computers (the 1940s) by George Boole, a 19th-century mathematican. Boole [1] developed an algebra which we now call *Boolean algebra*. Claude Shannon [2] adapted this algebra for digital switching circuits. In (two-valued) Boolean algebra, variables only take on one of two values, 0 or 1, i.e. if a variable does not equal 0, it must equal 1 and if it does not equal 1, it must equal 0. The 1 value corresponds to binary 1 and the 0 value corresponds to binary 0. Sometimes a 1 is called *true* and a 0 called *false* from the earlier propositional (Boolean) algebra. (Propositional algebra could be used, for example, to determine whether a conclusion is correct following a series of statements. Such statements could be true or false.) Also two-value Boolean variables can be used to show whether a particular result of a computation has occurred and in this sense, 'true' and 'false' keep their original meaning. Boolean algebra does not itself restrict variables to two values, but this is done here as only two-valued Boolean algebra is applicable to digital systems.

As an example of a simple switching system, consider a heating system controlled by a room thermostat and an external frost thermostat. When the heating is switched-on manually, heat is provided but only when the room temperature is below the setting on the room thermostat. Heat is also provided when the external frost thermostat indicates the external temperature is below $0°C$ and the room temperature is below the room thermostat setting (to protect against water in pipes freezing). We could allocate Boolean variables as follows:

(i) $H = 1$ if manual heating switch is on, otherwise $H = 0$
(ii) $R = 1$ if room temperature is below setting on room thermostat, otherwise $R = 0$
(iii) $F = 1$ if frost thermostat indicates external temperature below $0°C$, otherwise $F = 0$
(iv) $S = 1$ if heat is to be supplied.

Therefore $S = 1$ when either $H = 1$ and $R = 1$ or when $F = 1$ and $R = 1$. We have Boolean notations to indicate the 'and' operation and the 'or' operation, namely $+$ and $\cdot$. The Boolean expression for S becomes:

$$S = H \cdot R + F \cdot R$$

From this expression we will be able to develop the appropriate switching circuit, as we shall see later.

Suppose we had defined F as:

$F = 1$ if frost thermostat indicates external temperature below $0\,°C$, otherwise $F = 0$.

Then $S = 1$ when either $H = 1$ and $R = 1$ or when $F = 0$ and $R = 1$. In Boolean algebra, if a variable such as $F = 0$, the variable $\bar{F} = 1$ (and if $F = 1$, $\bar{F} = 0$). Hence $S = 1$ when either $H = 1$ and $R = 1$ or when $\bar{F} = 1$ and $R = 1$, i.e.

$$S = H \cdot R + \bar{F} \cdot R$$

As an example of Boolean variables applied to binary numbers, consider the addition of two binary digits as given in Chap. 1 section 1.3.1. SUM $= 1$ when either $A = 1$ and $B = 0$ or when $A = 0$ and $B = 1$. CARRY $= 1$ when $A = 1$ and $B = 1$. Hence the Boolean expressions for SUM and CARRY are:

$$\text{SUM} = A \cdot \bar{B} + \bar{A} \cdot B$$
$$\text{CARRY} = A \cdot B$$

Again we will be able to develop the circuits from these Boolean expressions. Circuits developed from Boolean expressions are considered in Chap. 3. Firstly, let us formally define the three fundamental Boolean (*logical*) operations.

2.2 BOOLEAN OPERATORS AND RELATIONSHIPS

2.2.1 NOT, AND and OR operators

(a) NOT operator

The NOT operator operates on a single variable say A, and is defined as follows:

If $A = 0$ then 'NOT' $A = 1$
If $A = 1$ then 'NOT' $A = 0$

i.e. the operation produces the opposite binary state to that of A. 'NOT' A is written as $\bar{A}$. $\bar{A}$ is the *complement* or *inverse* of A. A truth table can be used to show a Boolean function. This table lists all the possible values of the variables and the results of the operation. A NOT operation truth table is shown in Table 2.1. Note that a single variable can take on only one of two values, either 0 or 1, so there are two entries in the table.

Table 2.1   Truth table of NOT operation

A	$\overline{A}$
0	1
1	0

(b) AND operator

The AND operator operates on two variables, say A and B, and is defined as follows:

$$\text{If } A \text{ and } B \text{ are both a 1 then } A \text{ 'AND' } B = 1$$
$$\text{otherwise } A \text{ 'AND' } B = 0$$

A 'AND' B is written as $A \cdot B$. The operation is sometimes called Boolean multiplication and as in ordinary multiplication, the $\cdot$ is often omitted. We will include the $\cdot$ only where necessary for clarity. The AND operation truth table is shown in Table 2.2(a). Notice that in truth tables, the values of the 'input' variables are listed in increasing binary order. More variables can be introduced, for example $A \cdot B \cdot C$. The truth table for three variables is shown in Table 2.2(b). Three variables can take on any of eight combinations of values. Irrespective of the number of variables, the result is a 1 only if all the variables are a 1, otherwise the result is a 0, i.e.

$$\text{If } A \text{ and } B \text{ and } C \text{ and } D \text{ and } \cdots \text{ are all a 1, then } A \cdot B \cdot C \cdot D \cdots = 1$$
$$\text{otherwise } A \cdot B \cdot C \cdot D \cdots = 0$$

Table 2.2   Truth tables of AND operation

A	B	$A \cdot B$
0	0	0
0	1	0
1	0	0
1	1	1

(a) Two variables

A	B	C	$A \cdot B \cdot C$
0	0	0	0
0	0	1	0
0	1	0	0
0	1	1	0
1	0	0	0
1	0	1	0
1	1	0	0
1	1	1	1

(b) Three variables

The English word 'and' is taken literally, i.e. A and B and C, A and B and C and D, etc. The definition for several variables follows directly from the repeated application of the basic definition for two variables.

(c) OR operator

The OR operator operates on two variables A and B and is defined as:

$$\text{If } A \text{ or } B \text{ or both are a 1 then } A \text{ 'OR' } B = 1$$
$$\text{otherwise } A \text{ 'OR' } B = 0$$

A 'OR' B is written as $A+B$. This is sometimes called Boolean addition. The OR operation truth table is shown in Table 2.3(a). Again more variables can be introduced, for example $A+B+C, A+B+C+D$ i.e:

If A or B or C or D ⋯ is a 1 (including more than one) then $A+B+C+D+ \cdots = 1$
otherwise $A+B+C+D+ \cdots = 0$

Table 2.3(b) shows the OR operation with three variables. Irrespective of the number of variables, the result is a 1 if any of the variables is a 1. The English word 'or' is taken literally, i.e. A or B or C, A or B or C or D. The definition for several variables follows directly from the repeated application of the basic definition for two variables.

Table 2.3   Truth tables of OR operation

A	B	$A+B$
0	0	0
0	1	1
1	0	1
1	1	1

(a) Two variables

A	B	C	$A+B+C$
0	0	0	0
0	0	1	1
0	1	0	1
0	1	1	1
1	0	0	1
1	0	1	1
1	1	0	1
1	1	1	1

(b) Three variables

2.2.2 Basic relationships and laws

(a) Relationships
The following can be easily proved from the definition of the operators or their truth tables:

1.   (i) $A \cdot \bar{A} = 0$
      (ii) $A + \bar{A} = 1$
      (iii) $\bar{\bar{A}} = A$
2.   (i) $A \cdot 1 = A$
      (ii) $A \cdot 0 = 0$
      (iii) $A \cdot A = A$
3.   (i) $A + 1 = 1$
      (ii) $A + 0 = A$
      (iii) $A + A = A$

The relationships can be proved by substituting all possible combinations of values of the variables and deducing the result in each case, i.e. proof by perfect induction. Proof by perfect induction is particularly suitable for Boolean expressions containing a few Boolean variables as each variable can only take on one of two values, and it is feasible to try each value. For example, in the first relationship 1(i), $A \cdot \bar{A} = 0, A$ can be a 0, and then $\bar{A} = 1$. In that case, we have $0 \cdot 1 = 0$ from the truth table of the AND operation. The alternative value for A, a 1, and hence $\bar{A} = 0$, leads to $1 \cdot 0 = 0$. Therefore irrespective of the value of A, the result is a 0. It is left to the reader to prove the other relationships in a similar fashion. Where appropriate, the relationships can be extended to more than one variable, for example relationship 3(i), $A+1 = 1$, can be extended to $A+B+C+1 = 1$.

(b) Laws
There are three general algebraic laws relating to the way expressions can be written and their interpretation. These laws can be applied to both · and +:

(i) COMMUTATIVE LAW
This states that the order of variables is unimportant, e.g.:

$$A{\cdot}B = B{\cdot}A$$

and

$$A+B = B+A$$

(ii) ASSOCIATIVE LAW
This states that the grouping of variables is unimportant, e.g.:

$$A{\cdot}(B{\cdot}C) = (A{\cdot}B){\cdot}C = A{\cdot}B{\cdot}C$$

and

$$A+(B+C) = (A+B)+C = A+B+C$$

(iii) DISTRIBUTIVE LAW
This states that an operator 'distributes' its operation throughout variables within parentheses, e.g.

$$A{\cdot}(B+C) = A{\cdot}B + A{\cdot}C$$
$$A+(B{\cdot}C) = (A+B){\cdot}(A+C)$$

In the first instance above, the · operation operates on both B and C while in the second instance the + operation operates on both B and C. The first instance is true in ordinary algebra but the second is not true in ordinary algebra.

(iv) DE MORGAN'S THEOREM
De Morgan's theorem states that:

$$\overline{A+B+C{\cdots}} = \overline{A}{\cdot}\overline{B}{\cdot}\overline{C}{\cdots}$$
$$\overline{\overline{A}+\overline{B}+\overline{C}{\cdots}} = A{\cdot}B{\cdot}C{\cdots}$$

to any number of variables. De Morgan's theorem as given above can easily proved for two variables by substituting all combinations of the variables. Then repeated substitution can lead to a proof for any number of variables. For example, let us assume the first form of De Morgan's theorem has been proved for two variables, then replacing B+C for B in $\overline{A+B} = \overline{A}{\cdot}\overline{B}$, we get $\overline{A+B+C} = \overline{A{\cdot}(B+C)} = \overline{A}{\cdot}\overline{B}{\cdot}\overline{C}$ by applying De Morgan's theorem with two variables. This process can be repeated for any number of variables. Alternatively, we can note that $\overline{A+B+C}\cdots$ to any number of variables can only be a 1 if all the variables are a 0. Similarly $\overline{A \cdot B \cdot C} \cdots$ to any number of variables can only be a 1 when all the variables are a 0. Hence the two terms must be equivalent.

De Morgan's theorem is very useful in simplifying Boolean expressions, as we will see later. It can be generalized to:

$$f(A,B,C, \cdots \quad +,\cdot) = \overline{f}(\overline{A},\overline{B},\overline{C}, \cdots \quad \cdot,+)$$

i.e. the inverse function can be obtained by complementing all the variables, changing all ·'s to +'s and all +'s to ·'s.

(v) PRINCIPLE OF DUALITY

Each relationship, law or theorem has a dual, obtained by replacing every occurrence of 1 by 0, 0 by 1, + by · and · by +. Duals have been given above. For example, the dual of $A+0 = A$ is $A \cdot 1 = A$. Once we can prove one relationship, the dual relationship can be assumed to be true without proof. The existence of duality between the two operators AND and OR can be seen by changing all 1's to 0's and all 0's to 1's in the truth table of one operator, whereupon the truth table of the other operator is obtained. One must be careful not to confuse the principle of duality with De Morgan's theorem.

2.2.3 NAND and NOR operators

Of the three basic Boolean operators, AND, OR and NOT, either the OR operator or the AND operator is unnecessary. From De Morgan's theorem, $A+B = \overline{\overline{A} \cdot \overline{B}}$. Therefore all occurrences of $A+B$ can be replaced by $\overline{\overline{A} \cdot \overline{B}}$ and the OR operation can be eliminated. Alternatively, using $A \cdot B = \overline{\overline{A}+\overline{B}}$, all occurrences of $A \cdot B$ can be replaced with $\overline{\overline{A}+\overline{B}}$ and the AND operation can be eliminated. However, we cannot dispense with the NOT operator. An operator can be introduced which combines AND and NOT which is known as the NAND ('NOT-AND') operator.

(a) NAND operator

The NAND operator performs the AND operation followed by the NOT operation as described for two and three variables in Table 2.4. There is a

Table 2.4 Truth tables of NAND operation

A	B	$\overline{A \cdot B}$
0	0	1
0	1	1
1	0	1
1	1	0

(a) Two variables

A	B	C	$\overline{A \cdot B \cdot C}$
0	0	0	1
0	0	1	1
0	1	0	1
0	1	1	1
1	0	0	1
1	0	1	1
1	1	0	1
1	1	1	0

(b) Three variables

special symbol for NAND, $\uparrow$, i.e. A'NAND'B is written as $A \uparrow B$ but this is rarely used in engineering. Normally A'NAND'B is written as $\overline{AB}$.

Equally, the OR and NOT operations can be combined to created a 'NOT-OR' operator called a NOR operator.

(b) NOR operator

The NOR operator performs the OR operation followed by the NOT operation as described for two and three variables in Table 2.5. Again there is a special symbol, $\downarrow$, which is rarely used in engineering; A'NOR'B is written simply as $\overline{A+B}$.

Table 2.5   Truth tables of NOR operation

A	B	$\overline{A+B}$
0	0	1
0	1	0
1	0	0
1	1	0

(a) Two variables

A	B	C	$\overline{A+B+C}$
0	0	0	1
0	0	1	0
0	1	0	0
0	1	1	0
1	0	0	0
1	0	1	0
1	1	0	0
1	1	1	0

(b) Three variables

2.2.4 Exclusive-OR/NOR operators

The OR operation is sometimes called 'inclusive-OR' because the result is true when either of the two operands A and B is a 1, including both A and B a 1. The 'exclusive-OR' operator operating on two variables A and B is true if A or B is a 1 but not when both A and B are a 1, i.e. it excludes both A and B being a 1. A symbol for the exclusive-OR function is $\oplus$. The operation is described in Table 2.6. The operation can be derived as a function in terms of AND and OR from the truth table by examining the occurrences of 1's in the result. We can see that the result is a 1 when $A = 0$ and $B = 1$ or when $A = 1$ and $B = 0$. Therefore the exclusive-OR function is:

$$A \oplus B = \overline{A}B + A\overline{B}$$

The truth table of the inverse operation, 'exclusive-NOR', is given in Table 2.7. The exclusive-NOR function is true if both A and B are the same and

Table 2.6   Truth table of exclusive-OR operation

A	B	$A \oplus B$
0	0	0
0	1	1
1	0	1
1	1	0

Table 2.7   Truth table of exclusive-NOR operation

A	B	$\overline{A\oplus B}$
0	0	1
0	1	0
1	0	0
1	1	1

is false if A and B are different. The function is also called 'equivalence' ($\equiv$) and performs the comparison function of two binary digits. It is given, in terms of AND and OR as:

$$\overline{A\oplus B} = AB + \bar{A}\bar{B}$$

2.2.5 Logical devices

The electrical circuits which perform logical operations are called *gates*. The Boolean values are usually represented by voltages, one voltage to represent a 0 and another voltage to represent a 1. For example $+5\,V$ could represent a logical 1 and $0\,V$ could represent a logical 0. To give some immunity against electrical interference (noise, further details in Chap. 5 and Chap. 15) in the system, a voltage range is specified for each logic level. For example, a 0 could be represented by any voltage between $0\,V$ and $0.8\,V$, and a 1 could be represented by any voltage between $2\,V$ and $5\,V$. If a 1 is represented by a voltage which is more positive than the voltage representing a 0, the representation is known as *positive logic representation*. If a 0 is represented by a voltage which is more positive than the voltage representing a 1, the representation is known as *negative logic representation*. In the past, some computers used negative logic representation but now computers, including microprocessors, generally use positive logic representation. However, logic representation is only a convention; changing from one convention to the other in the same system involves changing all 1's to 0's and all 0's to 1's. An AND gate with positive logic representation becomes an OR gate in negative logic representation, and an OR gate becomes an AND gate.

Symbols widely used for logic gates are shown in Fig. 2.1. The actual circuit details of the logic devices are described in Chap. 5.

2.3 BOOLEAN EXPRESSIONS

2.3.1 Sum-of-product and product-of-sum expressions

A Boolean expression contains Boolean variables linked with Boolean operators. There are two standard forms of Boolean expressions, the *sum-of-product* form and the *product-of-sum* form. In the sum-of-product form, variables

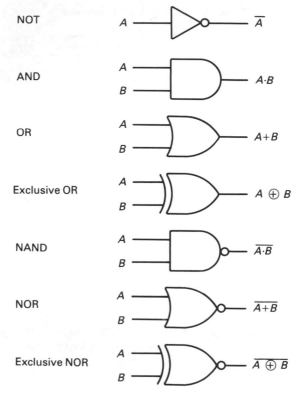

NOT

AND

OR

Exclusive OR

NAND

NOR

Exclusive NOR

Figure 2.1   Logical device symbols

are connected with AND operators to create Boolean terms which are then connected together with OR operations as in:

$$ABC+DEF+GHI$$

where A,B,C,D,E,F,G,H and I are Boolean variables.

In the product-of-sum expression, variables are connected together using OR operators to form terms which are then connected with AND operators as in:

$$(A+B+C)(D+E+F)(G+H+I)$$

An expression with every variable appearing in each term is called a *canonical* expression. For example:

$$f(A,B,C,D) = AB\bar{C}D + A\bar{B}CD + A\bar{B}C\bar{D}$$

is a canonical sum-of-product expression. A sum-of-product expression can be converted to canonical form by multiplying each term by $(A+\bar{A})\,(B+\bar{B})\,(C+\bar{C})$ $\cdots$, where $A,B,C \cdots$ are the variables not in the original term. Then the expression is expanded, for example the expression:

$$f(A,B,C)\ = AC + A\bar{B}$$

expands to:

$$= A(B+\bar{B})C + A\bar{B}(C+\bar{C})$$
$$= ABC + ABC + A\bar{B}C + A\bar{B}\bar{C}$$
$$= ABC + A\bar{B}C + A\bar{B}\bar{C}$$

One method of converting a product-of-sum expression to canonical form is to first find the inverse function, $\bar{f}$, by De Morgan's theorem, apply the above procedure, and then convert back to f.

The product term in a canonical sum-of-product expression is called a *minterm*. For example, ABC is a minterm in the canonical sum of product expression above. The sum term in a canonical product-of-sum expression is called a *maxterm*. Minterms and maxterms can be given numbers for identification purposes. These numbers are obtained by considering variables as binary 1's and their complements as binary 0's as shown in Table 2.8. Sometimes the maxterms are numbered with the variables as binary 0's and the complements as binary 1's ('inverse numbering') as this leads to a simpler conversion between sum-of-product and product-of-sum expressions.

Table 2.8   Minterm and maxterm notation

Minterm	Number	Product	Maxterm	Number	Sum
$\bar{A}\cdot\bar{B}\cdot\bar{C}$	000 0	P_0	$\bar{A}+\bar{B}+\bar{C}$	000 0	S_0
$\bar{A}\cdot\bar{B}\cdot C$	001 1	P_1	$\bar{A}+\bar{B}+C$	001 1	S_1
$\bar{A}\cdot B\cdot\bar{C}$	010 2	P_2	$\bar{A}+B+\bar{C}$	010 2	S_2
$\bar{A}\cdot B\cdot C$	011 3	P_3	$\bar{A}+B+C$	011 3	S_3
$A\cdot\bar{B}\cdot\bar{C}$	100 4	P_4	$A+\bar{B}+\bar{C}$	100 4	S_4
$A\cdot\bar{B}\cdot C$	101 5	P_5	$A+\bar{B}+C$	101 5	S_5
$A\cdot B\cdot\bar{C}$	110 6	P_6	$A+B+\bar{C}$	110 6	S_6
$A\cdot B\cdot C$	111 7	P_7	$A+B+C$	111 7	S_7

2.3.2 Conversion between canonical sum-of-product form and canonical product-of-sum form

Canonical sum-of-product terms and expressions can be converted into product-of-sum form and vice versa by algebraic means. Firstly, let us consider the conversion of individual terms:

(a) Relationship between minterms (product terms) and maxterms (sum terms)
By examining Table 2.8 we find that:

$$\bar{P}_0 = \overline{\overline{ABC}} = A+B+C = S_7$$

(For inverse numbering, $\bar{P}_0 = S_0$.) In general, the relationship between n variable minterms and maxterms is:

$$\bar{P}_i = S_{2^n-1-i} \tag{1}$$

(for inverse numbering, $\bar{P}_i = S_i$.)

(b) Minterm relationship
The Boolean summation (OR operation) of all minterms is given by:

$$\sum_{i=0}^{2^n-1} P_i = 1 \tag{2}$$

i.e.

Σ (all possible product terms) = 1

because one of the minterms must equal 1. If the function is f, then $f + \bar{f} = 1$ (one of the basic relationships). Therefore

Σ (minterms in f) + Σ (minterms not in f) = 1

and

$$\bar{f} = \Sigma \text{ (minterms not in } f) \tag{3}$$

(c) Canonical sum-of-product expressions to canonical product-of-sum expressions

Taking an example, let us convert the three-variable canonical sum-of-product function:

$f = \Sigma\ (P_0, P_2, P_3, P_4)$

into canonical product-of-sum form. We shall reduce the canonical notation to:

$f = \Sigma\ (0,2,3,4)$

From (3) we have:

$\bar{f} = \Sigma\ (1,5,6,7) = P_1 + P_5 + P_6 + P_7$

Therefore

$f = \overline{P_1 + P_5 + P_6 + P_7}$

and by De Morgan's theorem:

$f = \bar{P}_1 \bar{P}_5 \bar{P}_6 \bar{P}_7$

Hence, from (1) we have:

$f = S_6 S_2 S_1 S_0 = \Pi\ (6,2,1,0)$

(or with inverse numbering:

$f = \Pi\ (1,5,6,7)$

i.e. with inverse numbering, the equivalent product-of-sum expression contains the 'numbers' not in the sum-of-product expression.)

(d) Maxterm relationship

The Boolean multiplication (AND) of all maxterms is given by:

$$\prod_{i=0}^{2^n-1} S_i = 0 \tag{4}$$

i.e.

$$\Pi \text{ (all possible sum terms)} = 0$$

because one of the maxterms must equal 0. Also we have the basic relationship, $f\bar{f} = 0$. Therefore:

$$\Pi \text{ (sum terms in } f)(\text{sum terms not in } f) = 0$$

and

$$f = \Pi \text{ (sum terms not in } f) \tag{5}$$

(e) Canonical product-of-sum expressions to canonical sum-of-product expressions

As an example let us convert the three-variable canonical product-of-sum expression:

$$f = \Pi \, (1,2,3,4)$$

to canonical sum-of-product form. From (5) we have:

$$\bar{f} = \Pi \, (0,5,6,7) = S_0 S_5 S_6 S_7$$

Therefore:

$$f = \overline{S_0 S_5 S_6 S_7}$$

From De Morgan's theorem we obtain:

$$f = \bar{S}_0 + \bar{S}_5 + \bar{S}_6 + \bar{S}_7$$

From (1) we have:

$$f = P_7 + P_2 + P_1 + P_0 = \Sigma \, (7,2,1,0)$$

(or with inverse numbering:

$$f = \Sigma \, (0,5,6,7)$$

As in (c), with inverse numbering, the equivalent sum-of-product expression contains the 'numbers' not in the product-of-sum expression. Also we see that with this numbering, the inverse function ($\bar{f}$) in one form has the same numbers as the true function (f) in the other form.)

2.4 BOOLEAN MINIMIZATION

The aim of Boolean minimization is to reduce Boolean expressions to their simplest form. The simplest form is one with the least number of terms and the least number of variables in each term, if this is possible. There may be other criteria depending upon the application, for example number of gates required for the final implementation and how the gates are interconnected. It is usually preferable to have the number of gates between the inputs to the circuit and the outputs at a minimum to reduce the overall signal delay and the chances of unwanted transient signals occurring. The number of gates between the input and output defines the *levels of gating*. Two levels of gating is often a design aim, but may not always be feasible.

2.4.1 Boolean minimization by algebraic means

Minimization can be achieved through the use of Boolean relationships and theorems such as those given previously. The following are some methods that can be applied:

(a) Grouping of terms
Terms can be grouped together in a manner that leads to reduction through the use of a particular relationship, for example:

$$
\begin{aligned}
A + AB + BC \quad &= A(1+B) + BC \\
&= A + BC \qquad \text{since } 1+B = 1
\end{aligned}
$$

Terms can be repeated in an expression without affecting the expression and grouping may then be applied repeatedly using the same term grouped together with more than one other term, for example:

$$
\begin{aligned}
AD + ABD + \overline{AD}C \quad &= AD + AD + ABD + \overline{AD}C \\
&\quad \text{because } AD + AD = AD \\
&= AD(1+B) + AD + \overline{AD}C \\
&= AD + AD + C \\
&= AD + C
\end{aligned}
$$

(b) Multiplication of terms by redundant variables
The most common approach here is to multiply terms by $(X+X)$ where X is a variable not occurring in the term. This does not logically alter the expression and it may lead to simplification, for example:

$$
\begin{aligned}
AB + A\bar{C} + BC \quad &= AB(C+\bar{C}) + A\bar{C} + BC \\
&= ABC + AB\bar{C} + A\bar{C} + BC \\
&= BC(1+A) + A\bar{C}(1+B) \\
&= A\bar{C} + BC
\end{aligned}
$$

(c) Using De Morgan's theorem
Complex expressions can be often simplified by the repeated use of De Morgan's theorem, applied to various terms and groups of terms, for example:

$$
\begin{aligned}
\overline{(\overline{A\bar{B}C+\overline{A}CD})} + \overline{B\bar{C}} &= (\bar{A}+B+\bar{C}) + (\bar{A}+\bar{C}+\bar{D}) + B\bar{C} \\
&= (\bar{A}+B+\bar{C}+D) + B\bar{C} \\
&= (\bar{A} + B + \bar{C} + \bar{D}) \\
&= A\bar{B}CD
\end{aligned}
$$

It may also be possible to use the general form of De Morgan's theorem applied once to obtain the inverse function which may then immediately simplify.

(d) By substitution of all values

Sometimes it is easier to substitute all the possible values of variables in the expression and deduce the solution from the result. For example, the truth table of the expression $A+\bar{A}B$ is given in Table 2.9. From this, we can see that the expression, $A+\bar{A}B$, is a 1 when $A = 1$ or $B = 1$ or both A and B are a 1, so that the solution must be $A+B$.

Table 2.9   Truth table of function $A + \bar{A}B$

A	B	$A+\bar{A}B$
0	0	0
0	1	1
1	0	1
1	1	1

2.4.2 Karnaugh map minimization method

(a) The Karnaugh map

A *Karnaugh map* consists of a grid of squares, each sqaure representing one canonical minterm combination of the variables or their inverse, e.g. $\bar{A}\bar{B}\bar{C}$, $\bar{A}\bar{B}C$, $\bar{A}B\bar{C}$ etc. The map is arranged with squares representing minterms which differ by only one variable to be adjacent both vertically and horizontally. Therefore $\bar{A}\bar{B}\bar{C}$ would be adjacent to $\bar{A}B\bar{C}$ and would also be adjacent to $A\bar{B}\bar{C}$ and $\bar{A}\bar{B}C$. Figure 2.2 show the Karnaugh map for three variables. Squares on one edge of the map are regarded as adjacent to those on the opposite edge. The squares are labeled by one of two means, both of which are shown in the figure.

Firstly, the top left corner is labeled with the variables as shown and the two edges from this corner are labeled with 1,0 combinations, 1 to indicate the variable is true and a 0 to indicate the variable is false (complemented). For example, the top left square is allocated to $\bar{A}\bar{B}\bar{C}$ and all variables are false. Above the square, there is 00 to indicate that B and C are false and along the edge a 0 to indicate A is false. We note that the numbers on the top edge are in Gray code (Chap. 1, section 1.7). This will be also the case for maps with larger numbers of variables, on both edges.

The second form of labeling groups those squares which have a common variable. For example, the middle four squares all have the variable C true, and

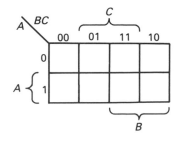

Figure 2.2   Three-variable Karnaugh map

this is labeled accordingly. The right four squares have *B* true as the common variable and the bottom row of four squares have *A* true as the common variable.

It is sometimes useful to know the minterm number associated with each square. Figure 2.3 shows two-, three- and four-variable Karnaugh maps with the minterm numbers included. Variables can, of course, be transposed. Two common arrangements are shown in the figure.

(b) Minimization technique

The expression to be minimized should generally be in sum-of-product form. If necessary, the conversion processes described previously are applied to create the sum-of-product form. The expression need not be in canonical form but let us first assume that it is in canonical form. The function is 'mapped' onto the Karnaugh map by marking a 1 in those squares corresponding to the terms in the expression to be simplified. The other squares may be filled with 0's. Thus, the function is described on the map.

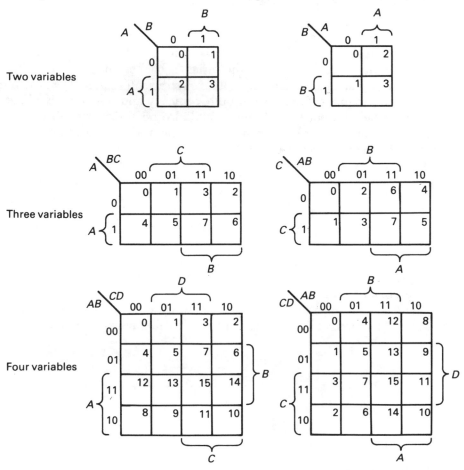

With position of variables changed

Figure 2.3   Two- three- and four-variable Karnaugh maps with minterm numbers

Pairs of 1's on the map which are adjacent are combined using the theorem:

$$P(A+\bar{A}) = P$$

where P is any Boolean expression. If two pairs are also adjacent, then these can also be combined using the same theorem. The minimization procedure consists of recognizing those pairs and multiple pairs. These are circled indicating reduced terms. Groups which can be circled are those which have two 1's, four 1's, eight 1's, etc. Figure 2.4 shows some possibilities on two, three and four

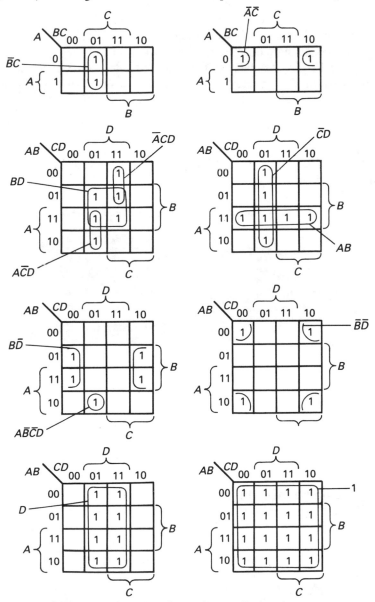

Figure 2.4   Examples of groupings on Karnaugh maps

variable Karnaugh maps. Note that because squares on one edge of the map are considered adjacent to those on the opposite edge, groups can be formed with these squares. Groups are allowed to overlap. The objective is to cover all the 1's on the map in the fewest number of groups and to create the largest groups to do this.

Once all the possible groups have been formed, the corresponding terms are identified. A group of two 1's eliminates one variable from the original minterm while a group of four 1's eliminates two variables and a group of eight 1's eliminates three variables. The variables eliminated are those which are different in the original minterms of the group.

For our first design problem, consider the problem of designing a combinational logic circuit which accepts two 2-bit numbers, A_1A_0 and B_1B_0, and generates a single output, Z, which is a 1 output only when A is greater than B. Table 2.10 can be derived from the problem specification. There are six instances when A is greater than B, namely when $A_1A_0 = 01$ and $B_1B_0 = 00$, $A_1A_0 = 10$ and $B_1B_0 = 00$ or 01, $A_1A_0 = 11$ and $B_1B_0 = 00$, 01 or 10. From the table, we can obtain the Karnaugh map for Z as shown in Fig. 2.5(a). This minimizes to:

$$Z = \bar{B}_1A_1 + \bar{B}_0A_0A_0 + \bar{B}_0\bar{B}_1A_0$$

A circuit realization is shown in Fig. 2.5(b).

Table 2.10   Truth table of a comparator

A_1	A_0	B_1	B_0	Z
0	0	0	0	0
0	0	0	1	0
0	0	1	0	0
0	0	1	1	0
0	1	0	0	1
0	1	0	1	0
0	1	1	0	0
0	1	1	1	0
1	0	0	0	1
1	0	0	1	1
1	0	1	0	0
1	0	1	1	0
1	1	0	0	1
1	1	0	1	1
1	1	1	0	1
1	1	1	1	0

(c) Don't care conditions

If a certain combination of variables cannot occur or it does not matter what the outputs are if the combination does occur, the combination is known as a *don't care* condition. Don't care conditions are marked on the Karnaugh map as X's. Each X can be considered as either a 0 or 1, whichever is best for minimization. A function with one or more don't care conditions is called an *incompletely specified function*.

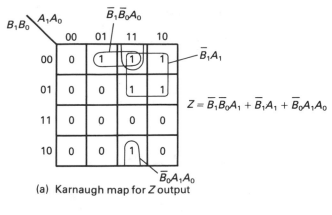

(a) Karnaugh map for Z output

$$Z = \bar{B_1}\bar{B_0}A_1 + \bar{B_1}A_1 + \bar{B_0}A_1A_0$$

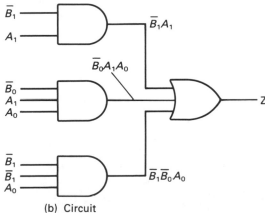

(b) Circuit

Figure 2.5 Comparator logic circuit design

Don't care conditions come about because of some physical constraint in the system. For example, consider the design of a circuit which generates the even parity bit for a 4-bit binary coded decimal (BCD) digit. (In practice, parity bits are not normally added to less than 8-bit words.) The circuit has four inputs to enter the BCD digit and one output, the parity bit. Assuming that a valid BCD digit is entered, the combinations 1010 (10 decimal), 1011 (11 decimal), 1100 (12 decimal), 1101 (13 decimal), 1110 (14 decimal) and 1111 (15 decimal) do not occur and can be considered as 'don't cares'. The parity bit is a 1 whenever there are an odd number of 1's in the BCD number, which creates an even number of 1's in all. The parity function is shown in Fig. 2.6(a). This function is minimized taking some of the don't cares as 1's and some as 0's, resulting in the reduced expression shown, and the circuit in Fig. 2.6(b).

(d) Function not in canonical form

It is not necessary to convert the original function into canonical form before minimization. Each term in the function can be mapped onto the Karnaugh map directly, noting that a term with one variable missing maps onto two adjacent squares, a term with two variables missing maps onto four squares,

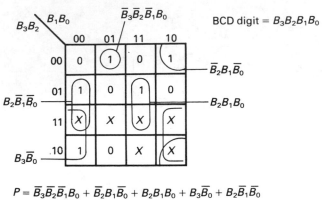

$$P = \bar{B}_3\bar{B}_2\bar{B}_1B_0 + \bar{B}_2B_1\bar{B}_0 + B_2B_1B_0 + B_3\bar{B}_0 + B_2\bar{B}_1\bar{B}_0$$

(a) Karnaugh map for output, P

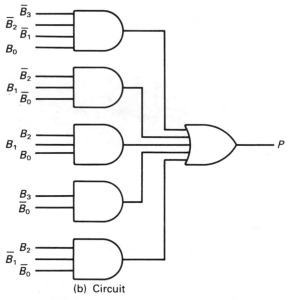

(b) Circuit

Figure 2.6 BCD parity generator logic circuit design

etc., just as the minimization procedure identifies a term with one variable omitted for two squares, a term with two variables omitted for four squares, etc.

(e) Large Karnaugh maps

A property of Karnaugh maps is that an n-variable map can be a direct extension of an $(n-1)$-variable map. A 4-variable map can be composed of two 3-variable maps. One is a mirror image drawn below the other. The fourth variable is assigned to the mirror image. A 5-variable map can be drawn taking a 4-variable map and placing another mirror image map next to it (or below it). Thus any size of Karnaugh map can be constructed by drawing a mirror image map by the side or below the original map. On 5-variable (and larger) Karnaugh maps, it is necessary to combine any sqaures in one half with squares in the mirror image as shown in Fig. 2.7. Generally it becomes increasingly difficult to

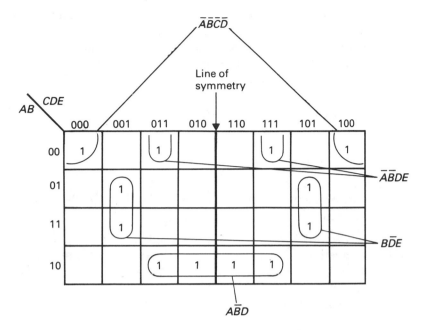

Figure 2.7   Five-variable Karnaugh map with examples of groups

recognize all possible groupings. The Quine-McCluskey method described in section 2.4.3 overcomes this problem.

(f) Technical terms

The following are some technical terms which can be applied to the Karnaugh map.

(i) PRIME IMPLICANT

This is the name given to the groups formed on the map. This may include groups not actually necessary in the final solution.

(ii) ESSENTIAL PRIME IMPLICANTS

This is the name given to the groups which include at least one 1 not covered by any other group. It is clear that the solution must include the essential prime implicants.

(iii) NON-ESSENTIAL PRIME IMPLICANTS

This is the name given to the prime implicants which are not essential but nevertheless cover 1's on the map. For example, it may be possible to cover a 1 in two ways, each with a different non-essential prime implicant. One of the non-essential prime implicants would be necessary in the solution to cover the 1.

(iv) REDUNDANT PRIME IMPLICANTS

Non-essential prime implicants which only cover 1's already covered by essential prime implicants are called *essentially redundant prime implicants* and are unnecessary. Sub-groups within a group are also redundant and need not be considered.

From these definitions, it can be seen that the minimal solution is given by all the essential prime implicants plus a careful selection of the non-essential prime implicants. An example is shown in Fig. 2.8. The expression to be minimized is:

$$f(A,B,C,D) = \bar{A}\bar{B}\bar{C}D + \bar{A}\bar{B}CD + \bar{A}B\bar{C}D + \bar{A}BC\bar{D} + \bar{A}BCD + A\bar{B}\bar{C}\bar{D} + A\bar{B}\bar{C}D + AB\bar{C}\bar{D} + AB\bar{C}D + ABC\bar{D}$$

The prime implicants are:

> Essential prime implicants: $A\bar{C}, \bar{A}D$
> Non-essential prime implicants: $\bar{A}BC, BC\bar{D}, AB\bar{D}$
> Redundant prime implicant: $\bar{C}D$

Complete cover of the 1's can be achieved by choosing the essential prime implicants together with the non-essential prime implicants $\bar{A}BC$ and $AB\bar{D}$ or the non-essential prime implicant $BC\bar{D}$. The minimal cover is obtained by choosing the non-essential prime implicant $BC\bar{D}$. Hence the minimal solution is given by $A\bar{C} + \bar{A}D + BC\bar{D}$.

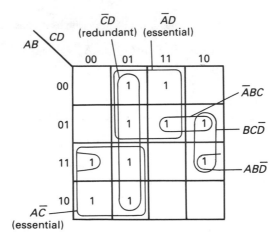

Figure 2.8 Prime implicants on a Karnaugh map

2.4.3 Quine–McCluskey minimization

The Quine–McCluskey minimization method uses the same theorem to produce the solution as the Karnaugh map method, namely $P(A+\bar{A}) = P$. This theorem is applied repeatedly using a formal tabular procedure which is particularly suitable for minimization of an expression containing a large number of variables. The procedure is also suitable for being carried out by a computer as well as manually.

First, the expression is represented in the canonical sum-of-product form if not already in that form. An example will be taken to explain the procedure. Suppose that the function to be minimized is:

$$f(A,B,C,D,E,F) = \overline{A}\,\overline{B}\,\overline{C}D\overline{E}\,\overline{F} + \overline{A}\,\overline{B}\,\overline{C}D\overline{E}F + \overline{A}\,\overline{B}\,\overline{C}DE\overline{F} + \overline{A}\,\overline{B}CDE\overline{F} +$$
$$\overline{A}B\overline{C}D\overline{E}\,\overline{F} + \overline{A}BC\overline{D}E\overline{F} + \overline{A}BCD\overline{E}\,\overline{F} + \overline{A}BCDE\overline{F} +$$
$$A\overline{B}\,\overline{C}D\overline{E}\,\overline{F} + A\overline{B}\,\overline{C}DE\overline{F} + A\overline{B}CD\overline{E}\,\overline{F} + A\overline{B}CDE\overline{F}$$

The function is converted into numeric notation described in section 2.3.1, i.e.:

$$f(A,B,C,D,E,F) = \Sigma\ (4,5,6,14,20,26,28,30,36,38,44,46)$$

The numbers are converted into binary form, i.e.:

$$f(A,B,C,D,E,F) = (000100 + 000101 + 000110 + 001110 + 010100 +$$
$$011010 + 011100 + 011110 + 100100 + 100110 +$$
$$101100 + 101110)$$

Then, the minterms are arranged in a column divided into groups. The minterm 00···00 (no 1's), if present, is placed in the first group. The minterms with one 1 in their numbers are placed in the second group. The minterms with two 1's in their numbers are placed in the next group, and so on until all the minterms are placed. The result of this operation for our example is shown in the leftmost column of Table 2.11.

Table 2.11   Quine–McCluskey minimization procedure

(4)	000100 ✓	(4,5)	00010X	(4,6,36,38)	X001X0
		(4,6)	0001X0 ✓	(6,14,38,46)	X0X110
(5)	000101 ✓	(4,20)	0X0100	(36,38,44,46)	10X1X0
(6)	000110 ✓	(4,36)	X00100 ✓		
(20)	010100 ✓				
(36)	100100 ✓				
		(6,14)	00X110 ✓		
		(6,38)	X00110 ✓		
(14)	001110 ✓	(20,28)	01X100		
(26)	011010 ✓	(36,38)	1001X0 ✓		
(28)	011100 ✓	(36,44)	10X100 ✓		
(38)	100110 ✓				
(44)	101100 ✓	(14,30)	0X1110		
		(14,46)	X01110 ✓		
(30)	011110 ✓	(26,30)	011X10		
(46)	101110 ✓	(28,30)	0111X0		
		(38,46)	10X110 ✓		
		(44,46)	1011X0 ✓		

The next step is the beginning of the minimization procedure proper. Starting with the first minterm of the first group, each minterm of one group is compared with each minterm in the group immediately below. Each time a number is found in one group which is the same as a number in the group below except for one digit, the pair of numbers are ticked and a new composite number is created. This composite number has the same digits as the numbers in the pair except the digit different which is replaced by an X. For example, 000100, the first and only number in the first group, can be combined with 000101 in the second group for form 0010X. The composite numbers are placed in the next column in groups as before. In our example, the number in the first group can be combined with all the numbers in the second group to form the first group of four numbers in the second column. Similarly, the four numbers in the second group of the first column combine with the numbers in the third group of the first column to produce the five numbers in the second group of the second column. The third and fourth groups of the first column combine to form the final group in the second column, and all terms in the first column have been ticked. Note that terms are compared with all terms of the group immediately below even though the term may already have been ticked from a previous comparison. Only one tick is shown on paired terms.

The above procedure is repeated on the second column to generate a third column. For pairs to be now ticked, the 'X's must be in the same position. For example, X00100 and X00110 combine to form X001X0. Subsequent columns are generated in the same manner until no more pairs can be found. In our case, three columns can be generated. Any repeated terms are deleted. The terms not ticked are the prime implicants of the expression. We have nine prime implicants, six in the second column and three in the third column.

The next step is to identify the essential prime implicants which can be done by using a *prime implicant* chart. The prime implicants label the rows of the prime implicant chart and the original minterms label the columns as shown in Table 2.12. For identification purposes, prime implicants are called a,b,c,d,e,f,g,h and i. Where a prime implicant covers a minterm, the intersection of the corresponding row and column is marked with a cross. Those columns with only one cross identify the essential prime implicants labeling the corresponding rows. We have three such cases:

a (4,5)	due to the single cross on column for minterm 5
e (26,30)	due to the single cross on column for minterm 26
i (36,38,44,46)	due to the single cross on column for minterm 44

Table 2.12   Prime implicant chart

								Minterms					
Prime implicants		4	5	6	14	20	26	28	30	36	38	44	46
a 00010X (4,5)	*	⊗	⊗										
b 0X0100 (4,20)		⊗				X							
c 01X100 (20,28)						X		X					
d 0X1110 (14,30)					X				⊗				
e 011X10 (26,30)	*						⊗		⊗				
f 0111X0 (28,30)								X	⊗				
g X001X0 (4,6,36,38)		⊗		X						⊗	⊗		
h X0X110 (6,14,38,46)				X	X						⊗		⊗
i 10X1X0 (36,38,44,46)	*									⊗	⊗	⊗	⊗

* = essential prime implicant

These prime implicants must be in the final answer. The single crosses on a column are circled and all the crosses on the same row are also circled, indicating that these crosses are covered by prime implicants selected. This procedure on our problem leads to circled crosses on minterm columns 4,30,36,38 and 46 in addition to 5,26 and 44. Once one cross on a column is circled, all the crosses on that column can be circled since the minterm is now covered. In our case this leads to crosses on all columns except 6,14,20 and 28 being circled. If any non-essential prime implicant has all its crosses circled, the prime implicant is redundant and need not be considered further. We have none of these.

Next, a selection must be made from the remaining non-essential prime implicants, by considering how the crosses not circled can be best covered. Generally one would take those prime implicants which cover the greatest number of minterms, that is, which have the most number of crosses on their row. If all the crosses on one row also occur on another row which includes further crosses, then the latter is said to *dominate* the former and can be selected. The dominated prime implicant can then be deleted. In our case, prime implicant c (01X100) dominates prime implicants b (0X0100) and f (0111X0). Similarly, prime implicant h (X0X110) dominates d (0X1110) and g (X001X0). These two dominating prime implicants cover all the remaining crosses and give us the solution, i.e.

$$a + e + i + c + h$$

or

$$00010X + 011X10 + 10X1X0 + 01X100 + X0X110$$

or

$$\bar{A}\bar{B}\bar{C}DE + \bar{A}BCE\bar{F} + A\bar{B}D\bar{F} + \bar{A}BD\bar{E}\bar{F} + \bar{B}DE\bar{F}$$

If necessary, one can also look for *column dominance*. If one column contains all the crosses on another column and other crosses, it is said to dominate the column with fewer crosses. The dominating column can then be deleted rather than the dominated row previously. This is because if the minterm with the fewer crosses is covered, the other minterm is covered automatically.

The above procedures to obtain the solution from the prime implicants are rather complicated and a much simpler approach is available, due to Petrick (and developed by Pyne and McCluskey). In the Petrick method all the prime implicants are regarded as single Boolean variables and a sum-of-product expression is formed. To take our example, we can deduce from the prime implicant chart that to cover minterm 4, either prime implicant a or b or g is needed. To cover minterm 5, prime implicant a is needed. To cover minterm 6, g or h is needed. Continuing along these lines, we obtain the following Boolean expression:

$$\text{Function} = \ (a+b+g)(a)(g+h)(d+h)(b+c)(e)(c+f)(d+e+f)(g+i)$$
$$(g+h+i)(i)(h+i)$$

This function can then be manipulated using any of the standard Boolean minimization procedures. Using algebraic manipulation we get:

$$
\begin{aligned}
\text{Function} &= aei(g+h)(d+h)(b+c)(c+f) \\
&= aei(h+hd+hg+gd)(c+bc+bf+cf) \\
&= aei[h(1+d+g)+gd][c(1+b+f)+bf] \\
&= aei(h+gd)(c+bf) \\
&= acehi+abefhi+acdegi+abefgi
\end{aligned}
$$

The minimized expression gives the possible combinations of prime implicants which would cover all the minterms. Normally, the combination with the smallest number of prime implicants would be taken, namely acehi, giving the same result as previously.

Don't care conditions can be handled in the Quine–McCluskey method. First, the don't care minterms are included in the function to be minimized and the normal procedure is followed. When the prime implicant chart is drawn, the don't care minterms are not included and are not considered further. Any prime implicants which cover only the don't care minterms can be deleted. Subsequent steps are as normal.

REFERENCES

1. Boole, G., *An Investigation of the Laws of Thought*. New York: Dover Publications, 1954 (Reprint of original publication in 1854).
2. Shannon, C.E., 'A Symbolic Analysis of Relay and Switching Circuits', *Trans. Am. Inst. Elect. Engrs.*, 57 (1938), 713–23.

PROBLEMS

2.1 Suppose in the heating system described in section 2.1, heat is provided when the frost thermostat indicates the external temperature is below $0°\text{C}$ irrespective of the room temperature. Derive the Boolean expression for S.

2.2 Expand the following expressions to canonical form:

(a) $\bar{A}B + A\bar{B} + \bar{C}$
(b) $(\bar{A} + B)(A + C)$

2.3 Convert the following sum-of-product canonical expressions to canonical product-of-sum expressions:

(a) $f(A,B,C) = \Sigma\,(1,4,5,6)$
(b) $f(A,B,C,D) = \Sigma\,(5,7,10,15)$

2.4 Minimize the following expressions algebraically:

(a) $(\bar{A}+BC)(\overline{\bar{B}+C})(\bar{A}\bar{B}C+B\bar{C})$
(b) $(A+BC)(A+\bar{B}C)(A+BC)$
(c) $X\bar{Y}\bar{Z} + XY\bar{Z} + X\bar{Y}Z$

2.5 Simplify the following by any method:

(a) $f(A,B,C)$ $= \bar{A}B+\bar{B}C+A$
(b) $f(A,B,C,D)$ $= \Sigma\,(0,4,6,8,9,10,11,15)$
(c) $f(A,B,C,D)$ $= A(BC+CD+C+B+\bar{C}) + \bar{A}$
(d) $f(A,B,C)$ $= \overline{AC} + (\overline{\bar{A}\bar{B}+C})(\bar{A}+C) + (\overline{\bar{A}\bar{B}\bar{C}})(A+B)$

2.6 Determine whether the following Boolean identities are valid, by algebraic means:

(a) $A + \bar{A}B = A + B$

(b) $(A + B)(\bar{A} + C) = AC + \bar{A}B$

(c) $\bar{A}\bar{C}D + \bar{A}CD + ABD = \bar{A}D + BD$

(d) $\bar{A}\bar{B}C + \bar{A}B\bar{C} + A\bar{B}\bar{C} + ABC = C(\bar{A}B + A\bar{B}) + \bar{C}(\bar{A}B + A\bar{B})$

(e) $XY + XZ + YZ = \bar{X}\bar{Y} + \bar{X}\bar{Z} + \bar{Y}\bar{Z}$

2.7 Reduce the following expressions using De Morgan's theorem:

(a) $f = \overline{\bar{A}\bar{B}C + \bar{A}BC}$

(b) $f = \overline{(\bar{A} + \bar{B} + C)(\bar{A} + B + \bar{C})}$

(c) $f = \overline{(A + \bar{B} + C)(\bar{A}B + \bar{C}D) + \bar{A}CD}$

2.8 Simplify the following expressions using the Karnaugh map method:

(a) $f = \bar{A}\bar{B}\bar{C}\bar{D} + \bar{A}\bar{B}C\bar{D} + \bar{A}BCD + A\bar{B}CD + AB\bar{C}D$

(b) $f = \bar{A}D + \bar{A}\bar{B}\bar{C} + A\bar{B}D + AB\bar{C} + \bar{A}\bar{B}C\bar{D}$

(c) $f = ABD + ABCD + \bar{A}\bar{B}C\bar{D} + A\bar{B}\bar{C}D + A\bar{B}D$
    Don't care $= \bar{A}B\bar{D}$

(d) $f = ABC + ABE + ABD + ADE + AE$

(e) $f(A,B,C,D) = \Sigma\,(1,3,4,5,9,11,12)$

(f) $f(A,B,C,D) = \Sigma\,(1,2,3,5,10,11)$
    Don't cares $= 4,9,13$

(g) $f(A,B,C,D,E) = \Sigma\,(2,7,9,10,13,15,18,19,23,26,27,28,29,31)$

2.9 Minimize the following functions using the Karnaugh map method:

(a) $f(A,B,C,D) = \Sigma\,(2,3,7,12,13,14,15)$

(b) $f(A,B,C,D) = \Pi\,(2,3,7,12,13,14,15)$

2.10 Extract the prime implicants from the Boolean expression:

$$f = \Sigma\,(10,11,15,21,24,25,26,28,29,30)$$

using the Quine–McCluskey method. Obtain the minimal set of prime implicants to cover the expression, with the aid of a prime implicant chart.

2.11 The output of a logic circuit is a 1 only when any of the following 6-bit numbers is present at its six inputs:

$$1,2,3,5,7,13,15,22,23,29,31,41 \qquad (\text{decimal})$$

Obtain the minimal logical expression for the circuit output signal. All numbers between 0 and 63 are valid except 39,45 and 47 which do not occur and can be considered as don't cares. Use the Quine–McCluskey method to obtain the prime implicants and an algebraic method to obtain the minimal solution.

2.12 A logic circuit accepts three 2-bit (positive) binary numbers A, B and C on six input lines, and produces a single output, Z, which is set to a 1 only when $A + B - C$ is equal to or greater than 4 (decimal). ($+$ and $-$ are arithmetic operations.) Show that the output is given by the Boolean function:

$$f(C_0,C_1,B_0,B_1,A_0,A_1) = \Sigma\,(5,7,11,13,14,15,31,39,45,47)$$

Where A_1, B_1 and C_1 are the most significant digits of A, B and C respectively. A_0, B_0 and C_0 are the least significant digits of A, B and C respectively. Minimize the above function using the Quine–McCluskey method.

Combinational Circuit Design

3.1 COMBINATIONAL CIRCUITS

A *combinational logic circuit* is one which has output values dependent upon the values of the input signals applied at that instant, i.e. the output(s) depend upon the combination of input values and do not depend upon any particular condition in the past. This contrasts with a *sequential logic circuit* whose output or outputs depend upon the input signals applied at that instant and also input/output values in the past. Chapter 4 considers sequential circuit design. Boolean expressions as described in the previous chapter are implemented using combinational logic circuits.

3.2 COMBINATIONAL CIRCUIT FUNCTION IMPLEMENTATION

3.2.1 TTL logic circuit family

Reference will be made to actual logic devices in the TTL (transistor-transistor-logic) logic family [1] which are widely used to implement digital systems. A full range of fundamental gates are manufactured, including those given in Table 3.1. Apart from the fundamental combinational logic circuit parts (AND gates etc.), other more complex integrated circuit parts exist for particular applications. The part numbers, apart from a manufacturer's prefix such as SN (semiconductor network), begin with the numbers 74 (for commercial versions; military versions use the numbers 54). These numbers may be followed by letters referring to particular internal circuit designs such LS (low-power Schottky), S (Schottky), AS (advanced Schottky), ALS (advanced low-power Schottky). These and other circuit designs are described in Chap. 5. The final numbers refer to the particular part within the logic family. Most of the devices in this family and similar families are manufactured in *dual-in-line* packages. The number of TTL gates fabricated within the package is often between 1 and 100. When the number of gates is less than 12, the technology is commonly called *small scale integration* (SSI). When the number of gates is between 12 and 100, the technology is called *medium scale integration* (MSI). (The term *large scale integration*, LSI, is used for devices with 100 to 1000 gates and *very large scale integration*, VLSI, when there are thousands of gates in the device.) The dual-in-

Table 3.1 Some gates in the TTL logic family

Gates		Number of gates in package	Device number
NOT		6 (Hex)	74LS04
AND	2-input	4 (Quadruple)	74LS08
	3-input	3 (Triple)	74LS11
	4-input	2 (Dual)	7421
OR	2-input	4 (Quadruple)	74LS32
NAND	2-input	4 (Quadruple)	74LS00
	3-input	3 (Triple)	74LS10
	4-input	2 (Dual)	74LS20
	8-input	1	74LS30
	13-input	1	74LS133
NOR	2-input	4 (Quadruple)	74LS02
	3-input	3 (Triple)	74LS27
	5-input	2 (Dual)	74LS260
EXCLUSIVE-OR	2-input	4 (Quad)	74LS86*
EXCLUSIVE-NOR	2-input	4 (Quad)	74LS266*
AND-OR-INVERT	2-wide 2/3-input	2 (Dual)	74LS51
	4-wide 2/3-input	1	74LS54

* Classified as MSI in reference [1].

line packages used commonly have 14, 16 or 20 pins for connections on the two longer sides of the package. Figure 3.1 shows the 14-pin package and some connections. Sixteen-pin and 20-pin packages have the same 0.3 in. width and 0.1 in. spaced pins.

A logic 1 in TTL is represented by the voltage 3.4V nominally, though it can be generated between 2.4V and 5V. A logic 0 is represented by the voltage 0.2V though can be generated between 0V and 0.4V. There are slight variations in the nominal voltages between device types. Voltages as low as 2V will be recognized as a logic 1 level by gates and voltages as high as 0.8V at the inputs of gates will be recognized as a logic 0 level, to allow extraneous electrical noise in the system. The overlaps between the recognized voltage ranges and the generated voltage ranges are shown in Fig. 3.2.

3.2.2 Using AND, OR and NOT gates

Circuit realization of any Boolean expressions can be done using the three fundamental gates, AND, OR and NOT gates. AND gates can be used where there are AND operations specified in the Boolean expression and OR gates used where there are OR operations. For example, a sum-of-product expression such as:

$$f(A,B,C,D) = \bar{A}BC + \bar{B}\bar{C} + AD$$

can easily be realized as shown in Fig. 3.3(a). The inverse variables $\bar{A}$, $\bar{B}$ and $\bar{C}$ are generated using NOT gates. The first product term, $\bar{A}BC$, is realized using a three-input AND gate. The second and third product terms are realized using two-input AND gates. The overall OR operation is performed using one three-input OR gate.

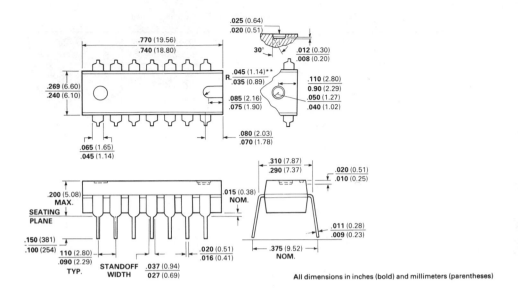

All dimensions in inches (bold) and millimeters (parentheses)

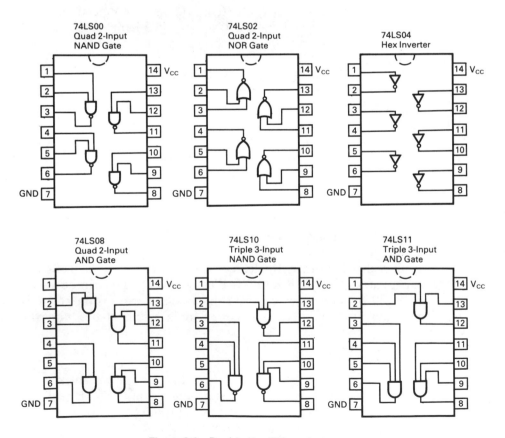

Figure 3.1 Dual-in-line TTL packages

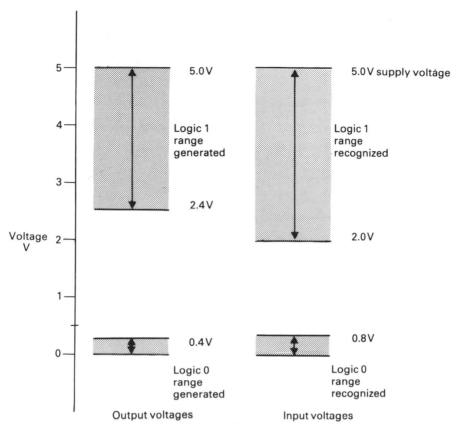

Figure 3.2 TTL voltages

The realization is *two level* because the signals pass through two gates from the input of the circuit to the output, if we ignore the gates for inverting the input signals. Alternative AND/OR implementations can sometimes be created by firstly factorizing the function. This may lead to less gates but a greater number of logic levels. Two-level implementations generally minimize the delay before a new output is generated. A further advantage of the implementation is that it is clear how the function has been implemented. This is particularly important to help any people other than the original designers subsequently working on the circuit, such as those making modifications or testing the circuit. Integrated circuit parts exist which contain composite two-level AND-OR/NOR gate combinations. In some applications, however, two-level implementations would require large numbers of gates and alternative schemes need to be produced, for example using iterative arrays (section 3.4.3).

3.2.3 Using NAND gates

NAND gates are universal in the sense that any logic function can be implemented using NAND gates only. A NAND gate implementation of the

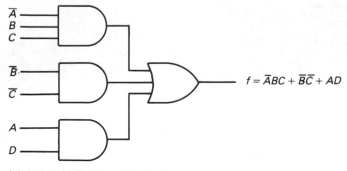

(a) Using AND gates and OR gate

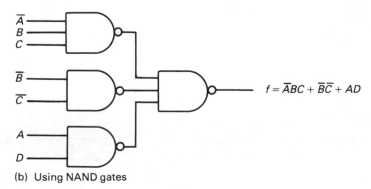

(b) Using NAND gates

Figure 3.3   Implementation of the function $f = \overline{A}BC + \overline{B}\overline{C} + AD$

previous sum-of-product is obtained by rearranging the function as follows; firstly apply double inversion:

$$f = \overline{\overline{\overline{A}BC + \overline{B}\overline{C} + AD}}$$

Then by De Morgan's theorem, we get:

$$f = \overline{(\overline{\overline{A}BC})(\overline{\overline{B}\overline{C}})(\overline{AD})}$$

This can be implemented as shown in Fig. 3.3(b). Inversion of input signals can be obtained by using a NAND gate with all its inputs tied together. The terms in the equation enclosed in parentheses are generated in the next level of gating and the overall NAND operation in the final level. Notice that the general configuration and the signals applied to the circuit are the same as those applied to an AND-OR gate arrangement. Therefore an AND-OR gate implementation can be directly converted into NAND gate implementation by inspection.

3.2.4 Using NOR gates

NOR gates are also universal and any logic function can be implemented with NOR gates only. Rearranging the above function to:

$$\overline{f} = \overline{\overline{(A+\overline{B}+\overline{C})} + \overline{(\overline{B}+C)} + \overline{(\overline{A}+\overline{D})}}$$

using De Morgan's theorem leads to a NOR implementation of the inverse function with two levels of gates disregarding gates for inverting A, B and D. NOR gate implementations are not now very common; either AND/OR or NAND gates are used for simple functions.

3.2.5 Mixed logic representation

We have seen that AND, OR and NOT gates can be used to implement a sum-of-product expression directly without any manipulation, or NAND gates can be used or even NOR gates can be used totally. It is also possible to employ both NAND gates and NOR gates in various combinations. However, it is preferable to design a circuit that can be easily understood from the logic diagram. This can be achieved with a system of logic diagrams, known as *mixed logic representation*, which shows the logic function intended in the mind of the designer irrespective of the actual gates used. Alternative symbols are used for AND, OR, NAND and NOR gates where the logic operation intended is different, as shown in Fig. 3.4. A small circle is used to indicate inversion as on the output of the NOT, NAND and NOR gate symbols. This circle is also applied to the inputs when the input variables are inverted before the main logical operation. For example, a two-input NAND gate has the function:

$$f(A,B) = \overline{AB}$$
$$= \overline{A} + \overline{B}$$

and so can be used as an 'OR' operation if the input variables are inverted as on the equivalent symbol shown. This symbol would be used if the designer had an OR operation in mind.

Figure 3.5 shows a mixed logic representation for the function $f(A,B,C) = ABC + \overline{B}\overline{C} + AD$ implemented using NAND gates.

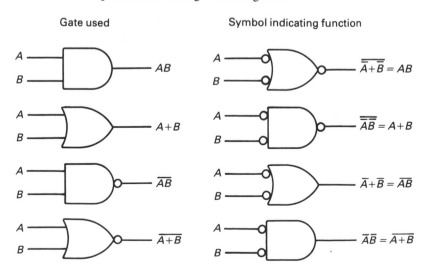

Figure 3.4   Mixed logic representation

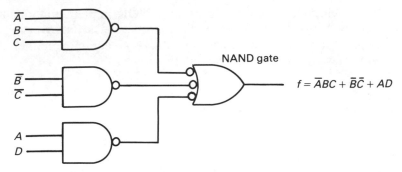

Figure 3.5   Mixed logic representation of function $f = \overline{A}BC + \overline{B}\overline{C} + AD$ using NAND gates

3.2.6 Multiple output combinational logic circuit design

In Chap. 2, two logic circuits were designed from a problem specification using the Karnaugh map minimization method (section 2.4.2). In each case, there are a number of logic inputs and one logic output. Now let us consider a circuit with more than one output. Suppose the three combinational functions:

$$f_1(B_3,B_2,B_1,B_0) = \Sigma\ (5,7,8,12,13,15)$$
$$f_2(B_3,B_2,B_1,B_0) = \Sigma\ (0,3,4,5,7,13,15)$$
$$f_3(B_3,B_2,B_1,B_0) = \Sigma\ (3,7,8,12,13)$$

are to be implemented, where the inputs to the circuits are B_3, B_2, B_1 and B_0. We could minimize each function separately and create three separate two-level circuits (plus inverters where necessary). However, it may be possible to share one or more of the first-level gates between functions. It may sometimes be better not to fully minimize the individual functions to obtain greatest gate sharing.

An informal approach to identify the appropriate Boolean expressions is to map each function onto individual Karnaugh maps and look for possible gate sharing. The Karnaugh maps for our functions are shown in Fig. 3.6(a). We can see that the term B_2B_0 is common to both f_1 and f_2. Similarly, $\overline{B}_3B_1B_0$ is common to f_2 and f_3. Finally, $B_3\overline{B}_1\overline{B}_0$ is common to both f_1 and f_3. This observation leads to the design shown in Fig. 3.6(b), where three gates are shared.

A formal approach can be used which ensures that the greatest gate sharing is achieved. First, we find the following prime implicants by examining the Karnaugh maps or in a more certain means by the Quine–McClusky method (Chap. 2):

(i)   The prime implicants common to all the functions, that is of the function $f_1 f_2 f_3$.

(ii) The prime implicants common to two of the three functions, that is, of the functions $f_1 f_2, f_1 f_3$ and $f_2 f_3$.

(iii) The prime implicants of the individual functions f_1, f_2 and f_3.

If there are more than three functions, the prime implicants of all combinations

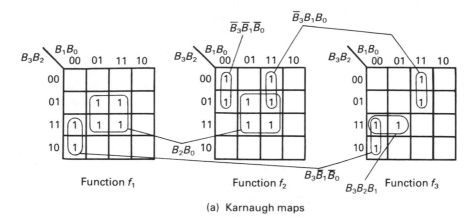

(a) Karnaugh maps

(b) Circuit

Figure 3.6   Circuit with three outputs

of functions must be found. In our case, the following prime implicants are found:

	Minterms	Prime implicants
$f_1 f_2 f_3$	7,13	(7),(13)
$f_1 f_2$	5,7,13,15	(5,7,13,15)
$f_1 f_3$	7,8,12,13	(7),(8,12),(12,13)
$f_2 f_3$	3,7,13	(3,7),(13)
f_1	5,7,8,12,13,15	(8,12),(12,13),(5,7,13,15)

f_2 0,3,4,5,7,13,15   (0,4),(3,7),(4,5),(5,7,13,15)
f_3 3,7,8,12,13   (3,7),(8,12),(12,13)

Then, a prime implicant chart is drawn with rows labeled with the prime implicants. The columns are divided into three groups, one for each function. One column is provided for each minterm within each group, as shown in Table 3.2. A cross is marked at the intersection of a row and a column if the prime implicant is in the function, i.e. if the minterm and all the other minterms in the prime implicant are included in the functioin.

Columns with only one cross identify essential prime implicants. Since essential prime implicants must be provided, all the crosses on essential prime implicant rows can be circled, indicating the associated minterms are covered. Once a cross has been circled, any other cross on the same column can also be circled as the minterms will be covered. In our case, we find four essential prime implicants.:

   (0,4),(3,7),(8,12),(5,7,13,15)

Prime implicants (8,12) and (5,7,13,15) will cover f_1 completely and prime implicants (0,4), (3,7) and (5,7,13,15) will cover f_2 completely. Prime implicants (8,12) and (3,7) are necessary for f_3, but we are left with minterm 13 to be covered. This minterm can best be covered with the prime implicant (12,13) rather than (13), leading to the same circuit as previously. If several non-essential prime implicants are present, it may be necessary to turn to Petrick's method (Chap. 2, section 2.4.3).

Table 3.2   Prime implicant chart for circuit with multiple outputs

Prime implicants																		
		Function f_1							Minterms Function f_2						Function f_3			
		5	7	8	12	13	15	0	3	4	5	7	13	15	3	7	8	12	13
(7)			⊗									⊗				⊗			
(13)						⊗							⊗						X
(0,4)	*							⊗		⊗									
(3,7)	*								⊗			⊗			⊗	⊗			
(4,5)										⊗	⊗								
(8,12)	*			⊗	⊗													⊗	⊗	
(12,13)					⊗	⊗													⊗	X
(5,7,13,15)	*	⊗	⊗			⊗	⊗				⊗	⊗	⊗	⊗					

* = essential prime implicant

3.2.7 Iterative circuit design

There are some design problems which would require a very large number of gates if designed as two-level circuits. One approach is to divide each function into a number of identical subfunctions which need be performed in sequence and the result of one subfunction is used in the next subfunction. Consider the following design problem.

Design an even parity generator circuit which produces the parity bit (B_7)

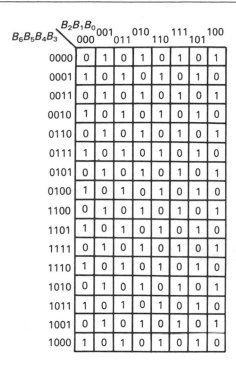

$B_6B_5B_4B_3$ \ $B_2B_1B_0$	000	001	011	010	110	111	101	100
0000	0	1	0	1	0	1	0	1
0001	1	0	1	0	1	0	1	0
0011	0	1	0	1	0	1	0	1
0010	1	0	1	0	1	0	1	0
0110	0	1	0	1	0	1	0	1
0111	1	0	1	0	1	0	1	0
0101	0	1	0	1	0	1	0	1
0100	1	0	1	0	1	0	1	0
1100	0	1	0	1	0	1	0	1
1101	1	0	1	0	1	0	1	0
1111	0	1	0	1	0	1	0	1
1110	1	0	1	0	1	0	1	0
1010	0	1	0	1	0	1	0	1
1011	1	0	1	0	1	0	1	0
1001	0	1	0	1	0	1	0	1
1000	1	0	1	0	1	0	1	0

Figure 3.7   Karnaugh map of parity generator

for a 7-bit code word $B_6B_5B_4B_3B_3B_2B_1B_0$, i.e. produces an output set to a 1 only when the number of ones in the code word is odd so as to have an even number of 1's in the (8-bit) word including the parity bit. The code word might be an ASCII representation of characters, for example. The parity function has seven variables as shown in the Karnaugh map in Fig. 3.7 and does not minimize. (It will not minimize for any number of bits in the code word.) Therefore the output function consists of a seven-variable canonical sum of product expression with sixty-four minterms. A two-level implementation requires sixty-four 7-input AND gates and a 64-input OR gate. Sixty-four input OR gates are not manufactured, so an equivalent configuration of cascaded OR gates would need to be formed, each OR gate having perhaps five to eight inputs. A NAND implementation would have the same difficulties.

A design based around the iterative approach is shown in Fig. 3.8(a). There are seven logic circuit cells. Each cell accepts one code word digit and the output from the preceding cell. The cell produces one output, Z, which is a 1 whenever the number of 1's on the two inputs is odd. Hence successive outputs are a 1 when the number of 1's on inputs to that point is odd and the final output is a 1 only when the number of 1's in the whole code word is odd as required. Each cell function can be described by the function:

$$O_i = B_i\bar{I}_i + \bar{B}_iI_i$$

where

$$O_i = i\text{th cell output}$$
$$I_i = i\text{th cell input}$$
$$B_i = i\text{th bit of code word}$$

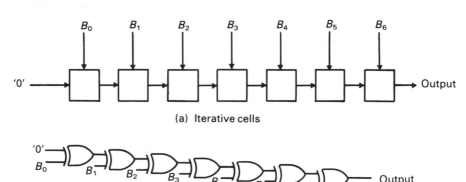

Figure 3.8   Parity generator using iterative cells

Thus, the cell function is the exclusive-OR function and the parity generator requires seven cascaded cells as shown in Fig. 3.8(b).

To create an iterative design, the number of cells and the number of data inputs to each cell need to be determined and also the number of different states that must be recognized by the cell. The number of different states will define the number of lines to the next cell (usually carrying binary encoded information). The above parity generator cell has the minimum number of inputs, one data and one from the previous cell, which results in the simplest cell design. The problem may decompose naturally in such a way that each cell has more than one output and several inputs. In a parity generator circuit, we could have chosen pairs of code word inputs, $B_{n+1}B_n$. Again one output is sufficient to indicate the state that there is an odd number of 1's so far, and hence one input to the next cell. The jth cell output function would now be:

$$O_j = B_{n+1}\bar{B}_n I_j + \bar{B}_{n+1}B_n I_j + B_{n+1}B_n \bar{I}_j + \bar{B}_{n+1}\bar{B}_n \bar{I}_j$$

3.2.8 Gate timing parameters

It will be useful at this stage to define some timing parameters of combinational circuits. The *propagation delay* is the delay between the application of new input signals to a logic gate or part and the generation of the resultant output. The propagation delay is typically measured at the 1.3 V points, as shown in Fig. 3.9 for a NOT gate. The propagation time for a 0 to 1 output change is not normally the same as the propagation time for a 1 to 0 output change in the same device. The propagation time for a 0 to 1 output change is typically 9 ns and the propagation time for a 1 to 0 output change is typically 10 ns (1 ns =

10^{-9}s) for a 74LS04 NOT gate. The differential between the two propagation times is greater in some other TTL gates. Notice that in practice logic voltages take a finite time to rise from a 0 to a 1 and fall from a 1 to a 0. These times are called the *rise time* and *fall time* respectively, measured at 10% and 90% points as shown. Using nominal values, the 10% point will be at $0.2\,\mathrm{V} + (1/10) \times (3.4 - 0.2)\,\mathrm{V} = 0.52\,\mathrm{V}$. The 90% point will be at $0.2\,\mathrm{V} + (9/10) \times (3.4 - 0.2)\,\mathrm{V} = 3.08\,\mathrm{V}$.

Propagation delay time, in particular, will define the speed of operation of logic circuits. The rise and fall times will depend upon the output circuit of the gate and the circuits connected to the output. Generally the rise and fall times will increase as greater loads are presented to the output and the propagation delay time will also be increased.

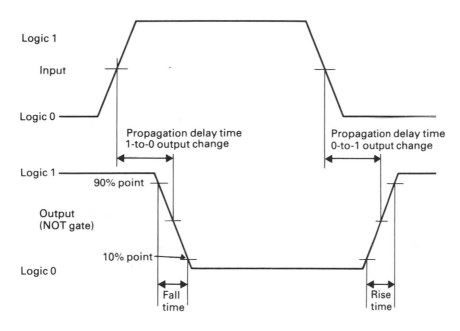

Figure 3.9   Rise time, fall time and propagation delay time

3.2.9 Race hazards in combinational circuits

A *race hazard* results in the generation of a 'logic spike', i.e. a transient logic signal, which may occur at the output of a gate when input signals change. It may be due to changes in signals passing through different paths to the output and experiencing different delays. A *static race hazard* is created by the delay between a signal and the complement signal. For example, a circuit implementation of the function $f(A,B) = AB + \bar{A}C$ is shown in Fig. 3.10(a). Consider the operation of the circuit when $B = C = 1$ and A changes state. $\bar{A}$ will be slightly delayed from A because of the extra gate delay of the NOT gate (ignoring the delay through the AND gates). During a 1 to 0 change, this extra delay causes both A

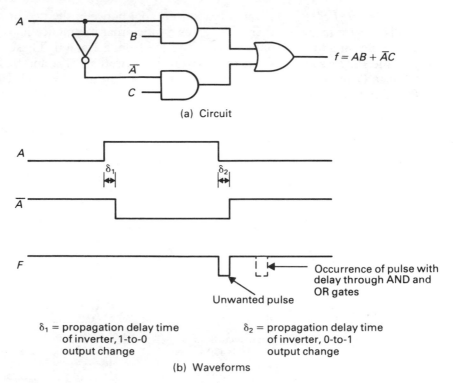

(a) Circuit

(b) Waveforms

δ_1 = propagation delay time
of inverter, 1-to-0
output change

δ_2 = propagation delay time
of inverter, 0-to-1
output change

Figure 3.10   Static race hazards

and A to be at a 0 transiently, resulting in a transient 0 output as shown in Fig. 3.10(b).

Static hazards can be eliminated as follows; first the function is mapped onto a Karnaugh map and groups (prime implicants) formed to specify the minimal solution. Then groups which do not overlap any other group are identified. These indicate potential race hazards. Additional groups are introduced crossing over these groups so that no group is not overlapped by another group. In our case, this means that one extra group, BC, is necessary between the two original groups, AB and $A\overline{C}$, as shown in Fig. 3.11(a). Finally this extra term is incorporated into the circuit as shown in Fig. 3.11(b). The inclusion of the logically redundant term maintains a '1' output during the A transition.

In general, all prime implicants must be included in the solution to avoid static hazards and perhaps the best method of identifying all the prime implicants is by the Quine–McCluskey method. Other types of race hazards exist (see Chap. 12).

3.3   MSI COMBINATIONAL LOGIC CIRCUIT PARTS

There are many MSI parts in the TTL family, including arithmetic circuits which we shall consider separately in section 3.4. Firstly, we shall consider two

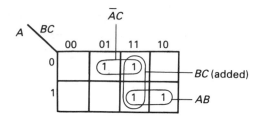

(a) Function with overlapping prime implicant added

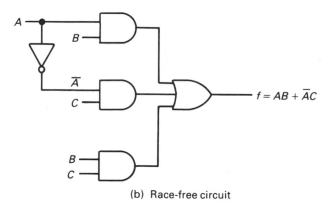

(b) Race-free circuit

Figure 3.11   Elimination of static race hazard in function $f = AB + \bar{A}C$

MSI parts, the decoder and the data selector, quoting part numbers in the TTL range.

3.3.1 Decoders/demultiplexers

A *decoder* is a logic circuit part which has a set of inputs, typically three or four, and a set of outputs. One output is activated for each possible binary pattern occurring on the inputs. Outputs are commonly *active low* meaning that they are normally at a 1 and become a 0 to indicate that the corresponding input pattern has been generated. With three inputs, there are up to eight (2^3) different possible binary input patterns and therefore eight outputs. The first output is activated when the pattern 000 occurs on the three inputs, the second output activated when the input pattern 001 occurs, the third output activated when the input pattern 010 occurs, and so on. With four inputs, there are up to sixteen different possible patterns and sixteen outputs. A decoder with three inputs and eight outputs is known as a 3-line-to-8-line decoder (e.g. 74LS138) and a decoder with four inputs and sixteen outputs is known as a 4-line-to-16-line decoder (e.g. 74LS154). The decoder may have additional *chip select* or enable inputs which must be activated to activate any of the outputs.

A *demultiplexer*, a component similar to a decoder, has one data input which is fed to one of a set of data outputs depending upon select inputs as shown in Fig. 3.12 with three select inputs to select eight data outputs. The first data

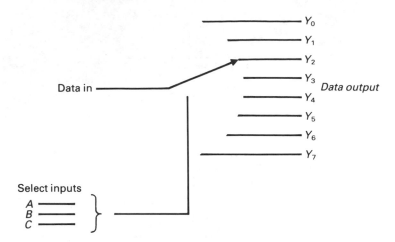

Figure 3.12   Demultiplexer

output is selected when the pattern 000 occurs on the select inputs and the second data output is selected when the pattern 001 occurs on the select inputs just as in the decoder. Whatever the logic level on the single data input, this occurs on the selected data output. The function of the data input is the same as the chip enable input of a decoder and consequently the two devices, decoder and demultiplexer, may be identical.

The truth table for a 74LS138 3-line-to-8-line decoder/demultiplexer is shown in Table 3.3 and the logic diagram is shown in Fig. 3.13. *A, B* and *C* are the binary encoded inputs. There are three enable inputs, G1, G2A and G2B shown on the decoder. The selected output is activated when $G1 \cdot \overline{G2A} \cdot \overline{G2B}$ is true. This expression becomes $G1 \cdot \overline{(G2A+G2B)}$ by De Morgan's theorem. In Table 3.3, G2A+G2B is called G2 and hence the device is activated when $G1\overline{G2}$ is true (when G1 = 1 and G2 = 0, i.e. when G1 = 1, G2A = 0 and G2B = 0).

Some decoders are designed to generate outputs corresponding to BCD (binary coded decimal) inputs. This simply means that there are only ten outputs corresponding to the number 0 to 9 and the patterns 10 to 15 (decimal) are not recognized. These decoders are called *BCD-decimal decoders* (e.g. 74LS42).

Decoders can be used to implement combinational logic expressions and may lead to a reduced number of packages. Each output of a decoder corresponds to one minterm. For example, the outputs of our 74LS138 3-line-to-8-line decoder generate the following minterms:

$$Y_0 = \overline{C}\overline{B}\overline{A}$$
$$Y_1 = \overline{C}\overline{B}A$$
$$Y_2 = \overline{C}B\overline{A}$$
$$Y_3 = \overline{C}BA$$
$$Y_4 = C\overline{B}\overline{A}$$
$$Y_5 = C\overline{B}A$$
$$Y_6 = CB\overline{A}$$
$$Y_7 = CBA$$

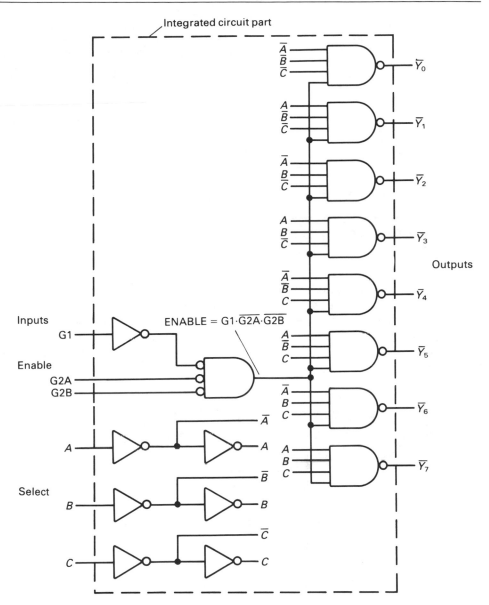

Figure 3.13 3-line-to-8-line decoder/demultiplexer

assuming A is the least significant bit and C is the most significant bit. Therefore canonical sum-of-product expressions can be implemented by feeding selecting outputs into an OR gate. For example, if the function:

$$F(C,B,A) = \overline{C}B\overline{A} + C\overline{B}\,\overline{A} + CBA$$

is required, Y_2, Y_4, and Y_7 are selected to feed in a three-input OR gate generating $Y_2 + Y_4 + Y_7$, as shown in Fig. 3.14. The decoder is permanently enabled. This solution requires two packages. The SSI solution using NAND

Table 3.3 Truth table of a 3-line-to-8-line decoder/demultiplexer (74LS138)

Inputs					Outputs							
Enable			Select									
G1	G2	C	B	A	$\overline{Y_0}$	$\overline{Y_1}$	$\overline{Y_2}$	$\overline{Y_3}$	$\overline{Y_4}$	$\overline{Y_5}$	$\overline{Y_6}$	$\overline{Y_7}$
X	1	X	X	X	1	1	1	1	1	1	1	1
0	X	X	X	X	1	1	1	1	1	1	1	1
1	0	0	0	0	0	1	1	1	1	1	1	1
1	0	0	0	1	1	0	1	1	1	1	1	1
1	0	0	1	0	1	1	0	1	1	1	1	1
1	0	0	1	1	1	1	1	0	1	1	1	1
1	0	1	0	0	1	1	1	1	0	1	1	1
1	0	1	0	1	1	1	1	1	1	0	1	1
1	0	1	1	0	1	1	1	1	1	1	0	1
1	0	1	1	1	1	1	1	1	1	1	1	0

G2 = G2A + G2B
X = don't care

gates would lead to two triple three-input NAND gate packages plus an additional package to generate all the complemented variables. In the decoder solution, the other decoder outputs are available, should several sum-of-product expressions be required, and it is easier to change a minterm. Also the enable inputs are available to generate more complex functions in conjunction with the *ABC* inputs.

3-line-to-8-line decoder/demultiplexer

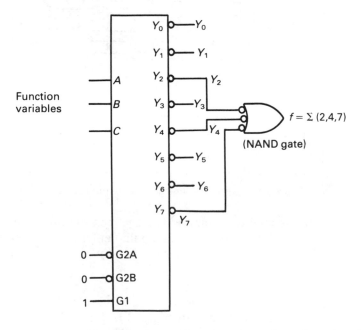

Figure 3.14 Generating a sum-of-product expression using a decoder

Decoders are more often used in logic systems to recognize a particular binary pattern by selecting only the output associated with the pattern. They are commonly used in microprocessor systems to activate memory modules containing memory devices. We shall consider microprocessor systems in Part 2. Briefly, an unique address (a binary number) is given to each memory location holding information. The first memory location is given the address 0 ⋯ 00000, the second location is given the address 0 ⋯ 00001, the third location 0 ⋯ 00010, and so on. If a memory device contains 1024 (2^{10}) memory locations, 10 address bits would be necesssary to identify the location within the device as there are 1024 different true and false combinations of 10 bits. The addresses would range from 0000000000 to 1111111111. There may be several memory modules. If there were eight identical memory modules, a further three address bits would be necesssary to identify the module as there are eight combinations of three bits. The module addresses would be 000, 001, 010, 011, 100, 101, 110 and 111. Suppose each memory module contains one memory device with 1024 locations. Thirteen address bits would be needed in all, three to select the memory module and eight to select the location within the memory module.

A 3-line-to-8-line decoder can be used to identify the individual memory module as shown in Fig. 3.15. The decoder output corresponding to the address of the module connects permanently to the memory device. The address lines from the microprocessor connect to the *ABC* select inputs of the decoder and a signal from the microprocessor which indicates that the address is valid connects to an enable input of the decoder. When the data is to be obtained or changed, the address of the location is generated by the microprocessor and appears on address lines from the microprocessor with the memory unit. The appropriate decoder output is activated which causes the data in the memory location to be transferred from the memory to the microprocessor and thus it can be obtained by the microprocessor. If new information is entered into the location, this is transferred from the microprocessor to the memory device. Different outputs of the decoder are necessary for different memory modules, and wire links can be provided between the decoder outputs and the memory device. Each module is then given a different link during manufacture or test. Alternatively, switches can be used. Eight switches are necessary in place of the wire links. Only one switch makes a connection, depending upon the address required.

3.3.2 Data selectors/multiplexers

A *data selector* or *multiplexer* is a logic circuit which allows one of several data inputs to be selected and fed to a single output as shown in Fig. 3.16. This is the reverse process to the data demultiplexer. As in the demultiplexer, the multiplexer has a set of select inputs, three if there are eight data inputs, four if there are sixteen data inputs. When one input is selected, the binary information on the data input is transferred to the output. The logic diagram of a 8-line-to-

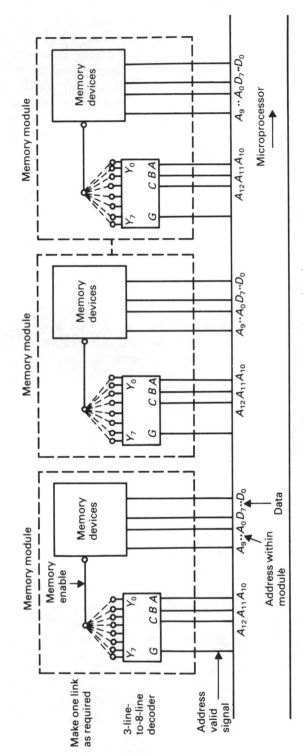

Figure 3.15 Memory module address decoder

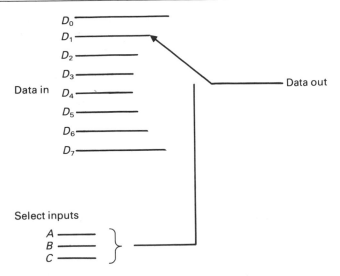

Figure 3.16 Multiplexer

1-line data selector/multiplexer (74LS151) is shown in Fig. 3.17 and its truth table in Table 3.4, where D_0 to D_7 are the data inputs. A single enable input, $\bar{E}$, is shown. Other data selectors include the 74150, which is a 16-line-to-1-line data selector; the 74LS153, a dual (two in a package) 4-line-to-1-line data selector; and 74LS157, a quad (four in a package) 2-line-to-1-line data selector.

Though not its primary design application (which is to select data from several sources and send to one destination), a data selector can be used to implement a combinational function by permanently connecting each data input either to a 0 or a 1 depending upon whether the associated minterm is required in the output function. The first data input is associated with the minterm, $\bar{C}\bar{B}\bar{A}$, the second with $\bar{C}\bar{B}A$, and so on. For example, the previous function:

$$f(C,B,A) = \bar{C}B\bar{A} + C\bar{B}\bar{A} + CBA$$

Table 3.4   Truth table of a 8-line-to-1-line data selector/multiplexer

Inputs				Outputs	
Enable		*Select*			
$\bar{E}$	C	B	A	Y	$\bar{Y}$
1	X	X	X	0	1
0	0	0	0	D_0	$\bar{D}_0$
0	0	0	1	D_1	$\bar{D}_1$
0	0	1	0	D_2	$\bar{D}_2$
0	0	1	1	D_3	$\bar{D}_3$
0	1	0	0	D_4	$\bar{D}_4$
0	1	0	1	D_5	$\bar{D}_5$
0	1	1	0	D_6	$\bar{D}_6$
0	1	1	1	D_7	$\bar{D}_7$

D_n is the nth data input
X = don't care

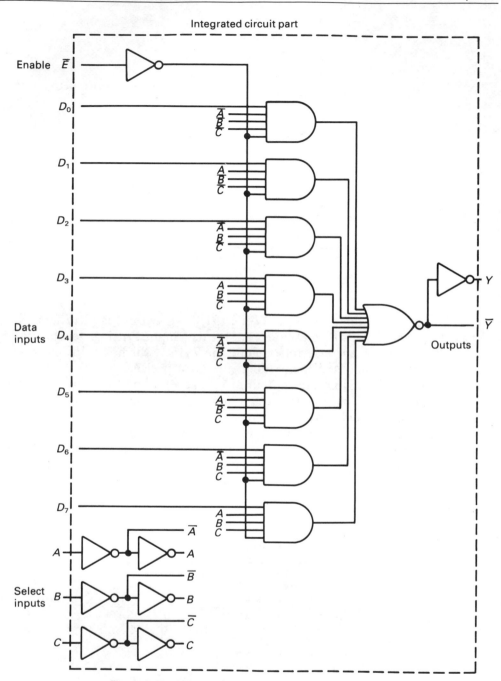

Figure 3.17   8-line-to-1-line data selector/multiplexer

can be implemented using a data selector as shown in Fig. 3.18. The inputs associated with the minterms in the function (2, 4 and 7) are permanently set to 1 and the rest set to 0. If the 74LS151 data selector is used, both the true and inverse functions are available. If a data selector is used having only the inverse output, to obtain the true function, $f = \Sigma\,(2,4,7)$ above, inputs 0,1,3,5 and 6 are set to 1 and the rest are set to 0 because $\bar{f} = \Sigma\,(0,1,3,5,6)$ from Chap. 2, section 2.3.3. Functions with four variables can be implemented with the 8-to-1-line data selector, by applying the fourth variable to selected data inputs instead of permanent logic 1 levels. An extra inverter is required should the fourth variable be complemented in the selected minterm. However, there is often a significant saving in packages by using a data selector rather than basic gates.

A data selector can be used as a memory address decoder. Taking the previous memory module example, in Fig. 3.19 the three memory module address lines connect to the *ABC* select inputs of the decoder and the enable input as before to the address valid line from the microprocessor. The single output of the decoder activates the memory device. The data input corresponding to the address of the module is connected to a permanent 0 (assuming that this activates the memory device) and all other data inputs connect to a permanent 1. Again wire links or switches can be provided on the data inputs for different module addresses.

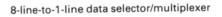

8-line-to-1-line data selector/multiplexer

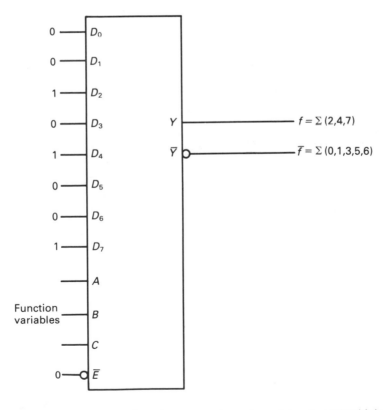

Figure 3.18   Generating a sum-of-product expression using a data selector/multiplexer

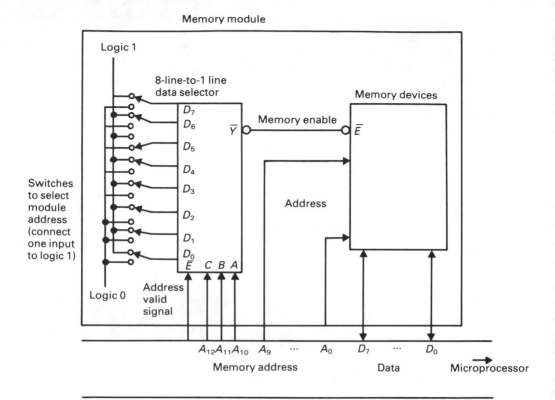

Figure 3.19   Memory module address decoder using data selector

3.3.3 Programmable logic arrays (PLAs)

A *programmable logic array* (PLA) is a logic circuit part containing a number of AND gates and OR gates which can be interconnected internally to implement sum-of-product expressions. Links are provided internally which may be selectively broken at the time of manufacture or subsequently by the user. In the latter case, the links are formed with 'integrated circuit' fuses which can be selectively blown to break the connection, using special PLA programming units. These types of PLAs are known as *field programmable logic arrays* (FPLAs). Once a link is broken, it cannot be re-made.

A logic diagram of a typical FPLA is shown in Fig. 3.20. There are sixteen inputs. Both true and complemented signals are generated from the inputs, each of which is connected via links to the inputs of 48 AND gates. The outputs of these gates connect via links to the inputs of 8 OR gates which generate the 8 outputs of the part. The inverse outputs can also be selected. In the unprogrammed state, all the connections are made, and those which are not required are broken by passing current through the device during a programming sequence. With this particular device, each of the device outputs, F_0 to F_7, can be programmed to any sum-of-product expression each containing up to 48 terms and up to 16 true or inverse variables in each term.

The actual PLA implementation of Fig. 3.20 uses only one line where 32 are indicated into each of the 48 AND gates (48 lines in all) and every true and complement variable connection is made to each line. (The link is a fuse and a diode or transistor; see Chap. 5 for details of diode and transistor logic.) Figure 3.21 shows the possible states for one pair of connections to a line. In the unprogrammed state, both connection links are made. In that case, both the true and complemented variables are applied to the AND gate. Clearly this would result in the AND gate being disenabled. Generally, this state is not used when

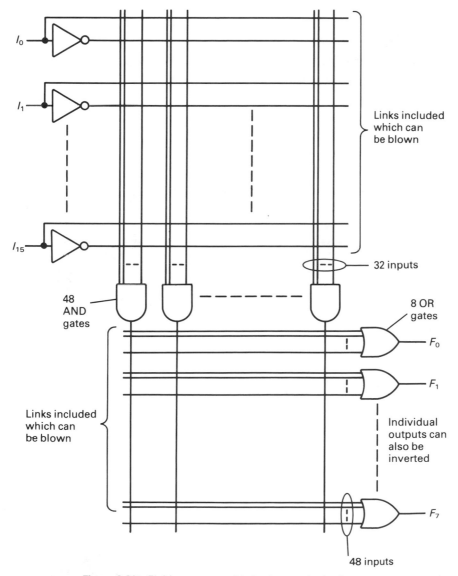

Figure 3.20   Field programmable logic array logic diagram

the device is programmed for use. In Fig. 3.21(b), the true variable is selected. In Fig. 3.21(c), the complement variable is selected. In Fig. 3.21(d), neither variable is selected. This is a 'don't care' condition. During the programming sequence, one of (b), (c) or (d) must be produced for each input of each AND gate. The subsequent OR gate connections are simply left made or broken as required.

The PLA is used for the memory decode function, particularly if the memory module address contains many bits. In fact eight separate address decode functions could be implemented simultaneously with the above PLA,

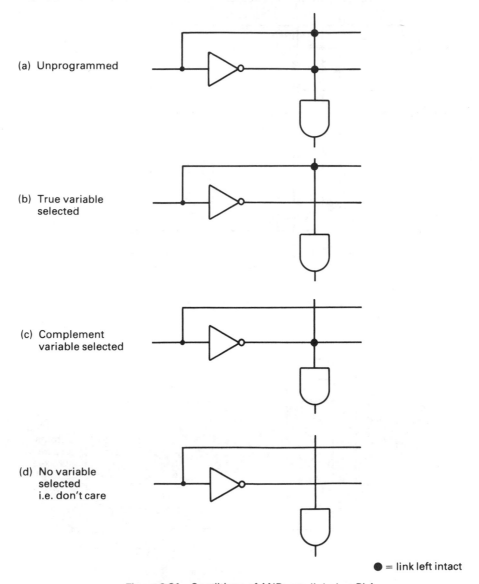

Figure 3.21   Conditions of AND gate links in a PLA

though this would then be sited in one place. Both canonical and non-canonical expressions can be implemented directly. Generally expressions are minimized to non-canonical expressions where possible because the number of gates available within the PLA is limited. For example, the problem in section 3.2.6 could be implemented using a PLA as shown in Fig. 3.22.

3.3.4 Read-only memories (ROMs)

A (semiconductor) integrated circuit memory is a logic part containing a circuit arrangement to maintain one bit of information. The circuit arrangement is repeated many times in the memory to store many bits. The primary use of a

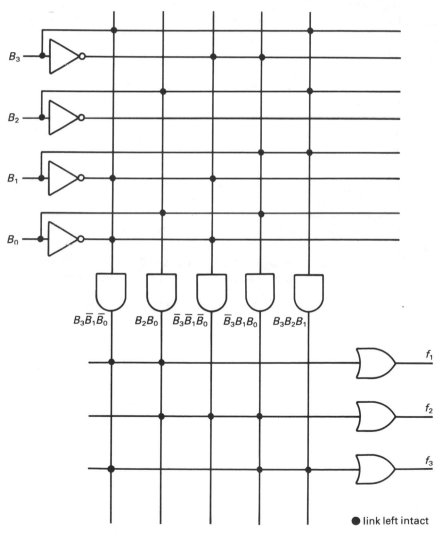

Figure 3.22 PLA solution for problem in section 3.2.6

memory is to store programs and data in a computer system such as a microprocessor system. The bits stored in a semiconductor memory are organized so that one bit or a fixed number of bits (a word) can be accessed at a time. Each bit or word is given an unique identification number known as an *address* as mentioned in section 3.3.1. This address is presented to the memory in order to identify the storage location for extracting the stored information (reading) or for inserting new information (writing). Semiconductor memories are considered in detail in Chap. 9.

One version of semiconductor memory called the *read-only memory* (ROM) has application as a combinational logic circuit. In a read-only memory, the information is defined during manufacture. In a variant of the read-only memory, the *field programmable read-only memory* (FPROM), the pattern may be defined by the user in much the same way as in a FPLA. The read-only memory has address inputs to select a particular memory location, data outputs carrying the information from the selected location, and enable inputs. For example, a read-only memory holding 1024 8-bit words requires a 10-bit address to identify one location (as $2^{10} = 1024$) and 8 data outputs. Typically there are two enable inputs, $\overline{CE}$, a general enable input, and $\overline{OE}$ which activates the data output circuits.

To use the device as a combinational logic circuit implementing a Boolean expression, the address inputs of the memory become the Boolean input variables and the data outputs become the required functions. Consider the previous function:

$$f(A,B,C,D) = \overline{A}BC + \overline{B}\overline{C} + AD$$

This function is described in truth table form in Table 3.5. The function has been expanded into canonical form as this is necessary for ROM implementation. Note that this is different from PLA implementation in which non-canonical form can be implemented. The truth table, if necessary, can be obtained from a Karnaugh map description of the function. The variables A, B, C

Table 3.5   Truth table of function $f = \overline{A}BC + \overline{B}\overline{C} + AD$

D	C	B	A	Function
0	0	0	0	1
0	0	0	1	1
0	0	1	0	0
0	0	1	1	0
0	1	0	0	0
0	1	0	1	0
0	1	1	0	1
0	1	1	1	0
1	0	0	0	1
1	0	0	1	1
1	0	1	0	0
1	0	1	1	1
1	1	0	0	0
1	1	0	1	1
1	1	1	0	1
1	1	1	1	1

and D specify the addresses of memory locations. The function output is the data at the addressed locations which can be programmed into the device. In our case, only one bit of each word is required to store the value of the function and only the first sixteen words of the memory, as there are only four variables A, B, C and D. Naturally, more complicated expressions can be realized, in particular, multiple independent expressions. Figure 3.23 shows a read-only memory solution for the three-output problem in section 3.2.6. Sixteen words each of 3 bits are necessary in the memory. A 16 word × 4-bit memory could be used with one bit in each location not used. (Memory devices generally have 1-, 4- or 8-bit words.)

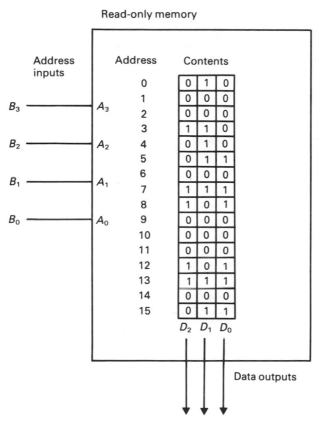

Figure 3.23 Using a ROM as a combinational circuit

3.4 BINARY ADDITION CIRCUITS

Binary arithmetic was introduced in Chap. 1, being fundamental to digital computers. Now we shall study the basic logic circuits that perform binary addition. Binary addition circuits can be combinational circuits because the binary sum output depends only on the values of input operands at that instant and not on any past values. Some very early binary addition circuits shared one internal circuit over successive digit additions, and therefore the outputs of the circuit would depend upon the previous digit additions. This process is sequential in nature internally such an adder circuit is classified as a sequential logic circuit. Sequential or serial adders are not considered here.

3.4.1 Half adder

As mentioned in Chap. 1, section 1.3.1, the circuit to add together two binary digits is known as a *half adder*. The half adder circuit accepts two inputs, A and B, and generates two outputs, SUM and CARRY according to Table 3.6. The Boolean expression for SUM and CARRY can be derived from this truth table, by examining the occurrences of 1's in the functions. For SUM there are two occurrences, when $A = 0$, $B = 1$ and when $A = 1$, $B = 0$. Therefore the SUM function is:

$$SUM = \bar{A}B + A\bar{B}$$

Similarly the CARRY function is obtained as:

$$CARRY = AB$$

The SUM function can be realized with two-level AND-OR gates and the CARRY function with a single AND gate as shown in Fig. 3.24. The SUM function, $\bar{A}B + A\bar{B}$, is the exclusive-OR function, and a single exclusive-OR gate could be used. Alternatively, the functions can be implemented using NAND gates as shown with NAND gate symbols in Fig. 3.25(a) and with mixed logic representation in Fig. 3.25(b).

Table 3.6   Half adder truth table

Inputs		Outputs	
A	B	SUM	CARRY
0	0	0	0
0	1	1	0
1	0	1	0
1	1	0	1

3.4.2 Full adder

A *full adder* is also mentioned in section 1.3.1 as a circuit to add two binary digits A and B together with a 'carry-in' from a previous addition. This addition is necessary when two binary words are added together. A full adder has three inputs, A, B and 'CARRY IN' (abbreviated here to C_{in}), and two outputs, SUM and 'CARRY OUT' (abbreviated to C_{out}). The truth table of the full adder is shown in Table 3.7.

From this truth table, we can deduce the Boolean expressions for both

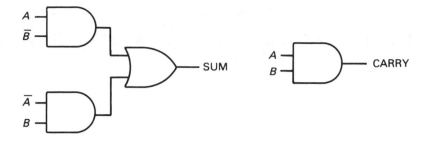

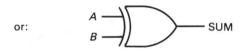

Figure 3.24   Half adder circuit

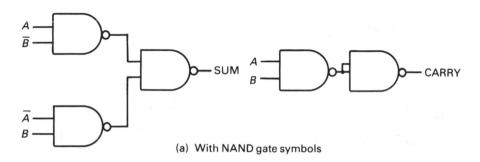

(a) With NAND gate symbols

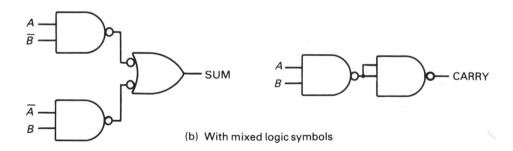

(b) With mixed logic symbols

Figure 3.25   Half adder using NAND gates

SUM and C_{out} as:

$$\text{SUM} = \overline{A}\overline{B}C_{\text{in}} + \overline{A}B\overline{C}_{\text{in}} + A\overline{B}\overline{C}_{in} + ABC_{\text{in}}$$
$$C_{\text{out}} = \overline{A}BC_{\text{in}} + A\overline{B}C_{\text{in}} + AB\overline{C}_{\text{in}} + ABC_{\text{in}}$$

The C_{out} function can be simplified to:

$$C_{\text{out}} = AB + AC_{\text{in}} + BC_{\text{in}}$$

Both SUM and C_{out} can be implemented with two level gating as shown in Fig. 3.26, assuming the complements of the input signals are available.

Table 3.7   Full adder truth table

	Inputs			Outputs	
A	*B*	C_{in}		SUM	C_{out}
0	0	0		0	0
0	0	1		1	0
0	1	0		1	0
0	1	1		0	1
1	0	0		1	0
1	0	1		0	1
1	1	0		0	1
1	1	1		1	1

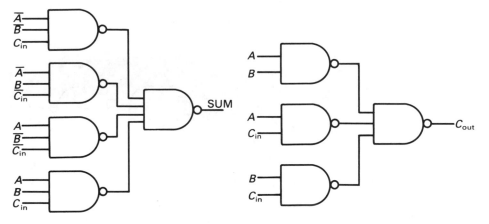

(a) With NAND gate symbols

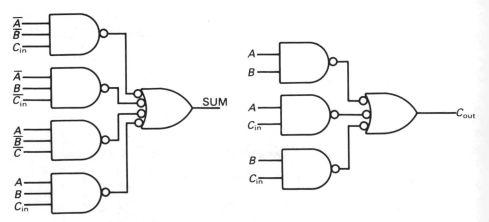

(b) With mixed logic symbols

Figure 3.26   Full adder using NAND gates

A full adder can also be formed from two half adders. Starting from the basic full adder expressions, we can derive:

$$
\begin{aligned}
\text{SUM} &= \bar{A}\bar{B}C_{\text{in}} + \bar{A}B\bar{C}_{\text{in}} + A\bar{B}\bar{C}_{\text{in}} + ABC_{\text{in}} \\
&= C_{\text{in}}(\bar{A}\bar{B} + AB) + \bar{C}_{\text{in}}(\bar{A}B + A\bar{B}) \\
&= C_{\text{in}}(\overline{\bar{A}B + A\bar{B}}) + \bar{C}_{\text{in}}(\bar{A}B + A\bar{B}) \\
&= C_{\text{in}}\,(\overline{A \oplus B}) + \bar{C}_{\text{in}}(A \oplus B) \\
&= C_{\text{in}} \oplus (A \oplus B)
\end{aligned}
$$

where $\oplus$ is the exclusive-OR (not equivalence) half adder SUM output function. From the original C_{out} expression, we can derive:

$$
\begin{aligned}
C_{\text{out}} &= \bar{A}BC_{\text{in}} + A\bar{B}C_{\text{in}} + AB\bar{C}_{\text{in}} + ABC_{\text{in}} \\
&= C_{\text{in}}(\bar{A}B + A\bar{B}) + AB(\bar{C}_{\text{in}} + C_{\text{in}}) \\
&= C_{\text{in}}(\bar{A}B + A\bar{B}) + AB \\
&= C_{\text{in}}\,(A \oplus B) + AB
\end{aligned}
$$

C_{out} can be obtained by 'ORing' together the CARRY outputs of both half adders. Hence a full adder can be implemented as shown in Fig. 3.27. Though a well quoted design solution for a full adder, it has the major disadvantage that there are several levels of gate. For example, if each half adder requires three levels, the overall number of levels is seven.

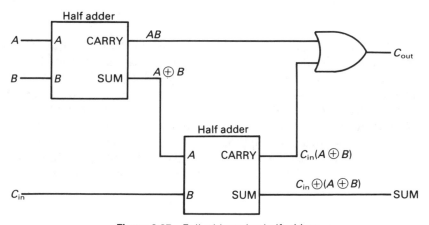

Figure 3.27 Full adder using half adders

3.4.3 Parallel adder

A circuit arrangement to add two binary words with all the bits of the words presented and processed together (i.e. in parallel) is known as a *parallel adder*. Figure 3.28 shows the general arrangement of a parallel adder using one full adder for each pair of binary digits. The two numbers to be added together, A and B have digits, $A_n \cdots A_1$ and $B_n \cdots B_1$ respectively. There are n full adders and each binary number has n digits. (In this section and the next section, the subscripts begin at 1 rather than the more conventional 0 to clarify the subsequent algebra.)

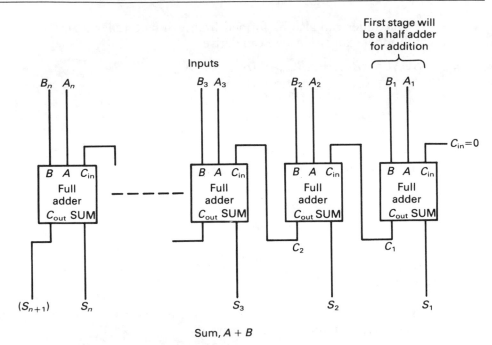

First stage will
be a half adder
for addition

Figure 3.28   Parallel adder

The first pair of digits, A_1 and B_1, enter the first full adder to produce the first sum digit, S_1 and a carry output, C_1. The carry input to the first full adder is set to a 0. The second pair of digits, A_2 and B_2 enter the second full adder together with the carry output from the first stage to produce the second sum digit, S_2, and the second carry output, C_2. This arrangement is continued for subsequent pairs of digits, resulting in the required sum digits being produced, $S_{n+1} \cdots S_1$. The final sum digit, S_{n+1}, is obtained from the carry output from the final state. (Note that the addition of two n-bit numbers leads to a possible $(n+1)$-bit answer.) This parallel adder is an example of an iterative logic circuit, each iterative cell of the circuit being a full adder. Parallel adders such as the above are available as complete parts (e.g. 74LS83 4-bit full adder).

Since the first stage $C_{in} = 0$, the first stage could be a half adder. However, a full adder in the first stage allows for subtraction. Subtraction using 2's complement arithmetic is done by adding the 2's complement negative of one operand (B), which can be accomplished with the parallel adder, by presenting the complement of B, i.e. $\bar{B}_n \cdots \bar{B}_1$ to the adder rather than $B_n \cdots B_1$. Simultaneously a 1 is applied to the first stage C_{in} input. Using a parallel adder for subtraction in this way is shown in Fig. 3.29 which follows from being able to produce the 2's complement of a number by inverting the digits and adding one. Hence the adder is easily modified into an adder/subtractor.

The parallel adder implements the addition directly as one would add binary numbers manually. The first digits are added, then the second digits with the carry from the first stage, continuing with subsequent stages in sequence. The second sum digit cannot be produced until the first carry digit has been

Inputs

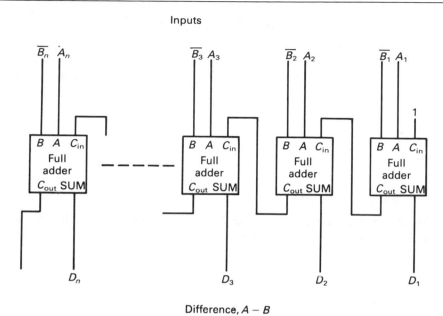

Difference, $A - B$

Figure 3.29 Subtraction using a parallel adder

produced. Similarly, the third sum digit cannot be produced until the second carry digit has been produced, and hence after the first carry digit has been produced. Therefore the overall addition time to produce the complete sum word will be the summation of each stage addition time, as the addition of each stage must occur separately in order. Hence the overall time is given by:

$(n) \times (C_{out}$ propagation delay time of one full adder)

where there are n digits in each binary number and n full adders. If each full adder has three levels of gating between the inputs and the carry output, and each gate used in the full adders has a propagation delay time of t seconds, the total time taken for the parallel adder to operate is:

$(n) \times (3t)$ seconds

Common logic gates such as TTL gates operate with propagation delay times the order of 5 to 20 ns. Using 20 ns gates, a 16-bit parallel addition would take 960 ns.

3.4.4 Carry-look-ahead adder

The aim of the carry-look-ahead adder is to increase the speed of operation of parallel addition by eliminating the 'ripple' carry between stages in the parallel adder. The full adders are still used, but separate logic is provided at each stage to generate each carry-in signal independently of the previous stages.

Table 3.8 shows the truth table of a full adder with two new output terms called *carry generate*, C_g, and *carry propagate*, C_p. C_g indicates that a C_{out} signal is generated by the adder stage itself, i.e. by A and B, which occurs when both A and B are a 1. C_p indicates that the value of C_{in} (1 or 0) is passed to C_{out} due to either A or B being 1. With the variables defined as described, we can see that:

$$C_g \quad = AB$$

and

$$C_p \quad = A \oplus B$$

and

$$C_{out} \quad = C_g + C_p C_{in}$$

An alternative definition for the carry propagate term includes the situation when both A and $B = 1$, overlapping the carry generate function. This definition leads to the same C_{out} and C_g functions but a simpler C_p given by:

$$C_p = A + B$$

The above expressions can be verified from the Karnaugh map of C_{out} shown in Fig. 3.30.

Table 3.8   Truth table for carry propagate and carry generate terms

Inputs			Outputs		New terms	
A	B	C_{in}	SUM	C_{out}	C_p	C_g
0	0	0	0	0	0	0
0	0	1	1	0	0	0
0	1	0	1	0	1	0
0	1	1	0	1	1	0
1	0	0	1	0	1	0
1	0	1	0	1	1	0
1	1	0	0	1	0	1
1	1	1	1	1	0	1

The carry generate and propagate terms are given by the inputs A and B of the stage. The C_{out} equation relates the carry out of the stage in terms of carry generate and carry propagate and from this, we can obtain the following carry out equations for each stage of a parallel adder:

For the first stage: $C_1 = C_{g1} + C_{p1} C_{in}$ (1)
For the second stage: $C_2 = C_{g2} + C_{p2} C_1$ (2)
For the third stage: $C_3 = C_{g3} + C_{p3} C_2$ (3)

.

.

.

For the final stage: $C_n = C_{gn} + C_{pn} C_{n-1}$ (*n*)

where C_{in} is the carry in of the first stage. $C_{in} = 0$ for addition. C_1 is the carry out of the first stage and carry in of the second stage, C_2 is the carry out of the second stage and carry in of the third stage, C_3 is the carry out of the third stage and carry in of the fourth stage, etc.

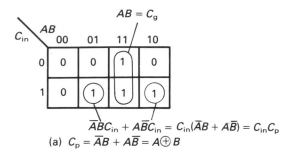

$$\overline{A}BC_{in} + A\overline{B}C_{in} = C_{in}(\overline{A}B + A\overline{B}) = C_{in}C_p$$

(a) $C_p = \overline{A}B + A\overline{B} = A \oplus B$

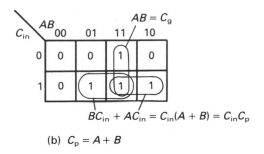

$$BC_{in} + AC_{in} = C_{in}(A + B) = C_{in}C_p$$

(b) $C_p = A + B$

Figure 3.30   Full adder C_{out} function on Karnaugh map showing C_g and C_p

Substituting (1) into (2) we get:

$$C_2 = C_{g2} + C_{p2}(C_{g1} + C_{p1}C_{in})$$

and then into (3):

$$C_3 = C_{g3} + C_{p3}(C_{g2} + C_{p2}(C_{g1} \mid C_{p1}C_{in}))$$

Continuing, we get an expression for the ith stage carry out as:

$$C_i = C_{gi} + C_{pi}(C_{gi-1} + C_{pi-1}(C_{gi-2} + C_{pi-2}(C_{gi-3} + C_{pi-3}(C_{gi-4} \cdots + C_{p1}C_{in})\cdots)$$

where

$$C_{gi} = A_iB_i$$
$$C_{pi} = A \oplus B \text{ or } A+B$$

and A_i, B_i are the inputs of the ith stage. This expression can be expanded into:

$$C_i = C_{gi} + C_{pi}C_{gi-1} + C_{pi}C_{pi-1}C_{gi-2} + C_{pi}C_{pi-1}C_{pi-2}C_{gi-3} + C_{pi}C_{pi-1}$$
$$C_{p-2}C_{pi-3}C_{gi-4} \cdots + (C_{pi} \cdots C_{p2}C_{g1})+(C_{pi} \cdots C_{p1}C_{in})$$

Consequently, the carry output for each stage can be generated from the C_g's and C_p's which are themselves generated from the inputs only. The logic required only needs these inputs with no ripple carry to slow the operation. The general scheme is shown in Fig. 3.31. The first three stages of carry out circuitry using AND and OR gates are shown in Fig. 3.32. The carry-look-ahead circuitry replaces the ripple carry connections of the parallel adder. Each carry generate

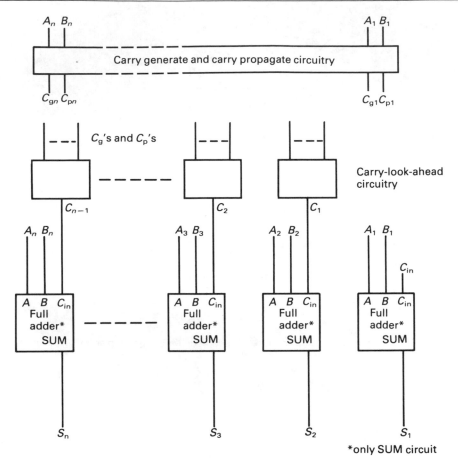

Figure 3.31   Carry-look-ahead parallel adder

term is produced with one AND gate and each carry propagate term is produced with one OR (or exclusive-OR) gate, resulting in one level of gating to generate these terms. The carry out terms can then be generated with an extra two levels of gating.

Normally, because of the considerable amount of logic required at the higher stages, not all stages are provided with true carry-look-ahead. One approach is to group, say, four stages together with carry-look-ahead within the group. The carry out from the group can be generated with look-ahead circuitry and connected to the carry in of the next higher group. Thus there is a form of 'ripple' carry between groups. This technique is employed in the 74LS283 '4-bit binary full adder with fast carry' logic part.

The ripple carry arrangement between stages can be replaced by group carry-look-ahead circuitry. The 'carry in' to each group is produced from 'group carry propagate' and 'group carry generate' signals from the carry-look-ahead adder groups. Each 'group carry generate' signal indicates that a carry is generated by the group, and the 'group carry propagate' signal indicates that a carry is propagated by the group. This technique is used in the 74S182 look-

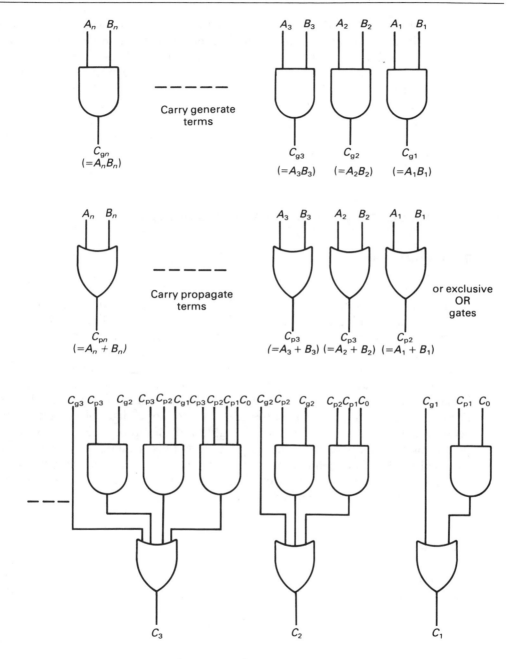

Figure 3.32 Carry-look-ahead logic

ahead carry generator and 74LS181 arithmetic unit combination.

The outputs of a parallel adder depend upon the combination of inputs applied at that instant and hence the combinational implementations using PLAs or ROMs are possible. A single PLA solution requires (preferably) the minimized sum-of-product Boolean expressions for each output. We can develop these expressions from the look-ahead equations, by substituting the carry generate and propagate expressions (AB and $A+B$ respectively) into the carry out expressions and substituting the result into sum expressions. However, the number of terms in higher expressions become excessive for a single PLA solution (see Problem 3.16). A ROM solution requires the result of every possible combination of input digits to be stored in the ROM. A 4-bit adder could be implemented using a ROM with $256(2^8)$ locations addressed by the two 4-bit operands (8 address bits).

3.5   BINARY MULTIPLICATION BY COMBINATIONAL LOGIC

3.5.1   Binary multiplication

As a further example of combinational logic design, let us consider binary multiplication by combinational logic. We shall assume that the numbers to be multiplied are positive binary numbers. The 'paper and pencil' method of binary multiplication of two unsigned binary numbers, A and B, is shown in Fig. 3.33. The traditional method to implement this multiplication is to use a parallel adder to successively add A to an accumulating sum when the appropriate bit of B is a 1. Starting with the least significant bit of B and with the accumulating sum initialized to zero, A is added to the accumulating sum if the B digit is a 1 but not if the B digit is a 0. Then, either A is shifted one digit place left or the accumulating sum is shifted one place right, and the process repeated with the next B digit, until the final product is generated. This is a lengthy process. Since the final product is dependent only on the values of A and B at the instant they are applied, there must be a purely combinational logic solution. Here we will consider three combinational logic methods.

3.5.2   Carry-save method

The carry-save method is used to add more than two numbers together in a way that ripple carries are eliminated, except in a final parallel addition. It is

```
A   110101
B   101011
    ───────
    110101
   110101
  000000
 110101
000000
110101
───────────
100011100111
```

Figure 3.33   Multiplication of two 6-bit numbers

particularly applicable to binary multiplication, though it can be applied whenever several numbers are to be added together. We use the fact that a full adder actually adds together three digits, which for the purposes of parallel addition, are called A, B and C_{in}, but it could be any three digits. Applying the carry-save method to the above binary multiplication of the numbers A and B, first we generate all the numbers to be added together. The digits of these numbers are given in Fig. 3.34(a) where A_n and B_n are the nth digits of A and B. Each of the above terms can be produced using AND gates.

Then, the numbers to be added together are divided into groups of three. We shall take the first three numbers of the six into one group and the remaining three numbers into the second group. The numbers in each group are added simultaneously using one full adder for each triplet of bits in each group without the carry being passed from one stage to the next. This process results in two numbers being generated for each group, namely, a sum word and a carry word, as shown in Fig. 3.34(b). Each carry word is shown moved one place right to give it the correct significance. The true sum of the three numbers in each case could be obtained by adding together the sum and carry words. The final product is the summation of Sum 1, Carry 1, Sum 2 and Carry 2. Taking three of these numbers, the carry-save process is repeated to produce Sum 3 and Carry 3 as shown in Fig. 3.34(c). Sum 2 is shown moved three places right to give the number the correct significance. The process is repeated taking Sum 3, Carry 3 and Carry 2 to produce Sum 4 and Carry 4 as shown in Fig. 3.34(d). Finally, the two numbers, Sum 4 and Carry 4, are added together using a parallel adder (Fig. 3.34(e)). To eliminate any ripple carry delay, the final parallel adder can use a carry-look-ahead scheme.

The method requires a considerable amount of logic but results in a substantial increase in speed of operation. In the above example, the traditional method could use one 6-bit parallel adder for five sequential additions plus an accumulator for storing the intermediate results. The carry-save method could be implemented as shown in Fig. 3.35 which would lead to the following operating delay:

> one AND gate delay

plus

> three full adder delays

plus

> one 8-bit carry-look-ahead adder delay

3.5.3 Binary multiplication using iterative arrays

An array of iterative cells can be used for the design of a binary multiplier. This approach is particularly suitable for integrated circuit construction. To take an example of the method, consider the multiplication of two 4-bit numbers, A

$$A_5B_0 \ A_4B_0 \ A_3B_0 \ A_2B_0 \ A_1B_0 \ A_0B_0$$
$$A_5B_1 \ A_4B_1 \ A_3B_1 \ A_2B_1 \ A_1B_1 \ A_0B_0$$
$$A_5B_2 \ A_4B_2 \ A_3B_2 \ A_2B_2 \ A_1B_2 \ A_0B_2$$
$$A_5B_3 \ A_4B_3 \ A_3B_3 \ A_2B_3 \ A_1B_3 \ A_0B_3$$
$$A_5B_4 \ A_4B_4 \ A_3B_4 \ A_2B_4 \ A_1B_4 \ A_0B_4$$
$$A_5B_5 \ A_4B_5 \ A_3B_5 \ A_2B_5 \ A_1B_5 \ A_0B_5$$

(a) Step 1 Generation of partial product digits

	110101		110101
Group 1	110101	Group 2	000000
	000000		110101
Sum 1	01011111	Sum 2	11100001
Carry 1	01000000	Carry 2	00101000

(b) Step 2 Carry-save addition of two three-word groups

Sum 1	01011111
Carry 1	01000000
Sum 2	11100001
Sum 3	11100010111
Carry 3	00010010000

(c) Step 3 Carry-save addition of three words from step 2

Sum 3	11100010111
Carry 3	00010010000
Carry 2	00101000
Sum 4	11011000111
Carry 4	01000100000

(d) Step 4 Carry- save addition of two words from step 3
      and one word from step 2

Sum 4	11011000111
Carry 4	01000100000
Final sum	100011100111

(e) Step 5 Final normal addition of two words from step 4

Figure 3.34   Multiplication of two 6-bit numbers by the carry-save method

and B, as set out in Fig. 3.36. The summation of the partial products is done by cells, each of which performs the following three-bit addition:

$$A_iB_j \, (+) \, K \, (+) \, M$$

where A_i, B_j, K and M are inputs to the cell. A_i and B_j are the *i*th and *j*th digits of the numbers A and B respectively. The AND operation with these digits is performed within the cell. The sumbol (+) represents binary addition and the three-bit addition is simply the full adder function. Two outputs are generated, SUM and CARRY.

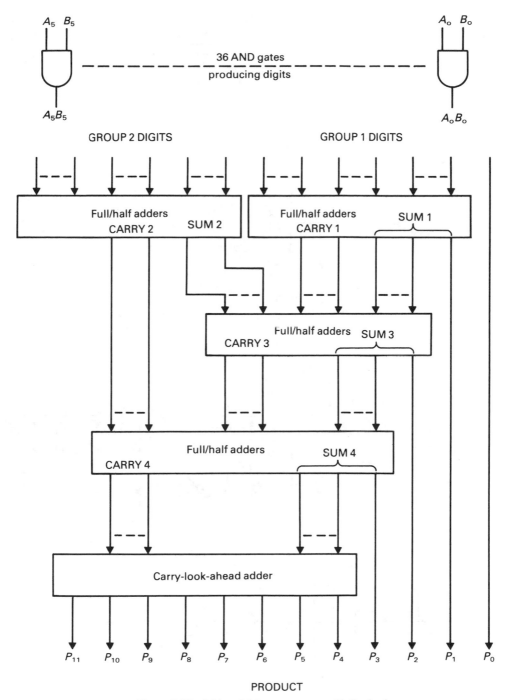

Figure 3.35   6-bit × 6-bit carry-save multiplier logic

The cells are interconnected as shown in Fig. 3.37. Each cell has been drawn for convenience with the A and B inputs at the top corners of the cell, the

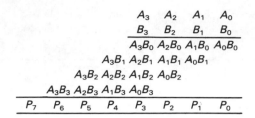

Figure 3.36   Multiplication of two 4-bit numbers

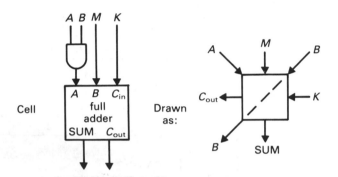

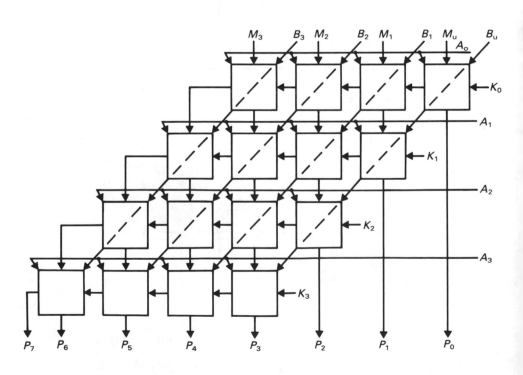

Figure 3.37   4-bit × 4-bit array multiplier

M input at the middle of the top and the K input at the middle of the right side. The B input also passes through, leaving at the bottom left corner to connect to other cells. In this application, $M_3M_2M_1M_0$ and $K_3K_2K_1K_0$ are set to 0000.

Each cell performs the summation of three digits, i.e. one partial product digit (A_iB_j), the output of another cell of the same significance but immediately preceding (partial product) word, and a carry output from the cell one significant place lower of the same word. The resultant sum is passed to the next cell of the same significance but one word further in the list of words to be added together. The carry output of the cell passes to the next cell of the same word but one greater in significance.

The time for the multiplier to produce the final product is given by:

$$10 \times \text{(time for one cell to produce valid summation)}$$

or for the multiplication of two n-digit numbers:

$$(3n - 2) \times \text{(time for one cell to produce valid summation)}$$

3.5.4 Simultaneous multiplier

The simultaneous multiplier implements multiplication by considering the multiplication functions as a normal combinational logic function, i.e. the outputs are given by the particular combination of inputs applied at that instant. The input combinations and corresponding output values can be listed by truth tables from which simplified Boolean expressions can be developed. This approach is only practical for numbers with a few bits. Take, for example, the multiplication of two 2-bit numbers, A_1A_0 and B_1B_0. The resultant product is the four-digit word, say $P_3P_2P_1P_0$. There are seven different valid values of the product word dependent upon A and B, which are given in Table 3.9. From this

Table 3.9   Truth table of a 2-bit $\times$ 2-bit multiplier

Inputs				Product			
B_1	B_0	A_1	A_0	P_3	P_2	P_1	P_0
0	0	0	0	0	0	0	0
0	0	0	1	0	0	0	0
0	0	1	0	0	0	0	0
0	0	1	1	0	0	0	0
0	1	0	0	0	0	0	0
0	1	0	1	0	0	0	1
0	1	1	0	0	0	1	0
0	1	1	1	0	0	1	1
1	0	0	0	0	0	0	0
1	0	0	1	0	0	1	0
1	0	1	0	0	1	0	0
1	0	1	1	0	1	1	0
1	1	0	0	0	0	0	0
1	1	0	1	0	0	1	1
1	1	1	0	0	1	1	0
1	1	1	1	1	0	0	1

table, we can derive the Boolean expressions for each output by plotting the 1's on Karnaugh maps. The minimal expressions for the product digits are:

$$P_0 = A_0 B_0$$
$$P_1 = \bar{A}_1 A_0 B_1 + A_1 A_0 \bar{B}_0 + A_1 \bar{B}_1 B_0 + A_1 \bar{A}_0 B_0$$
$$P_2 = A_1 \bar{A}_0 B_1 + A_1 B_1 \bar{B}_0$$
$$P_3 = A_1 A_0 B_1 B_0$$

The functions can be realized with two-level logic assuming the complements are available, or alternatively by PLA or ROM.

3.5.5 Two's complement multipliers

We introduced the multiplier to show combinational logic design. However, it should be noted that both the multiplier and multiplicand are considered as positive numbers. If the numbers employ the 2's complement notation, there are four possible combinations of A and B, namely:

(a) Both *A* and *B* positive
This produces the correct result.

(b)   *A* positive and *B* negative
Here we obtain:

$$A(2^n - B) = 2^n A - AB$$

(Adjacent terms are multiplied, not logically AND'ed.) The correct answer is $2^{2n} - AB$, i.e. the negative representation of AB to $2n$ digits.

One correction process is to add the difference between the required result and that obtained, ie. add $2^{2n} - 2^n A$ to $2^n A - AB$ to obtain $2^{2n} - AB$. Since $2^{2n} - 2^n A$ is the negative representation of $2^n A$ to $2n$ digits, we could subtract $2^n A$ from the multiplier result.

An alternative correction process is to 'sign extend' *B* by *n* digits, i.e. produce $2^{2n} - B$, before multiplying the numbers. Then we obtain:

$$A(2^{2n} - B) = 2^{2n} A - AB$$

The term $2^{2n} A = 2^{2n}(A-1) + 2^{2n}$. Therefore we obtain $2^{2n}(A-1) + 2^{2n} - AB$. $2^{2n}(A-1)$ is beyond the range of numbers in the computation, and therefore can be ignored, leaving the correct result, $2^{2n} - AB$.

(c) *A* negative and *B* positive
Here we obtain:

$$(2^n - A)B = 2^n - AB$$

The correct answer is $2^{2n} - AB$. One of the two correction factors in case (b) could be applied, with *A* and *B* transposed.

(d) Both A and B negative

Here we obtain:

$$(2^n - A)(2^n - B) = 2^{2n} - 2^nA - 2^nB + AB$$

The correct answer is AB. In this case, we can ignore 2^{2n} as it is outside the range of numbers in the computation, leaving a correction factor of $2^nA + 2^nB$ which could be added to the result. Alternatively, we could sign extend A to get:

$$(2^{2n} - A)(2^n - B) = 2^{3n} - 2^{2n}B - 2^nA + AB$$

Removing the first two numbers which are out of range of the computation, we get $-2^nA + AB$. This can be corrected to AB by adding 2^nA.

Note that in each case, the sign of the multipler and multiplicand need to be examined before any correction process is performed. The reader is referred to [2] for a description of another method of signed multiplication known as Booth's algorithm.

REFERENCES

1. *The TTL Data Book for Design Engineers* (6th European ed.). Dallas, Texas: Texas Instruments, Inc., 1983.
2. Lewin, D., *Theory and Design of Digital Computers.* London: Nelson, 1972.

PROBLEMS

3.1   Design a logic circuit to realize the function $f = AB + ACD + BCD$ using NAND gates.

3.2   Repeat Problem 3.1 using NOR gates.

3.3   Using the formal method described in section 3.2.6, derive the Boolean expressions to realize the following functions to enable greatest gate sharing:

$$f_1 = \Sigma(0,1,2,3,6,9,11)$$
$$f_2 = \Sigma(0,1,6,8,9)$$
$$f_3 = \Sigma(2,3,8,9,11)$$

Draw a gate realization.

3.4   Design an iterative logic circuit which detects when all of 32 data inputs are set to a logic 0.

3.5   A logic circuit accepts two 3-bit numbers and generates a logic 1 output only when the two 3-bit numbers applied to the circuit are equal. Design a two-level realization assuming that the complements of the inputs are available.

3.6 Repeat Problem 3.5 using an iterative logic circuit arrangement.

3.7 Design a circuit free of static hazards to implement the function $f = \overline{B}\overline{C}\overline{D} + AB\overline{C} + C\overline{D}$.

3.8 A logic circuit accepts two 3-bit positive numbers and generates a logic 1 output only when one 3-bit number is greater than the another 3-bit number. Design a two-level logic circuit realization assuming that the complements of the inputs are available.

3.9 Design a two-level combinational logic circuit which will produce a 1 only when the number of 1's in a set of three input variables *A, B* and *C* is even (i.e. a parity checker). The complements of the inputs are available.

3.10 A *majority* gate is a digital circuit whose output is a 1 if the majority of the inputs are a 1, otherwise the output is a 0. Design logic circuits for a 3-input majority gate and a 5-input majority gate.

3.11 The *excess-three* code, used to represent decimal digits, is a 4-bit code similar to binary code except that each code has a binary value three greater than the decimal number it represents. For example, the excess-three code for the binary number 0101 (5) is 1000 (8).

  (a) Design a logic circuit which will convert a 4-bit binary code to the equivalent 4-bit excess-three code. The binary codes 1010 to 1111 inclusive can be considered as don't cares.
  (b) Design a logic circuit which will produce a 1 only when the four output variables form a code which is not an excess-three code representing any of the decimal digits 0 to 9.

3.12 Design a 4-bit binary to Gray code converter using two-level logic.

3.13 Realize the functions in Problem 3.3 using a 4-line-to-16-line decoder and NAND gates.

3.14 Realize the functions in Problem 3.3 using a PLA.

3.15 A priority encoder logic circuit has eight inputs and produces three outputs according to Table 3.10. Obtain the minimal Boolean expression for each output.

Table 3.10 Priority encoder logic circuit truth table

Inputs								Outputs		
B_7	B_6	B_5	B_4	B_3	B_2	B_1	B_0	D_2	D_1	D_0
0	0	0	0	0	0	0	X	0	0	0
0	0	0	0	0	0	1	X	0	0	1
0	0	0	0	0	1	X	X	0	1	0
0	0	0	0	1	X	X	X	0	1	1
0	0	0	1	X	X	X	X	1	0	0
0	0	1	X	X	X	X	X	1	0	1
0	1	X	X	X	X	X	X	1	1	0
1	X	X	X	X	X	X	X	1	1	1

X = don't care

3.16 Develop sum-of-product expressions from the carry-look-ahead equations to implement the first three stages of a parallel adder using a PLA.

3.17 Devise a logic scheme to multiply two 8-bit binary numbers using the carry-save technique.

Sequential Circuit Design

4.1 SYNCHRONOUS AND ASYNCHRONOUS SEQUENTIAL CIRCUITS

In Chap. 3, we noted that combinational logic circuits have output values dependent upon the values of the input variables at a particular instant. For example, an AND gate has an output value of 1 only when at that instant the inputs are all at a 1. When the output depends upon not only the present values of the inputs but also on the past values of the inputs and outputs, the circuit is called a *sequential logic circuit*. Therefore sequential circuits must be capable of remembering information about the previous values.

Sequential circuits can exist in one of defined number of *states* and can change from one state to another state when new input values are presented to the circuit. The states are presented by variables from which the outputs are derived. It may be that the output and state variables are the same, which is the case for all sequential circuits described in this chapter. However, this correspondence does not always apply (see Chap. 12).

There are two classes of sequential circuit:

(i) Synchronous sequential logic circuit
(ii) Asynchronous sequential logic circuit.

A *synchronous sequential logic circuit* is one in which all changes in state (and output) are initiated directly by a clock signal applied to the circuit. The clock signal is a logic signal which changes from 0 to 1 and from 1 to 0 at fixed intervals. One type of clock transition (either 0 to 1 or 1 to 0) normally activates state and output changes.

An *asynchronous sequential logic circuit* is one in which the changes in state (and output) occur after inputs change and the changes do not depend upon an additional clock signal. In an asynchronous sequential logic circuit, changes in more than one output do not necessarily occur simultaneously. Changes in outputs may depend upon other output changes and propagation delays will occur.

Many digital systems are made to be synchronous in nature, for example a digital computer overall, though there may be particular instances of asynchronous operation internally. To create a synchronous system, a repetitive clock signal must be generated.

4.2 FLIP-FLOPS

The basic sequential logic circuit is the *flip-flop*. The flip-flop is used as the logic storage device in more complex sequential circuits. Flip-flops have two or more inputs dependent upon the type of flip-flop, and one or two outputs, Q and $\bar{Q}$. When the flip-flop is operating normally, $\bar{Q}$ always takes on the inverse logic value of Q, i.e. if $Q = 0$, $\bar{Q} = 1$ and if $\bar{Q} = 1$, $Q = 0$. The outputs remain permanently in a 0 or 1 state until new input values are applied. Then the output may 'flip' to a 1 if originally at a 0 or 'flop' to a 0 if originally at a 1 or remain at the original state.

There are three fundamental types of flip-flops, the *R–S flip-flop* the *J–K flip-flop* and the *D-type flip-flop*. The letters in the names are derived from the letters identifying the inputs.

4.2.1 *R–S* flip-flop

The R–S flip-flop has two basic inputs, the R input and the S input, abbreviated from reset and set. The R (reset) input is used to make the Q output become a 0 while the S (set) input is used to make the Q output become a 1. Just as a combinational logic circuit such as an AND gate can be described by a truth table, the operation of a flip-flop can be described by a truth table. The truth table of the R–S flip-flop is shown in Fig. 4.1(a). R–S flip-flops can be synchronous and incorporate an additional *clock* input for synchronizing output changes, or they can be asynchronous without the extra clock input. The truth table is the same in both cases, though in the synchronous flip-flop, the stated outputs are not attained until an activating clock transition has occurred.

It is necessary to describe present and past values in a sequential circuit such as flip-flop. We shall do this by appending the variable name with a subscript $+$ to indicate the value after new inputs have been applied (including the clock in synchronous flip-flops), otherwise the past value (before the clock has been activated in synchronous flip-flops) is assumed. Therefore Q_+ is the Q output after the stated inputs are applied, including the clock if present, while Q is the Q output before the stated inputs are applied. X marks an undefined output condition. In the R–S flip-flop, there is an undefined output when $R = S$ 1, an invalid combination of input values. Note that X is not a don't care (or cannot happen) condition. If $R = S = 1$, an output will be generated, but it is not defined and may be inconsistent (e.g. $Q = \bar{Q} = 0$). Normally, the input combination giving rise to an undefined condition would not be used.

A rectangular box symbol is used to represent flip-flops, with inputs and outputs labeled. Figures 4.1(b) and (c) show possible synchronous and asynchronous R–S flip-flop symbols. The clock input may be additionally marked to indicate the form of logic transition required to activate the device, and any restrictions. A restriction found in certain flip-flop implementations is that the other inputs should not alter while the clock is high. The actual flip-flop activation mechanism will be considered later when the internal flip-flop design is examined.

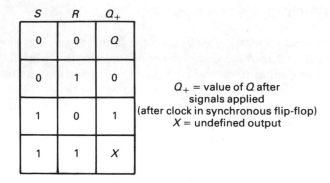

(a) Truth table

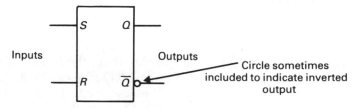

(b) Asynchronous *R–S* flip-flop symbol

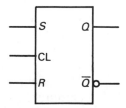

(c) Synchronous *R–S* flip-flop symbol

Figure 4.1   *R–S* flip-flop

4.2.2 *J–K* flip-flop

The *J–K* flip-flop is always synchronous. In addition to the clock input, the flip-flop has two inputs, *J* and *K*, which when activated independently cause the flip-flop to operate in the same manner as the *S* and *R* inputs of a *R–S* flip-flop, i.e. when $J = 1$ and $K = 0$, the *Q* output sets to a 1 and when $J = 0$ and $K = 1$, the output resets to a 0. The stated outputs are only attained after the device is 'clocked'. The undefined *R–S* flip-flop condition, $S = R = 1$, has been replaced in the *J–K* flip-flop with a specified action. With $J = K = 1$, the Q output complements, i.e. if $Q = 0$, $Q_+ = 1$ and if $Q = 1$, $Q_+ = 0$. The full *J–K* flip-flop truth table and symbol are shown in Fig. 4.2 (a) and (b) respectively. Remember that the first three entries in the truth table are the same as the first three entries in the *R–S* flip-flop truth table.

The *J–K* flip-flop is a very useful device in practice. By setting the *J–K* inputs to a 1 permanently, the output 'toggles' (changes state after each activation). This toggle operation is used in the design of binary counters. Counters are sequential circuits which produce defined output sequences when

J	K	Q_+
0	0	Q
0	1	0
1	0	1
1	1	$\bar{Q}$

(a) Truth table

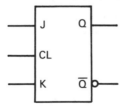

(b) Symbol

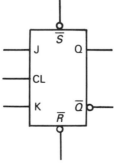

(c) *J–K* flip-flop symbol with asynchronous set and reset inputs

Figure 4.2 *J–K* flip-flop

input pulses are applied. Sometimes mention is made of a *toggle* or *T*-type flip-flop as a device having a single input, *T*, in addition to the clock input. A *T*-type flip-flop can be created from a *J–K* flip-flop by connecting the *J* and *K* inputs together and calling this connection the *T* input. Actual *T*-type flip-flops are not usually manufactured as such.

Asynchronous independent set and reset inputs can be incorporated into any synchronous flip-flop as shown in Fig. 4.2(c) for a *J–K* flip-flop. These inputs will set or reset the output irrespective of the signals applied to the *J*, *K* and clock inputs. The asynchronous set and reset inputs are commonly active low (action occurs when the signal is taken to a 0). This fact may be indicated by labeling the inputs as $\bar{S}$ and $\bar{R}$ and by marking the input with a small circle. Other features can be incorporated into the *J–K* flip-flop, for example several *J* and *K* inputs can be provided which are combined logically (either AND'ed or OR'ed or a combination) within the device. Occasionally, the *K* input is active low while the *J* input is active high, i.e. a $J–\bar{K}$ flip-flop. (This particular arrangement allows a $J–\bar{K}$ flip-flop to be easily configured as a *D*-type flip-flop by connecting both *J* and $\bar{K}$ together to form the *D* input; see next section.)

4.2.3 D-type flip-flop

The *D*-type flip-flop is always synchronous and is also used to store one binary digit. The flip-flop has one input, *D* (for data or delay), in addition to the clock input. The binary value applied to the *D* input at the time of the clock activation is transferred to the *Q* output. This action can be described in the very simple truth table shown in Fig. 4.3(a). The symbol of the *D*-type flip-flop is shown in Fig. 4.3(b).

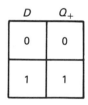

D	Q_+
0	0
1	1

(a) Truth table

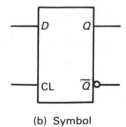

(b) Symbol

Figure 4.3   *D*-type flip-flop

4.3 FLIP-FLOP IMPLEMENTATION

In this section, the internal design of the major flip-flops is considered. We shall introduce some formal techniques of sequential circuit design. The finer technicalities of formal sequential circuit design will be considered in Chap. 12.

4.3.1 Asynchronous *R–S* flip-flop implementation

In designing an asynchronous R–S flip-flop, we are designing an asynchronous sequential logic circuit. This asynchronous sequential circuit has two inputs, R and S, and two outputs, Q and the complement, $\overline{Q}$. The first step we shall take in the design procedure is to draw a state diagram from the problem specification. A *state diagram* is a graphical representation of the logical operation of a sequential circuit. The diagram indicates the various states that the circuit can enter and the required input/output conditions necessary to enter the states.

A state diagram of the R–S flip-flop is shown in Fig. 4.4(a). This type of state diagram is known as a *Moore model state diagram*. Each large circle indicates a state. Inside each circle is the state number and the associated output of the circuit for that state. The lines between states indicate transitions from one state to the other state and the numbers next to the lines give the required input conditions. The effects of all input conditions must be considered in each state. Some input conditions cause no change in state which is indicated by a 'sling' line around the state circle. The states with sling lines around them are the stable states in an asynchronous sequential circuit. Stable states remain until an input condition occurs which causes a transition to another state which may be an unstable state. Transitions occur until another stable state is entered.

A state table is constructed from the information described in the state diagram. A *state table* lists the present states and the next states for each possible new input condition and the corresponding output. The state table for the R–S flip-flop is shown in Fig. 4.4(b). The two states are given in the first column. The next four columns give the new (next) state for each possible new input condition marked above the columns, i.e. $R = 0, S = 0$; $R = 0, S = 1$; $R = 1, S = 1$ and $R = 1, S = 0$. The input variables are labeled in this order to match the labeling of a Karnaugh map which will be constructed from the state table. There is only one independent output, Q, and this output corresponds directly to the two states. One state corresponds to the Q output being a 1 and one state corresponds to the Q output being a 0. A state table giving the variables representing the states, rather than the state numbers, is known as an *assigned state table*. The assigned state table for the R–S flip-flop is shown in Fig. 4.4(c). In our case, the state variable is the same as the output Q.

We next require a Boolean expression for the output. This expression can be derived from the assigned state table. The output function can be extracted directly as a Karnaugh map describing Q_+ as shown in Fig. 4.4(d) because for convenience, the state table is labeled with the relevant variables, R, S and Q, in the same order as a three-variable Karnaugh map. The Boolean expression becomes:

$$Q_+ = Q\bar{R} + S$$

which is known as the *characteristic equation* of the *R–S* flip-flop. The characteristic equation of a flip-flop describes the relationship between the new output in terms of the inputs applied and the current output.

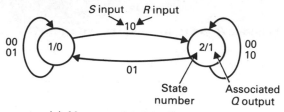

(a) Moore model state diagram

Present state	Next state S R inputs			
	00	01	11	10
1	1	1	X	2
2	2	1	X	2

(b) State table

Present state	Next state S R inputs			
	00	01	11	10
0	0	0	X	1
1	1	0	X	1

(c) Assigned state table

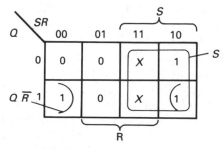

(d) Q_+ function

Figure 4.4   *R–S* flip-flop design procedure

Finally, a circuit realization is drawn from the Boolean characteristic expression. The circuit can use AND and OR gates as shown in Fig. 4.5. Though the procedure leads to a design, we have not taken into account possible malfunction due to new signal changes being fed back from the output to the input. Therefore it is now necessary to check that the circuit will operate under all valid input and output conditions and the appropriate stable outputs are generated. It is possible with our circuit to list all valid input and output combinations and then deduce the corresponding new output which is always correct. It is left to the reader to perform this verification.

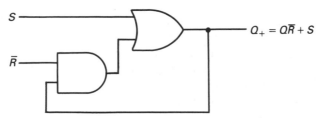

Figure 4.5   Asynchronous *R–S* flip-flop circuit

A more common circuit realization uses NAND gates totally as shown in Fig. 4.6, which follows from applying De Morgan's theorem to the characteristic equation, i.e.:

$$Q_+ = \overline{(\overline{Q\overline{R}})\overline{S}}$$

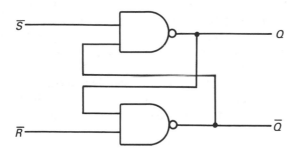

(a) With active low inputs

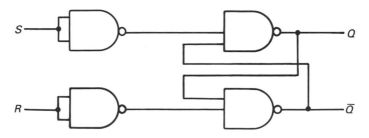

(b) With active high inputs

Figure 4.6   Asynchronous *R–S* flip-flop using NAND gates

The complement output expression is found from the Karnaugh map of Q_+ by grouping the 0's, i.e.

$$\overline{Q}_+ = \overline{Q}\overline{S} + R = (\overline{\overline{\overline{Q}\overline{S}}})\overline{R}$$

(Note that input combinations for the X's do not occur.) Active high inputs require extra NAND gates. Sometimes, active low R and S signals are used, in which case gates are not necessary to invert the input signals. If the undefined condition, $S = R = 1$, is applied, both Q and $\overline{Q}$ become a 1. If both S and R are then altered to a 0, the behavior of the circuit is unpredictable. Extra set and reset inputs can be incorporated by adding further R and S inputs to the cross-coupled NAND gates, leading to a very economical circuit design. Consequently, the circuit has been widely used, especially when the number of gates available in one package was low and hence it was particularly important to keep the number of gates in a system design to a minimum.

NOR gates alone can be used. Starting from the characteristic equation, by De Morgan's theorem we obtain:

$$\overline{Q}_+ = \overline{Q\overline{R} + S}$$
$$= \overline{(\overline{Q} + R) + S}$$

which leads to the circuit shown in Fig. 4.7. Notice that the R and S input signals are not complemented.

One application of the R–S flip-flop is as a *switch debouncer* for a switch used to generated logic 0 or a logic 1 depending upon the position of the switch. The contacts of most switches when the switch is operated have a tendency to vibrate, making and breaking contact several times over a period of perhaps a few milliseconds. This vibration can create transient 0's and 1's rather than a single logic transition. Figure 4.8 shows a simple circuit using a switch to generate a logic signal and the effect of switch contact bounce. Notice that there are several changes in the output when the switch is closed.

To avoid these transient changes in output, a switch debouncer circuit such as that shown in Fig. 4.9(a) can be employed. In this circuit, the R–S flip-flop consists of NAND gates and a two-way switch is necessary. When the switch connects $0\,\text{V}$ (accepted as a logic 0 voltage in TTL) to the $\tilde{S}$ input, the Q

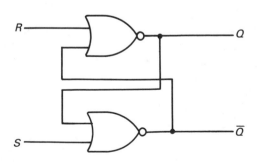

Figure 4.7   Asynchronous R–S flip-flop using NOR gates

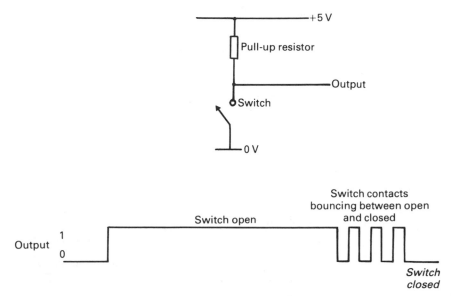

Figure 4.8   Switch bounce

output becomes a 1 and the $\overline{Q}$ output becomes a 0. Conversely, when the switch connects $0\,\text{V}$ to the $\overline{R}$ input, the Q output becomes a 0 and the $\overline{Q}$ output becomes a 1. The resistors ensure a logic 1 level in the open-circuit input condition. If the switch contacts vibrate during the change of switch position, assuming that the vibration is not sufficient to cause the switch arm to touch both contacts alternately, the output of the flip-flop will change only on the first contact made as shown in Fig. 4.9(b). For this application, a pair of NOT gates can be used as shown in Fig. 4.9(c). The switch connect $0\,\text{V}$ to one input. In this circuit, the output of one of the two NOT gates will always be connected to $0\,\text{V}$, depending upon the position of the switch. This is acceptable since at the same time the input of the gate is at a 1 and no conflict occurs between the output level and the voltage from the switch.

4.3.2 Synchronous *R–S* flip-flop implementation

A synchronous *R–S* flip-flop can be created by the simple modification to the asynchronous *R–S* flip-flop design as shown in Fig. 4.10. In this design, the clock signal controls the *R–S* input NAND gates so that when the clock signal is a 0 ('low'), the state of the flip-flop cannot be altered by any change on the *R–S* inputs. When the clock becomes a 1 ('high'), the *R–S* input signals are allowed to enter the flip-flop and the outputs change if a change is specified by the flip-flop truth table. By limiting the *R-S* input changes to when the clock is a 0, all changes in the output will occur as the clock signal changes from a 0 to 1, i.e. the output changes are synchronized by the rising transition of the clock signal.

It is important to note that the *R–S* input signals must not change while the clock input is a 1 if the synchronous operation is to be preserved. We will see

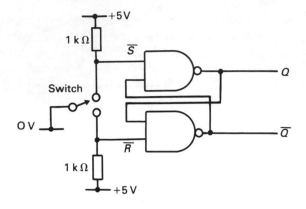

(a) Circuit using NAND gates

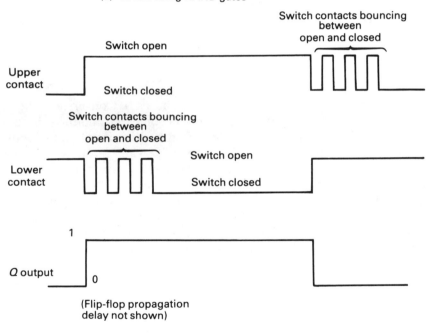

(b) Waveforms

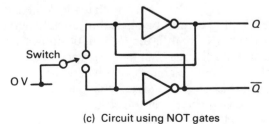

(c) Circuit using NOT gates

Figure 4.9   Switch debouncer circuits

later that this restriction can be removed by alternative circuit arrangements which are normally applied to *J–K* and *D*-type flip-flops. The particular merit of the *R–S* design presented here is the simplicity and economy of gates. Additional active low set and reset inputs can be incorporated as shown in dotted lines in Fig. 4.10.

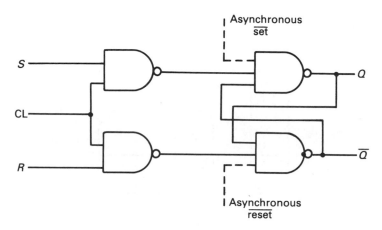

Figure 4.10   Synchronous *R–S* flip-flop

4.3.3 *J–K* flip-flop implementations

Again the first step we shall take is to draw the state diagram. A Moore model state diagram of the *J–K* flip-flop is shown in Fig. 4.11(a). From the diagram, we can derive the state table shown in Fig. 4.11(b) and the assigned state table shown in Fig. 4.11(c). This leads to the Karnaugh map shown in Fig. 4.11(d) and the characteristic equation for the *J–K* flip-Lop given by:

$$Q_+ = J\bar{Q} + \bar{K}Q$$

It is important to note that the state diagram given describes a synchronous sequential circuit, and we shall design a synchronous sequential circuit, as opposed to the asynchronous sequential circuit (such as the asynchronous *R–S* flip-flop circuit in Section 4.3.1). State changes occur due to clock signal transitions. Given a synchronous *R–S* flip-flop, the *J–K* flip-flop can be designed by adding extra gates to the *R–S* flip-flop so that it behaves as a *J–K* flip-flop. The clock applied to the circuit is applied to the clock input of the synchronous *R–S* flip-flop.

Let us firstly consider the effect of the inputs of an *R–S* flip-flop on flip-flop output, which can be one of four possible types: the output can remain at a 0 ('0 to 0'), the output can change from a 0 to a 1 ('0 to 1'), the output can change from a 1 to a 0 ('1 to 0') or the output can remain at a 1 ('1 to 1'). The required inputs to an *R–S* flip-flop to achieve these effects, as deduced from the *R–S* flip-flop truth table, are shown in Table 4.1. There are two possible *R–S* input combinations to achieve a '0 to 0' effect, either $R = 0, S = 0$ or $R = 1, S = 0$, so

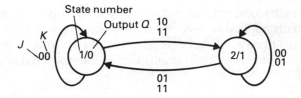

(a) Moore model state diagram

Present state	Next state JK			
	00	01	11	10
1	1	1	2	2
2	2	1	1	2

(b) State table

Present state	Next state JK			
	00	01	11	10
0	0	0	1	1
1	1	0	0	1

(c) Assigned state table

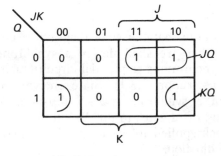

(d) Q_+ function

Figure 4.11   *J–K* flip-flop design procedure

the value of R does not matter and is entered in the table as a don't care X. Similarly, there are two possible R–S input combinations to achieve a '1 to 1' effect, either $R = 0, S = 0$ or $R = 0, S = 1$, so the value of S does not matter and is entered in the table as a don't care X.

Table 4.1 Q/Q_+ table for an R–S flip-flop

Required output change		Inputs	
Q	to Q₊	S	R
0	0	0	X
0	1	1	0
1	0	0	1
1	1	X	0

The required inputs to the R–S flip-flop can be found by applying Table 4.1 to the Q_+ function described in the Karnaugh map of Fig. 4.11(d). For example, when $J = K = Q = 0$ in Fig. 4.11(d), the output is to remain at a 0 ('0 to 0'), and the required inputs are $S = 0$ and $R = $ X. These values are entered on Karnaugh maps describing the reset and set functions. By continuing with this procedure, the two functions can be mapped totally, as shown in Fig.4.11(e). Simplifying, we obtain:

Set $= J\bar{Q}$
Reset $= KQ$

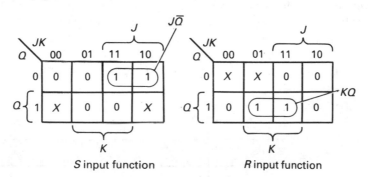

(e) R–S flip-flop input function

Figure 4.11 *continued*

Therefore the circuit implementation would appear to be as shown in Fig. 4.12. The true output, Q, and the inverse output, $\bar{Q}$, are cross-coupled to the input gates to produce the two input functions above. However, when checking for possible malfunction of the circuit, by examining all possible input and output conditions, we find that while the clock is high, the input gates are enabled allowing changes in J, K and Q to subsequently affect the flip-flop. In particular, if $J = K = 1$, the circuit would continuously oscillate. Therefore the circuit must be modified to prevent incorrect operation. The fundamental problem is the type of R–S flip-flop used, namely the type which must not have the R or S inputs change when the clock is at a 1. There are two principal methods which can be employed, namely the *edge-triggered* design and the *master–slave* design. Both of these designs alter the basic R–S flip-flop design.

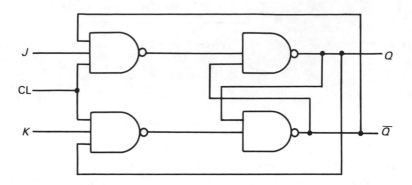

Figure 4.12   Incorrect *J–K* flip-flop design

(a) Edge-triggered flip-flop design

An edge-triggered flip-flop is activated by a logic transition on the clock input, say a 0 to a 1, or alternatively a 1 to a 0, but not both in one device. The former is called *positive edge-triggered* and the latter *negative edge-triggered*. The timing diagram for a negative edge-triggered *J–K* flip-flop is shown in Fig. 4.13. The shading indicates that the logic level does not matter.

The edge-triggered mechanism could be implemented by inserting a circuit in the flip-flop between the clock input and the original clock inputs of the AND gates to have the effect of producing one positive narrow logic 'pulse'

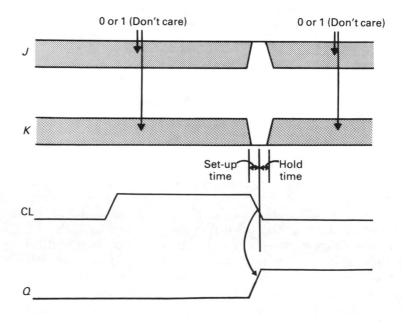

Figure 4.13   Timing diagram of a negative edge-triggered *J–K* flip-flop

(a signal which changes from a 0 to a 1 and then back to a 0, staying at a 1 for a very short time) on every positive clock transition. The pulse causes the flip-flop to operate. It is necessary for the duration of the pulse to be less than the time it takes for the output signals to be generated and fed back to the inputs. Figure 4.14 shows simple design using the delay through a NOT gate to produce a pulse. It is necessary to ensure that the pulse width is less than the delay around the flip-flop loop under all conditions. The implementation actually used in integrated circuits is usually a variant on the above.

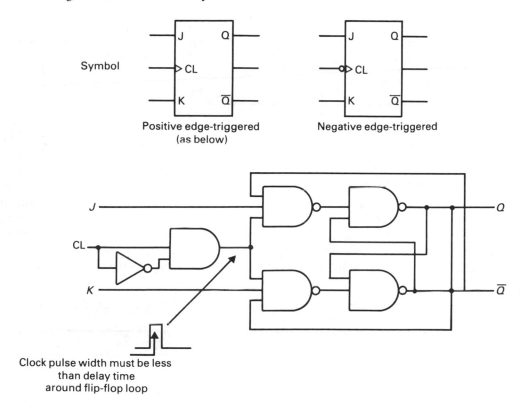

Figure 4.14   Edge-triggered *J–K* flip-flop

(b) Master–slave flip-flop design

In the master–slave flip-flop, the single *R–S* flip-flop above is replaced by two *R–S* flip-flops, one called the master flip-flop, and the other called the slave flip-flop. These are connected together as shown in Fig. 4.15. The *J–K* inputs enter the master flip-flop with the usual clock gating. The outputs of the master flip-flop are connected to the inputs of the slave flip-flop with additional gates and the outputs of the overall circuit are taken from the slave flip-flop. The cross-coupling between the inputs and the outputs of the overall circuit is provided as defined by the *J–K* flip-flop design. However, the overall feedback loop is broken by arranging that the *J–K* inputs enter the circuit when the clock is high (say) but only pass to the slave flip-flop when the clock is low. While the

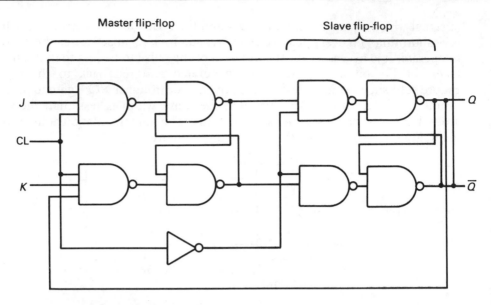

Figure 4.15   Master–slave *J–K* flip-flop

clock is low, the *J–K* inputs are inhibited from the master flip-flop but the master flip-flop can set or reset the slave. It is assumed that the *J–K* signals do not change when the clock is high. It is necessary for the NOT gate connecting to the slave flip-flop to have a higher switching threshold than the input NAND gates, so that there is no overlap between the master activation and the slave activation. The timing diagram for the master–slave flip-flop is shown in Fig. 4.16.

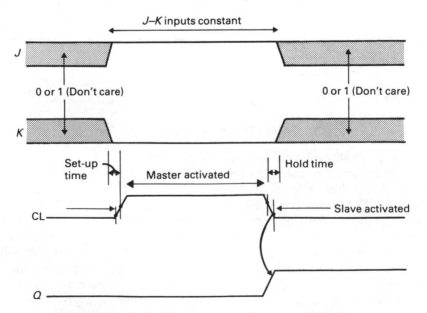

Figure 4.16   Timing diagram of a master–slave *J–K* flip-flop

If the *J–K* inputs did change during the high clock level, the master flip-flop would respond and the final result would depend upon the final input values rather than the states of the *J–K* inputs at the instant of the rising edge of the clock, losing the synchronous nature required. It is possible to modify the master–slave design to incorporate a *data lock-out* mechanism which allows the *J–K* inputs to change while the clock is high. However, most modern flip-flop are now edge-triggered. Examples of *J–K* flip-flops in the LS-TTL family include the 74LS109 dual positive edge-triggered *J–K* flip-flops, the 74LS73, 74LS76, 74LS78, 74LS112, 74LS113 and 74LS114 dual negative edge-triggered *J–K* flip-flops. Some of the edge-triggered flip-flops were master–slave in the original standard TTL series (e.g. 7473, 7476 and 7478 were master–slave *J–K* flip-flops).

4.3.4 *D*-type flip-flop implementation

For uniformity of approach, the procedure to implement a *D*-type flip-flop using an *R–S* flip-flop is shown in Fig. 4.17, performed in the same manner as for the *J–K* flip-flop. The characteristic equation is:

$$Q_+ = D$$

and the inputs to the *R–S* flip-flop are:

$$Set = D$$
$$Reset = \bar{D}$$

Hence a *D*-type flip-flop can be created from an *R–S* flip-flop by connecting a NOT gate from the *S* input to the *R* input, using the *S* input as the *D* input. The same arrangement can create a *D*-type flip-flop from a *J–K* flip-flop, connecting a NOT gate from the *J* input to the *K* input and using the *J* input as the *D* input. With these configurations, the clock activation mechanism of the resultant flip-flop will be the same as that of the original flip-flop.

Figure 4.18 shows a *D*-type flip-flop based on a synchronous *R–S* flip-flop employing cross-coupled NAND gates. In this implementation, the output would follow the data input while the clock is high and data would be stored at the instant that the clock falls to a low. The circuit is known as a *transparent* latch. Examples in the TTL family include the 74LS75 quad transparent latch and the 74LS373 octal transparent latch. In the 74LS75, pairs of latches share the same clock input and in the 74LS373 all eight latches share common clock. *D*-type flip-flops are also edge-triggered. Examples include the 74LS74 dual *D*-type positive edge-triggered *D*-type flip-flop and the 74LS534 octal *D*-type flip-flop, the latter with a common clock.

4.3.5 Timing considerations

In edge-triggered flip-flops, the *R–S*, *J–K* or *D* input signals must be applied before the activating clock transition for the circuit to operate correctly.

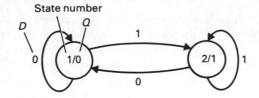

(a) Moore model state diagram

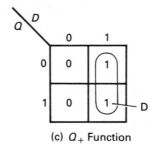

(b) Assigned state table

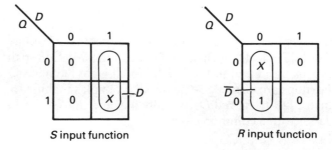

(c) Q_+ Function

(d) *R–S* flip-flop input functions

Figure 4.17 *D*-type flip-flop design procedure

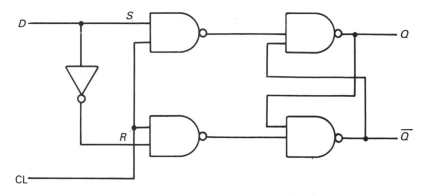

Figure 4.18 *D*-type flip-flop circuit (transparent latch)

The period before the transition during which the inputs must be stable is defined as the *set-up* time. Typically the set-up time of TTL flip-flops is in the region of 20 ns. Also these signals may need to be maintained at a steady level for a short period after the clock transition has occurred. The period after the clock transition during which the input must be stable is known as the *hold* time. The hold time is in the region of 5 ns for TTL. Some devices have no hold time, i.e. a hold time specified as 0 ns. Similar timing constraints exist for traditional master–slave flip-flops with the added constraint that the inputs must not change between the two clock transitions used to load the master and slave flip-flops (unless a data lock-out mechanism is incorporated into the flip-flop).

If the inputs do change during the set-up time or hold times, the resultant output could not be predicted. Worse, the flip-flop might enter a non-stable state with the output not at a defined logic level but at some intermediate voltage. Theoretically, this condition could, depending upon when exactly the inputs change, last for ever. In practice, the condition very occasionally lasts for several tens of nanoseconds. This is a particular problem when flip-flops are used with randomly occurring input signals.

4.3.6 Mealy model state diagram

Another type of state diagram is known as a *Mealy model state diagram*. In a Mealy model state diagram, the outputs are not associated with the states within the state circles. Instead, the new output is given next to the input values on the lines leaving the states. Thus in this type of state diagram, it would be admissible to have a state having more than one possible output value. The two types of state diagrams for flip-flops are very similar and one particular output is associated with each state. Figure 4.19 shows a Mealy model state diagram for the *J–K* flip-flop. In this chapter we will restrict our state diagrams to the Moore type in which the output values are given within the state circles. However, Mealy model state diagrams can be used, as shown (with implications) in Chap. 12. In the following, each state generally has different output values. The state numbers correspond to particular output values and are omitted, for clarity.

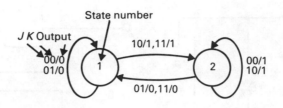

Figure 4.19   Mealy model state diagram of *J-K* flip-flop

4.4   SEQUENTIAL CIRCUIT DESIGN AND PARTS

In this section we will examine common sequential circuits including those often fabricated in MSI technology. Rather than simply present circuits, where appropriate, we shall introduce the common circuits via digital system requirements and specification using state diagrams. The circuits presented are mainly synchronous sequential circuits.

4.4.1   Registers

A *register* is a logic circuit capable of storing a number of binary digits and is normally implemented with a number of flip-flops. The most suitable flip-flop is the *D*-type flip-flop, and the discussion will concentrate on the use of *D*-type flip-flops for registers. Of course, other types of flip-flops can be used to store binary digits and can be made to behave as *D*-type flip-flops (for example as explained in section 4.3.4).

A *parallel-in parallel-out data register* stores a number of binary digits which are entered into the flip-flops of the register together and all digits are extracted from the flip-flops of the register together. A clock signal is used to cause the input data to be stored and the stored data becomes available at the outputs after the flip-flops have responded. Reset circuitry can be provided to clear the information held in the register, by using asynchronous reset inputs on the flip-flops, or synchronously by gating at the flip-flop inputs. Parallel-in parallel-out registers in the TTL family include the 74LS374 8-bit register (eight *D*-type flip-flops with a common clock).

4.4.2   Shift registers

Once we use a data register to store a binary pattern, possibilities exist by moving bits within the register. For example, we can multiply a binary number by two, by moving all the digits one place left, e.g.:

Number before operation $= 00000110\ (6_{10})$
Number after digits moved one place left $= 00001100\ (12_{10})$

Here the least significant digit is set to 0. Similarly moving the digits one place right divides the number by two, e.g.:

Number before operation $= 00011101\ (29_{10})$
Number after digits moved one place right $= 00001110\ (14_{10})$

Here the fractional part is lost, given an 8-bit register.

A data register configured to move the digits left or right is known as a *shift register*. In a shift register, all the digits can be moved from being stored in their current flip-flop to the adjacent flip-flop, on application of a clock signal. The logic circuit arrangement is probably now obvious to the reader from the above, but let us develop it formally. A state diagram and state table can be produced to describe the operations required, as given in Fig. 4.20 for a 3-bit shift register. In the state table, all possible values that could be held in the register are listed and the values that would appear after a clock pulse is applied. Only the outputs are shown in the state diagram as there is a direct correspondence between outputs and states. The circuit can exist in one of eight states corresponding to the eight possible values held in the register. The initial values held in the register are applied before the shifting operation.

Clearly we need three flip-flops to hold the 3-bit number and generate the outputs. We have specified *D*-type flip-flops although any synchronous type can be used. The appropriate signals need to be applied to the three *D* inputs of the flip-flops to cause the states given in the state table to be entered when clock pulses are applied. Since a *D*-type flip-flop takes on the value presented to the *D* input after the clock is applied, it is only necessary to apply the appropriate next state functions to each input. Figure 4.21(a) shows the Karnaugh maps of these functions taken directly from the next state columns of the state table. Minimizing, we obtain the functions shown and the circuit realization in Fig. 4.21(b).

The basic configuration of a shift register connects the output of each flip-flop to the input of the adjacent flip-flop. The data may be entered serially (one bit at a time) as shown in Fig. 4.22(a), or in parallel (all bits together) as in the parallel-in register using extra gates. In the serial input shift register, every time a clock signal is applied, each digit is moved ('shifted') to the adjacent flip-flop. In the shift register shown in Fig. 4.22(b) the shifting process is one place right, though the shift process may of course be configured for moving left. The values of the input applied to the first flip-flop at the time of each clock activation are shown as D_t, D_{t+1}, D_{t+2}, D_{t+3}, $\cdots$ It is assumed that all the flip-flops in the register are first set to zero. Notice that because all the flip-flops are activated simultaneously, the data transferred from one flip-flop to the next is the data present at that time, not the subsequent data, and all digits are moved one place right simultaneously.

Shift registers can be formed with *J*–*K* flip-flops, by connecting the *Q* and $\overline{Q}$ outputs of one flip-flop to the *J* and *K* inputs of the next flip-flop. The data can be also taken from the shift register in serial form from the final flip-flop if

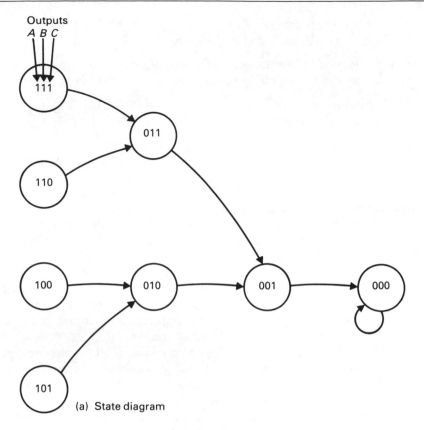

Outputs
A B C

(a) State diagram

Present state			Next state		
A	B	C	A_+	B_+	C_+
0	0	0	0	0	0
0	0	1	0	0	0
0	1	0	0	0	1
0	1	1	0	0	1
1	0	0	0	1	0
1	0	1	0	1	0
1	1	0	0	1	1
1	1	1	0	1	1

(b) State table

Figure 4.20   Shift register sequence

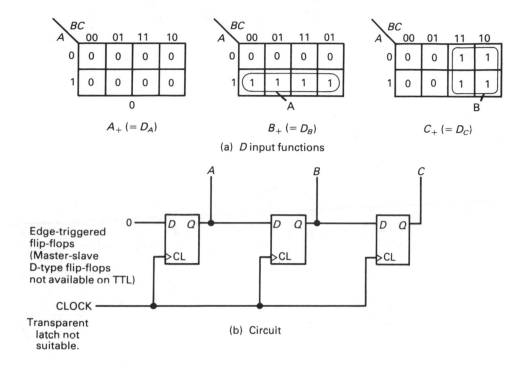

Figure 4.21   Shift register implementation

desired. Consequently, there are three variations, namely the serial-in serial-out register, the serial-in parallel-out shift register, and the parallel-in serial-out shift register. Shift registers in the TTL family include the 74LS194 4-bit parallel-in parallel-out bidirectional shift register, 74165/6 8-bit parallel-in serial-out shift register, the 74LS164 8-bit serial-in parallel-out shift register and the 7491 8-bit serial-in serial-out shift register.

When the output of the most significant (final) flip-flop of a shift register (i.e. the serial data output) is connected to the input of the least significant (first) flip-flop (i.e. the serial data input), the shift register is called a *ring counter*.

4.4.3 Generating control pulses using a shift register

A digital system is frequently controlled by sequences of timing pulses. Typically, a timing signal is required to activate a particular operation, say to transfer the contents of one register into another register. Suppose eight separate timing signals are required, each occurring in sequence and of one clock duration as shown in Fig. 4.23(a).

One design solution for generating these pulses is to initially load a 8-bit shift register with the pattern 10000000 and then shift the data right on application of a clock pulse. To achieve repetitive sequences, after 00000001 is reached we need to create the pattern 10000000 as shown in the state diagram

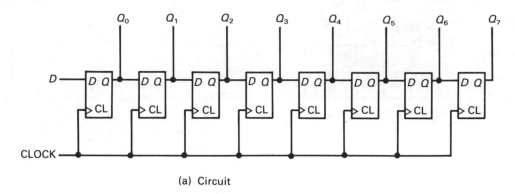

(a) Circuit

Clock pulse	D	Q_0	Q_1	Q_2	Q_3	Q_4	Q_5	Q_6	Q_7
	D_t	0	0	0	0	0	0	0	0
Φ_0	D_{t+1}	D_t	0	0	0	0	0	0	0
Φ_1	D_{t+2}	D_{t+1}	D_t	0	0	0	0	0	0
Φ_2	D_{t+3}	D_{t+2}	D_{t+1}	D_t	0	0	0	0	0
Φ_3	D_{t+4}	D_{t+3}	D_{t+2}	D_{t+1}	D_t	0	0	0	0
Φ_4	D_{t+5}	D_{t+4}	D_{t+3}	D_{t+2}	D_{t+1}	D_t	0	0	0
Φ_5	D_{t+6}	D_{t+5}	D_{t+4}	D_{t+3}	D_{t+2}	D_{t+1}	D_t	0	0
Φ_6	D_{t+7}	D_{t+6}	D_{t+5}	D_{t+4}	D_{t+3}	D_{t+2}	D_{t+1}	D_t	0
Φ_7	D_{t+8}	D_{t+7}	D_{t+6}	D_{t+5}	D_{t+4}	D_{t+3}	D_{t+2}	D_{t+1}	D_t
Φ_8	D_{t+9}	D_{t+8}	D_{t+7}	D_{t+6}	D_{t+5}	D_{t+4}	D_{t+3}	D_{t+2}	D_{t+1}

(b) Data flow

Figure 4.22   Serial-in parallel-out shift register

shown in Fig. 4.23(b). This can be implemented with a ring counter as shown in Fig. 4.23(c). The 1 in the pattern will continually move from one position to the next on application of a clock signal, generating the required pulses.

A variation of the recirculating shift register is with the inverse output of the most significant flip-flop passed to the input of the least significant flip-flop. This arrangement is known as a *Johnson counter* or *twisted ring counter* as shown in Fig. 4.24 with *J–K* flip-flops. (*D*-type flip-flops can be used by connecting the most significant flip-flop $\bar{Q}$ output to the least significant flip-flop *D* input.) The sequence followed begins with all 0's in the register. The final 0 will cause 1's to be shifted into the register from the left-hand side when clock pulses are applied. When the first 1 reaches the most significant flip-flop, 0's will be inserted into the first flip-flop, because of the cross-coupling between the output and the input of the counter.

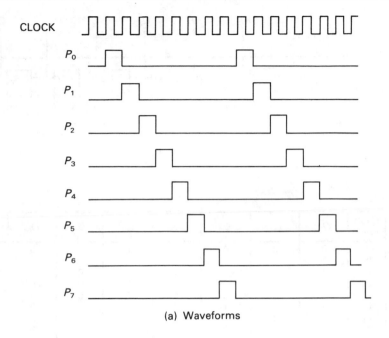

(a) Waveforms

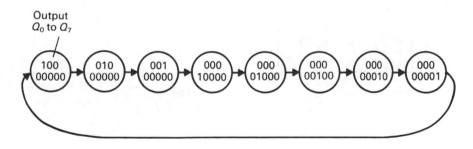

(b) State diagram

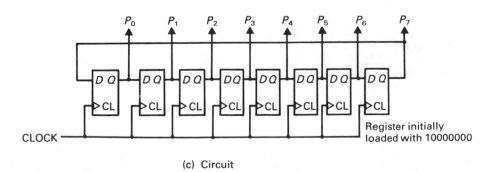

(c) Circuit

Figure 4.23   Generating timing pulses using a ring counter

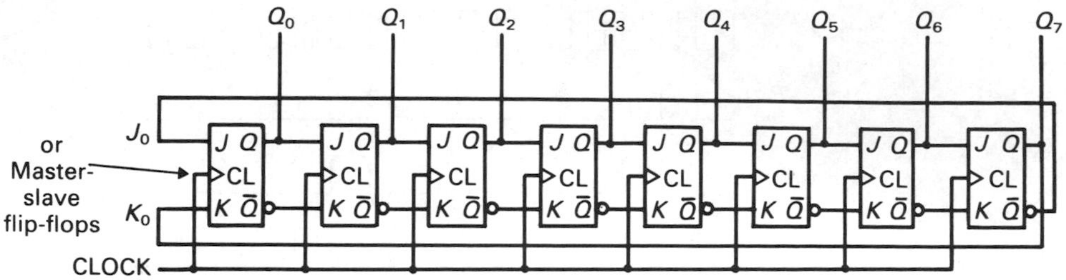

Q_0 Q_1 Q_2 Q_3 Q_4 Q_5 Q_6 Q_7

or Master-slave flip-flops J_0 ... K_0 ... CLOCK

(a) Circuit

Clock pulse	Q_0	Q_1	Q_2	Q_3	Q_4	Q_5	Q_6	Q_7
Φ_0	0	0	0	0	0	0	0	0
Φ_1	1	0	0	0	0	0	0	0
Φ_2	1	1	0	0	0	0	0	0
Φ_3	1	1	1	0	0	0	0	0
Φ_4	1	1	1	1	0	0	0	0
Φ_5	1	1	1	1	1	0	0	0
Φ_6	1	1	1	1	1	1	0	0
Φ_7	1	1	1	1	1	1	1	0
Φ_8	1	1	1	1	1	1	1	1
Φ_9	0	1	1	1	1	1	1	1
Φ_{10}	0	0	1	1	1	1	1	1
Φ_{11}	0	0	0	1	1	1	1	1
Φ_{12}	0	0	0	0	1	1	1	1
Φ_{13}	0	0	0	0	0	1	1	1
Φ_{14}	0	0	0	0	0	0	1	1
Φ_{15}	0	0	0	0	0	0	0	1

(b) Output pattern

Figure 4.24 Twisted ring (Johnson) counter

We notice now there are 16 different patterns generated with the eight flip-flops as opposed to eight different patterns with the ring counter holding a single 1. We can obtain 16 separate timing pulses by implementing the following functions:

$$P_0 = \overline{Q}_0\overline{Q}_7 \quad P_8 = Q_7Q_0$$
$$P_1 = \overline{Q}_1Q_0 \quad P_9 = Q_1\overline{Q}_0$$
$$P_2 = \overline{Q}_2Q_1 \quad P_{10} = Q_2\overline{Q}_1$$
$$P_3 = \overline{Q}_3Q_2 \quad P_{11} = Q_3\overline{Q}_2$$
$$P_4 = \overline{Q}_4Q_3 \quad P_{12} = Q_4\overline{Q}_3$$
$$P_5 = \overline{Q}_5Q_4 \quad P_{13} = Q_5\overline{Q}_4$$
$$P_6 = \overline{Q}_6Q_5 \quad P_{14} = Q_6\overline{Q}_5$$
$$P_7 = \overline{Q}_7Q_6 \quad P_{15} = Q_7\overline{Q}_6$$

as each is true only during the associated clock duration. Sixteen 2-input AND gates would be needed and hence there is a trade-off between number of flip-flops and additional decode gates.

When decode gates are used, it is usually important that 'glitches' do not occur. *Glitches* are unwanted logic pulses often associated with decode circuits due to more than one change occurring at the input of the gates supposedly simultaneously, but in fact at slightly different times. The principal advantage of the Johnson counter over other counter methods (see later) is that only one flip-flop output changes state at a time and consequently decode glitches will not be generated when the counter outputs are used in decode circuits such as the above. Note that, as with all counters, noise in the system may suddenly cause incorrect operation and a method of overcoming this problem must be provided such as by the use of reset circuitry.

4.4.4 Asynchronous binary counters

A counter is a sequential logic circuit whose outputs follow a defined sequence, such as the Johnson counter above. Another example of a counter is one whose outputs begin at 0000 and count in unit steps upwards, i.e. 0001, 0010, 0011, 0100, 0101, 0110, ···, 1111. This particular counter is called a *binary (up) counter*. The sequence moves from one number to the next after the application of a clock signal. After the maximum number is reached, the counter outputs return to the first number. Such counters play vital roles in digital systems. Whereas the D-type flip-flop is a natural choice for registers, J–K flip-flops are particularly suitable for counters as counter outputs often must change from 0 to 1 or from a 1 to a 0 (i.e. toggle). D-type flip-flops can also be used in counters by applying appropriate signals to the D inputs.

Counters, as all sequential logic circuits, can be asynchronous or synchronous in operation. In section 4.1, we defined a synchronous sequential logic circuit as one in which a clock signal initiates all changes in state, whereas an asynchronous sequential logic circuit is one in which no clock signal exists to synchronize changes. Though all counter circuits use an external clock signal to cause the states (and thus outputs) to change, the counter itself can be synchronous or asynchronous in operation internally. In the case of an asynchronous binary counter, the clock signal should be considered not as synchronizing signal but as a single input to an asynchronous sequential circuit. Firstly, we shall present asynchronous binary counter circuits. Formal asynchronous sequential circuit design is described in Chap. 12.

A 4-bit asynchronous binary-up counter is shown in Fig. 4.25(a). This counter employs falling (negative) edge triggered flip-flops or master–slave flip-flops whose slave outputs are triggered on the falling edge of the clock signal. Each flip-flop has its J–K inputs connected to a permanent logic 1, which configures the counter as a 'toggle' flip-flop. The counter clock signal controls only the first flip-flop. The output of the first flip-flop, A, complements (changes from a 0 to a 1 or from a 1 to a 0) each time there is a negative clock transition.

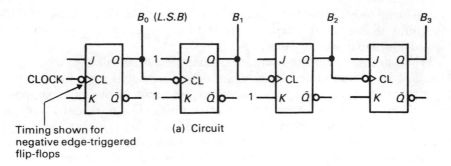

(a) Circuit

Timing shown for
negative edge-triggered
flip-flops

Clock pulse	B_3	B_2	B_1	B_0
Φ_0	0	0	0	0
Φ_1	0	0	0	1
Φ_2	0	0	1	0
Φ_3	0	0	1	1
Φ_4	0	1	0	0
Φ_5	0	1	0	1
Φ_6	0	1	1	0
Φ_7	0	1	1	1
Φ_8	1	0	0	0
Φ_9	1	0	0	1

(b) Output pattern

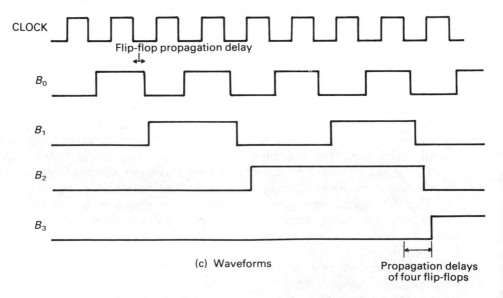

(c) Waveforms

Figure 4.25   Asynchronous binary counter

Output A is the least significant bit of the required counter sequence shown in Fig. 4.25(b). Output A is also fed into the clock input of the second flip-flop. The second flip-flop will toggle each time there is a '1 to 0' change in A. This transition occurs on every alternate output change in A and results in the required sequence for the next least significant bit, B, as shown. Similarly, the next bit C is generated by a '1 to 0' change in B.

The arrangement can be extended to any number of stages, with outputs taken from each flip-flop. The counter is asynchronous because each output depends upon a change in the previous output, and consequently there will be a small delay between output changes. The delays are cumulative, and the overall delay between the first output change and the last output change could be significant. The timing diagram for a 4-bit asynchronous counter is shown in Fig. 4.25(c). Typical flip-flop propagation delay times are in the order of 10 ns to 30 ns for TTL logic circuits. If the propagation delay time of each flip-flop is 10 ns, there would be a delay between the first output change and the fourth output change of 30 ns, when the output changes are due to change together (e.g. from 1110 to 0001). This delay will limit the rate at which clock pulses can be applied (the maximum frequency of operation). Normally a new activating clock transition is not applied to the circuit before all the flip-flop outputs have stabilized at their required outputs. Therefore in our case, activating transitions should not occur at intervals less than 40 ns (i.e. greater than 25 MHz) considering only the propagation delay alone. Flip-flops also have a maximum stated clocking frequency (closely related to the propagation delay time) which must not be exceeded. Asynchronous binary counters are sometimes called ripple counters as the clock 'ripples' through the circuit (cf. ripple carry parallel adders in Chap. 3).

A D-type flip-flop can be configured as a 'toggle' flip-flop by returning the $\bar{Q}$ output back to the D input. Hence as asynchronous binary counter can be formed in the same way as with $\mathcal{J}$–K flip-flops after the D to $\bar{Q}$ connections are made. Asynchronous binary counters exist in the TTL family, including the 74LS293 and 74LS197 4-bit asynchronous binary counters. Asynchronous binary counters generally require fewer internal gates than synchronous binary counters, as we shall see in section 4.4.5. However, delays between output changes may be significant (as discussed in section 4.4.8).

4.4.5 Synchronous binary counters

In the synchronous counter, the clock signal connects to all the flip-flop clock inputs. Consequently, all flip-flop output changes occur simultaneously (ignoring variations between flip-flops). Combinational logic is then provided attached to the flip-flop inputs to produce the required sequence.

The binary-up counter follows the sequence given in Fig. 4.26. The state table giving the present state and next state is derived as before. As with any counter sequence, each clock activation is required to cause one of the following 'effects' on each output:

Q to Q_+
'0 to 0'
'0 to 1'
'1 to 0'
'1 to 1'

All of these effects can be achieved by any of the major flip-flops, (i.e. R–S, J–K and D-type flip-flops). For example, Table 4.1 gives the inputs required for the R–S flip-flop. A similar table can be derived for the J–K flip-flop as shown in Table 4.2. In this table, the don't care conditions result from having two possible input conditions for each output condition. To have a '0 to 0' effect, either $J = K$ $= 0$ or $J = 0$ and $K = 1$. Therefore K could be a 0 or a 1. This is entered as an X. Similarily, to have a '0 to 1' effect, either $J = K = 1$ or $J = 1$ and $K = 0$. Therefore K is again entered as an X. To have a '1 to 0' effect, either $J = K = 1$

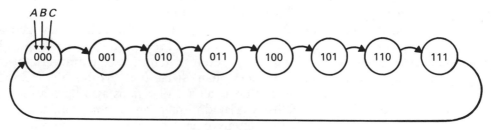

A B C

000 001 010 011 100 101 110 111

(a) State diagram

Present state			Next state		
A	B	C	A_+	B_+	C_+
0	0	0	0	0	1
0	0	1	0	1	0
0	1	0	0	1	1
0	1	1	1	0	0
1	0	0	1	0	1
1	0	1	1	1	0
1	1	0	1	1	1
1	1	1	0	0	0

(b) State table

Figure 4.26   Binary-up counter sequence

Table 4.2 Q/Q_+ table for an *J–K* flip-flop

Required output change		Inputs	
Q	to Q_+	J	K
0	0	0	X
0	1	1	X
1	0	X	1
1	1	X	0

or $J = 0$ and $K = 1$. Therefore J could be a 0 or a 1 and is entered as an X. To have a '1 to 1' effect, either $J = K = 0$ or $J = 1$ and $K = 0$. J is entered as an X.

Let us consider the use of J–K flip-flops for the counter. Three flip-flops are required for the three outputs A, B and C. There are six flip-flop inputs to consider, namely J_A, K_A, J_B, K_B, J_C and K_C. The Boolean functions for each of the six inputs can be found by deducing the required input values to achieve each new counter output from the previous counter output, using Table 4.2. For example, the first entry is $ABC = 000$, and changes to $A_+B_+C_+ = 001$. To make the required A = '0 to 0' effect, we need, $J = 0$, $K = X$, from Table 4.2. These are entered into the J_A and K_A Karnaugh maps respectively. All the entries of the six maps are entered in this way. The result is shown in Fig.4.27(a). The circuit is given in Fig. 4.27(b).

Clearly we can extend the design procedure for any number of variables. The final design can be deduced as follows: output changes occur on the activating edge of the clock signal. Examining the binary-up sequence given in Fig. 4.28(a), we see the first stage should toggle each time an activating clock transition occurs. This is achieved by applying a permanent 1 to both the J and K inputs of the first stage. The second stage should toggle if, at the time of the activating clock transition, the B_0 output is a 1. No change will occur when the B_0 output is a 0. This is achieved by applying B_0 to the J and K inputs of the second stage. The toggling action will occur on every alternate activating clock transition. It is important to note that the change in B_1 occurs because, immediately before, B_0 is a 1. Looking at the sequence, it can be seen that the third stage should toggle only when B_0 and B_1 are both 1. This can be achieved by applying B_0B_1 to the J and K inputs of the third flip-flop. Hence the first three flip-flops are configured as designed above.

Continuing, the toggle action for the fourth stage should occur when all of B_0, B_1 and B_2 are a 1. The combinational circuitry for the fourth stage could be one three-input AND gate. The toggle action for the fifth stage should occur when all of B_0, B_1, B_2 and B_3 are a 1 and thus requires a four-input AND gate. The sixth stage should toggle when all of B_0, B_1, B_2, B_3 and B_4 are a 1 and hence requires a five-input AND gate, and so on, as shown in Fig. 4.28(b). An alternative implementation is shown in Fig. 4.28(c) which reduces the number of inputs of the gates to two. However, this particular implementation has the disadvantage that the number of levels of gating increases with the number of stages which will limit the speed of operation.

A *binary-down counter* is a counter whose outputs form a counting sequence in reverse order to that of the up counter, e.g. 1111, 1110, 1101, 1100, 1011, 1010, ⋯ This can be obtained by connecting the $\bar{Q}$ output of one flip-flop to the next stage, rather than Q. Alternatively, the counter can be left connected as an up counter and the outputs taken from the $\bar{Q}$ instead of Q. (The reader may wish to confirm that complementing the output sequence, i.e changing all 0's to 1's and all 1's to 0's, will result in the count-down sequence.) If rising (positive) edge-triggered flip-flops are used in the counter circuits with the Q's taken as the counter outputs, to count up Q is fed to the next stage, while to count down, $\bar{Q}$ is fed to the next stage.

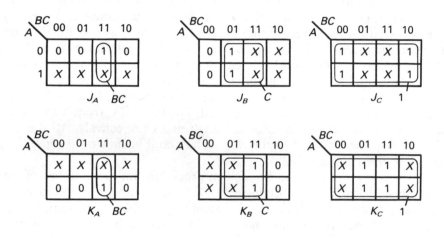

(a) *J–K* input functions

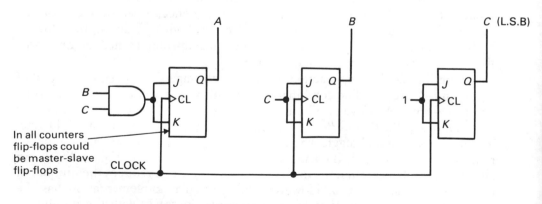

(b) Circuit

Figure 4.27   Binary-up counter implementation

A *bidirectional counter* is a counter which can count upwards or downwards depending upon some logic control signal. One bidirectional synchronous counter is shown in Fig. 4.29. In this circuit, there are two control signals, 'count-forward' and 'count-backward'. 'Count-forward' when set to a 1 selects the Q flip-flop outputs to feed to the next stage, while 'count-backward' when set to a 1 selects the $\bar{Q}$ flip-flop outputs. Counter outputs are always taken from the Q flip-flop outputs. If neither 'count-forward' nor 'count-backward' is a 1, the counter is inactive. Count-forward and count-backward are never set to a 1 together. Bidirectional counters are available as one part in integrated circuit

Clock pulse	B_5	B_4	B_3	B_2	B_1	B_0
Φ_0	0	0	0	0	0	0
Φ_1	0	0	0	0	0	1
Φ_2	0	0	0	0	1	0
Φ_3	0	0	0	0	1	1
Φ_4	0	0	0	1	0	0
Φ_5	0	0	0	1	0	1
Φ_6	0	0	0	1	1	0
Φ_7	0	0	0	1	1	1
Φ_8	0	0	1	0	0	0
Φ_9	0	0	1	0	0	1
Φ_{10}	0	0	1	0	1	0
Φ_{11}	0	0	1	0	1	1
Φ_{12}	0	0	1	1	0	0
Φ_{13}	0	0	1	1	0	1
Φ_{14}	0	0	1	1	1	0
Φ_{15}	0	0	1	1	1	1
Φ_{16}	0	1	0	0	0	0
Φ_{31}	0	1	1	1	1	1
Φ_{32}	1	0	0	0	0	0

(a) Pattern

Figure 4.28 6-bit synchronous binary counter

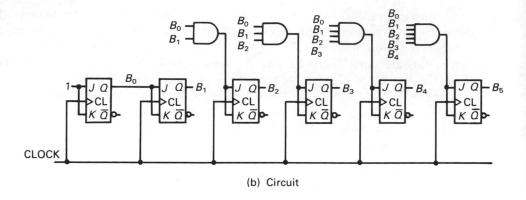

(b) Circuit

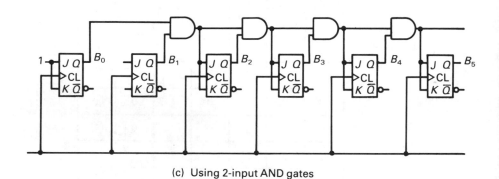

(c) Using 2-input AND gates

Figure 4.28   *continued*

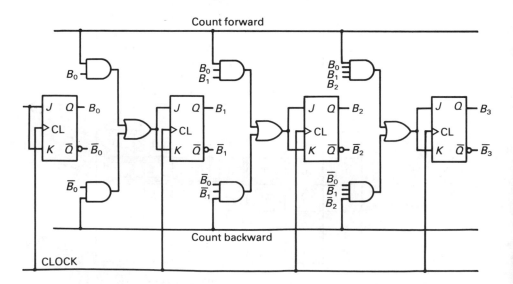

Figure 4.29   Bidirectional synchronous binary counter

construction, such as the TTL 74LS191/3 4-bit synchronous binary up/down counters. The 74LS191 has a single up/down control input. The flip-flops of the counters can be preset to initial values (i.e. loaded with data) using asynchronous set and reset inputs on the flip-flops activated with a 'load data' signal. Figure 4.30 shows additional logic circuitry to achieve this asynchronous load operation. The asynchronous load operation overrides any synchronous counting operation.

A synchronous load operation can be implemented as in the 74LS163 synchronous count-up counter. When the data input is a 0, $J = 0$ and $K = 1$ causing the output to become a 0, and when the data input is a 1, $J = 1$ and $K = 0$ causing the output to become a 1. The load operation takes place at the time of the activating clock transition and overrides the counting operation.

4.4.6 Design procedure for arbitrary code counters

Sometimes a counter is required which follows different sequences than simply counting in binary. Examples include binary counters which count only up to a number less than the maximum, and counters that follow specific codes sequences. It may be that an intuitive solution can be found. However, the procedure we have already presented to design binary counters can be applied to any sequence and to all types of flip-flops.

For example, consider the sequence described in state diagram shown in Fig. 4.31(a). The corresponding state table is given in Fig. 4.31(b). The subsequent design procedure is similar to that given previously. Four numbers do not appear in the sequence, 001 (decimal 1), 011 (3), 100 (4) and 111 (7).

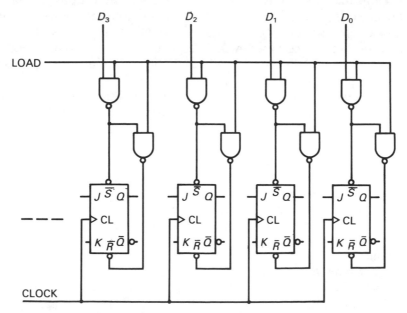

Figure 4.30 Asynchronous parallel load logic for a synchronous binary counter

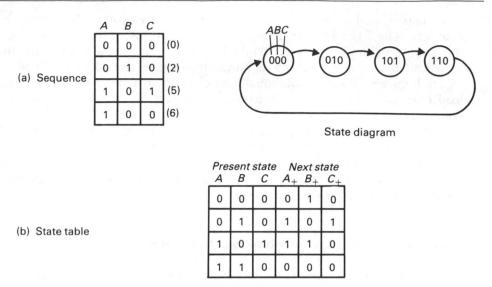

Figure 4.31   Arbitrary code counter sequence

One possible course of action is to consider these numbers as don't cares. The entries in the Karnaugh maps are then marked with X's. However, any of the unused numbers map appear upon switch-on and mapping the numbers as don't cares will mean that the subsequent behavior of the counter will depend upon the interpretation of the don't cares during the logic minimization process. For example, if the J and K functions were minimized as though the don't care were 1's, the outputs would toggle. The subsequent sequence followed would depend upon the mapping. It is possible that a completely different and unwanted sequence could be followed. If at any time one of the required numbers in the sequence appears, the correct sequence would then be entered. To ensure that the correct sequence is followed irrespective of the start-up conditions, each don't care needs to be considered separately and interpreted in a way that the correct sequence is found eventually.

Another approach to handle start-up conditions is to force the counter outputs into one of the correct numbers when the counter is first switched on by applying a general system reset signal to the asynchronous set and reset inputs of the flip-flops (if available).

In our problem, all don't cares are considered as such and the minimal solution is obtained as shown in Fig. 4.32(a). Finally, the circuit is drawn. One implementation is shown in Fig. 4.32(b). Figure 4.33 shows the design of the counter so that the next code after an unused code is 000. If an unused code appeared upon switch-on (or due to electrical noise), after one clock pulse the counter outputs would be 000, and subsequently would remain in the correct sequence.

A D-type flip-flop implementation requires only three inputs, D_A, D_B and D_C. Table 4.3 can be used to deduce the flip-flop inputs. The problem reduces simply to entering the new Q output, either A_+, B_+ or C_+ as appropriate, into the Karnaugh maps. The design is shown in Fig. 4.34. Notice that there is a

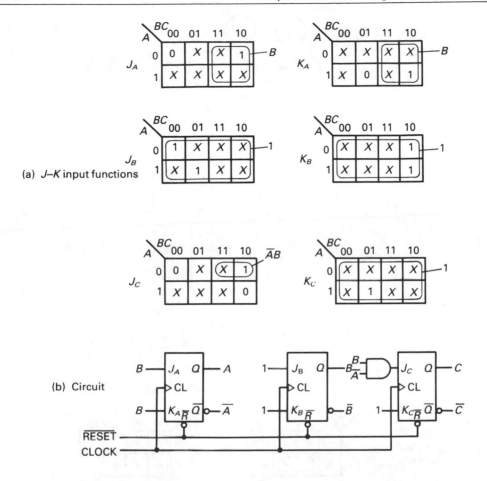

Figure 4.32   Design of an arbitrary code counter based on J–K flip-flops

common term, $\overline{A}B$, which allows a gate to be used for both D_A and D_C inputs. In general, the D-type flip-flop expressions will be more complicated than the J–K flip-flop expressions and more gates will be required for each expression. However, there are half the number of expressions so the number of gates may in fact be less. Also, larger numbers of D-type flip-flops are manufactured in one package.

Table 4.3 Q/Q_+ table for a D-type flip-flop

Required output change		Input
Q	to Q_+	D
0	0	0
0	1	1
1	0	0
1	1	1

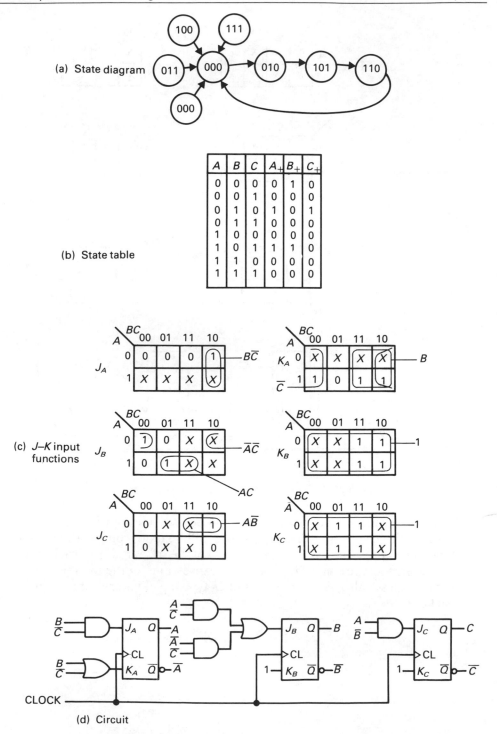

Figure 4.33 Arbitrary code counter design with unused codes mapped

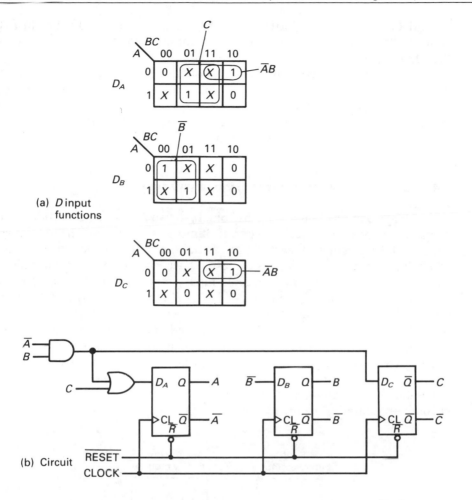

Figure 4.34　Design of arbitrary code counter based on *D*-type flip-flops

4.4.7 Alternative approach for arbitrary code counter design

We have presented counter designs using flip-flops and SSI gates. In practice, MSI binary-up counters are readily available, and this influences the design approach taken. For example, an arbitrary code counter can be designed using a standard binary counter and combinational logic to convert the binary output into the required output, if the number of states in the arbitrary code counter is the same as the binary counter. As mentioned in Chap. 3, read-only memories (ROMs) can replace combinational logic. To take an example, if an 8-bit Gray code counter (counter with outputs which follow the Gray code) is required, and 8-bit binary counter could be used together with a 256 (2^8) 8-bit word ROM as shown in Fig. 4.35. The first 8-bit memory location would hold the first Gray code (00000000), the second location addressed would hold the second Gray code (00000001), the third location would hold the third Gray code (00000011), the fourth location would hold the fourth Gray code (00000010), etc.

Apart from only requiring two components, a binary counter and a ROM, the method has the advantage that the sequence can be easily altered by inserting a new ROM holding a required sequence, However, the maximum speed of operation may be less than using the method in section 4.4.5 with gates because of the maximum speed of operation of the ROM.

4.4.8 Generating control pulses using binary counters

An application of binary-up and binary-down counters is to produce timing signals. Suppose the eight separate timing signals shown previously in Fig. 4.23(a) are required, each timing signal occurring in sequence and of one clock duration. Figure 4.36 shows a design based around a binary counter. Here each AND gate decodes one possible binary output combination from 000 to 111 ($\bar{B}_2\bar{B}_1\bar{B}_0$, $\bar{B}_2\bar{B}_1B_0$, $\bar{B}_2B_1\bar{B}_0$, $\bar{B}_2B_1B_0$, $B_2\bar{B}_1\bar{B}_0$, $B_2\bar{B}_1B_0$, $B_2B_1\bar{B}_0$, and $B_2B_1B_0$), and produces a 1 only when the combination occurs.

If an asynchronous binary counter is used in the above circuit, glitches can occur in the outputs because of delays between counter output changes. These glitches are shown in an idealized form in Fig. 4.37 and come about when more than one binary output must change. Figure 4.38 shows the actual patterns generated by the counter. Replacing the asynchronous counter with a synchronous counter is likely to eliminate glitches but there is still the finite

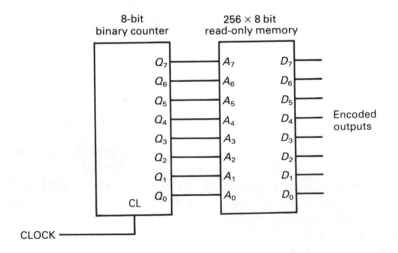

Figure 4.35 Arbitrary code counter based on a binary counter and a read-only memory

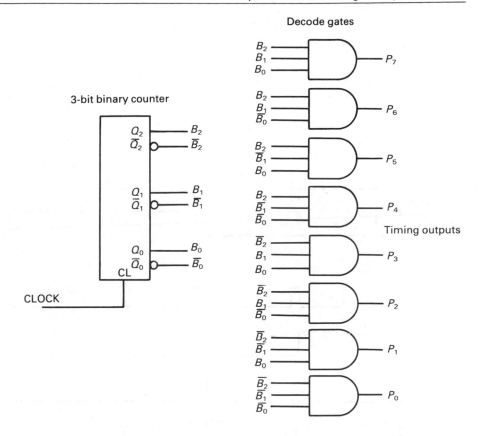

Figure 4.36 Generating timing pulses using a binary counter and decode logic

possibility that glitches are generated due to differences between flip-flop propagation delays. For example, the 74LS78 J–K flip-flop has a low-to-high output propagation delay time of 11 ns typically, and 20 ns maximum. The high-to-low output propagation delay time is 15 ns typically, and 30 ns maximum. Minimum delay times are not quoted. Pessimistically, the minimum times could be taken to be zero. Even between typical and maximum times, it is possible to generate glitches in decode outputs should the decode gates operate at high speed. The flip-flops of complete counter parts are likely to be more closely matched though actual figures are not normally given.

The Johnson counter approach described in section 4.4.2 would overcome the problem as only one output change occurs at a time in this counter. Alternatively, an enable signal could be applied to all decode gates to produce an output only after all possible glitch combinations have passed.

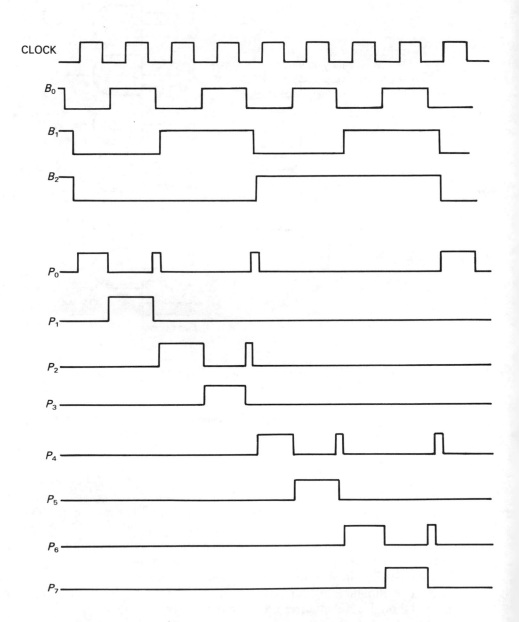

Figure 4.37 Glitches in decode outputs

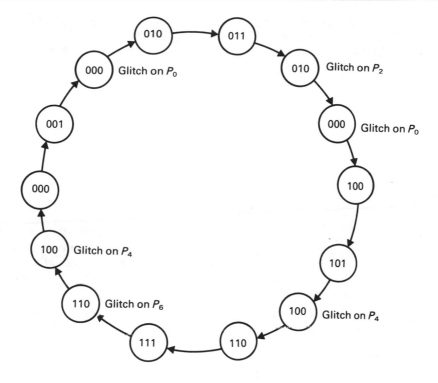

Figure 4.38   Outputs of asynchronous binary counter

PROBLEMS

4.1   Determine the truth table of the flip-flop shown in Fig. 4.39, assuming that $S = 0$, $R = 0$ cannot be followed by $S = 1$, $R = 1$, or vice versa. Comment. Modify this circuit so as to become a synchronous flip-flop.

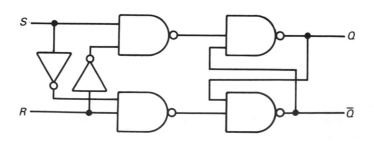

Figure 4.39   Logic circuit for problem 4.1

4.2 A design team is investigating possible new types of flip-flops and is considering a flip-flop they call an '*X–Y*' flip-flop with the truth table shown in Table 4.4. Show that the *X–Y* flip-flop can be designed around a *R–S* flip-flop by deriving the *R* and *S* input expressions.

Table 4.4 Truth table for Problem 4.2

Inputs		Output
X	Y	Q_+
0	0	0
0	1	1
1	0	$\overline{Q}$
1	1	$\overline{Q}$

4.3 Design a logic circuit using NAND gates to convert a shift register into either a ring counter or a Johnson (twisted ring) counter. Arrange that when a control signal, *A* (say), is a 1, the configuration is a ring counter, and when *A* is a 0, the configuration is a Johnson counter.

4.4 Design an asynchronous binary-down counter using positive edge-triggered *D*-type flip-flops.

4.5 Design a synchronous binary-up counter using *D*-type flip-flops.

4.6 Design a synchronous binary counter with outputs that follow the state diagram shown in Fig. 4.40, using *J–K* flip-flops.

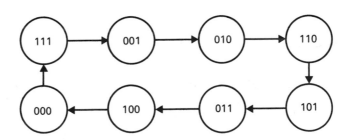

Figure 4.40   State diagram for Problem 4.6

4.7 Repeat Problem 4.6 using *D*-type flip-flops. Draw diagrams illustrating the logic levels taken by the outputs of the flip-flops for one complete cycle of the sequence.

4.8 Design a synchronous counter which follows one of the two state diagrams shown in Fig. 4.41, depending upon a control signal, *Z*. If *Z* = 1, state diagram (a) is followed. If *Z* = 0, state diagram (b) is followed. Use *J–K* flip-flops with asynchronous reset inputs and NAND gates. Numbers not in the sequences can be considered as don't cares. Use the reset inputs to initialize the circuit.

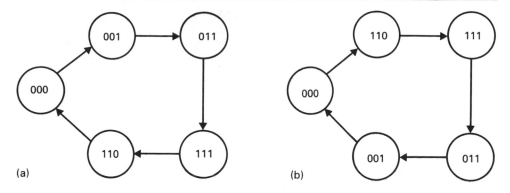

Figure 4.41   State diagrams for Problem 4.8

4.9 Design a synchronous counter to cycle repetitively through the numbers zero to five (i.e. binary 000 to 101). Ensure that the counter cannot cycle through any other sequence by mapping unused patterns to change the pattern 000 after one activating clock transition. Use $J-K$ flip-flops which do not have asynchronous set or reset inputs, and NAND gates. Modify the circuit so that the number five is omitted from the sequence when a control signal, A, is a 1.

4.10 Determine the sequence followed by the counter shown in Fig. 4.42. Draw the state diagram.

4.11 Design a circuit based upon a 4-bit binary-up counter and decode gates which will generate the recurring sequence of pulses on seven outputs $P_6 P_5 P_4 P_3 P_2 P_1 P_0$ described below:

$$P_6 P_5 P_4 P_3 P_2 P_1 P_0 = 1000001, 0000100, 0011000, 0100010$$

Determine whether any glitches might occur if an asynchronous binary counter were used.

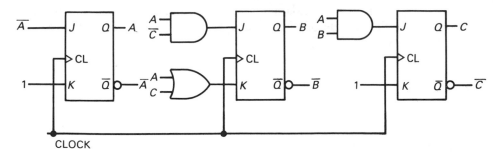

Figure 4.42   Logic circuit for Problem 4.10

Logic Circuit Implementation

5.1 LOGIC GATES

The circuit details of logic devices were mentioned briefly in section 2.2.4. Now we will take the subject a little further. Voltages are used almost universally to represent Boolean values and binary digits and clearly we need two voltages to represent the two Boolean/binary states. To recapitulate, if the voltage used to represent a 1 is more positive than the voltage used to represent a 0, the representation is known as positive logic representation. Conversely if the voltage used to represent a 1 is less than that used to represent a 0, the representation is known as negative logic representation. In this chapter we will assume a positive logic representation as this is most commonly chosen. It has already been noted that the representation chosen is only a convention and not intrinsic in the design of the gate.

A gate can have one input (NOT gate) or more than one input. The number of inputs is called the *fan-in*, e.g. a three-input AND gate has a fan-in of 3. The term *fan-out* is used to define the number of gates than can be connected to the output of a gate. Fan-out is limited by circuit considerations which we will consider later.

Logic gates can be designed using diodes and resistors, transistors and resistors, or diodes, transistors and resistors. Usually, the last combination of components is used. We shall firstly consider gates employing diodes and resistors as these are fundamental logic circuits. A knowledge of basic electronics would be helpful for this chapter; essential concepts will be explained only very briefly as necessary.

5.2 DIODE GATES

5.2.1 Diode AND gate

Let us review the p-n diode. Current flows in the forward direction through the diode (the same direction as the direction of the point in the symbol) when the voltage across the diode reaches about $+0.7$V. The diode is then said to be *forward-biased* or conducting. The voltage drop across a diode does not increase substantially above 0.7V as current is increased and commonly is assumed to be constant. Virtually no current flows when the applied voltage is less than 0.7 V or when a negative voltage is applied. When a negative voltage is applied, the diode is said to be *reverse-biased*. Figure 5.1 depicts a typical *p-n* diode voltage–current characteristic. In our analysis, we will assume an idealized characteristic in which conduction occurs at a voltage of 0.7 V and no conduction occurs below this voltage. The reader is referred to texts on electronics for a description of exactly how the diode achieves this behavior.

A three-input diode AND is shown in Fig. 5.2. Extra inputs can be formed by adding extra diodes. We shall take the input logic levels to be 0 V for a 0 and +5 V for a 1. When all the inputs are at 0 V, all the input diodes are forward-biased and current will flow from the +5 V supply through the resistor and diode and out of the input terminal. If the diodes are identical, the current will divide

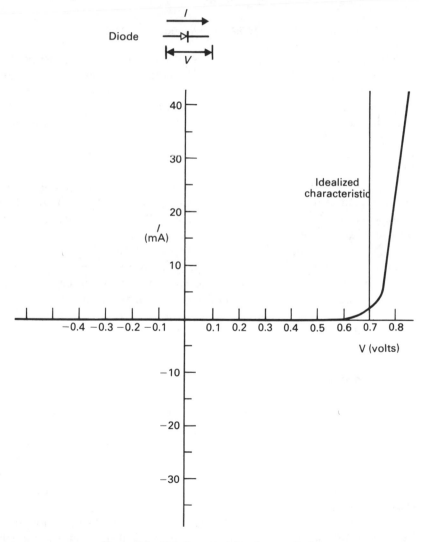

Figure 5.1 *V–I* characteristic of a *p–n* diode

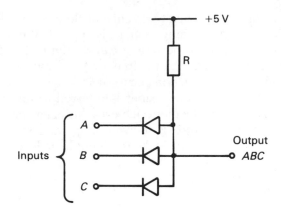

Figure 5.2   Three-input diode AND gate

equally between the diodes. Therefore the output voltage must be $+0.7\,\text{V}$ above the input voltage of $0\,\text{V}$, i.e. $0.7\,\text{V}$. This voltage will be taken as the output 0 level.

If one input is raised to $5\,\text{V}$ (representing a logic 1), the associated input diode will become reverse-biased, but the other diodes will still be forward-biased. Current will continue to flow through these diodes and the output will remain at a 0. If two inputs are raised to a 1 level, current will flow through the diodes associated with the inputs still at a 0, and the output will remain at a 0. Only when all the inputs are raised to a 1 level will this condition change. Then, the output voltage will rise. If $5\,\text{V}$ is applied on all the inputs, none of the diodes can conduct and the output voltage will also be at $5\,\text{V}$ (a logic 1). The circuit behaves as an AND gate since only when all the inputs are at a 1 level will the output be at a 1 level.

Notice that the output voltage representing a logic 0 is higher than the input 0 level by $+0.7\,\text{V}$, but the voltage at a 1 is $5\,\text{V}$ for both input and output. An extra $+0.7\,\text{V}$ at a 0 level is added to each output of similar circuits if they are cascaded, i.e. a second gate would have an output at a 0 level of $1.4\,\text{V}$, a third gate would have an output of $2.1\,\text{V}$. This is clearly unacceptable. Therefore many diode AND gates cannot be cascaded.

5.2.2 Diode OR gate

A three-input diode OR gate is shown in Fig. 5.3. Again extra inputs can be added by adding extra diodes. With all input signals at $0\,\text{V}$ (a logic 0), the output must be at $0\,\text{V}$ (a logic 0) since none of the input diodes can conduct. If any of the inputs rises to $5\,\text{V}$ (a logic 1), the associated diode will conduct and the output will also rise to $0.7\,\text{V}$ less than the input voltage, i.e. $4.3\,\text{V}$. This voltage will be taken as a 1. If more input signals rise to a 1 level, the output will remain at a 1 level. Consequently, the circuit behaves as an OR gate.

Notice in this circuit that the output level at a 0 is the same at $0\,\text{V}$ for both input and output, but the output voltage at a 1 level is lower than the input by

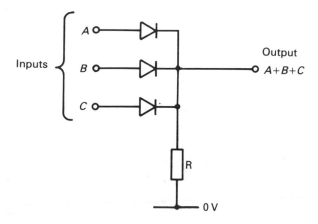

Figure 5.3   Three-input diode OR gate

0.7 V. Successive output voltages of cascaded OR gates are reduced by 0.7 V, i.e. a second gate would have an output at a 1 level of 3.6 V, a third gate would have an output of 2.9 V. Therefore, many diode OR gates cannot be cascaded either.

5.3 BIPOLAR TRANSISTOR GATES

The final fundamental Boolean operation, the NOT operation, cannot be produced with diodes and resistors alone. For the NOT operation, we need to use 'active' devices, nowadays transistors. In this section, we will consider the bipolar transistor as used in logic circuits. Commonly in logic circuits, transistors are operated in either a fully conducting state or a fully non-conducting state to produce the two logic voltages. The fully conducting state is known as the *saturated* or *turned-on* state and the fully non-conducting state is known as the *cut-off* state.

5.3.1 Transistor in cut-off and saturated conditions

Let us firstly review the bipolar transistor. A transistor has three connections, a *collector* connection, a *base* connection and an *emitter* connection. There are three currents associated with the connections, a collector current, I_C, a base current, I_B, and an emitter current, I_E. The direction of emitter current flow when the device is operated normally is shown by the arrow on the emitter part of the transistor symbol which may be either into the emitter terminal or out of the emitter terminal depending upon the type of transistor. In the type of transistor where the current flows out of the emitter, the current flows into the base and collector. This type is called an *n-p-n transistor* as shown in Fig. 5.4. In transistors where the current flows into the emitter, the current flows out of the

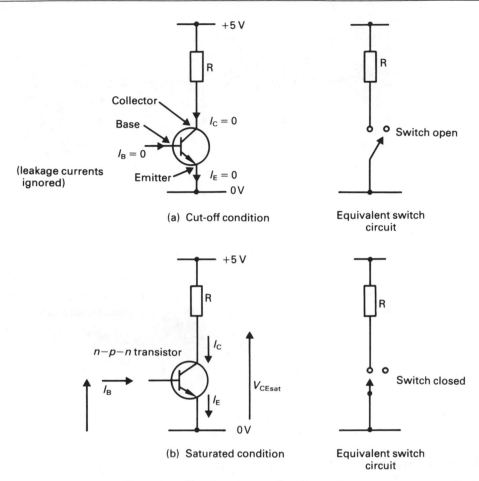

Figure 5.4   Transistor in cut-off and saturated conditions

base and collector. This type is called a *p-n-p transistor*. The names are derived from the '*n*' type and '*p*' type semiconductor materials used in their construction. Both the base–emitter 'junction' and the base–collector 'junction' consist of diodes.

The emitter current is given by the sum of the collector current and base current, i.e.:

$$I_E = I_C + I_B \tag{1}$$

While the base–emitter voltage is between $+0.6\text{V}$ and $+0.7\text{V}$ approximately, the collector current is determined by the relationship:

$$I_C = h_{\text{FE}}I_B \tag{2}$$

where h_{FE} is the d.c. current gain, a parameter of the particular transistor. The current gain is usually more than one hundred. Therefore the base current is much smaller than the collector current and the emitter current is approximately equal to the collector current. Again, the reader is referred to electronics texts for an explanation of the actual transistor mechanism.

In Fig. 5.4, a resistor is connected between the collector and the $+5\,\text{V}$ supply to provide a path for the collector current. When the base current is zero, the collector and emitter currents are zero (except for leakage currents; see below). The device is then said to be *cut off* and can be considered as an electrical switch in the open position between the collector and emitter. No voltage will be produced across the resistor as no current is flowing in the resistor (by Ohm's law, $V = IR$). The voltage at the collector, i.e. V_{out}, will be the same as the $+5\,\text{V}$ supply voltage. The cut-off state is generally achieved by applying $0\,\text{V}$ between the base and emitter, but certainly a voltage less than about $0.6\,\text{V}$ is necessary.

When a base–emitter voltage above $0.6\,\text{V}$ is applied, the base current increases and according to (2), the collector current increases. The voltage across the resistor increases and the collector voltage falls towards $0\,\text{V}$. Clearly the collector voltage cannot fall below $0\,\text{V}$. In fact, there is a minimum voltage across the collector and emitter of the transistor, known as the *saturation voltage* V_{CEsat}, which is approximately $0.2\,\text{V}$. If the base current is increased further, the relationship between collector current and base current given above, (2), does not hold, and the collector voltage and current remains approximately constant. Then:

$$h_{\text{FE}}I_B > I_C \tag{3}$$

and the transistor is said to be *saturated*. In the saturated state, the collector current is defined by the supply voltage ($+5\,\text{V}$) and the collector resistance (R_C) as follows:

$$I_C = (5 - V_{\text{CF.sat}})/R_{\text{C}} \tag{4}$$

A transistor in the saturated state generates a stable, low collector voltage which can be used to represent a logic 0. The voltage varies very little with increased load if the relationship (3) is kept true to maintain saturation. We shall assume that a base–emitter voltage of $0.7\,\text{V}$ is sufficient to saturate the transistor. In practice it may be between $0.7\,\text{V}$ and $0.9\,\text{V}$.

Leakage currents are very small currents (less than $10\,\mu\text{A}$) which flow between the three transistor terminals in addition to the above currents. We can identify three leakage currents: a leakage current between the emitter and base, a leakage current between the base and collector and a leakage current between the collector and emitter. When a transistor is saturated, collector and emitter currents are typically in the region of 1 to $10\,\text{mA}$ and base currents are in the region of 0.1 to $1\,\text{mA}$. Consequently the contribution due to leakage currents is not generally significant. The leakage currents can be significant in the cut-off state.

5.3.2 Transistor NOT gate

The transistor circuit shown in Fig. 5.5 is a NOT gate. If the input voltage is $0\,\text{V}$ (or less than about $+0.6\,\text{V}$), no base current or collector current will flow

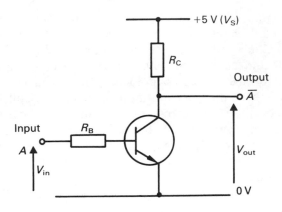

Figure 5.5   Transistor NOT gate

(except for leakage currents). Therefore the collector voltage will rise to 5 V. Conversely, if the input voltage is sufficiently above 0.7 V to cause the transistor to enter saturation, the output voltage will fall to 0.2 V (V_{CEsat}). Therefore the circuit can act as an NOT gate, with a 0 output represented by 0.2 V and a logic 1 output represented by 5 V. Input voltage levels can be the same.

The design values for the resistors can be calculated from Ohm's law as follows. If the input voltage is above 0.7 V, base current will flow into the base of the transistor and is given by:

$$I_B = (V_{in} - 0.7)/R_B$$

The maximum collector current is with the transistor saturated and is given by:

$$I_{Cmax} = (V_S - V_{CEsat})/R_C$$

For saturation, I_B must be greater than I_C/h_{FE} from (3). This can be achieved by choosing R_B sufficiently low for a given R_C, i.e. the following inequality must be met:

$$\frac{V_{in} - 0.7}{R_B} > \frac{V_S - V_{CEsat}}{R_C h_{FE}}$$

The calculation for R_B from the above assumes that no external load is present at the output to draw current. The effect of additional loads such as other gates, is considered later in section 5.4. Typically, a choice is made for R_B and R_C to give a collector current suitable for driving a number of additional gates.

5.3.3 Diode-transistor-logic (DTL) gates

The diode AND gate of section 5.2.1 and the transistor NOT gate of section 5.3.2 can be combined to form a *diode-transistor-logic* (DTL) NAND gate. A three-input DTL NAND gate is shown in Fig. 5.6. One output logic

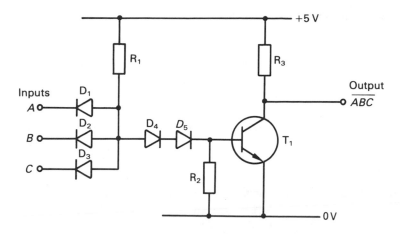

Figure 5.6   Three-input DTL NAND gate

level is with the transistor fully conducting, i.e. saturated, and the other with the transistor fully non-conducting, i.e. cut off. When the transistor is cut off, the output voltage is 5 V which represents a logic 1 and when the transistor is saturated, the output voltage is 0.2 V (V_{CEsat}) which represents a logic 0.

If one input signal is low (0.2 V) or more input signals are low, current will flow through R_1, the input diodes associated with the low inputs and out of the low input terminals. This current flow will cause the voltage on the lower end of R_1 to become 0.9 V (an input voltage of 0.2 V plus a voltage across the diodes of 0.7 V). One or two diodes are inserted between the input diode AND gate and the transistor NOT gate to ensure that the base of the transistor is now less than 0.7 V to cause the transistor to turn off and create a high output. R_2 is provided so that the transistor is properly kept cut off. (If one diode is provided the base voltage would be 0.2 V (0.9 V − 0.7 V). If two diodes are provided as shown, the base voltage is 0 V as insufficient voltage is available for the two diodes to conduct.)

If all the inputs are high (5 V), the input diodes will be reverse-biased. Current will flow through the R_1 resistor but then through the diodes D_4 and D_5 towards the base of the transistor. The current will divide at the base. Some will flow into the base and some will flow through the resistor R_2. The component values are chosen so that sufficient current flows into the base of the transistor to saturate the transistor under all load conditions. Hence the output falls to a logic 0 level.

Because two diodes are inserted in the circuit shown here, the input voltage must rise to at least +1.4 V before there is +2.1 V on the lower end of R_1 and 0.7 V across the base and emitter of the transistor sufficient to turn the transistor on. (If one diode is used, the input must rise only to +0.7 V before the transistor turns on.) Once the threshold is passed, current will stop flowing through the input diodes and instead all the current will flow through the interstage diodes D_4 and D_5.

5.3.4 Transistor-transistor-logic (TTL) gates

Some early integrated circuit parts employed DTL designs. However, in integrated circuit construction, transistors can often be as readily fabricated as diodes. Indeed, if diodes are required, transistors are commonly fabricated and used as diodes (for example, using the base and emitter with the collector connected to the base). Circuits can employ mainly transistors used as transistors. Such gates are known as *transistor-transistor-logic* (TTL) gates. The DTL gate can be modified to the TTL version by replacing the input diodes with one multi-emitter transistor which will operate logically as the original diodes. A multi-emitter transistor is one having several emitter regions. Each emitter–base junction can behave logically as a diode in a diode AND circuit. Electrically, transistor operation occurs as described in the following.

(a) Standard TTL

Standard TTL was first introduced in 1963 and has formed the basis of many subsequent logic circuits. A standard design TTL NAND gate using a multi-emitter transistor is shown in Fig. 5.7. There are three distinct parts in the circuit, an input stage using transistor T_1, an internal stage using T_2 and an output stage using T_3 and T_4.

Comparing the TTL circuit with the DTL circuit shown in Fig. 5.6, we can see that the diodes in the diode input circuit of the DTL circuit have been replaced by a multi-emitter transistor T_1. The three emitter–base junctions of the multi-emitter transistor correspond to the diodes D_1, D_2 and D_3 and the base-collector junction of the multi-emitter transistor correspond to the diode D_4. D_5 in the DTL circuit has been replaced by the transistor T_2 and the output transistor T_1 in the DTL circuit by transistor T_3 in the TTL circuit. An

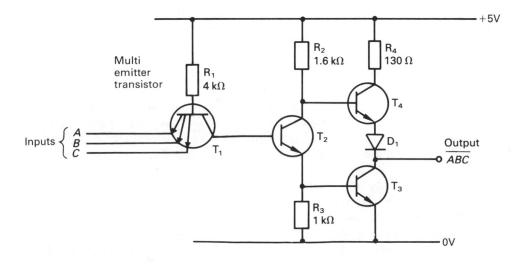

Figure 5.7 Standard TTL NAND gate

additional output transistor T_4 and the associated components are provided in the TTL circuit.

Firstly let us deduce the output 0 voltage level. In the DTL circuit, this level occurs when T_1 is saturated. In the TTL circuit the level occurs when T_3 is saturated and hence the logical 0 output voltage is V_{CEsat} of T_3 (say 0.2 V).

If one or more inputs are low (0.2 V), current will flow from the +5 V supply through the R_1 resistor into the base, out of the emitter (i.e. through the base–emitter 'diode') and out of the input terminals of the gate in a similar manner to the diode AND gate. However, because a transistor is used, 'transistor action' occurs and collector current will flow governed by the base current and the external circuitry. In this case, the base current is that flowing through R_1. The current flowing through the input terminals is actually an emitter current, the value of which is given by the sum of the base current and the collector current. Assuming that the base current is sufficient to saturate the transistor, the voltage across the emitter and collector is given by V_{CEsat}, or 0.2 V approximately. If the input is at 0.2 V, the base of transistor T_2 is at 0.4 V which will cause this transistor to be cut off. Therefore the collector current of transistor T_2 will fall to zero and the emitter falls to 0 V. This will in turn cause transistor T_3 to be cut off as the base of this transistor will be at 0 V. Transistor T_4 will conduct (but not generally saturate) and the emitter of this transistor will be at 0.7 V below its base. In this analysis, we will ignore the base current of T_4 (and leakage currents). Hence without any current through R_2, the base of T_4 will be at +4.3 V. The only physical diode in the circuit, D_1, will conduct and this will produce an output voltage of 3.6 V (4.3 V − 0.7 V). This voltage is taken as the nominal logic 1 level.

If all the inputs are high at 3.6 V, the base–emitter junctions of transistor T_1 are all reverse-biased. However, the collector cannot rise above 1.4 V because of the base–emitter junctions of transistors T_2 and T_3. Current will flow through R_1 across the base–collector junction of transistor T_1 and into the base of transistor T_2. Transistors T_2 and T_3 will become fully saturated. Transistor T_1 is operating now in an unusual mode. The emitter voltage is 3.6 V (a logic 1) , the collector voltage is at 1.4 V and the base voltage is at 2.1 V. Therefore the base–emitter junction is reverse-biased and the base–collector junction is forward-biased. In this situation, the roles of the emitter and collector are reversed. The emitter acts as a collector and the collector acts as an emitter. This is known as the *inverse mode*. The transistor may exhibit some current gain in the inverse mode though more likely this will be base–collector current attenuation, i.e. a current 'gain' of less than unity. (Generally, the inverse gain of T_1 is reduced by suitable transistor geometry incorporating components at the base to divert the base current from the base–collector junction.)

With transistors T_2 and T_3 fully saturated, the output voltage will be at V_{CEsat} of T_3, say 0.2 V. The base of T_4 will be at 0.9 V (the base–emitter voltage of T_3 plus V_{CEsat} of T_2). This voltage is insufficient to allow both D_1 and T_4 to conduct and these devices will be fully cut off. Notice that the diode D_1 is necessary in the circuit to prevent T_4 from conducting whilst T_3 is conducting. The 130 Ω resistor limits the current available at a high output level and makes the circuit output short-circuit protected. Typically only one output of a TTL integrated circuit package can be short-circuited to 0V at a time because of power dissipation limitations.

The circuit voltages given are only approximate. In particular, V_{CEsat} may be higher than 0.2V. We have deduced the logic levels as 0.2V and 3.6V. Manufactured TTL gates have a maximum generated 0 level voltage of 0.4V. Though not quoted, it is assumed that the minimum generated level voltage is 0V. The nominal generated 1 level voltage is sometimes quoted as 3.4V and can fall to 2.4V under load conditions (see later). The maximum generated 1 level voltage is +5V (the supply voltage). The input circuitry will recognize a voltage of up to 0.8V as a logical 0 and down to 2V as a logical 1. This allows some electrical 'noise' to be allowed on generated signals. We shall defer further discussion on noise for section 5.6.1 because it applies to all types of logic gates.

Figure 5.8 shows a TTL NOR gate circuit. The circuit without transistors T_2 and T_4 is identical to that of a TTL NOT gate (i.e. a NAND gate with a single input). Input A then generates $\bar{A}$ at the output. Similarly, the circuit with transistors T_2 and T_4 but without transistors T_1 and T_3 forms a NOT gate and the input B then generate $\bar{B}$ at the output. The circuits combine at the output stage so that if A or B or both are high, transistors T_3 or T_4 or both are conducting, causing T_5 to saturate and the output to be low. If A and B are both low, both transistors T_3 and T_4 are cut off and only transistor T_6 is conducting to produce a high output.

(b) Low-power and high-speed TTL (LTTL and HTTL)

The speed of operation and power consumption of logic devices using saturated transistors are closely related. Generally as the power consumption is increased by using smaller values of resistors, the speed of operation increases.

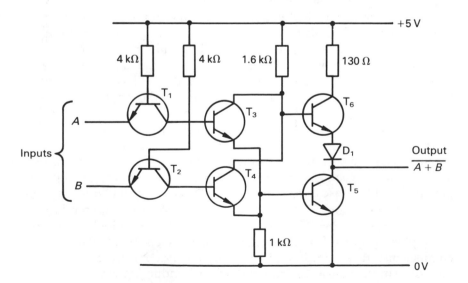

Figure 5.8   Standard TTL NOR gate

The product (propagation time) × (power consumption), called the *speed–power product*, is regarded as a figure of merit for a particular logic circuit family. Standard TTL has a speed–power product of 10 ns × 10 mW or 100 pJ. The component values in the basic design can be changed in order to either increase the speed of operation (i.e. reduce the propagation delay time) by decreasing resistor values, or to decrease the power consumption by increasing resistor values. The former has been done in high-speed TTL (HTTL) circuits and the latter in low-power TTL (LTTL) circuits. HTTL has a speed–power product of 6 ns × 22 mW or 132 pJ and LTTL has a speed–power product of 33 ns × 1 mW or 33 pJ. Both these circuits were introduced around 1967 but were superseded by Schottky versions in 1969–71. Schottky gates are considered in section 5.4.1.

5.3.5 Open-collector TTL gates

If we join the outputs of normal TTL gates together, with the intention that one gate will drive a common line as shown in Fig. 5.9, conflict will occur if different gates attempt to drive the output in opposite states. Indeed, it is possible that excessive current will flow (because saturated transistors present a low resistance perhaps in the region of 25 Ω between the collector and emitter for internal TTL transistors). Wiring outputs of *open-collector* gates together enables any one of the gates to drive a common line to a logical 0 without conflict. An open-collector TTL gate is similar to a normal TTL gate except that the upper output transistor and associated diode are removed which enables two or more similar gates to have their outputs joined together without the possibility of the output transistors being damaged.

A standard TTL open-collector gate is shown in Fig. 5.10(a). Figure 5.10(b) shows a number of open collector gates with their outputs wired together. A single *pull-up* resistor is used to produce 5 V (a logic 1) when all the individual output transistors are cut off. If at least one of the output transistors is conducting (output at a logic 0 level) the combined output will be at a 0 level (V_{CEsat}). The output will be at a logic 1 level only if all the output signals would normally be at a logic 1 level. Hence this arrangement creates an 'ANDing' operation of the output signals.

Figure 5.11 shows a logic diagram of the configuration. The value of the pull-up resistor is typically in the region 470 Ω to 4.7 kΩ. Though occasionally called a *wired-AND* configuration, the above is more commonly known as *wired-OR*, from the conceptual viewpoint that the overall operation is one of 'ORing' with active low signals. The wired-OR connection has found use in the past as it saves gates and can be expanded to incorporate perhaps up to ten gates in all without extra circuitry. Additionally, the wired-OR connection is applicable to *bus systems* in which several sources can drive the same line. Presently the wired-OR connection is not widely used for these purposes except for some particular signals in bus systems which are considered in Part 2.

The principal disadvantage or the wired-OR connection is that when the

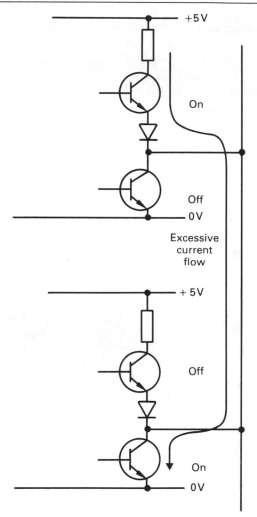

Figure 5.9   Normal TTL gates with outputs wired together

level on the output line switches from a 0 to a 1, the 1 level is brought about only by the pull-up resistor rather than an active device (transistor), which results is a slower transition. (The output capacitance must be charged to logical 1 level and the speed at which this occurs depends upon the current available. A pull-up resistor cannot generally provide the current of an active device because the minimum value of the resistor is limited by the maximum power dissipation of the open-collector output transistors.) The three-state gate overcomes this problem in bus systems.

5.3.6 Three-state TTL gates

A *three-state* (*Tri-state*†) gate has three output states, a normal logic 0 level, a normal logic 1 and a third state in which the output exhibits a very high

† *Tri-state* is a registered trademark of the National Semiconductor Corporation.

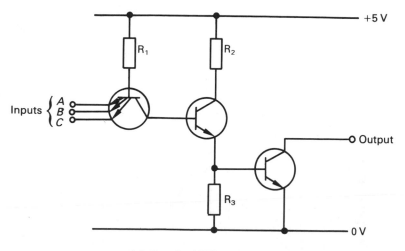

(a) Standard TTL open-collector circuit

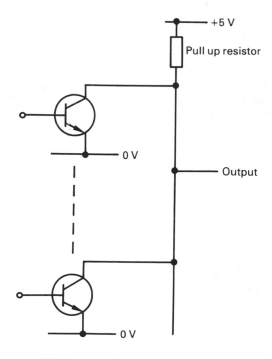

(b) Outputs wired together

Figure 5.10 Open-collector gates

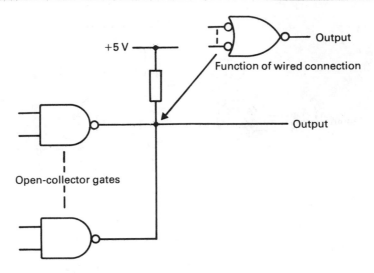

Figure 5.11 Wired-OR configuration

impedance (giving rise to typically less than $10\,\mu A$ leakage current.) The three-state device has replaced the open-collector gate in many bus systems in which several sources transmit data to one of several destinations, such as in a microprocessor system. Only one source transmits information at any instant. Figure 5.12(a) shows a symbol for a three-state NOT state gate, Fig. 5.12(b) the truth table of the device and Fig. 5.12(c) shows the general bus arrangement. Three-state gates are used at the source. The normal inactive state of these gates is with the outputs in the third state. When the device needs to drive the line, a control signal causes the device to revert to a normal two-state gate capable of producing both logic output levels.

The third state can be created through a simple modification to the standard TTL circuit, as shown in Fig. 5.13. The control input connects to an additional input of the multi-emitter input transistor and also through a diode D_2 to the upper transistor of the output stage. When the control input is high, D_2 is reverse-biased and the gate acts as a normal two-state gate. When the control input is low, without the extra diode, D_2, the output would normally become a logic 1 irrespective of the data input signal. However, with the diode, the upper transistor of the output stage is also cut off so that both output transistors are cut off. The only output current that can now flow is leakage current, and the circuit assumes a high impedance state. The circuit arrangement is enhanced in some three-state TTL gates by additional transistors.

5.4 HIGH-SPEED LOGIC CIRCUITS

The switching circuits so far described employ transistors existing in one of two states, either saturated (fully conducting) or cut-off and the transistors must

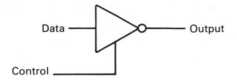

(a) Symbol

Data	Control	Output
0	0	High impedance
0	1	1
1	0	High impedance
1	1	0

(b) Truth table

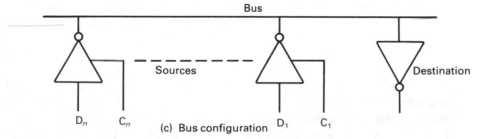

(c) Bus configuration

Figure 5.12   Tri-state gates

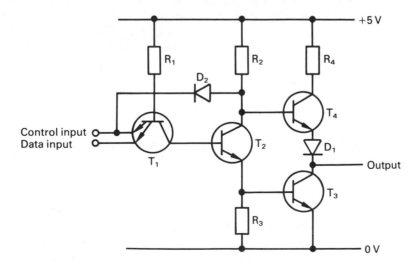

Figure 5.13   A circuit of a tri-state TTL gate

switch between these two states. When a transistor is saturated, more current enters the base than is necessary to maintain the collector current and causes 'excess' charge in the device which must be removed before the device can be taken out of the saturated state. This can take some time, perhaps several nanoseconds, and limits the speed of operation of the circuit but can be avoided by arranging that the transistor does not enter saturation. The two logic states can be fully cut off at some point before saturation; such circuits are known as non-saturating logic. Before discussing the intrinsically non-saturating logic designs, we shall consider a modification made to most of the transistors in the standard TTL which prevent these transistors saturating fully. This modification was first made to TTL in 1969 and led to a series of *Schottky TTL* gates.

5.4.1 Schottky TTL

When a transistor is saturated, the base–emitter voltage is V_{BEon} (say 0.7 V) and the collector–emitter voltage is at V_{CEsat}, approximately 0.2 V. A transistor can be prevented form entering saturation by preventing the collector voltage from falling to V_{CEsat} by 'clamping' the collector at a voltage above V_{CEsat}. An elegant way of doing this is to use a Schottky diode (a metal-semiconductor diode) as shown in Fig. 5.14(a). A Schottky diode has the special characteristic that when forward biased (metal side more positive), there is virtually no stored charge and also the voltage drop is less than V_{BEon}, at about 0.3–0.4 V. Hence when current is injected into the base of the transistor to cause conduction, and the collector voltage falls, the diode will begin to conduct when the voltage falls to 0.4 V (base voltage of transistor − forward bias of diode, 0.7 V − 0.3 V) and prevent the voltage falling any further. The circuit configuration of a bipolar transistor with a Schottky diode between the base and collector is known as a *Schottky transistor* which has the symbol shown in Fig. 5.14(b). In a Schottky TTL gate, most of the transistors are replaced by Schottky transistors. This results in a typical propagation delay (the time between the application of a new input signal which will create an output change and the resultant output change) of about 3 ns rather than 10 ns for standard TTL. Power consumption of Schottky TTL is about 19 mW compared to 10 mW for standard TTL, giving a speed–power product of 57 pJ compared with 100 pJ for Schottky TTL for standard TTL.

A low-power version of Schottky TTL was introduced in 1971, LSTTL, using larger internal resistor values, and resulted in a speed–power product of 9.5 ns × 2 mW = 19 pJ. A LSTTL NAND gate circuit is shown in Fig. 5.15. Notice that in this particular LSTTL circuit, the input circuitry has reverted to diode gate arrangement. Only one transistor is a non-Schottky transistor, T_5, which does not saturate because its collector keeps near +5 V and its emitter is always at least 1.4 V less than this. Only when the collector–emitter voltage of a transistor falls to V_{CEsat} does the transistor enter saturation. LSTTL has become the industry standard version of TTL. There have been further circuit

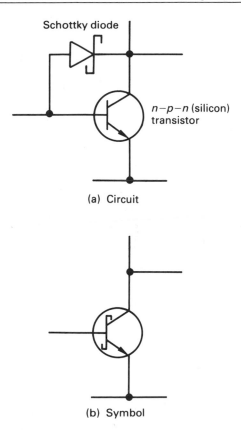

(a) Circuit

(b) Symbol

Figure 5.14 Schottky transistor

enhancements resulting in advanced Schottky TTL (ASTTL) and advanced low-power Schottky TTL (ALSTTL), both operating at twice the speed of their predecessor. ALSTTL also has half the power consumption of LSTTL. Figure 5.16 shows an ALS NOT gate (74ALSO4). In this circuit the input circuitry consists of a *p-n-p* transistor (T_1) and the low-level input current is much reduced over multi-emitter transistor and diode input circuitry as the input current constitutes a transistor base current (perhaps $20\,\mu A$). *P-n-p* input transistors are also used in some LSTTL parts to reduce low-level input currents. Table 5-1 lists the performance figures of the various TTL families.

5.4.2 Emitter-coupled logic (ECL)

Transistors are kept from saturation in *emitter-coupled logic* (ECL) designs to achieve very high speeds of operation by suitable choice of component values. Transistors in an ECL circuit are either cut-off or conducting to an extent, but not saturated. A basic ECL OR/NOR circuit is shown in Fig. 5.17. Three inputs are shown, *A, B* and *C*. Two outputs are provided, $A+B+C$ and $\overline{A+B+C}$.

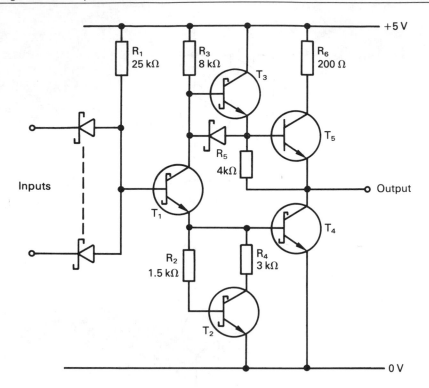

Figure 5.15   LSTTL gate

Table 5.1   Performance figures of various TTL series

Logic series	Propagation delay time (ns)	Power dissipation (mW)	Speed–power product (pJ)
74	10	10	100
74S	3	19	57
74LS	9.5	2	19
74AS	1.5	20	30
74ALS	4	1	4

Note that the supply voltages are $0\,V$ and $-5.2\,V$. The logic levels are not the same as TTL logic levels.

When all the inputs are at a low voltage, the associated input transistors, T_1, T_2 and T_3, are all cut off and current flows through T_4. When one input or more inputs are taken to some high voltage, the current switches from T_4 to the input transistor and T_4 is cut off. The voltage on the base of T_4 is mid-way between the two logic levels.

Suitable input voltages can be deduced by examination of the circuit. One condition is when all the input transistors T_1, T_2 and T_3 are cut off and in this condition, no current flows through these transistors and their collectors are at

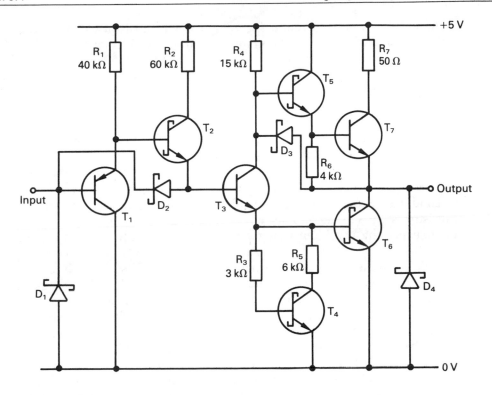

Figure 5.16   ALS NOT gate (74ALS04)

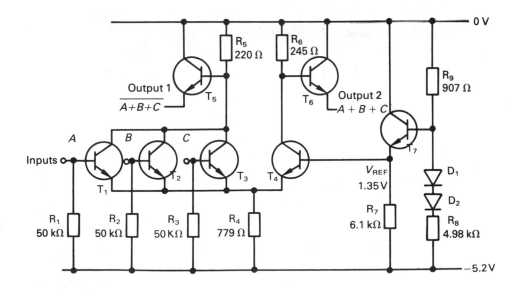

Figure 5.17   ECL OR/NOR gate

0 V (ignoring any base current of T_5). V_{BE} of each transistor when conducting is in the region 0.8 V to 0.9 V. Therefore the output voltage at the emitter of T_5 must be -0.9 V (assuming $V_{BE5} = 0.9$ V). This is the 1 level output voltage. Since input and output voltage 1 (and 0) levels must be nominally the same, the 1 level input voltage is also -0.9 V.

If the 1 level voltage is applied to one input, A, say, there must be a 0 output level on the NOR output. Transistor T_1 will conduct but the current is limited by the resistors R_4 and R_5 to prevent saturation. The lowest voltage allowed on the collector of T_1 is -0.9 V, the same as the base voltage, as below this voltage the transistor will begin to enter saturation. Therefore the 0 level output voltage must be -1.8 V (-0.9 V $- 0.9$ V), assuming again that $V_{BE5} = 0.9$ V. In all cases, T_5 conducts dependent upon any load applied to the output 1 terminal, but the transistor is not saturated. The reference voltage on the base of T_4 is set midway between the two input voltage levels, with our values, -1.35 V (-0.9 V $- 0.9$ V/2).

ECL circuits operate at very high speed. The 10K series ECL circuit has a propagation time of 2 ns with a power consumption of 25 mW, giving a speed–power product of 50 pJ. The faster 100K series has a propagation time of 0.75 ns with a rather large power consumption of 40 mW, resulting in a speed–power product of 30 pJ. ECL has the advantage that both the true and inverse outputs are available and outputs can be wired-ORed (see section 5.3.5). The supply current is nearly constant. However, ECL consumes substantially more power than TTL circuits, limiting manufacture in dual-in-line packages to SSI/MSI (small-scale integration/medium-scale integration) and is only used for very high-speed applications.

5.5 METAL-OXIDE-SEMICONDUCTOR (MOS) GATES

5.5.1 NMOS and PMOS

An alternative to employing bipolar transistors as used for TTL and ECL gates is to employ *metal-oxide-semiconductor field effect transistors* (MOSFET) particularly for LSI/VLSI (Large-scale integration/very large-scale integration, more than 100/1000 gates). Because of the importance of the MOSFET in microprocessors (Part 2) let us firstly briefly review characteristics of the MOSFET. The MOSFET can be constructed as *n-channel* (NMOS) or *p-channel* (PMOS) and for one of two modes of operation known as *enhancement mode* and *depletion mode*. There are three connections to MOS transistors, the *source*, the *gate* and the *drain*.

An *n*-channel enhancement-mode MOSFET is normally operated with the drain connected to a positive voltage with respect to the source. When the gate–source voltage, V_{GS}, is 0 V, no current flows between the source and drain. If V_{GS} is increased, a point is reached when conduction starts between the source and drain. The voltage at which conduction occurs is known as the *threshold voltage*, V_T. The current flow will increase as the gate–source voltage exceeds the threshold voltage. Hence the device can act as a logic device with two states, conducting and non-conducting. V_T can be about $+1$ V, allowing compatibility with TTL devices.

In the case of a depletion-mode *n*-channel MOSFET, V_T is negative. When $V_{GS} = 0$ V, conduction already occurs between the source and drain. Conduction stops when the gate–source voltage is less than the negative threshold voltage. Therefore, a two-state device can be obtained, only now a negative voltage is required on the gate to turn the device off, with respect to the source voltage. As before, the reader is referred to texts on electronics for an explanation of the MOSFET mechanism. *P*-channel MOSFETs operate similarly, but the polarity of all voltages is reversed.

A simple NMOS NOT gate with a resistor load is shown in Fig. 5.18(a). The positive supply voltage is V_{DD}. NAND and NOR gates are shown in Fig.5.18(b) and Fig. 5.18(c) respectively. The resistor load can be replaced by an enhancement-mode MOS transistor as shown in Fig.5.19(a). The enhancement-mode load transistor has the gate connected to the drain and the positive supply which will cause the load device to conduct only when the output is low. When the output is high, there is a threshold voltage drop across the device so that the output voltage is $V_{DD} - V_T$.

The voltage drop across the device can be eliminated by using a depletion-mode MOS load device with the gate connected directly to the source as shown in Fig. 5.19(b). In this case, the device will always conduct whether the output is low or high.

Separate gates are not manufactured in NMOS technology. However, the technology is used for LSI/VLSI devices such as microprocessors. PMOS was available before NMOS due to early difficulties in manufacturing NMOS, but NMOS devices intrinsically operate 2–3 times faster than PMOS and consequently PMOS is not now widely used alone for high-speed components.

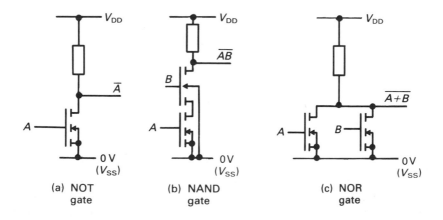

(a) NOT gate   (b) NAND gate   (c) NOR gate

Figure 5.18   Resistor load NMOS gates

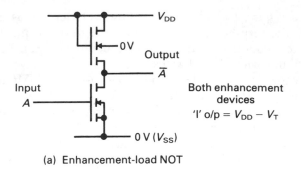

(a) Enhancement-load NOT

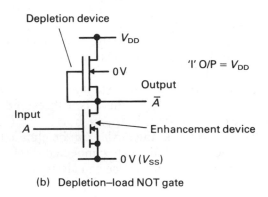

(b) Depletion–load NOT gate

Figure 5.19   NMOS gates with active loads

5.5.2 CMOS

Logic circuits can be implemented with n-channel and p-channel devices in a technology known as *complementary MOS* (CMOS). A CMOS NOT gate is shown in Fig. 5.20(a). An enhancement-mode p-channel transistor is connected to the positive supply (V_{DD}) and an enhancement mode n-channel transistor is connected to 0V. Both transistors are constructed to have similar threshold voltages of about 0.7V, though of opposite polarities. The logic levels are 0V and V_{DD} nominally, and V_{DD} can be typically between 3V and 15V.

When the input level is low (0V), the lower transistor will be turned off as the voltage across the gate and source of this transistor is 0V and below the threshold voltage. The voltage across the source and gate of the upper transistor is greater than the threshold voltage of this transistor. Therefore this transistor is turned on, and the output attains a high output voltage to within 100mV of the positive V_{DD} supply. When the input is high (V_{DD}), the voltage across the source and drain of the upper transistor is 0V. The device is turned off. The voltage across the source and drain of the lower transistor is greater than the threshold

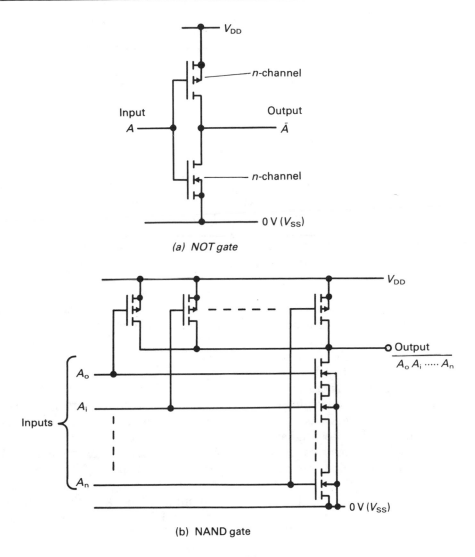

(a) NOT gate

(b) NAND gate

Figure 5.20 CMOS gates

voltage of the device, so this transistor is turned on. The output now attains a low voltage to within $100\,\text{mV}$ of $0\,\text{V}$.

The switching threshold is approximately mid-way between $0\,\text{V}$ and the supply voltage V_S, irrespective of the supply voltage (assuming this to be greater than about $1.4\,\text{V}$), because when the input is mid-way between $0\,\text{V}$ and V_S, V_{GS} of the upper transistor is equal in magnitude to V_{GS} of the lower transistor. With identical characteristics, the drain source voltage of both transistors must be the same and the output must be $0.5V_S$. This represents the cross-over point, above or below which a fast transition to a stable state occurs.

CMOS NAND and NOR gates are shown in Fig. 5.20(b) and Fig. 5.20(c) respectively. The particular advantage of CMOS circuits is that there is no d.c.

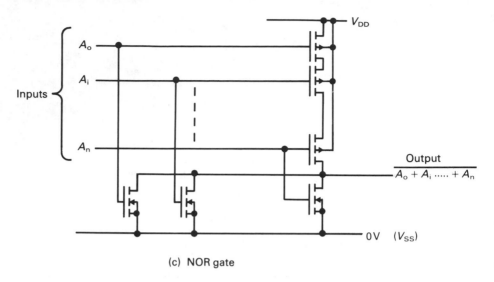

(c) NOR gate

Figure 5.20   *continued*

current path between V_S and $0\,V$ through the circuit in either logic state, and hence a very low static power consumption (with no logic transitions) due only to leakage currents. Unfortunately, during a logic transition both upper and lower transistors might conduct simultaneously. Also internal and external capacitances must be charged or discharged during the transition, and charging/discharging transient currents flow. This leads to the dynamic supply current and power consumption being directly proportional to the signal frequency.

CMOS versions of TTL circuits are manufactured, having similar logical characteristics and compatible input/output voltages. Many of the original 7400 series TTL gates have equivalent CMOS versions. For example the 74C00 is a CMOS equivalent to the TTL 7400 quad 2-input AND gate. In many applications, the CMOS versions can be chosen giving much lower power consumption than TTL. Power consumption of CMOS gates is in the region of $0.01\,\mu W$/gate with no logic transitions and about $1.25\,mW$/gate at $1\,MHz$. Speed of operation of CMOS versions of TTL gates has been generally slower than TTL having propagation delay times in the region of $50\,ns$. However, advances in CMOS technology for VLSI have resulted in improved speed.

5.6   GATE OPERATING CONDITIONS

5.6.1   Noise margins

Noise is the term given to unwanted electrical signals occurring in a system. It can come about from the normal operation of logic devices switching, which can generate interference on neighboring devices either by electromagnetic radiation or via associated power supply variations. Less commonly, the source of the noise can be external to the system. Logic gates must be designed to accept a certain amount of electrical noise in the system and continue to operate normally.

Noise margin is the name given to the voltage present as electrical noise in the system which can be tolerated. It is given in terms of the allowable noise voltage that can be added to a generated logic signal and still be recognized as a logic level, i.e.:

Noise margin at a logic 1 = (minimum 1 output voltage generated) −
(minimum 1 input voltage recognized)
Noise margin at a logic 0 = (maximum 0 output voltage generated) −
(maximum 0 input voltage recognized)

As an example, consider the typical input/output voltage transfer characteristic of a standard TTL gate shown in Fig. 5.21. The maximum generated logic 0 ouput voltage is 0.4 V. The minimum logic 1 output voltage is 2.4 V which occurs under full load conditions (see later). The switching point between a logic 0 and a logic 1 is roughly 1.4 V but this can change with temperature. However, it is guaranteed that the input will always recognize a logic 0 voltage of up to 0.8 V and a logic 1 voltage down to 2 V though such voltages cannot be generated by the output of a logic device. Therefore the noise margins in this case are given by:

Noise margin at a logic 1 = 2.4 V − 2 V = 0.4 V
Noise margin at a logic 0 = 0.8 V − 0.4 V = 0.4 V

The noise margins of ECL gates are musch lower, at about 125 mV.

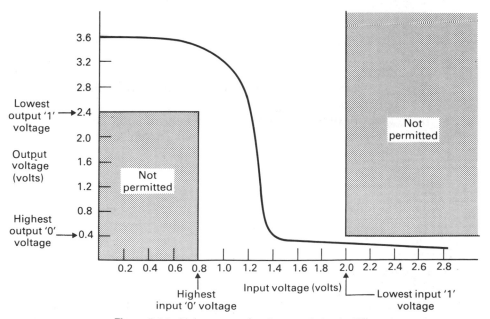

Figure 5.21 Voltage transfer characteristic of a TTL gate

The noise margins defined are applicable to continuous, fairly low-frequency noise. The behavior of the logic device under the influence of non-continuous or very high-frequency noise may be considerably different to that of low-frequency noise. The most likely high-frequency noise has the form of a narrow voltage pulse. If the duration of the pulse is sufficiently short, the device may not have time to respond to it. The behavior of a logic device under high-frequency noise conditions can be described by the a.c. noise margins as opposed to the (d.c.) margins.

5.6.2 Fan-out

As mentioned in the introductory section to this chapter, fan-out is the name given to the number of gates that can be attached to the output of a gate without causing the output gate to operate outside normal limits. Usually all the gates are of the same type or compatible types. Fan-out is determined by the maximum output current of the gate output stage and the maximum input currents of the gates attached to the output together with any leakage currents of the devices. The fan-out of a gate with a low output level is not necessarily the same as the fan-out of the gate with a high output level, as the maximum output current at each level is usually different and the input currents are usually different at each level. The fan-out at each level is given by:

$$\text{Logic 1 output fan-out} = \frac{I_{OH(max)}}{I_{IH(max)}}$$

$$\text{Logic 0 output fan-out} = \frac{I_{OL(max)}}{I_{IL(max)}}$$

where

$I_{OH(max)}$ = maximum high-level (1) output current that the gate can supply

$I_{OL(max)}$ = maximum low-level (0) output current that the gate can supply

$I_{IH(max)}$ = maximum high-level (1) input current of gate connected to output

$I_{IL(max)}$ = maximum low-level (0) input current of gate connected to output.

To determine the fan-out of a particular device, the above four currents need to be known, and can be found from the appropriate data sheets. The input and output currents for members of the TTL family are shown in Table 5.2. Measurements have been taken under different conditions in different series. The standard TTL series (not now often used) has a fan-out of:

$$\text{Logic 1 output fan-out} = \frac{I_{OH(max)}}{I_{IH(max)}} = \frac{800\,\mu A}{40\,\mu A} = 20$$

Table 5.2   Input and output currents of various TTL series

Logic series	Maximum 1 level input current $I_{IH(max)}$ (μA)	Maximum 0 level input current $I_{IL(max)}$ (mA)	Maximum 1 level output current $I_{OH(max)}$ (mA)	Maximum 0 level output current $I_{OL(max)}$ (mA)
74	40	-1.6	$-0.4/-0.8*$	16
74S	50	-2.0	-1.0	20
74LS	20	-0.36	-0.4	8
74AS	20	-2.0	-0.4	4/8*
74ALS	20	-0.1	-0.4	8

* depends upon devices. Conditions under which values obtained differ slightly from one family to another; see reference [1]

$$\text{Logic 0 output fan-out} = \frac{I_{OL(max)}}{I_{IL(max)}} = \frac{16\,\text{mA}}{1.6\,\text{mA}} = 10$$

The LSTTL series, in general, has a fan-out of:

$$\text{Logic 1 output fan-out} = \frac{I_{OH(max)}}{I_{IH(max)}} = \frac{400\,\mu\text{A}}{20\,\mu\text{A}} = 20$$

$$\text{Logic 0 output fan-out} = \frac{I_{OL(max)}}{I_{IL(max)}} = \frac{8\,\text{mA}}{0.36\,\text{mA}} = 22$$

Particular devices may have different input and output currents. The smallest fan-out value would determine the number of gates that can be attached to an output. Sometimes, the extra high-level fan-out if available can be utilized by connecting unused inputs of gates to used inputs. (Unused inputs should not be left unconnected, but connected to a logic voltage or the supply voltage.)

Logic circuit series can be intermixed if their logic level voltages are compatible, i.e. the output voltage range of a gate must be less than the input voltage range of the gate to which the output connects for both logic levels. Usually, TTL and equivalent CMOS families can be intermixed. The fan-out in these situations depend upon the actual I_{OL}, I_{OL}, I_{IL} and I_{IH} of the gates concerned. For example, LSTTL generally has a maximum I_{IH} of $20\,\mu$A and a maximum I_{IL} of $(-)0.36$ mA. Therefore a standard TTL gate could drive 44 LSTTL gates at a low level (i.e. 16 mA/0.36 mA) and 40 at a high level (i.e. $800\,\mu$A/$20\,\mu$A assuming $I_{OH(max)} = 800\,\mu$A).

5.6.3 MOS devices

A typical output characteristic of an NMOS device such a microprocessor is shown in Fig. 5.22. Note that the maximum output current at both low and high levels is much less than that of TTL devices and hence the number of

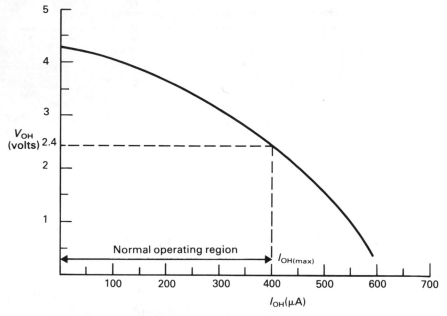

(a) '1' level output characteristic

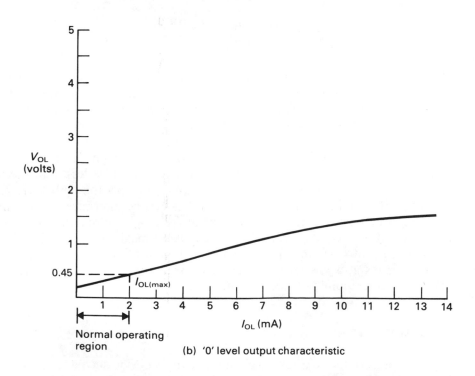

(b) '0' level output characteristic

Figure 5.22   Typical NMOS microprocessor output characteristics

TTL gates that can be attached to the output is very low, typically one standard TTL device or five LSTTL devices.

NMOS devices themselves present a very low current loading, normally in the region of $\pm 10\,\mu\text{A}$ for both high and low voltages. On first sight, it would seem that many NMOS devices could be attached before the loading limit is reached. However, all logic devices have an input capacitance which in the case of MOS devices, though perhaps only in the region of $10\,\text{pF}$, will often limit the number of MOS devices that can be connected to the output of a device. Capacitance on the output of a logic device will require the device to supply transient currents during logic transitions and will reduce the rise and fall times of the output signal. The rise and fall times each produce a delay which can be related to the capacitance by the equation:

$$\text{d}t = \frac{C_{\text{L}}\text{d}V_{\text{O}}}{I_{\text{O}}}$$

where

> C_{L} is the load capacitance including the self-capacitance of the device
> $\text{d}V_{\text{O}}$ is the logic swing
> I_{O} is the available current from the driver not taken by the d.c. load (assumed constant for the above equation).

If $\text{d}V_{\text{O}} = 2\,\text{V}$ and $I_{\text{O}} = 1\,\text{mA}$, the delay would be $0.2\,\text{ns/pF}$. The delay about $0.1\,\text{ns/pF}$ for the low-power Schottky TTL devices, $0.2\,\text{ns/pF}$ for advanced Schottky TTL devices, and usually between $0.1\,\text{ns/pF}$ and $0.6\,\text{ns/pF}$ for NMOS microprocessors.

For microprocessors, stated loads in test situations are in the region of $50\,\text{pF}$ to $150\,\text{pF}$, not including self-load (internal capacitance of the output). The maximum load is perhaps in the region of $300\,\text{pF}$ and there may be different delay rates in different ranges of load capacitances. If the capacitive load is greater than the stated test conditions, the delay can be calculated from the delay rate, and the processor operated slower if necessary. However, the reliability may be adversely affected due to the greater transient currents charging and discharging the capitances. One cannot sensibly load the output with a capacitance greater than the stated maximum.

Therefore from the above, during the design of a system, the maximum d.c. loading (at both low and high levels) and the maximum capacitive loading need to be calculated to ascertain whether the system will operate properly. Take as an example, the following output drive specification of a microprocessor:

> $I_{\text{OL}} = 2.0\,\text{mA}$ max.
> $I_{\text{OH}} = 400\,\mu\text{A}$ max.
> $C_{\text{L}} \;\; = 100\,\text{pF}$ max. without derating

Some possible combinations of devices that could be attached without exceeding the maximum load specifications are shown in Table 5.3 using the input current values given for LSTTL, assuming the input currents of each MOS device is

$\pm 10\,\mu$A and the input capacitance of each device is $10\,$pF. The determing factor in the first case is I_{OL} and in the other two cases, C_{L}.

If the lines are loaded differently, there will be a skew in the signals in addition to the delay. The specification of a microprocessor may define a maximum differential loading to obtain given timing (for example, a maximum load difference of $50\,$pF might be specified). There may also be effects due to the worsening rise and fall times on particular devices. If, for example, a load of $300\,$pF existed and $dt/C_{L} = 0.2\,$ns/pF, the rise and fall times would be $60\,$ns. Rise and fall times of this magnitude may be greater than allowed for proper operation.

The normal solution to the problem of loading is to use additional buffer

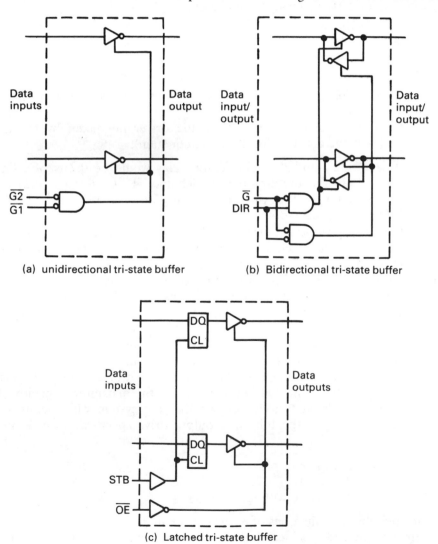

(a) unidirectional tri-state buffer   (b) Bidirectional tri-state buffer

(c) Latched tri-state buffer

Figure 5.23 Buffers

Table 5.3   Combinations of devices that can be attached to MOS device

Devices attached to output	Output current (mA) Logic level		Capacitance (pF) C_L
	0	1	
5 LSTTL devices	2	100	50
1 LSTTL device + 9 MOS devices	0.49	110	100
3 LSTTL devices + 7 MOS devices	1.2	130	100

gates, for example in a microprocessor system between the components of the system and the bus. This also provides a measure of protection in the event of a hardware malfunction. Integrated circuit parts are available with four, six and eight inverting or non-inverting three-state buffer gates. These buffers may be unidirectional, bidirectional or latched buffers. An 8-bit unidirectional three-state buffer is shown in Fig. 5.23(a), a bidirectional three-state buffer in Fig. 5.23(b) and a latched three-state buffer in Fig. 5.23(c). Unidirectional buffers can be used in particular when the signals can only pass from the device and not to the same device along the same lines. Bidirectional buffers can be used on all lines that carry signals to or from the device (such as data lines; see Chap. 6).

The differential nature of TTL input currents, I_{IL} and I_{IH}, is also reflected on the designed drive capability of all types of TTL buffers, with I_{OL} usually much larger than I_{OH}. Output stages of TTL buffers can provide currents in the region of 24 mA to 64 mA for a low output voltage and 5 mA to 15 mA for a high output voltage. The input currents of buffers are often lower than the input currents of normal TTL gates. Some buffer gates have Schmitt trigger inputs to increase the noise immunity. The characteristic of a Schmitt trigger input gate is shown in Fig. 5.24. The cross-over point for a rising input signal, V_{t+}, is higher than the cross-over point for a falling input signal, V_{t-}. This increases the effective noise immunity, that is the maximum amount of noise allowed on the signal before it causes a transition on the output, by the amount $V_{OL} - V_{t+}$ on a low voltage, and $V_{OH} - V_{t-}$ on a high voltage. Typically $V_{t+} = 1.7$V and $V_{t-} = 0.9$V, which would lead to a high-level noise immunity of 1.5 V (i.e. 2.4 V − 0.9 V) and a low-level noise immunity of 1.3 V (i.e. 1.7 V − 0.4 V).

REFERENCE

1. *The TTL Data Book for Design Engineers* (6th European ed.). Dallas, Texas: Texas Instruments, 1983.

PROBLEMS

In the following questions, assume that $V_{BEon} = 0.7$V and $V_{CEsat} = 0.2$V where necessary. Leakage currents can be ignored unless specified.

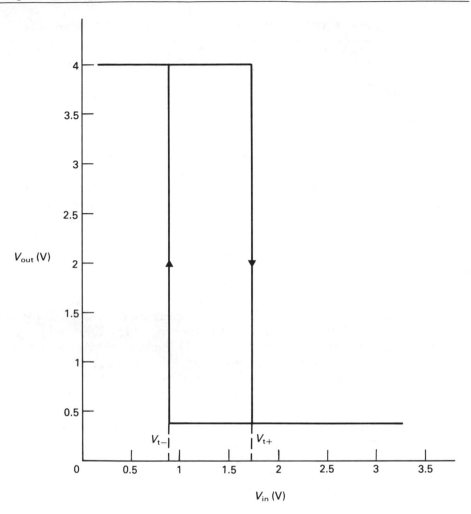

Figure 5.24   Transfer characteristic of TTL Schmitt trigger NOT gate

5.1   If the voltages applied to the diode AND gate shown in Fig. 5.2 are 2.5 V representing a logic 1 or 0 V representing a logic 0, what output voltages can be generated?

5.2   Repeat Problem 5.1 for the diode OR gate shown in Fig. 5.3.

5.3   Deduce the logical function performed by the circuit shown in Fig. 5.25 for (a) positive logic and (b) negative logic. Deduce the d.c. noise margins.

5.4   Repeat Problem 5.3 for the circuit shown in Fig. 5.26.

5.5   Choose suitable values for R_B and R_C in the transistor circuit shown in Fig. 5.5 to achieve the following specification:

High level input current, I_{IH}, $= 0.5\,\text{mA}$
High level output voltage, $V_{OH(min)}$, $= 3.5\,\text{V}$
High level fan-out $= 10$

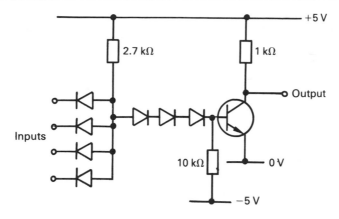

Figure 5.25 Circuit for Problem 5.3

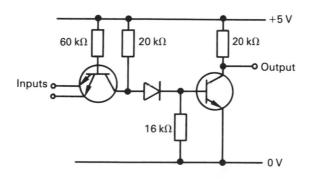

Figure 5.26 Circuit for Problem 5.4

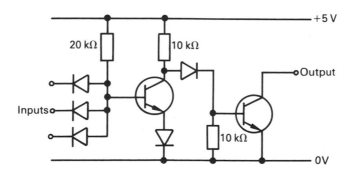

Figure 5.27 Circuit for Problem 5.7

Calculate the minimum value of h_{FE} to achieve a high level noise margin of 0.5 V.

5.6 Determine the maximum value for pull-up resistor of an open-collector TTL gate to achieve a fan-out of 10, given that $I_{IH} = 40\,\mu A$, the leakage current flowing through the collector of the TTL output transistor is $50\,\mu A$, and $V_{OH(min)} = 2.4\,V$.

5.7 Determine the high level fan-out of the open-collector gate shown in Fig. 5.27 given that the value of the pull-up resistor is $10\,\mathrm{k\Omega}$. What is the maximum value of this resistor to give a high level fan-out of 5? Each diode has a maximum leakage current of $100\,\mathrm{\mu A}$ when reverse biased. Make, and state, any necessary assumptions.

5.8 Determine the number of LSTTL devices that can be attached to the output of a STTL device (by reference to Table 5.2).

PART 2

MICROPROCESSOR SYSTEM DESIGN

Computer and Microprocessor Systems

6.1 STORED PROGRAM COMPUTER

In this chapter we shall describe the general features of microprocessor systems, making reference to several microprocessors. The 8-bit Z-80 microprocessor will be considered in Chap. 7 and the 16-bit 68000 microprocessor will be considered in Chap. 8. We firstly outline the basic features of digital computers, of which a microprocessor system is one implementation.

6.1.1 General scheme

A digital computer system contains the following fundamental parts:

(i)   Central processor unit (CPU)
(ii) Main (or primary) memory
(iii) Input circuits and devices
(iv) Output circuits and devices

as shown in Fig. 6.1. The *main* or *primary memory* provides a means of storing binary information in the form of binary words. One word consists of a fixed number of binary digits (bits), typically 8, 16 or 32, and each word is stored in one memory location. An 8-bit word is called a *byte*. Each memory location is given a unique number called an address as shown in Fig. 6.2. Memory locations are numbered consecutively. With n binary digits (bits) in the address, the address range is from 0 to $2^n - 1$, i.e. 2^n unique addresses. The number of address bits provided varies from computer to computer. Sixteen bits would give the ability to address 65,536 locations. Thirty-two bit addresses give the ability to address 2^{32} (4,294,960,000) locations.

The *central processor* is designed to obey instructions given to it. These instructions are encoded in a binary representation and stored in the main memory. Each instruction usually has between 8 and 64 bits depending upon the computer and the instruction. One or more memory locations are used to store one instruction. The instructions are called *machine instructions* and there are usually many different instructions available as defined by the *instruction set* of the computer. Operations that can be specified by instructions include data transfer operations transferring numbers from one location to another, arithmetic operations such as addition or subtraction, logic operations such as AND

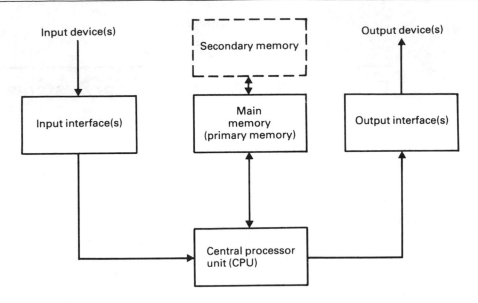

Figure 6.1   Digital computer

and NOT, and control operations such as to stop all operation. The arithmetic and logic operations are performed by the *arithmetic and logic unit* (abbreviated to ALU) within the processor.

The operation specified by the instruction often requires numbers (operands), usually one or two numbers. For example, a machine instruction may specify the addition of two numbers. Generally, these numbers can be held in the main memory, or in storage registers within the central processor. The result of the operation can be placed in the main memory or in internal processor registers depending upon the computer and the instruction. A list of instructions is created by the user to produce a desired action or result. This list is known as a *machine-language program* or *machine-code program* and is held in the main memory. After the processor has executed the first instruction in the program, it proceeds to the next instruction unless directed by the instruction to do otherwise.

The *input circuits and devices* are used to enter the program defined by the user. Numbers can also be input during the execution of the program. The output circuits and devices are used to convey results from the program. The input and output devices can also be used to control the overall operation of the computer system. The input circuits are required to translate the signals from the input devices to the system and similarly, the output circuits are required to translate the signals from the system to the output devices. These circuits are known as *interfaces*. Input and output for user communication is generally performed by the same device (usually a display terminal, commonly called a visual display unit, VDU). Because input and output are often closely coupled, the two terms, input and output, are abbreviated as input/output or I/O.

The memory of the system is usually divided into two parts for economic reasons, the primary memory containing locations which can be accessed at high

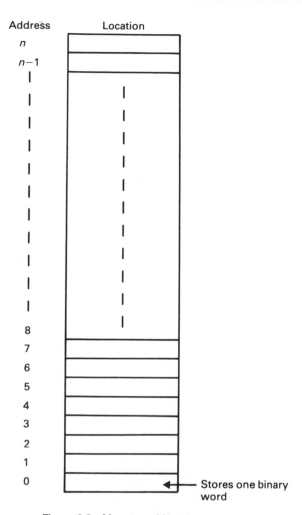

Figure 6.2   Memory addressing

speed in any order, and a *secondary* memory, often based on magnetic recording (magnetic disks and tape) capable of storing much larger amounts of information but not with very high-speed access. Generally the contents of the secondary memory must be transferred to the primary memory before the processor can access the information. The term *backing store* is sometimes used for secondary memory.

Briefly, the basic mode of operation of a digital computer system is to transfer the first instruction in the program from memory to the processor during a *fetch cycle* and then the processor performs the specified operation during an *execute cycle*, as shown in Fig. 6.3. The instruction is stored in an internal processor register called an *instruction register* and decoded (its purpose recognized) during the latter part of the fetch cycle. The subsequent operations in the execute cycle depend upon operation decoded. Should more than one memory word be necessary to hold a complete instruction, additional fetch

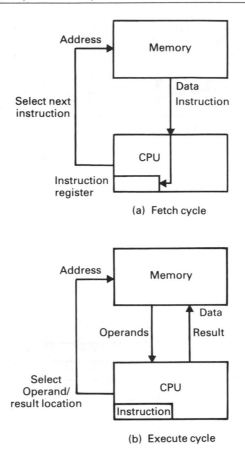

(a) Fetch cycle

(b) Execute cycle

Figure 6.3   CPU mode of operation

cycles are performed to form the instruction in the processor instruction register before the execute cycle can start. (This point is taken up later.) The fetch-execute cycle sequence is repeated for subsequent instructions.

Having a list of stored instructions which are executed in a sequential manner has been the mode of operation of most digital computers since their first conception in the 1940s. The system is called a *stored program computer*. One of the fundamental aspects of a stored program computer is that the memory is used to store both the program and the data. The concept is attributed to von Neumann and his co-workers at the Moore School of Engineering of the University of Pennsylvania in the period 1946–48. Hence this stored program computer is sometimes called a *von Neumann computer*, and particularly refers to the sequential nature of program execution. It is worth noting that attempts have been made to design digital computers which do not have this sequential operation, for example data flow computers described in Chap. 15. Such computers are referred to as non-von Neumann computers, though they may still have a stored program. However, the steps taken in the program are not defined by the order the instructions are placed in the program. (In a data flow computer, the order depends upon valid data being made available for the instruction.)

6.1.2 Processor instructions

The first point to note on the processor instructions is that the operation specified is reduced to a simple type, and more complex operations are achieved by forming an ordered list of instructions in the program. For example, we may write an apparently simple arithmetic computation on paper as:

$$\text{Result} = (2 + 6 - 4)/(8 \times 9)$$

However, we could not provide a unique machine instruction for this calculation and all other possible calculations. Instead, addition, subtraction, multiplication and division instructions can be provided operating upon two operands in the same manner as when using a calculator. Partial results need to be stored. Suppose all the numbers in the calculation are firstly stored in memory. A sequence might begin with an instruction to add the contents of the memory locations holding the numbers 2 and 6. Then the contents of memory location holding the number 4 would be subtracted to generate a partial result. The contents of the memory locations holding the numbers 8 and 9 would be multiplied together and the result of this operation divided into the first partial result. Clearly the same calculation using different numbers can be performed by firstly loading the appropriate memory locations with the desired numbers. Whether the described sequence could in fact be specified in practice would depend upon the computer instructions provided. As we shall see, it is often necessary to load at least one of the two operands into a processor register before an operation can be performed upon the operands.

Having accepted that (arithmetic and logic) instructions will specify a single operation upon one or two operands, we now consider the general format of processor instructions. The machine instructions are notionally split into two parts, an operation field and an operand field:

The operation field specifies the particular operation to be performed by the processor and the operand field specifies in some way the operands (numbers) that are to be used in the operation. Each of these fields contains encoded binary patterns. An operand may be given in the operand field as the actual binary number required and then it is known as a *literal*. Alternatively, the operand field may contain the address or addresses of storage locations from which the number or numbers may be obtained. This method of finding the operand is known as the *addressing* mechanism. There are various addressing mechanisms that can be invoked. It is usual to refer to the operand field as the address field even though in the case of a literal, it contains the actual number to be used rather than an address. The number obtained for the operation can always be regarded by the processor as an integer, for example an 8-bit integer, 16-bit integer or 32-bit integer. More advanced processors can also operate upon floating point numbers.

The most general machine instruction format is one with four addresses specifying the following:

(i)   Address of one operand
(ii) Address of second operand
(iii) Address of where the result of the operation is to be stored
(iv) Address of where the next instruction may be found.

Thus an instruction would be in the form:

OPERATION FIELD	FIRST OPERAND ADDRESS	SECOND OPERAND ADDRESS	RESULT ADDRESS	NEXT INSTRUCTION ADDRESS

The fourth address is always eliminated for machine instructions by arranging that the next instruction to be executed is immediately following the current instruction. The general movement of operands is shown in Fig. 6.4, assuming that all operands are stored in the main memory. To allow for non-sequential instruction execution, instructions are introduced into the instruction repertoire which can alter the sequence of instruction execution. Whether the sequence is altered may depend upon the results of arithmetic of logical operations. This leads directly to the decision-making power of computers because it permits programs to be executed which choose different instructions depending upon immediately preceding computations. (Four-address instruction formats are used in microprogrammed control units; see Chap. 13.)

The third address above can be eliminated by always placing the result of arithmetic or logic operations in the location where the first operand was found. The computer would then be a *two-address* machine with the implication that the result overwrites one of the original numbers. It leads to the instruction format:

OPERATION FIELD	FIRST OPERAND/RESULT ADDRESS	SECOND OPERAND ADDRESS

and the operand movement shown in Fig. 6.5.

The second address can be eliminated by also having only one place for the first operand which would be within the processor itself rather than in the memory. This location is known as an *accumulator*, as it accumulates the results. The computer would then be a *single address* or accumulator type of machine. The operand movement is shown in Fig. 6.6. However, having only one location for one of the operands and for the subsequent result is rather limiting, so a

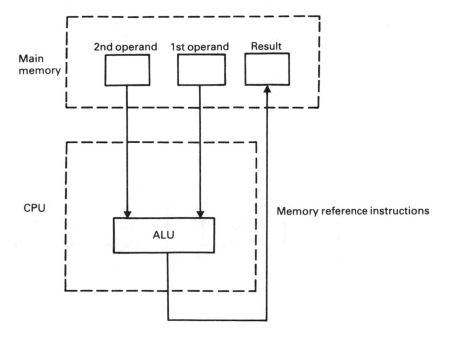

Figure 6.4   Data flow with three-address instruction format

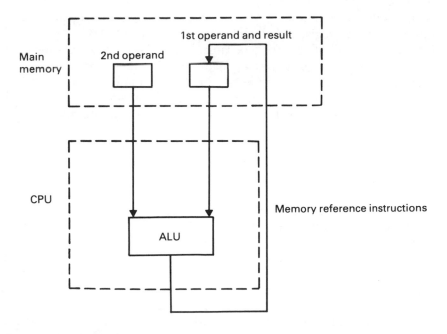

Figure 6.5   Data flow with two-address instruction format

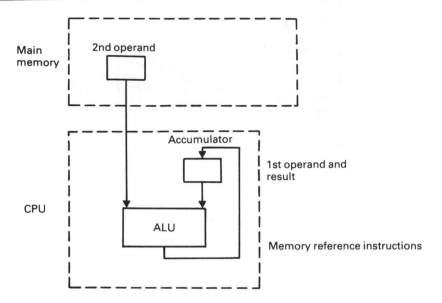

Figure 6.6   Data flow with one-address instruction format

small group of locations within the processor can be provided, i.e. processor registers. The term *one and a half address* machine has been used to cover this case but we shall simply call the architecture a *register file type*. The operand movement is shown in Fig. 6.7. Notice that once a set of registers is provided, it is desirable to be able to perform calculations between contents of registers rather than one register and a memory location. This results in a substantial increase in speed of operation because internal processor registers can usually be accessed much quicker than main memory locations. Also, although the registers used in the instructions need to be specified in some manner, they can be identified with a small *register address*, e.g. a 2-bit address for four registers, or 4-bit address for 16 registers, compared with 16 or more address bits usually required for main memory locations.

   All the addresses in the operand field can be eliminated by using two specific locations. These locations are specified as the first and second locations of a group of locations known as a *stack*. Usually the stack consists of a group of memory locations and the first location, or top of stack, is specified by a processor register known as the *stack pointer*. The computer using the 'top' two locations of a stack for storing the operands is called a *zero-address* machine. The operand movement using the top two locations of a stack is shown in Fig. 6.8. A zero-address machine has some advantages in some types of programming such as evaluating arithmetic expressions, but has generally lost favor in preference to register machines. Stack operations are incorporated into register machines, but primarily for interrupt and subroutine handling (see Chap. 7).

   There can be several hundred different instructions in the instruction set of the computer. Broadly speaking, instructions can be categorized into one of a number of groups (assuming one-, two- or three-address format):

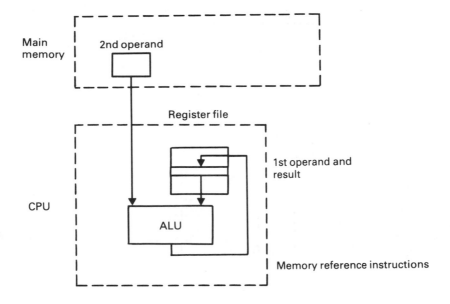

Figure 6.7   Data flow with 1½-address instruction format (register file instruction format)

(a) Transfer (also known as load/store and move)

Here the contents of one location are copied to another location. The locations may be memory locations or processor register locations, though direct transfer between memory locations is not always provided. The word 'transfer', though widely used, is misleading as the data is not removed from the source location, but left intact. The data held in the destination location before the execution of the transfer instruction is lost when the new data is transferred to the location.

(b) Arithmetic and logical

The arithmetic operations addition and subtraction are always in the instruction set. Logical operations are the Boolean operations AND, OR, NOT, exclusive-OR, exclusive-NOR, etc. AND, OR, NOT and exclusive-OR are often provided, operating upon pairs of bits in the two binary numbers held in the selected locations to produce the bits in the result.

(c) Shift and rotate

Shift and rotate operations involve moving each bit in a single binary number one or more places left or right in the same manner as the shift operation in a shift register. The rotate operations correspond to the operation of a ring counter (see Chap. 4, section 4.4.2).

(d) Jump/branch

These instruction alter the sequence of instructions executed. Some jump/branch instructions only alter the sequence if a specified condition prevails

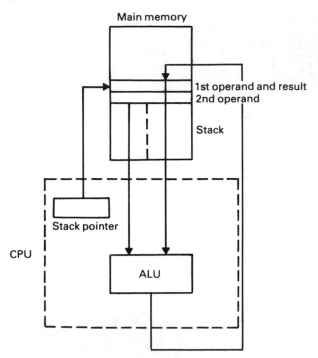

Main memory

1st operand and result
2nd operand

Stack

Stack pointer

CPU

ALU

Memory reference instructions

Figure 6.8   Data flow with zero-address instruction format

within the processor when the instruction is executed. Conditions normally relate to the last arithmetic/logical result before the jump/branch instruction.

(e) Input/output

Input instructions provide a means of transferring numbers from input interfaces/devices to processor registers. Output instructions provide a means of transferring numbers held in processor registers to output interfaces/devices.

(f) Control

A control instruction causes the processor to perform an operation such as stop completely, move automatically to the next instruction, wait for an external event to occur, or set a selected bit in a designated register used by the processor in connection with jump/branch operations or external events.

It is convenient to describe machine instructions using abbreviations for each field in the instruction, for example:

ADD R1,R2

could represent the instruction to add the contents of processor register R2 to processor register R1, placing the result in R1. The abbreviation ADD corresponds to the operation defined in the operation field. R1 and R2 correspond to the addresses in the operand address fields. These abbreviations form part of an assembly language which we will describe in section 6.3.2.

6.2 MICROPROCESSOR SYSTEM

6.2.1 General

A microprocessor system is a stored-program digital computer system with the four major parts described previously, but with an integrated circuit central processor called a *microprocessor*. The main memory is also usually fabricated in integrated circuit technology (i.e. semiconductor memory). The first microprocessor, the Intel 4004 introduced in 1971, was a 4-bit accumulator type. Second-generation microprocessors, typified by the Intel 8080 introduced in 1973, the Motorola 6800 introduced in 1974 and the Zilog Z-80 introduced in 1975, are 8-bit accumulator types. In all cases, additional registers are incorporated for particular purposes and some registers can be used to accumulate results. However, the true register type of processor in which instructions can operate on the contents of one of many registers were not widely found until later 16-bit microprocessors, for example the Motorola MC68000 introduced in 1978.

The microprocessor, memory and input/output interfaces are interconnected via a common set of electrical lines known as a *bus*, as shown in Fig. 6.9. The signals are TTL compatible, i.e. the signal voltages are within the range of TTL; see Chap. 5, section 5.6.1). Early microprocessors (e.g. Intel 4004) were not TTL compatible and required support devices to convert their signal voltages to TTL levels.

The main memory is semiconductor memory which employs a circuit arrangement to maintain one of two electrical states for each binary digit stored.

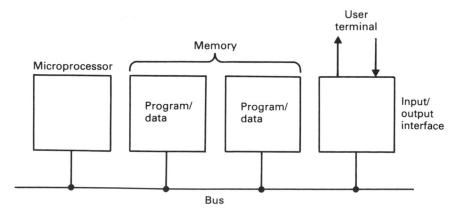

Figure 6.9 Fundamental parts of a microprocessor system

Reading the memory, i.e. examining the states and passing this information from the memory device to the processor, does not destroy the information stored. *Writing* to the memory, i.e. storing new information, of course destroys the original information. In a *random access memory*, RAM, information can be read from or written to the memory in any order with equal high speed.

It is essential that the main memory of a computer uses memory with the random access feature for both the program stored and any associated data. The main memory generally needs to be capable of both high-speed reading and high-speed writing in the case of program operands. However, the main memory may only need the feature of high-speed reading for program storage as instructions in a program are not altered when the program is being executed. This has led to the development of random access memory which is capable only of being read. The memory patterns held are defined either during manufacture of the device, or later by the user. Such devices are naturally called *read-only memories* (ROMs) although they are also random access. Thus to differentiate between the two types, the term RAM is limited to read–write memories.

The memory can comprise various types, *random access memory* (RAM), *read-only memory* (ROM), *programmable read-only memory* (PROM) and *erasable programmable read-only memory* (EPROM). Random access memory and at least one of the three types of read-only memory exists in most systems. Read-only memory is usually employed to store the *bootstrap program*, a program executed automatically when the computer is switched on. Memory may also include additional secondary memory such as *floppy disk storage*. EPROM devices use an electrical process to write information, allowing the user to 'program' the device. Ultra-violet light is used to remove the information (or an electrical process in electrically erasable PROM's). Further description of memory devices can be found in Chap. 9.

6.2.2 The microprocessor

The internal architecture of a representative microprocessor is shown in Fig. 6.10, using a single-address instruction format (i.e. an accumulator or A register is used to store intermediate results). An internal bus is used to connect the principal components to each other and to the external data bus. A microprocessor with a range of registers available rather than a single A register for arithmetic and logic operations may have a similar internal organization except that the two input operands to the ALU are selected from the register file and a A register is not sited in one ALU input path. The number of bits in each operand is that fundamentally associated with the processor, 4, 8, 16, etc. Negative numbers are considered in the 2's complement notation.

Other internal parts of the microprocessor include a control unit to generate the internal and external control signals and various registers. The *condition code register* consists of a number of single-bit *flags* which indicate some particular aspect of the result. For example, the *zero flag* is set to a 1 if the result is zero and set to a 0 if the result is not zero. Other flags found include the

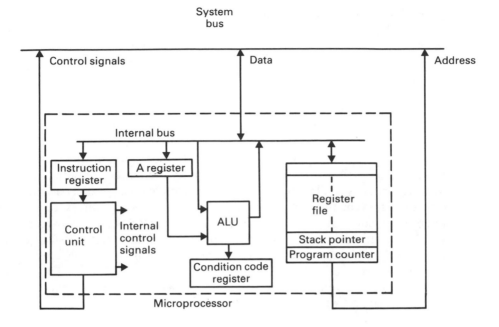

Figure 6.10 Microprocessor using a single-address instruction format

positive flag (result positive), *even parity flag* (result having an even number of 1's) and the *overflow flag* (result out of range and hence invalid). The *program counter* is an internal processor register, existing in computers to hold the memory address of the next instruction to be executed. Generally the contents of the program counter are automatically incremented (value increased by one) after a memory location holding the next instruction or next part of the instruction has been identified and the contents have been taken to the processor. The *stack pointer* holds the memory address of the top of the stack, for use in stack instructions. In addition to the program counter and stack pointer, registers in the so-called *register file* can often address the memory. Typically in 8-bit microprocessors, these registers can hold 16-bit numbers if the address bus is 16-bits.

6.2.3 Microprocessor fetch and execute cycles

A feature of microprocessor instructions is that they vary in length depending upon the instruction and the microprocessor, and in units given by the number of bits stored in one memory location. For example, the instructions of the 8-bit Z-80 microprocessor can be between one and five bytes. The first byte specifies the operation and subsequent bytes specify the addresses when necessary. The first byte of the instruction is called the *operation code*, abbreviated to *op-code*. During the fetch cycle, the op-code is fetched from the program memory. This is achieved by using the contents of the program counter to address the program memory and initiating a memory read cycle. The processor decodes the op-code when received and determines whether further bytes must be fetched. Bytes are then obtained in sequence from the memory as necessary. The contents of the program counter are used to address the memory and hence the value stored is incremented by one after each byte is fetched.

Once the complete instruction has been obtained, the processor can start the execute cycle. The addresses of any operands stored in memory are generally contained in the second and subsequent bytes of the instruction and these addresses have been obtained during the overall instruction fetch cycle. The execute cycle will include reading addressed operand bytes in memory if required, as well as performing the internal operation upon the operands obtained and any final write operation. The simple division of a computer system operation into an instruction fetch cycle and an instruction execute cycle in a microprocessor system, or any computer system in which instructions are of variable length, becomes a sequence of read cycles and a possible final write cycle. Often the term op-code fetch is used for the first read cycle which fetches the op-code.

The timing details of the Z-80 microprocessor fetch and execute cycles in terms of read and write cycles are considered in Chap. 7.

6.2.4 Bus

The bus signals contained in the external bus can be divided into the three groups:

   (i) Data lines
  (ii) Address lines
 (iii) Control lines

(a) Data lines
The data lines are used to transfer binary words between the processor, memory and input/output interfaces. The binary words may be machine instructions from the memory to the processor prior to performing the operation specified by the instruction, or may be data to or from the processor during the execution of the operation.

Microprocessors are described as 4-bit, 8-bit, 16-bit or 32-bit if the data operands are manipulated fundamentally in units of 4, 8, 16 or 32 bits respectively. The first microprocessors were 4-bit microprocessors and four data lines were provided (actually the same lines were also used for address signals). Instructions needed to be longer than four bits so multiple data transfers were necessary to obtain one instruction. For example, a 16-bit instruction could be obtained by four successive 4-bit transfers. Early 4-bit microprocessors had some 8-bit and 16-bit instructions, necessitating two and four 4-bit transfers respectively.

Eight-bit microprocessors have eight data lines. Commonly instructions of

8-bit microprocessors are between one and five bytes, requiring one to five data transfers to obtain the instruction. Normally, 16-bit microprocessors have sixteen data lines, and each instruction consists of one or more 16-bit words. It may be advantageous in some cases to design 16-bit microprocessors with eight data lines to reduce the number of lines. Using eight data lines also allows memory and input/output devices operating on eight bits to be easily accommodated. When 16-bit data is being processed with eight data lines, two successive 8-bit data transfers are necessary. Thirty-two bit microprocessors have 32 data lines (unless reduced in the same manner to 16 or 8 lines).

(b) Address lines

The address lines carry the address of the memory location being accessed during an instruction fetch or during the execution of data transfer to or from the memory location. Whereas the data signals may originate at the processor, memory devices or input/output interfaces, for simple instruction processing address signals always originate at the processor. (There are some instances when address signals originate elsewhere, i.e. when another device controls the bus lines; see Chap. 10, section 10.4.)

It is possible to combine the address lines or to combine some of the address lines with data lines to reduce the number of connections on the microprocessor device, though address and data are usually separated for connection to the other components. (An exception to this is in a microprocessor system using specially designed components to match combined address/data lines of the microprocessor.) The early 4-bit 4004/4040 microprocessors used four combined data/address lines. A 12-bit address was generated by the unusual arrangement of passing three consecutive 4-bit addresses along the bus. The address range was subsequently increased and the next generation of 8-bit microprocessors provided 16-bit addresses on 16 address lines, normally separate from the 8 data lines, though in one instance (the Intel 8085), the lower 8 address lines were shared with data. Figure 6.11 shows the use of a latched buffer to separate the data and address of the 8085. The signal $\overline{\text{ALE}}$ is activated (set to 0) when the data/address bus carries an address.

Sixteen-bit addresses give the capability to address up to 65,536 (2^{16}) locations. The early 16-bit microprocessors had 20 or 24 address lines. Trends have been to increase the number of address lines. For example, 32-bit microprocessors can have 32 address lines providing capability to address 4,294,960,000 (2^{32}) locations.

(c) Control lines

The control lines provide signals to synchronize the operation of the system, in particular the transfer of data along the data bus. There can be twelve or more control lines, each with a particular purpose. Most of the control signals originate at the processor, though one or two may be generated by the other components attached to the bus and sent to the processor.

The signals which originate at only one source device and pass to one or more destination devices can generated by two-state logic circuits. For the

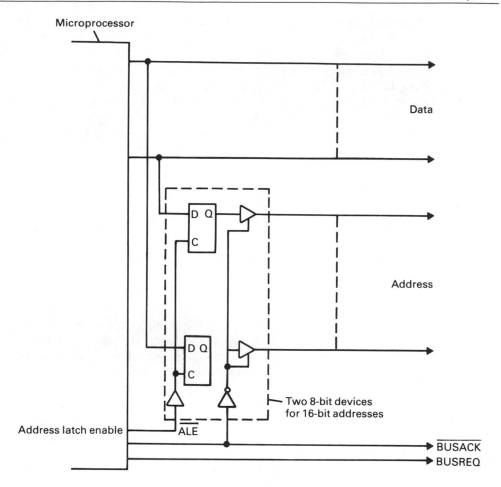

Figure 6.11   Demultiplexing data/address

components in addition to the microprocessor, semiconductor memory and MOS input/output parts, standard TTL gates can be used. MOS microprocessors and other MOS parts use equivalent MOS two-state circuits with active pull-up and active pull-down MOS transistors. In a simple system with no other device being able to address the memory or input/output, the address signals can be generated with two-state circuits. The control signals with one source (usually those from the processor) also can employ two-state circuits.

Those signals which may have more than one source and one or more destinations need to employ either open-collector gates or three-state gates. The data signals always employ three-state gates. The control signals with more than one source (generally those to the processor from the other bus devices) can use open-collector circuits. Open-collector signals must be active low, i.e. normally at a high level and brought low to indicate or cause some action. Open-collector signals would be used when multiple separate or simultaneous signal activations are possible, while three-state signals would be used when simultaneous activation is not allowed, such as passing data to and from the processor simultaneously. Note that the microprocessor itself is often of MOS technology and thus would use the equivalent MOS circuits. Usually MOS devices have a very low fan-out capability (about one TTL load) so additional TTL buffer gates are used between MOS microprocessors (and other MOS devices) and the bus, as described in Chap. 5, section 5.6.3.

6.2.5 Bus information transfer techniques

We now consider the techniques used to control the transfer of information in a bus system and the corresponding control signals. There are two basic information transfer techniques used. We shall call these methods the *synchronous bus transfer method* and the *asynchronous bus transfer method*:

(a) Synchronous transfer method
In the synchronous bus transfer method, a request signal together with data if appropriate, and address signals are generated by the source device, normally the processor. These signals are received by the appropriate destination device, normally a memory unit or input/output interface, whereupon data is accepted or generated. The time required for the transfer is known in advance and is taken into account by the source device before the next request is generated. The simple data transfer technique with one memory or input/output request timing signal and one active data direction signal (say read or write) is in this synchronous transfer category. Often it is arranged that all data transfers are of a fixed period, all memory operating with a common maximum access time and all the input/output interfaces operating within the same constraints.

The basic operation of synchronous data transfer requires the following information to be transferred along the control lines:

(i)   Direction of the data transfer, either to the processor or from the processor
(ii) Timing of the transfer
(iii) Whether the transfer involves a memory location or input/output interface (if these are differentiated).

Data (or an instruction) transferred to the processor is called a *read* cycle or transfer. Data transferred from the processor is called a *write* cycle or transfer. One signal may be generated to indicate a read transfer and another to indicate a write transfer. With separate signals for different transactions, the time of the transaction can be when the signal is generated. If the signals are combined, for example a combined read/write signal which is true for a read transfer and false for a write transfer (true = 1, false = 0), additional signals must be generated when the operation is to occur. Control signals are often active low, as indicated by a bar over the signal name.

In the Z-80, two signals are used to differentiate the direction of transfer and two for timing, i.e.:

$\overline{\text{RD}}$ Read enable

$\overline{\text{WR}}$ Write enable
$\overline{\text{MREQ}}$ Memory request
$\overline{\text{IOREQ}}$ Input/output request

Alternative is to combine $\overline{\text{MREQ}}$ and $\overline{\text{IOREQ}}$ into one signal:

IO/$\overline{\text{M}}$ Input-output/memory, a signal indicating whether the read or write transfer is to memory or input/output devices

together with $\overline{\text{RD}}$ and $\overline{\text{WR}}$ enable signals. This is used in the Intel 8-bit 8085 and the 16-bit 8086/8 in the 'minimum mode'.

It is not possible to also combine $\overline{\text{RD}}$ and $\overline{\text{WR}}$ without an additional timing signal. For example, in the Motorola 8-bit 6800 series, the control signals are:

VMA   Valid memory address activated when a stable address is on the bus, similar to $\overline{\text{MREQ}}$
R/$\overline{\text{W}}$ Read/write, a combined read-write signal, 1 for read, 0 for write, selected at the beginning of the transfer
E or Ø   General processor clock, timing synchronized to this signal

Input/output and memory are not generally differentiated in the Motorola 6800 (or the 68000).

Another approach is to have one definitive timing signal to each type of data transfer, i.e. memory read, memory write, input read and output write:

$\overline{\text{MEMR}}$ Memory read request
$\overline{\text{MEMW}}$ Memory write request
$\overline{\text{IO/R}}$ Input/output read request
$\overline{\text{IO/W}}$ Input/output write request

In this set, only one signal can be activated at any instant since they are mutually exclusive. The scheme is used by the Intel 8080 with the 8228 support device.

Yet another approach is to have separate data and address timing signals:

$\overline{\text{AS}}$ Address strobe, generated after the address is stable
$\overline{\text{DS}}$ Data strobe, generated after the data is stable

both for read and write at different times, together with a combined read/write and memory request signals:

R/$\overline{\text{W}}$ Read/write
$\overline{\text{MREQ}}$ Memory request

The method is particularly applicable to buses with time-shared data/address buses. In this case, $\overline{\text{AS}}$ and $\overline{\text{DS}}$ differentiate between address and data occurring on the same lines. It is used by the Zilog 16-bit Z8000 which has a time-shared data/address bus.

With the synchronous transfer technique, the processor must be operated at a frequency not greater than the speed which matches the slowest device. It may be that this clock frequency is not the maximum for the processor and the potential speed of the processor is not then being utilized. This problem can be alleviated with the introduction of a *ready* or *wait* signal, emitted from the destination device to the source device. One such signal is provided in all the above examples. The ready signal when activated causes the source to add extra dummy processor clock cycles (known as *wait* states) in the middle of the data transfer period. It is necessary to know how much extra time is required so that the wait state generator hardware within the destination can be designed to activate the ready/wait signal appropriately. The extra time actually given will be in units of one clock cycle. The processor will sample the ready/wait line during each clock cycle to ascertain whether another dummy cycle is necessary. Memory or input/output units attached to the bus which need extra time are provided with separate wait state generators arranged to generate the ready/wait signal as required for the unit as shown in Fig. 6.12. When a memory (or input/output interface) is selected by its address and associated control signals on the bus, the wait state generator is activated.

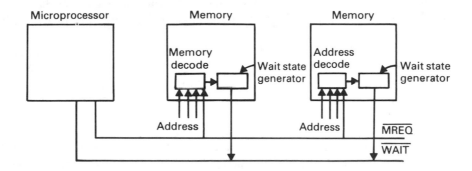

Figure 6.12   Generating wait states

(b) Asynchronous transfer method

The asynchronous bus transfer method uses two signals for timing the data transfer. The first signal from the source (the processor generally) to a destination (memory or input/output device) signifies the start of a data transfer. The transfer operation is only terminated by the second signal emitted from the destination, indicating that the transfer has been completed. This two-signal approach, as shown in Fig. 6.13, is known as *handshaking* and is similar to the synchronous mechanism modified with read/wait signal returned by the destination. The difference is that the timing of the transfer in full handshaking systems applies to all transfers and the duration of the transfer is dictated by the returning signal always. The return or acknowledge signal must be activated for the transfer to be completed, whereas with a ready/wait mechanism, the transfer is always completed unless delayed by the ready/wait signal.

For data operations, there would be a *data transfer acknowledge* signal produced by the memory or input/output interface indicating that the data transfer is complete, in addition to the 'direction' and 'type' signals of the synchronous method. If an asynchronous approach is taken to its logical conclusion, all control signals would have an acknowledge signal. For example,

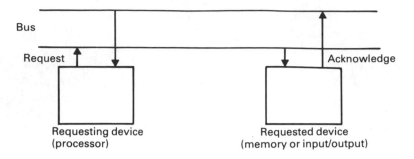

Figure 6.13   Asynchronous 'handshake' operation

the address strobe timing signals would have an address strobe acknowledge signal. This is not done, but there may be handshaking on certain control signals, for example the bus grant signal may have a bus grant acknowledge signal.

Generally if an acknowledge signal is not received within a fixed time specified by the bus design, 'time-out' error sequence is started automatically to ascertain the identity of the fault. (A microprocessor with a ready mechanism may have a maximum allowed period for waiting for a memory unit to be ready, maybe $10\,\mu s$.)

Asynchronous bus transfer systems have the advantage of matching the speed of data transfer with the source and destination, and of having an error detection mechanism, since if an acknowledge is not received there must be a fault which can be easily detected. (Not receiving a wait signal does not indicate a fault.) However, the method has the disadvantage of requiring more signals (the acknowledge signals) which must be allowed time to be generated and travel along the bus, so it may be that the speed of operation is slower.

The signals in an asynchronous bus include the signals described in the synchronous transfer method with the addition of acknowledge signals. For example, the Intel MULTIBUS system bus uses the signals:

$\overline{\text{MRDC}}$ Memory read command
$\overline{\text{MWTC}}$ Memory write command
$\overline{\text{IORC}}$ Input/output read command
$\overline{\text{IOWC}}$ Input/output write command

together with the acknowledge:

$\overline{\text{XACK}}$ Transfer acknowledge

The 68000 is provided with both synchronous and asynchronous signals. Generally the 68000 asynchronous signals:

$\overline{\text{AS}}$ Address strobe
$\overline{\text{UDS}}$ Upper data strobe (for data on data lines D_8 to D_{15})
$\overline{\text{LDS}}$ Lower data strobe (for data on data lines D_0 to D_7)
$\text{R}/\overline{\text{W}}$ Read/write (1 for read, 0 for write)

$\overline{\text{DTACK}}$ Data acknowledge

would be used. The synchronous signals are similar to those of the 6800 and are provided principally to enable 6800 input/output devices to be incorporated into the system.

The timing signals of synchronous Z-80 as modified with wait states and the timing signals of the asynchronous 68000 are considered in detail in Chap. 7 and Chap. 8 respectively.

6.3 PROGRAMMING ASPECTS

6.3.1 Machine-language programming

One can write programs directly in machine language. For example, a program sequence to add number 56 (hexadecimal) to the number held in memory location 100 (hexadecimal), placing the result in memory location 101, in Z-80 machine language, could be:

Machine operation	*Machine instruction encoding*		
	1st byte	*2nd byte*	*3rd byte*
Load contents of location 100 into A register	00111010	00000000	00010000
Add 56 (a literal) to the contents of A register	11000110	01010110	
Transfer contents of A register into location 101	00111010	00000001	00010000

Clearly, the patterns can more easily be represented in hexadecimal, i.e.:

3A 00 10
C6 56
32 01 10

where each pair of hexadecimal digits is held in one 8-bit memory location. The first pair of each instruction represents the op-code. The subsequent pairs of hexadecimal digits represent an operand or operand address. In the Z-80, the two bytes which make up the 16-bit operand addresses are stored in reverse order, i.e. the lower significant address byte is contained in the second byte of the instruction and the higher significant address byte is contained in the third byte of the instruction.

A keyboard for the hexadecimal digits 0 to 9 and the letters A to F can be provided on the system for entering the program in the hexadecimal representation. It is a very simple process of converting the hexadecimal representation into binary. Programming in 'hex' is suitable for very small microprocessor systems. *Single board computers* (a microprocessor system constructed on one printed circuit board) are usually provided with hexadecimal input. Small *monitor* programs are installed to enable the contents memory and processor registers to be displayed on a display terminal in the hexadecimal representation, or altered using the keyboard.

6.3.2 Assembly-language programming

Producing machine-language programs consisting of sequences of machine language instructions in hexadecimal is tedious, and a better means of writing programs is desirable. The problem is not limited to microprocessor systems and applies to computer systems in general. One improvement is to assign letter codes known as mnemonics to represent the operation part of the instruction, various symbolic conventions to represent the addressing modes, and decimal or hexadecimal number to represent the operand or address. This forms the essence of an *assembly language*. In an assembly language, each machine instruction is replaced by an alphanumeric representation which can be translated into machine language. The translation is done by a computer program known as an *assembler*.

The assembly process using the assembler is commonly performed within an operating system environment. An *operating system* is usually a complex program for controlling a computer system and supports software *packages* such as assemblers. The operating system maintains *files*, a name given to a collection of stored words for a particular purpose such as a program or data. Files are kept on disk storage (see Chap. 11) when not required. The process of creating an executable machine-language program begins with the creation of an assembly-language program held in an operating system file, known as a *source file*. The source file is created using another operating system software package known as an *editor*. The editor allows the user to type in the program at a terminal and to correct any mistakes easily. Once this process has been completed, the assembler is activated which then reads the specified assembly-language program file and generates a machine-language program file (the *object file*). Sometimes microprocessor assemblers generate a machine-language program in hexadecimal format rather than in binary and an additional process is necessary to convert the hexadecimal program into binary. This process can be done using an operating system package known as a *loader*. The loader will create a machine-language program in memory ready for execution.

Different manufacturers use different assembly-language mnemonics and different notations for similar machine instructions, and we shall follow the appropriate manufacturer's mnemonics when considering particular microprocessors. As an example, Zilog mnemonics for a data transfer instruction in the Z-80 is LD ('load'):

LD B,A

which copies the contents of the A register into the B register. Motorola uses the mnemonic MOV ('move') for a similar instruction, i.e. in the 68000:

MOV D1,D2

copies the contents of the D1 data register into the D2 data register. Notice that the order of operands is different.

Our three-line Z-80 program given in section 6.3.1 can be written in assembly language as:

```
LD A, (100)
ADD A,56H
LD (101),A
```

Parentheses are used to indicate a memory address, as opposed to a literal.

In addition to representing the operation and the operand fields of the machine instruction in a more recognizable form, assembly language incorporates various other features. Each *assembly-language statement* corresponding to one machine instruction is composed of several sections of fields. Commonly, the statement begins with a label field followed by an operation field, an operand field, and ends with a comment field. The label and comment fields are optional. The operation and operand fields relate to the machine instruction proper. Each field is separated by delimiters which may in general be spaces, commas, semi-colons or other specified non-alphabetic symbol. This leads to an assembly-language statement format:

Label : operation operand ; comment

where a colon is used to separate the label field from the operation, a space is used to separate the operation field from the operand field, and a semi-colon is used to separate the operand field from the comment field. Spaces can be used between fields to aid readability. An assembly-language program will consists of a sequence of the above statements together with other statements such as *directives*. Directives instruct the assembler to perform some action relating to the assembly process and will be considered later.

The label can be any sequence of alphanumeric characters but there may be restrictions. Commonly the first letter may not be any of the decimal digits 0 to 9. Labels serve to identify the statement, and more particularly, to identify the statement if control is passed to it via jump/call instructions. The same label is used in the operand field of the jump/call instruction in place of the actual address of the labeled statement (address of the equivalent machine-language instruction) and actual memory addresses need not be known when forming program loops such as in the Z-80 program:

```
       LD HL,4000
       LD B,10
Loop:  ADD A,(HL)
       INC HL
       DJNZ Loop
```

'Loop' is a label. (This program adds the contents of the memory locations 4000 to 4009 inclusive to the A register.)

The comment field allows the programmer to attach alphanumeric text to statements for documentation purposes. Comments do not affect the operation of the statement whatsoever, but are extremely useful to help a program algorithm being understood. This is particularly relevant when a program written by one programmer is to be taken by others and modified or incorporated into other programs. Comments should not simply describe the operation of the statement in terms of 'contents of register A is added to register

B' or 'register B is incremented' because the machine operation is clear from the operation mnemonic and operand description. It is much more useful to give a comment which describes the operation in terms of the problem variables and the intended problem calculation, for example, 'overflow variable set' or 'keyboard character received'.

The operation field consists of the mnemonic for the operation of the machine instruction. Typical mnemonics are three- or four-letter codes and are abbreviations of the actions required.

The operand field includes the addressing mode unless incorporated into the operation, and the addresses of operands. Generally special symbols are used to represent the addressing modes, either placed before the address or after it. Numbers used in the operand field are usually regarded as decimal numbers unless otherwise indicated. For example, numbers using binary, octal and hexadecimal representation might be indicated by the letters B, O, Q and H respectively, placed after the number. However, the exact convention depends upon assembly language. Hexadecimal numbers which begin with the letters A to F usually need to be have a zero prefix in order to distinguish them from names (see later).

Arithmetic expressions can usually be incorporated into the operand field. Such expressions can consist of numbers, symbolic names and arithmetic operators conventionally arranged. The expressions are evaluated by the assembler during the assembly process before the program is executed. The resultant values become the numbers to be used in the operand field of the statements.

The symbolic names mentioned above can be used to represent a number, operand or an address. A symbolic name is a sequence of alphanumeric characters selected by the programmer. The first letter of the name must be a letter of the alphabet so that the name may be differentiated from actual numbers. Other characters of the symbolic name may be either letters, digits or other symbols. There may be a restriction on the number of characters in the name. Names need to be declared in the assembly-language program, using *assembly-language directives*. A directive is a statement not corresponding to a particular machine instruction. Instead, an assembly-language directive specifies some other operation associated with the program assembly process or the running of the program, such as specifying the required start address of the assembled machine-language program, data areas and constants and variable definitions.

A common directive to declare a constant symbolic name is:

Symbolic name EQU expression

where EQU is the assembly language mnemonic for 'equate to'. The expression may be an ordinary arithmetic expression consisting of numbers and arithmetic operators. The symbolic name on the left-hand side of the EQU mnemonic is assigned the value of the expression. There are other assembly-language directives. Those used in a given program are usually grouped together at the beginning or at the end of the program.

Commonly the programmer will include several assembly-language directives into the assembly-language program to enable the assembler to perform correctly. A directive usually defines the start address of the final assembled machine-language program in memory. This directive in many assemblers is the origin directive, ORG with the format:

ORG Start address

where 'start address' may be an expression which evaluates to a suitable integer. For example, ORG 100H typically would cause the assembler to produce the machine-language program such that it will run correctly when loaded in memory beginning at location 100 (hexadecimal). The start address for execution may be different, i.e. the program may start some way into the program, and if so would need to be defined by another directive.

Sometimes it is desirable not to specify the start address of the assembled program explicitly, but to delay this decision until later. A common application is one in which several program modules are to be joined together to form one larger program. The final start address of each program module is not known until all the modules are in place. An assembler known as a *relocatable assembler* would be used (as opposed to an *absolute assembler*). A relocatable assembler assembles a program intended to be linked with others or for some other reason not have a fixed start address is used. The process of joining together program modules produced by the relocatable assembler and providing the final addresses is called *linking*. The software package to perform this task is called a *linker*. The overall sequence is shown in Fig. 6.14.

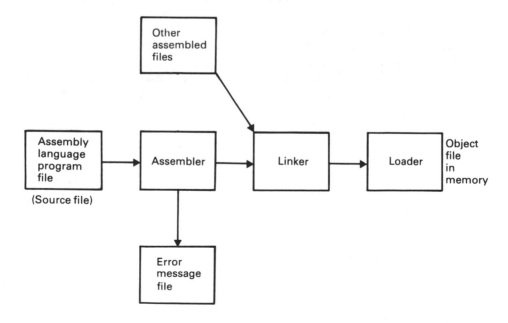

Figure 6.14 Assembly process

7

Z-80 Microprocessor

7.1 GENERAL

In this chapter we will examine the 8-bit Zilog Z-80 microprocessor[1], chosen because it is a very widely used 8-bit microprocessor. The Z-80 is a register/ accumulator type of machine having all of the instructions of an earlier microprocessor, the Intel 8080. Hence the Z-80 is capable of executing all 8080 programs. The main register set consists of a 8-bit accumulator (A register), and six further 8-bit general-purpose registers, B, C, D, E, H and L, which can be arranged as 16-bit register pairs, i.e. BC, DE and HL. The register pairs can be used to hold a 16-bit address of memory operands. HL is the principal pair for this type of operation. H holds the more significant (higher) address byte and L holds the less significant (lower) address byte. The register pairs can also hold 16-bit data and there are some 16-bit operations. There is a 16-bit program counter to hold the address of the next instruction to be executed and a 16-bit stack pointer to specify the top location of a memory *stack* (see later, section 7.4.7). There are some limitations to the manner in which the general-purpose registers can be used, depending upon the type of instruction. Input/output is mainly through the A register.

Arithmetic and logical operations are performed by the ALU (arithmetic and logic unit), taking one operand from the A register. The result is placed in the A register, overwriting the existing contents of the A register. The second operand, where appropriate, can be taken from any of the general-purpose registers. Memory locations can be specified through the use of the HL register pair to hold the address, but not explicity in instructions. Certain aspects of the result of an ALU operation are indicated in bits of the *condition code register*, also called the *flag register* (*F register*). Conditions include a zero result, a positive result, a result with even parity and a result which generates a carry or borrow.

All of the above registers are also available in the 8080 though the Z-80 provides some more instructions with these registers. In addition, the Z-80 incorporates two 16-bit *index registers*, IX and IY, particularly for accessing data arrays and also a complete additional general register set, A', F', B', C', D', E', H' and L', known as the *alternate register set*. Register pairs are represented by AF', BC', DE' and HL'. After the execution of two instructions (EXX which exchanges the use of BC, DE, HL with the alternate pairs, and EX AF, AF' which exchanges the use of AF with the alternate AF') the alternate register set can be used while maintaining the information in the normal register set. This has particular application in interrupt programming (see Chap. 10, section 10.3). Figure 7.1 shows the registers available in the Z-80.

In 8-bit microprocessors systems such as a Z-80 system, information is transmitted between the memory or I/O interfaces and the processor in units of one byte. Each addressed location in the memory holds one byte (8 bits). Similarly, instructions consist of one or more bytes (up to five bytes in the Z-80). The bytes of one instruction are stored in consecutive memory locations.

7.2 SYSTEM CONFIGURATION

7.2.1 Bus signals

There are 8 data signals (D_0 to D_7), 16 address signals (A_0 to A_{15}) and 13 control signals to or from the microprocessor. These signals would normally constitute the system bus. The 16 address signal enable 2^{16} (65,536) memory locations to be accessed. Memory and input/output can be differentiated. The fundamental control signals for data transfer are:

$\overline{RD}$ Read
$\overline{WR}$ Write
$\overline{MREQ}$ Memory request
$\overline{IORQ}$ Input/output request

The synchronous bus transfer mechanism is used. A $\overline{WAIT}$ signal is provided to extend the transfer with wait states if required. Often the wait state

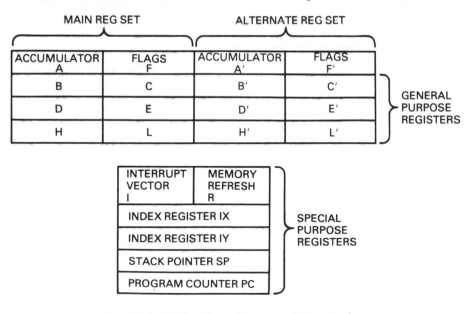

Figure 7.1 Z–80 registers (Courtesy of Zilog, Inc.)

mechanism is not used for small systems because of the hardware overhead. Usually it is possible to match memory and processor speeds. Input/output transfers have one wait state introduced automatically.

All processor signals are activated relative to the processor clock, Φ. The clock periods are called *T states* (T_1, T_2, T_3, etc.). Several T states are necessary to complete a data or instruction transfer. Each such transfer is called an *M cycle*.

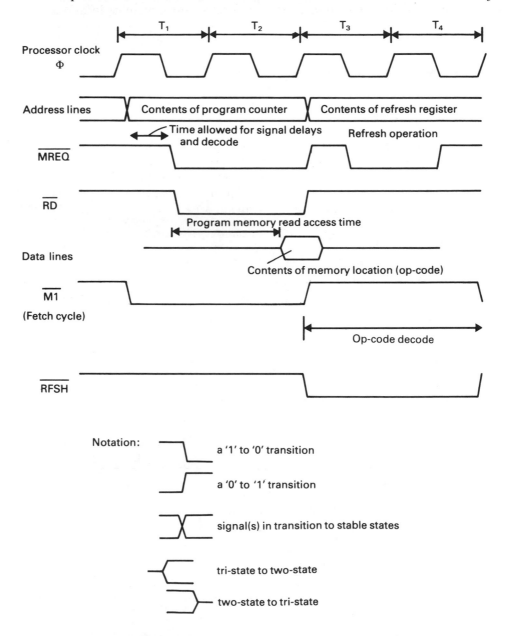

Figure 7.2   Z–80 fetch cycle (Courtesy of Zilog, Inc.)

The execution of an instruction requires one or more M cycles. There are three basic types of M cycles which can be used to fetch and execute a memory reference instruction, namely and instruction *op-code fetch cycle* which transfers the first byte of the instruction (the op-code) from memory to the processor, *memory (data) read cycle* which transfers subsequent operands or addresses of operands to the processor, and *memory write cycle* which transfers data from a processor register to memory.

The signal timing for an instruction fetch cycle is shown in Fig. 7.2 and consists of four T states. The control signal $\overline{M1}$ is a 0 throughout T_1 and T_2 to indicate that the cycle is an instruction fetch (the first M cycle). The first two T states are used to obtain the instruction. During these two states, the address lines carry the address of the instruction as contained in the program counter. After the address has settled, the memory request and read control signals are activated as shown. It is expected that the program memory will respond before the beginning of the third T state and place the *op-code* on the data lines, which is accepted by the rising edge of T_3. In the Z-80, an extra operation is included in the instruction fetch cycle to maintain dynamic memories known as *memory refresh* during T_3 and T_4, which will be explained in Chap. 9. A memory location is read during these states to maintain its information.

The signal timing for a memory data read cycle is shown in Fig. 7.3 and consists of three T states. Throughout the cycle, the address lines carry the address of the memory location which holds the required data. Again after the address has settled, the memory request and read control signals are activated as shown. It is expected that the memory will respond before the falling edge of T_3 and place the data on data lines. The data is accepted on the falling edge of T_3. In many microprocessors, instruction fetch and memory (data) read cycles are of

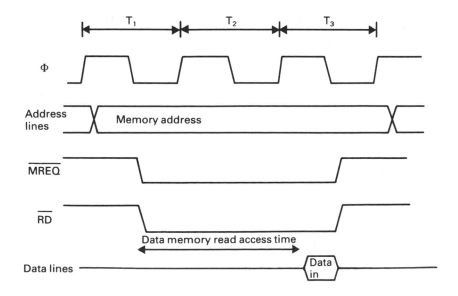

Figure 7.3 Z-80 read cycle (Courtesy of Zilog, Inc.)

the same form. Notice that in the Z-80, less time is made available for the memory to fetch the op-code. In the write cycle shown in Fig. 7.4, data is provided by the processor and $\overline{WR}$ is used by the memory to indicate that the data can be accepted.

If the memory requires more time in any of the cycles, the $\overline{WAIT}$ line is activated by the memory by the time that the falling edge of T_2 occurs. Then an extra T state is introduced between T_2 and T_3. Further wait states can be introduced as required by maintaining $\overline{WAIT}$ low, during each falling edge of the Φ clock.

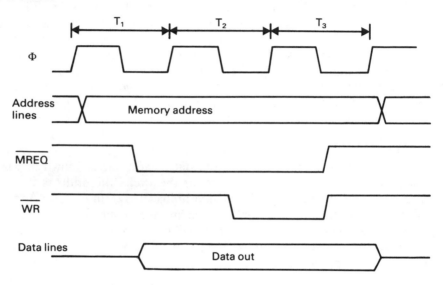

Figure 7.4   Z-80 write cycle (Courtesy of Zilog, Inc.)

7.2.2 A simple Z-80 microprocessor system

Let us briefly examine the logic components of a very simple microprocessor system shown in Fig. 7.5, designed to display a sequence on four light-emitting diodes (LEDs). There are four main parts, the microprocessor, program memory (EPROM), data memory (RAM) and an output interface.

A crystal-controlled oscillator is formed with two 74S04 inverters and a crystal to generate the processor clock, Φ, operating here at 1 MHz. When the system is switched on, a reset pulse must be generated to the $\overline{RESET}$ input of the processor to set the program counter to address 0. This is achieved here with an R–C network connected to the $\overline{RESET}$ input which causes the input to remain in the logic 0 voltage range for a few milliseconds after the power is applied. Processor inputs not used are connected to +5V through 10 kΩ resistors.

Two memory devices are provided, a program memory using a type 2716 EPROM (erasable programmable read-only memory) and data memory using a type 6116 RAM (random access memory). Both memories hold 2048 words each of 8 bit (i.e. 2k $\times$ 8). The devices have identical connections except that the EPROM does not require a write enable signal since the processor cannot write to an EPROM. Similar memory address decode circuits are employed. Address signals A_{11} to A_{15} select the memory module and A_0 to A_{10} select a location within the memory device. The memory module decode circuits each consist of an 8-bit comparator (74LS682) which compares the address generated on address lines A_{11} to A_{15} inclusive with a fixed binary number. When a match is found during memory request cycle ($\overline{MREQ}$ = 0), the output $\overline{P=Q}$ becomes low. This signal enables the memory device (i.e. the chip-enable input, $\overline{CE}$, of the memory is activated).

The processor read strobe signal, $\overline{RD}$, is applied directly to the output enable input of each memory device ($\overline{OE}$). When $\overline{RD}$ = 0, the data outputs of the memory are enabled. The processor write strobe signal, $\overline{WR}$, is connected to the write enable input of the RAM ($\overline{WE}$). When $\overline{WR}$ = 0, the memory will accept data into the addressed location. Memory module addresses are shown set to the range 0000H to 07FFH for the RAM and 0800H to 0FFFH for the EPROM.

Output information is displayed using four light-emitting diodes (LEDs). No user input is provided. The LEDs are driven by a quad TTL latch, type 74LS379. The LEDs have integral series limiting resistors. Each LED illuminates when a 1 is written to the appropriate bit of the latch. The address decode circuit is similar to the memory address decode circuit except $\overline{MREQ}$ is replaced by $\overline{IOREQ}$. Address selection is performed using A_1 to A_7 rather than A_{11} to A_{15}. The decode output signal is used to enable the latch. Data is entered into the latch using the write strobe signal, $\overline{WR}$. The output address is shown set to address 4H. The output interface will respond to two address 4H and 5H as A_0 is not used in the address decode mechanism.

7.3 INSTRUCTION ADDRESSING

Before considering the various instructions in the Z-80 instruction set, we shall outline four of the mechanisms available to access the operands. Further addressing mechanisms are considered in section 7.5.

7.3.1 Immediate addressing

We noted in the last chapter that the actual operand can be specified within the instruction. This is known as *immediate addressing*, as shown in Fig. 7.6. The operand is embedded in the instruction immediately following the operation field. In byte-orientated systems such as the Z-80, instructions are one or more bytes, each byte having a distinct memory address. The operation part of the instruction is normally held in the first byte and the operand is being specified. In 16-bit systems the first 16 bits in include the operation and some other

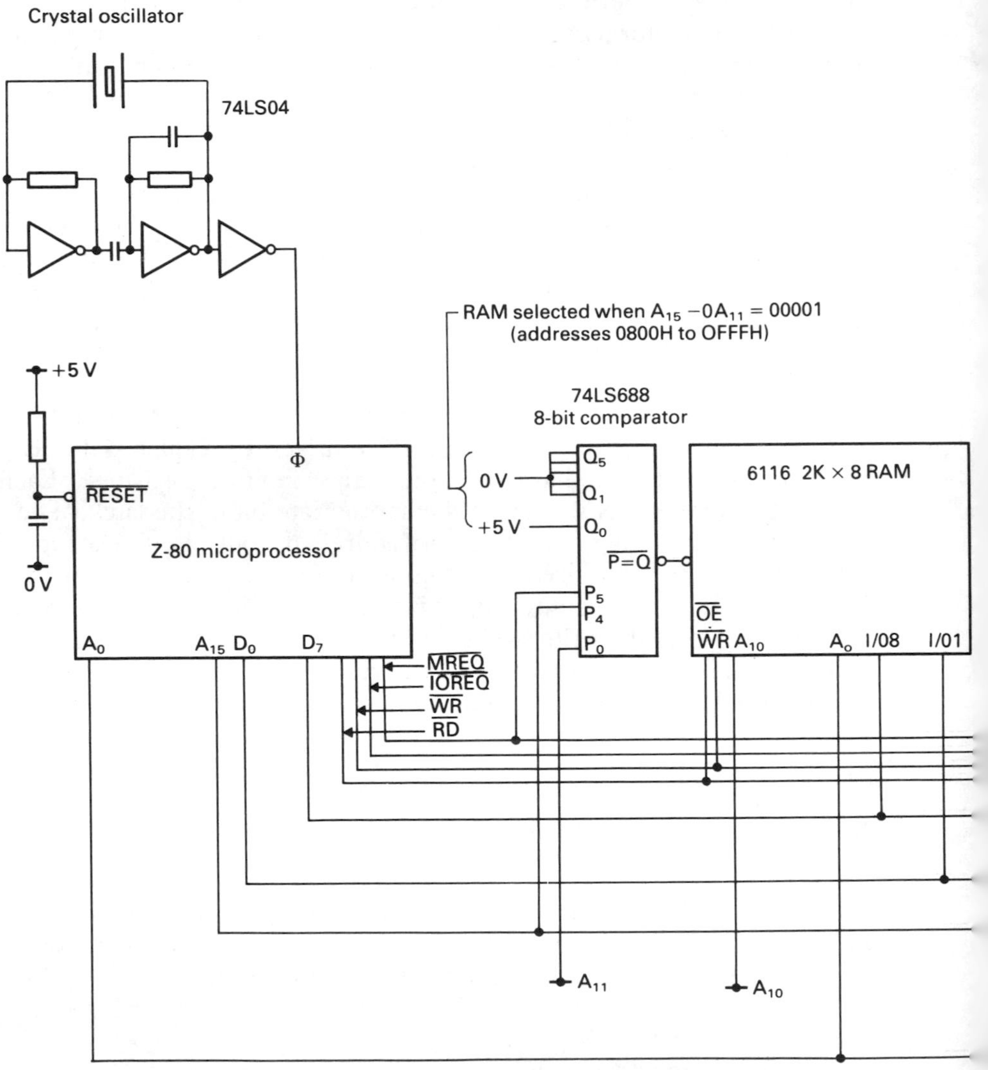

Crystal oscillator

74LS04

RAM selected when $A_{15} - 0A_{11} = 00001$
(addresses 0800H to OFFFH)

74LS688
8-bit comparator

+5 V

6116 2K × 8 RAM

RESET

0 V

Q_5

Q_1

Q_0

$\overline{P=Q}$

P_5

P_4

P_0

$\overline{OE}$

$\overline{WR}$ A_{10}

A_o I/08   I/01

0 V

+5 V

Φ

Z-80 microprocessor

A_0 A_{15} D_0 D_7

$\overline{MREQ}$
$\overline{IOREQ}$
$\overline{WR}$
$\overline{RD}$

A_{11}

A_{10}

Figure 7.5 Simple microprocessor system

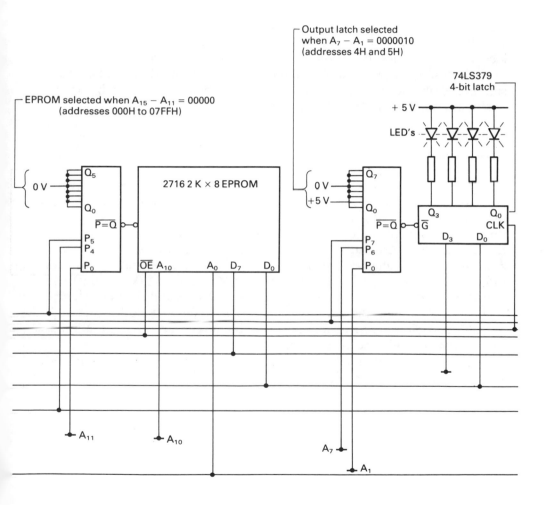

Output latch selected
when $A_7 - A_1 = 0000010$
(addresses 4H and 5H)

74LS379
4-bit latch

EPROM selected when $A_{15} - A_{11} = 00000$
(addresses 000H to 07FFH)

+ 5 V

LED's

Q_5

0 V

2716 2 K × 8 EPROM

Q_0

$\overline{P = Q}$

P_5
P_4

P_0

$\overline{OE}$ A_{10} A_0 D_7 D_0

Q_7

0 V

+5 V

Q_0

$\overline{P = Q}$

P_7
P_6

P_0

Q_3 Q_0

$\overline{G}$ CLK

D_3 D_0

A_{11}

A_{10}

A_7

A_1

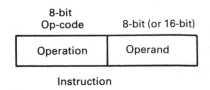

Figure 7.6   Z-80 immediate addressing

information, but the operand is still usually in the second word. Consequently, the address of the operand immediately follows the address of the operation location. Sometimes the term *literal* is used to describe the operand in immediate addressing because the number is 'literally' used. Immediate addressing is available to most classes of Z-80 instructions. The assembly-language notation is simply to write the literal.

7.3.2 Absolute Addressing

The fundamental method of obtaining the operand entails specifying the address of a memory location in the instruction as shown in Fig. 7.7. This method is known as *absolute addressing*. Since a memory location is used to store the operand, it is possible to alter the value stored. Hence one could compare the absolutely addressed operand with a variable. In the Z-80, absolute addressing is also called *extended addressing* as the address is a full 16-bit address rather than a shorter 8-bit address. The least significant (low-order) byte is stored in the 8-bit location following the op-code byte and the most significant (high-order) byte in the next 8-bit location. Extended addressing is only available in 8-bit load instructions involving the A register. It is noticeably absent from arithmetic and logic instructions.

The notation to show absolute or extended addressing is to enclose the address in parentheses, e.g. (300) would specify the memory location 300, the contents of which would be used as the operand. This notation is not used by other manufacturers. For example, Intel chose to use different operation mnemonics for immediate addressed and absolute addressed instructions (e.g. MVI and MOV) with the 8080/8085. Motorola chose to prefix literals with the

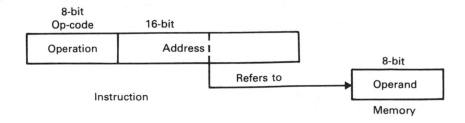

Figure 7.7   Z-80 absolute addressing

symbol to differentiate immediate addressing (using a literal) from absolute addressing. No special symbol is used to denote absolute addressing.

7.3.3 Register direct addressing

Another method entails specifying a register holding the operand, as shown in Fig. 7.8. This method is known as *register direct* addressing. Both register direct and absolute addressing are direct methods of locating the operand as opposed to some 'indirect' methods which require computation or multiple accesses to obtain the address of the operand. The register direct addressing method has the advantage over memory direct or absolute addressing of usually higher speed of access and a short instruction length, but has the disadvantage that there are only a limited number of processor registers available. The Z-80 has a good range of instructions in which register direct addressing can be applied, including 8-bit arithmetic, logic shift and rotate instructions, to all general-purpose registers (A, B, C, D, E, H, and L). Many register direct instructions have eight bits, but some have sixteen bits (e.g. shift and rotate).

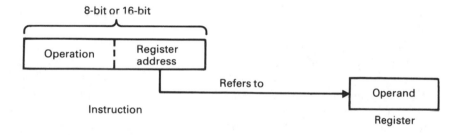

Figure 7.8   Z-80 register direct addressing

7.3.4 Indirect addressing

Considerable extra flexibility would be achieved in addressing operands if an addressing mode were provided in which the address was computed in some manner using operands provided as data in the program. Since all computations give results in registers (or memory locations), a useful addressing mode would be one which takes the contents of a register (or memory location) as the address of the operand. This method is known as *indirect addressing* and is illustrated in Fig. 7.9. Some early microprocessors did not have any form of indirect addressing, but all subsequent microprocessors have indirect addressing using the contents of a register, i.e. *register indirect* addressing. The main register pair used in the Z-80 for register indirect addressing is the HL register pair. Register H hold the high byte of the address while register L holds the low address byte. HL register indirect addressing can be applied to most instructions including all arithmetic, logic, shift and rotate instructions (see later).

The notation is (HL). i.e. the address of the operand is contained in HL.

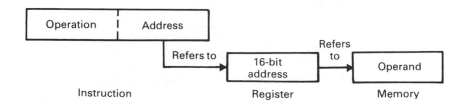

Figure 7.9 Z-80 register indirect addressing

To a limited extent, the other register pairs (BC and DE) can indirectly address operands. The use of the index registers will be considered separately.

7.4 INSTRUCTIONS

We now examine the range of Z-80 instructions. Opportunity was taken with the Z-80 to rationalize the assembly language mnemonics, so that the mnemonics are mostly different from those of the original 8080 (though much more consistent). We will describe Z-80 instructions using Z-80 mnemonics. In the following, user defined items will be enclosed in the symbols < and >. The notation *nn* is used to show a 16-bit address or 16-bit number and *n* is used to show a 8-bit number generally. The letter d (for displacement) is used to indicate the number of locations from a defined position. At least one space will be used to separate the operation mnemonic from the operand(s) and a comma will be used to separate operands, as the space and comma delimiters are commonly used in this manner.

7.4.1 Load instructions

Clearly it is necessary to provide a means of loading memory locations with numbers. It is also necessary to load processor registers with numbers. Finally it is necessary to be able to transfer the contents of memory locations to processor registers and vice versa. Depositing numbers in memory locations and processor registers is a prerequisite before any subsequent operation can be performed on the numbers, and transfer operations are necessary to rearrange the location of the numbers during various computational problems. This is particularly necessary because one operand of all computational operations must be in a processor register. Transferring the contents of one location to another does not affect the source location, i.e. it is a copying operation. Copying operations come under the 'load' type of instruction in the Z-80. Traditionally the source location has been a memory location and the destination location a processor register for 'load' operations, while copying between processor registers has been classified as a 'move' operation (for example in the 8080), but this distinction is not made in the Z-80 microprocessor instruction set.

The general form of load instruction is:

LD <destination location>, <source location>

Table 7.1 shows the possible combinations of source and destination locations for the 8-bit LD instruction. This table and subsequent tables list all valid addressing mechanisms for completeness, including index register addressing which will be considered in section 7.5. Remember that enclosing a register name or memory address in parentheses is used to indicate 'contents of'. The notable invalid combinations in the LD instruction are those involving (BC), (DE) and (*nn*) which can only be combined with A. The processor registers I (interrupt vector) and R (refresh counter) are not considered here.

The following program segment to transpose the contents of two memory locations 200 and 201, is given as a simple programming example involving load instructions:

```
LD A,(200)   ;load contents of memory location 200
LD B,A       ;transfer to B register
LD A,(201)   ;load contents of memory location 201
LD (200),A   ;transfer to memory location 201
LD A,B       ;transfer contents of location 200 to A register
LD (201),A   ;and then to memory location 201
```

Note that when the memory address is specified in the instruction, the contents of a memory location can only be copied to or from the A register. Hence in the above program, the contents of location 200 are first copied into the A register and then transferred into the B register before the A register is used to transfer the contents of location 201 to location 200. Finally, the contents of the B register are returned to the A register and then into location 201.

7.4.2 Arithmetic instructions

One of the fundamental operations of any digital computer is to add two numbers. The instruction must specify the operation (addition) together with information regarding where the two numbers may be found. In the Z-80, one operand is always held in the A register (for 8-bit arithmetic). The second operand is found in one of the locations specified as in the load instruction (see previous section), with the exception that (*nn*), (BC) and (DE) are not allowed. The result of the operation is placed in the A register, thus destroying the original contents of the A register.

The general form of the 8-bit arithmetic instruction is:

operation A, <second operand or address of second operand>

The two fundamental arithmetic operations are addition (ADD) and subtraction (SUB). For example, the instruction to add the contents of the B register to the contents of the A register (disregarding the value held in the carry flag) is:

Table 7.1   8-bit load group 'LD' (Courtesy of Zilog, Inc.)

Binary pattern of instruction, in hexadecimal

		IMPLIED		REGISTER							REG INDIRECT			INDEXED		EXT. ADDR.	IMME.
		I	R	A	B	C	D	E	H	L	(HL)	(BC)	(DE)	(IX + d)	(IY + d)	(nn)	n
REGISTER	A	ED 57	ED 5F	7F	78	79	7A	7B	7C	7D	7E	0A	1A	DD 7E d	FD 7E d	3A n n	3E n
	B			47	40	41	42	43	44	45	46			DD 46 d	FD 46 d		06 n
	C			4F	48	49	4A	4B	4C	4D	4E			DD 4E d	FD 4E d		0E n
	D			57	50	51	52	53	54	55	56			DD 56 d	FD 56 d		16 n
	E			5F	58	59	5A	5B	5C	5D	5E			DD 5E d	FD 5E d		1E n
	H			67	60	61	62	63	64	65	66			DD 66 d	FD 66 d		26 n
	L			6F	68	69	6A	6B	6C	6D	6E			DD 6E d	FD 6E d		2E n
REG INDIRECT	(HL)			77	70	71	72	73	74	75							36 n
	(BC)			02													
	(DE)			12													
INDEXED	(IX+d)			DD 77 d	DD 70 d	DD 71 d	DD 72 d	DD 73 d	DD 74 d	DD 75 d							DD 36 d n
	(IY+d)			FD 77 d	FD 70 d	FD 71 d	FD 72 d	FD 73 d	FD 74 d	FD 75 d							FD 36 d n
EXT. ADDR	(nn)			32 n n													
IMPLIED	I			ED 47													
	R			ED 4F													

SOURCE

DESTINATION

> ADD A,B (i.e. A = A + B)

The A register is not specified in the SUB instruction (nor logic instructions see later), e.g.:

> SUB B

A single-byte instruction is provided to add 1 to the contents of the A register, namely increment (INC). Another single-byte instruction is provided to subtract 1 from the contents of the A register, namely decrement (DEC). No operand is specified with either of these instructions.

The *carry flag* is one bit of the F register which is set to a 1 whenever a carry is generated from the most significant bit during the operation. An addition instruction is provided to add the two specified operands together with the value of the carry flag (ADC instruction) and a subtraction instruction which subtracts the two specified operands and subtracts the value of the carry flag (SBC instruction). With these instructions multi-byte arithmetic can be performed. 16-bit add and subtract instructions are provided where the 16-bit operands are found in register pairs. The result of these instructions is placed one of the register pairs.

The following program adds the contents of location 200 to the contents of location 201, putting the result in location 200, using the A and B registers:

```
LD A,(201)   ;load contents of memory location 201
LD B,A       ;transfer to B register
LD A,(200)   ;load contents of memory location 200
ADD A,B      ;add together
LD (200),A   ;return result into memory location 200
```

Note again that it is necessary to employ the B register to hold the contents of location 200 because it is not possible to add the contents of a memory location to the A register or to another memory location in the Z-80 by specifying the address in the instruction. (Alternatively, the HL register pair, and IX and IY registers could have been used to hold the memory address.)

7.4.3 Logic instructions

Logic operations, i.e. Boolean operations such as AND, OR and NOT, are always provided. The logical operation is performed on pairs of corresponding bits in the two operands to produce a result word. For example, the AND operation would logically AND together the most significant bits of the two operands to produce the most significant bit of the result. The next most significant bit would be generated from the logical AND operation on the next most significant bits of the two operands, and so on.

One original purpose of logical operations was to provide a mechanism to set up Boolean conditions and to test the conditions. The conditions are represented by single bits (flags) within the binary word. Different flags are assigned to represent different conditions. The Boolean OR operation can be used to set particular bits in a word by performing the logical OR operation of the data word with a mask pattern 00 ⋯ 010 ⋯ 00 where the 1 is in the position corresponding to the bit to be set, i.e. if this is in the fourth position corresponding to D_3, the operation is performed as shown in Table 7.2. Thus D_3 is set to a logical 1 but all the other bits are left unchanged. (To set the bit to a logical 0, leaving the other bits unchanged, the mask 11 ⋯ 10111 is used with a logical AND operation.)

Table 7.2   OR logical operation

Data word:	D_n	D_{n-1}	...	D_4	D_3	D_2	D_1	D_0
Mask pattern:	0	0	...	0	1	0	0	0
Result of OR operation:	D_n	D_{n-1}	...	D_4	1	D_2	D_1	D_0

An AND operation can be used subsequently to test whether the flag bit, D_3 in the above, is set or reset. Using the same masking pattern, 00 ⋯ 010 ⋯ 00, if the result of the AND operation is zero numerically, the bit must be reset (a logical 0), otherwise the bit must be set (a logical 1), as shown in Table 7.3. We now need to cause different sequences of program instructions to be executed depending upon whether a word is zero or not zero. This can be provided in the 'conditional jump' instruction (see later).

Table 7.3   AND logical operation

Data word:	D_n	D_{n-1}	...	D_4	D_3	D_2	D_1	D_0
Mask pattern:	0	0	...	0	1	0	0	0
Result of AND operation:								
if $D_3 = 0$	0	0	...	0	0	0	0	0
if $D_3 = 1$	0	0	...	0	1	0	0	0

The Z-80 is provided with the following logical operations:

	mnemonic
AND	AND
OR	OR
Exclusive OR	XOR
NOT	CPL (complement A register)

The form of instruction is as for arithmetic instructions. (Arithmetic and logical instructions are usually classified together in processor instruction sets.) Only the A register can be used for first operand/result and this is not specified. Table 7.4 shows the 8-bit arithmetic and logic instructions and the valid addressing modes for these instructions. General-purpose ALU operations are given in Table 7.5 (again for completeness).

Many microprocessors, including the Z-80, in addition to possessing logical operations are also provided with separate instructions for set, reset and test of Boolean flags within a binary word. The Z-80 'set bit' instruction, SET n, sets to a 1 bit n of any general purpose processor register (A, B, C, D, E, H, or L) or memory location specified by the contents of the HL register pair, (HL) or index register, (IX+d), and (IY+d), as shown in Table 7.6. Bits are numbered

Table 7.4   8-bit arithmetic and logic (Courtesy of Zilog, Inc.)

SOURCE

	REGISTER ADDRESSING							REG. INDIR.	INDEXED		IMMED.
	A	B	C	D	E	H	L	(HL)	(IX+d)	(IY+d)	n
'ADD'	87	80	81	82	83	84	85	86	DD 86 d	FD 86 d	C6 n
ADD w CARRY 'ADC'	8F	88	89	8A	8B	8C	8D	8E	DD 8E d	FD 8E d	CE n
SUBTRACT 'SUB'	97	90	91	92	93	94	95	96	DD 96 d	FD 96 d	D6 n
SUB w CARRY 'SBC'	9F	98	99	9A	9B	9C	9D	9E	DD 9E d	FD 9E d	DE n
'AND'	A7	A0	A1	A2	A3	A4	A5	A6	DD A6 d	FD A6 d	E6 n
'XOR'	AF	A8	A9	AA	AB	AC	AD	AE	DD AE d	FD AE d	EE n
'OR'	B7	B0	B1	B2	B3	B4	B5	B6	DD B6 d	FD B6 d	F6 n
COMPARE 'CP'	BF	B8	B9	BA	BB	BC	BD	BE	DD BE d	FD BE d	FE n
INCREMENT 'INC'	3C	04	0C	14	1C	24	2C	34	DD 34 d	FD 34 d	
DECREMENT 'DEC'	3D	05	0D	15	1D	25	2D	35	DD 35 d	FD 35 d	

Table 7.5   General-purpose AF operations (Courtesy of Zilog, Inc.)

Decimal Adjust Acc, 'DAA'	27
Complement Acc, 'CPL'	2F
Negate Acc, 'NEG' (2's complement)	ED 44
Complement Carry Flag, 'CCF'	3F
Set Carry Flag, 'SCF'	37

Table 7.6   Bit manipulation group (Courtesy of Zilog, Inc.)

	BIT	REGISTER ADDRESSING A	B	C	D	E	H	L	REG. INDR. (HL)	INDEXED (IX+d)	(IX+d)
TEST 'BIT'	0	CB 47	CB 40	CB 41	CB 42	CB 43	CB 44	CB 45	CB 46	DD CB d 46	FD CB d 46
	1	CB 4F	CB 48	CB 49	CB 4A	CB 4B	CB 4C	CB 4D	CB 4E	DD CB d 4E	FD CB d 4E
	2	CB 57	CB 50	CB 51	CB 52	CB 53	CB 54	CB 55	CB 56	DD CB d 56	FD CB d 56
	3	CB 5F	CB 58	CB 59	CB 5A	CB 5B	CB 5C	CB 5D	CB 5E	DD CB d 5E	FD CB d 5E
	4	CB 67	CB 60	CB 61	CB 62	CB 63	CB 64	CB 65	CB 66	DD CB d 66	FD CB d 66
	5	CB 6F	CB 68	CB 69	CB 6A	CB 6B	CB 6C	CB 6D	CB 6E	DD CB d 6E	FD CB d 6E
	6	CB 77	CB 70	CB 71	CB 72	CB 73	CB 74	CB 75	CB 76	DD CB d 76	FD CB d 76
	7	CB 77	CB 78	CB 79	CB 7A	CB 7B	CB 7C	CB 7D	CB 7E	DD CB d 7E	FD CB d 7E
RESET BIT 'RES'	0	CB 87	CB 80	CB 81	CB 82	CB 83	CB 84	CB 85	CB 86	DD CB d 86	FD CB d 86
	1	CB 8F	CB 88	CB 89	CB 8A	CB 8B	CB 8C	CB 8D	CB 8E	DD CB d 8E	FD CB d 8E

Table 7.6 *continued*

	BIT	REGISTER ADDRESSING A	B	C	D	E	H	L	REG. INDR. (HL)	INDEXED (IX+d)	(IX+d)
RESET BIT 'RES'	2	CB 97	CB 90	CB 91	CB 92	CB 93	CB 94	CB 95	CB 96	DD CB d 96	FD CB d 96
	3	CB 9F	CB 98	CB 99	CB 9A	CB 9B	CB 9C	CB 9D	CB 9E	DD CB d 9E	FD CB d 9E
	4	CB A7	CB A0	CB A1	CB A2	CB A3	CB A4	CB A5	CB A6	DD CB d A6	FD CB d A6
	5	CB AF	CB A8	CB A9	CB AA	CB AB	CB AC	CB AD	CB AE	DD CB d AE	FD CB d AE
	6	CB B7	CB B0	CB B1	CB B2	CB B3	CB B4	CB B5	CB B6	DD CB d B6	FD CB d B6
	7	CB BF	CB B8	CB B9	CB BA	CB BB	CB BC	CB BD	CB BE	DD CB d BE	FD CB d BE
SET BIT 'SET'	0	CB C7	CB C0	CB C1	CB C2	CB C3	CB C4	CB C5	CB C6	DD CB d C6	FD CB d C6
	1	CB CF	CB C8	CB C9	CB CA	CB CB	CB CC	CB CD	CB CE	DD CB d CE	FD CB d CE
	2	CB D7	CB D0	CB D1	CB D2	CB D3	CB D4	CB D5	CB D6	DD CB d D6	FD CB d D6
	3	CB DF	CB D8	CB D9	CB DA	CB DB	CB DC	CB DD	CB DE	DD CB d DE	FD CB d DE

Table 7.6 *continued*

	BIT	A	B	C	D	E	H	L	(HL)	(IX+d)	(IY+d)
				REGISTER ADDRESSING					REG. INDR.	INDEXED	
SET BIT 'SET'	4	CB E7	CB E0	CB E1	CB E2	CB E3	CB E4	CB E5	CB E6	DD CB d E6	FD CB d E6
	5	CB EF	CB E8	CB E9	CB EA	CB EB	CB EC	CB ED	CB EE	DD CB d EE	FD CB d EE
	6	CB F7	CB F0	CB F1	CB F2	CB F3	CB F4	CB F5	CB F6	DD CB d F6	FD CB d F6
	7	CB FF	CB F8	CB F9	CB FA	CB FB	CB FC	CB FD	CB FE	DD CB d FE	FD CB d FE

from 0 to 7. The reset instruction, RES *n*, sets the bit to a 0. The third bit instruction, BIT *n*, sets the *zero flag* to a 0 if the bit is 0 and sets the zero flag to a 1 if the bit is a 1. The zero flag is one bit of the F register and can be used subsequently to alter the program execution (see later).

7.4.4 Shift instructions

Sometimes we need to be able to move bits in a word left or right as shown in Fig. 7.10. Such operations can be achieved by shift left and shift right machine instructions which are always provided in the instruction set of a computer, including a microprocessor system. The shift right instruction known as a *logical right shift* causes all the bits in the addressed location to be moved one place right so that the contents of B_n moves into B_{n-1}, B_{n-1} into B_{n-2}, etc. The most significant bit is set to a 0 and the contents of the least significant bit is moved into the carry flag.

An alternative shift right instruction is one which keeps the most significant bit at its original value as well as shifting a copy into the next most significant bit. This would result in the number being divided by two, and thus this type of shift instruction is known as an *arithmetic shift instruction*.

A shift left instruction which is known as a *logical shift left* causes all the bits of the addressed location (processor register or a memory location) to be moved one place left so that the contents of bit B_0 is moved to B_1, B_1 to B_2, B_2 to B_3, etc. The most significant bit is moved into the carry flag. The least significant bit is set to a 0. This shift left operation causes the number to be multiplied by two

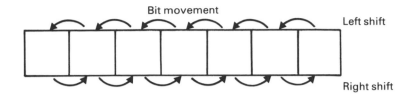

Figure 7.10   Shift operation

and consequently is also known as an *arithmetic left shift* instruction. The Z-80 provides an arithmetic shift left instruction but does not provide a separate logical shift left instruction as it would be the same as the arithmetic shift left instruction. (There can be a difference between a logical shift left instruction and an arithmetic shift left instruction in the manner that they affect the F register. For example, 68000 logic and arithmetic shift left instructions are different, see Chap. 8, section 8.3.6).

As an example of the use of the arithmetic shift instruction, consider the problem of multiplying a 4-bit number, n, by ten. This can be achieved very effectively by performing the following computation:

$$\text{Result} = (2 \times n) + (8 \times n) = 10n$$

The first product, $2n$, can be obtained by shifting n one place left arithmetically, and the second product $8n$ by shifting n three places left arithmetically. Hence if the number n is in memory location 200 and the result is to be placed in location 200, a Z-80 program could be:

```
LD   A,(200)  ;obtain number n
SLA  A        ;multiply n by 2
LD   B,A      ;generate second copy of 2n
SLA  B        ;multiply 2n by 2 to obtain 4n
SLA  B        ;multiply 4n by 2 to obtain 8n
ADD A,B       ;add 2n to 8n to obtain 10n
LD   (200),A  ;store result
```

where SLA is the mnemonic for the arithmetic shift left instruction. First the number n is obtained from memory and shifted one place left using the A register. The result of this shift process is copied into the B register and two more shift left operations are performed on the number in the B register. At this stage, $2n$ is stored in A and $8n$ is stored in B. The contents of A and B are then added together and the result returned to memory location 200.

Shift instructions can be circular, so that in a circular left shift, information shifted out of the most significant location or out of the carry register is placed in the least significant location. Similarly, a circular right shift would transfer the contents of the least significant bit or the carry register into the most significant bit. These types of shift instructions are known as *rotate* instructions.

The Z-80 shift and rotate operations are shown in Fig. 7.11. These may operate on any 8-bit register or memory location, as given in Table 7.7.

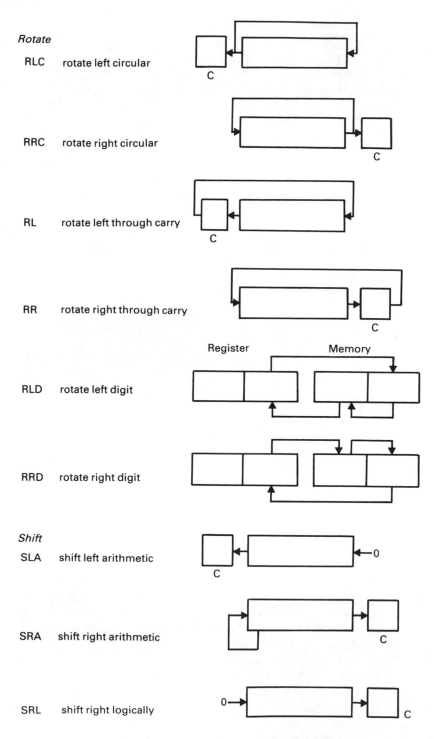

Figure 7.11   Z-80 rotate and shift operations

Table 7.7 Rotates and shifts (Courtesy of Zilog, Inc.)

Source and Destinction

TYPE OF ROTATE OR SHIFT		A	B	C	D	E	H	L	(HL)	(IX + d)	(IY + d)
	'RLC'	CB 07	CB 00	CB 01	CB 02	CB 03	CB 04	CB 05	CB 06	DD CB d 06	FD CB d 06
	'RRC'	CB 0F	CB 08	CB 09	CB 0A	CB 0B	CB 0C	CB 0D	CB 0E	DD CB d 0E	FD CB d 0E
	'RL'	CB 17	CB 10	CB 11	CB 12	CB 13	CB 14	CB 15	CB 16	DD CB d 16	FD CB d 16
	'RR'	CB 1F	CB 18	CB 19	CB 1A	CB 1B	CB 1C	CB 1D	CB 1E	DD CB d 1E	FD CB d 1E
	'SLA'	CB 27	CB 20	CB 21	CB 22	CB 23	CB 24	CB 25	CB 26	DD CB d 26	FD CB d 26
	'SRA'	CB 2F	CB 28	CB 29	CB 2A	CB 2B	CB 2C	CB 2D	CB 2E	DD CB d 2E	FD CB d 2E
	'SRL'	CB 3F	CB 38	CB 39	CB 3A	CB 3B	CB 3C	CB 3D	CB 3E	DD CB d 3E	FD CB d 3E
	'RLD'								ED 6F		
	'RRD'								ED 67		

	A
RLCA	07
RRCA	0F
RLA	17
RRA	1F

7.4.5 Jump instructions

Instructions are normally executed in consecutive order, i.e. instructions are executed in the order that they are placed in memory. To obtain any real computational power, we need to change the execution sequence, either always or sometimes dependent upon conditions set up within the program. Jump instructions are provided for this purpose and cause a change in the sequence of instructions executed after the jump instruction.

The *unconditional jump instruction* produces a change in the sequential execution by causing the next instruction to be taken from the memory location specified in the instruction. The format of the jump instruction differs from that of other machine instructions. The first field still specifies the operation, in this case 'JP', but the second field species the address of the next instruction to be executed, i.e.:

JUMP OPERATION	ADDRESS OF NEXT INSTRUCTION TO BE EXECUTED

There are four forms that the next address can be specified in the Z-80 JP instruction:

  (i)   The actual address
 (ii)   The address held in the HL register pair, i.e. (HL)
(iii) The address held in the IX index register, i.e. (IX)
(iv) The address held in the IY index register, i.e. (IY)

The *conditional jump instruction* only changes the normal sequential execution if a particular condition is satisfied. If the condition is not met, the next instruction executed is that following the jump instruction. There are various conditions, all based upon the contents of the condition code register. Both possible values can be used to select the jump.

The ALU condition code register (F register) containing the condition codes is notionally eight bits though bit 3 and bit 5 are not used. The other six bits as shown in Fig. 7.12 are as follows:

(a) Carry (C) bit 0

The carry flag is a combined carry/borrow flag. When an addition process has been performed, if a carry signal has been generated, the carry flag is set, otherwise the carry flag is reset. When a subtraction process has been performed, if a borrow is generated, the carry flag is set, otherwise the flag is reset. The generation of a carry/borrow signal does not necessarily indicate an error. For this, an overflow flag is provided.

(b) Overflow (P/V) bit 2

The overflow flag indicates that the result of an arithmetic operation has exceeded the allowable range. For 8-bit processors, the range is -128 to $+127$. If the result should be greater than 127 or less than -128, the overflow flag is set. For example, if the numbers 100 and 50 were added, the result would be:

Decimal	Binary	
100	01100100	
50	00110010	
0	10010110	$= -106$ in 2's complement representation

       ↑
   Carry

Bit 7	Bit 6	Bit 5	Bit 4	Bit 3	Bit 2	Bit 1	Bit 0
S Sign flag	Z Zero flag	Not used	H Half carry flag	Not used	P/V Parity/ overflow flag	N Subtract flag	C Carry flag

(V and N do not exist in the 8080)

Figure 7.12 Z-80 Flag register (Courtesy of Zilog, Inc.)

The result is incorrect (i.e. it is incomplete in its most significant bit) and the overflow flag will be set. Note that no carry has been generated in this particular case. It is also possible to generate a carry and produce a correct result (with no overflow signal generated).

The overflow flag is a combined overflow/parity flag. The flag is set during logic operations if the result has even parity (even number of 1's), and reset if the result has odd parity.

(c) Zero flag (Z) bit 6
This flag is set if the result of the operation is zero, otherwise the flag is reset.

(d) Sign flag (S) bit 7
This flag is set if the result of the operation is negative (most significant bit = 1), otherwise the flag is reset.

(e) Half carry or auxiliary carry (H) bit 4
This flag holds the carry from the fourth bit of the A register. The flag is a combined carry/borrow flag. It is used primarily in BCD arithmetic instruction DDA (decimal adjust) to produce a correct result after an addition or subtraction.

(f) Subtract flag (N) bit 1
This flag is also used by the DDA instruction. Neither of these last two flags can be used in conditional jump instructions, though it is possible to access them via the 16-bit load instruction.

There are eight conditional jump instructions in which the next instruction address is specified in the instruction, each of the form:

JP condition mnemonic, <address>

The conditions are:

Flag	*Mnemonic*	
Carry = 1	C	carry generated
Carry = 0	NC	carry not generated
Zero = 1	Z	result zero
Zero = 0	NZ	result not zero
Parity = 1	PE	parity even

Parity = 0   PO   parity odd
Sign = 0   P   positive
Sign = 1   M   negative

There is another form of jump instruction, JR, which uses relative addressing (see section 7.5.1).

It is important to note that the flags are not set or reset after every instruction but only after selected instructions, other instructions not affecting the flags. In particular, the LD instructions (except with the I or R registers) do not affect the flags. Generally, the 8-bit arithmetic instructions set or reset the flags appropriately. However the increment/decrement instructions do not affect the C flag. The logic instructions OR, AND and XOR (exclusive OR) set or reset the S and Z flags but always reset the C flag. The 16-bit arithmetic instructions, ADC and SBC set or reset the S, Z and C flags but the 16-bit ADD instruction only sets or resets the C flag. (N is also reset for ADD/ADC and set for SBC).

Since the conditional jump instructions use flags rather than the actual values of operands in the processor or memory, it is convenient to have arithmetic operations which affect the flags but do not overwrite either of their stored operands. One particular arithmetic instruction of this type provided is the *compare* instruction, which performs a subtract operation affecting the flags as appropriate, but without overwriting the destination register. The Z-80 has a compare instruction (CMP) which is the same as the subtract instruction, affecting the flags in the same way, except that the result is not placed in the A register, i.e. the original contents of the A register are not destroyed.

The following program given as an example of the use of jump instructions, adds together a series of six numbers in individual memory locations 200H to 205H inclusive, placing the result in the A register, by successively adding the numbers to the contents of the A register:

Location	Z-80 instruction		
0100	LD	L,00	;load memory start address into HL
0102	LD	H,02	
0104	LD	A,(HL)	;load memory contents into A register
0105	INC	L	;increment address to point to next memory ;location
0106	ADD	A,(HL)	;accumulate sum
0107	LD	C,A	;save sum in C register
0108	LD	A,L	
0109	CP	05	;set zero flag if last location added to sum
010B	LD	A,C	;return sum to A register
010C	JP	NZ,105	;repeat program is last location not reached

The program is loaded into memory starting at location 100. (Instructions are of variable length. The location addresses specified are the addresses of the first bytes of the instructions.) The successive addition process of the program is terminated when the lower significant byte of the memory address (L) has reached five.

7.4.6 Input/output

There clearly needs to be a mechanism of transferring data from the user to the program and memory, and from the program and memory to the user. The classical approach at the machine-language level is to provide special machine instructions which perform these transfers, and to insert these instructions into the program at the appropriate places. The instructions are known as *input/output instructions* and the technique is known as *programmed input/output*. Input/output instructions take the same instruction format as memory reference instructions except that the address of the location to be accessed is an input/output address rather than a memory address. Input and output devices are given identification input/output numbers in much the same manner as memory locations are given addresses. Input/output addresses are known as *port addresses* or *port numbers*. Since the number of input/output devices is usually quite small, the address may be such smaller than memory addresses. For example, an 8-bit port address would provide up to 256 independently addressed input/output devices. Consequently input/output instructions can be shorter than memory reference instructions.

The action of input/output instructions can be very similar to memory reference instructions. Some computers, including some microprocessors, notably Motorola microprocessors, use normal memory reference instructions to transfer data between processor registers and input/output devices. In this case, some of the memory addresses are allocated to input/output rather than to memory locations. The appropriate address decode circuitry has to be provided within the input/output interface. The method is known as *memory mapped input/output*, as the input/output devices are given memory addresses instead of input/output addresses (*I/O mapped*).

A particular advantage of memory mapped input/output is that all instructions available to reference memory are also available to reference input/output. Also additional instructions do not need to be included in the instruction repertoire for input/output. A particular disadvantage is that some of the memory address space is taken by the input/output devices and generally a block of memory address space much larger than that required for the input/output devices becomes unavailable for memory. Also any special nature of the input/output devices can be accommodated within input/output instructions. For example, input/output devices usually have a slower speed of operation than memory, and input/output instructions could automatically wait a little longer during the transfer to allow the device time to respond.

The Z-80 is provided with special input/output instructions. The general form of input instruction specifying the device address in the instruction is:

IN A,(<device address>)

which causes data to be transferred from the device specified to the A register. The general form of the output instruction specifying the device address in the instruction is:

OUT (<device address>),A

which causes the contents of the A register to be transferred to the device specified. In both cases, only the A register may be specified and the device address is 8 bits, providing up to 256 independently addressed devices. The contents of the A register is also transferred along the addresses lines A_8 to A_{15}, i.e. the contents of the A register is concatenated with the device address (A_0 to A_7) to form a 16-bit device address, but this feature is rarely used. There are other forms of input/output instructions available, the register indirect addressing form and the block transfer form which accesses a series of locations.

Often before an input/output instruction can be executed, it is necessary that an interface is ready, either to accept data or with valid data available. Some very simple interfaces may always be ready, but mostly interfaces have internal registers whose contents indicate their readiness. These registers are known as device/peripheral *status registers* and their contents are usually read under program control prior to an input or output data transfer. For example, a typical status register for a display terminal is shown in Fig. 7.13. This register is sited in the terminal interface within the computer system and indicates that data will be accepted by the interface if sent by the processor (bit 0 set to a 1), has been received at the keyboard and is ready to be read by the processor (bit 1 set to a 1), and various error conditions. The data received bit (bit 1) is automatically reset when the data is read by the processor under program control and only set again when new data is received (another key pressed) and the interface is ready. The three error conditions shown are related to the usual type of data transmission between the terminal and the interface, namely asynchronous serial transmission which is described in Chap. 10.

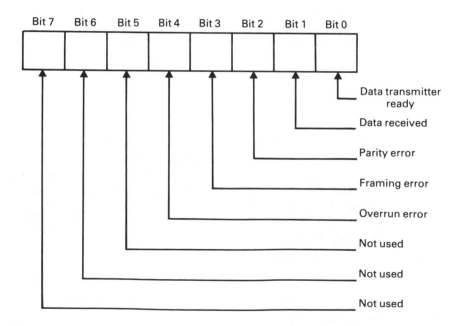

Figure 7.13   Terminal interface status register assignment

A typical programmed input sequence begins with a loop of instructions which tests whether the interface/device has data ready to be taken by the processor, as indicated by the data received bit in the status register being set to a 1. In the case of the keyboard of a terminal, the condition would be true if a key has been pressed after the last time the data was read and the subsequent new data is ready. A Z-80 instruction sequence could be:

```
L1: IN    A,(3)     ;read key status port
    BIT   1,A       ;check if ready bit set
    JP    Z,L1      ;if not repeat from L1
    IN    A,(2)     ;input character from data port
```

In this program, the status register of the interface (terminal interface, say) has been assigned the address 3 and the data register 2. The bit addressed instruction BIT 1,A sets the zero flag to a 1 when bit 1 of the status register is a 1 (i.e. when the interface has data ready). If bit 1 is a 0, the status word is read and test is repeated.

A typical programmed output sequence begins with a loop of instructions which tests whether the interface/device is ready to receive data as indicated by the data transmitter ready bit in the status register being set to a 1. Once this test becomes true, the loop is terminated and the program proceeds to the next instruction which is generally an instruction to output the required data. A Z-80 instruction sequence could be:

```
L2: IN    A,(3)     ;read display status port
    BIT   0,A       ;check if display is ready
    JP    Z,L2      ;if not, repeat from L2
    LD    A,B       ;obtain character from B
    OUT   (2),A     ;write character to display data port
                    ;continue
```

In this program, when bit 0 is a 1, the data held in the B register is transferred to the output interface, and subsequently to the output device.

The same port address is used for both data input and output in this example, though it refers to two different data registers within the interface, as shown in Fig. 7.14. The logical instruction AND 1 could be used in place of the bit addressed instruction BIT 0,A, and the logical instruction AND 2 could be used in place of the bit addressed instruction BIT 1,A.

We could join the two programs above to take data from a display terminal keyboard and to display the character on the screen. Transferring keyed data to the display is known as *echoplexing* and is used widely because the user can verify visually that the data keyed is correct. It is not done automatically in the *full-duplex mode* of terminals (see Chap. 10) and must be programmed if required. Joining the programs, we get:

```
L1: IN    A,(3)     ;read key status port
    BIT   1,A       ;check if ready bit set
    JP    Z,L1      ;if not, repeat from L1
    IN    A,(2)     ;input character from data port
```

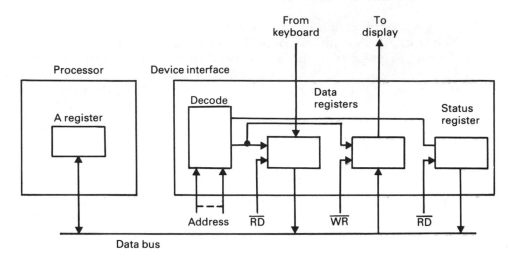

Figure 7.14   Terminal data and status registers

LD	B.A	;store character in B
L2: IN	A,(3)	;read display status port
BIT	0,A	;check if display is ready
JP	Z,L2	;if not, repeat from L2
LD	A,B	;retrieve character from B
OUT	(2),A	;write character to display data port
JP	L1	;repeat from start

The full range of input and output instructions are shown in Tables 7.8 and 7.9 respectively. The block input/output instructions enable a number of consecutive locations to be specified. In the block input/output instructions, HL is used to address the memory locations and B is used as a counter.

7.4.7 Subroutine instructions

Sometimes we wish to be able to jump to a 'subprogram' and return afterwards to the original program, and to repeat the process at different places in the main program jumping to the same subprogram. This would eliminate the need for multiple copies of the same subprogram and make the overall program better structured. It can be achieved with the *subroutine jump* and corresponding *subroutine return* instructions.

The overall scheme is shown in Fig. 7.15. The main program 'jumps' to the reusable subprogram in several places, each time returning to the main program immediately after the corresponding jump. The reused subprogram is known as a *subroutine*, and the machine instruction which causes the jump to the subroutine is called a subroutine jump or *call* instruction (the main program 'calls' the subroutine using the call instruction). To be able to return to the main program, we need to store the return address at the time of the subroutine jump. The return address is the address of the instruction in memory immediately

Table 7.8   Input Group (Courtesy of Zilog, Inc.)

			SOURCE PORT ADDRESS	
			IMMED.	REG. INDIR.
			(n)	(C)
INPUT 'IN'	R E G A D D R E S S I N G	A	DB n	ED 78
		B		ED 40
		C		ED 48
		D		ED 50
		E		ED 58
		H		ED 60
		L		ED 68
'INI' – input & Inc HL, Dec B	REG. INDIR	(HL)		ED A2
'INIR' – INP, Inc HL, Dec B, REPEAT IF B≠0				ED B2
'IND' – INPUT & Dec HL, Dec B				ED AA
'INDR' – INPUT, Dec HL, Dec B, REPEAT IF B≠0				ED BA

(Left margin label: INPUT DESTINATION; Right side bracket: BLOCK INPUT COMMANDS)

following the subroutine jump instruction. This address is stored automatically during the execution of the subroutine jump instruction. The return address needs to be used to jump back to the main program at the end of the subroutine (or whenever the return is made). A corresponding subroutine return jump instruction is provided for this purpose. Notice that the return address will depend upon the address of the location of subroutine call instruction and this will change with different calls.

Normally the return address is kept on a *stack*. A stack is a number of consecutive storage locations almost always in main memory. Information such as the return address can be placed in order in the stack and retrieved in reverse order, i.e. the first item put in the stack is the last out and the last in is the first out (first-in last-out, or FILO stack). A *stack pointer* holds the address of the top location of the stack as shown in Fig. 7.16. The Z-80 stack grows downwards, i.e. new information is added to locations with decreasing addresses.

The contents of the stack pointer are decremented by one as information is added to the stack and incremented by one as information is taken off the stack. The stack mechanism, in particular, allows subroutines calling subroutines (*nested subroutines*) to be arranged effectively. Nested subroutines are shown in

Table 7.9   Output group (Courtesy of Zilog, Inc.)

			SOURCE							REG. IND.
			REGISTER							
			A	B	C	D	E	H	L	(HL)
'OUT'	IMMED.	(n)	D3 n							
	REG. IND.	(C)	ED 79	ED 41	ED 49	ED 51	ED 59	ED 61	ED 69	
'OUTI' – OUTPUT Inc HL, Dec b	REG. IND.	(C)								ED A3
'OTIR' – OUTPUT, Inc HL, Dec B, REPEAT IF B≠0	REG. IND.	(C)								ED B3
'OUTD' – OUTPUT Dec HL & B	REG. IND.	(C)								ED AB
'OUTDR' – OUTPUT, Dec HL & B, REPEAT IF B≠0	REG. IND.	(C)								ED BB

BLOCK OUTPUT COMMANDS (OUTI, OTIR, OUTD, OUTDR)

PORT DESTINATION ADDRESS (OUT, immediate and reg. ind. columns)

Fig. 7.17. In the Z-80, the subroutine instruction has the mnemonic CALL, and has a similar format to a normal jump instruction, though only the actual jump address can be specified within the instruction. The CALL instruction can be conditional and all the jump conditions are available. The return instruction has the mnemonic RET. RET can be unconditional or, rather unusually though of some use in programming various places to leave the subroutine, it can be conditional with the same possible jump instruction conditions.

Two types of instruction are available for the user to form stacks or to use the stack required by the CALL and RET mechanism, namely the PUSH and POP instructions. The PUSH instruction causes the contents of a register pair to be copied on to the free space at the top of the stack and two is subtracted from the contents of the stack point, while the POP instruction copies the top two locations of the stack into a register pair and two is added to the contents of the stack pointer.

It is important to remember to load the stack pointer with the appropriate address before any subroutines are called. A suitable address must be sufficiently distant from the program to prevent the stack overwriting the program.

The full range of jump, call and return instructions are given in Table 7.10. The return from interrupt instructions are concerned with interrupt mechanisms which are considered in Chap. 10.

7.5   FURTHER ADDRESSING MODES

So far we can identify four methods of obtaining the operands for the instruction, namely:

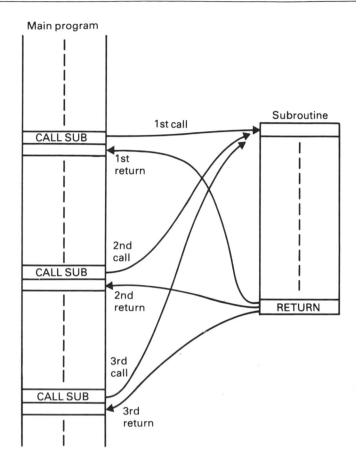

Figure 7.15   Subroutine cells

(i) By specifying the operand directly in the instruction
(ii) By specifying the memory location holding the operand
(iii) By specifying a processor register holding the operand
(iv) By specifying a register pair which holds the address of the operand.

There are other methods of obtaining the operand. The actual address used to access the operand is known as the *effective address.*

7.5.1 Relative addressing

It is sometimes convenient to specify the address of the operand in the instruction as a number of locations from some known location, the address of which is held in a processor register. This mode of addressing is known as *relative addressing.* There are two basic forms, differentiated by the register used to hold the reference location, namely:

(i) Program counter relative addressing
(ii) Base register relative addressing

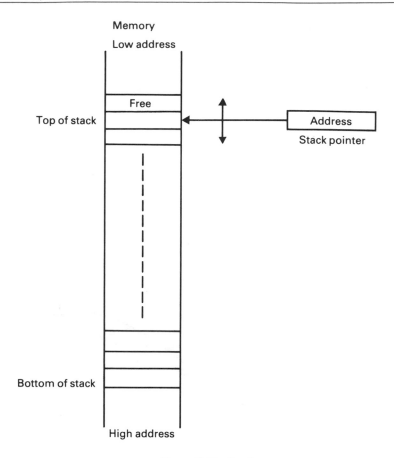

Figure 7.16　Stack

In each case, the operand field provides a displacement, d, which is added to the contents of the register. In program counter relative addressing, the displacement provided by the instruction is added to the contents of the program counter to form the actual (effective) address of the operand. Figure 7.18 shows program counter relative addressing. Program counter relative addressing is particularly suitable (and usually only available) for jump instructions because the jump address is likely to be close to the address of the jump instruction (for example in program loops). The displacement can be fairly small and the instruction shorter than otherwise.

Generally, the effective address is d locations from the address of the current instruction, where d may be positive or negative and is given in the operand field of the instruction. The program counter holds the address of the current instruction when it is being fetched. Hence the address of the operand is given by the value held in the program counter plus the displacement d. With normal sequential instruction execution, the program counter is incremented by one each time an instruction has been fetched from memory. Often this incrementing process is done immediately after the instruction has been fetched

Table 7.10　Jump, call and return group (Courtesy of Zilog, Inc.)

CONDITION

			UN-COND.	CARRY	NON CARRY	ZERO	NON ZERO	PARITY EVEN	PARITY ODD	SIGN NEG	SIGN POS	REG B≠0
JUMP 'JP'	IMMED. EXT.	nn	C3 n n	DA n n	D2 n n	CA n n	C2 n n	EA n n	E2 n n	FA n n	F2 n n	
JUMP 'JR'	RELATIVE	PC+e	18 e−2	38 e−2	30 e−2	28 e−2	20 e−2					
JUMP 'JP'		(HL)	E9									
JUMP 'JP'	REG. INDR.	(IX)	DD E9									
JUMP 'JP'		(IY)	FD E9									
'CALL'	IMMED. EXT.	nn	CD n n	DC n n	D4 n n	CC n n	C4 n n	EC n n	E4 n n	FC n n	F4 n n	
DECREMENT B, JUMP IF NON ZERO 'DJNZ'	RELATIVE	PC+e										10 e−2
RETURN 'RET'	REGISTER INDIR.	(SP)(SP+1)	C9	D8	D0	C8	C0	E8	E0	F8	F0	
RETURN FROM INT 'RETI'	REG INDIR.	(SP)(SP+1)	ED 4D									
RETURN FROM NON MASKABLE INT 'RETN'	REG. INDIR.	(SP)(SP+1)	ED 45									

NOTE – CERTAIN FLAGS HAVE MORE THAN ONE PURPOSE.

from memory and before the execution of the instruction. In this case, the number used to form the effective address during the execution of the instruction is one more than the current instruction address and the address of the location accessed is $d+1$ locations from the current instruction. The situation may be even more complicated in the case of multi-byte instructions in byte-orientated systems (e.g. a Z-80 system). In these cases, the program counter is incremented after each byte access, and may be incremented by two before the address calculation is done. However, this may not need to concern the user when using an assembler, as either the actual displacement from the current instruction would be specified in the assembly-language statement, or a label would be used to identify the operand location.

The Z-80 has program counter relative addressing provided only for jump instructions (as in normal). A special jump mnemonic is used to indicate relative addressing, JR. Only the unconditional jump instruction and conditional jump on the carry flag or the zero flag instructions are available in the relative form. (Another relative jump instruction is available, DJNZ, 'decrement B and jump if not zero'.) The number stored in the instruction is two less than the actual displacement, leading to a displacement range of -126 to $+129$.

Main program

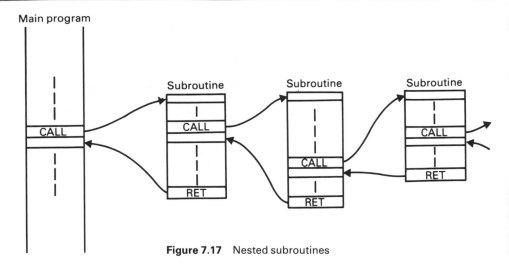

Figure 7.17   Nested subroutines

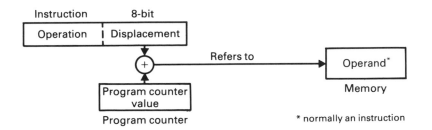

Figure 7.18   Program counter relative addressing

Base register relative addressing employs a general-purpose or dedicated central processor register to hold the address to be added to the displacement contained in the instruction. The base register is preloaded as required. All instructions using base register addressing subsequently would access operands loaded in memory locations relative to the address held in the base register. Consequently, a program can be written using addresses relative to, say, the beginning of the program, and the program can be loaded anywhere in memory without any need for the addresses specified in the instruction to be altered. The only requirement is that the base register is loaded with the appropriate starting address. Base register addressing, except in the form of index register addressing below, is not available in the Z-80.

7.5.2 Index register addressing

In *index register addressing*, the contents of the index register are added to a number held in the instruction, as shown in Fig. 7.19. Index register addressing

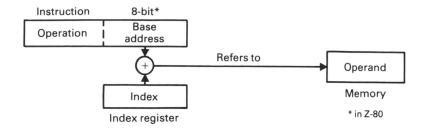

Figure 7.19 Index register addressing

is provided particularly to access consecutive memory locations. For this application, the address of the first memory location could be provided by the number in the instruction and the index register could hold the number of locations from the first location to the required location. Hence any particular item in the list of locations could be accessed by modifying the contents of the index register using the same index register addressed instruction. To access the locations in order, the index register addressed instruction could be within a loop and the index register incremented after each pass through the loop.

The Z-80 index addressing can be applied using the index registers, IX and IY (and IX', IY'). However, the number held in the instruction is only 8 bits, whereas the number held in the index registers can be 16 bits. Hence the addressing is not true index register addressing; rather, it is a form of base register addressing.

7.5.3 Implied addressing

There are some operations in which the addresses of the operands are fixed and defined by the operation. In these cases, no operand field is necessary. This is known as *implied addressing*. There are several examples of implied addressing in the Z-80, such as NOP (no operation) and HALT (stop all program execution).

7.6 FURTHER INSTRUCTIONS

The remaining Z-80 instructions not already given in tabular form can be found in Tables 7.11 to Table 7.17 inclusive. The instructions include 16-bit load and arithmetic instructions, exchange, block transfer and search, restart and CPU control. The restart instructions are single-byte call instructions with particular call addresses, 0, 8, 10, 18, 20, 28, 30, and 38 (hexadecimal). These instructions are intended for interrupt servicing (Chap. 10), in which the first instructions of the interrupt service routines are placed in the specified locations.

Table 7.11 16-bit load group 'LD' 'push' and 'pop' (Courtesy of Zilog, Inc.)

SOURCE

DESTINATION / REGISTER / PUSH INSTRUCTIONS

		AF	BC	DE	HL	SP	IX	IV	nn (IMM. EXT.)	(nn) (EXT. ADDR.)	(SP) (REG. INDIR.)
REGISTER	AF										F1
	BC								01 n n	ED 4B n n	C1
	DE								11 n n	ED 5B n n	D1
	HL								21 n n	2A n n	E1
	SP				F9		DD F9	FD F9	31 n n	ED 7B n n	
	IX								DD 21 n n	DD 2A n n	D E1
	IY								FD 21 n n	FD 2A n n	FD E1
EXT. ADDR.	(nn)		ED 43 n n	ED 53 n n	22 n n	ED 73 n n	DD 22 n n	FD 22 n n			
REG. IND.	(SP)	F5	C5	D5	E5		DD E5	FD E5			

POP INSTRUCTIONS

NOTE: The Push & Pop Instructions adjust the SP after every execution

Table 7.12　16-bit arithmetic (Courtesy of Zilog, Inc.)

<table>
<tr><td colspan="3"></td><td colspan="6" align="center">SOURCE</td></tr>
<tr><td colspan="3"></td><td>BC</td><td>DE</td><td>HL</td><td>SP</td><td>IX</td><td>IY</td></tr>
<tr><td rowspan="3">'ADD'</td><td colspan="2">HL</td><td>09</td><td>19</td><td>29</td><td>39</td><td></td><td></td></tr>
<tr><td colspan="2">IX</td><td>DD 09</td><td>DD 19</td><td></td><td>DD 39</td><td>DD 29</td><td></td></tr>
<tr><td colspan="2">IY</td><td>FD 09</td><td>FD 19</td><td></td><td>FD 39</td><td></td><td>FD 29</td></tr>
<tr><td colspan="2">ADD WITH CARRY AND SET FLAGS　'ADC'</td><td>HL</td><td>ED 4A</td><td>ED 5A</td><td>ED 6A</td><td>ED 7A</td><td></td><td></td></tr>
<tr><td colspan="2">SUB WITH CARRY AND SET FLAGS　'SBC'</td><td>HL</td><td>ED 42</td><td>ED 52</td><td>ED 62</td><td>ED 72</td><td></td><td></td></tr>
<tr><td colspan="3" align="center">INCREMENT 'INC'</td><td>03</td><td>13</td><td>23</td><td>33</td><td>DD 23</td><td>FD 23</td></tr>
<tr><td colspan="3" align="center">DECREMENT 'DEC'</td><td>0B</td><td>1B</td><td>2B</td><td>3B</td><td>DD 2B</td><td>FD 2B</td></tr>
</table>

DESTINATION (row label at left for the ADD/ADC/SBC/INC/DEC rows)

Table 7.13　Exchanges 'EX' and 'EXX' (Courtesy of Zilog, Inc.)

<table>
<tr><td colspan="3"></td><td colspan="5" align="center">IMPLIED ADDRESSING</td></tr>
<tr><td colspan="3"></td><td>AF'</td><td>BC', DE' & HL'</td><td>HL</td><td>IX</td><td>IY</td></tr>
<tr><td rowspan="3">IMPLIED</td><td colspan="2">AF</td><td>08</td><td></td><td></td><td></td><td></td></tr>
<tr><td colspan="2">BC, DE & HL</td><td></td><td>D9</td><td></td><td></td><td></td></tr>
<tr><td colspan="2">DE</td><td></td><td></td><td>EB</td><td></td><td></td></tr>
<tr><td>REG. INDIR.</td><td colspan="2">(SP)</td><td></td><td></td><td>E3</td><td>DD E3</td><td>FD E3</td></tr>
</table>

Table 7.14　Block transfer group (Courtesy of Zilog, Inc.)

<table>
<tr><td colspan="3"></td><td>SOURCE</td></tr>
<tr><td colspan="3"></td><td>REG. INDIR.</td></tr>
<tr><td colspan="3"></td><td>(HL)</td></tr>
<tr><td rowspan="4">DESTINATION</td><td rowspan="4">REG. INDIR.</td><td rowspan="4">(DE)</td><td>ED A0</td><td>'LDI' – Load (DE) ← (HL)
Inc HL & DE, Dec BC</td></tr>
<tr><td>ED B0</td><td>'LDIR' – Load (DE) ← (HL)
Inc HL & DE, Dec BC, Repeat until BC = 0</td></tr>
<tr><td>ED A8</td><td>'LDD' – Load (DE) ← (HL)
Dec HL & DE, Dec BC</td></tr>
<tr><td>ED B8</td><td>'LDDR' – Load (DE) ← (HL)
Dec HL & DE, Dec BC, Repeat until BC = 0</td></tr>
</table>

Reg HL　points to source
Reg DE　points to destination
Reg BC　is byte counter

Table 7.15   Block search group (Courtesy of Zilog, Inc.)

SEARCH
LOCATION

REG. INDIR. (HL)	
ED A1	'CPI' Inc HI, Dec BC
ED B1	'CPIR', Inc HL, Dec BC repeat until BC = 0 or find match
ED A9	'CPD' Dec HL & BC
ED B9	'CPDR' Dec HL & BC Repeat until BC = 0 or find match

HL points to location in memory
   to be compared with accumulator
   contents
BC is byte counter

Table 7.16   Restart group (Courtesy of Zilog, Inc.)

	OP CODE	
0000_H	C7	'RST 0'
0008_H	CF	'RST 8'
0010_H	D7	'RST 16'
0018_H	DF	'RST 24'
0020_H	E7	'RST 32'
0028_H	EF	'RST 40'
0030_H	F7	'RST 48'
0038_H	FF	'RST 56'

Table 7.17   Miscellaneous CPU control (Courtesy of Zilog, Inc.)

'NOP'	00	
'HALT'	76	
DISABLE INT '(DI)'	F3	
ENABLE INT '(EI)'	FB	
SET INT MODE 0 'IM0'	ED 46	8080A MODE
SET INT MODE 1 'IM1'	ED 56	CALL TO LOCATION 0038_H
SET INT MODE 2 'IM2'	ED 5E	INDIRECT CALL USING REGISTER 1 AND 8 BITS FROM INTERRUPTING DEVICE AS A POINTER

REFERENCE

1. *Z80-CPU Z80A-CPU Technical Manual.* Cupertino, California: Zilog, Inc., 1978.

PROBLEMS

7.1   Deduce what each of the following Z-80 programs achieves.

(a)
```
        Instruction
        LD    B,05
  L1:   ADD   A,(100)
        DEC   B
        JP    NZ,L1
```

(b)
```
        LD    HL, 400
        LD    A, 100
  L1:   LD    (HL), A
        INC   HL
        DEC   A
        CP    50
        JP    NZ,L1
```

(c)
```
        LD    A,00
  L1:   OUT   (18),A
        INC   A
        JR    L1
```

(d)
```
        LD    A,(400)
        SLA   A
        SLA   A
        LD    B,A
        SLA   B
        ADD   A,B
        LD    (400),A
```

7.2   Write a Z-80 program to append an even parity bit to a 7-bit number stored in memory location 100.

7.3   An 8-bit number is stored in each of the memory locations 100, 101, 102, 103 and 104. Write a Z-80 program to determine the largest number.

7.4   Write a Z-80 program to add together two 64-bit numbers. Each number is divided into four bytes. The bytes of one number are stored in the 8-bit memory locations 400, 401, 402 and 403, with the most significant byte first. The bytes of the other number are stored in memory locations 404, 405, 406 and 407, with the most significant byte first. The result is to be placed in memory locations 500, 501, 502 and 503.

7.5   Write a Z-80 program which will display the letters of the alphabet (A to Z) on a display terminal. The output data port address is 2. Data is interpreted as in the

ASCII code (see Table 1.4 in Chap. 1). The status register address is 3. Bit 1 of the status register is set to a 1 when data can be sent to the terminal.

7.6 Modify the program in Problem 7.5, to include the digits 0 to 9 before the letters.

7.7 Write a Z-80 program to input ASCII characters from a keyboard of a terminal, and convert any lower case characters to upper case representation (e.g. convert the code for 'a' to the code for 'A'), and display the character. The terminal data register has address 6 and status register has address 5. Bit 5 of the status register is set to a 0 when a character has been received at the keyboard, otherwise it is a 1. Bit 6 is set to a 1 when data can be sent to the display, otherwise it is a 0.

7.8 Explain the result of each instruction in the following program and hence determine the result of execution of the complete program.

```
        LD    B,05
        LD    HL,400
L1:  LD    (HL),00
        INC   HL
        DEC   B
        JP    NZ, L1
```

Determine the effect of substituting the instruction INC B for the instruction DEC B in the program. What is the effect of substituting the instruction SRL B for the instruction DEC B? All these instructions can effect the zero flag.

7.9 Show that the following program is equivalent to the last program given in section 7.4.6:

```
L1:  IN    A,(3)
        CPL
        AND   3
        JP    NZ,L1
        IN    A,(2)
        OUT   (2),A
        JP    L1
```

8

68000 Microprocessor

8.1 GENERAL

In this chapter, we will review the Motorola 68000 microprocessor as an example of a 16-bit microprocessor [1,2]. Sixteen bit microprocessors have, in general, 16-bit ALUs, 16-bit internal registers, 16-bit internal data paths and addresses up to 32 bits. These microprocessors are often register types of processors employing a register file containing many 16-bit registers, usually sixteen to thirty-two. The constraints of earlier microprocessors such as invalid source/destination locations with some instructions have in many cases been removed, leading to *orthogonal* instruction sets which allow all reasonable source and destination operands with all instructions. (Restrictions are introduced in the 68000. For example a register designated only for data operands cannot be used to hold memory addresses in indirect addressing. Such restrictions are part of the design philosophy.) Some 16-bit microprocessors have been designed with a view to 32-bit microprocessor developments. A 32-bit microprocessor can be simply an extension of a 16-bit microprocessor using 32-bit ALUs, 32-bit registers and 32-bit internal data paths.

The 68000 microprocessor is a register type of processor. The processor registers are shown in Fig. 8.1. There are eight 32-bit internal registers for data operands and seven 32-bit registers used to form memory addresses. The separation of a general register file into data registers and address registers is a particular design feature of the 68000 which is not found in other microprocessors. Other register types of microprocessors incorporate a single register file which can be used for both data operands and to form addresses (e.g. the Zilog Z-8000). Though the internal registers are 32-bits, this particular processor is designated a 16-bit microprocessor because ALU operations are performed in units of 16 bits. The data bus is 16-bit. Subsequent members of the 68000 (e.g. 68020) are true 32-bit microprocessors. The program counter has 32 bits though only 24 are used in the 16-bit 68000 (23-bit memory word address and one bit to identify the byte when necessary). There are two stack pointers, the *user stack pointer* and the *supervisor stack pointer*. Both stack pointers are given the identification A7. Only one can be used at a time depending upon whether the system is in a *user mode* or the *supervisor mode*.

The 68000 has five condition code flags found in the *user byte* of the *status register* shown in Fig. 8.2, namely:

C   Carry flag   (bit 0)

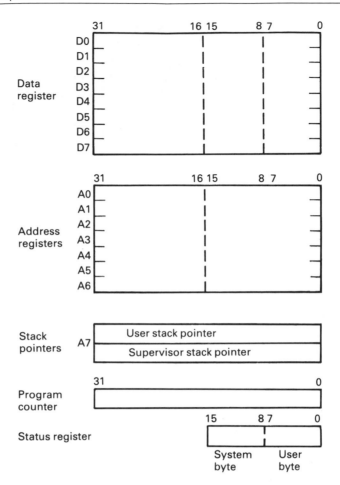

Figure 8.1 68000 processor registers (Courtesy of Motorola, Inc.)

V   Overflow flag   (bit 1)
Z   Zero flag   (bit 2)
N   Negative flag   (bit 3)
X   Extend flag   (bit 4)

These flags are set or reset, as usual, after the appropriate operations. The carry flag is set (to a 1) after an addition if a carry is generated from the most significant bit of the result. It is also set if a borrow is generated after a subtraction. The overflow flag is set if the result of the operation cannot be represented with the given number of digits, 8, 16 or 32 depending upon the instruction. It would indicate that the result is invalid. The negative flag is set if the result is negative, i.e. the most significant bit of the result is a 1. The *extend flag*, when affected, is affected in the same way as the carry flag and is included for multi-word arithmetic schemes in particular. The extend flag is not found in other microprocessors.

The system byte contains three bits (bits 8, 9 and 10) to enable interrupts (see Chap. 10), one bit (bit 13) to indicate the supervisor mode, and one bit (bit 15) to indicate the *trace mode*, a mode to aid program testing. The status register can be accessed by various instructions, though only the user byte (condition codes) can be changed by the user (i.e. in the user mode).

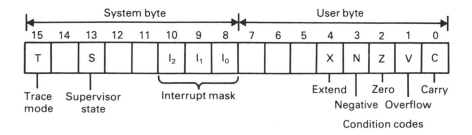

Figure 8.2   68000 processor status register (Courtesy of Motorola, Inc.)

8.2 SYSTEM CONFIGURATION

8.2.1 Memory organization

In an 8-bit microprocessor system, each location in memory has 8 bits and is identified by a unique address sent along the address bus. During instruction fetch and data transfer cycles, the processor generates one address word to access a memory location. There could be a similar arrangement for a 16-bit system using 16-bit memory locations and a unique address for each location. However, we need the ability to access individual bytes of each 16-bit memory location for 8-bit data, and parts of instructions if instructions can be multiples of 8 bits. Generally, an address is generated by the processor to identify the 16-bit word and additional signals are used to identify the byte in cases that an individual byte is to be accessed. The complete address of a memory location can be considered as a byte address. An even address could be the most significant byte and the odd address could be the least significant byte as in the Motorola 68000, or vice versa as in the 16-bit Intel 8086. Depending upon the system, the instructions can be 16 bits or multiples of 16 bits (e.g. 68000) or 8 bits and multiples of 8 bits (e.g. 8086). The 68000 imposes the restriction that instructions and multi-byte data cannot start at an odd byte address. The Intel 8086 does not impose this restriction and allows instructions and data to start at odd or even addresses.

8.2.2 Bus

The microprocessor, memory and input/output interfaces are connected as normally with a data/address/control bus. There are 16 data lines and 23 address lines addressing 2^{23} 16-bit words (16,777,216 bytes or 16 megabytes). Individual bytes of a word can be accessed using control signals. Twenty control signals are provided.

Memory and input/output are not differentiated and some memory addresses are used for input/output (i.e. the system is *memory mapped*). The information transfer in the 68000 uses the asynchronous method with one acknowledge signal for data transfers. Each data transfer is initiated by a request signal from the processor, and the transfer is terminated by an acknowledge signal from the device receiving the request, generally the memory or input/output device. Data can be transferred along the full 16-bit data bus or along either the lower 8 bits or the upper 8 bits.

The fundamental control signals for data transfer are:

$\overline{\text{AS}}$ Address strobe
$\overline{\text{UDS}}$ Upper data strobe
$\overline{\text{LDS}}$ Lower data strobe
$\text{R}/\overline{\text{W}}$ Read/write (= 1 for read, 0 for write)
$\overline{\text{DTACK}}$ Data acknowledge

Signals as shown are active low. The term used by Motorola to indicate that an activating signal level has occurred is *asserted*, i.e. one of the above signals is asserted when it is at a logical 0. The timing of the transfer is achieved with the three strobe signals. The address strobe is generated when the address lines carry a valid address and after all transients have decayed. The two data strobes in different combinations specify a byte transfer or a 16-bit word transfer. For no data transfer, both data strobes are high. For a byte transfer on the lower data lines, D0 to D7, the lower data strobe is at a 0 while for a byte transfer on the upper data lines, D8 to D15, the upper data strobe is at a 0. For a full 16-bit data transfer on the 16 data lines, both data strobes are low.

The signal timing for a read transfer (instruction fetch or data read transfer) is shown in Fig. 8.3. Each clock low or high period is designated an S state (S0, S1, S2, etc.). During a read transfer, the read/write signal is kept high (1). The appropriate word address is generated and a little time later, the address and data strobe signals are asserted. The other devices on the bus receive these signals and the one with the same address as that emitted responds by placing the contents of the specified location onto the data lines after some internal delay. At the same time, the addressed device must also generate a data transfer acknowledge signal, $\overline{\text{DTACK}}$, which is received by the processor. Once the processor has accepted the data, all processor output strobes are de-asserted. This action is recognized by the addressed device which then removes the data and de-asserts the acknowledge signal which terminates the read cycle. It may be that the memory or input/output interface cannot respond as soon as shown. If an acknowledge is not received by the start of state 5, extra wait states are introduced between state 4 and state 5 until the acknowledge signal is generated.

The signals for a write transfer are shown in Fig. 8.4. In the write cycle, the read/write signal is brought low (0). The address and address strobe signals are

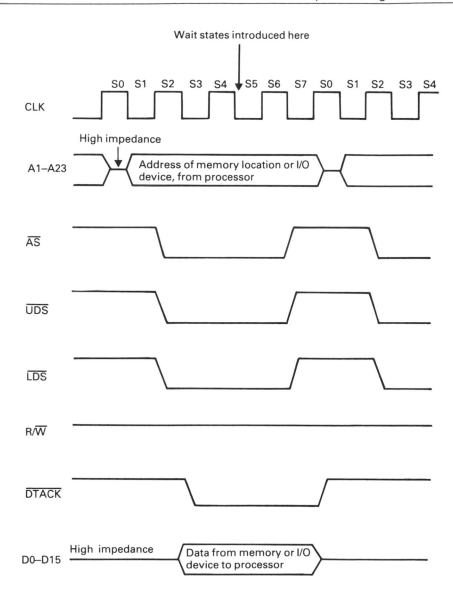

Figure 8.3   68000 read transfer signals (Courtesy of Motorola, Inc.)

asserted as before, but now the processor generates the data, and the data strobe signals a little time after to allow the data signals to settle. When the addressed device has accepted the data, it generates an acknowledge signal which causes the processor to release the data bus and de-assert the address and data strobes. As before, this causes the addressed device to de-assert its acknowledge signal, so terminating the write cycle.

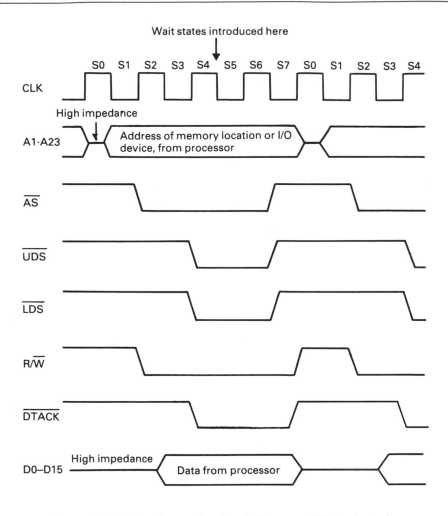

Figure 8.4 68000 write transfer signals (Courtesy of Motorola, Inc.)

8.3 INSTRUCTIONS

8.3.1 General

Many instructions can operate on bytes (8 bits), words (16 bits) or long words (32 bits). In these instructions, the operation mnemonic is commonly followed by:

.B   for a byte operation
.W   for a word operation
.L   for a long word operation

The default condition in the Motorola assembler is a word operation. A byte operation on a 16-bit location, if memory, uses the upper 8 bits and if a register, uses the lower 8 bits. A long word operation on memory contents uses two consecutive 16-bit locations. Bit data can be addressed in certain instructions and also binary coded decimal (BCD) instructions are provided.

The instruction can consist of between one and five words. The first word is designated the operation word specifying the operation and the data type. The operation word can also include literals and register designations. The encoding of the operation uses different numbers of bits within the word depending upon the operation. The first level of encoding is contained in the most significant four bits which selects one of fourteen different types of operations (two codes are not assigned). Additional bits are then used to identify the operation. Subsequent instruction words contain 8-bit, 16-bit or 32-bit literals (always the second or second and third words), or one or two 16-bit or 32-bit addresses or combinations. The general form of an instruction in assembly language is:

Operation <source operand>, <destination operation>

which can be preceded with a label field and followed by a comment field. The operation, if requiring two operands, takes both the source and destination operands and places the result in the destination. Note that the order of operands is the reverse of Z-80 instructions. The angle brackets < and > are not included in the instruction, but used here to indicate items in operand fields.

8.3.2 Addressing

(a) Modes

There are twelve addressing modes which can be applied. Not all addressing can be applied to all instructions. Table 8.1 shows the addressing modes and the encoding which is within the first word of the instruction. The first two modes are register direct (data and address register) addressing. The

Table 8.1 68000 effective address encoding (Courtesy of Motorola, Inc.)

Addressing mode	Mode	Register	Addressing Data	Memory	Control	Alterable
Data register direct	000	register number	X			X
Address register direct	001	register number				X
Address register indirect	010	register number	X	X	X	X
Address register indirect with postincrement	011	register number	X	X		X
Address register indirect with predecrement	100	register number	X	X		X
Address register indirect with displacement	101	register number	X	X	X	X
Address register indirect with index	110	register number	X	X	X	X
Absolute short	111	000	X	X	X	X
Absolute long	111	001	X	X	X	X
Program counter with displacement	111	010	X	X	X	
Program counter with index	111	011	X	X	X	
Immediate	111	100	X	X		

next five modes are address register indirect addressing. Note that data register indirect addressing is not provided as data registers should not hold addresses. The next two modes are absolute memory addressing (only word and long word). The next two are program counter relative addressing and the last one is immediate addressing. The addressing modes have been classified into four groups:

(i)   Data addressing – refers to a data operand
(ii) Memory addressing – refers to an operand held in memory
(iii) Alterable addressing – refers to an operand whose value can be changed
(iv) Control addressing – refers to a memory operand without an operand size

The *data addressing* group includes all addressing modes except address register direct, i.e. using an address register to hold the operand. The *memory addressing* group includes all addressing modes except register direct, i.e. using a register (either data register or address register) to hold the operand. The *alterable addressing* group includes all addressing modes except program counter relative and immediate addressing. The *control* group includes all addressing modes except register direct (data or address register) and address register indirect with postincrement/predecrement (see later).

Table 8.2 lists the instructions of the 68000 and the allowable addressing modes for each instruction. We will consider the instructions individually in the subsequent sections.

Table 8.2   68000 instructions and valid addressing modes

Allowed effective address modes

Immediate (source only)
Program counter with index
Program counter with displacement
Absolute long
Absolute short
Address register indirect with index
Address register indirect with displacement
Address register indirect with predecrement
Address register indirect with postincrement
Address register indirect
Address register direct
Data register direct

	Imm	PC idx	PC disp	Abs long	Abs short	Ar ind idx	Ar ind disp	Ar ind pre	Ar ind post	Ar ind	Ar dir	Dr dir	Size
ADDRESSING GROUPS													
Data	X		X	X	X	X	X	X	X	X		X	
Memory	X		X	X	X	X	X	X	X	X			
Control	X			X	X	X	X	X	X	X			
Alterable			X	X	X	X	X	X	X	X	X	X	
INSTRUCTIONS													
Data transfer													
MOVE Move	X	s	X	X	X	X	X	X	X	X	s	s	s	B/W/L
MOVEA Move to address register	s	s	s	s	s	s	s	s	s	s	s	s	W/L
MOVEM Move multiple registers			X	s	d	X	X	X	s	s			W/L
MOVEP Move peripheral data							X						W/L
MOVEQ Move quick		d											L

Table 8.2 68000 instructions and valid addressing modes

Allowed effective address modes

The effective-address-mode columns (left to right) correspond to the following modes:

1. Data register direct
2. Address register direct
3. Address register indirect
4. Address register indirect with postincrement
5. Address register indirect with predecrement
6. Address register indirect with displacement
7. Address register indirect with index
8. Absolute short
9. Absolute long
10. Program counter with displacement
11. Program counter with index
12. Immediate (source only)

Mnemonic	Description	1	2	3	4	5	6	7	8	9	10	11	12	Size
EXG	Exchange registers	X	X											L
SWAP	Swap register halves	X												W
LEA	Load effective address		d	s			s	s	s	s	s	s		L
PEA	Push effective address			s			s	s	s	s	s	s		L
LINK	Link stack		X											Unsized
UNLK	Unlink stack		X											Unsized
Arithmetic														
ADD	Add binary (with data register)	s	s	X	X	X	X	X	X	X	s	s	s	B/W/L
ADDA	Add to address register	s	X	s	s	s	s	s	s	s	s	s	s	W/L
ADDI	Add immediate	d		d	d	d	d	d	d	d			s	B/W/L
ADDQ	Add quick	d	d	d	d	d	d	d	d	d			s	B/W/L
SUB	Subtract binary (with data reg.)	s	s	X	X	X	X	X	X	X	s	s	s	B/W/L
SUBA	Subtract from address register	s	X	s	s	s	s	s	s	s	s	s	s	W/L
SUBI	Subtract immediate	d		d	d	d	d	d	d	d			s	B/W/L
SUBQ	Subtract quick	d	d	d	d	d	d	d	d	d			s	B/W/L
CLR	Clear operand (set to zero)	d		d	d	d	d	d	d	d				B/W/L
NEG	Negate	d		d	d	d	d	d	d	d				B/W/L
EXT	Sign extend	d												W/L
MULS	Signed multiply	X		s	s	s	s	s	s	s	s	s	s	W
MULU	Unsigned multiply	X		s	s	s	s	s	s	s	s	s	s	W
DIVS	Signed divide	X		s	s	s	s	s	s	s	s	s	s	W
DIVU	Unsigned divide	X		s	s	s	s	s	s	s	s	s	s	W
ADDX	Add with extend	X				X								B/W/L
SUBX	Subtract with extend	X				X								B/W/L
NEGX	Negate with extend	d		d	d	d	d	d	d	d				B/W/L
ABCD	Add decimal with extend	X				X								B
SBCD	Subtract decimal with extend	X				X								B
NBCD	Negate decimal with extend	d		d	d	d	d	d	d	d				B
CMP	Compare (with data register)	X	s	s	s	s	s	s	s	s	s	s	s	B/W/L
CMPA	Compare address	s	X	s	s	s	s	s	s	s	s	s	s	W/L
CMPI	Compare immediate	d		d	d	d	d	d	d	d			s	B/W/L
CMPM	Compare memory				X									B/W/L
TAS	Test and set	d		d	d	d	d	d	d	d				B
TST	Test operand	d		d	d	d	d	d	d	d				B/W/L
Logical														
AND	AND (with a data register)	s		X	X	X	X	X	X	X	s	s	s	B/W/L
ANDI	AND immediate	d		d	d	d	d	d	d	d			s	B/W/L
OR	Inclusive OR (with data register)	s		X	X	X	X	X	X	X	s	s	s	B/W/L

Note: For ADDX, SUBX, ABCD, and SBCD the two X marks indicate data register direct **or** address register indirect with predecrement (shown as "X or X").

Table 8.2   68000 instructions and valid addressing modes

Allowed effective address modes

Effective address mode legend (columns, listed top to bottom, each connected by a line to a column of the table below):

- Immediate (source only)
- Program counter with index
- Program counter with displacement
- Absolute long
- Absolute short
- Address register indirect with index
- Address register indirect with displacement
- Address register indirect with predecrement
- Address register indirect with postincrement
- Address register indirect
- Address register direct
- Data register direct

Mnemonic	Operation	Dn	An	(An)	(An)+	-(An)	d(An)	d(An,Xi)	(xxx).W	(xxx).L	d(PC)	d(PC,Xi)	#imm	Size
ORI	Inclusive OR immediate	d		d	d	d	d	d	d	d			s	B/W/L
EOR	Exclusive OR (with data register)	d		d	d	d	d	d	d	d				B/W/L
EORI	Exclusive OR immediate	d		d	d	d	d	d	d	d			s	B/W/L
NOT	Logical complement	d		d	d	d	d	d	d	d				B/W/L
Bit manipulation operations														
BTST	Bit test	d		d	d	d	d	d	d	d	d	d		B/L
BSET	Bit test and set	d		d	d	d	d	d	d	d				B/L
BCLR	Bit test and clear	d		d	d	d	d	d	d	d				B/L
BCHG	Bit test and change	d		d	d	d	d	d	d	d				B/L
Shift and rotate														
ASL	Arithmetic shift left	d		d	d	d	d	d	d	d				B/W/L
ASR	Arithmetic shift right	d		d	d	d	d	d	d	d				B/W/L
LSL	Logical shift left	d		d	d	d	d	d	d	d				B/W/L
LSR	Logical shift right	d		d	d	d	d	d	d	d				B/W/L
ROL	Rotate left (without extend)	d		d	d	d	d	d	d	d				B/W/L
ROR	Rotate right (without extend)	d		d	d	d	d	d	d	d				B/W/L
ROXL	Rotate with extend left	d		d	d	d	d	d	d	d				B/W/L
ROXR	Rotate with extend right	d		d	d	d	d	d	d	d				B/W/L
Jump and Branch														
JMP	Jump unconditional			d			d	d	d	d	d	d		Unsized
BRA	Branch always (unconditional)										d			B/W
B$_{cc}$	Branch conditional										d			B/W
DB$_{cc}$	Test condition, decr. and branch										d			W
S$_{cc}$	Set byte conditionally	d		d	d	d	d	d	d	d				
JSR	Jump to subroutine			d			d	d	d	d	d	d		Unsized
BSR	Branch to subroutine										d			B/W
RTR	Return and restore condition codes													Unsized
RTS	Return from subroutine													Unsized
Control														
RESET	Reset external devices*													Unsized
RTE	Return from exception*													Unsized
STOP	Stop program execution*													Unsized
NOP	No operation													Unsized
TRAP	Trap													Unsized
TRAPV	Trap on overflow													Unsized
CHK	Check D register against bounds	s		s	s	s	s	s	s	s	s	s	s	W
MOVE USP	Move user stack pointer*		X											L
MOVE to SR	Load new status register*	s		s	s	s	s	s	s	s	s	s	s	W
MOVE from SR	Store status register	d		d	d	d	d	d	d	d				W

Table 8.2 68000 instructions and valid addressing modes

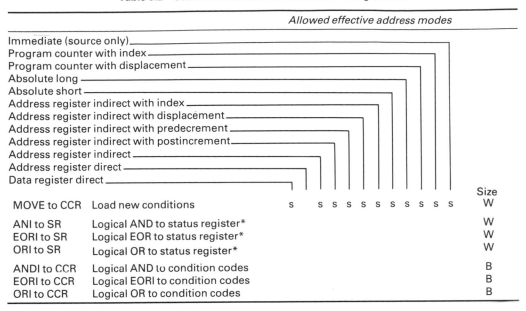

Allowed effective address modes

Immediate (source only)

Program counter with index

Program counter with displacement

Absolute long

Absolute short

Address register indirect with index

Address register indirect with displacement

Address register indirect with predecrement

Address register indirect with postincrement

Address register indirect

Address register direct

Data register direct

														Size
MOVE to CCR	Load new conditions	s		s	s	s	s	s	s	s	s	s	s	W
ANI to SR	Logical AND to status register*													W
EORI to SR	Logical EOR to status register*													W
ORI to SR	Logical OR to status register*													W
ANDI to CCR	Logical AND to condition codes													B
EORI to CCR	Logical EORI to condition codes													B
ORI to CCR	Logical OR to condition codes													B

Notes:

X = either source or destination or both (unless additional restruction, e.g. 'with data register' instructions must use a data register as either source or destination)

s = source

d = destination

cc = condition see Table 8.3

* = privileged, can only be executed in the supervisor mode.

B = Byte (8-Bit)

W = Word (16-bit)

L = Long (32-bit)

(b) Immediate addressing

The 68000 has the usual form of immediate addressing which allows a register or memory location to be loaded with a number specified within the instruction. The symbol # is commonly used to indicate immediate addressing. Hexadecimal numbers would be shown by prefixing the numbers with a $ symbol. The literal may be a byte (.B), a word (.W) or a long word (.L). An 8-bit literal (byte) is stored in the lower 8 bits of the word immediately following the operation word. A 16-bit literal occupies the full word following the operation word, while a 32-bit literal (long word) occupies two words immediately following the operation word. There are three *quick* forms of immediate addressed instructions, *quick add* (ADDQ), *quick subtract* (SUBQ), and *quick move* (MOVEQ), in which a literal is contained within the first 16-bit word of the instruction. Figure 8.5 shows the 68000 instruction format for immediate addressing except quick instructions. The mode and register fields specify the addressing mode of the destination. In the MOVEQ quick instructions, the destination must be a data register. In other immediate instructions, the destination may be found by one of several addressing modes.

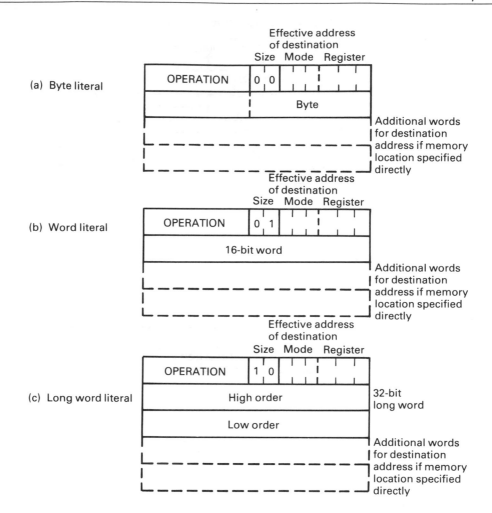

Figure 8.5   68000 immediate addressing (except quick instructions)

(c) Absolute addressing

The 68000 has two forms of absolute addressing, one using a *short* absolute address and one a *long* absolute address. The short address has a maximum of sixteen bits and the long address has a maximum of thirty-two bits. The short address can be encoded into an instruction with one less word. The address is sign extended to thirty-two bits which results in the address range being from 0 to 07FFF (hexadecimal) and from FF8000 to FFFFFF, i.e. the bottom 32 K bytes and the top 32 K bytes. A special symbol is not used to indicate absolute addressing; the address is given alone.

(d) Register direct addressing

The 68000 has separate address register direct addressing and data register direct addressing. Following this distinction, separate instructions are provided to operate on data operands (in memory or data registers) and addresses held in address registers. Some instructions can operate on either data registers or address registers (e.g. quick instructions). It is intended that data registers are used to hold data operands and address registers are used to hold addresses of memory locations.

(e) Indirect addressing

The 68000 uses only its address registers for register indirect addressing (Fig. 8.6). Parentheses surrounding the register name are used to indicate address register indirect addressing. There are four other forms of register indirect addressing which are mentioned in section 8.4.

8.3.3 Move instructions

The general instruction to copy the contents of one location into another location is called a *move* (MOVE) instruction. Either or both locations in the MOVE instruction can be memory locations or processor registers. For example, the instruction:

MOVE.L D2,D1

will copy the 32-bit contents of register D2 into register D1. MOVE is the assembler mnemonic representing the operation and the letter L indicates a *long word* (32-bit) operation. The MOVE instruction will operate on all three basic types of operands, byte (.B), word (.W) and long word (.L). The source may be

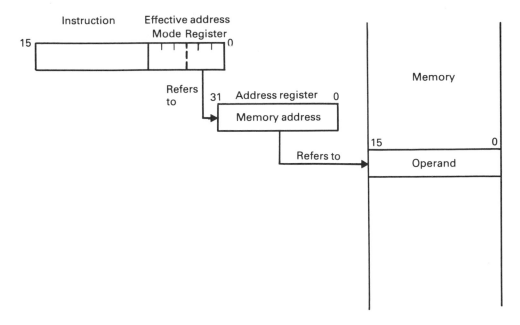

Figure 8.6   68000 register indirect addressing

specified by any addressing mode (except address register direct with byte operands which is not generally allowed), while the destination addressing must be both data and alterable, i.e. *data alterable* addressing. Therefore address registers cannot be loaded with this instruction. The MOVE instruction can be used with a literal.

The MOVE instruction sets the condition code flags appropriately. The N (negative) flag is set if the operand is negative. The Z (zero) flag is set if the operand is zero. V (overflow), C(carry) and the X (extend) flags are reset. Note that this is different from the Z-80 in which the equivalent LD does not affect the condition code flags.

There are several variations of the MOVE instruction. The quick move instruction (MOVEQ) enables a literal in the range -128 to 127 to be loaded into a data register with one 16-bit instruction. (The 8-bit literal is sign-extended to 32 bits before being placed in the destination register.) Other MOVE and associated transfer instructions generally operate upon addresses or the status register and are considered in section 8.5. The contents of two registers (data or address) can be exchanged using the EXG instruction, and the SWAP instruction exchanges the two 16-bit halves of a data register.

A 68000 program to exchange the contents of two memory locations 200 and 201 could be:

```
MOVE.B 200,D1
MOVE.B 201,200
MOVE.B D1,201
```

First, the contents of memory location 200 is copied into data register D1. Then in one instruction the contents of memory location 201 is copied into memory location 200. Finally, the original contents of 200 now in D1 is copied into memory location 201. Since the memory locations both hold 8-bit words, all the operations are specified as byte transfers. Two adjacent memory locations are used in word transfers. The upper 24 bits of D1 are not affected by word transfers.

8.3.4 Arithmetic instructions

The 68000 has instructions to perform the arithmetic operations of add, subtract, multiply and divide on data operands. One operand is always held in a data register. The other may be the actual number (immediate addressing), held in a processor register (register direct addressing) or a memory location (absolute addressing or address register indirect). The result replaces the contents of the register or memory location.

The binary ADD instruction can be used to add the contents of a memory location to a data register, for example:

```
ADD.L 2000,D1
```

which adds the contents of the 32-bit number held in memory locations 2000 to 2003 (2000 the least significant word) to the contents of data register D1.

Generally, ADD operates on a source operand and a destination operand, one of which must be a data register, placing the result of the addition in the destination location, i.e.:

ADD <source effective address>, <destination data register>
ADD <source data register>, <destination effective address>

Any of the three data types, byte, word or long word, can be used. All addressing modes are allowed for the source (except address register direct addressing with byte operands). For the destination, only memory addressing which is also alterable addressing, i.e. memory alterable addressing, can be used. Program counter relative and register direct addressing are precluded for addressing the destination. ADD using a literal is given a special instruction, ADDI. Subtract (SUB) has a similar form to ADD and the same variations as addition. As with the MOVE instruction, separate arithmetic instructions are provided for address register addition and subtraction.

The following adds the contents of memory location 200 to the contents of memory location 201, using D1:

MOVE.B   200,D1
ADD.B   D1,201

The corresponding 8-bit addition program given in Z-80 program in Chap. 7, section 7.4.2 requires five instructions.

Adding one or subtracting one is often required for counting purposes and special increment and decrement instructions are provided in most microprocessors. The 68000 accommodates this requirement, not by increment and decrement instructions, but by a short form of addition and subtraction called *quick add/subtract*. In these instructions (ADDQ and SUBQ), the number to be added or subtracted is given by three bits within the instruction. The range of numbers is between 1 and 8 decimal, where 8 is represented by 000. Figure 8.7 shows the quick instruction formats.

Multiplication and division were not provided in early microprocessors nor second-generation microprocessors such as the 8-bit Z-80 microprocessor, but are provided in 16-bit microprocessors. For multiplication, the result can be twice as long as the two numbers multiplied (assuming the numbers are of equal length). Sometimes only register direct addressing is provided with the multiplier and multiplicand held in 16-bit single-length registers and the product result held in a 32-bit double-length register. In the 68000, a memory location can be specified for one 16-bit operand but the other 16-bit operand must be in a data register occupying the lower 16 bits. The upper 16 bits of the data register are unused. The 32-bit result is placed in the data register.

Both multiplication and division can assume signed or unsigned numbers. A signed number employs the 2's complement representation for negative numbers, while unsigned numbers are regarded as positive binary numbers. Signed and unsigned number representation lead to two types of multiplication, signed multiplication and unsigned multiplication, and two types of division, signed and unsigned division. The 68000 has both forms of multiplication and division. For example:

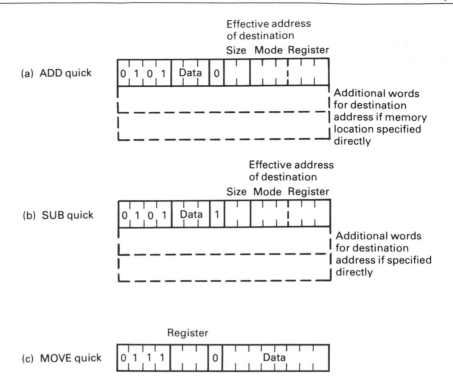

Figure 8.7   68000 quick instructions

MULS.W D1,D2

multiplies the lower 16 bits of data register D1 and the lower 16 bits of data register D2 forming a 32-bit product in D2, using signed arithmetic. '.W' indicates a 16-bit word operation and could be omitted as this operation only operates on 16-bit words. The unsigned multiplication mnemonic is MULU.

Division will generally operate on one single-length number (the dividend) and one double-length number (the divisor) to produce two results, one single- or double-length quotient and a single-length remainder. The 68000 produces only a single-length (16-bit) quotient. If the quotient is larger, the overflow flag is set to indicate an error. The signed and unsigned division instructions have the mnenonics DIVS and DIVU respectively.

A set of arithmetic instructions are provided which include the extend flag in the operation. The *add extended* instruction, ADDX, adds a source operand to a destination operand together with the extend bit, i.e. if the extend bit is set to 1, an extra 1 is added. The *subtract extended*, SUBX, subtracts a source operand from a destination operand and subtracts the value held in the extend flag, i.e. if the extend flag is set to 1, an extra 1 is subtracted. These instructions operate on the contents of two data registers or on the contents of two memory locations (but not on the contents of one data register and one memory location).

The extended flag, being the one-bit extension to any arithmetic (data operand) result, can be used particularly for multiple-word arithmetic. For example, to produce a 64-bit addition routine, first the lower 32 bits can be added together. Then the higher 32 bits can be added together with the extend flag as the carry from the first addition. Suppose that each 64-bit number is held in a pair of data registers, D1, D0 and D3, D2 respectively, and the result is to be placed in D3, D2. The 64-bit addition routine could be:

```
ADD.L    D0,D2
ADDX.L   D1,D3
```

The extend flag also finds application in BCD arithmetic, and BCD addition and subtraction instructions are provided.

8.3.5 Logic instructions

The logic operations of AND, EOR (exclusive OR), OR and NOT are provided in the 68000, for example:

```
AND.W 3000,D1
```

performs the logical AND operation using the 16-bit contents of memory locations 3000 and 3001 with the lower 16 bits of data register D1, placing the result in the lower 16 bits of D1. The upper 16 bits of D1 are not affected. The general form of logical operations is similar to that of arithmetic operations. One operand must be in a data register. In addition, only data addressing modes are allowed for the source and alterable memory addressing for the destination.

The 68000 has a number of bit test instructions. The bit is identified by a bit number either as a literal or in a data register. Test a bit, BTST, simply sets the zero (Z) flag appropriately. For example, in the instruction:

```
BTST #d, 5000
```

the # symbol indicates immediate addressing, d the bit number and 5000 the memory location containing the bit to be tested. The instruction sets the zero flag to a 1 if bit number d in the memory location is a 1 and sets the flag to a 0 if the bit is a 0. Either a data register or a memory location can be specified. If a memory location is specified, it is one byte (not a 16-bit word or two consecutive locations) and any bit of the byte can be tested. The number d is taken as a modulo 8 number, i.e. 8 is divided into the number as many times as possible and the remainder used. If a data register is specified, any of the 32 bits can be tested and the number is taken as a modulo 32 number. The bit number can also be specified by a number contained in a data register. This would allow the bit number to be altered during the execution of the program.

Other instructions operating on bits are *test a bit and set* (BSET) which in addition to the above also sets the selected bit if originally a 0; *test a bit and clear* (BCLR) which resets the bit to a 0; and *test a bit and change* (BCHG) which changes the bit from a 0 to a 1 or from a 1 to a 0 after the test.

The *test and set an operand* (TAS) is a special composite instruction which firstly examines the value held in a byte location, and sets the condition code flags N and Z appropriately. (Flags V and C are cleared and X is not affected)

Then the most significant bit (bit 7) of the location is unconditionally set to a 1. The instruction is intended for multiprocessor systems in which independent processors can set bits as flags without being stopped by other processors (see Chap. 15).

8.3.6 Shift and rotate instructions

The 68000 has a full range of shift and rotate instructions as shown in Fig. 8.8. In each case, if the operand is held in a register, multiple shift operations can be specified in one of two ways: as a literal in the instruction in the range 1 to 8, or as given by the contents of a register (range 0 to 63). All three data types, byte, word and long word are supported. As mentioned, there are two extension flags in the 68000, the traditional carry flag and an additional extend flag which generally holds the same value as the carry flag. Conceptually, the rotate instructions use the extend register in the loop rather than the carry register used in most other microprocessors. The shift instructions affect both the carry and the extend flags in the same way. The arithmetic shift (left or right) instruction sets or resets all of the condition codes appropriately, while the logical shift (left or right) instruction sets or resets all the codes except the overflow flag which is always reset to 0. Thus the arithmetic shift left and the logical shift left instructions are different.

The arithmetic shift left one place multiplies the operand by two, while the arithmetic shift right one place divides the operand by two, as mentioned in Chap. 7, 7.4.4. Suppose we wish to multiply an operand, n, held in D1, by 10 using the algorithm given in Chap. 7, namely to add together $2n$ and $8n$, each of which have been generated by shift operations. The program might be:

```
ASL.L      #1,D1
MOVE.L     D1,D2
ASL.L      #2,D2
ADD.L      D2,D1
```

We might wish to check that the result has not overflowed, by examining the value held in the V condition code flag.

The 68000, as mentioned, has multiply instructions and a program using a multiply instruction for the above $\times 10$ multiplication could be:

```
MOVEQ      #10,D2
MULU       D2,D1
```

if the number multiplied is a 16-bit operand. (The MULU instruction assumes 16-bit operands.) The MULU instruction always clears the V flag, irrespective of the result, as overflow would be impossible with 16-bit operands and a 32-bit destination.

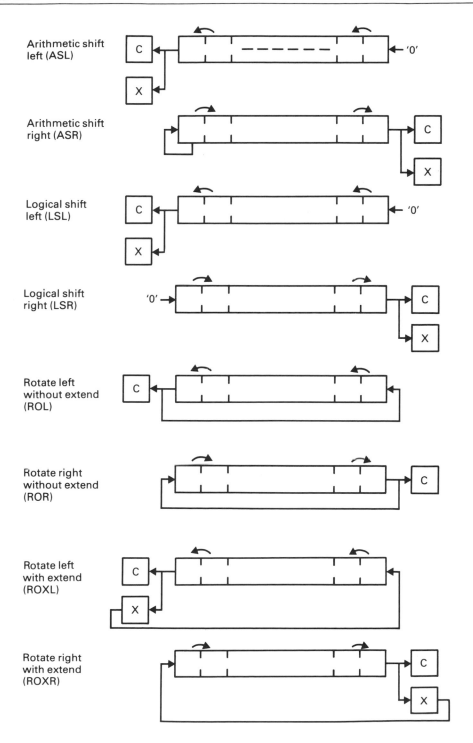

Figure 8.8   68000 shift and rotate instructions

8.3.7 Jump instructions

There are two forms of unconditional jump instruction in the 68000, the jump (JMP) instruction and the branch (BRA) instruction. In the jump instruction, the address of the new instruction must be an even byte address in memory, and a 24-bit address needs to be created (with the least significant bit zero). Only control addressing is allowed in the jump instruction. Therefore register direct addressing and address register indirect with increment/ decrement are not allowed, but address register indirect with displacement is allowed.

In the branch instruction, the address of the new instruction is given as a number of locations from the branch instruction, i.e. specified by *program counter with displacement* (program counter relative) addressing, as shown in Fig. 8.9. The displacement is interpreted as a 2's complement number which is added to the contents of the program counter plus two.

The conditional jump instruction only has the branch form and is similar, but only changes the normal sequential execution if a particular condition is satisfied as given in the instruction. If the condition is not met, the next instruction to be executed is that following the jump instruction. There are various conditions, all based upon the contents of the condition code register. Both true and false conditions can be used to select the jump. There are fourteen conditions as given in Table 8.3.

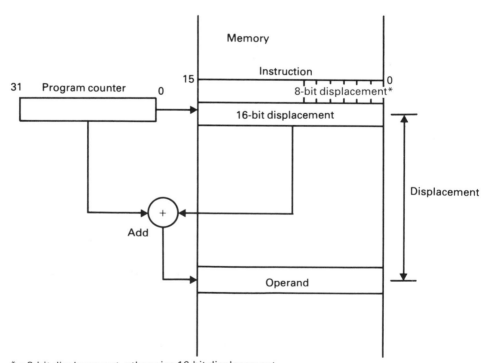

*.s 8-bit displacement, otherwise 16-bit displacement

Figure 8.9 68000 program counter with displacement addressing

The compare instruction is provided mainly for use with branch instructions, to perform the subtract operation without creating a result but affecting the flags. There are four forms of compare instructions. The first (CMP) subtracts the contents of the addressed location (memory or processor register) from the contents of a data register without affecting either. The second (CMPA) is similar except that it operates on an address register. The third (CMPI) uses a literal within the instruction to subtract from an addressed location (not an address register but indirect addressing allowed). The fourth (CMPM) subtracts the contents of one memory location from another using address register indirect addressing and afterwards increments the contents of the address register (postincrement addressing). This particular instruction allows sequences of locations to be accessed.

8.3.8 Subroutine instructions

The 68000 has two types of subroutine jump or call instructions, a *jump to subroutine* (JSR) which allows a full address to be used, and a relatively address *branch to subroutine* (BSR) instruction. These have the same forms as the unconditional jump and branch instructions, but in addition push the address of the instruction immediately following the call instruction onto the system stack, i.e. the top of the stack is loaded with the return address. This is achieved by decrementing the contents of the stack pointer and then loading the location addressed by the pointer with the return address.

There are two forms of return instruction which can be used with either call instructions, *return from subroutine* (RTS) and *return from subroutine and restore condition codes* (RTR). The return instructions do not have any operand/ address specification. The return from subroutine instruction transfers the contents of the top of the stack as specified by the stack pointer to the program

Table 8.3 68000 conditions in branch instructions (Courtesy of Motorola, Inc.)

Condition	Mnemonic	Logical test
Branch if greater than	BGT	$N \cdot V \cdot \overline{Z} + \overline{N} \cdot \overline{V} \cdot \overline{Z}$
Branch if greater or equal	BGE	$N \cdot V + \overline{N} \cdot \overline{V}$
Branch if less than	BLT	$N \cdot \overline{V} + \overline{N} \cdot V$
Branch if less or equal	BLE	$Z + N \cdot \overline{V} + \overline{N} \cdot V$
Branch if overflow	BVS	V
Branch if no overflow	BVC	$\overline{V}$
Branch if carry clear	BCC	$\overline{C}$
Branch if carry set	BVS	C
Branch if equal	BEQ	Z
Branch if equal not	BNE	$\overline{Z}$
Considering numbers as unsigned binary numbers		
Branch if high	BHI	$\overline{C} \cdot \overline{Z}$
Branch if low or same	BLS	$C + Z$
Branch if minus	BMI	N
Branch if plus	BPL	$\overline{N}$

counter and the stack pointer is then incremented by one. None of the flags are affected. Often the condition code register is saved on the top of the stack when a subroutine is first entered. The return and restore condition code instruction transfers the information at the top of the stack (assumed to be the stored condition codes) into the condition code register before transferring the next location on the stack into the program counter.

8.3.9 Input/output

The 68000 uses memory mapped input/output generally. One special input/output instruction is provided, the *move peripheral data* (MOVEP). This instruction copies the contents of a data register in units of 8 bits to a peripheral device which uses the lower 8 data lines, or the upper 8 data lines (one or the other for each device). Devices are given either even memory addresses or odd memory addresses accordingly and two or four bytes can be transferred to or from the data register during the execution of the instruction.

8.4 FURTHER ADDRESSING MODES

In this section we shall briefly review further addressing modes of the 68000.

8.4.1 Address register indirect with postincrement or predecrement

Index register addressing found in the Z-80 and other microprocessors is provided principally to access lists of locations in memory. In the Z-80, after a location has been accessed via the index register, the index register needs to be incremented to access the next item in the list. Two sequential operations can be identified:

(i)   Using the contents of a register to access a memory location
(ii) Incrementing the register contents after the memory location has been accessed, in preparation for accessing the next memory location.

These two operations are provided for address registers in one 68000 addressing mode called *address register indirect with postincrement*. Hence any address registers can be used as index registers very efficiently. A further mode is provided for accessing locations in the reverse order by decrementing the contents of the register before using the contents to access the location. This addressing mode is known as *address register indirect with predecrement*. The increment or decrement is by one, two or four, depending upon whether the access is to a byte, word or long word. These instructions are especially useful for stack operations. There are no special stack instructions such as PUSH and POP found in other microprocessor instruction sets.

A stack can be formed, for example, growing from a high memory address to a low memory address, with the stack pointer pointing to the last item placed on the stack (top of the stack), by using address register with predecrement to push data on to the stack. Address register with postincrement would be used to pull (pop) data off this stack. Stacks can also be formed growing towards high memory addresses, and queues can be formed. (A queue in memory is a list of locations, in which new items are placed at one end of the queue and items are taken off the other end. Two pointers are necessary to maintain a queue, one pointing to one end of the queue and the other pointing to the other end.)

The (Motorola) assembler notation for address register indirect with postincrement is (<address register>)+. The notation for address register indirect with predecrement is −(<address register>). For example, data in D1 can be pulled from a downward growing stack with the instruction:

MOVE (A1)+,D1

where the top address of the stack is held in A1. Data can be pushed back on to the stack with:

MOVE D1, −(A1)

8.4.2 Address register indirect with displacement

The form of base register addressing in which the contents of a register are added to a displacement within the instruction to form the effective address is provided in the 68000 as the *address register indirect with displacement*. The displacement within the instruction is a 16-bit integer. This is a true form of base register addressing and allows items in a table, for example, to be accessed. The base register would hold the address of the first item in the table and the displacement would give the number of locations from the first item to the required item.

The assembler notation for address register indirect with displacement is <displacement> (<address register>). For example, the fourth location in a list could be loaded into D2 with the instruction:

MOVE 3(A2),D2

where A2 hold the address of the first location in the list.

8.4.3 Address register indirect with index

In the *address register indirect with index*, the contents of the specified address register are added to a 8-bit literal within the instruction (displacement) together with the contents of another register (which may be a data register or address register) to form the effective address, as shown in Fig. 8.10. The second register is called an *index register* in this addressing mode. This addressing mode would allow, for example, a list of items in a table to be accessed in sequence. The address register could hold the address of the beginning of the table and the index register could hold the number of locations from the first item to the required item. To access items sequentially, the index register could be postincremented after each access.

The assembler notation for address register indirect with index is

displacement (<address register>,<index register>)

For example, 10 locations in a list starting from the second location could be added together and the result placed in D1 with:

```
       MOVEQ   #0,A3          ;initialize A3 to zero
       MOVEQ   #0,D1          ;initialize D1 to zero
L1:    ADD     1(A2,A3),D1    ;add item on list to D1
       CMPI    #9,(A3)+       ;check whether 10th item reached and
                              ;then increment A3
       BNE     L1             ;repeat if A3 ≠ 9
```

where A2 holds the address of the first location in the list and A3 is used as an index register. A3 may be specified as .L or .W.

8.4.4 Program counter with index

There are two forms of program counter relative addressing, *with displacement* (Fig. 8.9) and *with index* shown in Fig. 8.11. In program counter relative addressing with displacement, a 2's complement 16-bit literal in the instruction is sign-extended to 32 bits and added to the contents of the program counter to form the effective address. The program counter relative addressing with index is similar to the register indirect with index by using the contents of a register and a sign-extended 8-bit displacement to add to the contents of the program counter.

8.4.5 Implied addressing

The 68000 has 19 instructions which can be classified as using implied addressing, all using one of four particular registers as address registers, namely, the program counter (PC), the supervisor stack pointer (SSP), the user stack pointer (USP), and the status register (SR). The instructions are shown in Table 8.4.

8.5 FURTHER INSTRUCTIONS

8.5.1 Address register instructions

We have noted that the data operands and operand addresses held in data registers and address registers respectively have been provided in several cases

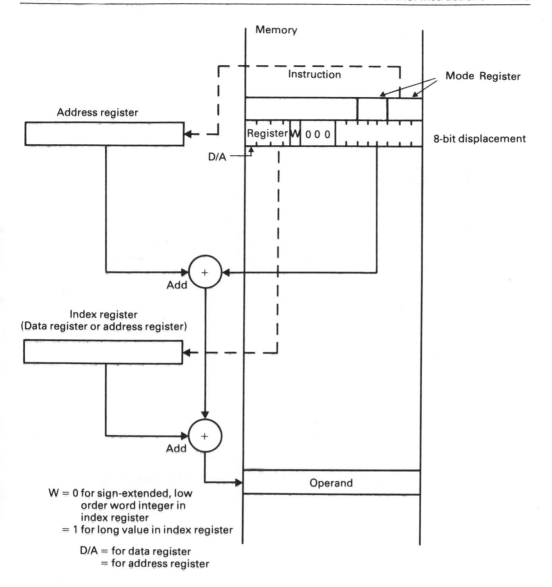

Figure 8.10   68000 address register indirect addressing with index

with separate instructions. Within the data transfer group, a number of MOVE type instructions are provided particularly for addresses. A MOVE instruction is provided to load the address register:

    MOVEA <effective address>, <address register>

Similarly, an ADD instruction is provided to add to an address register:

    ADDA <effective address>, <address register>

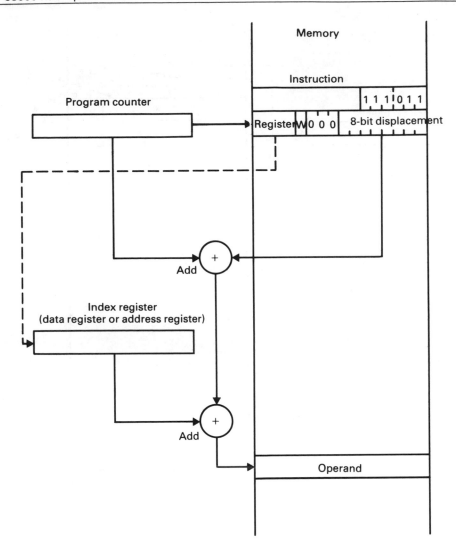

Figure 8.11   68000 program counter relative addressing with index

Table 8.4   Effects of instructions on condition codes (Courtesy of Motorola, Inc.)

Instruction	Condition codes					Notes
	X	N	Z	V	C	
Data transfer						
MOVE	–	*	*	0	0	
MOVEA	–	–	–	–	–	
MOVEM	–	–	–	–	–	
MOVEP	–	–	–	–	–	
MOVEQ	–	*	*	0	0	
EXG	–	–	–	–	–	
SWAP	–	*	*	0	0	1
LEA	–	–	–	–	–	

Table 8.4   Effects of instructions on condition codes

Instruction	Condition codes					Notes
	X	N	Z	V	C	
PEA	–	–	–	–	–	
LINK	–	–	–	–	–	
UNLK	–	–	–	–	–	
Arithmetic						
ADD	*	*	*	*	*	
ADDA	–	–	–	–	–	
ADDI	*	*	*	*	*	
ADDQ	*	*	*	*	*	
SUB	*	*	*	*	*	
SUBA	–	–	–	–	–	
SUBI	*	*	*	*	*	
SUBQ	*	*	*	*	*	
CLR	–	0	1	0	0	
NEG	*	*	*	*	*	
EXT	–	*	*	0	0	
MULS	–	*	*	0	0	
MULU	–	*	*	0	0	
DIVS	–	*	*	*	0	
DIVU	–	*	*	*	0	
ADDX	*	*	*	*	*	
SUBX	*	*	*	*	*	
NEGX	*	*	*	*	*	
ABCD	*	U	*	U	*	2
SBCD	*	U	*	U	*	3
NBCD	*	U	*	U	*	3
CMP	–	*	*	*	*	
CMPA	–	*	*	*	*	
CMPI	–	*	*	*	*	
CMPM	–	*	*	*	*	
TAS	–	*	*	0	0	
TST	–	*	*	0	0	
Logical						
AND	–	*	*	0	0	
ANDI	–	*	*	0	0	
OR	–	*	*	0	0	
ORI	–	*	*	0	0	
EOR	–	*	*	0	0	
EORI	–	*	*	0	0	
NOT	–	*	*	0	0	
Bit manipulation						
BTST	–	–	*	–	–	
BSET	–	–	*	–	–	
BCLR	–	–	*	–	–	
BCHG	–	–	*	–	–	
Shift/rotate						
ASL	*	*	*	*	*	
ASR	*	*	*	*	*	
LSL	*	*	*	0	*	
LSR	*	*	*	0	*	
ROL	–	*	*	0	*	
ROR	–	*	*	0	*	

Table 8.4   Effects of instructions on condition codes

Instruction	Condition codes					Notes
	X	N	Z	V	C	
ROXL	*	*	*	0	*	
ROXR	*	*	*	0	*	
Jump/branch						
JMP	–	–	–	–	–	
BRA	–	–	–	–	–	
Bcc	–	–	–	–	–	
DBcc	–	–	–	–	–	
Scc	–	–	–	–	–	
JSR	–	–	–	–	–	
BSR	–	–	–	–	–	
RTR	*	*	*	*	*	4
RTS	–	–	–	–	–	
Control						
RESET	–	–	–	–	–	
RTE	*	*	*	*	*	4
STOP	*	*	*	*	*	5
NOP	–	–	–	–	–	
TRAP	–	–	–	–	–	
TRAPV	–	–	–	–	–	
CHK	–	*	U	U	U	
MOVE USP	–	–	–	–	–	
MOVE to SR	*	*	*	*	*	6
MOVE from SR	–	–	–	–	–	
MOVE to CCR	*	*	*	*	*	7
ANI to SR	*	*	*	*	*	7
EORI to SR	*	*	*	*	*	7
ORI to SR	*	*	*	*	*	7
ANDI to CCR	*	*	*	*	*	7
EORI to CCR	*	*	*	*	*	7
ORI to CCR	*	*	*	*	*	7

Notes

1   N and Z set according to 32-bit result.
2   C and X set if decimal carry generated. Unchanged otherwise.
3   C and X set if decimal borrow generated. Unchanged otherwise.
4   Set according to contents of word on stack.
5   Set according to immediate operand.
6   Set according to source operand.
7   X Cleared if bit 4 of immediate/source operand zero. Unchanged
     otherwise.
     N Cleared if bit 3 of immediate/source operand zero. Unchanged
     otherwise.
     Z Cleared if bit 2 of immediate/source operand zero. Unchanged
     otherwise.
     V Cleared if bit 1 of immediate/source operand zero. Unchanged
     otherwise.
     C Cleared if bit 0 of immediate/source operand zero. Unchanged
     otherwise.
–   Not affected
*   Set according to result of operation.
U   Undefined

and subtract:

SUBA <effective address>, <address register>

and compare:

CMPA <effective address>, <address register>

Within the transfer group of instructions exist instructions which obtain the effective addresses and transfer this address to a specified location. For example:

LEA <effective address>, <address register>

computes the effective address and loads this address into the specified address register. Similarly:

PEA <effective address>, <address register>

computes the effective address and places this on to the stack. Only control address modes are allowed for these two instructions.

Two instructions, LINK and UNLK, are provided to form linked lists. The LINK instruction firstly transfers the contents of the address register onto the stack (using two 16-bit locations to hold the 32-bit address). The stack pointer is operated in a predecrement mode and points to the last item on the stack. The stack grows towards lower addresses. The value held in the stack pointer is then loaded into the address register. Finally a sign-extended displacement in the instruction is added to the stack pointer. The UNLK instruction firstly transfers the contents of the address register into the stack pointer giving a new top of stack address. Then the top of the stack is loaded into the address register and the stack pointer postincremented. LINK and UNLK operations are shown in Fig. 8.12 and Fig. 8.13 respectively.

8.5.2 Status register instructions

The instructions which can alter the contents of the full status register are *privileged*, i.e. can only be executed when in the supervisor mode, though those instructions which examine or copy the contents of the status register are not privileged. The method of altering the status register is via a separate form of MOVE instruction:

MOVE <effective address>, SR

The condition codes of the status register, however, can be altered in the user mode, using another separate form of MOVE instruction:

MOVE <effective address>, CCR

which copies the contents of the addressed location into the condition code byte of the status register. Both forms of MOVE can use only data addressing modes (i.e. all addressing modes except address register direct).

The contents of the status register can be copied into an addressed location by another separate form of MOVE instruction:

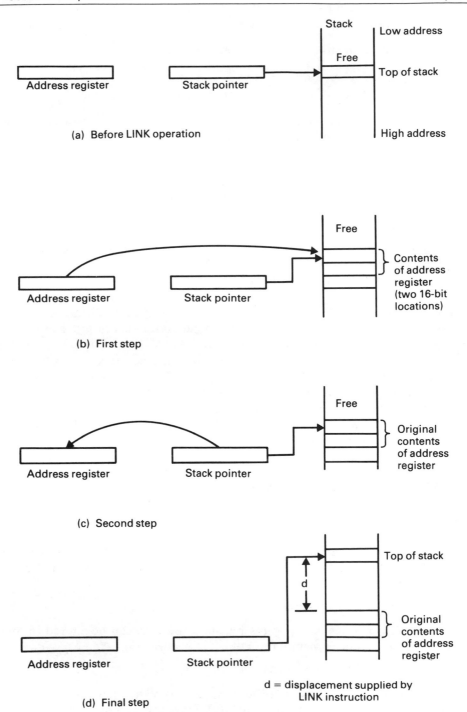

(a) Before LINK operation

(b) First step

(c) Second step

(d) Final step

d = displacement supplied by LINK instruction

Figure 8.12 LINK operation

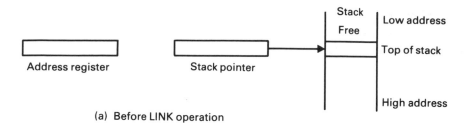

(a) Before LINK operation

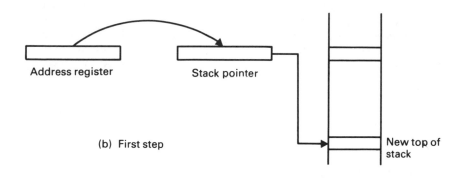

(b) First step

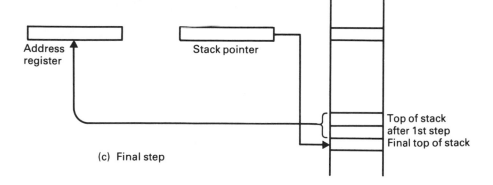

(c) Final step

Figure 8.13   UNLK operation

MOVE SR, <effective address>

using data alterable addressing only. These MOVE instructions have been
included within the control group of instructions in Table 8.2, together with
other control instructions.

REFERENCES

1. *MC68000 16/32-bit Microprocessor Programmer's Reference Manual* (4th ed.). Geneva, Switzerland: Motorola, Inc., 1984.
2. *MC68000 16-/32-bit Microprocessor Advance Information*, East Kilbride, Scotland: Motorola Ltd., 1985.

PROBLEMS

8.1   Produce a design for a simple 68000 microprocessor system similar to the Z-80 system design given in Chap. 7 (Fig. 7.5). Include a processor, $2\,K \times 16$-bit RAM unit using two $2\,K \times 8$-bit devices, $2\,K \times 16$-bit EPROM unit using two $2\,K \times 8$ devices, and a 4-bit output port. Design the appropriate address decode logic circuits and logic circuits to generate the required acknowledge signals. ($K=1024$.)

8.2   Describe the operation performed by each of the following 68000 instructions:

(a) MOVE D1,D1
(b) MOVE D1,100
(c) MOVE #45,D5
(d) MOVE (A1),(A2)
(e) MOVE A1,D1
(f) MOVE D1,(A2)+
(g) MOVE (A2)+,−(A1)

8.3   Determine whether each of the following is a valid 68000 instruction:

(a) MOVE D1,A1
(b) ADD D1,A1
(c) ADD A1,D1
(d) SUBQ #45,D3

8.4   Write a 68000 program to multiply a data operand held in D1 by 18. Use the method used in section 8.3.6. Compare with using a multiply instruction directly.

8.5   Write a 68000 program to add four 8-bit numbers held in memory locations 200, 201, 202 and 203 respectively, placing the result in memory location 204.

8.6   Write a 68000 program to determine the average of twelve 8-bit numbers held in consecutive (8-bit) memory locations beginning at location 400. Enter the result into memory location 500.

8.7   Write a 68000 program to exchange the contents of 100 memory locations starting at location 1500 with 100 locations starting at location 7000.

Semiconductor Primary Memory Devices

9.1 MEMORY REQUIREMENTS

The memory in a microprocessor system, or indeed in any computer system, serves one of two principal purposes. Firstly, it is used to store the machine language programs to be executed, and secondly it stores any data to be used in the program. The requirements for the memory can be summarized as follows:

(i) The memory needs to be able to store (memorize) binary patterns (0's and 1's) by electrical, magnetic or other means.

(ii) The memory needs to be able to store many binary patterns, arranged as binary words in accessible locations.

(iii) For storing a program currently being executed and storing its associated data, we need to be able to access any program/data location in the memory at will in any order with high speed, i.e. the memory must be *random-access*.

(iv) We need the capability of both reading and writing information in the case of data storage.

(v) For program execution, the capability of reading is sufficient.

Because random-access memory is relatively expensive, additional secondary memory is also employed in most computer systems. This memory is cheaper per bit but usually is not random-access and leads to a memory system divided into two parts:

(i) Main or primary random-access memory holding programs currently being executed, together with its data

(ii) Secondary memory, not necessarily and not normally random access, for holding further information.

The secondary memory is sometimes called *backing memory* or *backing store*. The processor has a direct connection to the primary memory and a connection is made between the primary memory and the secondary memory, in the case of a microprocessor system through the system bus, to enable information to be transferred between the primary memory and the secondary memory. This transfer is done in groups of binary words, typically 128, 256 or 512 words at a time as required. In this chapter, we will look at the main or primary memory. Chapter 11 is devoted to secondary memory based on magnetic recording.

The random-access memory widely used for almost twenty years till about

1970 was the so-called *core store* which used very small rings of magnetic ferrite material, magnetized in one of two circular directions to represent the two binary states. One ferrite ring or core was necessary for each binary digit and wires threaded the ferrite cores in order to magnetize the core (write information) or to sense the state of magnetization of the core (read information).

Since 1970, *semiconductor memory* has been increasingly used. Semiconductor memory is based on transistors and associated electronic components fabricated in integrated circuit construction and is always used as the main memory of a microprocessor system. There are two basic classes of components used in semiconductor memory, namely:

(i)   Bipolar transistors (*n-p-n and p-n-p*) and diodes
(ii) Metal-oxide-semiconductor (MOS) transistors

which leads to two classes of semiconductor memory, bipolar semiconductor memory and MOS semiconductor memory. Most semiconductor memory in microprocessor systems is of the MOS variety, though bipolar semiconductor memory is used for particular applications.

Semiconductor memory devices consist of a large number of individual memory cells of a common design, each of which maintains one of two states to represent the two binary values of one bit. The memory cell itself must have the following attributes:

(i)   Two states
(ii) A method of selecting the memory cell from many fabricated on one integrated circuit together with:
(iii) A method of setting the two binary states, i.e. writing
(iv) A method of sensing the two binary states, i.e. reading

We shall look at the ways the various cells achieve the above, but firstly we consider the common organization of these cells within the device.

9.2 MEMORY ORGANIZATION

Generally the cells are organized in a two-dimensional array and one or more cells are selected from the array. Once selected, the write or read process may be performed. One organization is to select one cell from the array for reading or writing. This is known as the *3-D organization*. As one bit is read or written at any instant, the organization is also given the notation $\times$ 1. For example, a 1024 $\times$ 1 memory would indicate a memory in which any one bit from the 1024 bits stored can be accessed and one bit of information passed to or from the memory.

The $\times$ 1 organization is shown in Fig. 9.1. A row select signal selects a complete row of memory cells. A data in/out column line connects to the cells as shown and is used to present new data to the cells or to obtain the existing data (write and read). *Static memory* cells (which will be described later) generally employ two data lines connecting to each cell, one for the true binary value and

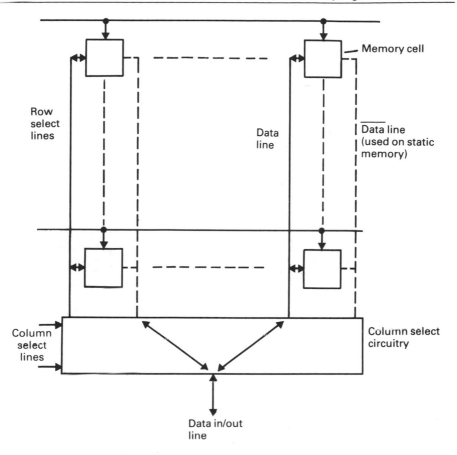

Figure 9.1 × 1 semiconductor memory organization

one for the complement value. One cell on the selected row is chosen by selecting one of the column data lines (or pair in the case of static memories). This enables either a writing process or a read process to be performed. Each cell is given a unique address which is divided into two parts, a *row address* which selects the row and a *column address* which selects a column. If the array is square the row and column addresses would have the same number of bits. The array need not be square, but a square array would give the least number of row and column circuits in total.

If we wish to read and write binary words consisting of several binary digits simultaneously, as would be normal, several memory devices of the × 1 organization could be used, each storing one digit of each word. For example, a 1024-word memory in which each word contains 8 bits could be formed with eight 1024 × 1 bit memory devices. An alternative organization is the × *n* organization which achieves simultaneous reading and writing of a complete word in one device. The usual arrangement for semiconductor memory is shown in Fig. 9.2. Here the memory array is arranged as before with a row select line connecting to a row of cells but rather than select one column data line, *n* column data lines are selected where *n* is the required number of digits to be

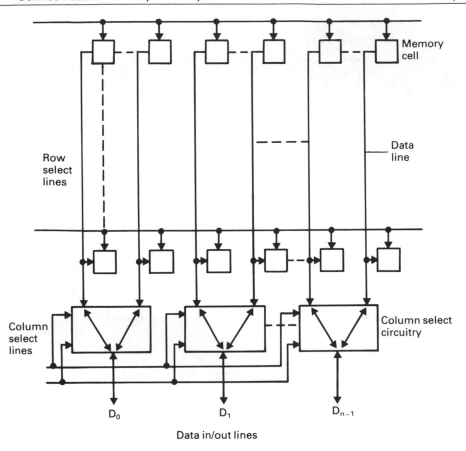

Figure 9.2   × *n* semiconductor memory organization

read or written simultaneously. The columns are formed into *n* groups with one column select circuit for each group. Each select circuit selects the corresponding column in its group. Typically *n* is 4 or 8. A 1024 × 8 bit memory device would hold 1024 bytes and all the bits of any one byte can be read or written simultaneously. Of course more than one memory device of this organization can also be used to increase memory capacity. Memory capacities of semiconductor memories are manufactured in large powers of 2. Since 2^{10} is 1024 or approximately 1000, the letter K is used to indicate the multiple of 2^{10}. For example, a 64K × 1 bit memory holds 64×2^{10} (2^{16}) bits.

9.3 METAL-OXIDE-SEMICONDUCTOR RANDOM ACCESS MEMORY

There are two classes of metal-oxide-semiconductor (MOS) random access memory, namely:

(i)   *Static MOS random access memory*
(ii) *Dynamic MOS random access memory*

classified by the type of internal memory cell circuit used.

9.3.1 Static MOS random access memory

Figure 9.3 shows a static MOS memory cell consisting of two 'cross-coupled' MOS transistors, T_1 and T_2, two load resistors and two separate MOS transistors, T_3 and T_4, to connect the memory cell to the digit and $\overline{\text{digit}}$ lines for selection, reading and writing. In this circuit, all the MOS transistors are enhancement types. (See Chap. 5, section 5.5 for details of MOS transistors.) When one of the two cross-coupled transistors is fully conducting, say T_1, the voltage of its drain falls to approximately 0 V. This causes the other transistor of the pair, T_2, to become non-conducting and its drain voltage rises to the supply voltage, 5 V. This voltage is applied to the base of T_1. As the voltage is above the threshold voltage of T_1, T_1 is maintained in the conducting state.

The circuit can be maintained in one of two states, either with T_1

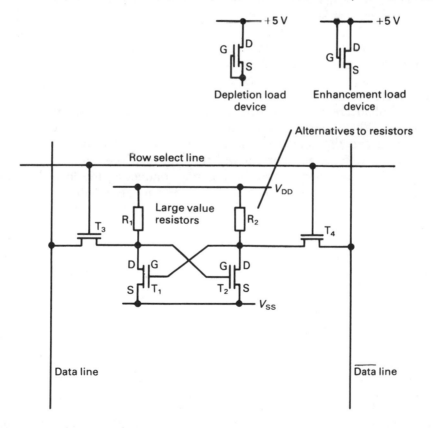

Figure 9.3 Resistor load static MOS RAM cell

conducting and T_2 not conducting, or with T_1 not conducting and T_2 conducting. These two circuit states represent the two binary values of one digit. Selection is performed using the two extra transistors, T_3 and T_4, which are placed into their conducting state by applying appropriate voltages on the row select lines. When selected, the information can be read from or written into the cell. One read amplifier is provided for each pair of digit lines sensing the voltage difference between the two outputs of the selected cell. To write to a selected cell, one side of the cell is brought down to $0\,\mathrm{V}$ and the other to $+5\,\mathrm{V}$ using a differential output write amplifier with true and inverse outputs driving the digit and $\overline{\text{digit}}$ lines respectively.

The resistors in the static MOS memory cell are fabricated as part of the integrated circuit construction and can have a very high value to reduce the power dissipation of the cell. (The power dissipation of each cell is given approximately by V_S^2/R where V_S is the supply voltage.) Resistor values as high as $500\,\mathrm{M\Omega}$ have been used. However, very high values result in slower operation because of the long time the output circuit then takes to charge the output capacitances. To counter this, sensitive read amplifiers can be used which record the state of the memory cell before the final output voltage has been reached. A $100\,\mathrm{mV}$ change may be sufficient to deduce the state of the circuit.

There are several variations in the static MOS memory cell described above. The load resistors can be replaced with either enhancement MOS transistor loads or depletion MOS transistor loads in a similar fashion as the MOS logic gates described in Chap. 5. In each case, the source of the load device is connected to the appropriate cross-coupled transistor and the drain is connected to the supply voltage.

Enhancement MOS load transistors have their gates tied to the supply voltage. When one cross-coupled transistor is conducting, the voltage between the gate and the source of the enhancement load device is greater than its threshold voltage, and current will flow through the load device. Conversely, when the cross-coupled transistor is not conducting the load device becomes non-conducting. It was noted in Chap. 5 that this results in the high output voltage being $V_S - V_t$ where V_t is the threshold voltage of the load device, perhaps $1.5\,\mathrm{V}$.

The depletion load has its gate connected to its source and to the cross-coupled transistors. Because the gate-source is always $0\,\mathrm{V}$, the depletion device is always conducting, though only with leakage currents when the associated cross-coupled transistor is non-conducting.

9.3.2 Dynamic MOS random access memory

The second class of semiconductor MOS random access memory is the dynamic memory which uses a capacitor charged to a potential to represent one state and uncharged to represent the other state. The approach can be traced back to the early 1970s when methods were sought to reduce the number of components in the memory cell. This would clearly increase the number of memory cells that could be fabricated in one device. A characteristic of MOS transistors is that the gate current, due to the leakage across the gate electrode and the surrounding silicon dioxide, is extremely small. Therefore once the gate electrode is charged to some potential and then disconnected, it takes several milliseconds for the potential to decay. For example, if the load resistors or devices were removed from the static MOS design, the binary state of the device would be maintained for a few milliseconds due to the charge of the capacitance of one of the cross-coupled transistors. If, before the state is lost, the memory cell is refreshed, i.e. read and a full state reinstated, and repeated at regular intervals, a practical memory cell can be formed. One of the first dynamic MOS memory cells was of this type, using the two MOS cross-coupled transistors without load devices, and two select devices, four transistors in all. This approach can be developed using the charge on the gate–source capacitance of a single MOS transistor to maintain the conducting state of the MOS transistor and additional transistors to select the memory cell for reading and writing. This requires one MOS transistor as the storage element, one to select the cell for reading and one to select the cell for writing, three transistors in all.

The memory cell can be reduced to a specially formed capacitor and one select MOS transistor as shown in Fig. 9.4. This form was introduced in 1973. The select transistor, when conducting, allows both reading or writing to take place using a single digit line. The select signal selects a row of cells as in other memory designs described. One digit line is provided for each column of cells (digit not required in dynamic cells). Each digit line has a read amplifier and write amplifier attached. There were some problems to overcome with this particularly attractive design with regard to reading. To create a small memory cell, the storage capacitor needs to be physically very small and hence with a small value of capacitance. When the cell is selected and the capacitor connects to the digit line, the voltage originally on the storage capacitor reduces because of the capacitive attenuator formed by the storage capacitor and intrinsic capacitance of the digit line which is connected in parallel. Designs in the 1970s called for storage capacitances in the order of 0.04 pF. The capacitance of the digit line may be in the order of 0.5 pF giving an attenuation of $0.04/0.54 = 1/13.5$ or a reduction to 7.4% of the original storage voltage. The original

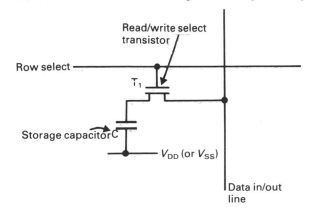

Figure 9.4 Dynamic memory cell

voltage is usually between 3.75 V and 5 V. With these voltages the final read voltage is between 278 mV and 370 mV. The voltage must be allowed to decay from these values. To sense such low voltages, sensitive read amplifiers were necessary, and generally these amplifiers needed to be fabricated using MOS technology.

The general read amplifier design often chosen has a central portion consisting of two MOS transistors configured in a similar way to the static memory cell, with their drains and gates cross-coupled. A simple example is shown in Fig. 9.5. Outputs are taken from both drains of the read amplifiers. Columns of memory cells are divided into two halves and one read amplifier is placed between the two halves for each column. Let us consider the action of one read amplifier which is repeated for all the read amplifiers simultaneously. One row line is selected on one side of the read amplifier to select a memory cell. The cell connects to one output of the read amplifier. One *dummy* memory cell is provided on each side of the read amplifier. The dummy cell on the other side to the selected cell is connected via the column line to the associated read amplifier output. The dummy cell has been charged so as to create a voltage

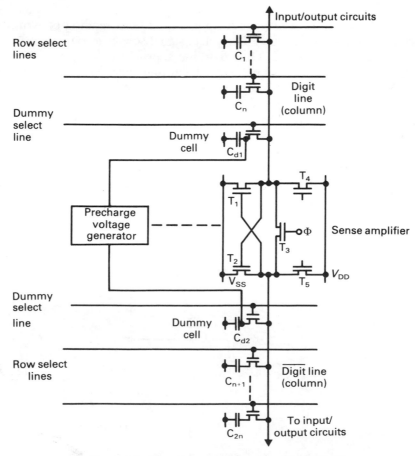

Figure 9.5   Simple dynamic memory sense amplifier

half-way between the two possible voltages of store cells, i.e. ½ $V_{storage}$ where $V_{storage}$ is the 1 level voltage and 0 V is the 0 level voltage.

The read amplifier is placed in an unstable state by, in this case, joining both outputs together temporarily using additional MOS transistors. One single transistor, T_3, is used in the simple design shown. When the outputs are released, the cross-coupled transistor circuit relaxes into a stable state with one transistor conducting and the other not conducting. If the selected memory cell is in a charged state (representing a 1), the voltage on that side of the read amplifier will be higher than on the other side having the dummy cell and the read circuit will relax with high output voltage on the selected memory cell side and low on the dummy cell side. If the selected cell is at an uncharged state (representing a 0), this is followed by the read amplifier and 0 V re-imposed. In fact the regenerative action will result in the selected cell being recharged to the starting voltage, say 5 V, or discharged to 0 V and thus a read operation will also perform an automatic refresh action.

Notice that the use of dummy memory cells takes into account the voltage attenuation because both the selected memory cell and the dummy cell have the same (half) column line capacitance and each voltage will be attenuated by the same factor. Writing is performed by using the same read amplifier as these also fully charge or discharge the selected cells.

Dynamic memories will loose their information over a period of time as the charge on the storage capacitors discharge. Typically the worst-case time for the charge to decay to a level it cannot be distinguished is 2 ms. Therefore the cells must be *refreshed* at 2 ms periods or sooner. Refreshing the cells means reading and rewriting the same information. With the read amplifier design above, a refresh operation can be the same as a normal read operation without any need to look at the read outputs from the device, and all the cells on a row can be refreshed together. This would need to be repeated for all the cells, and the whole process repeated every 2 ms. Refresh represents an overhead to the memory system as while the memory is being refreshed, it cannot be used for normal read or write operations. However, it is usually an insignificant fraction of the overall available time. For example, if a read/refresh operation takes 500 ns, there are 128 rows and the maximum refresh period is 2 ms, the percentage of the available time spent in refresh is:

$$\% \text{ time in refresh} = (500\,\text{ns} \times 128 \times 100\%)/2\,\text{ms} = 3.2\%$$

Often, it can be arranged that refresh can take place at times when the memory is not being used for normal read/write operations. If this is done, there is no overhead to the use of dynamic memories whatsoever.

9.3.3 Memory signals

(a) Memory data sheet standards

There are various notations used by manufacturers to describe memory timing signals. A standard has been laid down by the IEEE Task Force, P662, on Semiconductor Memory Terminology and Specifications, in co-operation with the JEDEC JC42 Committee on Semiconductor Memories [1], and some but not all memory manufacturers have followed this standard. In the IEEE standard, upper case letters are designated for particular signals. For example, the data input is D and the data output is Q. A bidirectional data input/output line is labeled DQ. The time between two timing signals is described by a mnemonic consisting of a series of upper case letters, beginning with the letter T. The next letter or group of letters refer to the leading (first) timing signal. This is followed by a letter indicating the type of logic transition of the leading signal. The next letter or group of letters refer to the following (second) timing signal, and this is followed by a letter indicating the type of transition of this signal. The following types of transitions are identified:

L   to a low logic level
H   to a high logic level
V   to a valid state
X   to an invalid state
Z   to high impedance (tri-state)

For example, the timing parameter TDVWL is the time from the data signal D becoming valid to the write strobe W going to a low state. The bar over an active low signal is omitted in the timing parameter name. In the following memory timing waveforms, we will give the IEEE signal names in parentheses where other names are very common. Timing parameters will use the IEEE notation.

(b) Static memory
A number of logic signals need to be applied to semiconductor memory parts. For a write operation, the following basic information needs to be passed to the part:

(i)   The address of the memory cell(s)
(ii)   The data to be written into the memory cells
(iii) A write strobe signal to initiate the operation

For a read operation, the following information needs to be present:

(i)   The address of the memory cell(s)
(ii)   A read data strobe signal to initiate the operation

together with a data path for the resultant information read from the selected cells. Figure 9.6 shows the internal arrangement of a typical static memory and Fig. 9.7 the timing signals. A general chip enable, $\overline{\text{CE}}$, is also present. The enable signal must be activated before the part will respond to any other signal.

The write strobe is labeled $\overline{\text{WE}}$, write enable. To activate a write transfer, the chip is selected by setting $\overline{\text{CE}}$ low. A high to low transition is applied to $\overline{\text{WE}}$. (A write transfer would also be activated if $\overline{\text{WE}}$ is set low before $\overline{\text{CE}}$. Then a high to low $\overline{\text{CE}}$ transition activates a write transfer). These signals are applied after the address has been presented to the part and the signals have stabilized. The data entered into the addressed cells will be that present on the data lines at the

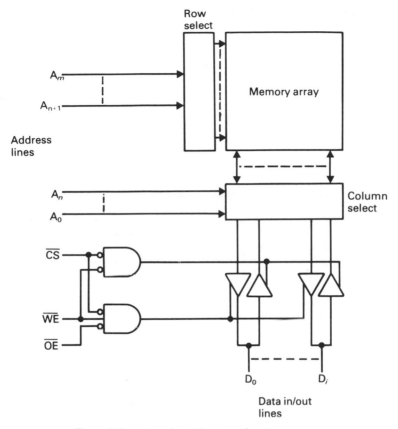

Figure 9.6   Internal architecture of static memory

time of the low to high write enable signal transition (or $\overline{CE}$ high to low transition if this occurs later).

The read strobe is called $\overline{OE}$, output enable. For a read transfer, the chip is selected by setting $\overline{CE}$ low after the address is applied and then a $\overline{OE}$ high to low transition is applied. Some time later, the data from the addressed memory cells appear on the data output lines. In some memory devices $\overline{OE}$ is not present. In these cases, $\overline{CE}$ acts as a read strobe when $\overline{WE} = 1$.

In the timing waveforms shown, it is assumed that the address must remain valid throughout the memory cycle. This type of memory is known as a *asynchronous memory*. Some memories, known as *synchronous memories*, incorporate internal address latches which are activated by the falling edge of $\overline{CE}$. In these memories, the address need remain valid only till the hold time from the falling edge of $\overline{CE}$. Similarly, other applied signals can be latched internally, including the data input. The data input latch would be activated by the falling edge of $\overline{WE}$.

(c) Dynamic memory
Dynamic memories require the same information and control but this is usually provided in a different way. The memory address is split into two parts, a

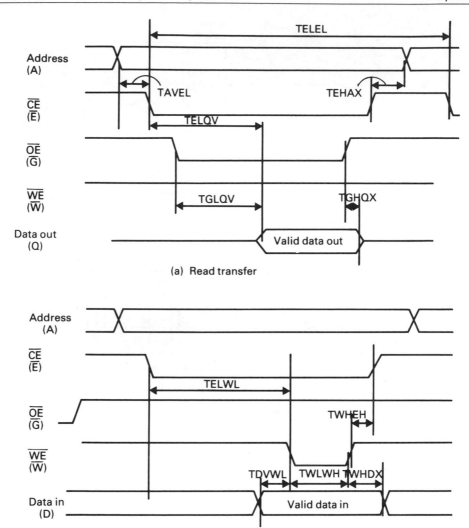

(a) Read transfer

(b) Write transfer

Symbol	Parameter
TELEL	Cycle time (of $\overline{CE}$)
TAVEL	Address to $\overline{CE}$ set-up time
TEHAX	$\overline{CE}$ to address hold time
TELQV	$\overline{CE}$ to data out valid time ($\overline{CE}$ access time)
TGLQV	$\overline{OE}$ to data out valid time ($\overline{OE}$ access time)
TGHQX	$\overline{OE}$ to data invalid time
TELWL	$\overline{CE}$ to $\overline{WE}$ set-up time
TDVWL	Data in to $\overline{WE}$ set-up time
TWLWH	$\overline{WE}$ pulse width
TWHDX	$\overline{CE}$ to Data in hold time
TWHEH	$\overline{WE}$ to $\overline{CE}$ hold time

Figure 9.7 Representative static memory read and write timing

row address and a column address corresponding to the row and column of the required cells. Since the row address can be selected before the column address, the two addresses are arranged to enter the part on the same address lines at different times to reduce the number of address lines. This technique is known as *address multiplexing*. The general arrangement is shown in Fig. 9.8. Typically seven or eight row/column address lines are provided. Eight row and column addresses would give 256 rows and 256 columns that could be addressed. Two address strobe signals are provided:

$\overline{RAS}$ Row address strobe signal
$\overline{CAS}$ Column address strobe signal

Only one other control signal is shown:

$\overline{WE}$ Write enable

with independent data input and output. Using the $\times$ 1 organization, dynamic memories up to 256K $\times$ 1 bit can be contained in 16-pin dual in-line packages.

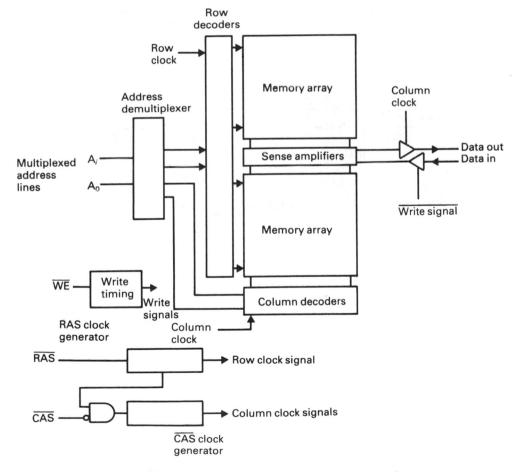

Figure 9.8 Internal architecture of dynamic memory device

The × 8 dynamic memories normally do not employ address multiplexing and use larger 24–28 pin packages.

Each address strobe signal is activated when the appropriate row or column address is stablized on the address lines, first the $\overline{RAS}$ signal and then the $\overline{CAS}$ signal, as shown in Fig. 9.9. Notice that the action is triggered on the falling edge of the two strobe signals and both $\overline{RAS}$ and $\overline{CAS}$ are kept low to the end of the memory cycle.

The read cycle is selected by ensuring that $\overline{WR}$ is set to a 1 when the $\overline{CAS}$ becomes low. The time before the data bit appears on the data output line is dependent upon the $\overline{CAS}$ transition to a low (but see below). When the output becomes valid, it remains valid while $\overline{CAS}$ is low and becomes high impedance (tri-state) when $\overline{CAS}$ is brought high (outputs are not usually latched internally).

For a write operation, $\overline{WR}$ is set to a 0. If this is done before the $\overline{CAS}$ signal transition to a low, the data bit on the data line is strobed (entered) with

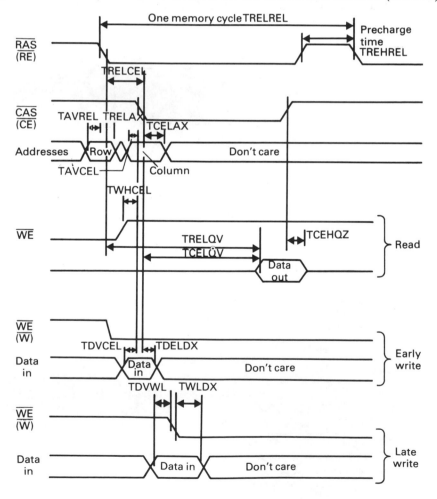

Figure 9.9   Dynamic memory read–write timing

$\overline{CAS}$ so the data must be valid then. If $\overline{WR}$ is set to a 0 after the $\overline{CAS}$ transition, the data bit is strobed with $\overline{WR}$, so that the data must be valid then. The latter case is known as *late* or *delayed write*, and the former case is known as *early write*. These mechanisms provide greater flexibility in read–write operations. The normal microprocessor memory operation is early write, which allows the data-in and data-out lines to be joined together. In both modes, $\overline{RAS}$ must be maintained at a low throughout the cycle.

Certain timing factors must be satisfied. Generally the signals $\overline{RAS}$ and $\overline{CAS}$ are internally gated so that the time relationship of these signals is not critical for the memory to operate. In particular, $\overline{CAS}$ may be applied before the device is ready to select the column, and the signal is internally inhibited until the correct time. This is known as *gated CAS*. Assuming that the delay between $\overline{RAS}$ and $\overline{CAS}$ is not greater than some maximum value, typically, 50 ns, and not less than some minimum value, typically 20 ns, the access time is measured from the falling edge of $\overline{CAS}$. If, however, $\overline{CAS}$ is applied later, the access time will be determined by the 'access time from $\overline{CAS}$', plus the delay between the two strobes. To achieve the minimum access time, $\overline{CAS}$ must be applied within the window above (for example 20 ns to 50 ns), but the device will still operate, though slower, if $\overline{CAS}$ is applied later.

Set-up times and hold times as in flip-flops need to be satisfied. Typically the row address set-up time is zero and the row hold time 20 ns. To give the maximum possible time to establish the column address, the column address set-up time is often negative, for example −10 ns, which means that the column address need not be stable until 10 ns after the $\overline{CAS}$ has been applied. The column address hold time is typically 45 ns. The $\overline{WR}$ set-up and hold times referenced to the falling edge of $\overline{CAS}$ are zero. This means that $\overline{WR}$ may be applied before or after $\overline{CAS}$ though this results in different modes of operation (early write and late write). Also the device requires time to precharge internal circuits before the next memory operation can take place, typically 100 ns. However, the data remains valid during this time while $\overline{CAS}$ is low.

Refresh operations can be initiated by one of several methods. The usual method is to use the falling edge of $\overline{RAS}$ to cause a refresh as this causes the read amplifiers to refresh a selected row. A number of refresh operations can be initiated in succession by $\overline{RAS}$ low transitions with $\overline{CAS}$ kept high. This is known as $\overline{RAS}$-only refresh. The level on $\overline{WR}$ is irrelevant. A row address has to be provided for each refresh operation.

An alternative mode, known as *hidden refresh*, utilizes the fact that while $\overline{CAS}$ is low, valid data once appearing will remain on the data output line. Subsequent refresh cycles can be initiated by falling transitions of $\overline{RAS}$ while $\overline{CAS}$ is low, without disturbing the output data. The usual plan is to perform one or more refresh cycles immediately after each memory reference cycle while keeping the original data output valid. The first cycle consists of a normal $\overline{RAS}$–$\overline{CAS}$ cycle but with $\overline{CAS}$ remaining low at the end of this cycle. One or more $\overline{RAS}$ cycles are then performed, with refresh addresses provided to refresh rows of memory. The timing of $\overline{RAS}$-only and hidden refresh modes are shown in Fig. 9.10.

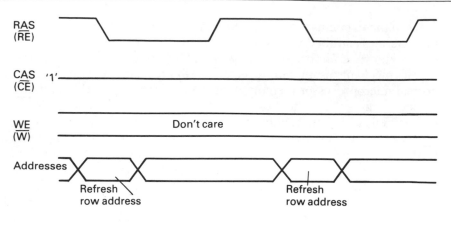

(a) RAS only refresh

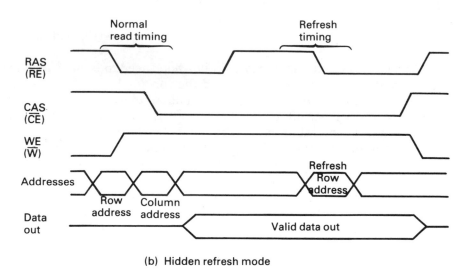

(b) Hidden refresh mode

Figure 9.10   Dynamic memory refresh timing

9.3.4 Dynamic memory subsystem design

Dynamic memories pose additional problems over static memories when designed into a memory subsystem, for two reasons:

(i)   Multiplexed address inputs (when used)
(ii) Necessity of refresh

We firstly consider the additional circuitry for multiplexed address input parts.

The circuitry required needs to perform the following sequence:

1. Gate row address (A_0 to A_7, say) from processor to the memory address inputs
2. Set row address strobe, $\overline{RAS} = 0$
3. Gate column address (A_8 to A_{15}, say) from the processor to the memory address inputs
4. Set column address strobe, $\overline{CAS} = 0$
5. Set $\overline{CAS}$ and $\overline{RAS} = 1$
6. Allow a precharge time before next cycle.

The row and column addresses are the lower and upper parts of the full address (or vice versa). For a 64K memory device, both the row and column addresses are eight bits. The row could be the processor address signals A_0 to A_7 and the column address could be the processor signals A_8 to A_{15}. Each 8-bit address could be connected to the memory address lines using eight 2-to-1 line multiplexers (typically two integrated circuits). Let us firstly assume that the processor address does not extend beyond A_{15}. Figure 9.11 shows the arrangement for a Z-80 microprocessor. The memory request signal, $\overline{MREQ}$, is used as the row address strobe with the multiplexer set to choose the row address. After one processor clock period, the multiplexer select signal is changed to select the column address and after a suitable delay, a column address strobe signal is generated from the multiplexer select signal. Signals to the memory devices have series resistors to limit signal reflections (see Chap. 16, section 16.2).

If the processor address space is larger than one memory device (e.g. greater than 2^{16} with 64K $\times$ 1 devices), the memory device selection needs to be performed in addition to the above. The normal approach is to connect higher address lines to the $\overline{RAS}$ inputs of individual devices, or sometimes both $\overline{RAS}$ and $\overline{CAS}$ for a two-dimensional decode.

Now consider the second aspect, that of memory refresh. Except for self-refresh devices (see later) it is necessary to provide all row refresh addresses, usually in succession, to the devices within the refresh period of, say, 2 ms. The Z-80 incorporates an internal refresh counter to produce the refresh address during every instruction fetch cycle. The contents of the refresh counter are placed on to the lower 7-bits of the address bus and the refresh counter is automatically incremented between refresh operations. Without processor support, an external refresh counter needs to be provided, which is periodically incremented and gated on to the address lines in place of the normal read–write address. If no particular regular occasion is known when the processor is not requiring the memory, the normal approach is to use the wait mechanism of the processor to hold up the processor periodically, as necessary, to perform a refresh activity.

There are support devices available called *dynamic memory controllers* which provide most of the required circuitry, including the address multiplexer, refresh counter, processor and refresh request arbiter and row/column address strobe circuitry. These devices are bipolar because of the required high speed of

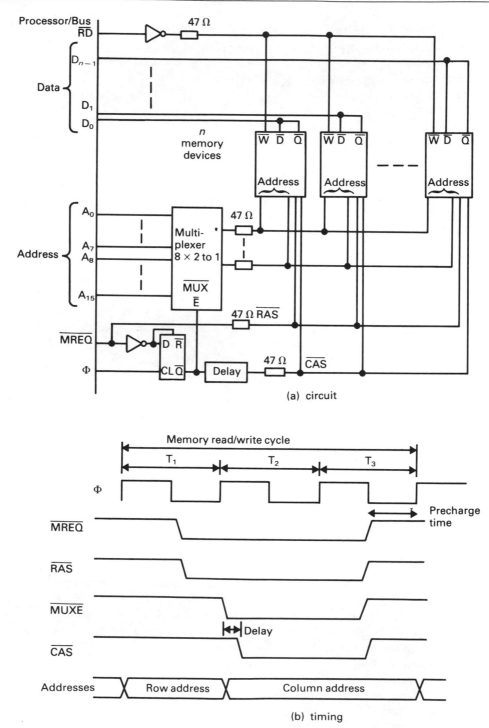

(a) circuit

(b) timing

Figure 9.11   Simplified dynamic memory system

operation, and all read, write and refresh operations are handled by the device. If a read or write request is received while the controller is performing a refresh operation, a wait request is generated, delaying the processor until the refresh operation has been completed. Refresh operations occur once every (refresh period/number of row) seconds, say $2\,\text{ms}/128$ or $15.6\,\mu\text{s}$ on average. If a refresh operation is requested by the controller after a processor read or write cycle has been accepted, the refresh operation will be held in abeyance until the read or write operation has been completed. Then the refresh operation takes place. In the event of simultaneous requests, special arbitration logic resolves the conflict.

(a) Self-refresh memories

Additional circuitry can be incorporated into dynamic memory parts to provide automatic or assisted refresh capability. The simplest form is known as *pin 1 refresh*. Pin 1 on 16-pin dual in line packages is used by some manufacturers to activate an internal refresh mechanism with a signal $\overline{\text{RFSH}}$. When $\overline{\text{RAS}}$ is high, $\overline{\text{RFSH}}$ is taken low to perform a refresh operation. Each low-going transition of $\overline{\text{RFSH}}$ causes the outputs of an internal refresh counter to be connected to internal row address inputs and a refresh operation take place (basically a read operation). On the subsequent rising edge of $\overline{\text{RFSH}}$, the counter is incremented by one in preparation for the next refresh operation which is initiated as required. With repeated use of $\overline{\text{RFSH}}$, either in burst or distributed between normal memory cycles, all rows in the memory can be refreshed. This mechanism is sometimes known as *automatic refresh*. Hidden refresh can be accomplished with $\overline{\text{RFSH}}$ in place of $\overline{\text{RAS}}$.

Pin 1 refresh may include a true *self-refresh* feature whereby successive refresh operations take place if $\overline{\text{RFSH}}$ is held low for, say, longer than $8\,\mu\text{s}$. From then on, refreshes with refresh counter increments take place automatically every 12–$16\,\mu\text{s}$ to ensure that the whole memory is refreshed totally within the specified time interval ($2\,\text{ms}$, say). Self-refresh is generally useful for power-down situations where the memory is powered by a battery while the normal supply is unavailable. It is simply necessary then to keep $\overline{\text{RFSH}}$ low in order to maintain the data stored. Note that when $\overline{\text{RFSH}}$ has returned to a high level, a refresh cycle may just have started and thus a period needs to elapse before a new memory cycle can begin, to allow the refresh cycle to complete. Typically this period will be the same as for a normal memory read or write operation.

Pin 1 refresh, though convenient, does require a previously unused pin for 64K devices. An alternative which leaves pin 1 free and available for a multiplexed address input in larger devices (e.g. 256K) is to use a previously unused combination of $\overline{\text{RAS}}$ and $\overline{\text{CAS}}$, namely $\overline{\text{CAS}}$ low and $\overline{\text{RAS}}$ going low to trigger an internal refresh mechanism.

A *pseudo-static* or *quasi-static* memory is a dynamic memory with additional internal circuitry providing automatic or self-refresh and with an organization which gives the device the external attributes of a static memory, so that it can be treated as such in a system design. Address multiplexing is not done. Pseudo-static memories offer higher capacity and lower cost than static memories, without the overhead of the external refresh and address multiplexer circuitry.

9.4   READ-ONLY MEMORY

9.4.1   General

Read-only memory is a type of memory which is capable of having its stored information read but not altered (written to). Such memory is non-volatile, that is, the stored information is not lost if the power is removed. When the power is returned to the memory device, the previous stored information is still available. Consequently, read-only memory finds applications where the program or unalterable data needs to be available when the computer is first switched on. Examples include:

(i) *Bootstep memory*, the memory used to store the program which is first executed when the computer is switched on. This program is usually fairly short and causes a larger program to be brought into the primary memory from the secondary memory.

(ii) *Control memory* storing the processor microprogram. In a microprogrammed design of processor, a microprogram is created which defines the sequence of steps which are necessary to execute the machine instructions of the processor. This microprogram is stored in a fast memory which needs only to be read-only for the basic microprograms of the processor, but must be non-volatile. Most microprocessors, if microprogrammed, have internal read-only control memory. See Chap. 13 for further details of microprogrammed processor designs.

In addition to the above applications, read-only memory is used particularly in microprocessor-based systems where the microprocessor is applied in dedicated applications such as in washing machines or cash dispensers. In these applications, the whole program can be kept in a read-only memory. Similarly, video terminals are usually microprocessor based. The microprocessor program controlling the operation of the terminal can be kept in read-only memories within the terminal. The dot-matrix pattern of each displayable character is kept in another read-only memory.

Locations in a read-only memory can still be accessed in any order at high speed, i.e. read-only memory is still random-access, though the term random-access is normally associated with memory capable of both reading and writing. If it is necessary to differentiate clearly between memory capable of both reading and writing, and read-only memory, the term *read–write memory* (RWM) can be used for the former. There are several classes of semiconductor read-only memory. We shall firstly consider the class of read-only memory called *fixed read-only memory* in which the information is incorporated during manufacture and cannot be altered subsequently.

9.4.2   Fixed read-only memory

The memory cell in a fixed read-only memory (ROM) can use bipolar transistors or diodes or MOS transistors. A memory using bipolar transistors or diodes is a bipolar memory. Both bipolar memory and MOS memory employ the same basic technique. The memory cells are arranged in a two-dimensional array with row select lines and column output lines in the X direction and Y direction respectively, as in the previous semiconductor memories except there is no data input. One row of memory cells is selected using a row select signal. If a 1 is to be stored in a memory cell, a direct connection is made between the row select line and a column digit output line in that memory cell. Therefore after selection is made, a signal will appear on the column output lines. If a 0 is to be stored, no direct connection is made between the row and column lines and no signal appears on the column line when the cell is selected. The configuration for a 0 and a 1 can, of course, be reversed.

Figure 9.12 shows a typical MOS fixed read-only memory. In this particular case, rather than make a direct connection physically, an electrical connection is made by manufacturing the cell transistor with a low threshold voltage. For no electrical connection, the transistor is manufactured with a high threshold voltage. Bipolar transistor fixed read-only memories are also available, which use actual links in series with diodes or transistors.

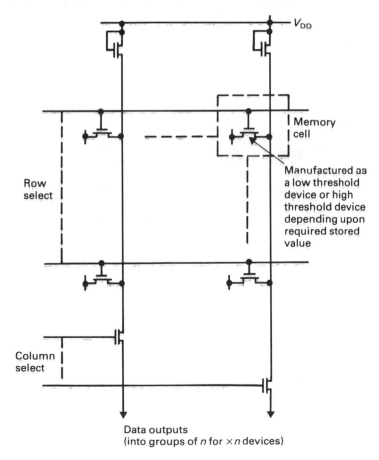

Figure 9.12   An MOS read-only memory array

9.4.3 Programmable read-only memory

In a *programmable read-only memory* (PROM), the connection is broken during a programming sequence. The devices can be supplied to the customer with all the connections left intact. The customer can then perform the programming sequence to blow selected fuses. A bipolar transistor programmable read-only memory is shown in Fig. 9.13. The connection between the row and column lines is made through a bipolar transistor and a semiconductor fuse. This fuse is blown intentionally in those cells which are to have a 0 stored, and left intact if a 1 is to be stored (assuming a 1 is represented by a direct connection and a 0 is represented by no connection). The fuse is composed of a material such as polysilicon. It is blown by selecting the cell and passing a relatively high current, perhaps 50mA, through the cell using the row and column lines. Special programmer units are available for this purpose. Programmable read-only memories of this type are always bipolar because of the high currents involved during programming. Programmable read-only memories which can be programmed by the customer are known as *field-programmable read-only memories*, FPROMs.

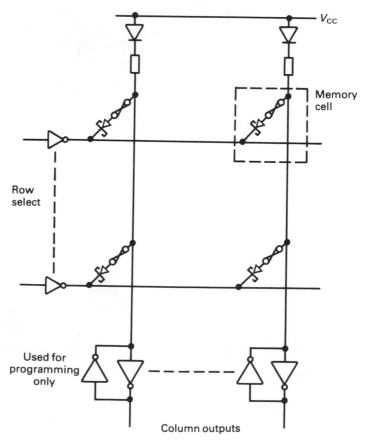

Figure 9.13   Schottky diode PROM array

9.4.4 Erasable programmable read-only memory

Erasable programmable read-only memories, EPROMs, are programmable read-only memories which have a mechanism for altering the stored information. There are several mechanisms that can be used. Often the mechanism is such that the memory cannot be used for high-speed writing and thus cannot be regarded as normal read–write memory. A very successful type of erasable programmable memory uses ultra-violet light shone on to the surface of the integrated circuit to erase the information and an electrical programming sequence to reprogram the memory with new information. This type of erasable programmable read-only memory is normally associated with the term EPROM, but may be differentiated from other types by the term U-V EPROM. The U-V EPROM has had an extremely significant effect on the development of microprocessor systems.

The original U-V EPROM was developed by Intel using PMOS technology and introduced in 1971. The memory cell consists of one enhancement mode MOS transistor with no connection made to the gate electrode. The gate is surrounded completely by a silicon dioxide insulating layer. In the natural unprogrammed state (in this case representing a logic 1), no conduction occurs between the source and drain of the device. In the programmed 0 state, charge is placed on the isolated gate and causes the transistor to conduct as the voltage on the gate is above the threshold voltage of the device.

To program the device, $-30\,\mathrm{V}$ is applied between the source and drain. This causes electrons to avalanche through the drain towards the source. The silicon dioxide layer between the gate electrode and the drain-source channel is made only about $1000\,\text{Å}$ thick. Electrons travel through this silicon dioxide layer on to the isolated gate, giving the gate electrode an electrical charge. The gate electrode is charged sufficiently to produce conduction between the drain and source. Then, the programming voltage can be removed. Because of the very good insulation properties of silicon dioxide, the charge on the gate leaks away very slowly and the conducting state will remain for a very long time. It is expected that at room temperature, the charge will keep the device in a recognized 0 state for decades. In manufactured devices, the condition is guaranteed for 10 years at $125\,^{\circ}\mathrm{C}$, and 70% of the charge expected is then to remain.

The charge can be removed by exposing the integrated circuit chip to ultra-violet light which gives the built-up charge sufficient energy to leak away. The package is provided with a transparent quartz lid so that the radiation from a U-V lamp can penetrate and reach the chip. For sufficient energy to be imparted to the electrons, the radiation needs to have a wavelength of less than $4000\,\text{Å}$, and typically a wavelength of $2537\,\text{Å}$ is used. The dosage required may be $15\,\mathrm{W\text{-}sec/cm^2}$ (U-V intensity $\times$ exposure time) which could be achieved with a $10{,}000\,\mathrm{\mu W/cm^2}$ rated lamp for 15 seconds. Selection of the memory device is performed using an additional MOS transistor in series with the device and driven by X AND Y select lines. For programming, appropriate programming voltages are applied to both X and Y lines for about $1\,\mathrm{ms}$. For reading, lower voltages are used.

Subsequent developments have taken place. The original PMOS devices have been replaced with NMOS devices (except for some CMOS EPROMs) and a more compact design developed. The separate MOS selection transistor can be combined with the storage device into a single structure as in the NMOS U-V EPROM design shown in Fig. 9.14. This memory cell consists of

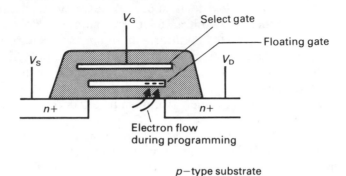

(a) Construction

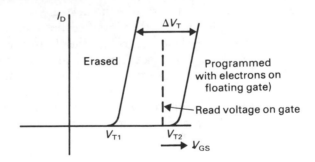

(b) Characteristic

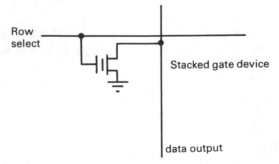

(c) Memory cell

Figure 9.14 Stacked-gate FAMOS memory cell

an MOS transistor with two gate electrodes, one stacked above the other. The row select signal connects to the upper electrode. The lower electrode is unconnected and totally electrically isolated by the silicon dioxide. The column output is taken from the drain of the MOS transistor. In the unprogrammed state, which is taken to represent a 1, the MOS transistor is conducting because the row select voltage is chosen to be greater than the natural threshold voltage of the MOS transistor. Programming a 0 into the memory cell involves charging the lower electrode negatively. This is achieved by applying a voltage of $+16\,$V on the drain of the transistor with respect to the source and $+26\,$V on the select electrode. The drain–source potential causes electrons to flow from the source to the drain. As electrons cross the channel between the source and drain, some acquire sufficient energy to pass through the silicon dioxide layer between the channel and the lower floating electrode, finally reaching the floating electrode. The process will slow down as more electrons land on the floating electrode and an equilibrium state is reached. (The voltages quoted are for 64K byte devices; larger 'scaled-down' devices have lower voltages.)

When the programming voltages are removed, the charge on the lower electrode will decay very slowly indeed, as before, because the insulating properties of silicon dioxide are extremely good and it takes many years for the charge to decay significantly. The effect of a charged lower electrode is to alter the threshold voltage of the overall MOS transistor by an amount given by:

$$\Delta V_{\mathrm{T}} = -\Delta Q_{\mathrm{FG}}/C$$

where ΔQ_{FG} is the added charge on the floating gate and C is the capacitance between the floating gate and the select gate [2]. The threshold voltage becomes larger than the row select voltage, and the transistor will not conduct when selected. The charge is removed by shining ultra-violet light on to the top of the exposed integrated circuit which gives the electrons on the floating gate sufficient energy to return to the channel of the memory cells. The charge will be removed in all the cells simultaneously. Special U-V EPROM programmer units and eraser units are manufactured. Typically, it takes 300 ns to program one word of the memory and 15–20 minutes to erase the whole contents. U-V EPROMS include the type 2716 2K $\times$ 8-bit EPROM, 2732 4K $\times$ 8-bit and 2764 8K $\times$ 8-bit. Such devices require a 21–25 V programming voltage (depending upon the device) to be applied during the programming sequence, though only a $+5\,$V supply is required during read-only operation.

Clearly the necessity of ultra-violet light to erase the memory prevents in-circuit reprogramming and may be inconvenient at times. This is eliminated in the *electrically erasable programmable read-only memories*, EEPROMs. One EEPROM design is a modification of the above U-V EPROM to allow electrons to tunnel through the silicon dioxide in both directions depending upon the applied voltages. Tunneling with reasonable voltages requires a very thin oxide layer (25 Å). The thin oxide layer can be placed directly underneath the two gate electrodes or, as shown in Fig. 9.15, with the electrodes extended to cover the drain, it can be placed above the drain. This structure is used in the Intel 2816 2K $\times$ 8-bit electrically erasable PROM [3].

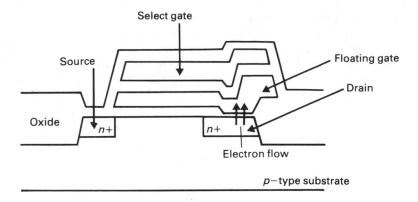

(a) Construction of FLOTOX device

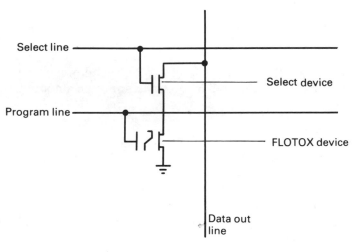

(b) Memory cell

Figure 9.15   Floating-gate tunnel oxide (FLOTOX) memory cell

REFERENCES

1. *Memory Applications Handbook*. Santa Clara, California: National Semiconductor Corp., 1978.
2. Woods, M. H., 'An E-PROM's Integrity Starts With its Cell Structure',*Electronics International*, 53, no. 18 (August 14, 1980).
3. Johnson, W.S., G.L. Kuhn, A.L. Renninger, and G. Perlegos, '16-K EE-PROM Relies on Tunneling for Byte-erasable Program Storage', *Electronics International*, 53, no. 5 (February 28, 1980).

PROBLEMS

9.1 A matrix of semiconductor memory cells has a $\times n$ organization with the same number of rows as columns. The memory stores 1024 words with each word having 16 bits. Draw a suitable memory layout giving the overall number of rows and columns, and the internal divisions.

9.2 The memory cells in a 16k $\times$ 1 bit static RAM consist of two cross-coupled MOS transistors and two resistive loads connected to 5 V. Determine the minimum resistance of the loads if the total power dissipation of the device is not to exceed ¼ watt. The voltage across an MOS transistor when conducting can be taken as 0 V. Internal circuits apart from the memory cells need not be considered.

9.3 The value of the storage capacitors of a dynamic memory device is 0.01 pF. Each digit line has a capacitance of 0.5 pF. The voltage on a capacitor is +4.5 V before it is selected. Determine the voltage after the cell is selected.

9.4 The refresh period of a dynamic cell is given by the empirical equation:

$$t_{\text{refresh}} = Ae^{-BT}$$

where T is the device junction temperature (°C)
   A is a constant
   $B = 0.05/°C$ (a constant)
The refresh period is to be 2 ms when the ambient temperature is 70 °C which creates a junction temperature of 100 °C in the device. Determine the necessary refresh period measured at an ambient temperature of 25 °C if this temperature creates a junction temperature of 27 °C in the device.

9.5 A 64K $\times$ 1 bit dynamic MOS RAM is organized internally as 256 row $\times$ 256 column matrix of memory cells. There is one sense amplifier per column. The cycle time (read, write or refresh) is 300 ns and the maximum period between refresh operations of one column is 2 ms. What is the percentage time that must be spent in the refresh activity? How much of this type of memory can be employed with a microprocessor that automatically produces one refresh cycle every 1.5 μs without using additional refresh circuitry?

10

Input/Output Circuits and Operation

10.1 GENERAL

We have described a microprocessor system as having three major parts, namely the microprocessor proper, the main program/data memory and the input/ output circuitry. In this chapter, we will consider the last of these, the input/ output circuitry together with methods of controlling this circuitry. The input/ output circuitry is necessary to interconnect the system to components outside the system, collectively called the peripherals of the system. In particular, the peripheral used by the user to communicate with the system is essential in all systems and must be connected. Usually in a computing application, the user communication peripheral is the video display terminal. There may be other peripherals in the system. For example, a printer is essential in most computing applications. Peripheral devices and circuits are necessary to connect the system to experimental equipment in laboratories or industrial equipment in industrial control applications.

In Chap. 7, section 7.4.6, we identified one method of transferring information between the input/output interface and the microprocessor called *programmed input/output*. In programmed input/output, input machine instructions are used to transfer data to processor registers (or possibly to memory locations) from an input interface, and output machine instructions are used to transfer the contents of processor registers (or possibly memory locations) to output devices. We also noted that it is often necessary to check that the input device has data ready before an input instruction to read the data is issued. Similarly, it is often necessary to check that an output interface can accept data before issuing an output instruction to send data to the output interface. These checks are done by examining particular bits of the *status register* of the interface, which indicate the readiness of the interface to supply or accept data. The process of checking the readiness of individual input/output interfaces is known as *polling*. Some very simple interfaces may always be ready, and hence will not need polling.

In this chapter, we will firstly describe some common interfaces, and then alternative methods to polling for transferring data between the processor or memory and the input/output interfaces.

10.2 INPUT/OUTPUT INTERFACES

10.2.1 Parallel interface

In a *parallel interface*, data is transmitted with one wire assigned to one bit of data. For 8-bit transfers, 8 data wires are provided between the parallel interface and the device. If data is transmitted to and from the device, 16 lines could be provided, 8 for transmission to the device and 8 for transmission from the device. A simple application of a parallel input interface would be to connect to switches such as shown in Fig. 10.1. A switch arm in one position would result in

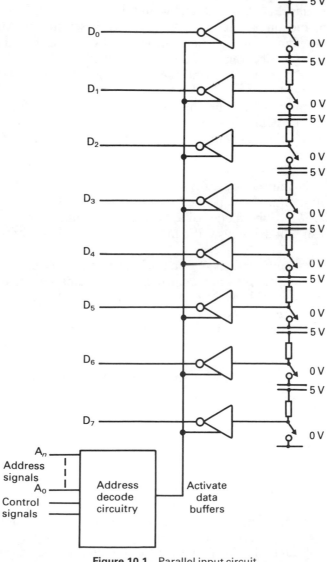

Figure 10.1   Parallel input circuit

a 1 being read and in the other position, a 0 being read. In the particular circuit shown, when a switch is closed, a 0 is generated at the input of the data buffers, and when a switch is open, the pull-up of resistor to +5 V causes a valid 1 to be generated. During the execution of an input instruction, the interface address together with the timing signals are generated in much the same way as in a memory read operation (in exactly the same way for memory mapped systems). The address and timing signals are recognized by the interface address decode circuit which causes the interface to place a binary word on the data bus. The bits of the word as set according to the state of the switches. The processor then accepts the data.

A simple application of a parallel output interface would be to drive indicator lamps. Each output line would drive one lamp. When the appropriate output instruction is executed, a binary word is sent to the interface. A 1 could specify the illumination of the lamp and a 0 could specify the lamp not to be illuminated (or vice versa). The scheme would necessitate a flip-flop to be associated with each lamp to maintain the specified state after the instruction has been completed.

An appropriate parallel output interface is shown in Fig. 10.2. The data of the output instruction is sent to the interface via the data bus together with the timing signals via the control bus, and the output address via the address bus. The address decode circuit responds to the address and the timing signals, and causes the data to be placed in the flip-flops that drive the indicator lamps. In Fig. 10.2, the indicators are light-emitting diodes and each diode is connected to the Q output of a flip-flop, such that when $Q = 1$ the diode will not emit light and when $Q = 0$ the diode will emit light. The input data is complemented by inverters so that a 1 sent to the interface causes a light-emitting diode to emit light.

The data output lines of a parallel output interface can be used to control a variety of components. For controlling a.c. mains-operated devices such as motors and solenoids, solid-state switches such as triacs and thyristors can be interfaced to the outputs of the interface. It is normal practice to switch on triacs and thyristors only when the a.c. mains is at zero volts to reduce radio-frequency interference to a minimum. A comparator can be used to detect the zero-crossing which occurs twice in every mains cycle. Composite solid state switches or solid state relays (SSRs) are manufactured incorporating zero-crossing detection circuitry in sealed modules for industrial applications. Sealed modules are also available for opto-isolated digital inputs, which provide electrical isolation between the logic inputs and the a.c. mains.

Commonly, parallel interfaces are designed using special LSI devices known as *parallel input/output* devices (PIOs) (or *peripheral interface adapters*, PIAs), which incorporate most of the necessary circuits to interface to a microprocessor except a full address decode circuit. Typically, two or three separate 8-bit parallel interfaces (*ports*) can be fabricated in one integrated circuit. Each port can be pre-programmed as input or output or bidirectional, or in some cases with individual lines as input or output. To effect this, the contents of internal control registers of the interface device are set to particular

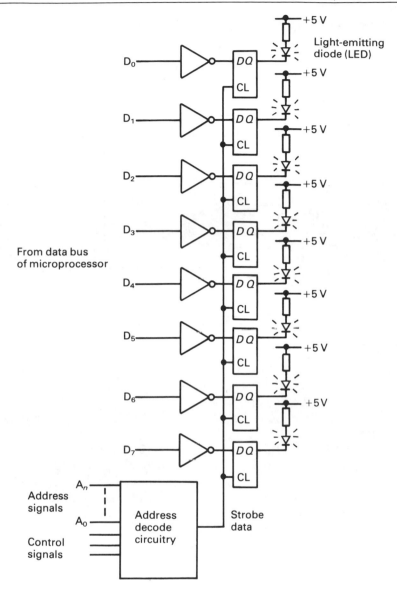

Figure 10.2 Parallel output circuit

values during a software initialization process prior to the port being used for data input and output.

Figure 10.3 shows a simplified implementation of one line of the interface to produce programmable input/output lines. The circuit would be repeated seven more times for a typical 8-bit input/output port. The control flip-flop, FF1, is used to set up the line as input or output as required prior to normal data transfer operations. For input (FF1 Q output = 1), the data from the peripheral device is loaded into a data input flip-flop, FF2, and enters the system bus via a

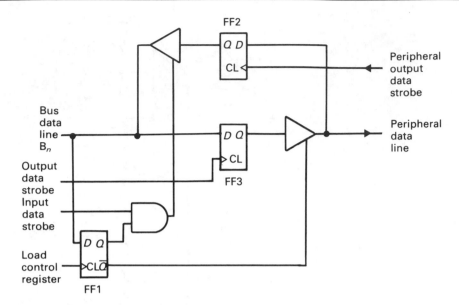

Figure 10.3   One data line of a parallel input/output device

tri-state buffer when enabled by an input data strobe. In some applications, the data input flip-flop is not used and the input data not held permanently within the port. For output (FF1 $\overline{Q} = 1$), data generated by an output machine instruction enters the port from the bus and is loaded into the data output flip-flop, FF3, using the output data strobe. The output to the peripheral device is via a buffer.

A typical LSI PIO device is the Z80-PIO [1] which consists of two 8-bit ports as shown in Fig. 10.4. Each port can be programmed for input, output, bidirectional or control, and has ready/strobe handshaking signals available. In the output mode, information can be sent to the selected port. The ready signal will be activated when the data is ready for the output device attached to the PIO. The output device accepts the data. If the device issues an acknowledgment on the strobe line, the ready signal is reset (and an interrupt request is generated as described in section 10.3 if interrupts are enabled). In the input mode, the processor performs a read operation which causes the ready signal to be activated. The input device attached to the port then may enter data to the PIO port and activate the strobe line to latch the data internally. The strobe will, as in the input mode, reset the ready signal (and generate an interrupt). Only port A may use the bidirectional mode as both A and B handshaking signals are used. In the bidirectional mode all the lines of port A can transfer data either into or out of the port using handshake signals. The A handshaking signals are used for output and the B handshaking signals are used for input. Data may only be output from the PIO to a peripheral device when the A strobe signal is inactive (i.e. when data is not being presented to the PIO from a peripheral device). Port B must be set in the control mode when port A is set in the bidirectional mode. In the control mode, individual lines of the port may be set up for input or for output but not both. The handshaking signals are not used.

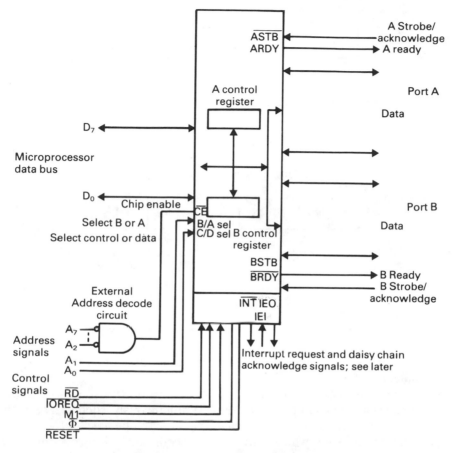

Figure 10.4   Two-port PIO (Z-80)

Each port of the PIO has two I/O addresses, one associated with the input/output data and one associated with control registers within the PIO as governed by two inputs *B/A Sel* (select port B or port A) and *C/D Sel* (select control or data). Typically C/D *Sel* would be driven by the least significant address bit from the processor, A_0, and B/A *Sel* would be driven by the next least significant bit, A_1. Other address bits would be used by the address decode circuitry which enables the chip generally. Prior to using the port of the PIO for data transfers, the operating mode must be selected by loading the control word shown in Fig. 10.5(a). This control word is differentiated from other control words by having the first four bits set to 1. A second control word shown in Fig. 10.5(b) must be sent if the control mode is selected, to define the lines for input and the lines for output. Other control words are sent to set up the interrupt mechanism (section 10.3) if used.

10.2.2 Serial interface

In a *serial interface*, information is transmitted along one wire. The information usually consists of more than one bit, and the bits are sent along the

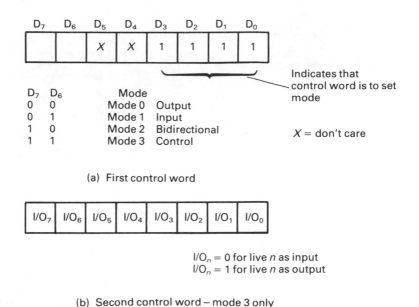

(a) First control word

I/O$_n$ = 0 for live n as input
I/O$_n$ = 1 for live n as output

(b) Second control word – mode 3 only

Figure 10.5   Z80–PIO control words to select operating mode

single wire one after the other, i.e. separated in time rather than in 'space' as in a parallel interface.

The term *full-duplex* is used to describe the transmission system where transmission occurs in both directions simultaneously, such as a serial transmission system with one line for each direction. The *half-duplex* describes the transmission system where transmission occurs in both directions but only one way at a time, as would be constrained by a single shared line. If transmission can be only in one direction the term *simplex* is used. Serial transmission particularly finds application for peripherals such as video terminals and printers connected locally or at some distance, and is also a widely used method of connecting computers in a network.

(a) Asynchronous serial transmission

The form of serial interface used for local connections to terminals and some printers is the *asynchronous* serial interface which transmits units of one binary character. A character consists of a fixed-size data word, usually between 5 bits and 8 bits, which is prefixed with a 0 level *start bit* and terminated with one 1 level *stop* bit. (One and one-half stop bits or two stop bits can also be used.) Multiple characters are sent in this format and any time may elapse between the end of one character and the beginning of the next character. The quiescent logic level is a 1. A single character to be sent to the peripheral device is first sent to the system interface usually by the execution of a programmed output instruction. The character is converted into the asynchronous serial format by the interface and then transmitted along one wire to the device (with a 0V return path provided by another wire). The interface within the device converts the serial format back to parallel form for internal use. A single character sent from the device is converted into asynchronous serial format by the device interface and transmitted along another wire to the system interface. The system interface converts the serial form back to parallel form which is usually read under programmed control.

From a programmer's point of view, it does not matter whether a parallel or serial interface is employed; it is just a means of transmitting the data between the device and the system. Clearly the parallel method should be faster than the serial method and for high-speed devices, a parallel interface may be mandatory.

The data bits are usually encoded in 7-bit ASCII code shown in Chap. 1, Table 1.4. A parity bit is attached, making an 8-bit word. The asynchronous serial transmission format for the transmission of the ASCII code for the letter R (1010010) with even parity and one stop bit is shown in Fig. 10.6. The least significant bit is sent after the start bit. Speeds of transmission may be typically 9600 bits/sec for video terminals which are usually connected to the system via an asynchronous serial interface. At 9600 bits/sec, 960 characters could be transmitted in one second, assuming one start bit, 8 data bits, one stop bit and no delay between character transmissions. One stop bit is widely used except for very slow mechanical devices and transmission rates (usually only for the obsolete printing terminal known as the Teletype operating at 110 bits/sec, i.e. 10 characters/sec with two stop bits). Sometimes the term *baud* is used to mean bits/sec. Strictly the baud rate is the number of pieces of information per second.

The electrical connection between the device and the serial interface usually conforms to a standard known as RS232C/V24. In this standard, a logic 1 is represented by a voltage greater than $+3\,V$ (typically between $+5\,V$ and $+15\,V$) and a logic 0 is represented by a voltage less than $-3\,V$ (typically between $-5\,V$ and $-15\,V$). By not having $0\,V$ to represent either level, an unconnected line can be differentiated from a connected line. The normal quiescent state with no information being transmitted is that of a logic 1. The RS232C standard

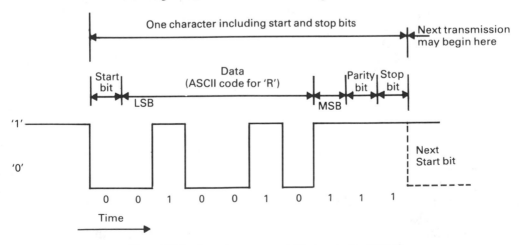

Figure 10.6   Asynchronous serial transmission format

not only specifies the voltages to be used but also connectors, allocation of pins on connectors and definition of signals. This enables all RS232C asynchronous serial interfaces to be compatible and peripherals with RS232C interfaces to be interchangeable electrically. Table 10.1 lists the signals and the pins numbers on the RS232C 25-way connector [2]. On simple systems, only pins 2, 3 and 7 are used for transmitted data, received data and the earth return respectively.

Table 10.1 RS 232C signals

Contact	Description	Contact	Description
1	Protective earth	14	Secondary transmitted data
2	Transmitted data	15	Transmitter signal element timing
3	Received data	16	Secondary received data
4	Request to send (RTS)	17	Received signal element timing
5	Clear to send (CTS)	18	Unassigned
6	Data set ready	19	Secondary RTS
7	Signal earth	20	Data terminal ready
8	Received line signal detector (RLSD)	21	Signal quality detector
9	Unassigned	22	Ring indicator
10	Unassigned	23	Data signaling-rake selector
11	Unassigned	24	External transmitter clock
12	Secondary RLSD	25	Unassigned
13	Secondary CTS		

Special integrated circuit parts known as *universal asynchronous receiver/ transmitters* (UARTs) are available to convert the parallel data as would be handled by the processor and memories to serial data in the described asynchronous format, and vice versa. These parts can be considered as having two internal sections, a transmitter to convert parallel data presented to it into asynchronous serial data, and a receiver to accept asynchronous serial data and convert this to parallel data. The transmitter inserts the start, stop and parity bits prior to transmission and the receiver checks the format and parity of the received data. The transmitter and receiver can operate simultaneously. UARTs are available to suit particular microprocessors. (These parts are also known as *asynchronous communications interface adapters*, ACIAs or *asynchronous communications elements*, ACEs). The serial output of a UART is converted from TTL levels to RS232C levels using an RS232C driver, and an RS232C receiver is used to convert RS232C levels to TTL levels for the UART.

In a UART designed for microprocessor applications, options for number of stop bits (1, 1½ or 2), odd, even or no parity and size of the data word are set by loading internal registers of the UART under program control. The transmitting and receiving data rates are governed either by an external oscillator or internal oscillator, operating at some multiple of the data rate. Frequently, the data rate can be modified under program control. An internal status register is provided which can be read under program control. The contents of the status register indicate the readiness to transmit and receive data and any errors.

A dual asynchronous receiver/transmitter (DART) part is available in the Z-80 family, consisting of two independent receiver/transmitters, (port A and port B) shown in Fig. 10.7. One port of the DART might be used for a user

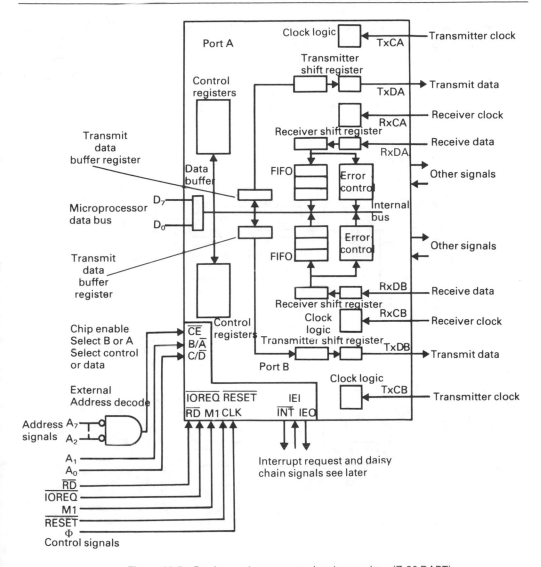

Figure 10.7 Dual asynchronous receiver/transmitter (Z-80 DART)

terminal, and the other port might be used for a printer (if connected via an asynchronous serial method). The receiver section of each port incorporates a three-stage first-in first-out buffer in addition to a holding buffer, which allows up to four characters to be received in succession and stored awaiting the processor to read the first character. As with the Z80-PIO, control registers must be set up prior to using a port for data transfers. The address decode is similar to that of the PIO, having B/A port select and C/D (control/data) select inputs.

Each port of the device has three read registers RR0, RR1 and RR2, which may be read to give status and other information. There are five write registers WR0, WR1, WR2, WR3, and WR4, which can be loaded to set up the port. The partial assignment of bits in RR0, RR1, WR0, WR3, WR4 and WR5 relevant to using programmed input/output with *polling* are shown in Fig. 10.8. Other bits in these registers and the other registers are concerned with the interrupt mechanism (section 10.3) in particular. The same external control address is given for all registers. To read the contents of a read register other than RR0, a write operation must precede the read operation to load the first three bits of WR0 selecting the read register. To write to any of the write registers other than

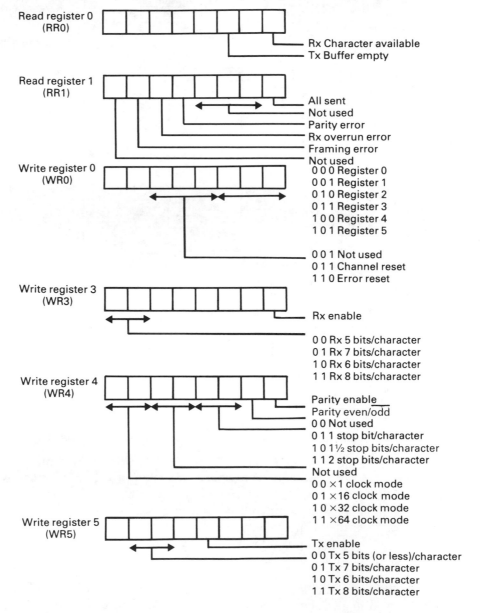

Figure 10.8   Some Z-80 DART read and write registers (simplified)

WR0, two bytes must be sent. The first three bits of the first byte select the WR register. The second byte sent is loaded into the selected WR register. To write to WR0 only requires one byte, with the first three bits $(D_2D_1D_0)$ set to 000 and the other bits set according to the WR0 operation required. (It is not possible to select another register and perform a channel reset by setting $D_5D_4D_3 = 011$ as channel reset automatically initializes $D_2D_1D_0$ to 000.)

The Rx character available bit in RR0 is set when at least one character is available in the receive buffers. The Tx buffer empty bit is set when the transmit buffer is empty. The first bit in RR1 is set when all characters have passed completely through the transmitter. The other bits in RR1 give receiver error conditions. The bits shown in WR3 and WR5 allow 5, 6, 7 of 8 data bits to be selected in the receive format and the transmit format independently. An external clock source is necessary set to $1 \times$ bit rate, $16 \times$ bit rate, $32 \times$ bit rate or $64 \times$ bit rate (with the most significant bit and the next most significant bit of WR4 set appropriately). The reader is referred to [3] for further information on the DART.

General-purpose UART parts exist for microprocessor and non-microprocessor applications. The data format of the general-purpose UART is not set under program control but by applying the appropriate logic levels to inputs of the UART. A general-purpose UART is shown in Fig. 10.9. In this UART, there are three strobe inputs, one to read data from the UART, one to write data to the UART, and one to enable separate three-state status outputs. The status outputs form a status word and can be connected directly to the data bus. The external address decode circuitry generates each of the three strobe signals when the corresponding machine instruction is executed. The data format can be altered by using switches as shown. The particular advantage of the general-purpose UART is that the switches provide a convenient manual means of selecting the data format.

(b) Synchronous serial interface

In *synchronous serial transmission*, a block of characters is transmitted one bit at a time without start or stop bits. This technique is used when the time of transmission is important as it does not carry the overhead of two or three non-data bits on each character and consequently is 20% or 27% (2/10 or 3/11) quicker for the same bit rate. The actual rate that data is sent is reduced slightly because it is necessary to insert extra 'synchronization' characters in the transmission for the receiving circuitry to accept the data correctly. Various formats are possible. One is to insert three 'sync' characters at the beginning and at the end of the transmission and periodically between data characters during the transmission. Naturally, these 'sync' characters must not be valid data characters otherwise they would be mistaken for data. In ASCII transmissions, the control code 0010110 (SYN) can be used.

As with asynchronous serial transmission, there are LSI parts for implementing synchronous serial interfaces, which are known as *universal synchronous/ asynchronous receiver and transmitters*, USARTs. As the name suggests, such parts can be programmed for either synchronous or asynchronous transmission.

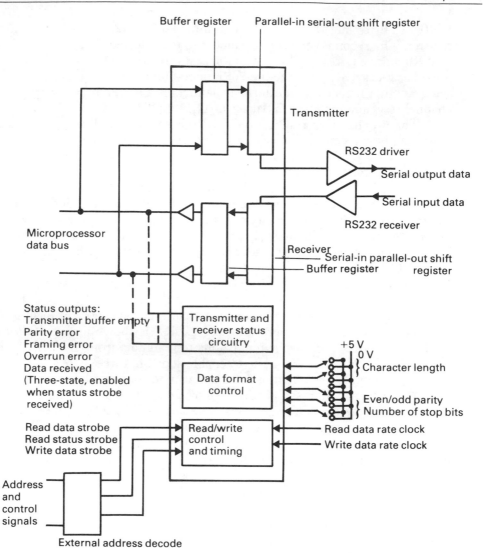

Figure 10.9   General-purpose UART

Microprocessor parts may be called *serial input/output* parts, SIOs (cf. PIOs) or *programmable communications interface* parts.

10.2.3 Analog interface

Digitally represented quantities can vary only in discrete steps, i.e. the smallest difference between two values is given by the least significant bit. Although microprocessor systems, as all computer systems, are inherently digital and operate on digital quantities, there are instances when inputs and outputs are not digital in nature, but are totally variable quantities such as continuously variable voltages. Such quantities are known as *analog* quantities.

For every digital number, there must be a corresponding nominal voltage (assuming the analog quantity is a voltage). If the binary number is an unsigned binary number with n digits, the range of numbers is from 0 to $2^n - 1$. Each of the distinct numbers is equivalent to one analog voltage. The number 0 will correspond to the minimum voltage, usually $0V$, and the maximum number, $2^n - 1$, will correspond to the maximum voltage, and there are 2^n increments.

If the binary number is a signed number using the 2's complement representation, generally negative and positive numbers correspond to negative and positive voltages respectively. The maximum negative number that can be represented in binary is -2^{n-1} which would generally correspond to maximum negative voltage. The maximum positive voltage corresponds to the maximum positive number $2^{n-1}-1$. Again there are 2^n increments. Notice that the maximum negative number is one greater in magnitude that the maximum positive number.

An *analog output interface* is one which generates analog quantities, usually voltages, which are proportional to the digital numbers transferred to the interface. Applications for such interfaces include connections to variable speed motors, variable position valves for computer control of industrial plant. An *analog input interface* is one which accepts analog quantities, again usually voltages, and converts these to proportional digital values which can be transferred to the system by program control or otherwise. Applications for such interfaces include connection to measuring equipment.

The circuit to translate a digital quantity to its equivalent voltage or current is known as a *digital-to-analog converter (D/A converter or DAC)*, and the circuit for the reverse process of translating a voltage or current to the equivalent digital quantity is known as an *analog-to-digital converter (A/D converter or ADC)*. The electrical methods of achieving D/A conversion are not considered here; the reader is referred to texts on electronic circuits for details. The most common method of A/D conversion in microprocessor systems is the *successive approximation method*.

Notice that because the analog voltage of an input can take on any value within the allowable range, this range must be divided into subranges one for each binary value. All the voltages within each subrange will convert to the same binary value. Typically each subrange extends from ½ LSB (least significant bit) below the nominal value to ½ LSB above the nominal value. A generated analog output will nominally be the exact equivalent of the binary input. In practice, some variation is present and allowable but not to extend beyond ±½ LSB.

The outputs of the A/D converter are presented to the system data bus in parallel form via a parallel input interface, and the system data bus is presented to a D/A converter via a parallel output interface as shown in Fig. 10.10. Programmed input/output is commonly used to transfer data to a D/A converter and from an A/D converter. D/A conversion to produce an analog signal typically requires 1 to $10\,\mu s$ depending upon the *settling time* of the converter. A/D conversion usually takes longer than D/A conversion. After an output

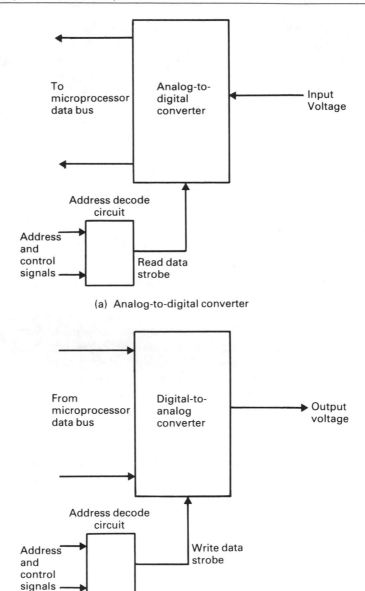

(a) Analog-to-digital converter

(b) Digital-to-analog converter

Figure 10.10   Analog/digital and digital/analog converters

instruction is issued to a D/A interface, there will be some time before the required voltage is generated, and similarly when an input instruction is issued to an A/D interface, there will be some time before the digital result is available. These factors are usually accomodated in a programmed input/output environment by the use of a status register whose contents hold single-bit flags indicating when the conversion is complete.

The number of bits in a converter is chosen to provide the required accuracy. Integrated circuit D/A and A/D converters are readily available with 8, 10 and 12 bits. An 8-bit converter would suit an 8-bit microprocessor system if the converter is of sufficient accuracy (say $\pm \frac{1}{2}$ LSB or $\pm 0.2\%$). Converters can be designed with 14 and even 16 bits, but with increasing numbers of bits, increment in voltage steps become smaller and become difficult to distinguish from unwanted electrical noise in the system. For an 8-bit system, the data would need to be transferred in two parts for converters having 9 to 16 bits. Generally, the conversion becomes slower as more bits are provided in the converter.

In the above, we have assumed that the analog input has remained constant while the conversion is taking place. If the input varies, the conversion may not be performed correctly. Often, there is a maximum rate of change of the input signal for the converter to function correctly, and hence the corresponding maximum input frequency can be calculated (see Problem 10.8). To convert higher-frequency signals, an additional circuit known as a *sample and hold circuit* is inserted before the A/D converter. The sample and hold circuit accepts the analog input signal under program control and subsequently holds the signal constant at the output of the circuit for a period required to perform the conversion.

Finally, to prevent loss of information in the sampling process, it is necessary to perform the sampling at a frequency at least twice the greatest frequency within the sampled signal (Shannon's sampling theorem). Generally, a low pass filter is inserted to attenuate frequencies above those of interest and then the signal is sampled at greater than twice the maximum frequency of interest.

10.3 INTERRUPTS

10.3.1 Mechanism

We have described the programmed input/output approach as one involving the use of machine instructions to cause data transfer between processor registers (or memory) and input/output devices, and one which usually necessitates a status check before the transfer. We have shown the status check in a loop of instructions which are continuously repeated while waiting for the device to become ready. If we wished to execute another program while waiting for the device to become ready, we could insert status check instructions at various places in the program and at a sufficeint frequency to ensure no new input data is lost (if transferring data from an input device) or the required output rate is achieved (if transferring data to an output device).

An alternative method is the *interrupt mechanism*, so called because the device or input/output circuit interrupts the normal program execution when it is ready, rather than waiting to be serviced. This interruption is done using special signals between the processor and the input/output interface. The two basic signals necessary to implement an interrupt scheme are shown in Fig. 10.11(a), namely an *interrupt request* signal from the interrupting device to the processor and an *interrupt acknowledge* signal from the processor to the device. The interrupt request signal is generated by the device interface when it is ready either to receive data or to part with new data. The interrupt acknowledge signal is generated by the processor when it is willing to respond to the interrupt.

For example, if the interrupt mechanism is used in a keyboard interface, when a key is pressed, input data is produced and transmitted to the interface. Subsequently, the data is ready to be accepted by the processor. An interrupt request signal is generated by the interface and sent to the processor. The processor will accept an interrupt usually at the end of the execution of the current instruction and will then act in a prescribed manner. (The precise time

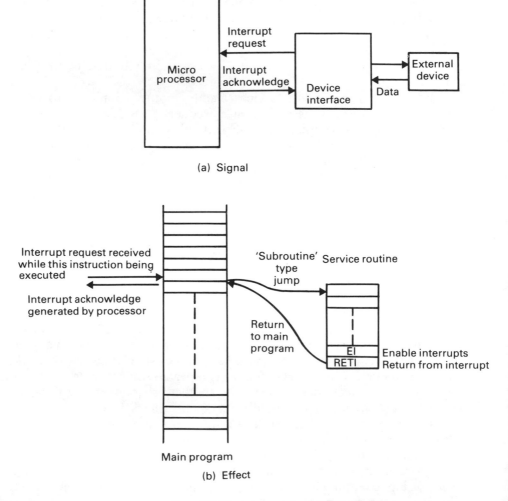

(a) Signal

(b) Effect

Figure 10.11   Interrupt mechanism

that the interrupt acknowledge is issued and the moment the processor will act in other ways depends upon the processor.)

The basic action that must take place once the interrupt has been accepted by the processor is to provide a mechanism to cause the execution of a routine performing relevant actions associated with the interrupting device. Typically, the routine will transfer data to or from the interrupting device and is known as a *service routine* as it services the interrupt device. In all case, when the processor accepts the interrupt request, it automatically stores the address of the instruction it would have next executed (the *return address*) on the stack and then executes the service routine. After the service routine has been executed, control is returned to the program being executed before the interrupt occurred by the use of an *interrupt return* instruction, sited at the end of the service routine in Fig. 10.11(b). The return-from-interrupt instruction (RETI in the Z-80) retrieves the return address from the stack for the jump back to the main program.

The process can be compared to a subroutine call, except the jump is caused by an asynchronous hardware event. In the scheme shown, interrupts are automatically disabled immediately an interrupt is received, and must be enabled as required by a machine instruction (given in Fig. 10.11 as the Z-80 enable interrupt instruction, EI). The interrupt enable instruction only takes effect after the next instruction, which allows it to be placed before the return instruction. As with a subroutine call, interrupts can cause nested routines to be executed which would occur should interrupts be enabled during the body of the service program and further interrupts occur before the return to the main program.

The interrupt mechanism is particularly suitable if the input/output device or circuitry external to the processor is ready at a time which is indeterminate and not synchronized with the processor. It would usually be at a time that the processor is performing other duties. The interrupt scheme is also especially suitable in a multi-programming environment (one which interleaves the execution of several logically separate programs). Though the interrupt scheme is described for external devices, it can be used for internal hardware conditions of the processor, for example, a particular arithmetic overflow condition.

10.3.2 Finding the interrupt service routine

The interrupt acknowledge sequence is generally accompanied by one of several additional mechanisms which cause the processor to perform a specified interrupt service routine. A simple mechanism is one which creates an unconditional jump to a known memory location. The jump address may be fixed by the design of the processor. Several interrupt request inputs may be provided for more than one device, each with a different jump address.

A more flexible mechanism is the *vectored interrupt mechanism*. Here the address of the service routine (the jump address) is provided to the processor in some manner. It can be done by using a defined memory location to hold the service routine address (i.e. memory indirect addressing).

In another vector method, the device itself provides the service routine address (vector) along the data lines when requested by the processor. The implementation of this interrupt scheme could use three-state gates at the device interface with the processor bus reading the data lines. The inputs of the gates can be connected permanently to a logic 1 or logic 0 according to the required vector address, as shown in Fig. 10.12. The outputs are brought out of high impedance into two-state by the interrupt acknowledge signal together with the device request being active. Then the data is read automatically by the processor. (Multiple interrupting devices require additional circuitry and signals to identify the jump address; see section 10.3.3.)

In an 8-bit data bus system using the data bus to transmit the vector, the service address would be limited to the first 256 locations. Additional jump instructions can be placed here. As such instructions are multi-byte instructions, the number of usable service addresses would be reduced. To avoid this problem, the 8-bit address can be multiplied by, say, four (i.e. two extra least significant 0's are added) by the processor before being used as the service address. The scheme can be further refined by concatenating the address sent by the device with the contents of a processor register before being used (as used by the Z-80; see section 10.3.4). Rather than sending the interrupt service address, other information could be sent, for example the input/output address of the device. In one microprocessor system (Intel 8080), a machine instruction is sent and interpreted as such by the processor.

Finally, the processor can be designed to use the vector sent by the device to identify a memory location which holds the start address of the service routine (for example the 68000; see section 10.3.4). Upon receipt of the vector, the address is fetched from memory and a jump operation to the service routine occurs automatically.

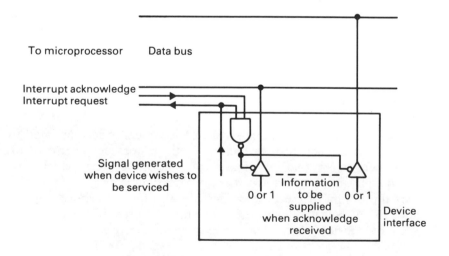

Figure 10.12   Device-supplied interrupt information scheme

10.3.3 Multiple interrupting devices

If more than one interrupt device is to be connected to the system, an interrupt request line can be provided by the processor for each device (but see later). It is possible for two or more devices to request service simultaneously, or a second and subsequent devices to request service while the first is being serviced. These situations can usually be accommodated in the hardware after assigning a particular level of priority to each device. Each device is given a *priority number*. Frequently, the lower the priority number, the higher the priority of the device. The interrupt device with the lowest priority number (highest priority) is accepted first. Those interrupts with the same priority will be accepted according to the time they are received. Actual simultaneous requests are resolved by the hardware, which makes a choice. Once a device interrupt is accepted, all other device interrupts at the same or lower priority that may occur are ignored by the processor automatically resetting a processor interrupt enable flag, unless subsequently altered by the programmer. There are various ways that the priority can be established.

(a) Polled interrupts

The *polled interrupt* method is perhaps the simplest method of handling multiple devices with different or the same priority. In the polled method, a single interrupt request is generated from the group of possible interrupting devices by, say, a single wired-OR (open-collector) interrupt request signal. The acknowledge sequence involves interrogating each device in turn by programmed instructions to determine whether the device has an interrupt request outstanding. One possible hardware implementation of this method is to provide one addressable interrupt request flag in each device interface capable of an interrupt request. Each flag is set if an interrupt is requested. The flags are read under program control in priority order, the highest-priority device first. The process of reading a flag resets it. An alternative scheme is to have a centralized interrupt request register with bits set in this register if the appropriate interrupts are requested. The least significant bit could be assigned the lowest priority request and the most significant bit the highest priority request. A program sequence can identify the interrupt request and its priority.

(b) Daisy chaining interrupt signals

An interrupt request/acknowledge pair of signals can be used with more than one device by using a *daisy chain* method. In the daisy chain method, one of the signals is passed through all the devices in a sequence dictated by the priority of the devices. A system of a daisy-chained acknowledge signal and a common wired-OR request signal is shown in Fig. 10.13. The highest-priority device is closest to the processor and the lowest-priority device is farthest away. When a request is generated by a device, the request is received by the processor directly. The processor generates an acknowledge signal which is sent to the first device on the daisy chain. This device, if not the interrupting device, passes the acknowledge signal on to the next device. The process continues until the device causing the interrupt is reached. This device prevents the signal passing any

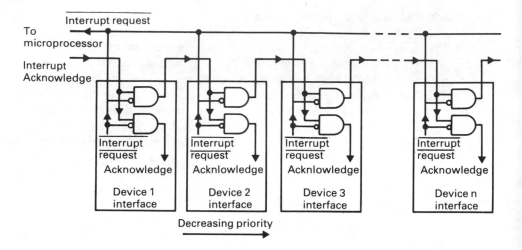

Figure 10.13 Interrupt priority scheme using daisy-chained interrupt acknowledge signals

further and responds accordingly. If more than one device generates an interrupt signal, the highest-priority device obtains the acknowledge signal first and is selected. After this device has been serviced, the next device receives the acknowledge signal and is serviced. The device-supplied vector scheme can be used to cause the correct service routine to be selected in each case.

The system with a daisy-chained request signal and a common acknowledge signal has the lowest-priority device closest to the processor and the highest priority device farthest away. When a device makes a request, the request is passed along the daisy chain and reaches the processor. The processor issues an acknowledge signal which is received by all devices. The highest-priority device making a request has an inactive request daisy chain input (say a logic 0) and an active daisy chain request output (say a logic 1). This condition causes the device to respond to the acknowledge signal. Lower-priority devices issuing requests will have both daisy chain request input and output lines active (a logic 1), which inhibits the requesting device from responding to the acknowledge.

(c) Interrupt mask register

Added flexibility and speed can be incorporated into priority schemes by selectively enabling certain usually higher-priority devices immediately after a request has been accepted. This is often done by using an interrupt mask register arranged as shown in Fig. 10.14. The interrupt requests accepted are those with the corresponding mask register bit set. This scheme is an extension of a single interrupt enable flag mentioned previously which causes all interrupts to be accepted.

(d) Interrupt controllers

An interrupt controller is a device for handling multiple interrupts outside the processor. A typical device can support up to eight randomly occurring

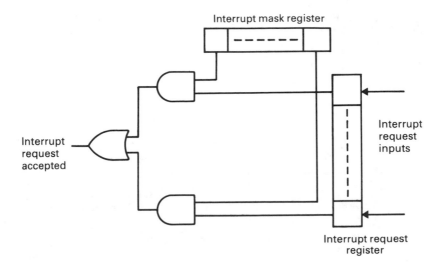

Figure 10.14　Interrupt scheme using an interrupt mask register

interrupts, and devices can be cascaded to provide more inputs. Devices normally have the ability to set priority levels for inputs and various programmable options are provided, including programmable interrupt vectors. Apart from assigning a fixed priority to inputs, interrupt controllers have the ability to assign *rotating priority*, as shown in Fig. 10.15. With rotating priority, the inputs can be considered as forming a ring. When an interrupt is received and acknowledged, the input immediately assumes the lowest priority, and those following it in the ring assume linearly increasingly higher priority with the highest priority assigned to the input immediately behind the current one. When another request is received, the same procedure is taken with this input assigned the lowest priority, and all other inputs reassigned. This scheme prevents any one input from taking a permanent or dominant portion of the available time and all inputs have a chance of being serviced. The maximum time that any one input request need wait is that given by seven other service cycles if there are eight inputs. Rotating priority is also used in multiple bus master schemes; see Chap. 15, section 15.2.3.

Interrupt inputs can generally be one of two types, *level triggered* or *edge triggered*. With level-triggered inputs, the presence of a logic state, say a 1, causes an interrupt request to be generated and the request will remain as long as the input is activated. Consequently, if after the first interrupt acknowledge cycle is complete and the input is still activated, a second request is generated. This will continue until the input is deactivated, which may or may not be a desirable feature depending upon the application. For example, repetitive interrupts could be used to continually re-execute a service routine until the interrupt is released. It also allows for wired-OR interrupt requests. In edge-triggering, interrupts are activated by a logic transition, say a 1 to a 0 transition, and cannot be reactivated until the input returns to a 1 and another transition to a 0 occurs.

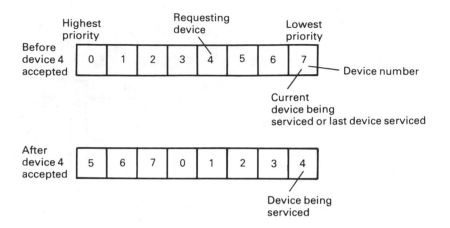

Figure 10.15 Rotating priority

10.3.4 Examples of interrupt schemes

In this section we will review the interrupt schemes in the Z-80 and 68000 processors.

(a) Z-80 interrupt schemes

The Z-80 has two interrupt inputs, $\overline{\text{INT}}$ and $\overline{\text{NMI}}$. $\overline{\text{INT}}$ can be masked. The non-maskable interrupt, $\overline{\text{NMI}}$, cannot be disenabled and will always generate an interrupt if activated. In all cases, the return address is stored on the stack. Interrupt acknowledgment is indicated by both of the processor signals $\overline{\text{M1}}$ and $\overline{\text{IORQ}}$ both being low (0), a condition that does not occur otherwise. A separate interrupt acknowledge signal is not generated.

The non-maskable interrupt input is negative edge triggered and a 1 to 0 transition on the input causes an internal flip-flop to be set. This flip-flop is examined by the processor near the end of the execution of each instruction. If the flip-flop is set, i.e. an interrupt has been requested, an unconditional jump to memory location 66 is executed. The non-maskable interrupt service routine should be stored starting at this location. The non-maskable interrupt would typically be used for very important events such as impending loss of power.

The maskable interrupt is level triggered. A 0 level on the interrupt line ($\overline{\text{INT}}$) indicates an interrupt request, and the processor examines the maskable interrupt line near the end of the execution of each instruction. (Actually, the line is examined on the rising edge of the last clock cycle of the instruction and at the same time the non-maskable interrupt flip-flop is examined.) The processor can engage one of three modes of operation for the maskable interrupt request. The first mode, mode 0, emulates the 8080 interrupt mechanism, by executing a machine instruction placed on the data bus by the interrupting device. The second mode, mode 1, causes an unconditional jump to memory location 38. In mode 2, the vectored interrupt mode, the device supplies a 7-bit vector along the data bus during the acknowledge sequence. The eighth (least significant) bit is assumed to be a 0. The eight bits are concatenated with the contents of an 8-bit internal interrupt register I (holding the most significant eight bits) to form a 16-bit address. The memory location with this address is taken to hold the lower eight bits of the service routine address and the next location the upper eight bits of the service address.

On power-up, mode 0 is selected. Any mode can be selected by executing special machine instructions, one for each mode (instructions IM0, IM1 and IM2 respectively). Maskable interrupts can be disabled with the instruction DI and enabled with the instruction EI. There are two interrupt return instructions, the return from interrupt instruction, RETI, and the return from non-maskable interrupt, RETN.

Z-80 input/output devices, in particular the Z-80 PIO device, the Z-80 CTC (counter timer circuit), and the Z-80 SIO (serial I/O controller), incorporate interrupt capability using a daisy chain method in which an interrupt enable signal is daisy chained and both the request and acknowledge signals are common signals as shown in Fig. 10.16. Devices make requests using the common request line and at the same time set their enable out line, IEO, to a 0, disenabling lower-priority devices. An acknowledgment is generated after a suitable time for the daisy chain signals to settle. During this time, requests cannot be made ($\overline{\text{M1}}$ is set low, which is used to inhibit requests). Acknowledgment is indicated by both $\overline{\text{M1}}$ and $\overline{\text{IORQ}}$ low. The highest-priority requesting device has its enable input active which allows the device to respond to the acknowledgment. The device response will be to send a vector along the data bus as part of the mode 2 interrupt mechanism.

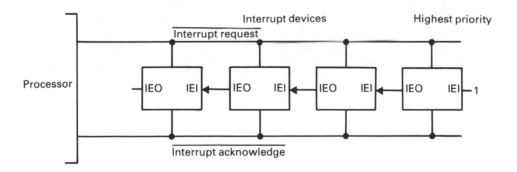

Figure 10.16   Interrupt scheme with daisy-chained interrupt enable

(b) 68000 interrupt scheme

The 68000 interrupt mechanism is part of a larger internal/external interrupt mechanism called *exception processing* by Motorola [4]. An *exception* may be due to:

(i) A reset signal applied to the processor
(ii) An external interrupt applied to interrupt inputs of the processor

(iii) An abnormal condition occurring during the execution of an instruction or the execution of an instruction to detect an abnormal condition (both classified as an *instruction trap*)

(iv) The occurrence of an unimplemented instruction (binary patterns not used as instructions)

(v) Privilege violation, i.e. the attempted execution of a privileged instruction while in the user state

(vi) The trace mode selected which causes an exception after the execution of every instruction

(vii) Bus error detected by external logic which informs the processor via the $\overline{BERR}$ processor input

When an exception occurs, an 8-bit *vector number* is generated. For an interrupt, the vector number is supplied by the interrupting device. The vector number is multiplied by four, which is then considered as a byte memory address, and identifies the first byte of a pair of 16-bit memory locations holding an *exception vector* (an address). The first vector, 0, is the reset vector which is assigned to initialize the system stack pointer and program counter to the addresses stored in the memory locations. Hence, four 16-bit locations are used for this vector number.

The 68000 has three interrupt request inputs, $\overline{IPL0}$, $\overline{IPL1}$ and $\overline{IPL2}$. These are not used as individual interrupt lines but are used to present to the processor a binary number which identifies the interrupting device, from 1 to 7, 0 indicating no interrupt. Hence, additional logic is necessary to produce this number from the individual request signals of the devices. The logic must also resolve any multiple requests. A TTL priority encoder part is available to perform the whole function, producing a binary number corresponding to the priority of the highest-priority request. The encoder connects to the processor as shown in Fig. 10.17. The actual request/acknowledge signals may be daisy-chained. The number presented is compared by the processor with a number

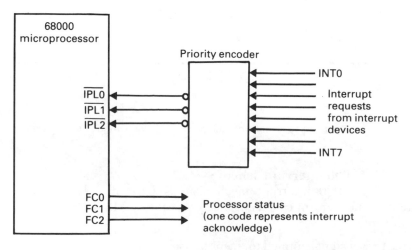

Figure 10.17   68000 interrupt request and acknowledge signals

stored in an internal interrupt mask register. If the request number is equal to or less than that stored in the interrupt mask register, the interrupt is ignored. If it is greater, an interrupt acknowledge sequence is generated at the end of the current instruction (except level 7 which always produces an interrupt).

First the current contents of the processor status register (which include the condition codes and the interrupt mask register) are saved in a non-addressable internal register. Then the processor leaves the user state and enters the supervisor state. The trace facility which is provided for test purposes is disabled. The interrupt level of the interrupting device is loaded into the interrupt mask register. Interrupt acknowledge is indicated by the binary code 111 on three function code outputs of the processor labeled FC0, FC1 and FC2. The function code outputs are used for several purposes in addition to interrupt acknowledge to indicate one of various processor states. The interrupt number is copied on to the lower address, A1, A2 and A3. The address strobe, $\overline{AS}$ is set to a 0, the lower data strobe, $\overline{LDS}$, is set to a 0 and R/$\overline{W}$ is set for read (1). (The upper data strobe $\overline{UDS}$ is also set to 0.)

The interrupt acknowledge sequence causes the device to place a vector number onto the data lines D0 to D7 and to assert the data transfer acknowledge signal ($\overline{DTACK}$ = 0). The processor accepts the vector and de-asserts the address and data strobe signals. This is recognized by the device which then de-asserts $\overline{DTACK}$.

The current contents of the program counter and the status register are loaded on to the supervisor stack. Then the processor starts the interrupt service routine as defined by the vector number. As mentioned, the 8-bit vector number is multiplied by four to identify the memory location holding the exception vector, which in this case is the start address of the interrupt service routine. Some vector numbers are also assigned for other types of exceptions, but could be also used for interrupts, if desired.

The 68000 is provided with three control lines for interfacing to the 8-bit 6800 microprocessor peripherals, and will generate a vector number itself rather than take an external vector number if one of the control lines (VPA) is asserted. Motorola call this mechanism the *autovector operation*. The autovector numbers are 25 to 31 corresponding to interrupt levels 1 to 7 respectively. Vector number 24 is used if a bus error occurs.

10.4 DIRECT MEMORY ACCESS (DMA)

10.4.1 Mechanism

In programmed input/output, the processor initiates the data transfer to or from the input/output device, and takes full control of the transfer. There are two major disadvantages with this approach. Firstly, the processor cannot generally do any other meaningful processing while the data transfer is taking place. Secondly, the speed of transfer is limited by the speed of executing machine instructions. For multiple transfers, several machine instructions normally need to be executed between each data transfer to load the data into memory if input, or to read data from memory if output. These disadvantages can be overcome by the direct memory access (DMA) mechanism. The DMA mechanism uses additional hardware to take full control of the multiple transfers after initial activation by the processor.

The general scheme is shown in Fig. 10.18. A part known as a *DMA controller* is instructed by the processor to transfer a consecutive sequence of memory locations to the input/output device or vice versa. Once so instructed, the DMA controller uses the microprocessor bus to transfer data at a rate dictated by the input/output device without any further control from the processor. The mechanism requires that before the transfer command is received by the DMA controller, the controller is given the address of the starting location in memory (and possibly in the input/output device) and the number of transfers. This is done by loading internal registers of the controller, usually under program control. Once loaded, the DMA controller is allowed to take over the bus and inititiate the first and subsequent data transfers. After the first transfer has taken place, the DMA controller increments the stored address(es) and the next transfer is initiated. The process continues until the number of transfers is reached as specified. Then, the DMA controller signals the processor that the transfers have been completed.

Notice that while the DMA transfer is occurring on the bus, the processor cannot use the bus. Similarly, if the processor is using the bus when the DMA controller requires it, the controller must wait until the processor has finished

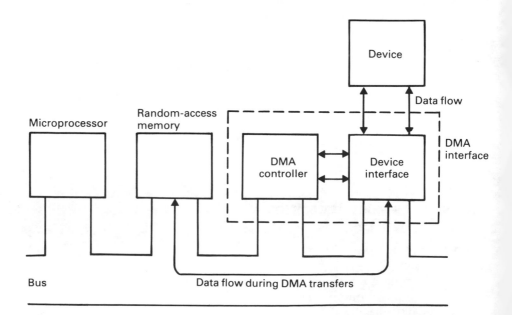

Figure 10.18 Direct memory access system

using the bus (until the end of a machine cycle in the case of the Z-80). The processor then relinquishes control of the bus to the DMA controller and must then wait for the bus to be free again. Normally the processor will be executing a program while the DMA transfer mechanism is in progress and the DMA controller will 'steal' processor cycles to use the bus at intervals (*cycle stealing*). The effect on the processor is to slow its execution, by an amount dependent upon the frequency of the cycles stolen.

There are variations on this general approach. For example, the set-up addresses and count may be held in memory and the controller sufficiently intelligent to fetch them. The controller may have additional modes, for example, a *scan* mode in which data is taken from the source, but rather than being transferred to the destination, the data is compared with the contents of a previously loaded DMA register. If a match is found, the DMA controller signals the processor accordingly. An alternative scan mode may signal the processor when a match is not found. This latter mode could be useful in testing memory, by loading a block memory locations with the same value as the internal DMA register. Any discrepancy in this scan would indicate an error in the memory circuits.

The DMA mechanism is particularly applicable to input/output devices such as magnetic disk memory units (see Chap. 11) as the transfer of information between the central system and these devices requires that a block data is transferred as an uninterrupted stream of bytes at a speed dictated by the speed of revolution of the disk. In this case, the device interface shown in Fig. 10.18 typically incorporates a special-purpose device controller (e.g. a floppy disk controller) which generates the required signals for the disk unit, and works in conjunction with a general purpose DMA controller.

10.4.2 Processor–DMA controller signals

There are two or three special signals between the processor and the DMA controller to handle the mechanism, in addition to the normal data and address signals. In particular, it is necessary that at any instant, only one device is controlling the bus, either the processor or the DMA controller. This leads to a pair of *handshaking* signals between the two devices, one to the processor from the DMA controller to request the use of the bus and one from the processor to the DMA controller granting use of the bus. DMA requests for the bus are presented for each data transfer. Each request must be granted quickly when the DMA mechanism is used with time-critical devices such magnetic disk memory units.

(a) Z-80 DMA signals
The Z-80 uses two signals to transfer the control of the bus, namely:

$\overline{\text{BUSRQ}}$ Bus request, for the requesting device to the processor
$\overline{\text{BUSAK}}$ Bus acknowledge from the processor to the device

A bus request will be accepted only at the end of a machine cycle and the acknowledge issued then. At the same time as the acknowledge is issued, the processor releases the bus (into tri-state). The timing is shown in Fig. 10.19. Whenever $\overline{\text{BUSRQ}}$ is brought low, this is only noticed by the processor on the rising edge of the last clock cycle (T state) of an M cycle, and the acknowledge signal, $\overline{\text{BUSAK}}$, is brought low on the rising edge of the next clock cycle when the bus is released into tri-state. The DMA controller may then use the bus and the bus control signals for data transfers. The bus is available for any duration. (Note that the Z-80 refresh capability is suspended during the time that the processor has released the bus.) The DMA controller indicates that it has finished with the bus by returning $\overline{\text{BUSRQ}}$ to a high level. This is recognized by the processor on the rising edge of the next clock cycle, and returns $\overline{\text{BUSAK}}$ to a high level. At the same time the bus is taken over by the processor.

(b) 68000 DMA signals

The 68000 is provided with a general mechanism for handling any device which wishes to use the bus instead of the processor, of which the DMA controller is one possibility. Other devices include further processor units in a multiple processor system (see Chap. 15). Three signals are used:

(i)   bus request signal ($\overline{\text{BR}}$) from the requesting device to the processor
(ii) A bus grant signal ($\overline{\text{BG}}$) from the processor to devices that might wish to use the bus and the requesting device in particular
(iii) A bus grant acknowledge signal ($\overline{\text{BGACK}}$) from the device back to the processor.

The bus request signal is activated (*asserted* in 68000 terminology) by the

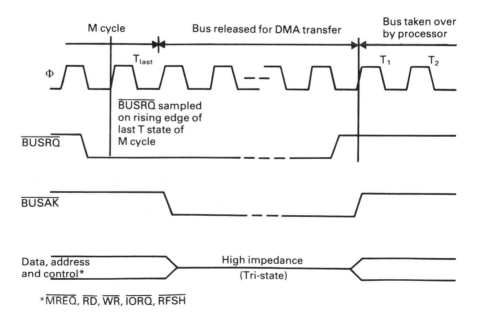

Figure 10.19   Z-80 bus request/acknowledge cycle

device wishing to use the bus. For now let us assume that there is only one such device. If the processor is executing a bus cycle, the grant signal is generated after internal synchronization and the bus cycle is continued to its conclusion. If the processor has just decided to start a cycle but not yet asserted the address strobe $\overline{AS}$, the cycle is still started and will be completed. The bus grant signal is asserted one clock cycle after $\overline{AS}$ is asserted in this case. The bus grant signal indicates that the processor will release the bus at the end of the current bus cycle.

The device requesting the bus recognizes the grant signal and waits for the bus to be released before generating the bus grant acknowledge signal, $\overline{BGACK}$. The device detects that the bus has been released from conditions of two processor signals:

(i)   The address strobe signal, $\overline{AS}$ is inactive, which shows that the processor is not using the bus

(ii)   The data transfer acknowledge signal, $\overline{DTACK}$, is inactive which indicates that no memory or peripheral device is using the bus.

In addition, the bus grant acknowledge signal, $\overline{BGACK}$, cannot be generated if it is already being generated by another device.

REFERENCES

1. *MOSTEK Microcomputer Components Data Book.* Carrollton, Texas: Mostek, 1979.
2. Wilkinson, B., and D. Horrocks, *Computer Peripherals.* London: Hodder and Stoughton, 1980.
3. *Z-80 DART Dual Asynchronous Receiver/Transmitter Product Specification.* Cupertino, California: Zilog, Inc., 1979.
4. *MC68000 32-/16-bit Microprocessor Advance Information,* East Kilbride, Scotland: Motorola, Ltd., 1985.

PROBLEMS

10.1   The parallel input circuit of Fig. 10.1 is used in a Z-80 microprocessor system. Design a suitable address decode circuit, assigning port address 18 to the circuit.

10.2   Three processor address lines, A_2, A_1 and A_0, are connected to $\overline{CE}$, C/D select and B/A select inputs of a Z-80 PIO respectively. Determine the addresses of the data and control registers of the PIO, assuming that the remaining address lines are set to 0. Write a Z-80 program to initialize the PIO such that port A acts as an input port and port B acts as an output port.

10.3   A Z-80 PIO is used in a microprocessor-controlled combination lock on a safe. Port A is set up for input and port B is set up for output. The lock is controlled by bit 1 of port B. Four switches numbered 0, 1, 2 and 3 are attached to bits 0, 1, 2 and 3 of port A respectively. The safe lock will open only after the following sequence:

> All switches are set in open position
> Switch 0 is set in closed position
> Switch 0 is set in open position
> Switch 3 is set in closed position
> Switch 2 is set in closed position
> Switch 2 is set in open position
> Switch 3 is set in open position

Any other sequence will set an alarm controlled by bit 2 of port B. Write a suitable Z-80 control program for the lock. The addresses of data and control registers of port A are 2 and 3 respectively. The addresses of data and control registers of port B are 6 and 7 respectively. The switches are configured as in Fig. 10.1.

10.4 Write a Z-80 program to initialize port A of a Z-80 DART to operate with the following data format:

> Seven data bits
> 1 stop bit
> Even parity bit

and a ×64 clock mode. The addresses of the data and control registers are 2 and 3 respectively.

10.5 Write a Z-80 program to read data from a DART and output the characters back to the DART (i.e. echoplexing). Choose suitable DART addresses.

10.6 Design suitable address decode logic for the general-purpose UART shown in Fig. 10.9, assigning port address 25 for data and port address 26 for the status register.

10.7 Determine the maximum negative and maximum positive voltages in a 2's complement 8-bit A/D converter if the incremental steps are $10\,mV$.

10.8 If the input to an n-bit A/D converter must not change by more than ½ LSB, determine an expression for the maximum input signal frequency.

10.9 Sketch the logic required to pass an interrupt request signal through interrupt devices in a daisy-chained request and common acknowledge interrupt scheme.

11

Magnetic Secondary Memory

11.1 INTRODUCTION

In Chap. 9, we identified two types of memory, primary memory and secondary memory, and examined semiconductor primary memory. Now we shall consider secondary memory. Most secondary memory is based upon magnetizing a material in a form of a magnetic disk or reel of magnetic tape to represent the binary information, and we shall only consider this type. This type of magnetic secondary memory has the feature of being able to store large amounts of data relatively economically, is non-volatile and often the recorded information can be physically removed, but operates much slower than semiconductor memory and is not random-access. The material magnetized, i.e. the recording medium, is usually either in the form of a disk or tape. Firstly we shall review the mechanism of creating a magnetized material and the possible schemes for representing binary information using magnetized materials.

11.2 MAGNETIC RECORDING

11.2.1 Principles

In magnetic recording, a material is magnetized in one of two directions to represent the binary information. (The direction is not necessarily directly equivalent to the two binary states; special magnetic codes are commonly used, as we shall see later.) There are two operations required: firstly a mechanism of magnetizing a material, the so-called write operation; and secondly a mechanism of sensing the magnetism, the so-called read operation.

(a) Write operation

To permanently magnetize a material, it is necessary for the material to have a magnetic flux density (B)–magnetic field strength (H) characteristic with hysteresis as shown in Fig. 11.1. This indicates that after a magnetic field has been applied to the material, there is a remanent magnetic flux density, B_r. Such materials are known as *hard magnetic materials*. Other materials, such as iron, may be able to be magnetized while the field is applied, but the magnetic flux reduces to (nearly) zero when the field is removed. These materials are known as

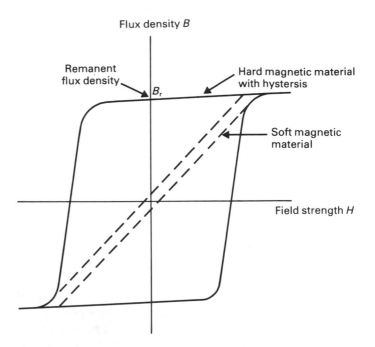

Figure 11.1   *B–H* curves of magnetic materials

soft magnetic materials and are not suitable for permanent magnetic recording storage media.

The usual method of producing the magnetic field to magnetize a material is to use an electromagnet, in the form of a *write head*. The write head is made from a very soft magnetic (ferrite or laminated high-permeability metal) ring, and carries a coil of thin wire as shown in Fig. 11-2(a). The ring has a small air gap designed so that when a current flows through the wire, the magnetic flux generated prefers to enter a recording medium placed immediately below rather than cross the air gap which causes a small area of the recording medium to become magnetized. Often writing is saturated, i.e. the maximum magnetic flux is generated within the recording medium. This occurs when the field strength is above the point that the plateau is reached on the *B-H* characteristic.

(b) Read operation

Sensing the state of magnetization of the recording medium can be achieved using a read head constructed in a similar fashion to a write head, and indeed often the one head performs both functions, reading and writing. (Large tape systems use separate read and write heads however.) Referring to Fig. 11.2(b), when a magnetized area is placed below the read head, some flux is diverted through the core of the head and the read coil. Moving the recording medium will cause this flux to change and a change of flux passing through the coil induces a voltage across the coil (Faraday's law, $v = N d\phi/dt$ where N is the number of turns on the coil and ϕ is the flux). The induced voltage can be detected as a *read voltage*. With this mechanism it is necessary to have relative

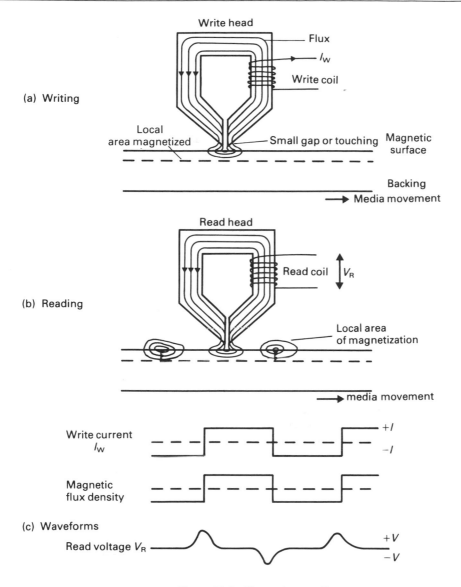

Figure 11.2 Magnetic recording

movement between the medium and the head to obtain a read voltage. Normally the medium is continuously moving for both reading and writing. Figure 11.2(c) shows the form of read voltage obtained. The voltage reaches a peak at the point that the magnetization reverses direction in the recording medium, assuming a step change and no effects due to more distant magnetization changes. Naturally, the amplitude of the read pulse depends upon various factors such as the physical construction of the read head, the number of turns on the coil and the distance the recording medium is from the head. Typically, read voltages are in the range 1 to 100 mV.

11.2.2 Vertical recording

In *vertical recording*, also called *perpendicular recording*, the medium is magnetized perpendicular to the surface rather than in the same plane and hence columns of magnetized material are created. A north pole is on one surface and south pole on the opposite surface or vice versa. These columns tend to reduce in width and the recording density that can be achieved is substantially greater than with traditional *horizontal recording*. Vertical recording can be performed, for example, through the use of a write head which one pole piece (one side of the gap) on one side of the media and the other pole piece on the opposite side of the media. We will assume traditional horizontal recording in the following discussion.

11.2.3 Recording codes

The surface to be magnetized is logically divided into a number of tracks for recording purposes. One or more read/write heads are used to record on these tracks while the surface moves beneath the heads. Each track is divided into elemental areas known as *bit cells*. The magnetization state(s) in the bit cell represent one binary digit. The relationship between the magnetic states and the binary information is given in a recording code. There are many recording codes, each with their own attributes, advantages and disadvantages. A fundamental requirement is high recording density, measured in bits/inch. For high recording density, there should be the minimum number of changes in magnetic states in the bit cell, since there is a minimum surface length required to support a magnetic state. However, in practice, detection of the magnetic state is the limiting factor rather than minimum surface length. Consequently, other factors such as ease of signal detection may be more important than having the minimum number of flux changes.

(a) Non-return-to-zero (NRZ) code

A simple method of representing binary information is to magnetize each bit cell totally in one of two lateral directions with one direction representing a 0 and the other direction representing a 1, as shown in Fig. 11.3(a). This method is called *non-return-to zero* (NRZ) since the whole area is either magnetized in one direction or the other and is never returned to an unmagnetized state (zero magnetization). Adjacent areas are magnetized in a similar fashion with, ideally, an immediate change of direction of magnetization at the boundaries if opposite binary states are recorded.

For writing, a current, I, is applied through the write coil to record a 1 and a current, $-I$, to record a 0 (I being the current required to magnetize the medium). Reading will produce pulses at the edges of bit cells that have opposite magnetizations. To reproduce the original data stream, positive read pulses could be arranged to set a flip-flop and negative read pulses could be arranged to reset the flip-flop using positive and negative signal detectors. The output of the flip-flop would then follow the magnetization states and hence the data pattern.

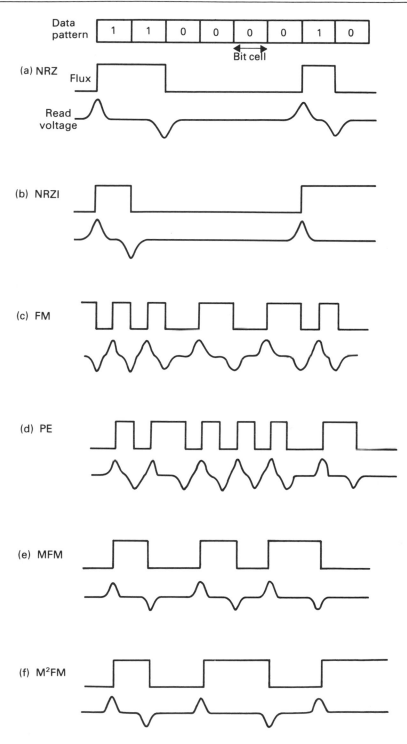

Figure 11.3   Recording codes

However, NRZ has a number of major disadvantages. Firstly, it presupposes that the speed of the medium is very accurately known and does not alter, since a single bit stream produced (assuming only one track recorded) requires an external clock signal to strobe the serial data into a holding register. Any alteration in the speed of the medium either during writing or reading would soon result in bits being missed or unintentionally put into the holding register, since any error in clocking would be cumulative. Secondly, the range of read signal frequencies is very large, extending from the bit cell rate resulting from a 010101 ⋯ data pattern, down to virtually d.c. (no change) if a long string of 0's or a long string of 1's is recorded. In practice, long strings of 1's or 0's do not occur, but the range may still be very large. This means that the read amplifier must have a wide *bandwidth* (a measure of the range of frequencies that can be amplified), and results in a poor *signal-to-noise ratio* (a measure of the fraction of the amplifier output corresponding to the signal compared to the output due to electrical noise). If the signal bandwidth is allowed to extend to d.c., further thermal considerations often come into play due to the design of the amplifier.

Finally, an error in one bit propagates until the next read pulse is encountered, which could be many bit cells away. For example if a data pattern 11000010 is written and upon reading, the third digit, a 0, is misread such that the read pulse is missed, this would be taken as a 1. All subsequent 0's (which do not generate read pulses) till the next recorded 1 would also be interpreted as 1's. The resultant read data pattern becomes 11111110. The error can be detected since every positive read pulse should be followed by a negative read pulse which does not occur with single bit errors.

(b) Non-return-to-zero-inverted (NRZI)

The error propagation property of NRZ coding can be eliminated by using the NRZI (*non-return-to-zero-inverted*, or *non-return-to-zero-one*) code. On NRZI, a 1 is represented by change of magnetization, in either direction at the beginning of the cell and a 0 by no change in magnetization as shown in Fig. 11.3(b). This results in a read pulse in a positive or negative direction when a 1 is stored and no read pulse when a 0 is stored. Consequently, 1's and 0's have quite different read signals and single bit errors do not propagate. The bandwidth is still large and a clock signal is required to reconstitute the data.

An independent external clock signal can probably be eliminated with multi-track recording (principally tape systems and large fixed-head disk systems) where several tracks are recorded or read simultaneously. Then one track can be used for odd parity so that there is at least one read pulse from one of the tracks in every word read, which can be used to resynchronize the clock circuitry. This feature and the high recording density due to a maximum of one flux change per bit cell, has lead to the use of NRZI in tape systems in particular. In single-track systems, the addition of an odd parity bit in every word recorded guarantees a read pulse in every word read back which can also be used for synchronization. However, the ability to generate an accurate clock signal is of paramount importance in high-speed, high-density systems and consequently other codes have been developed having at least one flux change in every bit cell or small groups of bit cells. The term *self-clocking* codes is used to describe this feature. The two fundamental self-clocking codes are frequency modulation (FM) and phase encoding (PE).

(c) Frequency modulation (FM)

The NRZI code can be modified to incorporate self-clocking by the inclusion of a flux transition at the beginning of every cell and placing the 1 flux transition half-way across the cell. This code is known as *frequency modulation* (FM) or *double frequency* (DF) and is shown in Fig. 11.3(c). A 0 is recorded as a single flux transition occurring at the beginning of the cell and a 1 is recorded as two flux transitions, one at the beginning of the cell and one, in the opposite direction, half-way across the cell. This leads to one read pulse for a recorded 0 and two read pulses for a recorded 1. Hence there are two dominant frequencies, f (equivalent to the bit cell rate) and $2f$, and the read bandwidth is narrow. The first pulse occurring is assumed to be at the beginning of the bit cell. This and subsequent pulses at the beginning of the cells are used to provide self-clocking.

Since there can be two flux changes per bit cell, the media and circuitry must be able to accommodate this. Therefore, we would expect the recording density to be reduced by half using this recording code compared with NRZI. However, the self-clocking feature particularly aids the data recovery process, making the code very attractive for single-track recordings.

(d) Phase encoding (PE)

Phase encoding (PE), also known as *phase modulation* (PM), results in similar features to FM code. In PE, a 1 is represented by a change of magnetization in one direction and a 0 by a change of magnetization in the other direction, both changes occurring half-way across the bit cell, as shown in Fig. 11.3(d). Extra changes are necessary between consecutive 0's or consecutive 1's, and these are placed at the beginning of the bit cell. In the phase encoding known as Manchester I, a north-to-south change in magnetization at the beginning of the cell represents a 1 and a south-to-north change represents a 0. Any extra changes occur at the middle of the cell. In the phase encoding known as *Manchester II* ($+180°$) a south-to-north change at the middle of the cell represents a 1 and a north-to-south change represents a 0, with extra changes if necessary occurring at the beginning of the cell. The Manchester II code is normally used. PE has the same bandwidth as FM, with one or two read pulses generated per bit cell.

By incorporating an additional flux change in each bit cell, the effective recording density is reduced. Doubling the number of flux changes does not necessarily halve the recording density since other factors such as self-clocking may enable a higher density. However, it is a significant factor, especially among a range of codes which otherwise may be similar (say all self-clocking). In a desire to reduce the number of flux changes while maintaining the ability of self-clocking, codes have been devised to remove flux changes provided for self-clocking when there are already flux changes for data representation in particular cases. Such codes can be classified as *group* or *adaptive self-clocking* codes since the flux changes used are adapted to the data pattern. The major adaptive self-clocking codes are modified frequency modulation (MFM), modified-modified frequency modulation (M^2FM) and group coded recording (GCR).

(e) Modified frequency modulation (MFM)

Modified frequency modulation (MFM), also known as *delay modulation* (DM), is shown in Fig. 11.3(e), and is based on FM. Recall that in FM, a 1 is represented by a flux change at the mid-point of the bit cell and a 0 by no flux change. This is also used in MFM. In FM, an additional flux change is provided at the beginning of every cell. In MFM, this clocking flux change is only inserted if there is a 0 in the previous and present bit cells, i.e. between two consecutive 0's when otherwise there would be no flux changes at the middle of the cells. Consequently the maximum length between flux changes is two cell lengths and the minimum is one cell length. The corresponding read pulses are sufficient to synchronize the read circuitry.

An alternative equivalent definition for MFM is as follows: 1 is represented by a change in flux at the mid-point of the cell and a 0 is represented by a change in flux at the end of the cell if the 0 is followed by another 0, otherwise by no flux transition.

(f) Modified-modified frequency modulation (M^2FM)

In *modified-modified frequency modulation* (M^2FM), a 1 is recorded as a flux change at the middle of the bit cell and a 0 by no change as in FM. However, the clocking flux change at the beginning of the cell is only included for 0's and only then if there is no flux change in the previous cell (at the beginning or mid-point). This is different from MFM with three or more consecutive 0's recorded. In M^2FM, only alternate flux changes are inserted, as shown in Fig. 11.3(f).

The minimum number of flux changes occurs in M^2FM with the pattern 001, giving a flux change spacing of $2\frac{1}{2}$ cells. The maximum number of flux changes occurs with a string of 1's, giving a flux change in every cell. Consequently, the bandwidth is slightly wider than MFM.

(g) Group coded recording (GCR)

Another approach to reducing the number of flux transitions while maintaining self-clocking is to translate the incoming data into new bit patterns which when recorded using a standard non self-clocking code, always results in a flux change at intervals. The new bit pattern will be, by necessity, longer than the original pattern but this will be more than fully compensated by the self-clocking ability. The technique is known as *group coded recording* (GCR).

The usual GCR code is one designed to use NRZI code, known as *modified NRZI* (MNRZI) [1]. The difficulty with the basic NRZI code is that consecutive 0's produce no read pulses. In MNRZI, this is avoided by encoding the data so that long strings of 0's do not occur. The incoming data is divided into 4-bit

Table 11.1 MNRZI recording pattern

4-bit data				5-bit recording				
0	0	0	0	1	1	0	0	1
0	0	0	1	1	1	0	1	1
0	0	1	0	1	0	0	1	0
0	0	1	1	1	0	0	1	1
0	1	0	0	1	1	1	0	1
0	1	0	1	1	0	1	0	1
0	1	1	0	1	0	1	1	0
0	1	1	1	1	0	1	1	1
1	0	0	0	1	1	0	1	0
1	0	0	1	0	1	0	0	1
1	0	1	0	0	1	0	1	0
1	0	1	1	0	1	0	1	1
1	1	0	0	1	1	1	1	0
1	1	0	1	0	1	1	0	1
1	1	1	0	0	1	1	1	0
1	1	1	1	0	1	1	1	1

words and these are translated into 5-bit words according to Table 11.1, which has the property that there are no more than two consecutive 0's in the pattern, including when concatenated with adjacent encoded words. The 5-bit words are recorded in the NRZI code which results in read pulses occurring at least every three bit cells. This is sufficient to provide read circuitry synchronization.

11.2.4 Read/write circuitry

A single isolated flux transition results in a read pulse with the peak of the read pulse corresponding to the position of the flux transition on the recording medium. For each pulse generated by the read head, the read circuitry needs to produce a logic signal. Simply amplifying the read signal and constraining the signal to a particular amplitude (by clipping) is rarely satisfactory. Usually the amplitude of the read pulse can vary widely during playback by a factor of five or six due to physical factors. In particular, any change in distance between the recording medium and the head will greatly alter the amplitude. Amplitude variations would result in variable width pulses with simple amplify-clip circuits. One approach to reduce this effect is to incorporate circuitry which adjusts the read amplifier gain so as to reduce the gain when the signal amplitude increases (i.e. automatic gain control). Automatic gain control generally requries a preamble recorded on the medium to set up the circuitry.

Irrespective of the amplitude of the signal, the position of the peak remains broadly constant at low recording densities. The peak indicates the position of the flux change. We are particularly interested in the flux changes and their position. Therefore read circuits are often designed to detect the peak of the read signal, by differentiator circuits or otherwise. At higher recording densities, a phenomenon known as *peak-shift* occurs where the position of the peak of the signal moves, due to the effect of adjacent pulses. The amplitude also reduces.

The effect depends upon the recording pattern as shown in Fig. 11.4 [2]. The results can be deduced by summing together the signals of isolated pulses.

Fairly low-density FM and NRZI recording systems may not exhibit significant peak-shift and additional circuitry to accommodate peak shift may be unnecessary. However, high-density systems commonly provide either *write pre-compensation* or adaptive *read post-compensation*, using the fact that the peak shift can be predicted by the recording pattern. Consider write pre-compensation for MFM recording (widely used on floppy disks; see section 11.3). Figure 11.5 shows four bit patterns that exhibit peak shift in the MFM code [3]. In two patterns, the peak is shifted to the right and in two it is shifted to the left, i.e. in two it appears earlier in the cell time than the mid-point, and in two it appears later. The reasons can be identified by the closeness of the adjacent flux changes to that of the cell under consideration. If the nearest flux change is to the right, the peak shifts to the left. Conversely if the nearest flux change is to the left, the peak moves to the right. If there are flux changes equidistant on both sides, there is no peak shift. In the patterns with don't cares, X's, the flux changes do not appreciably affect the peak shift and can be ignored. The actual amount of peak

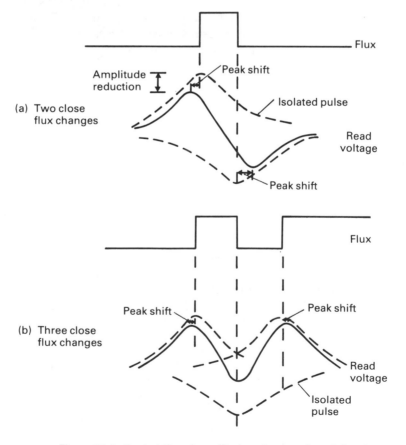

Figure 11.4 Peak shift and amplitude reduction of read signal

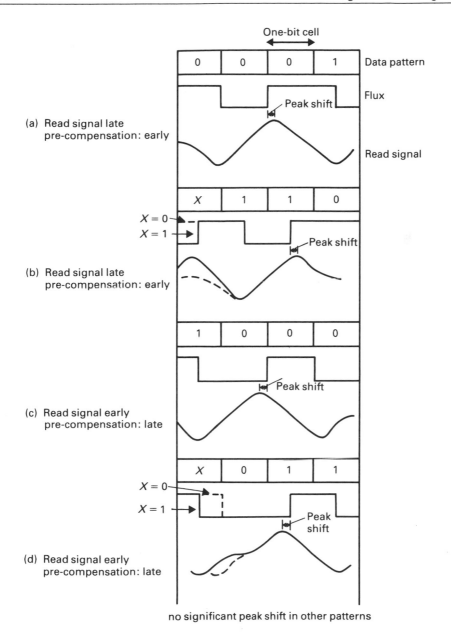

One-bit cell

| 0 | 0 | 0 | 1 | Data pattern |

Flux

(a) Read signal late
pre-compensation: early

Peak shift

Read signal

| X | 1 | 1 | 0 |

X = 0
X = 1

Peak shift

(b) Read signal late
pre-compensation: early

| 1 | 0 | 0 | 0 |

Peak shift

(c) Read signal early
pre-compensation: late

| X | 0 | 1 | 1 |

X = 0
X = 1

Peak
shift

(d) Read signal early
pre-compensation: late

no significant peak shift in other patterns

Figure 11.5 Write pre-compensation for MFM recording

shift is the same in all cases because it is caused by the nearest flux change which is one cell length away. In a floppy disk system having a $2\,\mu s$ bit time, for example, the peak shift is typically 10% or 200 ns. To write pre-compensate, the current to the write head is switched 200 ns early or late in opposition to the peak shift, resulting in a read signal with no peak shift. This mechanism can be achieved by loading the bit serial write data into a 4-bit holding shift register.

The patterns that cause peak shift, four in our example, are recognized using decode logic (Fig. 11.6). The position of the write current transition is then adjusted in these cases so as to write early when the peak shift is late and to write late when the peak shift is early. Write pre-compensation is incorporated into some LSI floppy disk controllers.

An alternative scheme is read post-compensation, utilizing the fact that a flux transition in one cell will cause the peak in the next cell to shift. Read signals are strobed with a logic signal which can be delayed or brought early in response to the information recorded in the previous cell.

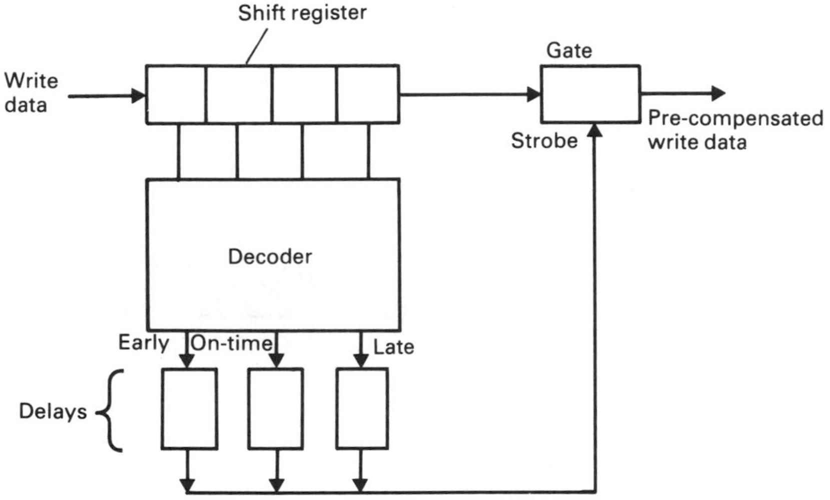

Figure 11.6   Write pre-compensation circuitry

11.3 FLOPPY DISK STORAGE SYSTEMS

11.3.1 General

The *floppy disk* storage system was originally developed by IBM in the late 1960s as a testing aid for their type 3330 rigid disk systems. The original specification called for a small, low-cost and reliable disk system which could be used to store diagnostic programs for fault detection in the rigid disk system. These diagnostic programs can be read-only. The floppy disk system was introduced as part of the 3330 system in 1970. However, it was three years before the device was introduced as a storage peripheral in its own right, with the introduction of the IBM 3740 commercial data entry system in 1973 which incorporated an 8 in. diameter floppy disk system for data storage. Subsequent developments included the introduction of a 5¼ in. diameter floppy disk by Shugart in 1976 and more recently 3 in. and 3½ in. diameter floppy disks.

A floppy disk system (8 in. or 5¼ in.) is shown in Fig. 11.7 and uses an exchangeable flexible disk which is held permanently in a square envelope. (An outer protective paper sleeve is removed before the disk is used.) The disk is manufactured from mylar with a coating of a magnetic material such as ferrite oxide. The envelope has openings for movable combined read/write heads, the drive spindle and for index/sector hole sensing (see later).

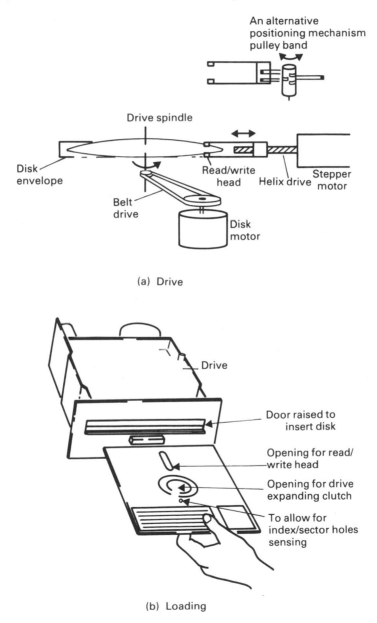

(a) Drive

(b) Loading

Figure 11.7 Floppy disk

The disk is never taken out of the envelope. The whole disk and envelope can be inserted or removed from the disk unit (the so-called disk drive) after opening a hinged door on the drive. When the door is closed, the read/write heads may be actuated, but not otherwise. Location of the disk on the spindle is done by an expanding clutch or other means to achieve correct registration. The disk is usually only inserted with the drive motor turned off. (Early floppy disk drives left the motor continuously running.)

For reading or writing, the disk is rotated by the drive spindle at a fairly slow speed, normally 360 rpm for the 8 in. disk and 300 rpm for the 5¼ in. disk, and the read-write head is positioned on the surface, making direct contact when reading or writing. Writing is performed on concentric tracks. The head is positioned over the required track using a spiral cam/wheel, pulley band or other mechanism. When not reading or writing, the head is brought off the surface to reduce wear of both the media and the head and after a few seconds, the motor is automatically turned off.

Originally a single head and surface was used. By 1977, a double head system, recording on both surfaces had been perfected. The original single-track density floppy disk was 48 tracks/in. Not all the disk surface is used as the linear recording density increases towards the middle if, as is usual, the same number of bits are recorded on each track. In the original *single-track density* system, 35 tracks are recorded on a 5¼ in. disk and 77 tracks on an 8 in. disk. The recording code used on the standard bit density floppy disk is FM but the storage capacity can be increased through the use of MFM or M²FM codes. These codes give double bit densities (i.e. *double density* disks as opposed to *single density* disks). The track density can be increased, for example, to the *double-track density* of 96 tracks. One limiting factor is the stability of the recording media, mlyar, which is subject to deformaties by mechanical stress, thermal and other environmental causes.

The smaller 3/3½ in. floppy disks are enclosed in rigid plastic cases with sliding openings for the read/write heads. These smaller disks are less prone to thermal changes of the media and greater track density can be achieved.

The rotational speed of the disk need not be kept constant for all tracks. In the variable-speed disk drives, greater recording capacity is obtained by recording and reading data on tracks further towards the outer edge with increased disk rotational speed which will maintain the bit density in terms of bits/in. more uniformly. Variable-speed mechanisms have been applied to floppy disk drives.

11.3.2 Recording formats

Each track is divided into a number of sectors, as shown in Fig. 11.8. Each sector holds a convenient fixed number of bytes. It is necessary to be able to identify each sector. This can be done by one of two methods, known as *hard sectoring* and *soft sectoring* respectively.

In hard sectoring, the disk is provided with a small hole at the beginning of

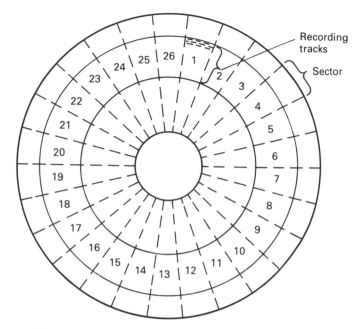

26 sectors shown; there can be a different number of sectors
(For example 10, 18, 52)

Figure 11.8   Floppy disk format

each sector, punched near the spindle hole. For example, with 10 sectors, there
would be 10 sector holes around the disk. These holes are sensed photoelectri-
cally as the disk revolves and a count is kept in hardware. The first sector is
identified by an additional hole known as an index hole, punched near the first
sector hole. The index hole can be used to reset the sector count. When the
required sector is reached, the appropriate reading or writing takes place.

In soft sectoring, the disk is provided only with the index hole, identifying
the first sector. Each sector is identified by a pre-recorded address which
includes a special address mark written near the beginning of the sector. To
locate a sector, a track is read until the required sector is found. The tracks can
be divided into sectors which have addresses in sequential order or non-
sequential order. The latter may reduce the access time in some applications.
Hard- and soft-sectored disks are not interchangeable. Most disks are soft
sectored.

Each disk has other information recorded during a programmed *formatting
procedure*. The format for hard- and soft-sectored disks is different; the hard-
sectored format does not include sector address information. Between sectors,
synchronizing patterns are recorded. Sectors of 128 or 256 bytes are common.
The information recorded on each sector of a soft-sectored disk consists of two
parts, an identification part and a data part. The identification part (ID) begins
with a special ID address mark (a special recording pattern), followed by the
track address, sector address and terminated with two CRC (*cyclic redundancy*

character) error detection bytes. The length of the sector and the head number in the case of double-sided systems may be incorporated. The data field begins with either a data or a deleted data address mark (special recording patterns), followed by the data bytes and terminated with two CRC bytes.

The CRC bytes are added to provide a means of detecting many but not all possible errors due to the read/write mechanism. Faults in the recording media often result in a string of bits being misread or incorrectly formed during writing (the so-called burst error). Suppose the block of characters recorded in a sector is treated as a sequence of bits of one large number rather than distinct bytes, and this large number is divided by a predefined binary number both before recording and after recording. The remainder resulting from the division would be the same if no errors have occurred during recording. If one or more errors have occurred, it is likely that the remainder will be different.

In the CRC method, the division process is performed using modulo-2 arithmetic (carry/borrow values are ignored in modulo-2 arithmetic). The remainder from the division process becomes the CRC word which is attached to the field during writing. Upon reading, the division process is checked. The checking process involves dividing the block of characters read, including the appended CRC word, by the predefined binary word. (In practice a logical equivalent process is performed.) If the division results in a non-zero remainer, a read/write error has occurred. The CRC calculation is performed on all data bits and special address/data marks. The predefined word used is called a generating polynomial and is described in an algebraic notation; for example $X^{16} + X^{12} + X^5 + 1$, which means the word 10001000000100001 (= $1 \times 2^{16} + 1 \times 2^{12} + 1 \times 2^5 + 1$). This particular generating polynominal is widely used on floppy disks and will detect 16-bit error bursts.

11.3.3 Drive and controller

With disk systems in general, the electronic circuitry connecting the disk to the computer is divided into two physical parts, the drive electronics and the controller logic. However, in floppy disk systems, only the analog circuitry required for the read/write heads and for positioning is placed in the drive, sufficient to provide a logic level interface to the controller. The controller takes over complete control, even to the level of stepping the head actuator. In larger disk systems, sector and track selection logic is incorporated into the drive electronics. The controller then provides the required sector and track to the drive, and data in the case of a write operation, or in the case of a read operation, some time later the drive returns the required data. In floppy disk systems, there is often no intelligence built into the drive electronics which is largely analog in nature and simply provides an analog/digital interface. The general scheme is shown in Fig. 11.9. There are about nine signals between the controller and the drive to enable the head to be stepped across tracks, to read serial data and to write serial data.

The recording pattern for one data byte can be described by two

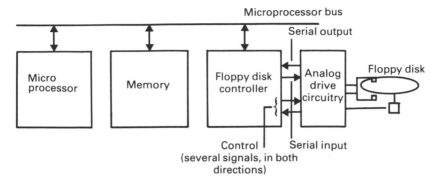

Figure 11.9 Floppy disk system

hexadecimal numbers, one giving the clock transitions at the beginning of the cell and one giving the data transitions at the middle of the cell. FM has a clock pattern FF (11111111) except for the special address/data marks which have missing clock transitions. The example in Fig. 11.10 shows the result of combining clock and data patterns.

The floppy disk drive generally requires combined clock and data pulses on one serial input line and generates combined clock and data pulses on one output line. The formation of the appropriate serial input and interpretation of the serial output is a function of the controller. The separation of clock and data in the serial output of the drive may be performed by analog circuitry external to the actual (digital) controller device. FM and MFM/M²FM recording codes can be implemented using separate data and clock pulses.

The floppy disk controller system generally uses a programmable LSI disk controller device. Such parts interface to the microprocessor bus as an input/output peripheral device with several internal addressable read/write registers. Typically a pre-programmed recording code (e.g. FM or MFM) can be selected. The controller accepts data bytes from the disk during a read operation and provides data bytes during a write operation. The transfer of these bytes can be via programmed input/output instructions or via DMA. Programmed input/output is feasible with floppy disk systems because of their relatively low data rate, 125 K bits/sec for 5½ in. single-density floppy disks, 250 K bits/sec for 5¼ in. double-density floppy disks or 8 in. single density floppy disks, and 500 K bits/sec for double-density 8 in. floppy disks. These rates represent one byte transfer every 64 μs, 32 μs and 16 μs respectively. (Specific disk controllers may require different data rates.)

The controller usually has a range of commands available. Examples are given in Table 11.2. (This table is based upon the Intel 8272 Single/Double Density Floppy Disk Controller [4].) Each command from the processor to the controller typically consists of a number of bytes specifying the command, and providing parameters required to complete the command. Internal disk controller registers store the bytes. In the case of a read command, an internal data register is loaded from the disk and must be read by programmed input instructions or by DMA before the next byte is found on the disk (unless additional buffer registers are provided). In the case of a write command, the

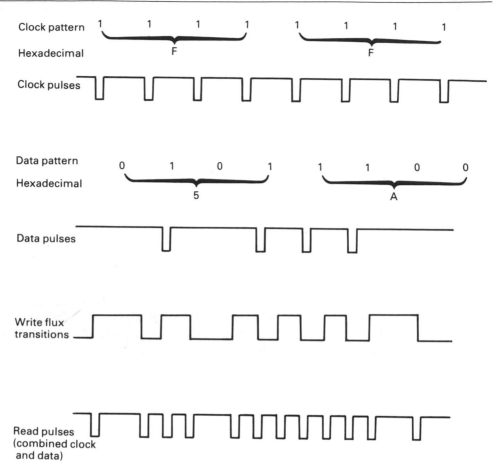

Figure 11.10   Floppy disk write and read pulses

data register is loaded by the processor and subsequently written on to the disk. The register must be reloaded with the next byte before the next location on the disk is found (unless additional buffer registers are provided). Otherwise, an error flag is set in the controller and the next transfer is not carried out. The controller usually has the ability to handle tracks which are unusable. These bad tracks, once recognized, can be indicated on track 00 (the outermost track) and withdrawn from service. Two spare tracks can be provided by the controller. When a bad track is encountered, it is skipped over with subsequent tracks renumbered. Clearly, track 00 must not be faulty with this scheme.

Errors occurring during the execution of a command are indicated in an addressable status register within the controller. Typical errors are:

Read error
Write error
CRC error

Table 11.2 Typical LSI floppy disk controller commands

Command	Parameters supplied	Result
Initialize (may be part of subsequent commands)	Head load time Head unload time Step rate	Internal register loaded with information
Seek track	Track address Step rate	Head stepped inward or outward at predefined rate to specified track Some registers re-initialized
Read data	Recording code Head load settling time Track address Sector address Number of bytes/sector Number of sectors or final sector address	Head loaded on to track Wait specified settling time Read ID fields when specified sector reached Read CRC bytes and check Load data into internal data register Generate control signals When all data bytes read, read CRC bytes and check Unload head and wait specified unload time Set status register
Read deleted data	As read data	As read data but will read sector only if deleted data address mark present
Read ID	None	First ID field read; used to give present position of head
Read track	As read data	As read data but returns contents of data fields of complete track
Write data	As read data	As read data except data in data register loaded on to disk Before data written, a data address mark is written Data is continually loaded onto disk until specified number of bytes reached or external signal received. In the latter case, sector then filled with zeros.
Write deleted data	As write data	As write data but will write deleted data address mark instead of normal mark
Format track	Number of bytes/sector Number of sectors/track Gap length Data pattern	Write a complete track, including address marks, data marks, ID fields according to agreed format. The data byte specified is repeated in each data field.
Scan	As read data	Data read on specified track is compared with that supplied by processor until a specified relationship is found (equal, less or greater). Then command is terminated and location identified in a status register. If relationship not found, indication given at end of command.

Address/data mark undetected
Sector address undetected
Seek error (sector/track not found)
Hard error
Clock bit missing (when expected)
Drive not ready
Write protected (A disk can be protected from alteration by covering a slot in the envelope with tape before inserting the disk in the drive in a typical system.)

11.4 WINCHESTER DISK STORAGE SYSTEMS

Large-capacity *hard disk* systems incorporating a flying head mechanism have been used in computer systems for many years. The Winchester system is a recent form of flying-head disk system. In a traditional flying-head disk system, the disk is manufactured from a material such as aluminium treated with a magnetic coating. The diameter of the disk is typically 14 in. and several disks can be mounted on one spindle. The read/write heads are kept close but not touching the rigid disk as it revolves at high speed, typically 3000 to 4500 rpm. The head are spring-loaded and forced away from the surface by the air layer generated when the disk is revolving at high speed. It is necessary to retract the heads away from the surface completely when the system and disk motor are turned off because otherwise the head would crash into the surface. The flying-head mechanism allows very close head–media separation, typically in the region 50–100 μin., and can be designed so that the head retracts sufficiently for the disk to be removed from the drive and replaced with another disk. Such systems are known as *cartridge disks* as the disk is contained in a plastic cartridge case. It is essential to keep the whole assembly clean and free from foreign particles which might cause a head crash, including the smallest airborne particles. For example, a smoke particle is about 250 μin., several times the head-media separation, and might easily cause a head crash if sucked under the head.

The key feature of the Winchester type of flying-head system is that the head does not retract completely from the disk when the disk system is turned off, but lands on the surface in a controlled manner, taking off from the surface when the disk is turned on. To prevent damage, the disk surface is lubricated and additionally a special outside track is used as a landing zone and not for recording. When the disk is stationary, the head rests on this landing zone. When the disk motor is turned on, the disk rapidly accelerates and the head experiences a sliding contact with the surface for about $1/3$–$1/2$ of one revolution, taking off at about 400 rpm. When the system is switched off, a brake is applied to the disk spindle and the head lands as the speed reduces below about 400 rpm. This technique allows greater precision in the head actuator and disk assembly and a reduced flying distance of 20 μin. or less can be achieved, greatly increasing the bit densities. To achieve this flying distance, the head assembly must be very lightly loaded, typically 8–10 gm rather than around 350 gm in previous flying-head systems.

As it is very important in a Winchester system to exclude airborne particles, the complete system is sealed except for a highly efficient air filter. Some particles are generated internally through the action of the head landing on the surface and dislodging oxide. These particles must be removed from the unit as soon as possible. The whole system should then be very reliable and be able to withstand the occasional head crash.

Though Winchester development began as a replacement technology to large flying-head disk systems, it soon became apparent that it could be developed as a low-cost mass storage system suitable for microprocessor systems using 8 in. and 5¼ in. diameter disks. A typical 8 in. Winchester could have sixty-eight 128-byte sectors per track and 600–1600 tracks per surface. Capacities for 8 in. disks can be greater than 12 M bytes/surface.

11.5 MAGNETIC TAPE SYSTEMS

In a magnetic tape system, the recording medium is a reel of magnetic oxide-coated mylar tape which is fed past a set of read/write heads. There are various forms of tape system, from the large reel tape units found on large computer systems to the very small reel cassette tape units found on home computers. Tape systems differ in their data format from disk systems. In a disk system, each unit of information written or read is one sector, say 128 or 256 bytes. This is a fixed value, though it may be possible to transfer the contents of a number of consecutive sectors one after the other if required. In tape systems the length of the data stream is not fixed but may be any reasonable length. The complete contiguous stream of bits is called a *record*. A record is separated from adjacent records by *inter-record gaps* (IRGs) which are provided to enable the tape to stop and start between records (except tape streamers; see later).

A cassette tape system uses ¼ in. wide magnetic tape enclosed in a case similar to an audio cassette tape system; indeed, audio cassettes are used for digital storage on home computers, which use commercial audio cassette recorders with no modification. Recording is via the intermediate use of two sound tones to represent binary information. Digital techniques are applied to higher-quality, purpose-designed digital cassette systems.

An example of an audio cassette system is the *Kansas City standard* system in which a 1 is represented by 8 cycles at 2400 Hz and a 0 is represented by 4 cycles at 1200 Hz. The information is recorded using the RS232C format. In audio systems, the responsibility of finding a record or a correct place for writing is often left to the user who may need to resort to the use of a tape counter.

In higher-quality digital cassette systems, each record has an address header followed by the data items and CRC words. A preamble is included at the start of the record to synchronize the read/write circuitry, and a similar postamble is inserted at the end of the record. Digital cassette tape standards are laid down which specify, among other factors, the bit density, total tape length, the minimum and maximum data length in a record, preamble and postamble, CRC error detection word, and the inter-record gaps. The PE recording code is often used.

In 1972, 3M Corporation introduced a small ¼ in. wide tape cassette designed for data storage, known as a *cartridge tape*. A cartridge tape has a slightly larger case than a normal cassette and embodies an integral drive band to move the tape, rather than the conventional pinch roller and capstan or direct reel motor drive. The drive band of the cartridge is driven by an external motor and wraps partly around the tape on each reel, gripping the tape. This scheme results in constant tape tension whether the tape is stationary or in motion. Originally four tracks were recorded and 300 ft of tape provided. Subsequent developments include greater tape length and a 0.15 in. wide tape. More tracks can also be provided.

Tape systems are not a convenient backing store for frequent accessing because of the long time involved in winding and rewinding the tape to select the records. Tapes are much more suited as back-up or archival storage. Particularly relevant to microprocessor systems is the use of cartridge for back-up to Winchester disks. Protection against lost data due to disk crashes or otherwise can be afforded by dumping the contents of the Winchester disk at the end of each day after all transactions and computations have been done. Simply taking a copy of a hard disk for safety can be done using a tape operation known as *streaming*. Streaming was first introduced on larger ½ in. tape systems to back-up disks. Now the idea has been extended to ¼ in. cartidge tape systems.

Firstly, consider the conventional mode of operation of tape systems, which can be described as start-stop. The length of the IRG must be sufficient to enable the tape mechanism to stop between records. On larger ½ in. tape systems, the tape transport incorporates vacuum chambers (10½ in. reels) or tension arms (7 in. and 8½ in. reels) to buffer the inertia of the heavy reels from the tape. Without the requirement for rapid start/stop, these complicated and expensive mechanical arrangements are not necessary, and a much simpler system can be used. This is the rationale behind tape streamers. Simply dumping the contents of a disk on to a tape does not require rapid start/stop. In a streamer, any interblock gaps are written while the tape is moving from one block to the next. If it is necessary to position the tape at the beginning of a block, a sequence of stopping, reversing and shunting forward to the required place is performed. This is a time-consuming process but done infrequently. The tape format and recording can actually be the same as used in the start/stop mode to allow interchangeability. The tape system can be designed to operate in two modes, a slow speed start/stop and a higher speed streaming mode.

The ¼ in. cartridge tape can also be designed to operate in an equivalent streaming mode. A GCR code can be used and tracks recorded in a serpentine fashion with alternate tracks recorded in opposite directions to eliminate rewind at the end of the tape during reading or writing.

REFERENCES

1. Tamura, T., M. Tsutsumi, H. Aoi, N. Matsuishi, N. Nakagoshi, S. Kawano and M. Makita, 'A Coding Method in Digital Magnetic Recording', *IEEE Trans. Magnetics*, MAG 8 (1972), 612–14.
2. Wilkinson, B., and D. Horrocks, *Computer Peripherals*. London: Hodder and Stoughton, 1980.
3. Franchini, R. C., and D. L. Wartner, 'A Method of High Density Recording on Flexible Magnetic Discs', *Computer Design* (Oct. 1976), 106–9.
4. *Component Data Catalog*. Santa Clara, California: Intel Corp., 1982.

PROBLEMS

11.1 Encode the data pattern 011101000 in each of the following magnetic recording codes:

(a)   Non-return-to-zero-inverted (NRZI)
(b)   Frequency modulation (FM)
(c)   Phase encoding (PE)
(d)   Modified frequency modulation (MFM)

Sketch the read signal in each case.

11.2 Calculate the percentage decrease in recording density if the group coded recording code given in Table 11.1 is used in instead of NRZI recording.

11.3 Determine the shortest and the longest length of magnetization in one state for each of the following codes:

(a)   NRZI
(b)   PE
(c)   FM
(d)   MFM
(e) M^2FM
(f)   MNRZI

The efficiency of a magnetic recording code is given by:

$$\text{Efficiency} = \frac{\text{bit density}}{\text{flux density}} \times 100\% = \frac{100}{\text{number of flux changes per bit}}\%$$

Determine the efficiency of each recording code.

11.4 Devise a group coded recording code encoding 8-bit data words such that there are no more than three zeros recorded included when encoded patterns are concatenated.

11.5 Show that the peak shift in M^2FM occurs with the three data patterns:

011X
110X
0001

where X indicates that the bit can be either a 0 or a 1. Specify the peak shift as either early or late (see Fig. 11.5). Identify the one pattern in which the peak shift is less than the others. Peak shift occurs in the second bit.

11.6 An 8 in. floppy disk has an inside track diameter of 4.058 in. and an outside track diameter of 7.2746 in. A variable-speed drive is used. The inside track speed is 360 rpm. Calculate the outside speed to maintain the same bit density on both tracks.

11.7 The head of a floppy disk has a life of 5000 hours continuous contact. Estimate the life of the head if the disk has 11 sectors, revolves at 300 rpm and there are on average two disk accesses every second.

11.8 Draw the clock and data pulses associated with the data pattern 01100111 recorded in FM, MFM and M^{2}FM. State the hexadecimal numbers describing the clock pattern and data pattern.

PART **3**

FURTHER ASPECTS OF DIGITAL SYSTEM DESIGN

Formal Sequential Circuit Design

A method of developing a sequential logic circuit beginning with a state diagram was introduced in Chap. 4 to obtain the basic J–K flip-flop circuit configuration and to design synchronous binary counters. The method will be considered further in this chapter.

12.1 SYNCHRONOUS SEQUENTIAL CIRCUIT DESIGN

12.1.1 General model

The general model for a synchronous sequential circuit is shown in Fig. 12.1. There are a number of inputs to the circuit, x_0, x_1 $\cdots$, x_n and a number of outputs, Z_0, Z_1, $\cdots$, Z_m. In addition, internal signals are generated, Y_0, Y_1, $\cdots$, Y_k which are stored (shown using D-type flip-flops) and fed back to the input. The signals fed back to the input are labeled here y_0, y_1, $\cdots$, y_k. Thus the sequential circuit is divided into two parts, a combinational logic section and a storage section. The internal Y variables are combinational functions of the y variables and the system input variables.

The whole circuit exists in a particular state as defined by the y variables, and hence these variables are called *state variables* or *present-state variables*. With three state variables and three flip-flops, there could be eight different states. The present state variables and applied input variables produce the Y signals which will produce a change in the present state variables after the activating clock transition has occurred. Hence the Y variables could be called the *next-state variables*. The output variables are combinational functions of the present state variables, and the applied input variables in some cases. Sometimes state variables are also the system outputs, as in the case of synchronous counters.

We expect the system input changes, if any, to occur at one instant between the activating clock transitions, perhaps just before a transition. There must be a sufficient delay between the occurrence of new input values and the clock transition to allow the next-state variables to be set up in time for the clock transition. Multiple changes in the inputs between activating clock transitions have no effect on the state of the circuit; only the value of the inputs at the time of the activating clock transition can cause a state change. The type of clock transition (rising edge or falling edge) which causes a state change is that which

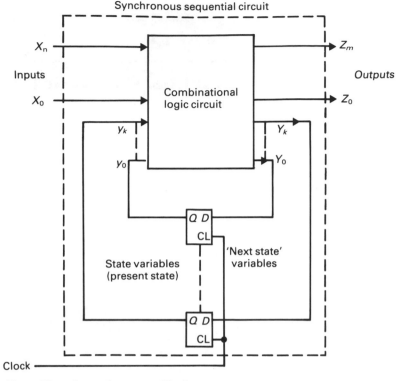

Synchronous sequential circuit

Note: Though not shown specifically,
flip-flops are normally edge-triggered.

Figure 12.1   General model of a synchronous sequential circuit

activates the particular flip-flops used. However, multiple input changes between activating clock transitions may be reflected on the output if the output is a combinational function of both the state variables and the input variables.

12.1.2 Design procedure

Consider the following problem: a synchronous sequential circuit has one output, Z, and one input, x. The output is to be at a logic 1 whenever the sequence 0010110 (the ASCII code for 'SYN') occurs in serial form on x. The output is to become a 1 during the last bit of the sequence. Overlapping sequences are not to produce a 1 output. A synchronizing clock signal is provided. Design the circuit.

This sequence detector problem, though chosen to illustrate the formal techniques of traditional synchronous sequential circuit design, has application in computer design. Data transmitted serially, i.e. along one wire one bit at a time for high-speed transmission, may use the synchronous serial format rather than the common asynchronous serial format. In the synchronous serial format, start and stop bits are not introduced and many characters are transmitted without any data gaps. Timing is achieved by inserting SYN characters at intervals. These SYN characters are intercepted by the receiving circuitry. The problem here is in effect to design the intercept circuitry. Such circuitry is usually incorporated into integrated circuit synchronous serial transmitter/ receiver circuit parts.

The first step we shall take is to draw the state diagram. This step is usually the most difficult because the state diagram usually needs to be deduced from the problem specification. Clearly the state diagram must be correct, otherwise the subsequent implementation will be incorrect. We can use the Moore model state diagram or the Mealy model state diagram. Recall that in a Mealy model state diagram, the output is associated with the corresponding input values on the paths connecting the present and new states. In the Moore model state diagram, the output is associated with the state only. Hence in the Mealy model, the output will generally be a combinational function of both the system input variables and the (present) state variables representing the state. In the Moore model, the output will only be a combinational function of the state variables. Here we will create two designs, one based on the Mealy model, and one based on the Moore model to show implications of each model.

(a) Mealy model state diagram

The Mealy model state diagram of our sequence detector is shown in Fig. 12.2(a). There must be an initial state from which other states are entered when the required bits in the sequence are encountered. Since there are seven digits

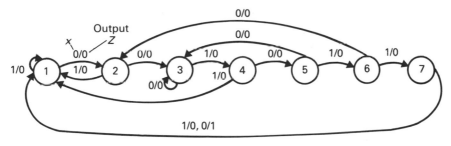

(a) Mealy model state diagram

Present state	Next state x		Output Z x	
	0	1	0	1
1	2	1	0	0
2	3	1	0	0
3	3	4	0	0
4	5	1	0	0
5	3	6	0	0
6	2	7	0	0
7	1	1	1	0

(b) State table

Present state $Y_3Y_2Y_1$	Next state $Y_3Y_2Y_1$		Output Z x	
	0	1	0	1
000	001	000	0	0
001	011	000	0	0
011	011	010	0	0
010	100	000	0	0
100	011	101	0	0
101	001	111	0	0
111	000	000	1	0

(c) Assigned state table (Y matrix)

Figure 12.2 Sequence detector using Mealy model state diagram

in the sequence, there are seven fundamental states and the move from one state to the next is after the next bit in the sequence has occurred at the input.

In the state diagram, the path caused by the occurrence of the correct sequence is from left to right except the final path from state 7 to state 1. If the input is a 0 for the final path, the output becomes a 1. This output will remain for only one clock duration (approximately, depending upon the state variable timing). The other paths in the state diagram are for incorrect sequences. Not all intermediate paths return to the initial state 1. When determining return paths, the bit patterns received at each state must be examined to see if the last part corresponds to the beginning of the required sequence. In our problem, at state 3, if a 0 is received, the circuit stays in state 3 because at least three 0's have been received, of which the last two may be the first two 0's in the correct sequence. Similarly, the return path from state 5 is to state 3, not state 1, as two 0's have been received. The return path at state 6 upon receiving a 0 is to state 2, not state 1, because the 0 received may be the first 0 in the correct sequence. It is specified that overlapping sequences are not allowed. In our case, the final 0 in the sequence cannot also be the first 0 in a new sequence. Therefore, the return path from 7 to 1 when a 0 is received is to state 1, not state 2.

The state table is obtained from the state diagram and this is shown in Fig. 12.2(b). The output is due to the present state and the new system input. The next step is to minimize this table if possible, i.e. to reduce the number of states in the table to a minimum. We will consider minimization separately. The state table for our problem does not minimize.

Then state variables are assigned to represent the states. We need a minimum of n state variables when the number of states lies between $2^{n-1} + 1$ and 2^n. One (binary) variable is needed for two states, two variables when there are 3 or 4 variables, three variables for 5 to 8 states, four variables for 9 to 16 states, five variables for 17 to 32 states, etc. Therefore in our case, we need three variables to represent the seven states. An arbitrary approach can be used to assign the state variables to the states. Here we will make the arbitrary assignment as shown in Table 12.1. This particular choice will allow rapid translation of state variables on to Karnaugh maps. However, it may not necessarily lead to the minimum number of gates. This matter will be raised later. After an assignment is made, the state numbers in the state table are replaced by the equivalent state variables to produce an assigned state table as shown in Fig. 12.2(c). The assigned state table is known as a *Y matrix*. Note that the present states are represented by the assigned y (present-state) variables and the next states are represented by the assigned Y (next-state) variables.

We now need to decide on the implementation. Examining our model of a synchronous sequential circuit shown in Fig. 12.1, we see that flip-flops are required to store the state variables. Combinational circuits generate the next-state variables and output from the system input variables and stored state variables. We could use small-scale integrated circuits (SSI) for the combinational section and SSI flip-flops for storage.

Firstly, let us choose D-type flip-flops and gates. Three D-type flip-flops are required for the three state variables. It is necessary to determine the next-

Table 12.1   State variable assignment for synchronous sequential circuit problem

y_3	y_2	y_1	State
0	0	0	1
0	0	1	2
0	1	1	3
0	1	0	4
1	0	0	5
1	0	1	6
1	1	1	7

state variables, i.e. the Boolean expressions for the D inputs. Karnaugh maps can be drawn for each of D_1, D_2 and D_3. The flip-flop Q output of a D-type flip-flop is the same as the applied D input, after clock activation. Therefore, the new values of y_1 (i.e. the values of Y_1) are entered on to the D_1 map, the new values of y_2 (i.e. Y_2) are entered on to the D_2 map and the new values of y_3 (i.e. Y_3) are entered on to the D_3 map. The output expression is also derived from the state table. The Karnaugh maps for the three state variables and the output, Z, are shown in Fig. 12.3(a). The expressions are minimized. Because this is a multi-output combinational circuit, common terms are sought. One such term is found in D_1 and D_3 ($y_3 \bar{y}_2 x$) and chosen in D_1 rather than the reduced term, $y_3 \bar{y}_2$. Another common term, $\bar{y}_3 y_2 \bar{x}$, is found in D_1 and D_2. Finally, from the minimized expressions, we obtain the circuit implementation, as shown in Fig. 12.3(b). This circuit is drawn to emphasize the correspondence with the synchronous sequential circuit model.

(b) Moore model state diagram

The Moore model state diagram for our sequence detector is shown in Fig. 12.4(a). Note that an extra state (8) is introduced. States 1 to 6 and the interconnecting paths are identical to those in the Mealy model state diagram. The state table is shown in Fig. 12.4(b) and the assigned state table in Fig. 12.4(c). Three state variables are again adequate. The new state, 8, is assigned the number 110. A D-type flip-flop design based on the assigned state table is shown in Fig. 12.5. Note that the output is only a function of the state variables, y_3, y_2 and y_1. Compared to the Mealy model design, we observe that the number of states is increased. This is often the case, though in our particular example, no extra flip-flops are necesssary. Traditionally, the Mealy model has been selected for synchronous designs because it results in the minimum number of states and hence the minimum number of flip-flops.

If the inputs only change at the time of the activating clock transition, the output will be the same in both designs. However, if the input does change (even transiently, say due to noise) at other times, the output may also change in the Mealy model design but not in the Moore model design. In the Mealy model, the output is a function of both the state variables and the system input variables. In the Moore model design, the output is only a function of the state variables which can only change at the time of the activating clock transition.

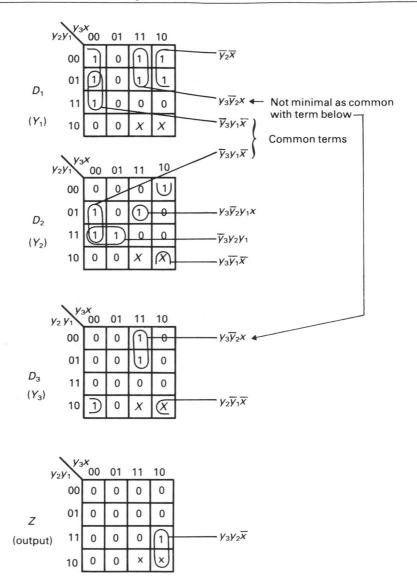

$$D_1 = \bar{y}_2\bar{x} + y_3\bar{y}_2x + \bar{y}_3y_1\bar{x}$$
$$D_2 = \bar{y}_3y_1\bar{x} + y_3\bar{y}_2y_1x + \bar{y}_3y_2y_1 + y_3\bar{y}_1\bar{x}$$
$$D_3 = y_3\bar{y}_2x + y_2\bar{y}_1\bar{x}$$
$$Z = y_3y_2\bar{x}$$

(a) Next state and output functions

Figure 12.3   Sequence detector design using *D*-type flip-flops (Mealy model)

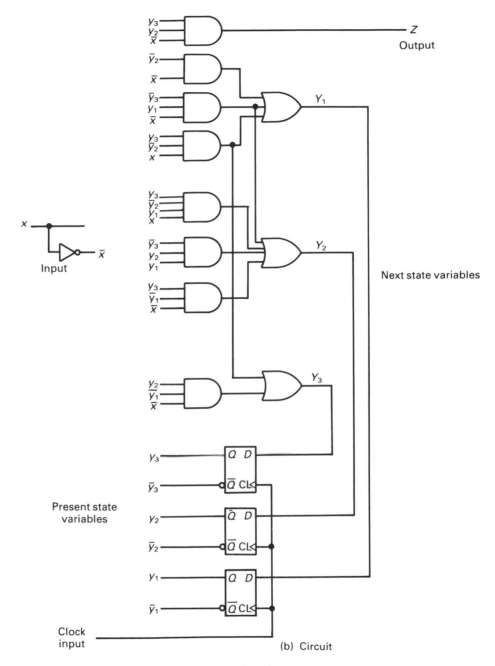

Figure 12.3 *continued*

(c) Alternative implementations

Consider another problem: a synchronous sequential circuit has one output, Z, and two inputs, x_1 and x_2. The output will be at a 1 whenever the input sequence on x_1 and x_2 both consist of 0011 in the same time sequence. The

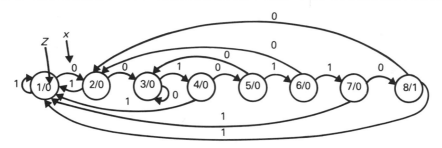

(a) Moore model state diagram

Present state	Next state x		Present output, Z
	0	1	
1	2	1	0
2	3	1	0
3	3	4	0
4	5	1	0
5	3	6	0
6	2	7	0
7	8	1	0
8	2	1	1

(b) State table

Present state $y_3y_2y_1$	Next state $Y_3Y_2Y_1$ x		Present output, Z
	0	1	
000	001	000	0
001	011	000	0
011	011	010	0
010	100	000	0
100	011	101	0
101	001	111	0
111	110	000	0
110	001	000	1

(c) Assigned state table (Y matrix)

Figure 12.4 Sequence detector using Moore model state diagram

output will become a 1 during the last bit period of the sequence. Design the circuit.

This problem is similar to the previous sequence detector, except that there are two synchronous inputs rather than one. The Mealy model state diagram is shown in Fig. 12.6(a) and the state table in Fig. 12.6(b). There are four states so that two state variables are adequate. The assigned state table is shown in Fig. 12.6(c). Notice that there are four next-state columns and four output columns, because there are four combinations of the two inputs. The combinations are listed in the order which corresponds to the labels of a Karnaugh map. A design using D-type flip-flops is shown in Fig. 12.7. Notice that there is a direct correspondence of entries in the assigned state table and four variable Karnaugh maps.

As a first alternative, let us choose J–K flip-flops rather than D-type flip-flops. Table 4.3 in Chap. 4 lists the required input values for each of the possible output effects (0 to 0, 0 to 1, 1 to 0 and 1 to 1) and is used to deduce the required J–K inputs. There are two next-state variables for each flip-flop, one for the J input and one for the K input. For each present-state entry and each state variable, we note the present output (y) to next-stop output (Y) change. For example, in the first state, the present to next-state change is a 0 to 0 for y_1.

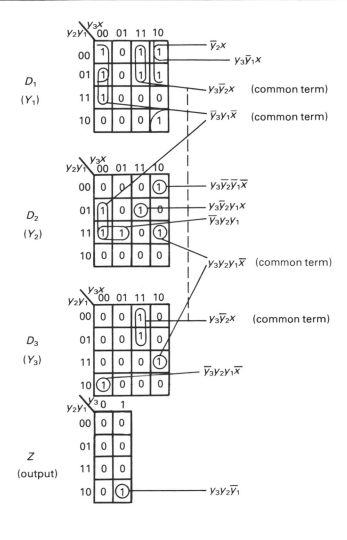

$$D_1 = \bar{y}_2 x + y_3 \bar{y}_2 x + \bar{y}_3 y_1 \bar{x}$$
$$D_2 = y_3 \bar{y}_2 \bar{y}_1 \bar{x} + y_3 \bar{y}_2 y_1 x + \bar{y}_3 y_2 y_1 + \bar{y}_3 y_2 y_1 \bar{x} + \bar{y}_3 y_1 \bar{x}$$
$$D_3 = y_3 y_2 y_1 \bar{x} + \bar{y}_3 y_2 y_1 \bar{x} + y_3 \bar{y}_2 y_1$$
$$Z = y_3 y_2 \bar{y}_1$$

(a) **Next state and output functions**

Figure 12.5   Sequence detector design using *D*-type flip-flops (Moore model)

Therefore the top left-hand entry of the J_1 Karnaugh map is a 0 and a don't care (*X*) for K_1 to achieve this change according to the table. All other changes are examined to complete each Karnaugh map. The final realization using *J–K* flip-flops is shown in Fig. 12.8.

We could use synchronous *R–S* flip-flops. Then Table 4.1 in Chap. 4 is

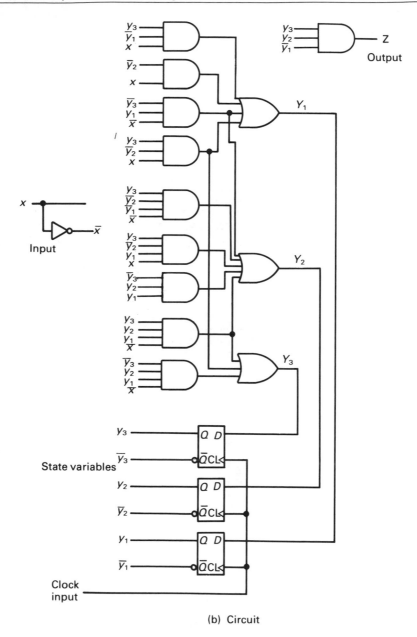

(b) Circuit

Figure 12.5   *continued*

used to deduce the required *R–S* inputs. The *R–S* flip-flops must not be simple cross-coupled NAND/NOR gates. An edge-triggered or master–slave version is necessary for stable operation. (There is only one suitable *R–S* flip-flop available in the TTL 7400 family, namely the old 74L71 master–slave flip-flop which has three '*S*' and three '*R*' AND-gated inputs.)

A completely different approach is to replace the combinational circuitry

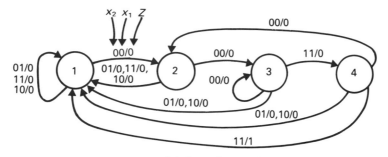

(a) State diagram (Mealy model)

Present state	Next state x_2,x_1				Output x_2,x_1			
	00	01	11	10	00	01	11	10
1	2	1	1	1	0	0	0	0
2	3	1	1	1	0	0	0	0
3	3	1	4	1	0	0	0	0
4	2	1	1	1	0	0	1	0

(b) State table

Present state y_2y_1	Next state, Y_2Y_1 x_2,x_1				Output Z x_2,x_1			
	00	01	11	10	00	01	11	10
00	01	00	00	00	0	0	0	0
01	11	00	00	00	0	0	0	0
11	11	00	10	00	0	0	0	0
10	01	00	00	00	0	0	1	0

(c) Assigned state table (Y matrix)

Figure 12.6 Two-input sequence detector

with a read-only memory (ROM) in conjunction with a storage register (e.g. *D*-type flip-flops) as shown in Fig. 12.9(a). Each memory location of the ROM is addressed by the input variables, x_2x_1, and state variables, y_2y_1. The ROM outputs are the next-state variables, Y_2Y_1, and the circuit output, Z. The memory contents are found directly from the assigned state table as shown in Fig. 12.9(b). The approach is particularly elegant and one which is easy to check or modify by ROM replacement. Since large-capacity read-only memories are manufactured, state minimization may be unnecessary, and indeed undesirable because it then masks the original sequence.

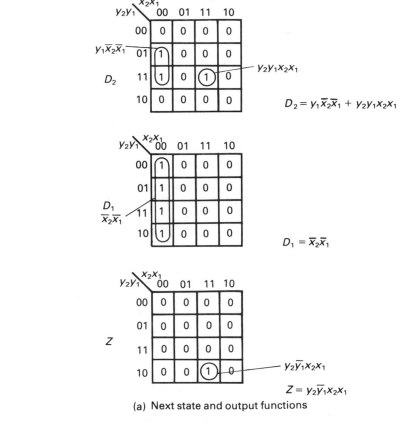

$$D_2 = y_1\bar{x}_2\bar{x}_1 + y_2y_1x_2x_1$$

$$D_1 = \bar{x}_2\bar{x}_1$$

$$Z = y_2\bar{y}_1x_2x_1$$

(a) Next state and output functions

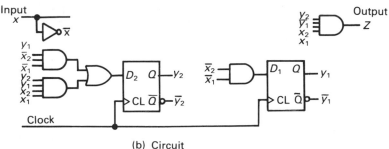

(b) Circuit

Figure 12.7   Two-input sequence detector design using *D*-type flip-flops

12.1.3 State minimization

The minimum number of states is usually a requirement for SSI/MSI implementation, to reduce the number of gates. State minimization methods are available which depend upon recognizing states which are identical or can be made identical.

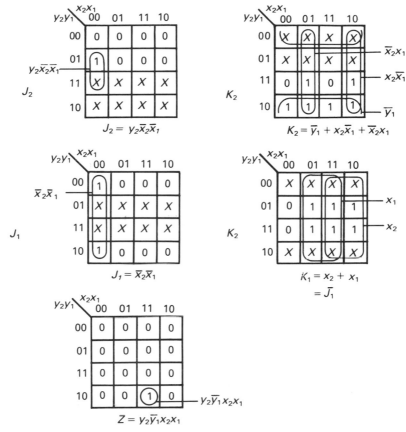

$$J_2 = y_2\bar{x}_2\bar{x}_1$$

$$K_2 = \bar{y}_1 + x_2\bar{x}_1 + \bar{x}_2x_1$$

$$J_1 = \bar{x}_2\bar{x}_1$$

$$K_1 = x_2 + x_1$$
$$= J_1$$

$$Z = y_2\bar{y}_1x_2x_1$$

(a) Next state and output functions

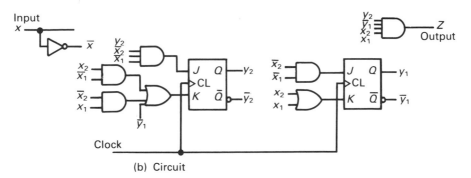

(b) Circuit

Figure 12.8 Two-input sequence detector design using *J–K* flip-flops

Consider the state table given in Table 12.2 based on a Mealy model. Here there are two input variables, x_1 and x_2, eight states and one output, Z. States cannot be the same or made the same if their outputs are different for the same conditions. For example, state 5 has a 1 in the $x_2x_1 = 11$ output column whereas all other states have a 0 in that column. This is known as an *output incompatible*

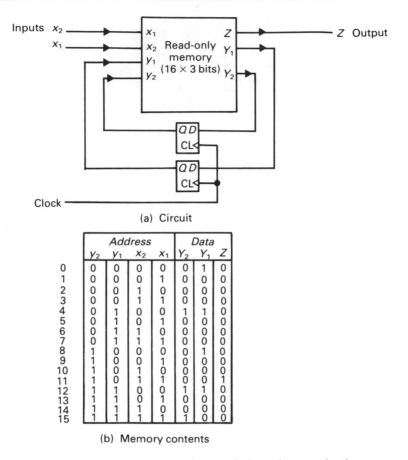

(a) Circuit

	Address				Data		
	y_2	y_1	x_2	x_1	Y_2	Y_1	Z
0	0	0	0	0	0	1	0
1	0	0	0	1	0	0	0
2	0	0	1	0	0	0	0
3	0	0	1	1	0	0	0
4	0	1	0	0	1	1	0
5	0	1	0	1	0	0	0
6	0	1	1	0	0	0	0
7	0	1	1	1	0	0	0
8	1	0	0	0	0	1	0
9	1	0	0	1	0	0	0
10	1	0	1	0	0	0	0
11	1	0	1	1	0	0	1
12	1	1	0	0	1	1	0
13	1	1	0	1	0	0	0
14	1	1	1	0	0	0	0
15	1	1	1	1	1	0	0

(b) Memory contents

Figure 12.9 Two-input sequence detector design using a read-only memory

state. Therefore state 5 cannot be combined with any other state. All the other states have compatible outputs and it may be possible to combine some of these states together.

A procedure is to look at every combination of pairs of states which are output compatible and note for each pair, the required states which must be identical for the pair to be equivalent. This is shown in Table 12.3 for our problem. Then the required equivalent pairs are examined. All output incompatible pairs are identified and the associated possible equivalent pair is deleted. If this results in other pairs being incompatible, these are also deleted. The process is continued until all incompatible pairs are deleted, leaving possible equivalent pairs.

Creating a state diagram in which states are equivalent may occur because the state diagram is deduced intuitively from the problem specification. There can be more than one state diagram which describes a circuit, some with more states than others.

In our state diagram, the following pairs are equivalent:

$$1 \equiv 2$$

Table 12.2 State table; candidate for minimization

Present state	Next state x_2x_1				Output Z x_2x_1			
	00	01	11	10	00	01	11	10
1	1	2	2	4	0	0	0	0
2	1	3	1	4	0	0	0	0
3	1	3	2	4	0	0	0	0
4	1	8	1	5	0	0	0	0
5	1	5	6	5	0	0	1	0
6	3	8	7	5	0	0	0	0
7	2	8	6	5	0	0	0	0
8	3	8	7	8	0	0	1	0

Table 12.3 Equivalent pairs in Table 12.2

Possible equivalent pairs	Required equivalent pairs	Incompatible
1,2	(2,3)	
1,3	(2,3)	
1,4	(2,8), (1,2), (4,5)	x
1,6	(1,3), (2,8), (2,7), (4,5)	x
1,7	(1,2), (2,8), (2,6), (4,5)	x
2,3	(1,2)	
2,4	(3,8), (4,5)	x
2,6	(1,3), (3,8), (1,7), (4,5)	x
2,7	(1,2), (3,8), (1,6), (4,5)	x
3,4	(3,8), (1,2), (4,5)	x
3,6	(1,3), (3,8), (2,7), (4,5)	x
3,7	(1,2), (3,8), (2,6), (4,5)	x
4,6	(1,3), (1,7)	x
4,7	(1,2), (1,6)	x
5,8	(1,3), (6,7)	
6,7	(3,2)	

$$1 \equiv 3$$
$$2 \equiv 3$$
$$5 \equiv 8$$
$$6 \equiv 7$$

The remaining state, 4, is incompatible with any other state. Since $1 \equiv 2$, $1 \equiv 3$ and $2 \equiv 3$, we can say that $1 \equiv 2 \equiv 3$. In fact, if only two of these equivalent pairs are found, say $1 \equiv 2$ and $1 \equiv 3$, it is correct to deduce the third pair, 2 is equivalent to 3 and hence all three are equivalent, if every next state is specified in the state table. This produces three identical entries. It is not allowable to make this deduction if the state table has don't cares. State tables with don't cares are discussed in the section 12.1.5.

We now need to select a group of equivalent states which as a set includes all the original states. There may be more than one selection which will cover all the states. In our case, the minimization procedure results in only one possible selection:

$$(1 \equiv 2 \equiv 3),(4),(5 \equiv 8),(6 \equiv 7)$$

which could be called, say:

A, B, C, D

Then a new reduced state table is drawn in terms of these states, as shown in Table 12.4. Each occurrence of 1, 2 or 3 has been replaced by *A*, each occurrence of 4 by *B*, each occurrence of 5 or 8 by *C* and each occurrence of 6 or 7 by *D*. The design procedure then follows the usual pattern using the reduced state table to form the *Y*-matrix.

Table 12.4   Minimized state table

Present state	Next state x_2x_1				Output, Z x_2x_1			
	00	01	11	10	00	01	11	10
A	A	A	A	B	0	0	0	0
B	A	C	A	C	0	0	0	0
C	A	C	D	C	0	0	1	0
D	A	C	D	C	0	0	0	0

12.1.4 State assignment

So far, the assignment of state variables to states has been done arbitrarily. It may be that one paritcular assignment will result in less components in the final design. However, there is no known method to obtain directly an assignment which will result in a minimum component count for every problem. It even differs for different implementations. The number of assignment combinations grows very rapidly with the number of states and it is impractical to try every combination except in very small problems. After choosing the minimum number of state variables, we can employ two rules of thumb which tend to lead to fewer components:

(i)   Choose codes which differ by one variable (are adjacent on a Karnaugh map) for states that lead to the same next state.
(ii) Where (i) is not possible, choose codes which differ by one variable for next states of a present state.

Usually neither of these rules can be applied completely. By applying the rules to the Mealy model 'SYN' sequence detector problem, one assignment becomes as shown in Table 12.5. It is left to the reader to rework the design procedure.

12.1.5 Incompletely specified systems

An incompletely specified system is one in which there is at least one condition that cannot occur, or if it does occur, the response of the system is irrelevant. This is the same as 'cannot happen' or don't care conditions in combinational circuits. As an example, consider the following incompletely specified problem.

Table 12.5 State assignment using empirical rules

State	Assignment $y_3y_2y_1$
1	000
2	001
3	011
4	010
5	101
6	110
7	100

A synchronous sequential circuit has a single input, x, and a single output, Z. A binary sequence is applied to the input and the output is required to become a 1 only when the serial input sequence 00110010 is detected and then only during the last clock pulse period of the sequence. The sequence 0010 cannot occur except as part of the sequence to be detected. Design the circuit.

A Mealy model state diagram for this problem is shown in Fig. 12.10(a), deduced in a similar manner as previous diagrams (and purposely not minimal to illustrate the technique of minimizing incompletely specified systems). As in the previous sequence detector, the main flow is from left to right with incorrect numbers causing paths backwards, not all of which return to state 1. Because the sequence 0010 cannot occur except as the latter part of the correct sequence, there is a 'cannot happen' situation at state 4. A 0 cannot occur here since this would form 0010. The state table is given in Fig. 12.10(b). The cannot happen condition at state 4 with x input at a 0 is marked in both the next state and the output columns as an X. Minimizing results in the following equivalent pairs, interpreting the X's differently in the cases where state 4 is involved:

$$
\begin{array}{llll}
1 \equiv 2 & 2 \equiv 3 & 3 \equiv 4 & 4 \equiv 5 \\
1 \equiv 3 & 2 \equiv 4 & 3 \equiv 5 & 4 \equiv 6 \\
1 \equiv 4 & 2 \equiv 5 & 3 \equiv 6 & 4 \equiv 8 \\
1 \equiv 5 & 2 \equiv 6 & 3 \equiv 7 &
\end{array}
$$

Generally in incompletely specified systems, it does not follow automatically that if $A \equiv B$ and $B \equiv C$, then $A \equiv C$ because the don't care/cannot happen conditions might be interpreted differently for $A \equiv B$ and $B \equiv C$. Therefore only pairs are formed. In our case, there is a completely circular equivalence of $1 \equiv 4$, $1 \equiv 5$ and $4 \equiv 5$. Consequently we can say that $1 \equiv 4 \equiv 5$. The X in the state table is interpreted as either 6 or 2 and one equivalent pair is $2 \equiv 6$.

We need to choose those pairs which as a set cover all the original numbers, and also do not require other pairs to be equivalent which are not in the selection. This leads to the following selection (by trial and error):

$$(1 \equiv 5), (2 \equiv 6), (3 \equiv 7), (4 \equiv 8)$$

The reduced state table with these four states is shown in Fig. 12.10(c), the reduced state diagram in Fig. 12.10(d) and the assigned state table in Fig. 12.10(e). A solution using D-type flip-flops is shown in Fig. 12.11.

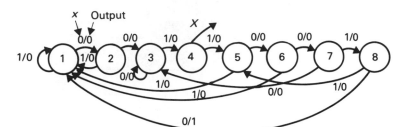

(a) State diagram

Present state	Next state *x* 0	1	Output *x* 0	1
1	2	1	0	0
2	3	1	0	0
3	3	4	0	0
4	X	5	X	0
5	6	1	0	0
6	7	1	0	0
7	3	8	0	0
8	1	5	1	0

(b) State table

Present state	Next state *x* 0	1	Output *x* 0	1
1/5	2	1	0	0
2/6	3	1	0	0
3/7	3	4	0	0
4/8	1	1	1	0

(c) Reduced state table

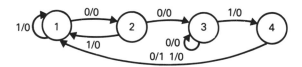

(d) Reduced state diagram

Present state $y_2 y_1$	Next state $Y_2 Y_1$ 0 *x* 1	Output *x* 0 1
00	01 00	0 0
01	11 00	0 0
11	11 10	0 0
10	00 00	1 0

(e) Assigned state table

Figure 12.10   Incompletely specified problem

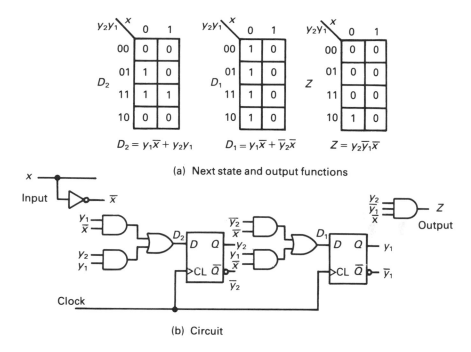

$$D_2 = y_1\bar{x} + y_2 y_1 \qquad D_1 = y_1\bar{x} + \bar{y}_2\bar{x} \qquad Z = y_2\bar{y}_1\bar{x}$$

(a) Next state and output functions

(b) Circuit

Figure 12.11   Implementation of incompletely specified problem using *D*-type flip-flops

The original state diagram was deduced intuitively using more than the necesssary number of states so that the formal minimization techniques can be shown. Clearly, it is possible (and desirable) to deduce the minimal state diagram (Fig. 12.10(d)) directly without needing to minimize formally. For more complex problems, the minimal state diagram may not be obvious.

12.2 ASYNCHRONOUS SEQUENTIAL CIRCUIT DESIGN

12.2.1 Asynchronous circuit design difficulties

The general model of an asynchronous sequential logic circuit is shown in Fig. 12.12. As opposed to a synchronous sequential logic circuit, a general asynchronous sequential logic circuit does not use a clock signal to time all events. The system inputs are called *primary variables*. The inputs may change at any time unless some restriction is placed on them. An asynchronous sequential logic circuit, as a synchronous sequential logic circuit, can exist in a particular state, though in an asynchronous sequential circuit some of the states only last for a short time between changes from one permanent or *stable* state to another stable state. The transitory states are called *unstable* states. The states are indicated by the *y* state variables, called here the *secondary variables*. The *Y*

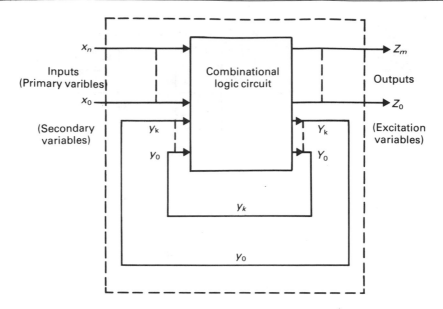

Figure 12.12   General model of an asynchronous sequential circuit

signals generated from the combinational circuit part of the system cause a change in the state and are called here the *excitation variables*. The excitation variables are fed back into the combinational logic, and enter the combinational circuit as secondary variables. The circuit is in a stable state when the primary inputs are stable and all internal signals have been established. In the stable state, the excitation variables and the secondary variables are the same. The excitation variables can be imagined to be generated with no delay through the combinational logic circuit and a lumped delay introduced between the excitation variables and the secondary variables. The terms primary variables, excitation variables and secondary variables derive from relay switching circuit design [1].

Though the design of asynchronous sequential logic circuits follows similar lines to that of synchronous sequential circuits, the lack of any synchronization presents additional constraints and design problems over the synchronous circuits. If, for example, two excitation signals are fed back to the inputs and it is intended that both these signals should change together, say from 00 to 11, after an input change, it is most likely in practice that one signal will change before the other due to different delays in the circuit. For a short period we may have the combinations 01 or 10. One of these combinations may be sufficient to cause the circuit to enter an unwanted state, producing new excitation signals and subsequent incorrect operation. Similarly, if the system primary inputs change together, an incorrect sequence could be followed. To avoid this problem, asynchronous sequential circuits are designed so that internal signals fed back to the input do not change simultaneously. In addition to disallowing simultaneous changes, sufficient time must elapse between any changes to allow the system to settle.

Preventing simultaneous changes in system inputs is more difficult as this may occur naturally. It is necessary to assume that simultaneous input changes do not occur (or to prevent such changes) to be able to design an asynchronous sequential circuit that will work reliably. In some cases, we might be able to consider a change of two inputs from, say, 00 to 11, as either a change from 00 to 01 and then from 01 to 11, or as a change from 00 to 10 and then from 10 to 11, i.e. limiting the change to one signal at any instant. If so, it is still necessary that the time between the changes is sufficient for the circuit to distinguish the input changes. We can compare the problem to the input set-up and hold times that must be satisfied in a flip-flop such as a D-type flip-flop (which internally can be considered as an asynchronous sequential circuit). If we applied a signal change on the D input at exactly the same time as the activating clock transition, the operation of the flip-flop would be indeterminant. If simultaneous input changes are likely to occur in a problem, asynchronous sequential circuit design should not be used [2].

An asynchronous sequential circuit design must also not generate *critical race hazards*. As mentioned in Chap. 3, section 3.2.9, a race hazard is a logic configuration which leads to the unwanted generation of logic spikes due to signals passing through different paths to the output and the signal delays have been different. A critical race hazard is one which subsequently causes the system to operate incorrectly (i.e., to enter unwanted stable states). Race hazards can be tolerated in an asynchronous sequential circuit if they cause perhaps different unstable states to be entered but finally the same stable state to be reached; indeed, allowing non-critical race hazards can give reduced logic components.

Race hazards can be classified into three types:

(i)   Static race hazards
(ii) Dynamic race hazards
(iii) Essential race hazards

A *static race hazard* can be created a race between a signal and its complement and is considered in Chap 3. It was noted that these race hazards can be completely eliminated by the introduction of all the prime implicants in the Boolean expression being implemented. Note, however, that static race hazards are concerned with 1-to-0 logic transitions on input signals (in sum-of-product expressions) and not with 0-to-1 transitions. In an asynchronous sequential circuit, it is only necessary to correct for a static race hazard if a 1-to-0 change will occur. Often, there are several transitions that cannot occur if the circuit is functioning correctly. We can of course correct for all static race hazards, but this would often lead to more components than actually necessary [3].

A *dynamic race hazard* results in three transitions in a signal when only one is intended, for example a change from 0 to 1 to 0 to 1 instead of a 0-to-1 change. Such hazards may be due to multilevel gate implementations in which signals interact as they pass through several gates between the input and output. If circuits are designed with only two levels of gating and static hazards have been eliminated, dynamic hazards do not occur.

Both static hazards and dynamic hazards are combinational circuit hazards, but generally are only significant in asynchronous sequential circuits (as opposed to purely combinational logic circuits or synchronous sequential circuits). In contrast, an *essential race hazard* is found only in asynchronous sequential circuits, and is caused, as we shall see, by the interaction between a primary and a secondary signal change. Essential race hazards can be eliminated by introducing delays in the circuit.

12.2.2 Design procedure

For our first example of an asynchronous sequential circuit design, consider a circuit with one input, x, and one output, Z. A series of pulses is applied to the input and every alternate pulse is to be passed to the output. This is shown diagramatically in Fig. 12.13(a). The pulse duration and separation are variable.

A Moore model state diagram for this circuit is shown in Fig. 12.13(b). A Moore model state diagram is often used for asynchronous sequential circuit design because a stable state is clearly identified in the Moore model by a 'sling' path around the state. A transition from a stable state will only occur when the input changes from the sling value.

The next step is draw the state table giving the information in tabular form. The asynchronous sequential circuit state table as shown in Fig. 12.13(c) is known a *primitive flow table*.† The stable states are indicated by circles around the stable state numbers in the next-state columns. The circled stable states will be the same as the number in the present-state column. The output pertains to the stable state. The primitive flow table should then be minimized where possible. We will consider the minimization methods later. Our table does not minimize.

Then secondary variables are assigned. In doing this assignment, we must take care not to make an assignment which results in more than one variable change between states. A *transition map* may help us here. A transition map is a map labeled in the same way as a Karnaugh map, and using the secondary variables. States are chosen for each square on the map. Then, the transitions from one state to another are marked on the map and if any show a diagonal path across two variable changes, a new assignment must be made. A transition map for our problem giving a satisfacory assignment is shown in Fig. 12.13(d), and the assigned flow table in Fig. 12.13(e). Swapping state assignments for 1 and 2 would result in an unsatisfactory map. It may be necessary in some problems to introduce dummy states, i.e. to have a non-minimal number of states, in order to achieve a satisfactory assignment.

Finally a circuit is developed. There are two principal circuit implementations, one using purely combinational logic gates and one using combinational

---

† The word *primitive* is used to indicate that there is only one stable state in each row; the table can sometimes have more than one stable state per row, as we shall see.

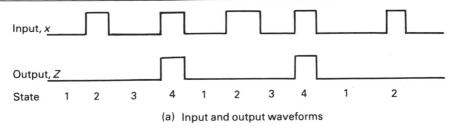

(a) Input and output waveforms

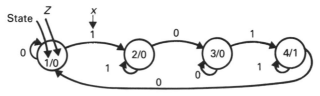

(b) State diagram (Moore model)

Present state	Next state x 0	1	Output Z
1	①	2	0
2	3	②	0
3	③	4	0
4	1	④	1

(c) Primitive flow table

(d) Transition map

Present state $y_2 y_1$	Next state $Y_2 Y_1$ 0 x 1	Output Z
00	00 01	0
01	11 01	0
11	11 10	0
10	00 10	1

(e) Assigned Primitive Flow Table

Figure 12.13 Asynchronous sequential circuit

logic with asynchronous R–S flip-flops. (The asynchronous R–S flip-flops are implemented with combinational logic gates, e.g. a pair of cross-coupled NAND gates.)

(a) Combinational logic gate implementation

For a purely combinational logic gate implementation, the Boolean expressions for the excitation variables, Y_2 and Y_1, are obtained directly from the assigned primitive flow table, as shown in Fig. 12.14(a). Redundant prime implicants are added to eliminate static hazards.

The output function can be obtained in a three-step procedure. First the stable states are identified in the primitive flow table and mapped onto a Karnaugh map. The unstable states (transitions between stable states) can then be included as either the same as the present stable state output or the same as the next stable state output. If there is a change, a don't care could be mapped. If an early output change is desired, the next output value can be chosen so as to produce the final output during the transition between stable states. If a late change is desired, the present output value can be chosen, causing the output during the transition to be the same as the output before the transition. Our unstable outputs are mapped to be the same as the next stable state outputs. The final map is then minimized, taking care to eliminate static hazards if spikes must not occur in the output.

The complete logic circuit is shown in Fig. 12.14(b). Notice that the Y (excitation) outputs are fed back to the inputs of the gates as the y (secondary) variables. In a stable state, $Y = y$.

We must now consider essential race hazards. A possible critical essential race hazard is found in the circuit as a race between primary input, x, and the secondary variable, y_1, as indicated in Fig. 12.14(b). A change in x from 0 to 1 causes y_1 to change from 0 to 1, and if this returns before $\bar{x}$ is generated, incorrect operation will result. The particular circuit implementation shown makes this unlikely (but not impossible). If required, a delay circuit can be added to the y_1 output.

The essential race hazard can be identified on our primitive flow table as occurring during the transition from stable state 1 to stable state 2. The hazard will cause a transition from stable state 1 to stable state 4 rather than the required change to stable state 2. Stable state 4 would, in fact, normally be entered after a change in the input from 0 to 1, then back to 0 and again to 1. If in any primitive flow table, three changes in an input (for example 0 to 1 to 0 to 1) result in a different state after the final change than after the first change, an essential race hazard is present, which is known as Unger's rule [4]. We may apply Unger's rule to detect the presence of essential race hazards, though it is then necessary to locate the problem and add the appropriate delay if necessary.

Since essential race hazards (as all race hazards) are due to gate propagation delays and their variations, we should examine the specification of the gates used. Often typcial and maximum propagation delays are given but not the minimum delays. For example, typical LSTTL gates (such as the 74LS00, 74LS04, 74LS10 and 74LS20) have the following propagation delay times:

Typical Maximum

t_{PLH} Propagation delay time low-to-high level output 9 ns   20 ns
t_{PHL} Propagation delay time high-to-low level output 10 ns   20 ns

If we were to assume a minimum propagation delay time of 0 ns for the gates in our circuit except the inverters, and a non-zero propagation delay time for the inverter, the secondary variables would always arrive back to the input before the inverter has generated its output and a critical essential race hazard would exist. The appropriate delay in this case would be the same as the maximum propagation delay time of the inverter. Occasionally, a minimum propagation

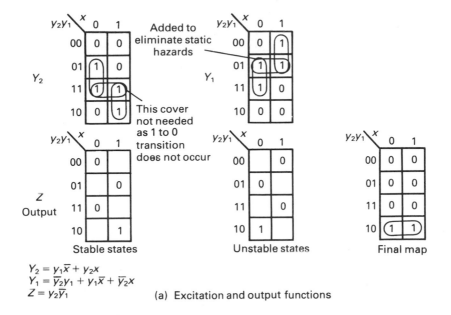

$$Y_2 = y_1\bar{x} + y_2x$$
$$Y_1 = \bar{y}_2y_1 + y_1\bar{x} + \bar{y}_2x$$
$$Z = y_2\bar{y}_1$$

(a) Excitation and output functions

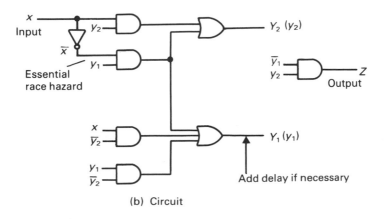

(b) Circuit

Figure 12.14 Asynchronous sequential circuit design using gates

delay time is given (e.g. the Fairchild Advanced Schottky TTL type 74F00 quad 2-input NAND gate has a stated minimum T_{PLH} and T_{PHL} of 1.5 ns (maximum $T_{\text{PLH}} = 3.9$ ns and maximum $T_{\text{PHL}} = 3.6$ ns) [5]. In addition to gate propagation delays such as the above, interconnection delays should also be considered (about 2 ns/ft).

(b) Designing with combinational circuits and asynchronous *R–S* flip-flops

The *R–S* flip-flop design approach assigns one flip-flop for each secondary variable. The inputs to these flip-flops are determined by the required change of *y* to *Y*. Using Table 4.1 with *y* as *Q* and *Y* as Q_+, we obtain one function for each flip-flop input as shown in Fig. 12.15(a). The final circuit shown in Fig. 12.15(b) uses cross-coupled NAND gate *R–S* flip-flops. A particular advantage of the *R–S* flip-flop method is that is is not necessary to correct for static hazards because all the prime implicants are present in both the set and reset functions, which will be the case in all problems. Hence, the *R–S* flip-flop method often requires less components.

In the *R–S* flip-flop method, both true and inverse *y* outputs are available for feeding back to the flip-flop inputs. If the set and reset functions of the flip-flop include true and inverse variables, it is possible that both set and reset are a 1 together during a transition, causing both the *y* and $\bar{y}$ outputs to be both 0. This might create a critical race hazard, though this is unlikely with two-level circuits. The inverse *y* output can be generated using a separate gate if necessary [6].

12.2.3 State minimization

Consider a second asynchronous circuit problem. An asynchronous sequential circuit has two inputs, x_1 and x_2, and one output, *Z*. The output is to change state (from a 0 to a 1 or from a 1 to a 0) if any change from 0 to 1 occurs on either of the two inputs. Design the circuit assuming that the input signals never change simultaneously.

As before, the first step is to draw the state diagram. A Moore model state diagram for the problem is shown in Fig. 12.16. The primitive flow table is shown in Fig. 12.17(a). The dashes indicate disallowed conditions (requiring simultaneous changes in two primary variables).

Next we can minimize where possible. As in synchronous sequential circuits, we look for states which are equivalent. Following the same procedure as in the synchronous design of examining pairs of states with the same output, and listing the required equivalent pairs, we find that two pairs are equivalent without any required equivalent pairs, namely (2,3) and (6,7). These pairs are the same (rather than equivalent). No other pairs can be found as equivalent.

Next, we can use a technique known as *merging* which utilizes the disallowed conditions in the next-state columns. A disallowed condition is a form of can't happen condition and can assume any state for minimization. For example, in our primitive flow table, states 2 and 3 can also be combined by merging:

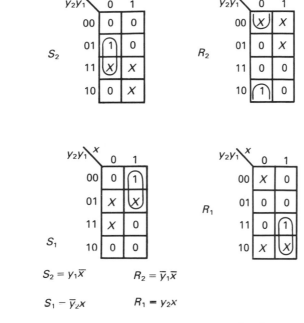

$$S_2 = y_1\bar{x} \qquad R_2 = \bar{y}_1\bar{x}$$

$$S_1 - \bar{y}_2 x \qquad R_1 = y_2 x$$

(a) Input functions for R–S flip-flops

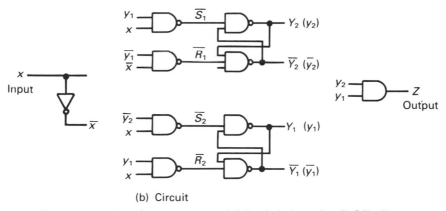

(b) Circuit

Figure 12.15 Asynchronous sequential circuit design using *R–S* flip-flops

Present state	*Next state*		*Output*		*Present state*	*Next state*		*Output*
2	5	— 4	2	1				
3	5	3 4	—	1	= 2/3	5	3 4	2 1

Similarly, states 6 and 7 can be combined. But in addition, states can also be merged even if their outputs are different because the outputs are uniquely

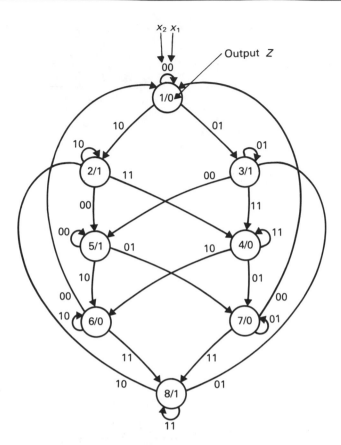

Figure 12.16 Asynchronous sequential circuit Moore model state diagram requiring minimization

defined by the inputs and the secondary variables. Consequently, states 1 and 8 can be combined and states 4 and 5 can be combined. This leads to the reduced flow table shown in Fig. 12.17(b). More than two states can be merged, but all the corresponding can't happen conditions (dashes) must be equivalent. The merging procedure results in four states;

$$(1,8), (2,3), (4,5), (6,7)$$

which we shall call *A, B, C,* and *D* respectively. The original state numbers are kept in the merged state diagram.

The subsequent procedure is the same as outlined previously. A transition map for assignment is given in Fig. 12.17(c), the assigned flow table in Fig. 12.17(d), secondary variables In Fig. 12.17(e) and output function in Fig. 12.17(f). We can identify several possible essential race hazards by Unger's rule. For example, starting at stable state 1 (*A*), one change in x_1 leads to stable state 3 (*B*), while two further changes in x_1 lead to state 7 (*D*). It is left to the reader to find the other essential race hazards by using Unger's rule.

In the above problem, a satisfactory secondary variable assignment can be made for the merged flow table. Often this is not possible, and either the original

Present state	Next state $x_2 x_1$				Present output
	00	01	11	10	
1	①	3	–	2	0
2	5	–	4	②	1
3	5	③	4	–	1
4	–	7	④	6	0
5	⑤	7	–	6	1
6	1	–	8	⑥	0
7	1	⑦	8	–	0
8	–	3	⑧	2	1

(a) Primitive flow table

Present state	Next state $x_2 x_1$			
	00	01	11	10
A	①	3	⑧	2
B	5	③	4	②
C	⑤	7	④	6
D	1	⑦	8	⑥

A = 1/8
B = 2/3
C = 4/5
D = 6/7

(b) Merged flow table

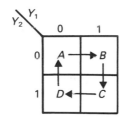

(c) Transition map

Present state $y_2 y_1$	Next state $Y_2 Y_1$ $x_2 x_1$			
	00	01	11	10
00	00	01	00	01
01	11	01	11	01
11	11	10	11	10
10	00	10	00	10

(d) Assigned flow table

Figure 12.17 Asynchronous sequential circuit minimization and design

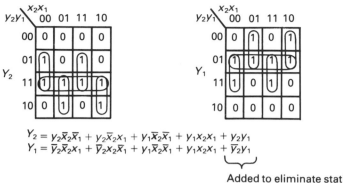

$$Y_2 = y_2\bar{x}_2\bar{x}_1 + y_2\bar{x}_2x_1 + y_1\bar{x}_2\bar{x}_1 + y_1x_2x_1 + y_2y_1$$
$$Y_1 = \bar{y}_2\bar{x}_2x_1 + \bar{y}_2x_2\bar{x}_1 + y_1\bar{x}_2\bar{x}_1 + y_1x_2x_1 + \bar{y}_2y_1$$

$\underbrace{\qquad}$
Added to eliminate static hazards

(e) Secondary variables

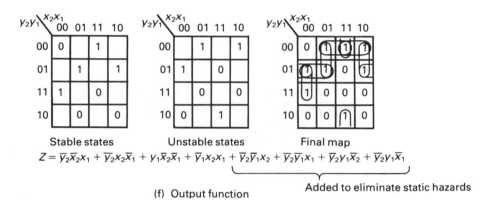

Stable states   Unstable states   Final map

$$Z = \bar{y}_2\bar{x}_2x_1 + \bar{y}_2x_2\bar{x}_1 + y_1\bar{x}_2\bar{x}_1 + \bar{y}_1x_2x_1 + \bar{y}_2\bar{y}_1x_2 + \bar{y}_2\bar{y}_1x_1 + \bar{y}_2y_1\bar{x}_2 + \bar{y}_2y_1\bar{x}_1$$

$\underbrace{\qquad\qquad\qquad\qquad}$
(f) Output function   Added to eliminate static hazards

Figure 12.17 *continued*

primitive flow table must be used, or dummy states introduced between state transitions so that only one secondary variable changes at a time. For example, consider the merged flow table shown in Fig. 12.18(a) which has three states (1,2), (3,4) and (5) given the letters *A*, *B* and *C* respectively. A satisfactory assignment cannot be made without modifying the state table. A transition map is shown in Fig. 12.18(b). We note that the transition from state *A* to state *C*, with the assignment chosen, requires both secondary variables to change. In two cases (the first and final next-state columns), there is only one stable state in the next-state column and any race hazard is not critical. In the third next-state column, there are two stable states and a hazard exists. One solution is to generate a fourth state *D* as shown in Fig. 12.18(c). The *A–C* transition when $x_2x_1 = 11$ now passes through state *D*. The other *A–C* transitions are similarly mapped though state *D* to maintain race-free transitions. The remaining entry is considered as can't happen.

If we do have a final state table which does not use all combinations of secondary variables, the next states of any unused row should be mapped with suitable unstable states to lead to a used state, so that a predicted action occurs upon switch-on.

Present state	Next state x_2x_1			
	00	01	11	10
A	①	3	②	5
B	1	③	④	5
C	1	–	2	⑤

(a) Merged flow table

(b) Transition map

Present state	Next state x_2x_1			
	00	01	11	10
A	①	3	②	5
B	1	③	④	5
C	1	–	2	⑤
D	1	–	2	5

(c) Assigned flow table

Figure 12.18 Introducing a dummy state into the flow table

12.2.4 Pragmatic approach to asynchronous sequential circuit design

The above design techniques are really only suitable for designs with relatively few components. Once the problem requires several state variables (secondary variables), obtaining a satisfactory race-free design can become difficult. The difficulties of asynchronous sequential circuit design have lead design engineers to avoid asynchronous designs when possible. Generally, asynchronous designs would be used if the required speed of operation could not be achieved with a synchronous design.

One approach is to convert the asynchronous signals into synchronous signals using a timing or clock signal. An asynchronous signal can be synchronized with a clock signal using a D-type flip-flop (clock signal to clock input of flip-flop and asynchronous signal to D input). However, this suffers from the disadvantage that the set-up and hold times of the flip-flop must be satisfied for proper operation. For example, if the set-up and hold times of a flip-flop used to synchronize an asynchronize signal were 20 ns and 5 ns respectively and the asynchronous input changed between 20 ns before and 5 ns after the clock signal being applied, the output could not be predicted. Worse, the flip-flop might enter a non-stable state with the output not at a defined logic level but at some intermediate point. This condition could, theoretically, last for ever, but in practice lasts for a considerable time (tens of nanoseconds). To reduce the probability of this output, two flip-flops in cascade can be employed as shown in Fig. 12.19, though there is still a finite probability of the circuit entering an unstable state. Once the asynchronous inputs have been synchronized with the clock signal, the design can be synchronous. Set-up and hold times of some flip-flops in the TTL family are listed in Table 12.6.

A microprocessor application of the above technique is in the synchronization of asynchronuous ready signals from memory units to the processor, the processor being a synchronous device internally. External interrupt signals can also be synchronized for the processor. Similarly, the asynchronous bus transfer technique described in Chap. 6 for communication between units in a microprocessor system is an example of handshaking in which units operate synchronously internally, but with no synchronization between them. Synchronization circuits can be used to capture the external asynchronous signals.

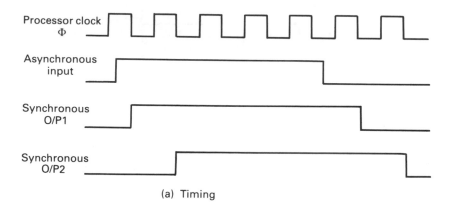

(a) Timing

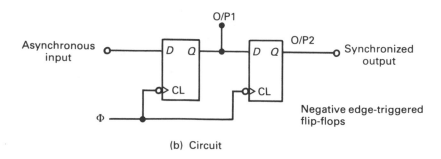

(b) Circuit

Figure 12.19   Double flip-flop synchronization circuit

Table 12.6 Set-up and hold times of various TTL flip-flops

Flip-flop	Type	Set-up time (ns)	Hold time (ns)
7474	D	20	5
74109	J–K	10	6
74111	J–K	0	30
74LS74	D	20/25 (D=1/D=0)	5
74LS76/78/112/114	J–K's	20	0
74LS109	J–K	20	5
74S74	D	3	2
74S112	J–K	3	0
74ALS74	D	15	0
74ASL109	J–K	15	0

REFERENCES

1. Lewin, D., *Design of Logic Systems*. Wokingham, England: Van Nostrand Reinhold, 1985.
2. Lind, L.F., and C.C. Nelson, *Analysis and Design of Sequential Digital Systems*. London: Macmillan, 1977.
3. Fletcher, W.I., *An Engineering Approach to Digital Design*. Englewood Cliffs, N.J.: Prentice-Hall, Inc., 1980.
4. Unger, S.H., 'Hazards and Delays in Asynchronous Sequential Switching Circuits', *IRE Trans. Circuit Theory*, CT6 (1959), 12–25.
5. *Fairchild Advanced Schottky TTL*. Mountain View, California: Fairchild Corp, 1979.
6. Dunderdale, H., *An Introduction to Formal Methods in Logical Design, Sequential Systems*. University of Salford (UK), 1970.

PROBLEMS

12.1 A synchronous sequential logic circuit has two inputs, x_1 and x_2, and one output, Z. The output is required to become a 1 only during the presence of the final number in the sequence 00, 01, 10, 11 applied to the two inputs.

Draw a Mealy model state diagram for the circuit and derive the state table. Hence design a circuit to perform the desired function using the minimum number of $J–K$ flip-flops and combinational circuits.

12.2 A synchronous sequential circuit has one input, x, and one output, Z. The output will be a 1 whenever the input sequence consists of 0110 or 1001, otherwise the output will be a 0.

Draw a state diagram for this circuit and construct a state table. Simplify where possible and design the circuit using D-type flip-flops and combinational circuits.

12.3 A synchronous sequential circuit has two inputs, x_1 and x_2, and one output, Z. The output is to be set to a 1 only when any group of four bits on one input is identical to the group of four bits on the other input, occurring in the same clock sequence.

Draw a Mealy model state diagram for the circuit and a state table. Determine a suitable state variable assignment by considering present and next states. Derive input equations for D-type flip-flop realization, and an output equation. Then give a complete circuit diagram.

Show how the combinational circuit can be realized using a read-only memory (ROM). List the contents of the ROM and give the overall circuit configuration.

12.4 Minimize the synchronous sequential circuit state table given in Table 12.7. Draw the reduced state table and sketch the equivalent state diagram. Assign state variables and obtain input and output equations for synchronous R–S flip-flop realization. Draw the logic circuit.

Table 12.7   State table for Problem 12.4

Present state	Next state x_2x_1				Output, Z x_2x_1			
	00	01	11	10	00	01	11	10
1	1	2	2	4	0	0	0	0
2	1	3	1	4	0	0	0	0
3	1	3	2	4	0	0	0	0
4	1	8	7	5	0	0	0	0
5	1	5	6	5	0	0	1	0
6	3	8	7	5	0	0	0	0
7	2	8	6	5	0	0	0	0
8	3	8	7	8	0	0	1	0

12.5 An asynchronous sequential circuit has one output, z, and two inputs x_1 and x_2. An output logic pulse is generated when a logic pulse has occurred on x_1 and a logic pulse has occurred on x_2 (in either order). The input pulses are of variable width and occur at undefined intervals but cannot overlap. The output pulse has the same duration as the last input pulse that occurs. Second and subsequent pulses on one input before a pulse on the other input has activated the output do not have any affect.

Draw an annotated Moore model state diagram for the circuit and derive the primitive flow table. Minimize the table where possible.

Modify the state diagram to generate a single output pulse if overlapping input pulses occur. Describe the modification. State any assumptions considered necessary.

12.6 An electronic door switch is controlled by two 'push-button' switches, A and B. The door will open after switch A has been depressed and released twice and subsequently switch B has been depressed and released once. Any other sequence will cause an alarm to be activated. The sequence to open the door will also switch the alarm off if it has been activated. Switch A is depressed and released once to lock the door.

Draw an annotated Moore model state diagram for the door lock.

Processor Design

In Chap. 6, the internal operation of a microprocessor was briefly described. Now we shall consider the internal operation in greater detail. The techniques described apply to processors in general.

13.1 INTERNAL OPERATION OF PROCESSOR

13.1.1 Fetch/execute cycles

Let us recapitulate the mode of operation of a central processor. As noted in Chap. 6, section 6.1.1 (and subsequently developed in section 6.2.3 for microprocessors and Chap. 7, section 7.2.1, for the Z-80 microprocessor), the operation of a processor can be divided into two parts:

(i) Fetch cycle
(ii) Execute cycle

In the fetch cycle, the instruction to be executed is brought from the memory into an internal processor register known as the *instruction register*. (In the first instance, we will assume that the whole instruction is held in one memory word and is transferred in one action.) The fetch cycle itself may require several distinct steps. Referring to Fig. 13.1(a), a typical internal architecture of a register type of processor, the program counter holds the address of the instruction at the beginning of a fetch cycle. First, the contents of the program counter are placed on the address lines and the appropriate control signals are generated by the processor when the address signals are stable. The address signals together with the control signals are fed to all the memory units. The unit holding the memory location whose address coincides with the address transmitted is activated and the contents of the addressed location are placed on the data lines sometime later. The delay before the data is present depends upon the access time of the memory but is typically 200–500 ns. The processor waits either a set time unless modified by a wait signal from the memory, or it always waits until an acknowledge signal is received from the memory, depending upon the design. The former is assumed here. (The Z-80 uses the former method and the 68000 uses the latter method.)

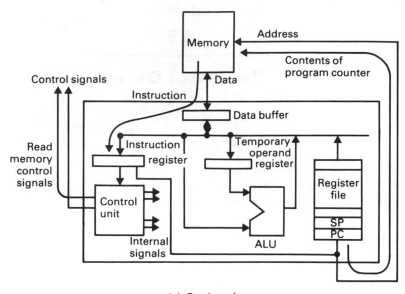

(a) Fetch cycle

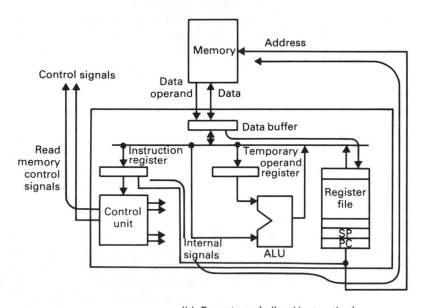

(b) Execute cycle (load instruction)

Figure 13.1 Processing operation

After the data signals have settled on the bus, i.e. after all transients have died down and valid logic levels have been established, the processor accepts the data. This 'data' is the required machine instruction and is placed in the internal instruction register. Generally, the program counter is then incremented by one in preparation for the next instruction fetch cycle.

We have noted in sections 6.2.3 and 7.2.1 that the instruction may be composed of more than one bytes or words, each byte/word requiring a memory read operation. If this is the case, the fetch cycle is repeated for each byte or word of the instruction. The first byte or word specifies the operation and will indicate how many further bytes/words are necessary to fetch to complete the instruction fetch cycle. In 8-bit microprocessors, the first byte fetched is the op-code and the first fetch cycle is the op-code fetch cycle. The op-code fetch cycle would be followed by memory read cycles to obtain additional bytes of the instruction, when necessary. A similar process occurs in 16-bit microprocessors, but the transfers are often in 16-bit words. The fetch cycle is complete when all the bytes/words have been transferred into the processor, and the fetch cycle is then followed by the execute cycle.

Referring now to Fig. 13.1(b), in the execute cycle the operation specified in the instruction is executed. This may involve several distinct steps which will be different for different instructions. As an example, consider the instruction (in Z-80 notation):†

LD A,(100) ;copy the contents of location 100 into the A register

To execute the instruction, firstly location 100 is addressed by placing the address 100 on the address lines together with, at the correct time, the control signals. The appropriate memory unit becomes activated and some time later the contents of the addressed location are placed on the data lines. The contents of the memory location are accepted by the processor and directed to the A register, whereupon this simple read instruction has been executed, and the next instruction can be fetched.

In the write instruction:†

LD (100),A ; copy the contents of the A register into memory
            ;location 100

the execute cycle begins by placing the contents of the A register on to the data line and the address 100 on the address lines. The appropriate control signals are generated. Some time later the memory unit addressed will accept the data, whereupon the instruction execution cycle is complete.

In general, the execution phase will involve an effective address calculation which may involve extra steps. For example, indirect addressing involves an extra memory read cycle to obtain the address of the operand from memory before the operand itself can be accessed. Therefore, the execute cycle may be composed of several memory read cycles or read cycles and a write cycle. It is

---

† In the Z-80, these instructions are 3-byte instructions and hence in each case, an op-code fetch and two further memory read cycles are necessary to form the complete instruction in the instruction register. The two additional cycles fetch the 16-bit operand address 100. In general terms, these actions are still part of the instruction fetch cycle, i.e. the instruction fetch cycle consists of an op-code fetch cycle and two memory read cycles. Each additional memory read cycle will increment the program counter in anticipation of the next cycle.

convenient to divide the execute cycle into several subcycles, each of which is either a read cycle or a write cycle. The op-code fetch cycle is simply a special case of a read cycle.

The processor operates using a periodic clock signal. All internal operations are initiated by the clock and all timing is related to the clock. A microprocessor clock signal is either generated internally or externally using a crystal to create the correct frequency. There are two basic design approaches to activate read or write cycles using the processor clock. The simplest arrangement is to have one clock period for each cycle, either the instruction fetch, read or write cycle. A direct transfer instruction would need two clock periods whereas a complex indirect addressing instruction may require many clock cycles. The Motorola 8-bit 6800 microprocessor uses this method.

An alternative is to have a number of clock periods for each of the fetch, read or write cycles. The Z-80 and the 68000 use this method. The division of major cycles into subcycles has the advantage of being able to activate the various steps within each cycle in sequence and to time the steps more finely.

13.1.2 Z-80 timing signals

In the next section we will describe the steps taken in fetching and executing an instruction using a register transfer notation and the Z-80 as the example. Firstly, we review the timing of the Z-80. The basic Z-80 timing signals are given in Chap. 7, section 7.2.1. The reader is referred to Figs. 7.2, 7.3 and 7.4. To recapitulate, each clock period is called a T cycle, T_1, T_2, T_3, etc. Each fetch, read, write or other machine cycle is called an M cycle, i.e. M1, M2, M3, etc. Each M cycle is composed of a number of T cycles. The address read strobe action is produced by two signals, $\overline{\text{MREQ}}$ and $\overline{\text{RD}}$ (memory request and memory read). The memory request signal is activated (i.e. brought low to activate a memory operation) when the address lines have settled. The read signal indicates a read operation and is enabled at the same time. $\overline{\text{MREQ}}$ and $\overline{\text{RD}}$ are related to the '1' to '0' transition of T_1, i.e. the falling edge of T_1 (actually about 50 ns later). This allows a maximum of one clock high time for the address lines to settle and for delays in the units and interconnection circuitry. Delays may be different for individual address lines, causing skew between line signals. In any system design, the worst-case situation must be accommodated.

The time before the required instruction appears on the data lines depends upon the memory read access time. The data is sampled by the processor on the rising edge of T_3. The data needs to be valid some time before this for the processor to accept the data. This *data set-up* time is typically 50–60 ns. Therefore the time allowed for the program memory to produce the required instruction is given by:

(1½ clock periods) − (bus stabilization and skew delay) − (interconnection delay) − (memory unit delays) − (processor data set-up time)

The instruction operation is then decoded during T_3 and T_4. Also during T_3 and T_4, a refresh operation takes place. This operation supports dynamic memory devices (Chap. 9) by providing a memory address which can be used to refresh the memory. A 7-bit refresh address is held in the processor counter, R, which is incremented after each instruction fetch. (Dynamic memories require a row address, not a full address to perform a refresh operation.) A processor signal, $\overline{\text{RFSH}}$ is generated at the same time as the refresh address and not after the address has stablized. ($\overline{\text{MREQ}}$ is generated after the address has stabilized). $\overline{\text{RD}}$ and $\overline{\text{WR}}$ are not generated during the refresh operation.

Once the M1 cycle is complete, the processor moves on to the M2 cycle, the first cycle of the execute period. Both read and write cycles require three T states. In the read cycle, the time provided for the data memory to respond is two T states less connection delays, logic delays, skew times and set-up times. The memory is expected to supply the data held in the addressed location by the falling edge of T_3. The processing time (or instruction time) of a simple read instruction including the fetch cycle takes seven T cycles. If the processor clock operated at 4 MHz, for example, one clock period would be 250 ns and the instruction would take 1.75 μs.

In a write cycle, the memory address lines carry the address of the location to be accessed and the memory request address strobe signal appears as before. To activate a memory write operation, the signal $\overline{\text{WR}}$ is used. This occurs after the data signals produced by the processor have settled on the data lines. The data output is related to the falling edge of T_1, with an allowed delay of nearly one clock period less the amount of delay from the falling edge of T_1 to the data becoming valid. Notice that the memory address and data are not put on the bus simultaneously here. The $\overline{\text{WR}}$ signal begins on the falling edge of T_2 and this is when the data is loaded into the memory. The period of $\overline{\text{WR}}$ is one T state. Therefore the write access time needs to be sufficiently less than this to take all delays into account.

In the above, it is assumed that the memory will respond by the allotted time. If the memory is unable to respond in the time available, a wait mechanism can be used. To activate this mechanism, a $\overline{\text{WAIT}}$ signal must be generated by the memory and is fed to the processor. The processor 'samples' the WAIT line on the falling edge of Φ in T_2. If WAIT = 0, a dummy wait state is introduced between T_2 and T_3. The $\overline{\text{WAIT}}$ line is again sampled during the wait state, and further wait states introduced if the memory is not ready. Wait states can be introduced in instruction fetch and execute read/write cycles.

Input/output instructions produce timing signals similar to those of read/write instructions, with the addition of one permanent dummy T cycle (wait state) introduced between T_2 and T_3 to allow extra time for the input/output interface to decode the address and perform any action required, including asking for additional wait states in order to produce further delay. (This is done using the $\overline{\text{WAIT}}$ signal from the input/output unit to the processor.) $\overline{\text{MREQ}}$ is replaced by $\overline{\text{IOREQ}}$ and the memory address by an 8-bit port address.

Naturally, the more complicated machine instructions require many more T cycles and M cycles. There may be one to six M cycles and two to six T cycles per M cycle, giving over twenty T cycles for a really complicated instruction.

13.1.3 Register transfer logic

An essential part of the above mechanism is the transfer of the contents of one register to another register. We can specify this action in a register transfer notation. For example:

$$A \leftarrow B$$

means transfer the contents of register B into register A. The notation specifies a *data flow* action. Obviously, some control signal must be generated to initiate the action. We shall specify the control signal within the register transfer notation by prefixing the data flow action with a symbol identifying the control signal and a colon. For example:

$$T: A \leftarrow B$$

indicates that when a control signal, T, is true (1), the data flow occurs. The *control flow* component could be a Boolean expression, for example, $T_1 T_2$, which would indicate that the data flow occurs when both T_1 and T_2 are true.

To transfer the contents of one register to another register requires gating between the registers. The transfer can be activated by the control signal alone. Alternatively, the transfer can be synchronized with a central clock signal which could be specified as:

$$T\Phi: A \leftarrow B$$

where Φ is a clock signal. In this example, the transfer occurs when both T and Φ are true. The transfer mechanism might be implemented as shown in Fig. 13.2. Here, register B is composed of rising edge-triggered *D*-type flip-flops, and hence the transfer occurs on the rising edge of the last signal to become true.

Since commonly a number of registers will exist in the system and many if not all combinations of transfers are to be provided, an internal bus configuration is convenient. A single bus can connect all inputs and outputs of the registers with the appropriate gating on the inputs and outputs of each register. The data flow component can include operations between stored operands. The operations are performed by one or more units in addition to registers. The most common additional unit is the arithmetic and logic unit (ALU) which performs the arithmetic and logical operations on data operands within the processor. Arithmetic addition would be specified by:

$$T: A \leftarrow B + C$$

which specifies two operations, firstly the addition of the contents of the B and C registers, and secondly the transfer of the result to the A register. All this occurs when T is activated. We now need to differentiate between arithmetic addition and the Boolean OR operation. Here, in the data component, we will use the + symbol in indicate arithmetic addition. The symbols $\vee$ and $\wedge$ can be used to indicate the Boolean OR and AND operations respectively. The Boolean symbols + and · can be used to indicate the OR and AND Boolean operations in the control component. The · can be implied.

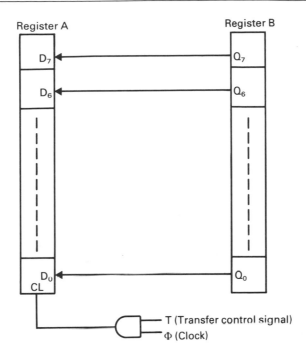

Figure 13.2   Register transfer mechanism

An internal bus can be used in a central processor to interconnect the ALU, registers and other functional units as shown in Fig. 13.3 using some of the Z-80 registers and control signals. The external data bus connects to the internal bus through a data buffer. During an instruction fetch cycle, the internal data bus is used in the transfer of an instruction from the external data bus to the instruction register (IR) connecting to the internal bus. The internal bus also carries various operands as the operands are transferred between internal registers during the execute cycle. The address bus will only connect to registers allowed to hold addresses, and a separate internal address bus could have been provided for this purpose. The registers used to hold an address in the Z-80 are the program counter, refresh counter, stack point register and register pairs within the general purpose register group. We show the result of arithmetic and logic operations as produced by the ALU to be sent only to the A register.

Now we have outlined the basic register transfer notation, let us apply it to some of the instructions of the Z-80 assuming the above architecture. We shall use the term *micro-operation* to describe each operation specified in the register transfer notation. (The lists of micro-operations developed might be different in the actual Z-80, and are not available to the user.) The abbreviations used are given in Fig. 13.3.

An internal address buffer, ABF and data buffer, DBF, are introduced. The function of ABF is to hold addresses that are to be placed on the address bus. Therefore:

ABUS ← ABF

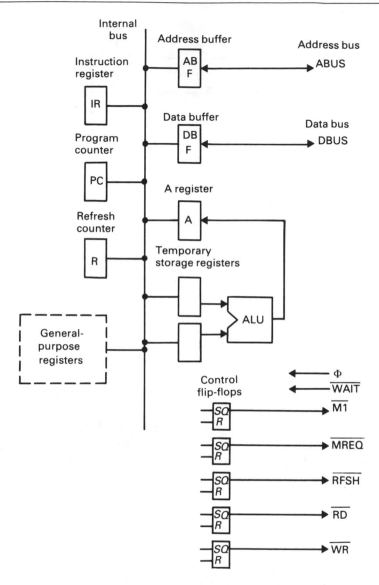

Figure 13.3   Processor architecture for register transfer notation

is an implicit action though it will be included in the lists of micro-operations. DBF holds data to be placed on the data bus, i.e.

DBUS ← DBF

The transfer of data from the external bus to the internal bus does not use DBF (though such transfers would use internal buffer gates). ABF and DBF registers are not explicitly mentioned in the Z-80 architecture but probably exist. The inclusion of these registers enables the address/data on the external bus to remain stable while using the internal bus for other purposes.

Abbreviations:
Processor inputs:
ABUS = External address bus
DBUS = External data bus
WAIT = WAIT input
Φ = System clock output

Internal registers:
ABF = Address held in internal address buffer
DBF = Data held in internal data buffer
IR = Instruction register
PC = Program counter
R = Refresh counter

Processor outputs:
M1 = Machine cycle one output
MREQ = Memory request output
RFSH = Refresh output
RD = Memory read strobe output
WR = Memory write strobe output

Figure 13.3 *continued*

We shall extend the register transfer notation to include the generation of external signals ($\overline{M1}$, $\overline{MREQ}$, $\overline{RFSH}$, $\overline{RD}$ and $\overline{WR}$). For convenience, the output signals are generated by flip-flops and therefore can be considered as single-bit registers. Also each transfer occurs on the rising edge of the control signal specified, i.e. the registers are rising edge triggered. Examining the fetch, read and write waveforms (Fig. 7.2, 7.3 and 7.4), we can see that actions are always related to either the rising edge of Φ or the falling edge of Φ in a particular T state. We could specify T state signals T_1, T_2, T_3, etc., that are true during the whole of the corresponding period. Then Φ or $\overline{Φ}$ could be logically ANDed with the T signal in the control component.

Alternatively, the T state signals could already be generated with rising and falling edges corresponding to the transfer times and then either T or $\overline{T}$ needs to be specified in the control component. We shall mainly choose this approach. Hence, the T state signals necessary are as shown in Fig. 13.4.

(a) Instruction fetch

The Z-80 instruction op-code fetch cycle (machine cycle 1, M1) can be specified in our register transfer notation as shown in Table 13.1. The control variable F signifies a fetch cycle is activated. Notice that the program counter is incremented after the contents have been placed on the address bus and well before the end of the cycle. This will have particular significance in instructions that use the contents of the program, e.g. relative jump instructions. In these instructions, the new value held in the program counter will be used to compute the jump address. The final T_1 state is the first T state of the next machine cycle. We have assumed that it is not necessary to disenable ABUS at the end of the fetch cycle.

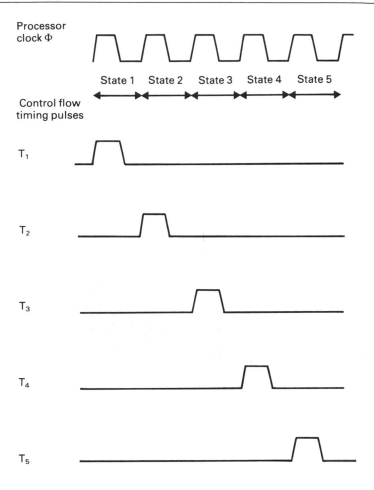

Figure 13.4 T-state timing pulses

An alternative to using flip-flops to generate the outputs is to generate the outputs directly from the T states which would lead to the instruction fetch cycle shown in Table 13.2. Possible wait states will be considered later. We can see that the notation can include more than one data action for each control component. The actions are separated with commas here. The control component can also have more than one control variable, as shown particularly in the second form shown. The control variables are connected with Boolean operations. For example, the first step is performed when either T_1 or T_2 are true, i.e. during the first two T cycles (assuming T variables true throughout state). The program counter is incremented immediately after the contents are used to fetch the instruction. Flip-flops are used in the following sequences.

The instruction fetch cycle here only fetched the op-code byte. If the instruction includes additional bytes, further memory read cycles (M2, M3, etc.)

Table 13.1   Instruction op-code fetch cycle (M1)

FT_1:	ABUS ← ABF ← PC, $\overline{M1}$ ← 0
$F\overline{T}_1$:	PC ← PC + 1
$F\overline{T}_1$:	$\overline{MREQ}$ ← 0, $\overline{RD}$ ← 0
FT_3:	IR ← DBUS
FT_3:	ABUS ← R, $\overline{MREQ}$ ← 1, $\overline{RD}$ ← 1, $\overline{M1}$ ← 1, $\overline{RFSH}$ ← 0
$F\overline{T}_3$:	$\overline{MREQ}$ ← 0, R ← R + 1
$F\overline{T}_4$:	MREQ ← 1
$\overline{F}T_1$:	$\overline{RFSH}$ ← 1

Table 13.2   Instruction op-code fetch cycle using T state signals without flip-flop storage

$F(T_1+T_2)$:	ABUS ← ABF ← PC, M1 ← 0
$F(T_1\Phi)$:	PC ← PC + 1
$F(T_1\overline{\Phi} + T_2)$:	MREQ ← 0, RD ← 0
$F(T_2\overline{\Phi})$:	IR ← DBUS,
$F(T_3 + T_4)$:	ABUS ← REFR
$F(T_3\overline{\Phi} + T_4\Phi)$:	$\overline{MREQ}$ ← 0, R ← R + 1
$F(T_3 + T_4)$:	RFSH ← 0

Table 13.3   Read cycle

$E_{read}T_1$:	ABUS ← ABF
$E_{read}\overline{T}_1$:	$\overline{MREQ}$ ← 0, $\overline{RD}$ ← 0,
$E_{read}\overline{T}_3$:	MREQ ← 1, $\overline{RD}$ ← 1, REG ← DBUS

REG = selected internal register

Table 13.4   LD A, n fetch operand cycle

$E_{LDn}T_1$:	ABUS (← ABF) ← PC
$E_{lDAn}T_1$:	PC ← PC + 1
$E_{LDAn}\overline{T}_1$:	$\overline{MREQ}$ ← 0, $\overline{RD}$ ← 0,
$E_{lDAn}\overline{T}_3$:	MREQ ← 1, RD ← 1, A ← DBUS

are necessary to obtain the rest of the instruction. The micro-operations for a memory read cycle could be as shown in Table 13.3. Again wait states are not included. The program counter must be incremented during each read cycle if fetching part of an instruction (but not if it is used otherwise; see below).

(b) Execute cycle

(i) LOAD INSTRUCTIONS
Some instructions can complete the execution of the instruction internally without any further read or write cycles. For example, the LD A,n instruction, where n is a literal, has one additional byte holding the literal. The read cycle to fetch the literal simply needs to cause the A register to be loaded with the fetched literal. Table 13.4 lists the steps required. This particular read cycle can be selected once the op-code has been decoded. Hence a separate execute cycle is not evident. However, a directly addressed LD instruction loading a register requires two additional bytes to hold the 16-bit memory address. In all there are four M cycles, M1 to fetch the op-code, M2 to fetch the lower address byte, M3 to fetch the upper address byte and M4 to perform the memory read operation. M2, M3 and M4 are given in Table 13.5.

The steps for a general memory write cycle are shown in Table 13.6. The final T_1 state is the T_1 of the next cycle. Z_{high} indicates that the register outputs enter a high-impedance state. The instruction transferring the contents of the A

Table 13.5 LD A,(nn) cycles to fetch operand

M2   (Operand data read of low bute, ODL)
$E_{LDA(nn)}T_1$:   ABUS $(\leftarrow ABF) \leftarrow PC$
$E_{LDA(nn)}T_1$:   PC $\leftarrow$ PC + 1
$E_{LDA(nn)}\overline{T_1}$: $\overline{MREQ} \leftarrow 0, \overline{RD} \leftarrow 0$,
$E_{LDA(nn)}\overline{T_3}$: $\overline{MREQ} \leftarrow 1, \overline{RD} \leftarrow 1, IR_{lower} \leftarrow DBUS$

M3   (Operand read of high byte, ODH)
$E_{LDA(nn)}T_1$:   ABUS $(\leftarrow ABF) \leftarrow PC$
$E_{LDA(nn)}T_1$:   PC $\leftarrow$ PC + 1
$E_{LDA(nn)}\overline{T_1}$: $\overline{MREQ} \leftarrow 0, \overline{RD} \leftarrow 0$,
$E_{LDA(nn)}\overline{T_3}$: $\overline{MREQ} \leftarrow 1, RD \leftarrow 1, IR_{upper} \leftarrow DBUS$

M4   (Memory read, MR)
$E_{LDA(nn)}T_1$:   ABUS $(\leftarrow ABF) \leftarrow IR$
$E_{LDA(nn)}T_1$:   PC $\leftarrow$ PC + 1
$E_{LDA(nn)}\overline{T_1}$: $\overline{MREQ} \leftarrow 0, \overline{RD} \leftarrow 0$,
$E_{LDA(nn)}\overline{T_3}$: $\overline{MREQ} \leftarrow 1, \overline{RD} \leftarrow 1, A \leftarrow DBUS$

Table 13.6 Write cycle

$E_{write}T_1$:   ABUS $\leftarrow$ ABF
$E_{write}\overline{T_1}$: $\overline{MREQ} \leftarrow 0$, DBUS $\leftarrow$ DBF
$E_{write}\overline{T_2}$: $\overline{WR} \leftarrow 0$
$E_{write}\overline{T_3}$: $\overline{MREQ} \leftarrow 1, \overline{WR} \leftarrow 1$
T_1':   DBUS $\leftarrow Z_{high}$

$T_1' = T_1$ of next cycle

register to a memory location, LD (nn),A, has an op-code byte and two bytes holding the address, as in the instruction performing the transfer from the memory to the A register above. Hence there are four M cycles, an op-code fetch (M1) followed by M2 to fetch the lower address byte, M3 to fetch the upper address byte as above, and finally M4 to write the contents of the A register into the addressed byte, as given in Table 13.7.

(ii) ARITHMETIC INSTRUCTIONS
Although the architecture described would allow, in principle, the operation:

$$ET_1: A \leftarrow B + C$$

most processors have two address instruction formats which limit the destination of an ALU operation to be one of the source locations. Single address formats would further limit the one source and destination register to be the A register. Such processors would only need to provide one path from the A register to the ALU and one return path. (In the Z-80, the first operand of any 8-bit arithmetic operation must be held in the A register and the result is placed in the A register.)

Let us consider the operation:

$$ET_1: A \leftarrow A + B$$

The statement implies one step operation. It corresponds to the execute cycle of the machine instruction:

Table 13.7   LD (nn),A write (M4) cycle

M4	(Memory write, MW)
$E_{LD(nn)A}\overline{T_1}$:	ABUS $\leftarrow$ ABF $\leftarrow$ IR
$E_{LD(nn)A}\overline{T_1}$:	$\overline{MREQ} \leftarrow 0$, DBUS $\leftarrow$ DBF $\leftarrow$ A
$E_{LD(nn)A}\overline{T_2}$:	$\overline{WR} \leftarrow 0$
$E_{LD(nn)A}\overline{T_3}$:	$MREQ \leftarrow 1, \overline{WR} \leftarrow 1$
T_1':	DBUS $\leftarrow Z_{high}$

ADD A,B

However, a number of actions are necessary. First the contents of the A register are placed on the internal data bus (assuming that the connection from the A register is through the internal data bus). Then the data on the internal data bus enters the ALU. The contents of the B register need to be placed on the internal data bus and then enter the second input of the ALU. Finally, the output of the ALU has to be passed via the internal data bus to the A register. Since the inputs to the ALU must generally remain stable during the ALU operation, further temporary buffer registers are necessary at the input of the ALU. We will assume that these registers are loaded when the ALU input is selected. One buffer may be sufficient, holding the first operand to be entered. We could decompose the ADD operation into the following elementary steps:

$E_{ADDAB}t_1$:   Intbus $\leftarrow$ A
$E_{ADDAB}t_2$: ALU_{in1} $\leftarrow$ Intbus
$E_{ADDAB}t_3$:   Intbus $\leftarrow$ B
$E_{ADDAB}t_4$: ALU_{in2} $\leftarrow$ Intbus
$E_{ADDAB}t_5$:   A $\leftarrow ALU_{out}$

where E_{ADDAB} is a control signal from the control unit indicating that an ADD instruction has been decoded. The first two steps could be combined in practice, and also the third and fourth steps:

$E_{ADDAB}t_1$: $ALU_{in1} \leftarrow$ A
$E_{ADDAB}t_2$: $ALU_{in2} \leftarrow$ B
$E_{ADDAB}t_3$:   A $\leftarrow ALU_{out}$

In fact it may be possible to combine all the steps in one time interval. The Z-80 does this by performing the ADD A,B instruction (and other ALU instructions between registers) within the M1 cycle.

Arithmetic instructions using memory operands which require cycles in addition to the fetch cycle have further M cycles. Apart from fetching the operands as above and writing the results, in some cases, an M cycle is devoted to an internal (arithmetic) operation.

(iii) CONDITIONAL MICRO-OPERATION

So far, we have omitted wait states. Wait states are introduced if the memory is not ready to read or write. They provide a delay until the memory is ready. We need a notation to describe a micro-operation which is executed if $\overline{WAIT} = 0$, but not otherwise, i.e. a conditional micro-operation. For example:

If Boolean condition THEN micro-operation

In this notation, if the Boolean condition has been satisfied, the stated micro-operation is performed, but not otherwise. However, this is not sufficient, as we need to be able to repeat a micro-operation until a Boolean condition becomes false (i.e. until $\overline{\text{WAIT}} = 1$). One approach would be to introduce a 'conditional jump' operation, i.e.:

$$T_2: \text{IF } \overline{\text{WAIT}} = 0 \text{ THEN } T_{next} = T_2$$

Here we are controlling the next T cycle to be executed. If $\overline{\text{WAIT}} = 0$, then the next T cycle after the first T_2 is another T_2 cycle. Alternatively, since it is not desirable to allow continuous wait states to be generated, as would occur if the memory never responded, a fixed number of conditional operations could be included, say ten. If after this time the wait line is still a 0, an error flag could be set.

Conditional micro-operations are also necessary to implement conditional machine instructions, i.e. conditional jump/branch/call instructions. These conditions are indicated in the F register. All conditions, whether externally or internally generated, need to be made available for the control unit (see next section).

13.2 CONTROL UNIT DESIGN

We have seen generally that the processing of every machine instruction consists of an instruction fetch cycle and an execute cycle. In the Z-80, the instruction fetch cycle is further decomposed into an op-code fetch cycle and possible extra read cycles. In the Z-80, the execute cycle can consist of an internal operation at the end of the op-code fetch cycle (for example, in the case of register/register arithmetic operations) or more generally can be decomposed into read cycles and a possible final write cycle. Op-code fetch, read and write cycles are called *machine cycles*. Each machine cycle consists of a number of fundamental micro-operations. Each of these micro-operations require signals to be generated by the control unit of the processor to initiate the micro-operations. There are two basic approaches in the design of a control unit:

 (i) Random logic design
(ii) Microprogrammed design

13.2.1 Random logic design

In the random logic approach, gates and counters are interconnected to generate the signals. Each design requires a unique set of gates and counters and interconnections. One implementation is to use a ring counter or shift register holding a circulating 1 to generate the T state signals as shown in

Fig. 13.5. A signal sets the first flip-flop of the shift register to a 1 output and the remaing flip-flops to a 0 output. Then the clock pulses may be applied (at twice the frequency of Φ to achieve the waveforms given in Fig. 13.4). Further gating is then necessary to produce the require control signals.

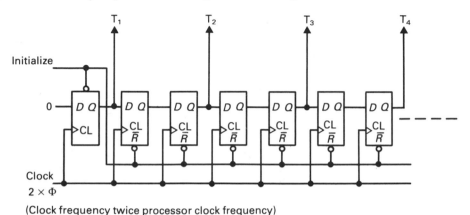

(Clock frequency twice processor clock frequency)

Figure 13.5   Using a shift register to generate control pulses

13.2.2 Microprogrammed design

The microprogrammed approach utilizes the fact that each step in itself is a basic 'instruction' and these instructions need to be executed in sequence. Each step is encoded into a *microinstruction*. A sequence of microinstructions is formed for each machine instruction and stored in a control memory within the internal control unit of the processor. The sequence of microinstructions is known as a *microprogram* and a sequence is executed for each machine instruction. The method leads to a clear-structured and flexible design and has been adopted in the design of some microprocessors (e.g. Motorola 68000, National Semiconductor 16032) but not all (e.g. Motorola 6809 and Zilog Z8000 use a random logic design). A combination of the two approaches can be taken (e.g. Intel 8086).

The technique of microprogramming was first suggested by Wilkes in the early 1950s [1] though it was not commonly put into practice for the design of digital computers until the 1960s. The original Wilkes scheme used a microinstruction encoded into two fields, one known as a *micro-order* (or *microcode*) giving the signals to be generated for the step, and one giving the address of the next microinstruction to be executed. The general arrangement of a microprogrammed control unit is shown in Fig. 13.6. The instruction is fetched into the instruction register using a standard microprogram. The machine instruction 'points' to the first microinstruction of the microprogram for that machine instruction. This microinstruction is executed and subsequent microinstructions in the microprogram. The sequence can be altered by conditions occurring within or outside the processor. In particular, microprogram sequences of

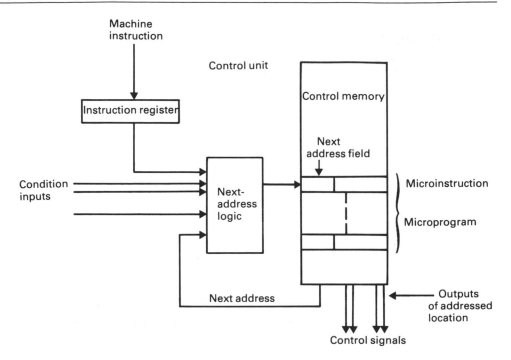

Figure 13.6   Microprogrammed control unit

conditional branch machine instructions may be altered by conditions indicated in the processor condition code register. One scheme causes the next micro-instruction to be skipped over if a condition prevails, i.e. a microprogram counter is incremented by two rather than by one. Also subroutine microinstructions can be provided to reduce the size of the microprogram. Just as a stack is used to hold the return address of machine instruction subroutines, a control memory stack can be provided to hold the return address of a microinstruction subroutine return.

There are two basic types of micro-order format:

(i)   Horizontal micro-order format
(ii)   Vertical micro-order format

In the *horizontal* micro-order format (the original Wilkes scheme), one bit is provided for each logic signal that can be generated by the microinstruction, as shown in Fig. 13.7(a). For example, if there were 100 possible signals, there would be 100 bits in the micro-order. To generate a particular signal, the corresponding bit in the micro-order would be set to a 1. More than one signal could be generated simultaneously if required by setting more bits to a 1.

In the *vertical* micro-order format, the bits are encoded into fields to reduce the number of bits in the micro-order, as shown in Fig. 13.7(b). Bits are formed into groups specifying signals that cannot be activated together. For example, if four data transfer request signals, memory read, memory write, input read and output write, were provided, these would be all mutually exclusive and cannot

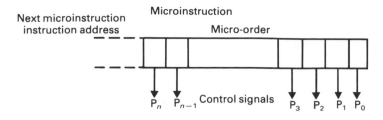

(a) Horizontal micro-order format

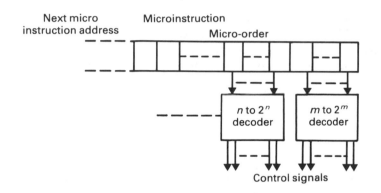

(b) Vertical micro- order format

Figure 13.7   Micro-order formats

occur together. These together with up to three other signals could be encoded into three binary digits. One encoded pattern, say 000, must be reserved for no signal at all.

The horizontal method is the most flexible but results in a long micro-order whereas the vertical method is more efficient but requires logic to decode the patterns and hence the speed of operation is reduced. Examples can be found of both approaches. Texas Instrument's 99000 microprocessor uses an almost totally unencoded microinstruction word of 152 bits, while Intel's 8086 uses an encoded field of 21 bits. Motorola's 68000 uses a two-level approach in which a 10-bit microinstruction points to a 70-bit 'nano' instruction. The horizontal and vertical formats can be used in one microinstruction, if desired.

Since a complete microprogram must be executed for each machine instruction, it follows that the speed of operation of executing each micro-instruction must be much faster than that of the required machine instruction. Therefore, the control memory must operate much faster than that of the main memory holding the machine instruction. In a processor with a fixed set of machine instructions, the control memory can be read-only memory (see Chap. 9). If a read–write memory (or programmable read-only memory) is used for the control memory, the possibility exists of altering the machine instruction set through writing new microprograms (a technique known as *microprogramming*) which leads to the concept of *emulation*. In emulation, a computer is microprogrammed to have exactly the same instruction set as another computer and behave in exactly the same manner, so that machine instruction programs written for the emulated computer will run on the microprogrammed computer. Emulation is not applicable to complete microprocessor devices such as the Z-80 or 68000. Special TTL processor parts known as *bit-slice* microprocessors exist to form microprogrammable systems.

13.2.3 Bit-slice microprocessors – an example

We shall review a design of representative microprogrammed system using two devices in the Am2900 series, namely the Am2901A bit-slice ALU and the Am2910A microprogram sequencer. These devices are manufactured in bipolar transistor technology by Advanced Micro Devices Inc. [2] (and also manufactured by Motorola as the MC2901A and MC2910A respectively). A clock signal is applied to the component parts (i.e. the system is synchronous). Microinstructions can be executed at 100 ns intervals, given suitable control memory and high-speed registers.

The system (somewhat simplified for our purposes) is shown in Fig. 13.8. Four Am2901A's can be used to creat a 16-bit ALU. Carry generate and propagate signals are produced for high-speed carry-look-ahead. The system microinstructions are held in the microprogram memory, which are addressed by a 12-bit address generated by the Am2910. Each microinstruction has the format shown in Fig. 13.9. The function of each bit will be explained shortly. The format is divided into a several sections, the next microinstruction address field, the Am2910 microcode, condition select field, and Am2901 ALU microcode, the operand select and address fields.

Referring to Fig. 13.8, logic consisting of Am2930 program control units [2] is provided to fetch the next machine instruction and load the machine instruction register (IR). A programmable read-only memory (PROM) is used to decode the operation, producing the first 12-bit microinstruction of the appropriate microprogram. The Am2910A microcode has 4-bits specifying one of sixteen different operations which are listed in Table 13.8. Many operations are conditional upon two inputs, $\overline{CC}$ and $\overline{CCEN}$ ($\overline{CC}$ enable). The condition test fails if $\overline{CCEN} = 0$ and $\overline{CC} = 1$. The test passes if $\overline{CCEN} = 1$ or $\overline{CC} = 0$. In our system, we have allocated seven conditions, selected by a 3-bit field in the microinstruction. (Only one condition can be selected in any microinstruction.) Three conditions are 2901A ALU conditions loaded in an ALU status register and four conditions are unassigned. One pattern (say 000) is reserved for unconditional 'pass', achieved by connecting the corresponding multiplexer data input to a permanent logic level. The output of the condition multiplexer drives the $\overline{CC}$ input. The ALU conditions are carry out, overflow and zero result. Other conditions could include hardware error conditions. $\overline{CCEN}$ is not used (though it would be available to force an operation unconditionally).

The Am2910A generates the 12-bit address of the next system microinstruction. One of three possible sources internal to the Am2910A or one of three external sources can be selected as holding the next system microinstruction,

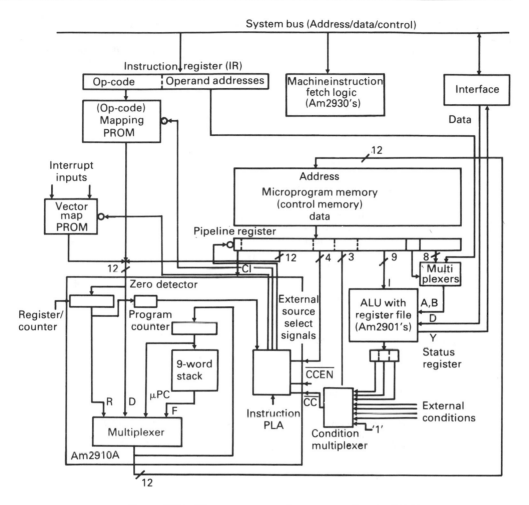

Figure 13.8   Microprogrammed processor using Am2910A

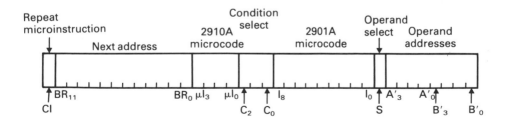

Figure 13.9   Microinstruction format of system in Fig. 13.8

depending upon the microprogram. The three internal sources are a 12-bit register/counter, the microprogram counter, or an address stored in an nine-word 12-bit stack. One or these sources, or an external source, is selected by the internal multiplexer shown. The three external sources are the mapping PROM,

Table 13.8 Microinstructions of AM2910A Microprogram Controller

$I_3I_2I_1I_0$	Mnemonic	Operation	Register/ counter contents	Condition Inputs Fail*		Pass*		Register/ counter	Source select
				Y	STACK	Y	STACK		
0000 (0)	JZ	Jump to zero or reset Unconditionally set program counter to 0	X	0	CLEAR	0	CLEAR	HOLD	PL
0001 (1)	CJS	Conditional jump to subroutine, pipeline If test passes, address of next instruction in pipeline register. Return address placed on stack. If test fails, address in microprogram counter (generally the next sequential instruction)	X	PC	HOLD	D	PUSH	HOLD	PL
0010 (2)	JMAP	Jump MAP instruction (unconditionally) Address of next instruction in external mapping PROM	X	D	HOLD	D	HOLD	HOLD	MAP
0011 (3)	CJP	Conditional jump pipeline If test passes, address of next instruction in pipeline register (BR_{11}-BR_0) If test fails, address in microprogram counter	X	PC	HOLD	D	HOLD	HOLD	PL
0100 (4)	PUSH	Push/conditional load register/counter If test passes, return address placed on stack, reg/counter loaded with address in pipeline register. Move to next instruction	X	PC	PUSH	PC	PUSH	**	PL
0101 (5)	JSRP	Conditional jump to subroutine, R/PL If test passes, address of next instruction in pipeline register. Return address placed on stack If test fails, address of next instruction in register/ counter.	X	R	PUSH	D	PUSH	HOLD	PL
0101 (6)	CJV	Conditional jump vector, If test passes address of next instruction in external vector PROM/register. If test fails, address in microprogram counter	X	PC	HOLD	D	HOLD	HOLD	VECT
0111 (7)	JRP	Conditional jump R/PL, If test passes, address of next instruction in pipeline register	X	R	HOLD	D	HOLD	HOLD	PL

Table 13.8 *continued*

$I_3I_2I_1I_0$	Mnemonic	Operation	Register/ counter contents	Condition Inputs Fail* Y	STACK	Pass* Y	STACK	Register/ counter	Source select
		If test fails, address in register/counter. i.e. as (5) but no return address stored.							
1000 (8)	RFCT	Repeat loop if reg./counter ≠ 0. If reg./counter not zero, reg./counter decremented. Address of next instruction on top of stack. If reg./counter zero, address in microprogram counter. Also stack pointer decremented.	≠ 0 = 0	F PC	HOLD POP	F PC	HOLD POP	DEC HOLD	PL PL
1001 (9)	RPCT	Repeat pipeline register, counter ≠ 0 As (8) but branch address in pipeline register.	≠ 0 = 0	D PC	HOLD HOLD	D PC	HOLD HOLD	DEC HOLD	PL PL
1010 (10)	CRTN	Conditional return for subroutine If test passes, address of next instruction on top of stack If test fails, address in microprogram counter	X	PC	HOLD	F	POP	HOLD	PL
1010 (11)	CJPP	Conditional jump pipeline reg., Pop stack If test passes, address or next instruction in pipeline register. Stack pointer decremented (stack pop-ed). If test fails, address in microprogram counter.	X	PC	HOLD	D	POP	HOLD	PL
1100 (12)	LDCT	Load counter and continue. Reg/counter loaded with value at its inputs (normally the pipeline register).	X	PC	HOLD	PC	HOLD	LOAD	PL
1101 (13)	LOOP	Test end of loop conditionally. If test passes, address of next instruction in microprogram counter. Stack pointer decremented (stack pop-ed). If test fails, address on top of stack.	X	F	HOLD	PC	POP	HOLD	PL
1110 (14)	CONT	Continue microprogram counter incremented	X	PC	HOLD	PC	HOLD	HOLD	PL

Table 13.8 *continued*

$I_3I_2I_1I_0$	Mnemonic	Operation	Register/counter contents	Condition Inputs				Register/counter	Source select
				Fail*		Pass*			
				Y	STACK	Y	STACK		
1111 (15)	TWB	Three-way branch. If test passes, address in microprogram counter. Also stack pointer decremented. If test fails and reg./counter zero, address of next instruction in pipeline register If test fails and reg./counter not zero, reg./counter decremented, address of next instruction on top of stack.	$\neq 0$ $=0$	F D	HOLD POP	PC PC	POP POP	DEC HOLD	PL PL

Notes:

PL = pipeline register   MAP = mapping PROM   VECT = vector register
R = register/counter   PC = microprogram counter   F = top of stack
D = source external to   DEC = decrement   X = don't care
    Am2910A
*   Test passes if $\overline{CCEN} = 1$ or $\overline{CC} = 0$, Test fails if $\overline{CCEN} = 0$ and $\overline{CC} = 1$
**   If $\overline{CCEN} = 0$ and $\overline{CC} = 1$ hold; otherwise load.

an interrupt vector PROM and the next instruction field of a microinstruction which is held in a pipeline register. The last source is referred to simply as the pipeline register. Three signals are provided to enable the outputs of one of the external sources.

The pipeline register is not strictly necessary in the system, but is included to increase the speed of operation. In any stable system state, two microinstructions are present in the system, one selected in the microprogram memory and one in the pipeline rgister. When the Am2910A issues a system microinstruction address, the microinstruction next executed will not be the microinstruction selected by the AM2910A in the microprogram memory, but the previous microinstruction which is held in the pipeline register. The general pipeline technique is discussed in section 13.3

The Am2910A microprogram counter is an incrementer followed by 12-bit register. The same microinstruction may be executed repeatedly by setting the CI input low. If CI is high, sequential instructions are executed, unless modified by jump/subroutine call instructions. Non-sequential instruction execution is achieved via the jump instructions and subroutine call instructions (see Table 13.8). The subroutine jump instructions use the internal stack to store the return address. In our system, we have chosen to drive the CI line with the most significant bit in the system microinstruction, so that any instruction can be executed repeatedly. Normally, this feature would only be used on conditional microinstructions in which the condition can alter, otherwise the system would never move on to another microinstruction.

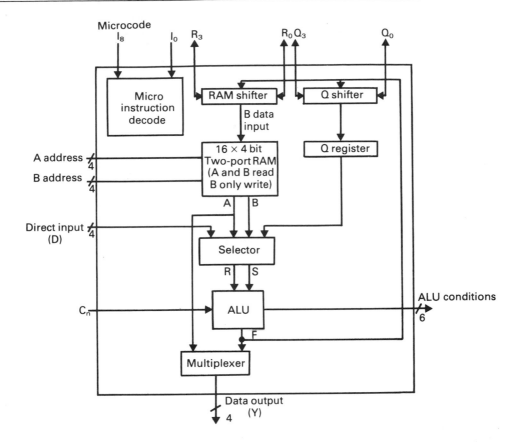

Figure 13.10   Am2910A 4-bit bit-slice microprocessor

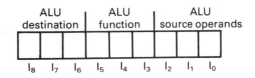

Figure 13.11   Am2901A microcode format

The Am2901A is a 4-bit device containing a 4-bit ALU, a 16-word, 4-bit register file, together with binary shifters, 4-bit accumulator extension register and a microinstruction decode circuit as shown in Fig. 13.10. A 9-bit microcode having the 3-field format shown in Fig. 13.11 is applied to the device. Table 13.9 lists the interpretation of the binary patterns in each of the three fields. Three bits $(I_2I_1I_0)$ are used to select the pair of source operands. Three bits $(I_5I_4I_3)$ are used to select the ALU function. The final three bits $(I_8I_7I_6)$ direct the result of the ALU to the RAM and/or the Q extension register. Additional shift functions can be specified in the final three bits.

Table 13.9 Am2901A Microinstruction decode

	Microcode			ALU source operands	
I_2	I_1	I_0		R	S
0	0	0	(0)	A	Q
0	0	1	(1)	A	B
0	1	0	(2)	0	Q
0	1	1	(3)	0	B
1	0	0	(4)	0	A
1	0	1	(5)	D	A
1	1	0	(6)	D	Q
1	1	1	(7)	D	0

(a) ALU source operand decode

	Microcode			ALU function
I_5	I_4	I_3		
0	0	0	(0)	$R + S + C_n$
0	0	1	(1)	$S - R - C_n$
0	1	0	(2)	$R - S - C_n$
0	1	1	(3)	R or S
1	0	0	(4)	R AND S
1	0	1	(5)	$\overline{R}$ AND S
1	1	0	(6)	R Exclusive-OR S
1	1	1	(7)	R Exclusive-NOR S

(b) ALU function decode

	Microcode			RAM function		Q register function		Y output	RAM shifter		Q shifter	
I_8	I_7	I_6		Shift	Load	Shift	Load		R_0	R_3	Q_0	Q_3
0	0	0	(0)	X	None	None	$Q \leftarrow F$	F	X	X	X	X
0	0	1	(1)	X	None	X	None	F	X	X	X	X
0	1	0	(2)	None	$B \leftarrow F$	X	None	A	X	X	X	X
0	1	1	(3)	None	$B \leftarrow F$	X	None	F	X	X	X	X
1	0	0	(4)	Down	$B \leftarrow F/2$	Down	$Q \leftarrow Q/2$	F	F_0	Input	Q_0	Input
1	0	1	(5)	Down	$B \leftarrow F/2$	X	None	F	F_0	Input	Q_0	Input
1	1	0	(6)	Up	$B \leftarrow 2F$	Up	$Q \leftarrow 2Q$	F	Input	F_3	Input	Q_3
1	1	1	(7)	Up	$B \leftarrow 2F$	X	None	F	Input	F_3	X	Q_3

(c) ALU destination decode

Notes:

$+$ = arithmetic addition

$-$ = arithmetic subtraction

carry (C_n) = carry in to ALU

Up = towards most significant bit

Down = towards least significant bit

X = don't care, shift pin TTL input (output high impedance)

INPUT = shift pin TTL input (output high independance)

Shift pins, R_0, R_3, Q_0 and Q_3 are input/output, i.e. a TTL input internally connected to a three state output.

The pair of source operands can be various combinations of A, B, Q and D, as given in Table 13.9(a). A and B are operands held in the internal RAM. D represents the external (direct) input. In addition, one operand can be the number zero. Both operands are read simultaneously into the ALU (including the RAM operands). The ALU result (F) can be shifted one place left or right if desired, which allows the result to be multiplied by 2 or divided by 2. The final result, shifted or not shifted, can then be loaded into the B location in the RAM, or both the B location and the Q register simultaneously. The ALU output is also produced at device Y outputs ($Y_3Y_2Y_1Y_0$). In one case, the A operand can be selected at the Y outputs instead of F.

The RAM and Q shifters (implemented using multiplexers rather than shift registers) each have two input/output lines, indicated in Fig. 13.10 as R_0R_3 and Q_0Q_3 respectively. These lines are used to enter most or least significant bits for the shifting process. In a right (down) shift, i.e. towards the least significant bit, R_3 and Q_3 are used to enter the most significant bit in the result. In a left (up) shift i.e. towards the most significant bit, R_0 and Q_0 can be used to enter the least significant bit in the result. When not used for input, i.e. R_3 and Q_3 in the left shift and R_0 and Q_0 in the right shift, the lines become outputs and indicate the most significant bits (R_3, Q_3) or least significant bits (R_0, Q_0) being discarded in the shift process. Normally, these input/output lines are connected to adjacent Am2901 devices to produce shift operations across the full number of bits of the operand.

13.3 OVERLAP AND PIPELINING

Overlap and the associated concept, *pipelining*, are methods of increasing the speed of operation of the central processor and are applied to the internal design of more advanced microprocessors. Overlap and pipelining really refer to the same technique, that of dividing a *task* into a number of *operations* which need to be performed in sequence. Each operation is performed by its own logical unit rather than a single unit performing all the operations. The units are connected together in a serial fashion with the output of one unit connecting to the input of the next unit. The overall operation is such that while one unit is performing an operation on the *n*th task, the preceding unit is performing an operation on the (*n*+1)th task. The unit attached before that is performing the operation on the (*n*+2)th task, as shown in Fig. 13.12.

The mechanism can be compared to a conveyor belt on an automobile assembly line, in which automobiles are in various stages of completion. Each automobile must pass through all stages to be completely assembled. Similarly in overlap/pipelining, tasks are presented in succession to the first unit. After the first operation on the first task is completed, the second task is presented, then the third, in the same way as parts enter an assembly line. Results from one operation are passed to the next unit as required. One complete task is completed after all the units have processed the operations of the task.

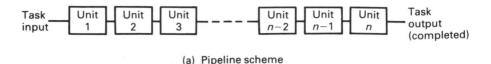

(a) Pipeline scheme

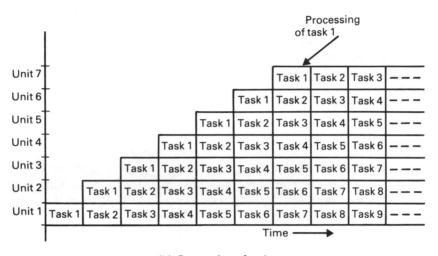

(b) Processing of tasks

Figure 13.12   Pipelining

Suppose each unit has the same operating time to complete an operation, the first task is complete and a succession of tasks are presented. Then the time to perform one complete task is the same as the time for one unit to perform one operation of the task, rather than the summation of all the unit times. Ideally each operation should take the same time, but if this is not the case, the overall processing time will be that of the slowest unit, with faster units having to be delayed.

Let us take a specific example, that of the overlap of the fetch and execute cycles of the processor. In the first instance, we shall assume one fetch cycle fetching a complete instruction and one execute cycle, and not any further decomposition. The technique requires that there are two separate units, a fetch unit and an execute unit, which are connected together as shown in Fig. 13.13(a). The address of the first instruction is presented to the fetch unit (by the program counter) and the fetch unit proceeds to fetch the first instruction. Once this is complete, the instruction is passed to the execute unit which decodes the instruction and proceeds to execute the instruction. While this is being done, the fetch unit fetches the next instruction. The process is continued with the fetch unit fetching the nth instruction while the execute unit is executing the $(n-1)$th instruction, as shown in Fig. 13.13(b). The overall processing time is given by:

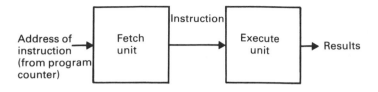

(a) Fetch and execute units

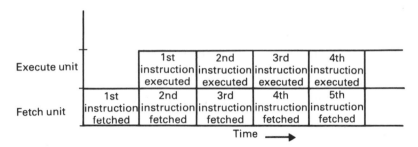

(b) Fetch/execute timing

Figure 13.13   Fetch/execute overlap scheme

$$\text{Processing time} = \sum_{i=1}^{n+1} \text{Max}(T(F_i), T(E_{i-1}))$$

where:

$T(F_i)$ = time of ith fetch unit
$T(E_i)$ = time of ith execute unit

and

$T(F_{n+1}) = T(E_0) = 0.$

Clearly, the execute unit may operate at a different time to the fetch unit. In particular, it is likely to require more time for complicated instructions, and this will dominate the overall processing time. To reduce this effect, the execute unit could be split into further separate units. Firstly, a separate instruction decode unit could be provided after the fetch unit, followed by an execute unit. This scheme is known as a *three-level overlap*. However, it is usually not possible for the fetch unit to fetch an instruction and an execute unit to fetch any required operands of the previous instruction at the same time if the program and data are held in the same memory, as only one unit can assess the memory at any instance.

One method to overcome this problem is to fetch more than one instruction at a time using memory *interleaving*. In memory interleaving, the memory is divided into modules which allows one word from each module to be accessed simultaneously (see also Chap 14, section 14.2.1). Memory addresses of individual locations are numbered across the modules as shown Fig. 14.16. The number of modules is a power of two, so that the memory addresses in the first module, which identify all the words accessed, might be obtained from any memory address by setting the least significant bits to 0 (one bit for two modules, two bits for four modules, etc.).

To fetch two instructions simultaneously, two memory modules are required. The two instructions can then be used in three-level overlap as shown in Fig. 13.14(a). In three-level overlap, there are three units, a fetch unit which fetches two instructions, a decode unit which decodes one of the instructions and fetches any operands, and an execute unit which executes one instruction as shown in Fig. 13.14(b). After the memory bus has been used by the fetch unit to fetch two instructions, it is available by the decode unit for fetching operands. The execute unit now does not use the bus.

Further decomposition can be made. For example, we could have five stages:

  (i)   Fetch instruction
 (ii)   Decode instruction
(iii)   Fetch operand(s)
 (iv)   Execute operation (ADD, etc.)
  (v)   Store result

The term pipelining is usually applied when several units are connected together.

Complex arithmetic operations could be decomposed further, into several separate operations. Floating point arithmetic, particularly, can naturally be decomposed into several sequential operations. Consider the addition of two floating point numbers A and B, where A and B are each represented by a mantissa and exponent and the addition produces a floating point result. The addition requires a number of steps:

  (i)   Normalization, if not already done (remove leading 0's in mantissas and adjust the exponents accordingly)
 (ii)   Compare exponents and determine which is larger
(iii)   Adjust small exponent to become the same as the larger exponent and adjust mantissa accordingly
 (iv)   Add mantissa
  (v)   Normalize result

We can provide a separate unit for each step with the units connected in a pipeline. With this scheme, a series of floating point additions can be performed at increased speed over a single floating point unit. For example, suppose the processing time of each unit is:

  (i)   Pre-normalization $t_1 = 200\,\text{ns}$
 (ii)   Comparison $t_2 = 100\,\text{ns}$
(iii)   Exponent adjustment $t_3 = 150\,\text{ns}$

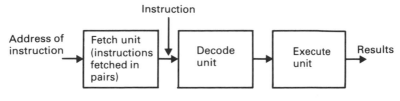

(a) Fetch, decode and execute units

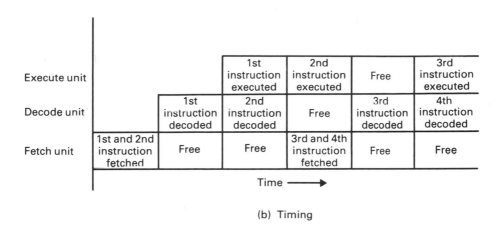

		1st instruction executed	2nd instruction executed	Free	3rd instruction executed
Execute unit					
Decode unit	1st instruction decoded	2nd instruction decoded	Free	3rd instruction decoded	4th instruction decoded
Fetch unit	1st and 2nd instruction fetched	Free	Free	3rd and 4th instruction fetched	Free	Free

Time ⟶

(b) Timing

Figure 13.14   Three-level instruction fetch/decode/execute overlap

(iv) Mantissa addition $t_4 = 250\,$ns
(v)   Post-normalization $t_5 = 200\,$ns

The processing time if the operations are performed within a single unit would be $t_1 + t_2 + t_3 + t_4 + t_5 = 900\,$ns. With the pipeline and a series of floating point additions, the processing time is 250 ns (the processing time of the slowest unit). To gain full use of a pipeline system in an ALU, all the arithmetic operations would need to be integrated into a single pipeline. Units not necessary for a particular operation could be switched out of the pipeline temporarily.

Two methods of implementing the control mechanism of a pipeline (or overlap) can be identified, namely:

(i)   Asynchronous method
(ii) Synchronous method

as shown in Fig. 13.15. In the asynchronous method, a pair of handshaking signals are used between each unit and the next unit. One signal is a ready signal from a unit to the next unit which informs the next unit that it has finished its present operation and is ready to pass the task and any results onwards. The second signal is an acknowledge signal from the unit receiving the ready signal

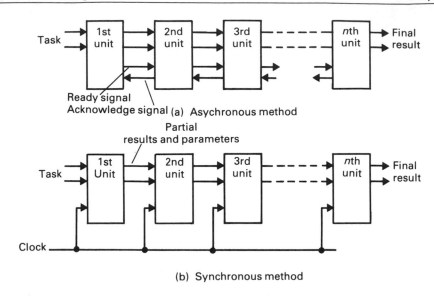

Figure 13.15 Transfer of information between units in a pipeline

back to the previous unit generated when it is ready to accept the task and results. In the synchronous method, one timing signal causes all outputs of units to be transferred to the succeeding units. The timing signal occurs at fixed intervals. In the floating point addition pipeline above, this would be every 250 ns.

The asynchronous method provides the greatest speed of operation. Also, in the synchronous method, *clock skew* can cause mal-operation. Clock skew is the variation in the delay of a clock signal arriving at different units, due to the time it takes for signals to pass along interconnection tracks (about 5–7 ns/m). In the example shown in Fig. 13.16, a pipeline consists of several *D*-type flip-flops, and the CLOCK signal is increasingly delayed before it reaches successive flip-flops. It is possible that CLOCK will be delayed sufficiently to cause subsequent data to be passed across to the next the flip-flop, rather than present data.

Overlap and pipelinging assume that there is a sequence of tasks to be performed in one order and that there is no interaction between tasks, other than passing the results of one unit on to the next unit. However, although programs are written as a linear sequence, the execution of one instruction will often depend upon the result of a previous instruction, and also the order of execution may be changed by jump/branch instructions. Therefore we have two possible causes for breakdown of the pipeline, namely:

(i) Data dependencies between instructions
(ii) Conditional instructions

As regards (i), little can be done to reduce the problem without constraining the programmer. For example, suppose we wish to compute the value of C = 2×(A + contents of memory location 100) with the program sequence (in Z-80 notation):

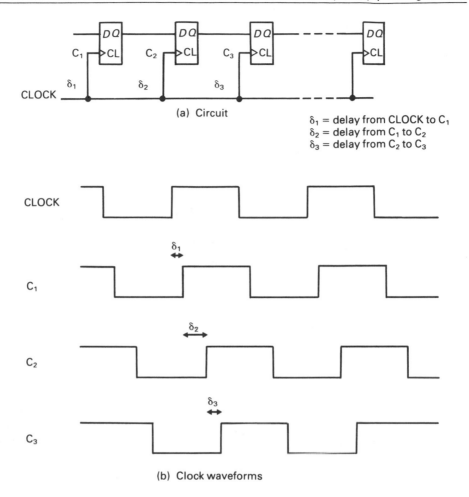

δ_1 = delay from CLOCK to C_1
δ_2 = delay from C_1 to C_2
δ_3 = delay from C_2 to C_3

(a) Circuit

(b) Clock waveforms

Figure 13.16   Clock skew in a pipeline

```
ADD  A,(100)  ;A = A+contents of location 100   (not a Z-80 instruction)
SLA  A        ;A = 2A
LD   C,A      ;C = A
```

and these instruction are in a five-stage pipeline as shown in Fig. 13.17. (The Z-80 does not have a pipeline.) It would be incorrect to begin shifting A before the add instruction, and similarly, it would be incorrect to load C before the shift operation. Hence each instruction must produce its result before the next instruction can begin. Should the programmer know a pipeline organization exists in the computer used and the operation of the pipeline, it may be possible to rewrite some programs to separate data dependencies. Otherwise, when a data dependency does occur, the pipeline is held up until the required results are generated.

As regards (ii), schemes do exist to reduce the number of times the pipeline breaks down. One approach is to allow the branch instruction, and other

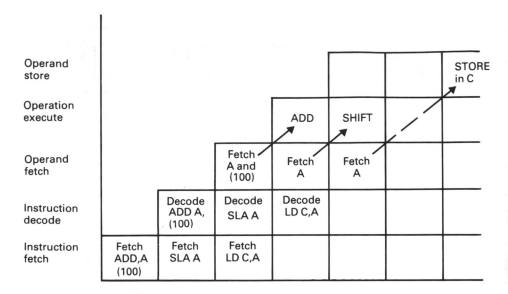

Figure 13.17 Five-stage pipeline with data dependencies

instructions that follow, to be processed as normally. When the branch instruction is completely executed, it would be known which instruction to process next. If this instruction is not the next instruction in the pipeline, which is most unlikely, all the instructions in the pipeline are abandoned and the pipeline is cleared. The required instruction is fetched and must be processed through all the units in the same way as when the pipeline is first started.

Jump/branch instructions might typically occur every 10–20 instructions and would reduce the speed of operation accordingly in the above mechanism. For example, if a seven-stage pipeline operated at 100 ns steps and an instruction which subsequently cleared the pipeline occurred every 10 instructions, the average instruction processing time would be:

$$(9 \times 100\,\text{ns} + 1 \times 700\,\text{ns})/10 = 160\,\text{ns}$$

Methods to alleviate this problem include:

(i) Prediction logic to fetch the most likely next instruction after a jump/branch instruction
(ii) Instruction buffers to fetch both possible instructions.

The first method is generally successful because normally jump/branch instructions are used in program loops and cause a repetition of branching back to the same instruction many times before leaving the loop. After the first branch, it can be predicted with a good probability that the next time the instruction is encountered, the branch will be to the same location.

The instruction fetch/execute overlap technique is now applied to the many microprocessors, including 8-bit microprocessors, to substantially increase the speed of operation. The bus timing described earlier needs to be modified if the processor uses overlap/pipelining because the instruction and the associated operand transfers on the bus will not be in sequence. It may be possible to have a number of instruction fetch cycles between operand transfers.

REFERENCES

1. Wilkes, M. and C. Stringer, 'Micro-programming and the Design of Control Circuits in an Electronic Digital Computer', *Proc. Camb. Phil. Soc.*, 49 (1953), 230–38.
2. *Am2900 Family Data Book*. Sunnyvale, California: Advanced Micro Devices, Inc., 1985.

PROBLEMS

13.1 With the Z-80 timing shown in Fig. 7.2, 7.3 and 7.4, determine the maximum allowable memory read and write access time in each case, assuming the following:

(i) Data set-up time = 10 ns
(ii) Bus stabilization and skew time = 50 ns
(iii) Interconnection delay time = 30 ns
(iv) Clock high and low period = 0.5 μs

Other factors may be ignored. List these factors.

13.2 Write a microprogram using the register transfer notation in section 13.1.3 to perform the Z-80 machine instruction LD A, (HL).

13.3 Design a microinstruction format to generate the Z-80 signals $\overline{M1}$, $\overline{MREQ}$, $\overline{RFSH}$, $\overline{RD}$ and $\overline{WR}$. Encode the microprogram in Table 13.1 using the format.

13.4 Write a microprogram for the Am2900 system described in section 13.2.3 to emulate the following Z-80 instructions, making your own assignment of registers in the Am2901 register file:

ADD A,B
ADC A,B
SUB B
SBC A,B

Z-80 signals need not be generated. The carry flag is selected with $C_2C_1C_0 = 001$ in the microinstruction (Fig. 13.9).

13.5 A microprocessor has two internal units, an instruction fetch unit and an instruction execute unit, with fetch/execute overlap. Compute the overall processing time of eight sequential instructions, in each of the following cases:

(a) $T(F_i) = T(E_i) = 1\,\mu$s for $i = 1$ to 8
(b) $T(F_i) = 0.5\,\mu$s, $T(E_i) = 1\,\mu$s for $i = 1$ to 8

(c) $T(F_i) = 1\,\mu s$, $T(E_i) = 0.5, 0.75, 1.25, 1.50, 1.25, 1, 0.75$ and $0.5\,\mu s$ for $i = 1$, 2, 3, 4, 5, 6, 7 and 8 respectively

where $T(F_i)$ = the time to fetch the ith instruction, and $T(E_i)$ = the time to execute the ith instruction.

Memory Management

14.1 PRIMARY–SECONDARY MEMORY MANAGEMENT

14.1.1 Memory management schemes

In a computer system, the memory is often composed of a primary main memory and a secondary memory (backing store). In a microprocessor system, the primary memory is always semiconductor memory and the secondary memory is usually disk memory. This memory hierarchy needs schemes to arrange that the required information is in the main memory when it is to be read or altered. The general term for the schemes is known as *memory management*.

The simplest memory management method is to employ *overlaying*, in which programs or sections of programs are transferred into primary memory as required, overwriting existing programs. Each transfer is specifically programmed. Overlaying is used in microprocessor systems, particularly small floppy disk based systems. For example, one of the first widely used microprocessor operating systems†, CP/M [1], and similar subsequent operating systems such as MS-DOS generally employ overlaying. A large software package which could not reside in the main memory in a complete form because of the limited available main memory would be divided into a main file and one or more overlay files. The overlay files would be called from within the main file, and would typically overwrite the main file when transferred into the main memory. This process would be repeated with other files as they are required. It is necessary to copy files in the disk memory before they become overwritten if true copies are not already present on the disk. The overlay method normally places a heavy burden on the programmer, since interaction between sections in different overlays can cause continual and excessive disk transfers ('disk thrashing') and errors can be very difficult to locate.

A better approach is to have an automatic process of transferring blocks of words into and out of the primary memory, which relieves the burden of programming transfers specifically, and preferably takes into account the likely blocks required in the near future, to limit disk thrashing. Automatic transfer mechanisms were devised for computers well before microprocessors were

† An operating system is the controlling program of a computer system; see also Chap. 6. section 6.3.

developed and rely on having two addresses associated with each word stored, the actual address used by the memory units and another address which is produced by the processor when executing the user programs. A translation mechanism is provided in hardware (with software back-up support) to perform the translation of program addresses into the actual addresses used in the memory units. Each program address has a corresponding memory address somewhere in the memory system but the memory address may change as programs are transferred into and out of the memories, which allows programs to be transferred automatically without alteration of program addresses. There are two basis schemes, namely:

(i) Paging system
(ii) Segmented system

Firstly we will consider the paging system.

14.1.2 Paging system

In a paging system, the actual address in memory is called a *real* address and the program address is called a *virtual* address. The term *virtual (paged) memory system* is used to describe the system. The memory space is divided into blocks of equal size, typically 128 words, 256 words, 512 words or 1024 words. Each block is called a *page*. An address is composed of a page number and a line number. The virtual and read addresses have the same line number but a translation is necessary to convert a virtual page number to a real page number. Page numbers are concatenated with the line number to form the complete address. A hardware mechanism is provided to translate the virtual page number into the real page number. The hardware mechanism operates only on pages in the primary memory. If the required real page number is not found in the translation mechanism, a software replacement algorithm (method) must be executed to find the required page in secondary memory, to transfer this page into the primary memory, and to choose the best existing page to be transferred back into secondary memory providing space for the new page.

Figure 14.1 shows how the virtual and real pages might be allocated. In this example, each page contains 512 words. There are 8 pages in the primary memory and 24 pages in the secondary memory; in a real system, there would be many more pages in each memory, but a small number is chosen here to clarify the assignment of addresses. The primary memory page address range is from 0 to 7 inclusive, and the secondary memory page address page is from 8 to 31 inclusive.

Both the real and virtual addresses are divided into two fields, a page field and a line (within a page) field. Since there are 512 words in a page, both line fields contain 9 bits. The page field of the real address contains 5 bits to enable any of 32 pages to be specified. The virtual page field can have a different number of bits. In our example the virtual page filed has the same number of bits as the real page field, and hence there are 32 possible virtual pages.

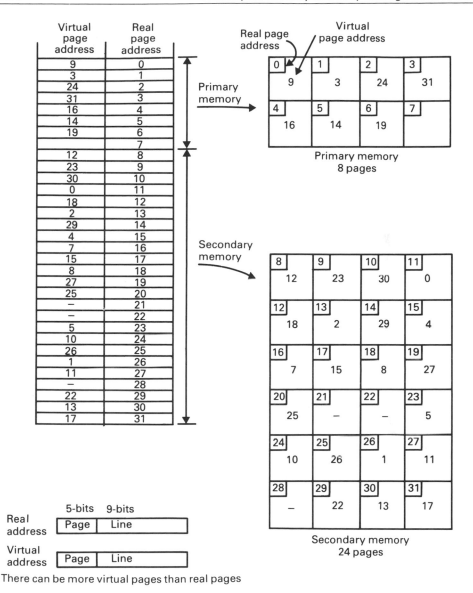

Figure 14.1   Real and virtual addresses in a paged system

In an assignment of virtual pages to real pages shown in Fig. 14.1, some virtual pages are unassigned (not used). Real page 7, the last page in the primary memory is currently free. Suppose virtual page 3 is requested by the processor. First hardware is activated to check whether the page is in the primary memory. The hardware finds the page currently residing in real page 1 and the page can be referenced. However, suppose virtual page 7 is now requested by the processor. The check shows that the page is not currently residing in the primary memory. Then, a software mechanism is activated to search for the location in the secondary memory. In this case, the page is found in real address 16 in secondary memory. The page is transferred into the free (real) page 7 in primary memory, and subsequently referenced by the processor. Now the primary memory is full. If a reference is made to another page in the secondary memory, an existing page in the primary memory must be returned to the secondary memory before the new page is transferred into the primary memory. Hence, a free page must be always be maintained either in the primary memory or in the secondary memory (unless a copy is always held in secondary memory).

There are two basic hardware methods to translate the virtual page into a real page:

(i) Direct mapping
(ii) Associative mapping

The *direct mapping* approach is shown in Fig. 14.2(a). All the real page addresses are stored in a high-speed random access memory in locations whose addresses are the virtual addresses of the associated real addresses. Consequently, a real address can be found directly from the memory.

The *associative mapping* approach is shown in Fig. 14.2(b). A special type of memory is used called an *associative memory*, also called a *content addressable memory*, CAM. In a content addressable memory, a location is identified by its contents rather than an assigned address. The binary word applied to the data inputs of the CAM is compared with all the stored words simultaneously by the internal logic of the device. If any word is found to be the same as the applied word, an appropriate match signal is generated by the device. CAMs are designed to operate at high speed using bipolar technology. Delays from data input to match output can be less than 30 ns, but the devices are relatively expensive.

When used for associative mapping, the content addressable memory is coupled to normal random access memory, giving two parts to the memory. If a match is found in the first part, the corresponding second part is read out. Each location in the first part stores the virtual page address and the second the corresponding real page address. When the virtual address is generated by the processor, it is compared with all the first parts simultaneously using the logic within the associative memory. If a match is found, the corresponding real address held in the second part is read out. The real address is then sent to the primary memory. A *page fault* occurs whenever the page referenced is not already in the primary memory.

14.1.3 Replacement algorithms

There are various replacement algorithms that can be used to select the page to remove from the primary memory to make room for the incoming page.

(a) Random replacement algorithm

In the *random replacement algorithm*, pages to be taken out of the primary

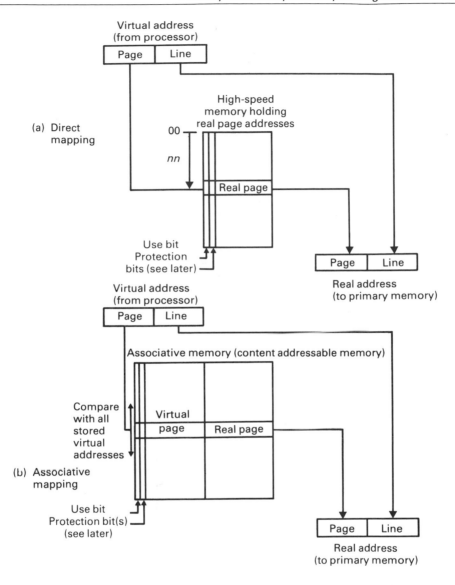

Figure 14.2 Translation of virtual addresses into real addresses in a paged system

memory are chosen in a random order. This method would not be really suitable for most programs which normally access locally, i.e. the next location required is usually near the last.

(b) First-in-first-out replacement algorithm
In the *first-in-first-out replacement algorithm*, the page existing in the primary memory for the longest time is transferred out. A list of pages current in the primary memory is maintained in a (first-in-first-out) queue. As a new entry is inserted all the entries move down one place and the last is taken out to be used for replacement.

For example, suppose the following pages are requested in the order shown:

3, 4, 3, 6, 8, 3, 7, 6, 8, 3, 2, 6

and the primary memory can only hold four pages at any instant. The pages in the primary memory when a page fault occurs is shown in Fig. 14.3. Initially, the primary memory is empty, and page faults occur when pages are first referenced.

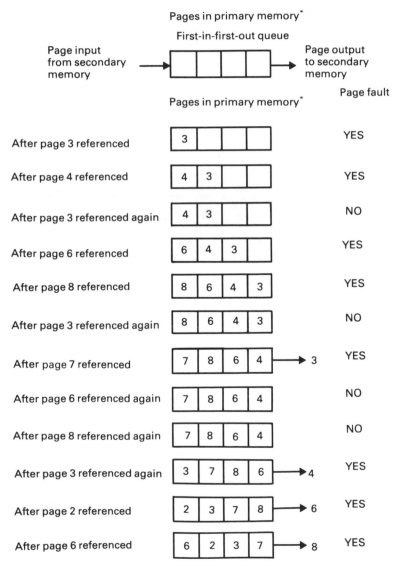

* Actual pages in primary memory not reordered

Figure 14.3 Pages in primary memory using first-in-first-out replacement algorithm

Each time a new page is referenced, the page entries are moved one place right (conceptually, not actually). When the memory is full and a page fault occurs, the page returned to the secondary memory is the page at the rightmost end of the queue. (Free space is left in the secondary memory.) We see that with our sequence of page references, the first-in-first-out algorithm produces eight page faults.

The algorithm can be implemented using a circular list holding the page entries as shown in Fig. 14.4. A pointer indicates the current rightmost end of the queue and the leftmost entry of the queue is immediately before the pointed entry. At page fault time, the page replaced is that indicated by the pointer. The pointer is then incremented to point to the next entry.

The first-in-first-out algorithm can be modified to avoid unnecessary transfers by moving over pages in the queue which have been referenced (and hence are likely to be accessed again especially if in program loops). This is known as *first-in-not-used-first-out*. It requires the addition of a *use* bit set by hardware when the page is referenced. A pointer points to a page in the circular list. When a replacement is necessary, the use bit is examined. If the use bit = 0, the page is replaced and the pointer advanced to the next page. If the use bit = 1, it is reset and the pointer advanced to the next page. This is repeated until a use bit is already reset. The corresponding page is then transferred out of the primary memory and replaced with the incoming page. The pointer is then advanced one place. Whenever a page is referenced subsequently, the associated use bit is set. The bit is not set upon first loading the page. The algorithm using a circular list is shown in Fig. 14.5.

The first-in-not-used-first-out algorithm applied to the previous sequence is shown in Fig. 14.6. Here we see that there are six page faults.

(c) Least recently used (LRU) replacement algorithm
In the *least recently used replacement algorithm*, the page which has not been

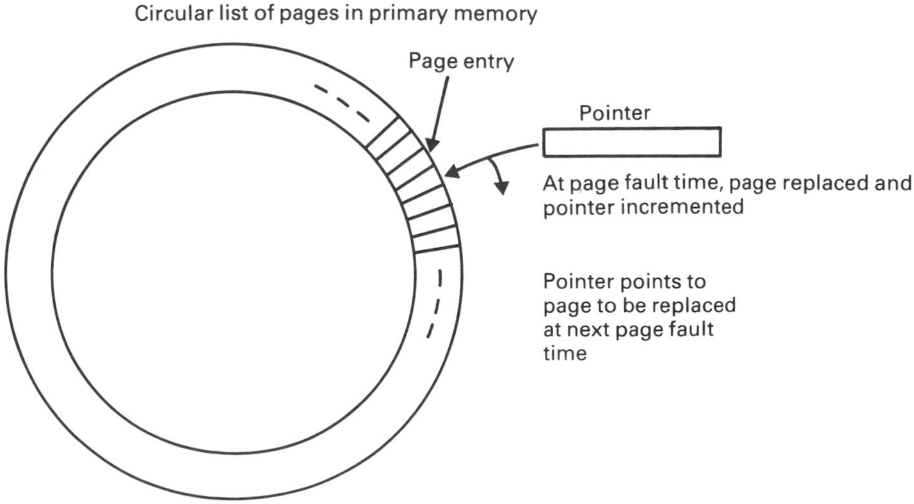

Circular list of pages in primary memory

Figure 14.4   First-in-first-out replacement algorithm using a circular list

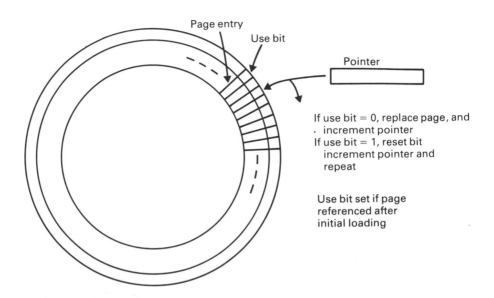

Figure 14.5   First-in-not-used-first-out replacement algorithm

used for the longest time is transferred out. One implementation of the least recently used algorithm is to hold the list of pages in the primary memory in the order that they have been referenced. Whenever a reference is made, the order of the list has to be updated. This means that the page is placed at the top of the list and all the other pages are moved down one place. The algorithm applied to our sequence is shown in Fig. 14.7. Again we have six page faults. The number of page faults with each algorithm, of course, depends upon the actual sequence.

The LRU algorithm poses some practical problems for a true implementation if there are very many pages in the primary memory, as would be the case in a virtual memory system. For example, a counter could be associated with each page and incremented every time the page is referenced to record the number of references, which would enable the least recently used page to be found. This approach would necessitate very many counters and substantial logic and would not be feasible for a large system. Alternatively, an associative memory could be used to record the primary memory pages. (It is left as an exercise to devise an associative memory solution.) Again, the associative memory would need to have substantial capacity. As associative memory is expensive, the top portion (say 16 or 32 entries) could be in an associative memory and the rest maintained by software.

The use bit of each page, if necessary for the replacement algorithm, is incorporated into the virtual address/real address hardware translation table, together with additional bits for memory protection. (Protection bits might, for example, make pages read-only or prevent a page being removed from the primary memory if the page is part of an active user program in a multi-programming environment.)

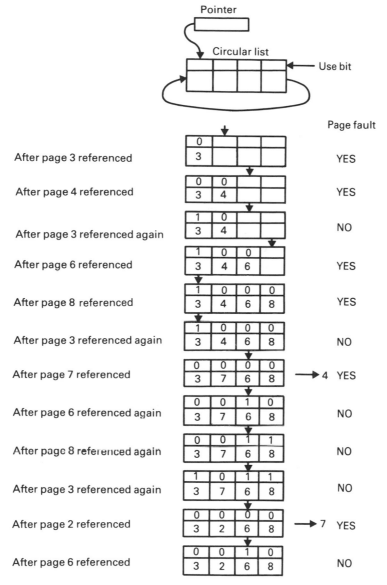

					Page fault
After page 3 referenced	0				YES
	3				
After page 4 referenced	0	0			YES
	3	4			
After page 3 referenced again	1	0			NO
	3	4			
After page 6 referenced	1	0	0		YES
	3	4	6		
After page 8 referenced	1	0	0	0	YES
	3	4	6	8	
After page 3 referenced again	1	0	0	0	NO
	3	4	6	8	
After page 7 referenced	0	0	0	0	→ 4 YES
	3	7	6	8	
After page 6 referenced again	0	0	1	0	NO
	3	7	6	8	
After page 8 referenced again	0	0	1	1	NO
	3	7	6	8	
After page 3 referenced again	1	0	1	1	NO
	3	7	6	8	
After page 2 referenced	0	0	0	0	→ 7 YES
	3	2	6	8	
After page 6 referenced	0	0	1	0	NO
	3	2	6	8	

 * Actual pages in primary memory not reordered

Figure 14.6 Pages in primary memory using first-in-not-used-first-out replacement algorithm

The page size is typically 512 words. If a small page size is chosen, the time taken in transferring a page between the primary memory and secondary memory is short and a large selection of pages from various programs can reside in the main memory. However, a small page size necessitates a large page table for any particular main memory size, and information to link pages to programs increases. The secondary memory, if a disk memory as normally, also constrains

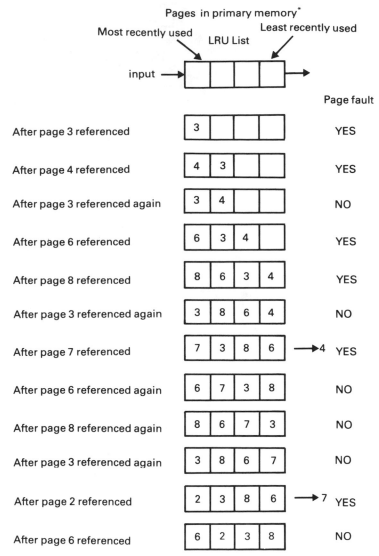

Pages in primary memory*

Most recently used   Least recently used

LRU List

input →

Page fault

After page 3 referenced	3				YES
After page 4 referenced	4	3			YES
After page 3 referenced again	3	4			NO
After page 6 referenced	6	3	4		YES
After page 8 referenced	8	6	3	4	YES
After page 3 referenced again	3	8	6	4	NO
After page 7 referenced	7	3	8	6	→4 YES
After page 6 referenced again	6	7	3	8	NO
After page 8 referenced again	8	6	7	3	NO
After page 3 referenced again	3	8	6	7	NO
After page 2 referenced	2	3	8	6	→7 YES
After page 6 referenced	6	2	3	8	NO

* Actual pages in primary memory not reordered

Figure 14.7 Pages in primary memory using least recently used (LRU) replacement algorithm

the page size to that of a sector or a multiple of a sector (unless additional sector buffer storage is provided to enable one page from several in a sector to be selected). Making the sector small increases the proportion of recorded information given over to sector identification on the disk. A large page size requires a small page table but the transfer time is generally longer and unused space at the end of each page is likely to increase. (This is known as the *internal fragmentation*.) The number of words in each page chosen is a compromise between the various factors.

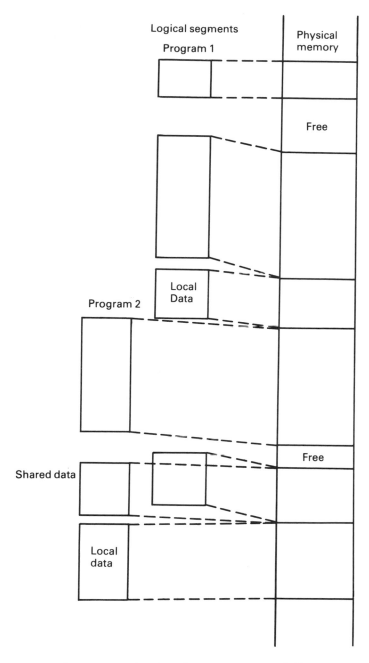

Figure 14.8   Mapping of segments onto available memory

14.1.4 Segmented system

In a *segmented* system, the memory space is not divided into equal sized pages but into variable sized blocks of contiguous locations called *segments*. This approach may be better for programs and data which are naturally generated in various sizes. Segments may be allowed to overlap. Each address is composed of a segment number and a displacement within the segment (called an *offset*). Rather than concatenate the two, in a segmented scheme the segment and the offset are added together to form the read address. The term *logical* address is sometimes used in segmented systems to describe the virtual address, and the term *physical* address used to describe the real address. Figure 14.8 shows how segments in two programs might be assigned space in the memory. Segments can be shared between different programs. Segments can also partially overlap if required.

Figure 14.9 shows the usual method of translating logical addresses into physical addresses. The logical address is divided into two fields, a segment number field and an offset field. The segment number field specifies the logical segment and the offset specifies the number of locations from the beginning of the segment. The logical segment field selects a physical segment from a segment table using direct mapping here. The selected location in the table holds the address of the first location in the physical memory. This address is called the *base*. The base is added to the offset to form the physical address.

The 16-bit 8086 microprocessor introduced in 1978 is perhaps the first

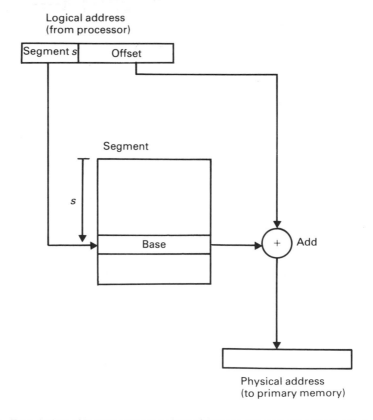

Figure 14.9 Translation of logical addresses into physical addresses in a segmented system

example of a microprocessor to incorporate segmentation within the device [2]. This microprocessor contains four segment registers called the code segment register (CS), the data segment register (DS), the stack segment register (SS) and the extra segment register (ES) respectively. The address generated by the program is a 16-bit offset, without a segment number. A 16-bit offset allows segments up to 64K bytes. The particular segment is selected by context. Instruction fetch cycles always use the code segment register with the offset provided by the program counter (called instruction pointer, IP). Most data operations normally assume the use of the data register, though any register can be selected. Stack instructions always use the stack register. The extra segment is used particularly for results of string operations. The translation mechanism is shown in Fig. 14.10. The segment register have 16-bits. Four least significant 0's are added, giving a 20-bit base address, and a 20-bit physical address.

The segment table can incorporate additional information, for example use and protection bits. Protection from referencing a location beyond the end of a particular segment can be achieved by adding a segment length field in the table. Also several segment tables can be provided. A system with these features is shown in Fig. 14.11. In this system, the contents of a segment table pointer (a register) are first added to the logical segment number before accessing the segment table. The segment table holds the base together with the length of the segment, flags to enable replacement algorithms to be implemented, and

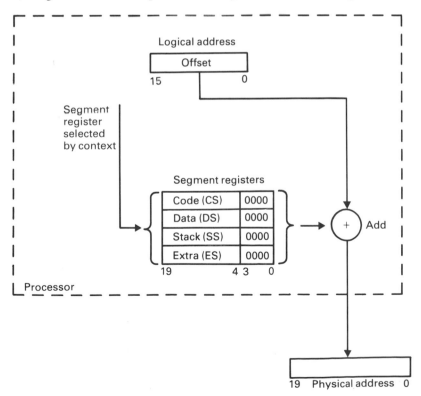

Figure 14.10 8086 segmentation

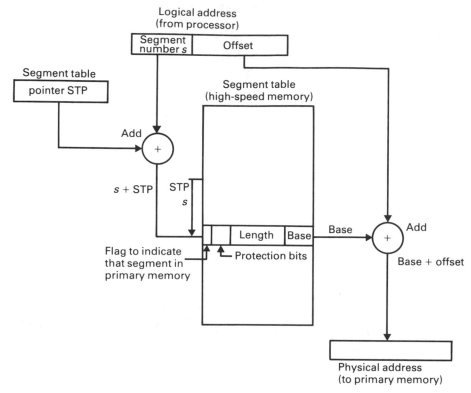

Figure 14.11   Translation of logical addresses into physical addresses in a segmented system incorporating more than one segment table

memory protection flags (see later). The length is compared with the displacement to check that a valid logical address is present. The displacement must be not greater than the length, otherwise a segment error signal is generated. The base is extracted and added to the displacement to form the full physical address. As with the paged system, all processor-generated addresses must be translated before a memory location can be accessed and hence the mechanism must operate at high speed.

The replacement algorithm in a segmented system can be similar to the replacement algorithms in a paged system, but the algorithm needs to take the varying size of the segments into account when allocating space for new segments. Too small spaces which cannot be used should not be generated. This is known as *external fragmentation*. The *first-fit* algorithm [3] for finding space in the primary memory requires two items to be associated with each segment:

(i) Pointer to next free space, NEXT
(ii) Length of free space between segment and next segment, LENGTH

as shown in Fig. 14.12. These two items are stored at the beginning of each free space in memory. The algorithm to find a space for a segment from the secondary memory is as follows:

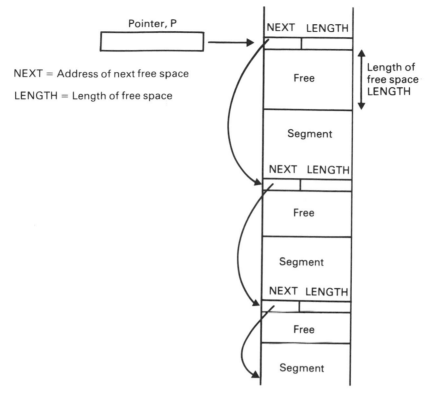

Figure 14.12   First-fit algorithm

Step 1   Set a memory pointer, P, to select the first free space.
Step 2   If length of free space, LENGTH, is greater than incoming segment, insert segment in space, followed by LENGTH specifying remaining free space and NEXT. Alter previous NEXT to point to new free space. Leave algorithm.
Step 3   If length of free space is equal to the segment, as step 2 but update information relating to free space. Leave algorithm.
Step 4   If length of free space is less than segment, move to next segment and repeat step 2 or 3.

To prevent external fragmentation, step 2 can be modified to:

Step 2   If length of free space is greater than incoming segment + size of space not usable (perhaps 8–16 words), insert segment in space, alter length of free space accordingly and leave algorithm.

14.1.5 Memory management units

We now turn our attention to how a memory management scheme, either a paged memory management scheme or a segmented memory scheme, can be implemented in a computer system. We shall concentrate on a microprocessor system, in particular. The hardware to implement a memory management scheme is known as a *memory management unit* (MMU). An MMU may be a processor support device or an integral part of the processor, and provides two principal functions:

(i)   Memory translation
(ii) Memory protection

As we have seen, memory address translation involves taking the address emitted from the processor, the virtual or logical address, and converting this address to a different address known as the real or physical address. The physical address is passed to the memory units. Memory protection involves stopping this translation and preventing any address or address strobe signals being passed to the memory units if there has been a violation of an accepted memory operation. For example, some areas of memory may be designated as read-only and a write operation would be an invalid operation; there are several other possible invalid operations.

Consider a segmentation system (though much is also true for a paged system). (The following is based upon the Z8010 MMU support device for the 16-bit Z8001 microprocessor [4].) The processor provides a logical address given by a segment number together with an offset (displacement). The MMU converts this logical address into a physical address, for example as shown in Fig. 14.13. First the segment number 'points' to an MMU register holding the

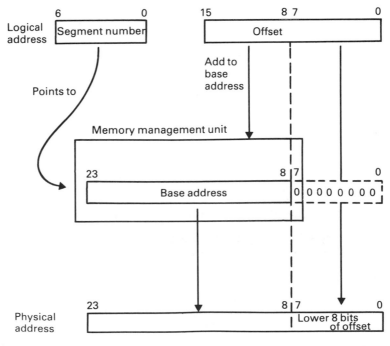

Figure 14.13   Generating a physical address using a segmented MMU

segment starting address, the base address. The offset address is added to this base address to obtain the physical address. The base address generally has its lower significant digits set to zero so that the lower part of the offset need only be concatenated with the address formed by the addition of the base address and the higher significant part of the offset address. In our example, the lower 8 bits of the base address are all zero.

Since every memory access requires the logical-to-physical address translation in this scheme, the translation must be very fast within the MMU. If the segment number is 7 bits, there are 128 base addresses possible. These base addresses are stored in internal MMU registers and accessed directly through the segment number. The resultant base address is added to the upper offset internally and the physical address is produced at the output of the MMU. The lower offset address need not pass through the MMU for this operation.

The second function of the MMU, that of memory protection, requires additional fields in the internal MMU memory. A limit (segment length) field is provided to enable a maximum segment size to be specified. If the offset is greater than the limit size, an error flag in the MMU error-condition register is set and the processor informed. MMU and processor status information is saved automatically to enable recovery from error conditions. Typically, any segment can be assigned as:

(i)   Read-only
(ii) Execute-only
(iii) System-only

Assigning a segment as read-only allows data to be protected from alteration. Assigning a segment as execute-only means that it can only be referenced during a fetch cycle, which prevents, for example, unauthorized copying of programs since execute-only code is unable to be read as data.

For the system-only assignment, it is necessary for the processor to have two operating modes, a normal mode which is for ordinary users and a system mode dedicated to the operating system. Generally when in the normal mode, there will be certain instructions which cannot be executed and the only method to enter the system mode is through a system call to the operating system, either intentionally or via a software or hardware interrupt, or error condition. Hence, functions such as input/output can be totally controlled by the operating system without interference from user programs.

Rather than having an 'only' assignment, it is possible to have an 'excluded' assignment, for example:

(i)   CPU excluded
(ii) DMA excluded

In CPU excluded, the segment cannot be accessed by the central processor, leaving all other possible 'bus masters' such as DMA controllers. In DMA excluded, the DMA controllers are excluded. This leaves the central processor and other bus masters, generally other processors in a multiprocessor system.

Any attempted violation of the above assignments would cause the MMU to set the appropriate error flags in the MMU error condition register and to signal the processor, generally with a special 'segment trap' signal. Information such as segment number and offset of the violation and of the current processor instruction and status information will be saved.

There may be other error conditions indicated. For example, if a segment is being used as a stack, it is convenient to know when the end of the allocated memory space is being reached before the end is actually reached. Since stacks generally grow downwards, access to, say, the first 256 locations in the segment would indicate an approach to the end of the stack. A flag may be set accordingly by the MMU which would be used to prevent a stack overflowing its memory space.

There is the possibility of multiple violations. For example, a central processor violation might occur and while this is being handled, a DMA violation might occur during an autonomous transfer. To cater for this situation, DMA violations are sensed and indicated but the status information not saved because this might overwrite status information being used by the central processor violation service routine. Similarly, if a second error condition or violation occurs while the first is being serviced, an additional 'fatal error' flag is set.

Typically two flags are associated with each logical/physical address entry in the MMU segment table to help choosing segments for returning to the secondary memory, namely:

 (i) Written flag
(ii) Accessed flag

The written flag is set if a write operation has taken place to the segment. Thus if this flag is not set when the segment is considered for returning to the secondary memory, the transfer need not be done (assuming a copy is kept on the secondary memory when it was transferred to primary memory). It is only necessary to delete the primary memory copy.

The accessed flag indicates that a memory access has been made to the segment. This can be used to determine which segments are active and which are dormant and not used. The dormant segments would be returned to the secondary memory first when space is needed in the primary memory for incoming active segments. All accessed flags can be reset when a transfer is made.

The interconnection of a separate MMU to a processor involves all the data lines (for loading control registers) and at least the higher significant bits of the address lines. The lower address lines are not used for address translation if base addresses are used with the lower significant bits set to zero. Processor status information needs to be passed to the MMU and this may use a dedicated group of status lines from the processor. The usual data transfer control signals will be needed.

There are two possible methods of treating the MMU, as part of the processor or as part of the memory as shown in Fig. 14.14(a) and (b). A MMU which is an integral part of a processor must be configured as (a). If the MMU is part of a particular memory block as shown in (b), each memory would have its

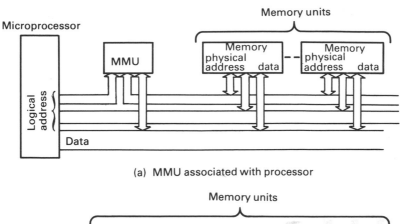

(a) MMU associated with processor

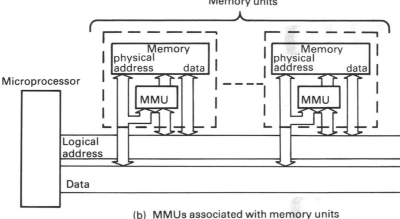

(b) MMUs associated with memory units

Figure 14.14 Connection of memory management units (MMUs) to processor

own MMU and all MMUs together with non-managed devices, such as input/ output interfaces, connect through the processor bus or a derivative. However, if the MMU is considered as part of the processor, all memory and input/output devices connect to the physical address side of one or more MMUs and the processor connects to the logical address side of the MMU. This means that address translation also applies to input/output devices. In either case, each MMU is set up in a similar fashion to programmed input/output interfaces. Input/output instructions are used to load the command registers, load the MMU memory or read the status register.

14.2 PROCESSOR—PRIMARY MEMORY MANAGEMENT

14.2.1 Cache memory

In the last section we considered the problem of efficiently handling the transfer of information between primary and secondary memory. A significant factor is the difference in speed of operation of primary and secondary memory. Secondary memory is often several orders of magnitude slower than primary memory. There is also a mismatch between the speed of operation of the processor and that of the primary memory; processors (except early microprocessors) are generally able to perform operations on operands faster than the access time of the primary memory. Though semiconductor memory exists which can operate at speeds comparable with the operation of the processor, it is not economical to provide all the primary memory using very high-speed semiconductor memory. The problem can be alleviated by introducing a small block of high-speed memory called a *cache* between the primary memory and the processor. The general scheme is shown in Fig. 14.15. The cache consists of semiconductor memory operating at the speed required by the processor. The cache might hold, say, 512 words. Program and data are first transferred to the cache and then the processor accesses the cache. Any new data is first written to the cache and either written at same time to the primary memory or subsequently when the location is replaced with new information from the primary memory.

A cache is generally successful because programs usually exhibit a feature that memory references for instructions are near previous memory references for instructions and, to a lesser extent, memory references for data are near previous memory references for data (*principle of locality*), and particular instruction and data references are often repeated. For example, a purely sequential list of instructions which is executed only once is rare; more often, loops of instructions are programmed and the loop is executed many times. The length of a loop is usually quite small. Therefore once a cache is loaded with information from the main memory, it is used more than once before new information is required from the main memory.

The principle of locality also makes primary memory–secondary memory management schemes efficient. However, the principle is particularly significant in cache systems. If every memory reference to the cache required a transfer of one word between the primary memory and the cache, no increase in speed would be achieved; in fact the speed would probably drop. However, suppose the reference is repeated n times in all during a program loop and after the first reference, the location is always found in the cache, then the average access time would be:

Average access time $= (M + nm)/n$

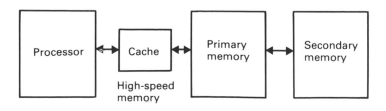

Figure 14.15   Cache memory scheme

where M = time to transfer the word between primary memory and cache
   m = time to access the cache
   n = number of references

If $M = 400$ns, $m = 50$ns, and $n = 10$, the average time would be 90ns rather than 400ns without the cache, i.e. 444% increase in speed with a cache operating at 8 times the main memory, assuming no additional timing factors with the introduction of the cache, and the processor can handle the increased speed.

We have assumed that it is necessary firstly to reference the cache before a reference to the primary memory is made to fetch a word. It may be necessary to make a second reference to the cache after the word is fetched into the cache, though for a read operation it is likely that the word can be sent to the cache and processor simultaneously. Write operations require an additional scheme which we shall describe later. Also, any word altered must be transferred back to the primary memory eventually and this transfer will reduce the average time.

The primary memory can be and is usually interleaved (see also Chap. 13, section 13.3), to match the speed of transfer of the primary memory with the cache. In interleaving, the memory is divided into modules and one word from each module is transferred to or from the memory and, in this application, the cache simultaneously. An interleaved system is shown in Fig. 14.16. Normally, the number of modules is a power of two to simplify the memory addressing. The primary memory addresses are numbered across the modules. For example, with four modules, the addresses in the first module would be 0, 4, 8, 12, 16, etc. The addresses in the second module would be 1, 5, 9, 13, 17, etc. The addresses in the third module would be 2, 6, 10, 14, 18, etc., and the addresses in the fourth module would be 3, 7, 11, 15, 19, etc.

The number of modules is chosen to produce a suitable match in the speed of operation of the memories. For example, if the cache has an access time of 50ns and the primary memory has an access time of 400ns, eight blocks would

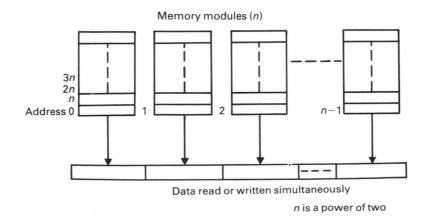

Memory modules (n)

$3n$
$2n$
n
Address 0   1   2 $n-1$

Data read or written simultaneously

n is a power of two

Figure 14.16   Memory interleaving

allow eight words to be transferred to or from the cache in 400 ns, and subsequently be accessed in sequential order by the processor in another 400 ns. Hence the average access time of these words when first referenced would be 800 ns/8 = 100 ns. Should the words be referenced ten times in all, the average access time would be:

$$\text{Average access time} = (100 + 10{\times}50)/10 = 60\,\text{ns}$$

making the same rather broad assumptions as before. However, it does indicate that substantial speed improvements can be achieved by using the cache.

The probability that the required word is already in the cache depends upon the program; typically 80–90% of references will find their words in the cache. A *hit* occurs when a location is immediately found in the cache, otherwise a *miss* occurs and a reference to the primary memory is necessary. The *hit ratio* is defined as:

$$\text{Hit ratio} = \frac{\text{number of times required word found in cache}}{\text{Total number of references}}$$

For example, if the hit ratio is 0.85, the primary memory access time is 400 ns and the cache access time is 50 ns, then the average access time is:

$$1{\times}50 + 0.15{\times}400 = 110\,\text{ns}$$

assuming again that the first access must be to cache before an access is made to the primary memory.

14.2.2 Mapping schemes

The problem of mapping the information held in the primary memory into the cache is similar to primary–secondary memory virtual memory systems, though any cache mapping scheme must be totally implemented in hardware to achieve improvement in the system operation. Various strategies are possible.

(a) Direct mapping

In *direct mapping schemes*, the least significant bits of the memory address in the primary memory and the cache are the same. The most significant bits of the address are stored in the cache and read after the least significant bits have been used to access the cache word.

Firstly, consider the example shown in Fig. 14.17. The address from the processor is divided into two fields, a *tag* and an *index*. The tag identifies a page in the primary memory and the index identifies the word within the page. Upon a memory reference, first the index is used to access a word in the cache. Then, the tag stored in the accessed word is read and compared with the tag in the address. If the two tags are the same, indicating that the word is the one required, the access is made to the addressed cache word. If however, the tags are not the same, a reference is made to the primary memory to find the required word. The word is then transferred into the cache and the access made to the word.

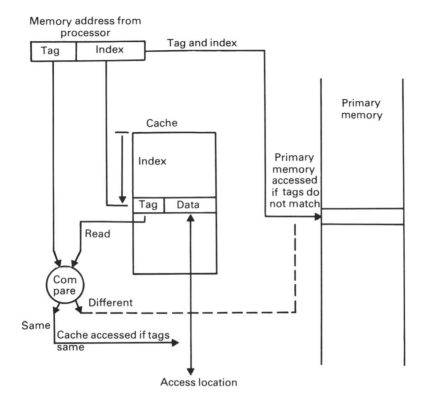

Figure 14.17 Cache with direct mapping

In the above scheme, one word is transferred to the cache at a time. In Fig. 14.18, several words are transferred together by interleaving. We shall call the words transferred a *block*. The primary memory address is composed of a tag, a block, and a word within a block. All the words within a block in the cache have the same stored tag. The block/word part of the address is used to access the cache and the stored tag compared with the required tag address. If the tags are not the same the block containing the required word is transferred to the cache. In this scheme, the corresponding blocks in every page would map into the same block in the cache.

(b) Associative mapping

Associative mapping requires the cache to be composed of associative memory as also used in the primary memory–secondary memory associative mapping scheme (section 14.1.2). The incoming memory address is compared with all the stored addresses simultaneously using the internal logic of the associative memory as shown in Fig. 14.19. If a match is found, the corresponding data is read out. When used as a cache, single words from anywhere within the primary memory could be held in the cache (assuming that the associative part of the cache is capable of holding a full memory address).

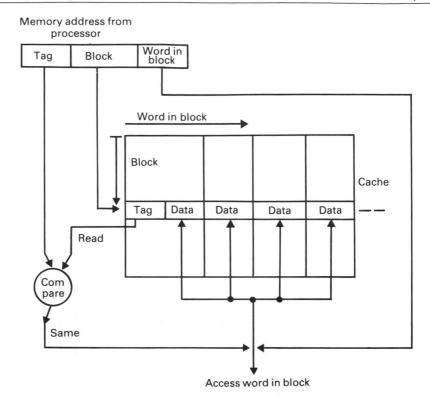

Memory address from
processor

| Tag | Block | Word in block |

Figure 14.18   Direct mapped cache with block organization

(c) Set-associative mapping

In the direct scheme above (Fig. 14.17), all words stored in the cache must have different indices. The tags may be the same or different. The *set-associative mapping* scheme allows more than one word in the cache with the same index and different tags as shown in Fig. 14.20. Each word has a stored tag completing the identification of the word. The tags are stored in associative memory. First the index of the address from the processor is used to access the words. Then, all tags are compared with the incoming tag associatively. If a match is found the location is accessed, otherwise, as before, an access to the primary memory is made.

14.2.3 Write mechanism and replacement policy

As reading the required word in the cache does not affect the cache contents, there can be no discrepancy between the cache word and the copy held in the primary memory after a memory read instruction. However, writing can occur to cache words and in these cases it is possible that the cache word and copy held in the primary memory may be different. It is necessary to maintain both the cache and the primary memory copy identical if input/output transfers

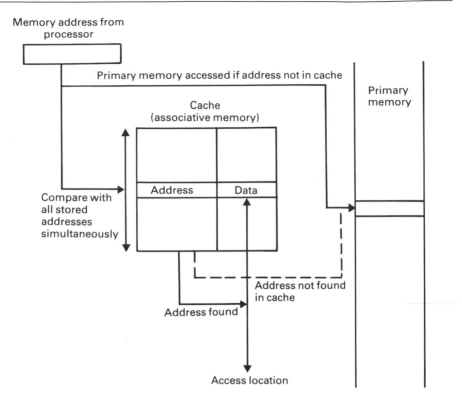

Figure 14.19   Cache with fully associative memory to store addresses

(such as DMA, Chap. 10, section 10.4) operate on the primary memory contents. There are two mechanisms to update the primary memory during a memory write instruction.

(a) Write-through

In the *write-through* mechanism, every write operation to the cache is repeated to the primary memory. The additional write operation to the primary memory will of course take much longer than to the cache. Fortunately, there are usually several read operations between write operations (typically between 3 and 10) and these read operations to the cache can take place while the main memory write operation is in progress.

(b) Write-back

In the *write-back* mechanism, the write operation to the primary memory is only done at a block replacement time. A tag (bit) is associated with each cache word, which is set whenever the word is altered. At replacement time, the tags are examined to determine whether it is necessary to write the block back to the primary memory.

When the required block or word is not held in the cache, it is necessary to transfer the block or word needed from the primary memory into the cache,

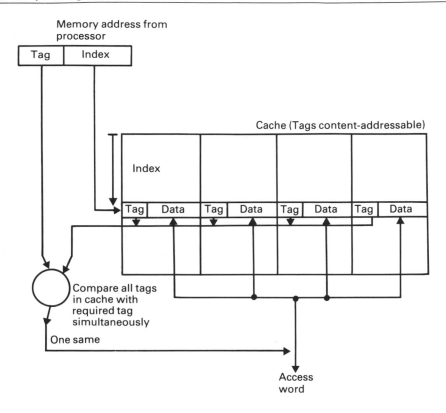

Figure 14.20 Cache with set-associative mapping

displacing an existing block or word. The existing block or word in the cache can be chosen by a random replacement algorithm, first-in-first-out algorithm, or least recently used algorithm as used in virtual memory systems. The least recently used algorithm can be implemented fully because the number of blocks involved is small. The replacement mechanism must be implemented totally in hardware, and additional tags in the cache are provided to assist the replacement algorithm.

REFERENCES

1. *An Introduction to CP/M Features and Facilities.* Pacific Grove, California: Digital Research, 1978.
2. *The 8086 Family User's Manual.* Santa Clara, California: Intel Corp., 1979.
3. Bear, J.L., *Computer System Architecture.* Rockville, Maryland: Computer Science Press, Inc., 1980.
4. Stevenson, D., *An Introduction to the Z8010 MMU Memory Management Unit.* Cupertino, California: Zilog, Inc., 1979.

PROBLEMS

14.1 In a paged systems, suppose the following pages are requested in the order shown:

3, 4, 6, 10, 3, 5, 3, 5, 4, 5, 3

and the primary memory can only hold four pages at any instant. List the pages in primary memory after each page is transferred using the first-in-first-out replacement algorithm and the least recently used replacement algorithm. How many page faults occur in each case?

14.2 In the *working set algorithm*, the last n pages referenced are kept in memory, where n is the 'working set'. At replacement time, the page deleted from the working set and transferred to secondary memory is the one not referenced in the last n references. It is possible to have less that the full set held. For example, if the last five references were pages 2, 5, 6, 8 and 2, the pages in the set would be 6, 8 and 2. Apply the working set algorithm to the sequence:

3, 4, 3, 6, 8, 3, 7, 6, 8, 3, 2, 6

(also used in section 14.1.3), assuming the maximum number of pages in the primary memory is four.

14.3 A computer employs a 64K 16-bit word primary (main) memory and a cache of 512 words. Determine the number of bits in each field of the address, in the following organizations:

(a) Direct mapping with a block size of one word
(b) Direct mapping with a block size of eight words
(c) Set-associative mapping with a set size of four words.

14.4 Determine the average access time in a computer system employing a cache, given that the primary memory access time is 500 ns, the cache access time is 75 ns and the hit ratio is 90%. The write-through policy is used. 20% of memory requests are write requests.

14.5 Repeat Problem 14.4 assuming a write-back policy is used, and the block size is 16 words fully interleaved.

Multiprocessor Systems

15.1 GENERAL

The von Neumann stored program computer, as described in Chap. 6, section 6.1, is the basis of digital computer designs described so far. The fundamental concept has been refined and improved over the years by the introduction of measures to increase the speed of operation such as pipelining the processor (Chap. 13) and the use of cache memory (Chap. 14). Improvements in technology have seen a dramatic increase in the speed of operation. Traditionally, emitter-coupled logic (ECL) gates have been used in computers to achieve very high speed of operation. ECL gates operate with propagation delay times in the order of 0.9 ns. Higher-speed devices can be devised. However, the fundamental speed of electrical signals, about two-thirds of the speed of light, will eventually limit the speed of operation. Light travels at 3×10^8 m/s, i.e. takes 3.3 ns to travel 1 m. The time required for the logic signals to pass from one logic component to another logic component therefore can become significant with high-speed gates and it is necessary in very high-speed computers to reduce the interconnection distances to a minimum. The demand for increased speed of operation has led to proposals for alternative architectures which we shall examine in this chapter.

One apparent method to increase the speed of operation is to provide more than one processor in the system and operate the processors simultaneously. Such systems are known as *multiprocessor systems* or *parallel processor systems*. The term *tightly coupled multiprocessor system* is used to describe multiprocessor systems in which the processors are physically close and can operate on a common problem. An alternative is the *loosely coupled multiprocessor* or *computer network* in which complete computers are interconnected, perhaps over long distances. The design goals of loosely coupled systems are different to those of tightly coupled systems. Tightly coupled systems are designed principally to obtain increased speed of operation, or sometimes to obtain increased reliability (as there is the potential of using alternative processors or memory components in the system). In contrast, loosely coupled systems are often formed to share hardware resources such as printers or software packages or data. We shall restrict our discussion to tightly coupled systems.

To achieve an improvement in speed of operation, it is necessary to be able to divide the computation into tasks or processes which can be executed simultaneously. Suppose that the computation can be divided at least partially into concurrent tasks. A measure of the performance is:

$$\text{Speed-up factor} = \frac{\text{execution time using one processor}}{\text{execution time using } p \text{ processors}}$$

Let us firstly make the assumptions that:

(i) Either one processor or all p processors are actively executing tasks
(ii) There is no extra computation or other overhead when divided into concurrent tasks.

If the time to execute the computation on a single processor is t seconds and fraction of the computation that can be divided into concurrent tasks is α, then the time to perform the computation with p processors is given by:

$$(1-\alpha)t + \alpha t/p$$

Therefore, the speed-up factor is given by:

$$\text{Speed-up factor, } S, = \frac{t}{(1-\alpha)t + \alpha t/p} = \frac{1}{(1-\alpha) + \alpha/p}$$

Figure 15.1 shows this function plotted with $\alpha = 80\%$, $\alpha = 90\%$, $\alpha = 95\%$ and $\alpha = 100\%$. We see that indeed a speed improvement is shown, but the fraction of the computation that is executed by concurrent tasks needs to be a substantial part of the overall computation if a significant increase in speed is achieved.

The speed-up factor omits, in particular, any overhead due to processors communicating with each other, which is likely to be necessary, and any

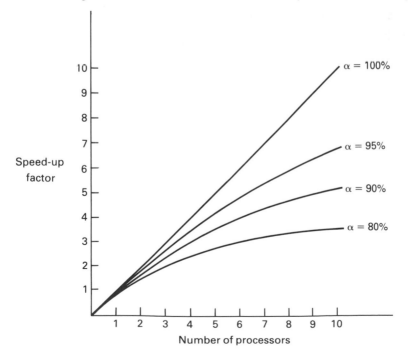

Figure 15.1 Speed-up factor against number of processors

overhead at the point that multiple tasks are generated. Generally these overheads, especially the latter, will be a function of the number of processors and will increase as more processors are used. Also, it is unlikely that all the available processors can be utilized simultaneously. It is more likely that the number of processors that can be utilized will vary throughout the computation. However, some improvement in speed should be possible.

A normal single-processor von Neumann computer generates a single stream of instructions acting upon single data items. Flynn [1] called this type of computer a *single instruction–single data (SISD) computer*. In a general multiprocessor system, more than one instruction stream is generated, one for each processor. Each instruction acts upon different data. Flynn called this type of computer a *multiple instruction–multiple data (MIMD) computer*. Apart from these two extremes, it is possible to design a computer in which a single instruction stream is generated by a single control unit, and the instruction is broadcast to more than one processor. Each processor executes the same instruction, but using different data. The data items form a vector and the instruction acts upon the complete vector in one instruction cycle. Flynn called this type of computer a *single instruction–multiple data (SIMD) computer*. Such computers are particularly suitable for vector and matrix computations. The fourth combination, *multiple instruction–single data (MISD) computer*, in which several instructions simultaneously act upon the same data item, does not exist (unless one classifies pipelined architectures in this group). Flynn's classifications are shown in Fig. 15.2. We give Flynn's classifications as the terms have been widely used in the past. In the following, we shall consider the general-purpose MIMD computer, particularly when implemented using microprocessors. There are various schemes to interconnect processors in a tightly coupled MIMD system. We will concentrate particularly upon the time-shared bus architecture.

15.2 TIME-SHARED BUS ARCHITECTURE

15.2.1 General

The time-shared bus system shown in Fig. 15.3 is particularly suited as a multiprocessor extension to a normal single-processor microprocessor system. A bus connects all the major units, processors, memory units and input/output interfaces. Individual processors can access selected memory units, though only one data or instruction transfer can occur on the bus at any instant. The time-shared bus scheme has been taken up by microprocessor manufacturers, and there are several standard buses which can support multiple processors. To reduce bus contention, each processor can be given local memory, which can act as a cache. The local memory can attach to the associated processor using a local bus as shown in Fig. 15.4.

The local bus could, of course, carry more than one processor, if suitably designed. More commonly, the local bus might carry *co-processors* and DMA

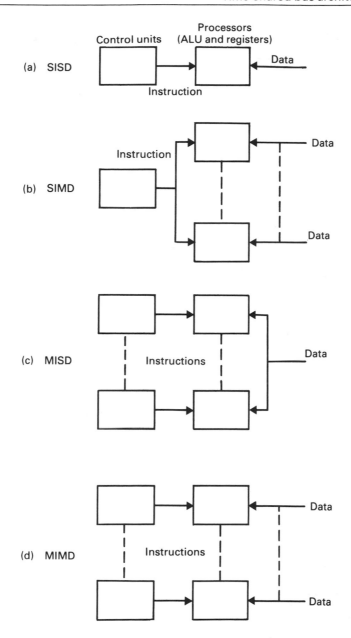

Figure 15.2 Flynn's classifications (1966)

devices which are allowed to use the local bus though overall control is always returned to the processor. Co-processors are devices designed to enhance the capabilities of the central processor and operate in cooperation with the central processor. For example, an arithmetic co-processor enhances the arithmetic ability of the central processor by providing additional arithmetic operations, such as floating point operations and high-precision fixed point operations

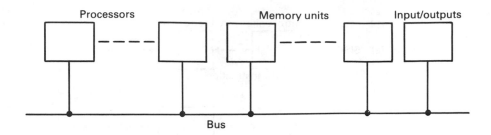

Figure 15.3   Single time-shared bus multiprocessor system

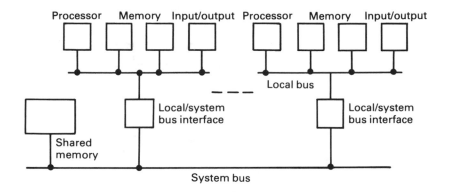

Figure 15.4   Multiple microprocessor system with local buses and system bus

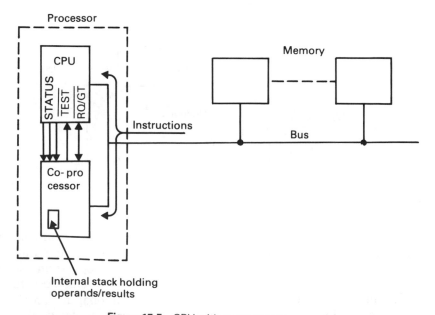

Figure 15.5   CPU with co-processor

including addition, subtraction, compare, multiplication and division. Arithmetic co-processors also include floating point trigonometric functions such as sine, cosine, and tangent, inverse functions, logarithms and square root. The co-processor can perform designated operations at the same time as the central processor is performing other duties.

Usually not all the binary patterns available for encoding machine instructions are used internally by the microprocessor, and it is convenient to arrange the arithmetic co-processor to respond to some of the unused bit patterns as they are fetched from the memory. The main processor would expect the arithmetic processor to supply the result of any such operations, and in this way the arithmetic co-processor is seen simply as an extension to the processor. It would be designed for particular processors. An example of a co-processor is the Intel 8087 numeric co-processor [2] designed to match the 16-bit Intel 8086 processor.

Figure 15.5 shows an 8087 co-processor attached to an 8086 central processor and a common bus. The 8086 central processor fetches instructions in the normal way. All instructions are monitored by the 8087 co-processor. Instructions which begin with the binary pattern 11011 are assigned in the 8086 instruction set for external co-processor operation and are grouped as an ESC (escape) instruction. If an ESC instruction is fetched, the 8087 prepares to act upon it. The ESC instruction also indicates in subsequent bits whether an operand is to be fetched from memory. If so, the address of the operand is provided in the third and fourth byte of a multi-byte instruction, and the 8086 fetches the address of the operand; otherwise, the 8086 will continue with the next instruction. The 8087 recognizes the ESC instruction and performs the encoded operation. If an operand address is fetched by the 8086, the address is accepted by the 8087. The 8087 will subsequently fetch the operand. It is possible for both processors to be operating simultaneously, with the 8086 executing the next instruction. The operations provided in the 8087 co-processor include long word length fixed point and floating point operations. The 8087 has an internal 8-word, 80 bit-word stack to hold operands. Some co-processor instructions operate upon two operands held in the top two locations of the stack. Results can be stored in the stack or memory locations by co-processor instructions.

The operations typically are performed about 100 times faster than if the 8086 had performed them using software algorithms [2]. However, once the 8087 has begun executing an instruction, the two processors act asynchronously. When the 8087 is executing an instruction, its $\overline{\text{BUSY}}$ output is brought high (active high). BUSY is usually connected to the $\overline{\text{TEST}}$ input of the 8086. The $\overline{\text{TEST}}$ input can be examined via a 8086 WAIT instruction. If $\overline{\text{TEST}} = 1$, the WAIT instruction causes the 8086 to enter wait states, until $\overline{\text{TEST}} = 0$. Then, the next instruction is executed. Typically, the WAIT instruction would be executed before an ESC instruction to ensure that the co-processor is ready to respond to the ESC instruction. Hence the two processors can be brought back into synchronism. Other signals connect between the two processors, including bus request and grant signals to enable the two processors to share the bus. The

8086 has an internal 6-byte queue used to hold instructions prior to instructions being executed. The state of the queue is indicated by queue status outputs which the 8087 uses to ensure proper operation of ESC instructions. (The 8087 can also be connected to the 16-bit 8088 processor which has a 4-byte queue.)

Some arithmetic processors, for example the Intel 8231A Arithmetic Processing Unit [2], are simply memory mapped or input/output mapped devices which respond to particular commands from the central processor. Results are held in an internal stack which can be examined by the processor under program control or under an interrupt scheme. These arithmetic processors do not require special ESC instructions in the central processor instruction set, and can be attached to most microprocessors. The general scheme is shown in Fig. 15.6.

We have seen that the burden of input/output operations can be largely taken away from the (central) processor by DMA devices. DMA devices can be improved to take the shape of a processor in their own right, and these are called *input/output co-processors*. An example of an input/output co-processor is the Intel 8089 [2] designed to cooperate with the 8086 processor. An input/output processor is a DMA controller with the added feature of being able to execute its own arithmetic, logic and control instructions held in a memory. The input/output processor can be attached to the same bus as the processor in a similar fashion to arithmetic co-processors, and use the same memories. Alternatively, the input/output processor be provided with its own dedicated memory on a separate bus connected to the main bus via a bus interface such as shown in Fig. 15.7. The latter method eliminates memory conflicts during DMA transfers.

15.2.2 Transferring control of the bus

In the above, we have seen various bus configurations. We now outline the fundamental signals necessary in transferring control of the bus from one

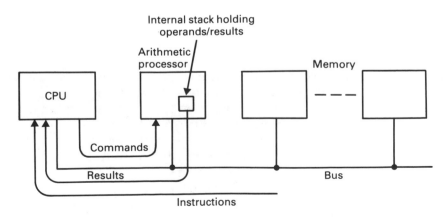

Figure 15.6   CPU with I/O (or memory) mapped arithmetic processor

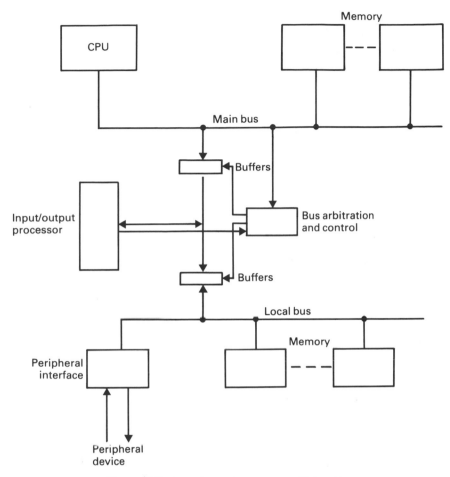

Figure 15.7   Input/output processor with local bus

processor to another processor in a general multiprocessor time-shared bus system (Fig. 15.3). The device which controls the transfers of data (or instructions) on the bus is known as the *bus master*. In a single-processor system, the processor is the normal bus master, though DMA controllers (Chap. 10, section 10.4) can also be temporary bus masters. In a bus system with more than one processor as in Fig. 15.3, any processor is capable of being a bus master and each competes for the use of the bus. At any instant, only one bus master can control the bus. As in a single-processor system, there are two fundamental signals involved in transferring control of the bus, namely a bus request signal from the requesting bus master to the current master and the bus acknowledge/grant signal from the current bus master to the requesting master. The requesting master generates the bus request signal when it wishes to gain control of the bus. When the current bus master is ready to release the bus, it generates the bus grant signal and releases control of the bus by causing all its bus drivers to enter into the high-impendance state (tri-state). The bus is then available for the requesting master. All microprocessors have such signals principally for

DMA devices. Additional signals can be provided for multiprocessors applications. We have mentioned the 68000 bus transfer signals in Chap. 10, section 10.4.2. In the following, we shall draw further examples from the Intel 8086 and Zilog Z8000 16-bit microprocessors.

In some cases the current bus master may be completing a very important task which cannot be interrupted. Conversely, a very important task may need to be done by a requesting bus master, and the current bus master should relinquish control at the earliest opportunity. To cater for these types of situations, a bus master priority scheme is necessary to decide on the appropriate action, similar to interrupt priority schemes (Chap. 10). Each bus master is allocated a priority number. Masters which have the ability to demand control of the bus over other bus masters are given a higher priority, say a lower priority number. Therefore bus master priority number 2 can take over from bus master priority number 3 but not from bus master priority number 1. (Note that the 68000 use a higher priority number for a higher priority.) In addition to deciding whether to exchange control of the bus from one master to another, the possibility of receiving two or more requests simultaneously must be handled. This problem generally requires bus request arbitration logic either centrally located or distributed among masters. It may be that the request signals must be synchronized with a clock signal. Since individual bus masters may have their own clock which will not necessarily be synchronized with each other, an additional independent bus clock signal is provided on the bus for synchronization.

The principal difference of a multiprocessor bus transfer mechanism to a single-processor system bus transfer mechanism is that in a single-processor system, control is always returned to the processor whereas in a multiprocessor system, any processor can maintain control of the bus, and transfer can occur between any pair of processors.

15.2.3 Time-shared bus priority schemes

Priority schemes can be a parallel priority scheme or serial priority scheme.

(a) Parallel priority scheme

In the parallel priority scheme, the bus request signal from each of the bus masters, including the bus request signal of the current bus master, enters a centralized priority resolution circuit. The highest priority signal applied (that of the current master when there are no other requests) is accepted and the corresponding bus grant signal is returned to the master. There is one bus grant signal corresponding to each bus request signal, as shown in Fig. 15.8.

When a higher priority signal is received, the bus grant signal is switched to the higher requesting master. The current master recognizes that it has lost its grant signal and releases control of the bus at the end of the current cycle. A common $\overline{\text{BUS BUSY}}$ line is also released. This latter signal indicates to the requesting master, together with its grant signal being received, that it may now take over the bus.

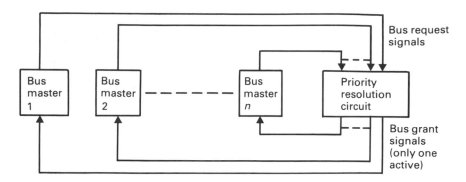

Figure 15.8 Parallel priority scheme

We could permanently (statically) assign one input of the arbitration circuit as the lowest priority and the other with increasingly higher priority, none of which can alter. In this case, the centralized arbitration circuit can consist of a 2^n-to-n line priority encoder connecting to an n-to-2^n line decoder, given 2^n processors. For eight processors, a TTL 74148 8-to-3 line priority encoder connected to a 74LS138 3-to-8 line encoder could be used, as shown in Fig. 15.9. The priority encoder generates a binary coded output identifying the highest priority input. This number enters the decoder which generates one output corresponding to the binary input number. The 74138 outputs are assigned in reverse order as shown because the 74148 has active low inputs and outputs and the 74138 has active high inputs and active low outputs.

(b) Serial priority schemes

Various forms of serial priority schemes have been devised based upon daisy-chaining a signal between bus masters in a similar fashion to daisy-chained signals in interrupt schemes. For example, the bus request signal can be daisy-chained and the bus acknowledge signal can be applied to all bus masters. Alternatively, the bus acknowledge signal can be daisy-chained and bus request applied to all bus masters. A third daisy-chain method is to daisy-chain a bus enable signal and apply bus request and acknowledge signals to all bus masters (as done in the Z-80 interrupt mechanism of interface devices; see Chap. 10, section 10.3.3). A variation to employing a common acknowledge signal is to use a common bus busy signal which is activated by the current bus master. Releasing this signal indicates that the request has been accepted and the bus is free for the requesting signal, as in the parallel scheme above. In all cases, priority is implemented depending on the wiring of the daisy chain.

The serial priority arrangement using a daisy-chained request enable signal is shown in Fig. 15.10 as used by the Intel 8086 [3]. (The 8086 does not generate the following bus transfer signals directly; these are generated by the 8289 bus arbiter device [3], connected to the 8086.) The priority input signal, $\overline{\text{BPRN}}$, is a 0 when no higher priority master is requesting the bus. The bus request output signal, $\overline{\text{BPRO}}$, from each master connects to the priority input of the bus master directly one lower in priority. If a master wishes to make a bus request to the current master, it sets $\overline{\text{BPRO}}$ to a 1. This signal will propagate

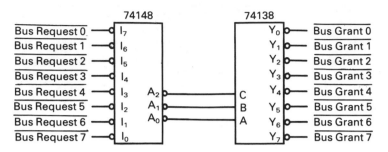

Bus request maintained low while bus being used
and corresponding bus grant low

Bus request inputs		Bus grant outputs	
74148		**74138**	
I_7 I_6 I_5 I_4 I_3 I_2 I_1 I_0	A_2 A_1 A_0	Y_0 Y_1 Y_2 Y_3 Y_4 Y_5 Y_6 Y_7	
0 X X X X X X X	0 0 0	0 1 1 1 1 1 1 1	
1 0 X X X X X X	0 0 1	1 0 1 1 1 1 1 1	
1 1 0 X X X X X	0 1 0	1 1 0 1 1 1 1 1	
1 1 1 0 X X X X	0 1 1	1 1 1 0 1 1 1 1	
1 1 1 1 0 X X X	1 0 0	1 1 1 1 0 1 1 1	
1 1 1 1 1 0 X X	1 0 1	1 1 1 1 1 0 1 1	
1 1 1 1 1 1 0 X	1 1 0	1 1 1 1 1 1 0 1	
1 1 1 1 1 1 1 X	1 1 1	1 1 1 1 1 1 1 0	

Figure 15.9   Parallel arbitration logic with fixed priority

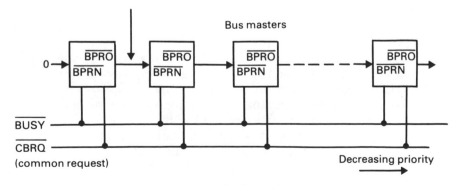

Figure 15.10   8086 bus transfer signals (daisy-chained request)

down the daisy chain. If the requesting master is of higher priority than the current master, the signal will eventually reach the current master, which then prevents the signal continuing down the daisy chain. Obviously if the requesting master is of lower priority, the bus request signal never reaches the current master and control of the bus is not exchanged.

Assuming the request is received, the current bus master concludes its current bus cycle and releases control of the bus. It then deactivates the open-collector bus busy signal, $\overline{\text{BUSY}}$, which passes to all other bus masters. Releasing $\overline{\text{BUSY}}$ is detected by the requesting master which takes over control of the bus and activates $\overline{\text{BUSY}}$ itself. Simultaneous requests are handled by arranging that the bus master which takes over control has its bus request priority input not activated, which indicates that no higher priority master is requesting the bus. Of course, its bus request output must be activated. In an 8086 system, the current bus master relinquishes control of the bus when it is not using the bus. To enable lower priority devices opportunity to access the bus, a bus signal named common bus request, CBRQ, is provided which is activated by all bus masters requesting the bus. CBRQ indicates to the current bus master that a master wants the bus, not necessarily a master of higher priority to the current master. If the requesting master is of lower priority, no daisy-chaincd enable signal will be received by the current master. However, in these circumstances, the master can be arranged to release the bus to a lower priority master after each bus transfer. The higher priority master can regain control of the bus later if it requires use of the bus.

The major disadvantage of the above scheme is the speed limitation due to the time required for the daisy-chained request-enable signal to pass from one master to another. In fact, the higher the priority of the requesting master, the farther the request signal needs to travel to reach the current master. The time delay with at least one gate delay through each intermediate master leads to this scheme being practical for either slow systems or those with only a few bus masters (three for the 8086 operating at 10 MHz).

An alternative daisy-chain scheme is with a common wired-OR request signal connecting to all bus masters and a daisy-chained acknowledge. An example is the Z-8000 multimicroprocessor bus transfer signals [4] shown in Fig. 15.11. In this scheme, the current bus master receives a bus request signal, μRQ, from the requesting master on the common request line and $\overline{\mu\text{ST}}$ is set to 0. An accept signal is passed along a daisy chain, first to the highest priority master and eventually the highest requesting master. This device will prevent the signal continuing down the chain and takes control of the bus. When the bus is being used, a bus busy signal, $\overline{\mu\text{ST}}$ (multimicro status) is set to 0. Requests cannot be made if the bus is being used as indicated by this signal and must wait until the bus is not being used. Therefore, bus masters must release the bus when not using the bus.

The serial priority technique and the parallel technique using encoder–decoder implementation assign fixed priority to bus masters, which may not be particularly suitable for a multiprocessor system. It may be preferable to give all

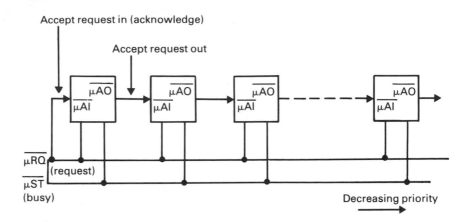

Accept request in (acknowledge)

Accept request out

$\overline{\mu RQ}$
(request)

$\overline{\mu ST}$
(busy)

Decreasing priority

Figure 15.11 Z-8000 bus transfer signals (daisy-chained acknowledge)

processors an equal right to use the bus, by using rotating priority (as used in interrupt controllers, Chap. 10, section 10.3.3).

15.3 OTHER MULTIPROCESSOR ARCHITECTURES

There are various alternative architectures to the time-shared bus architecture. Here we will outline some architectures which have been investigated.

15.3.1 Multiport memory architecture

The multiport memory architecture, shown in Fig. 15.12, uses one multiport memory unit connecting to all the processors. Input/output can also be a shared resource. Multiport memory is designed to enable more than one location to be accessed simultaneously, in this case by different processors. If there are, say, 16 processors, 16 ports would be provided into the memory, one port for each processor. Multiport memory can be implemented using normal single-port random access memory with the addition of arbitration logic at the memory–processor interface to allow processors to use the memory on a first-come, first-served basis (or with a defined priority). Using normal memory components, it is necessary for the memory to operate substantially faster than the processors to prevent processors being delayed.

15.3.2 Crossbar switch architecture

In the shared bus system, processor–memory contention can arise which will slow the speed of operation. Similarly, delays can arise in a multiport

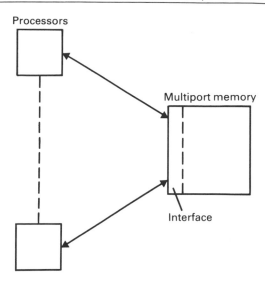

Figure 15.12   Multiport memory multiprocessor system

memory system if the access time of the memory is insufficient to support multiple requests. In the crossbar switch system, a direct path is made between each processor and any memory unit, as shown in Fig. 15.13 using electronic switches, which eliminates this contention and can allow processors and memory to operate at their maximum speed. There are two basic methods of operation, namely the master–slave approach and the approach with no central control. In the crossbar switch without central control, each processor controls its own switches and arbitration logic resolves conflicts.

A small crossbar switch system using master–slave approach is shown in Fig. 15.14 [5], constructed as an experimental research vehicle. Three Z-80 processors and three memory modules are provided. All the crossbar switches are controlled by one processor, the master processor. This processor also has responsibility for overall control of the system and delegating tasks to the slave processors. Each processor is also provided with local read/write memory, permanent bootstrap memory and input/output devices. Input/output is provided locally on all processors so that a particular input/output device becomes inextricably linked with a particular processor. The crossbar switches employ 74LS03 open-collector gates for low cost.

Direct control of the slave processors by the master, and communication between processors, are necessary. The former is achieved by programmed output circuitry controlling inputs to the slaves, such as reset, halt and interrupt. Additionally, programmed input circuitry is used to examine important status conditions of the slave processors and the address lines. For slave-to-master communication, a dedicated interrupt mechanism is chosen for a slave signalling the master. Circuitry is provided with each slave processor to generate a slave interrupt request whenever a memory address is produced by the slave processor which is outside the current memory module range. A simple jump, intentional

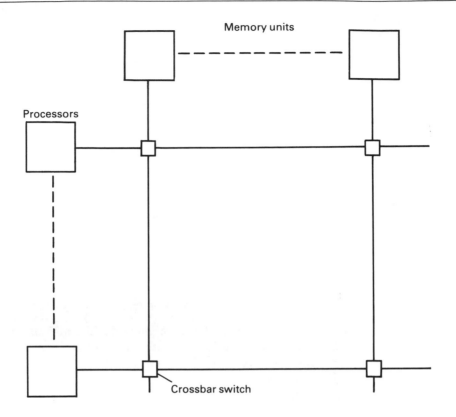

Figure 15.13 Crossbar switch multiprocessor system

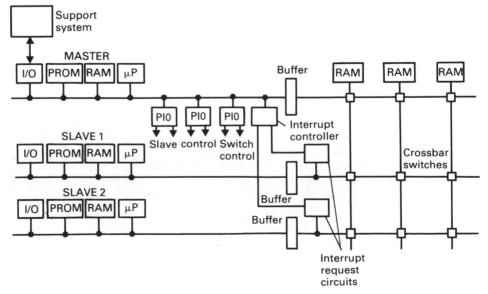

Figure 15.14 Cardiff crossbar switch multiprocessor system

or otherwise, to outside the current address space will cause this. Typically, a jump instruction would be placed at the end of slave processes.

A floppy disk based system is provided, which connects to the master system via serial transmission links, for program development and general support.

15.3.3 Restricted direct connections

Clearly, the crossbar switch approach becomes impracticable for large numbers of processors. A limited number of direct connections could be made. For systems designed with VLSI (very large scale integration) in mind, processors/memory elements can be laid out in an array and connections only made to the four adjacent elements, as shown in Fig. 15.15. The architecture may suit particular applications, such as digital filtering.

The processing elements could be formed with reduced-instruction-set computers (RISC). A reduced-instruction-set computer has a very limited number of instructions, perhaps 16. The instructions typically have a single address format and are short length (perhaps as small as 8 bits), leading and to a very high instruction execution rate, and to possible VLSI fabrication of many processors on one chip.

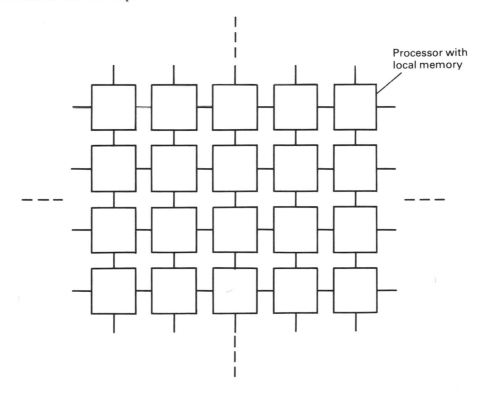

Figure 15.15   Array of processor–memory elements

15.4 MAPPING A PROBLEM ONTO A MULTIPROCESSOR SYSTEM

In this section, we will review some software techniques used in multiprocessor systems.

15.4.1 Concurrent processes

For the computation of a single problem on a multiprocessor system, the general approach is to divide the problem into sections (*processes* or *tasks*) which can be performed simultaneously on separate processors. Assuming this can be done, which may require a completely new look at the problem, additional software constructs are necessary to program the complete system. Firstly, the simultaneous parts of the problem need to be specified. (There will normally be parts which cannot be divided into processes.) One method is to take a standard sequential programming language such as FORTRAN or PASCAL and introduce a construct which generates separate processes and another construct to re-form the program into one sequence. The constructs FORK and JOIN could be used in FORTRAN. FORK is used in the program to indicate separate paths and JOIN used to terminate the paths, as shown in Fig. 15.16. The program continues when all the separate processes are been completed. The constructs PARBEGIN and PAREND are applicable to PASCAL and PASCAL-like languages. In the PARBEGIN–PAREND construct [6], the statements between the two constructs are executed simultaneously. The statements might be compound statements (statements containing one or more statements grouped together and considered as one). The greatest speed improvement would occur when the number of processes is equal to the number of processors available and all processes take the same time.

15.4.2 Process data transfer and synchronization

Once more than one process is formed, it is natural to expect that the same data may need to be accessed by several processes, and data may need to be transferred between the processes. This has led to various mechanisms which attempt to maintain order in data transfer. Clearly, it is necessary to avoid the situation in which one process(or) has begun accessing data and another processor starts to act on the same data. Given a shared memory system this could arise if mechanisms were not provided to prevent it. Similarily, shared peripherals must only be used by one process at a time.

The classic operating system problem called *deadly embrace* must be solved. A deadly embrace occurs when two or more processes are waiting for resources held by the other process and none of the processes can proceed. For example one process, A, may be allocated resource 1 and process B may be allocated resource 2. Process A makes a request for resource 2 but is placed in abeyance because resource 2 is being used by process B. Process B then makes a request for resource 1 and is similarly placed into abeyance. Neither process can

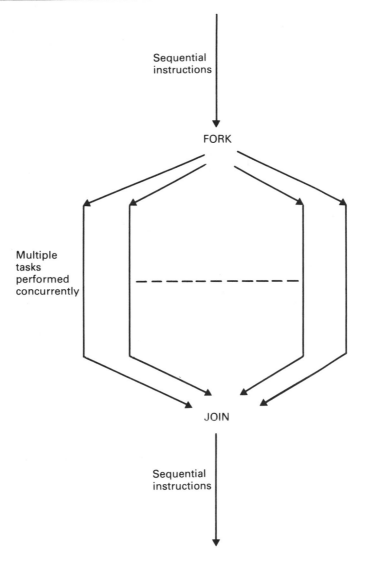

Figure 15.16 FORK and JOIN constructs

continue. Deadly embrace can occur with several processes each making a request upon another process's resource, in such a manner that none of the processes can proceed.

Let us briefly review some software techniques for transferring data between process(or)es and to effect synchronization.

(a) Semaphores

A *critical section* is that part of a program executed by a process which must be performed only when no other process is executing its critical section, i.e. only one, if any process, must execute its critical section at any instant. In the critical section, the shared resource is accessed.

A *binary semaphore* is a one-bit flag which is reset to a 0 (say) to indicate that a process is executing a critical section to access a shared resource and the resource is not available to other processes. The flag is set to a 1 when the process is not executing its critical section and hence the resource is free to be used. Two operations are provided to operate on the semaphore, $P(s)$ and $V(s)$ where s is the semaphore. A $P(s)$ operation is inserted at the beginning of each critical section and a $V(s)$ operation is inserted at the end of each critical section. $P(s)$ firstly checks the current value of the semaphore s. If s is a 1, indicating that no process is executing its critical section and the resource is available, s is reset to a 0 and the process continues into the critical section to access the resource. If s is already a 0, indicating that a process is in its critical section and the resource is currently being used, the $P(s)$ operation is held in abeyance until s is a 1, indicating that the resource is available. The $V(s)$ operation sets s to a 1 and the process continued. If one $P(s)$ has been held in abeyance, this is also completed and the critical section entered. If several $P(s)$ operations are in abeyance, one is chosen to proceed, either on a first-come, first-served basis of according to a priority scheme.

It is possible for processes to encounter their $P(s)$ operations at the beginning of their critical sections simultaneously. To avoid the incorrect operation of several processes reading a 0 value for the semaphore and subsequently entering their critical sections, it is necessary for the $P(s)$ operations to be indivisible, that is, not stopped once started, and during the $P(s)$ operation the semaphore is denied access by any other process.

The semaphore can of course be defined to be a 1 if in critical section (resource not available) and a 0 if not in the critical section (resource available). *General semaphores* can be integer variables which can take on values greater than one. In this case the operation P on a semaphore s causes s to be decremented by one. If s is then greater than or equal to zero, the process is allowed to continue, otherwise the process is stopped and placed on a queue associated with s. The operation V on a semaphore s causes s to be incremented by one. If S is then greater than zero, the process continues. If s is equal to zero or less than zero, a process waiting on the queue is allowed to continue, together with the process associated with V.

To implement binary semaphores, it is necessary to be able to examine the value of a stored flag (binary semaphore) and alter it if necessary without any other processor accessing the flag. This can be achieved by providing indivisible composite machine instructions, instructions which must be completed before another processor can access the memory location. The usual indivisible machine instruction is a *test and set* instruction which examines a stored value and sets it to a 1 if a 0. (Notice this is the reverse of the binary semaphore defined above.) The 68000 has a suitable test and set instruction, TAS. This instruction operates upon the most significant bit of the addressed operand.

(b) Monitors
Unfortunately, though semaphores can effect synchronization, the unintentional omission of a P or V operation could creat havoc. Hence a higher-level

mechanism is desirable, for example a monitor. A *monitor* [7] (in this application) is a suite of procedures which provide the only method to access shared data. Reading or writing shared data can only be done by using a monitor procedure and only one process can use a monitor procedure at any instant. If a process requests a monitor procedure while another process is using a monitor procedure, the requesting process is suspended and placed on a queue. After the process has finished using the monitor, the first process in the queue, if any, is allowed to use a monitor procedure.

Synchronization is effected by the use of two operations, wait and signal (or similar operations). Each wait and signal operation is associated with a particular process, i.e. wait(p) and signal(p) are associated with process p. When a process executes a wait operation, the process is suspended and placed on the queue. When another process executes a signal operation, the process on the queue associated with the signal/wait operations is executed, and any others suspended by the wait operation. The sequence of processes executed from the queue may be first-in, first-out or from some defined priority. When all the suspended processes have been executed, the process signaling the suspended processes is excuted.

(c) Rendezvous

In the rendezvous mechanism, data transfer and synchronization are achieved together. In one form [8], if process A wishes to transmit data x to process B, the transmitting process includes the statement:

B!x

and the receiving process includes the statement:

A?y

Either statement may be reached first. The first statement reached causes the associated process to be suspended until the second statement is reached. When both statements have been reached, the rendezvous occurs. The transfer is effected and the value of x is assigned to variable y. Though a process is suspended until the rendezvous can take place, the processor executing the process is free to perform other duties. The rendezvous technique could be used, for example, in arrays of reduced-instruction-set computers to communicate between processors, using handshaking signals between computers.

15.5 NON-VON NEUMANN COMPUTERS

15.5.1 General

The von Neumann computer executes instructions in sequence (unless otherwise directed by control instructions). To solve a problem or to perform any other task on such computers, it is necessary to form a sequential list of steps. The extensions of the basic concept to incorporate additional processors with a view to increased speed of operation does not fundamentally alter the sequential nature of each processor. The stored-program von Neumann computer can be described as a *control flow* computer, i.e. the actions taken by the computer are dictated by the sequential control mechanism of the computer. There are alternatives to the control flow computer, for example:

(i)   Dataflow/data driven computer
(ii) Demand driven computer
(iii) Pattern driven computer

In all three types, instructions are still required for the computer and these instructions are stored in a memory. However, the instructions are not executed in sequence generally and hence a program counter is inappropriate.

In *dataflow* computers, instructions are executed when all the data operands for the instruction are available. These data operands are often generated as results of previous instructions, but could be input. Once an instruction has been executed, any results from the instruction are made available to other instructions should they want the results, and the process is repeated. The order of execution of instructions generally depends upon the generation of results from previous instructions, and not in the order they might be placed in the program memory.

In *demand driven* (or *reduction*) computers, an instruction is executed when the result it produces is required by other instructions. In *pattern driven* computers, instructions are executed when particular patterns or conditions are matched. Here we shall consider only the dataflow computer.

15.5.2 Dataflow computers

To take an example of the dataflow computational method, consider the computation of $A/B + B \times C$. It is convenient to represent the computation in a graphical form known as a *data dependence graph* or *dataflow graph* [9], as shown in Fig. 15.17. The inputs to the program are the variables A, B and C shown entering at the top. Operations (add, multiply and divide in our example) are shown as circles or *nodes*. Generally, operations take one or two operands and pass on one or two results. The paths between nodes are *arcs* which indicate the route taken by the results of the operations. The general flow of data is from top to bottom. We notice that B is required by two instructions. An explicit COPY operation is used to generate an additional copy of B. The dataflow program for this program is a list of nodal instructions. The actual order in which the instructions are executed will depend upon when the operands are made available. Assuming than all the input variables are presented together, both the multiplication and division can occur simultaneously if there is more than one processor in the system.

Data operands/results move along the arcs contained in *tokens*. Figure 15.18 shows the movement of tokens between nodes. After the inputs are applied, the token containing the A operand is applied to the division node, the

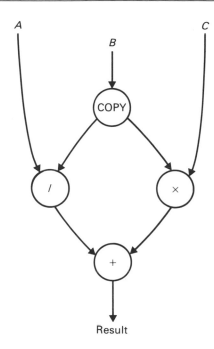

Figure 15.17   Dataflow graph of computation $A/B + B \times C$

token containing the B operand is applied to the COPY node and the token containing the C operand is applied to the multiply node. Only the COPY node is activated ('fired') as its single-input token is present at the node. The other nodes require a result token of the COPY node. After the tokens have become available, both the multiply and divide nodes have all their tokens and are fired. It may be that the multiplication is completed before the division, in which case the final node waits for the division to complete before it can commence.

Clearly one can build up in-line computations of this sort for the dataflow computer, but practical computations usually require additional features. For example, in control-flow computations, conditional instructions provide decision making power. Similarly, conditional instructions are provided in dataflow computers. Generally these instructions take one or two operands and one conditional input. They pass forward one or two results which depend upon the value of the data input and the value of the condition. Condition instructions can be regarded as switches, passing the data input tokens to one of the outputs. Two forms are shown in Fig. 15.19. In the MERGE instruction, there are two input data tokens and one output. If the condition is true, the left-hand side input token is passed on to the output, and if the condition is false, the right-hand side input token is passed on to the output. In the BRANCH instruction, the single-input token is passed on the left output path if the Boolean condition is true or passed on the right output path if the condition is false. It is not necessary to use both outputs. Figure 15.20 shows the implementation of the MERGE instruction using BRANCH instructions. Note that outputs can be

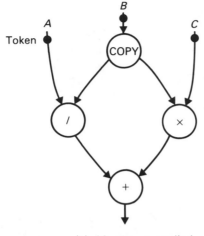

(a) After inputs applied

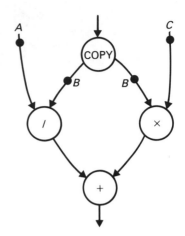

(b) After copy instruction executed

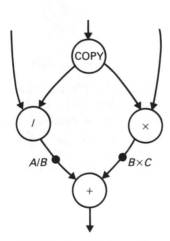

(c) After both divide and
multiply instructions
executed

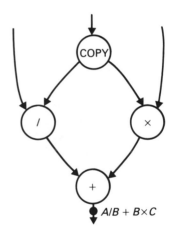

(d) After addition instruction
executed

Figure 15.18   Movement of data tokens in computation $A/B + B \times C$

joined together if there is no conflict between node outputs. Figure 15.21 shows
a dataflow graph for the computation to find the maximum of three numbers
using MERGE operations.

Program iteration loops of conventional programming languages can be
produced by feeding results back to input nodes. Commonly loops are formed in
conventional languages using loop variables which are incremented each time
the body of the computation is computed. The loop is terminated when the loop
variable reaches a defined value. This method can be carried over to dataflow

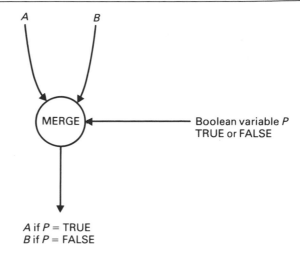

(a) MERGE instruction

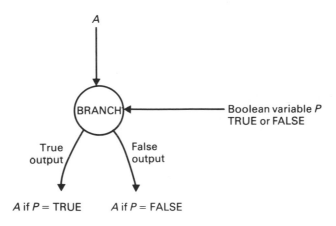

(b) BRANCH instruction

Figure 15.19 Conditional dataflow instructions

programs as shown in Fig. 15.22. However, a problem occurs as it is possible for the two loops in Fig. 15.22 to become out of step. This problem can be resolved by introducing a rule that nodes are only fired when the previous output token or tokens of the node have been used by successive nodes. In our example, the lower COPY node in the counting loop in particular would synchronize the two loops. This technique rather limits the system, so a queue could be formed at the output of each node to hold tokens waiting to be used. Then it is necessary to identify different tokens produced by different iterations so that the correct tokens are used together. A solution is associate tags with individual tokens. This mechanism can also be used to allow function routines.

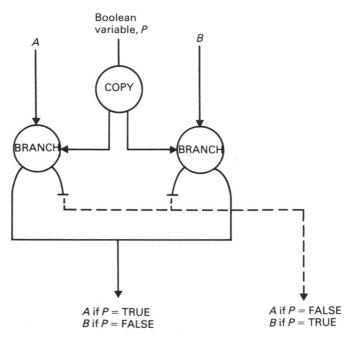

Figure 15.20   Implementation of MERGE using BRANCH instructions

15.5.3 Dataflow system architecture – an example

Figure 15.23 shows the architecture of the dataflow computer constructed at Manchester University by Gurd and Watson [10]. The system uses a pipelined ring architecture. The processor executes 166-bit packages consisting of two data operands, a tag, an operation code (op-code), and one or two destinations (i.e. the address of the next instruction or instructions). A system/computation flag is associated with all packages to differentiate between a computational package to be executed by the processor and a package carrying a system message (such as to load a value into memory). Data operands can be 32-bit integers or floating point numbers. Once executed, one or two result token packages are generated. A token package contains one data operand, a tag and the destination address (i.e. the address of the next instruction), 96 bits in all. Each token package enters a 2-way switch. The switch enables data to be input or output. Assuming the token package is to pass to another node, the package is directed to a first-in, first-out token queue and on to a matching unit. Here a search is made to identify another token to complete the tokens necessary to fire a node (if the node requires two tokens). This is done by comparing the destination and tag of the incoming token with all stored tokens. If a match is found, a token-pair package is formed, otherwise the incoming token is stored in the matching unit awaiting its matching token. Token-pairs are passed on to the program store which holds the nodal instructions and the full executable package formed. Executable packages are sent to free processors in an array of

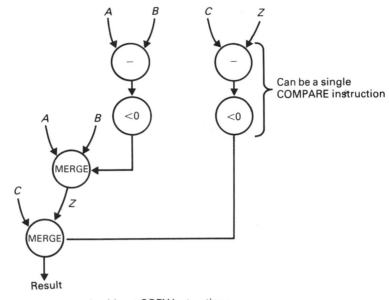

Can be a single
COMPARE instruction

(a) Dataflow graph without COPY instructions

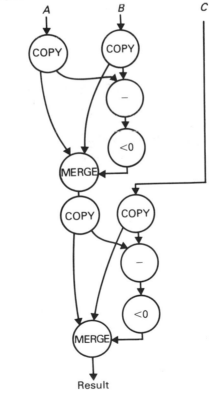

(b) Dataflow graph with COPY instructions

Figure 15.21   Computation to find maximum of three numbers *A, B* and *C* using MERGE instructions

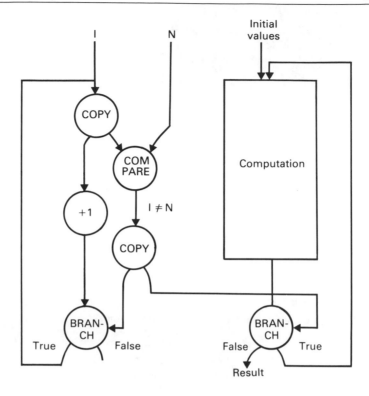

Figure 15.22 Dataflow loops

15 processors when possible.

Token-pair packages and executable packages are expected to be formed every 300 ns on average and token packages produced by processors at an average rate of one every 200 ns, but this will depend on the program. These figures indicate that three tokens must enter the matching unit in the period that two token pairs are generated, or one in every three tokens for single-input nodes. Similarly, as executable packages enter the processor array at a rate of one every 300 ns, every two executable tokens must generate three token packages if the generation rate is one every 200 ns. In fact the processors are microprogrammed devices (Am2900 series; see Chap. 13) requiring 4.5 μs per machine operation and a throughput of one executable package every 300 ns is achieved if all 15 processors are active.

REFERENCES

1. Flynn, M.J., 'Very High Speed Computing Systems', *Proc. IEEE*, 12 (Dec. 1966), 1901–1909.
2. *Component Data Catalog*. Santa Clara, California: Intel Corp., 1982.

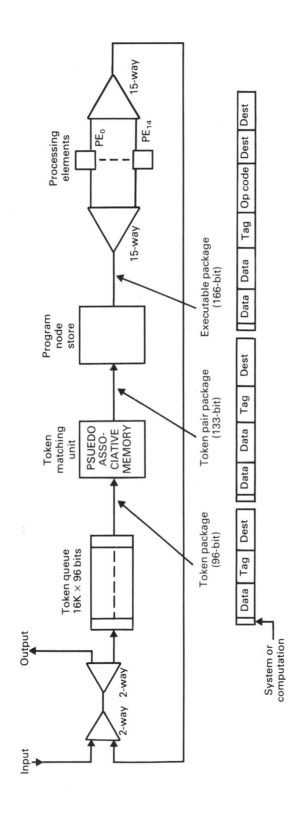

Figure 15.23 Manchester dataflow computer architecture

3. *The 8086 Family User's Manual.* Santa Clara, California: Intel Corp., 1979.

4. *AmZ8000 Family Reference Manual.* Sunnyvale, California: Advanced Micro Devices, Inc., 1979.

5. Wilkinson B., and H. Abachi, 'Cross-bar Switch Multiple Microprocessor System', *Microprocessors and Microsystems*, 7, no. 2 (1983), 75–9.

6. Dijkstra, E.W., 'Cooperating Sequential Processes', in *Programming Languages*, ed. F. Genuys. London: Academic Press, 1968.

7. Grimsdale, R.L., 'Programming Languages', in *Distributed Computing*, ed. F.B. Chambers, D.A. Duce and G.P. Jones. London: Academic Press, 1984.

8. Hoare, C.A.R., 'Communicating Sequential Processes', *Comm. ACM*, 21 no. 8 (1978), 666–77.

9. Gurd, J.R., 'Fundamentals of Dataflow', in *Distributed Computing*, ed. F.B. Chambers, D.A. Duce and G.P. Jones. London: Academic Press, 1984.

10. Gurd, J.R., and I. Watson, 'Data Driven Systems for High Speed Parallel Computation. Part 2: Hardware Design', *Computer Design*, 9, no. 7 (July 1980), 97–106.

PROBLEMS

15.1 Introduce a multiprocessor overhead quantity, q, into the speed-up factor given in section 15.1. Assume that q is proportional to the number of processors.

15.2 The efficiency ratio, ρ, is defined as:

$$\rho = \frac{\text{Summation of each processor operating times}}{\text{Number of processors} \times \text{system operating time}}$$

Determine an expression for the efficiency of a multiprocessor system in terms of number of processors, N, and times that each processor is operating, t_1, t_2, etc. Suppose the system is operating such that one processor is operating for a time t_1 and then all N processors are operating for a time t_N. Derive the corresponding expression for the efficiency.

15.3 Design a central parallel priority logic circuit to control 20 processors, using standard logic components.

15.4 Draw a dataflow graph to compute the function

$$T = 2n^2/[(2n-1)(2n+1)].$$

Show the movement of tokens through the graph.

Engineering Aspects

16.1 GENERAL

This chapter can be considered as a continuation of Chap. 5. Three problems have been selected, each relating to obtaining a working system. In particular, we shall be concerned with problems of interconnected logic devices. A microprocessor system will be used as the example of a digital system, though most of the discussion is applicable to digital systems in general.

The first problem is concerned with *signal reflections* occurring at the ends of wires or printed circuit tracks. When a logic transition reaches a termination point, say the input of a gate, an effect known as signal reflection occurs which causes a part of the signal to travel back towards the source. The reflected signal may add to or subtract from the original signal and the process may repeat at each end several times, though over a period of time the reflected signal will decay to zero. Reflections, if too large, may cause incorrect logic operations.

The second problem is concerned with the unwanted transfer of a portion of a logic signal transition from one line to an adjacent line due to the proximity of the lines. This again may cause incorrect operation.

The final problem is concerned with the effects of electromagnetic interference or noise both externally generated and generated by the system itself. The dominant internal noise is caused by devices switching which can produce a significant transient signal on the power supplies. Noise must be considered in all digital designs.

Reliability of digital systems, an additional engineering consideration, is discussed separately in Chap. 17 because of the extent of this subject.

16.2 TRANSMISSION LINE REFLECTIONS

16.2.1 Transmission lines

Let us firstly review the electrical characteristics of interconnection wires or tracks in a digital system. The term *transmission line* is given to an interconnection path in electrical systems when the series resistance and inductance and the resistance and capacitance to earth are regarded as distributed along the length of the path. Generally, the line carries a changing electrical signal, or a signal that can change, and the distributed nature of the inductance and capacitance of the lines has a significant effect on the signal. In a transmission line, the distributed resistance, inductance and capacitance are (normally) constant, and as a signal passes along the line, it is presented with a constant impedance called the *characteristic impedance* of the line. The characteristic impedance, Z_0, is given by:

$$Z_0 = \frac{\text{transient line voltage}}{\text{transient line current}}$$

Notice that the voltage and currents are transient values. When the signal is stable at a d.c. voltage, the corresponding line current is not defined by the characteristic impedance but by the output resistance of the source, the input resistance of the destination and the series resistance of the line (and the resistance to earth). We shall ignore the transmission line series resistance and resistance to earth as these have a negligible effect upon the analysis in our case.

The characteristic impedance of a line can be related to the distributed inductance and capacitance as follows; let the line inductance per unit length be L and the line capacitance per unit length be C. In a small element of the line, dx, the inductance is Ldx and the capacitance is Cdx. If the transient current is i, the voltage generated across the distributed inductance Ldx is given by:

$v = Lidx/dt$ (from $v = di/dt$)

Also the current due to the transient voltage, v, across the capacitance Cdx is given by:

$i = Cvdx/dt$ (from $i = Cdv/dt$)

by substituting, we get:

$v/i = Z_0 = L/C$

The propagation velocity of a signal, V_p, is given from the above equations as:

$V_p = dx/dt = 1/\sqrt{LC}$ m/s

or the delay, d, of:

$d = \sqrt{LC}$ s/m

The distributed inductance and capacitance of a line will depend on the dimensions and shape of the line, and the proximity to the return ground. The distributed capacitance will also depend on the relative permittivity of the surroundings. Normally the surroundings are nonmagnetic so that the relative permeability is unity.

The distributed inductance and capacitance of simple line configurations, and hence the characteristic impedance, can be found from standard formulas derived by electric and magnetic field theory. We shall quote for two configurations [1] which may be of use in digital design. Firstly, a pair or round wires of radius r and separated by a distance d has an inductance, capacitance and characteristic impedance given by:

$$L = \frac{\mu_0 \ln (d/r)}{\pi} \qquad \text{henries/m}$$

$$C = \frac{\pi \epsilon_0 \, \epsilon_r}{\ln (d/r)} \qquad \text{farads/m}$$

$$Z_0 = \sqrt{\frac{\mu_0}{\epsilon_0 \, \epsilon_r}} \; \frac{\ln (d/r)}{\pi} \qquad \text{ohms}$$

respectively. Secondly, a single wire of radius r separated from a ground plane by a distance h has an inductance, capacitance and characteristic impedance given by:

$$L = \frac{\mu_0 \ln (2h/r)}{2\pi} \qquad \text{henries/m}$$

$$C = \frac{2\pi \epsilon_0 \epsilon_r}{\ln (2h/r)} \qquad \text{farads/m}$$

$$Z_0 = \sqrt{\frac{\mu_0}{\epsilon_0 \, \epsilon_r}} \; \frac{\ln (2h/r)}{2\pi} \qquad \text{ohms}$$

respectively. Z_0 is computed from $Z_0 = L/C$. The permeability constant, μ_0, is $4\pi \times 10^{-7}$. Nonmagnetic surrounding media is assumed. The permittivity constant, ϵ_0, is approximately $1/(36\pi \times 10^9)$. The relative permittivity of the media, ϵ_r (also called the dielectric constant) is typically 4.5 for printed circuit material epoxy glass.

The characteristic impedance of printed circuit tracks similarly depends on the width of the track, the distance from the ground plane if any, and the dielectric constant of the printed circuit board. The characteristic impedance is typically in the region of $80\,\Omega$ to $200\,\Omega$.

Whatever the physical configuration and track size, the propagation velocity is only dependent upon the relative permittivity of the media surrounding the track or wire according to the equation:

$$V_p = 1/\sqrt{\mu_0 \epsilon_0 \epsilon_r} = c/\sqrt{\epsilon_r}$$

where c is the velocity of light in a vacuum. The propagation velocity is often in the range $5\,\text{ns/m}$ to $7\,\text{ns/m}$ ($1.5\,\text{ns/ft}$ to $2\,\text{ns/ft}$).

16.2.2 Reflections

Now, let us investigate the effects of logic signal changes from a voltage representing one logical state to another voltage representing the other logical state. To understand the effects that occur, consider a source which generates a logic transition from 0 volts to V_f volts. This transition passes along a line of characteristic impedance Z_0 to a destination with an input impedance Z_t as shown in Fig. 16.1(a). As the signal passes along the line, the equation:

$$Z_0 = V_f/I_f$$

must be satisfied, where I_f is the current flowing in the line due to V_f. The subscript f signifies the 'forward' direction. The voltage (and current) travel along the line as a step function, as shown in Fig. 16.1(b). When the transient reaches the destination, it is presented with an impedance Z_t, so then the voltage

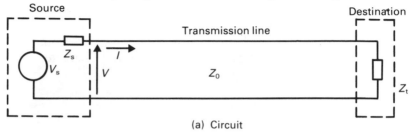

(a) Circuit

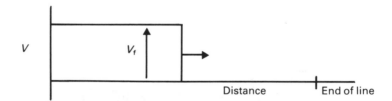

(b) Signal on line before reaching destination

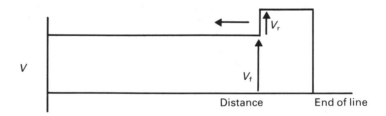

(c) Signal on line after reflection $Z_t > Z_0$

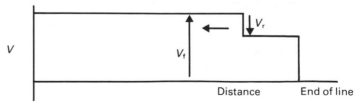

(d) Signal on line after reflection, $Z_t < Z_0$

Figure 16.1   Transmission line reflections

and current must be determined by Z_t. If Z_t is not equal to Z_0, the voltage and current must immediately change. The change that occurs will result in a transient signal known as a *reflection*, traveling backwards along the line towards the source. The reflection may be positive or negative and add to the original voltage or subtract from the original voltage. We shall see that it will add to the original forward signal if Z_t is greater than Z_0, as shown in Fig. 16.1(c), and subtract from the original forward signal if Z_t is less than Z_0, as shown in Fig. 16.1(d).

The amplitude of the reflected 'wave' can be obtained as follows. At the instant that the signal arrives at the destination, we have the current flowing into Z_t given as:

$$I_t = I_f + I_r$$

where I_f is the current of the forward (original) wave and I_r is the additional current producing the reflected wave. The corresponding voltages are given by:

$$V_t = V_f + V_r$$

where

$$I_t = V_t/Z_t$$

and

$$I_f = V_f/Z_0$$

and

$$I_r = -V_r/Z_0$$

Combining the above, we get:

$$V_r = V_f \left(\frac{Z_t - Z_0}{Z_t + Z_0} \right)$$

The term $(Z_t - Z_0)/(Z_t + Z_0)$ gives the fraction of the reflected wave to the forward wave and is called the *voltage reflection coefficient*, ρ. The voltage reflection coefficient has a value between -1 through zero to $+1$. It is zero when Z_t equals Z_0 and then no reflection occurs. If $Z_t = 0$ (a short-circuit), the reflection coefficient is -1 and a maximum negative reflection occurs, i.e. the reflected signal is of the same amplitude as the forward wave and subtracts from the forward wave to produce no signal. If $Z_t = \infty$ (an open-circuit), a maximum positive reflection occurs, i.e. the reflected wave is of the same amplitude as the forward wave and adds to the forward wave to produce double the original signal.

The actual voltage reflected down the line is given by V_t (which is equal to the sum of V_f and V_r). Rearranging the above equations, we get:

$$V_t = (1 + \rho)V_f = 2 \left(\frac{Z_t}{Z_t + Z_0} \right) V_f$$

i.e. the final reflected signal can be between zero and double the original signal.

In practice, zero or double the original signal will never occur because perfect short-circuit or open-circuit conditions cannot occur.

When the reflected wave reaches the source, a second reflection occurs if $Z_0 \neq Z_t'$, where Z_t' is the output impedance of the source. Reflections may continue at both ends of the line though each reflection will be reduced and eventually a steady state is reached in which the line voltage and current are governed by ohmic resistances. The signal at each end will change in amplitude at t-second intervals if reflections occur, where t is the time taken for the signal to travel down the line in either direction. Often the signal changes manifest as a damped oscillation or ringing, as shown in Fig. 16.2, and it is usually necessary that this ringing does not cause the noise margins of the logic circuits to be exceeded.

16.2.3 Graphical analysis

Input and output impedances of logic devices are generally nonlinear and accurate analytical prediction of the reflections is not easy. A convenient method is by graphical construction. Firstly let us consider the simple potential divider circuit shown in Fig. 16.3(a). A voltage step from $0\,\text{V}$ to $+5\,\text{V}$ is applied to the circuit, and a current I flows through both R_s and R_1. A graphical construction to determine the voltage V_1 across R_1 is shown in Fig. 16.3(b). The two axes indicate current and voltage. Two lines are drawn, one with a slope of $-1/R_s$ and one with a slope of $1/R_1$. The intersection of these two lines defines the current I and the voltage V_1 by geometry as shown.

The technique can be applied to a transmission line circuit such as shown in Fig. 16.4(a). A voltage step is applied to the circuit as before, and a current I_0 flows. Initially a step voltage V_0 appears at the input of the transmission line. At this time, the step voltage 'sees' the characteristic impedance of the line, Z_0. We can obtain the voltage V_0 by graphical construction, as in Fig. 16.4(b). Two lines are required, one with a slope of $-1/R_s$ and one with a slope of $1/Z_0$. The intersection of the lines give V_0 and I_0. This event is marked on the graph as

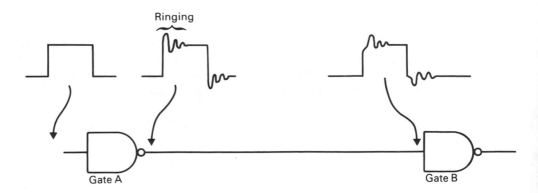

Figure 16.2 Interconnected gates suffering from transmission line reflections

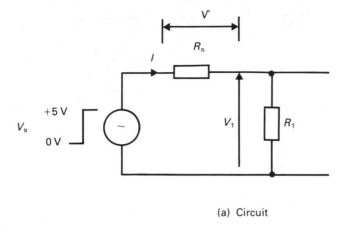

(a) Circuit

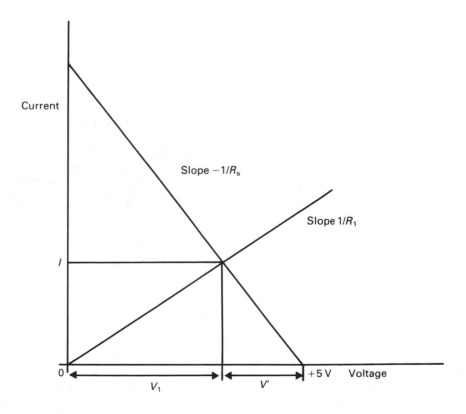

(b) Graphical construction

Figure 16.3 Graphical analysis of potential divider

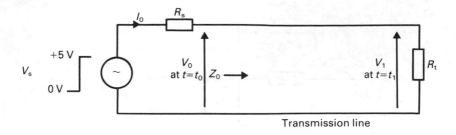

(a) Circuit

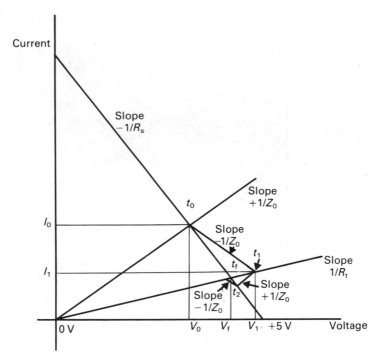

(b) Graphical construction

Figure 16.4   Graphical analysis of transmission line

occurring at time t_0. The step voltage travels along the transmission line, always 'seeing' an impedance Z_0, and hence a constant amplitude is maintained. When the step voltage reaches the end of the line, it sees a resistance, R_t. A change in voltage will occur if $R_t \neq Z_0$. The new voltage can now be ascertained by graphical construction using a line of slope $-1/Z_0$ and a line of slope $1/R_t$. One end of the $-1/Z_0$ line must start at the t_0 point. The intersection of the two lines is marked as occurring at t_1 and defines the new voltage at the end of the line, V_1. Assuming a different voltage is generated and hence a reflection occurs, a step waveform travels back towards the source, reaching the source at time t_2. This point is identified by drawing a line of slope $1/Z_0$ from t_1 to intersect the line of slope $1/R_t$ as shown. This process can be continued by drawing lines alternately of slope $-1/Z_0$ and $1/Z_0$, to find successive voltages at the source and destination as the signal travels forward and backward along the line until steady-state point t_f is reached.

We can now extend the technique for nonlinear resistances. Take the example of a low-power Schottky (LS) TTL gate A connected to another LSTTL gate B (see Fig. 16.2). The input and output characteristics of the gates are plotted on graph paper. We shall arbitrarily choose the positive current axis for the current flowing into a device and the negative axis for the current flowing out of the device. There is one input characteristic for the destination gate B. The two output characteristics of the source gate A, one for a logic 0 output and one for a logic 1 output, are plotted separately.

Suppose firstly a 1-to-0 transition is to be investigated. Figure 16.5(a) shows the characteristics of the TTL gates and the subsequent graphical construction. The static 0 and 1 levels are identified by the cross-over of the input and output characteristics. From the static 1 point, a *load line* is drawn with a slope of $-1/Z_0$ where Z_0 is the characteristic impedance of the line. The intersection of the load line with the 0 output characteristic gives the initial low output voltage at the driving gate A. From this intersection, a line is drawn with a slope of $+1/Z_0$ to reach the input characteristic. The line is constructed for the signal as it travels from gate A to gate B, and gives the initial voltage appearing at gate B after the signal has passed along the line once. From this point on the input characteristic, a line is drawn with a slope of $-1/Z_0$ to strike the 0 level output characteristic. This gives the voltage after the first reflection at gate A. Subsequent lines are drawn between the input and output characteristics with alternate slopes $+1/Z_0$ and $-1/Z_0$ respectively until the static 0 point is reached. Each line indicates one transversal of the signal along the line.

The appropriate voltages and signal waveforms can be found from the intersection of the lines with the characteristics. These points are marked t_0, t_1, t_2, etc., in Fig. 16.5(a). The odd subscripts indicate the times when the signal is at gate A and the even subscripts the times when the signal is at gate B. The result in our example is shown in Fig. 16.5(b) and (c) for the signal at A and B respectively. We can see that the waveform at gate A falls within the 0 voltage range after t_2 seconds, i.e. after one complete transversal of the signal to the destination and back to the source. The signal at gate B initially undershoots (falls below the static 0 level) but then rises and finally settles at the static 0 voltage. In practice, the actual waveforms are not straight with abrupt changes as shown, but will have finite rise and fall times with rounded peaks and troughs.

A similar process is followed to obtain the reflections for a 0-to-1 transition starting at the static 0 point and drawing a load line to meet the 1 output characteristic. Subsequently, lines with alternate slopes of $-1/Z_0$ and $+1/Z_0$ are drawn. This has been done in Fig. 16.6(a). The resultant waveforms are shown in Fig. 16.6(b) and (c).

The method is applicable to all types of gates including non-saturating logic such as emitter-coupled logic gates which have relatively high input and output impedances. Characteristics of gates can vary between manufactured devices and this would have a significant effect on the validity of the results.

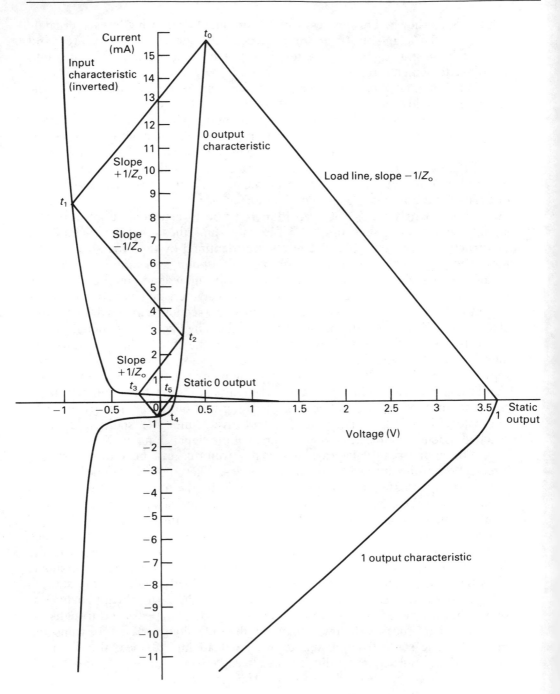

(a) Graphical construction

Figure 16.5   Graphical analysis of 1–to–0 transition with TTL gates

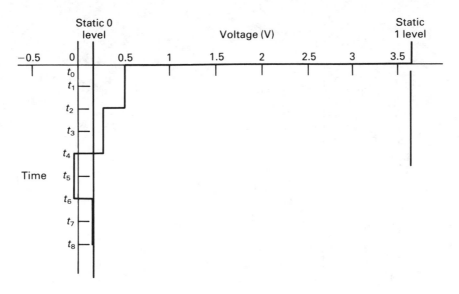

(b) Idealized waveform at source (gate A)

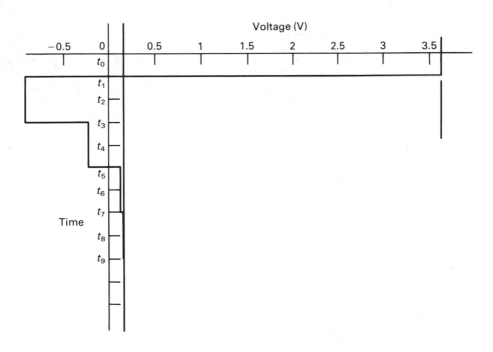

(c) Idealized waveform at destination (gate B)

Figure 16.5 *continued*

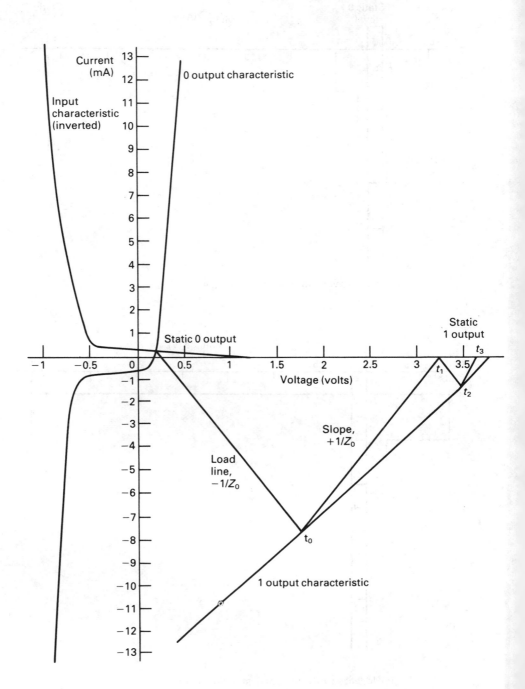

Figure 16.6 Graphical analysis of 0–to–1 transition

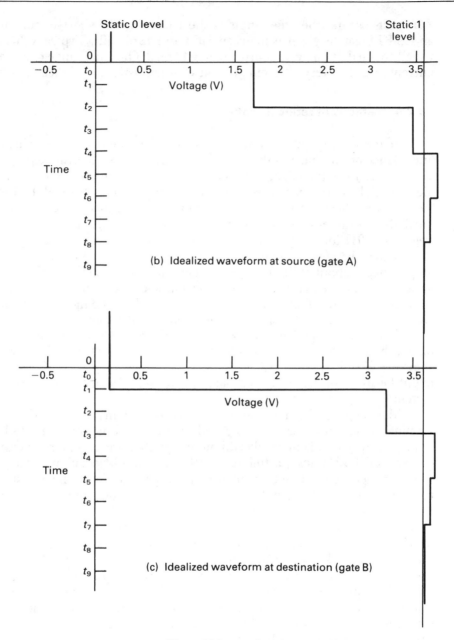

(b) Idealized waveform at source (gate A)

(c) Idealized waveform at destination (gate B)

Figure 16.6 *continued*

Given no additional knowledge of the actual gates in the system, the typical characteristics would be used. In some cases, individual device characteristics can be very different from typical device characteristics. For example, the LSTTL logic 1 output characteristic is significantly different from device to device within the same device type. The characteristic falls approximately in a linear fashion from the static 1 output to 0 V as the output is increasingly loaded.

Zero volts occurs when the output is short-circuit. The short-circuit current of an LSTTL gate is given as between 5 mA and 42 mA [2]. Typical values are not usually quoted but may be approximately 14 mA. The wide range of short-circuit current leads to a very different possible characteristics in practice.

16.2.4 Methods of reducing reflections

If the driving gate has an output impedance equal to the characteristic impedance of the line and the input impedance of the receiving gate is equal to the characteristic impedance, no reflections occur at either end of the interconnection. (The reader may care to show this graphically.) Normal TTL gates do not possess these impedances. The output impedance of an LSTTL gate (including a three-state gate with its output not in high impedance) is in the region of 30 Ω for a logic 0 and 300 Ω for a logic 1 output. The logic 1 output impedance changes to about 50 Ω for currents below about 2 mA. The input impedance is about 100 Ω for input voltages less than 1.5 V and about 10 kΩ for input voltages greater than 1.5 V. The input circuitry of TTL gates usually includes clamping diodes which prevent undershoot being below about -1 V. Without clamping diodes, a large undershoot might occur.

The output impedance of a gate can be increased artifically in an attempt to match the line characteristic impedance, by using an external series resistor as shown in Fig. 16.7(a). A typical value for the resistor is 47 Ω. Series resistors might be used for critical signals such as the ready signal in a microprocessor system.

Matching at the receiving end in bus systems can be done by line termination resistors placed at the end of the bus. For example, the bus on a multi-board system is normally laid out on parallel tracks on a motherboard. At the end of these tracks, a full-value reflection would occur if not terminated since an open-circuit line is an infinite impedance and the worst case for reflections. (Note that MOS devices exhibit very high input impedance and cause almost maximum reflections.) Termination resistors attached to the ends of the lines can take the form of a single resistor connected to $+5$ V (pull-up) or to 0 V (pull-down) as appropriate. Typical values for the former case may be in the region of 2.7 kΩ and in the latter case in the region of 10 kΩ. The smallest value is determined by the drive currents available. Open-collector gates naturally require pull-up resistors to $+5$ V. Three-state gates could use either pull-up or pull-down resistors. When the output line is in high impedance (tri-state), a pull-up resistor would cause a 1 to be generated, while a pull-down resistor would cause a 0 to be generated.

An alternative approach, particularly to achieve improved matching, is to use a resistor divider network with one resistor connected to $+5$ V and one connected to 0 V as shown in Fig. 16.7(b). Typical values are 3.3 kΩ connected to $+5$ V and 4.7 kΩ connected to 0 V. Values may be lower to improve the matching with the characteristic impedance, perhaps as low as 220 Ω and 330 Ω respectively if the gates can supply the required d.c. currents (20 mA with 220/330 Ω resistors). The effective resistance of this termination is 132 Ω, close to

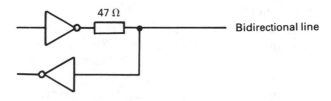

(a) Series matching

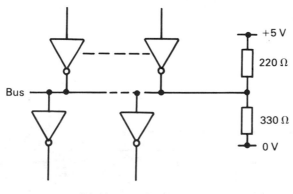

(b) Line termination

Figure 16.7   Methods of reducing transmission line reflections

the typical characteristic impedance of lines. More complex terminations using diodes and voltage sources are possible. Termination can be applied to critical signals or to all bus signals, but in each case, the d.c. current of the termination resistors must be taken into account when accessing the d.c. loading.

16.3 CROSS-TALK

Cross-talk is the effect of one signal transition coupling on to an adjacent line due to the capacitance and mutual inductance between the lines. Suppose a gate A is connected to gate B with a line close to a line connecting gate C to gate D. A logic pulse is generated by gate A to pass to gate B. The connection of A to B runs close, in the worst case parallel, to the connection of gate C to gate D as shown in Fig. 16.8(a), and causes a signal to appear on the C–D line. The signal coupled on to C–D is backward wave, i.e. a current flows in the opposite direction to that caused by the signal on A–B. This can be deduced by considering the two lines as inductors with a mutual inductance between them and capacitors as shown in Fig. 16.8(b). The current flowing in the coupled inductor opposes that flowing in the 'primary' circuit. When a logic transition is generated on the A–B line, a current (and voltage) transition appears on the C–D line starting with the A–B transition and lasting for the time it takes for the A–B transition to propagate down the A–B line, ignoring reflections.

The detailed analysis is rather complicated. We shall restrict our analysis to a simple single lumped impedance [3]. Consider two lines with a mutual impedance, Z_m, between them sited in one place at the middle of the two lines as shown in Fig. 16.9(a). The characteristic impedance of each line is Z_0. Gate A has an output impedance of Z_{out} and a voltage source V_{out}. The gate is connected to the A–B line which presents the output with a load impedance Z_0 as in the equivalent circuit for transient signals shown in Fig. 16.9(b). The actual voltage generated by gate A is thus:

$$V_1 = \left(\frac{Z_0}{(Z_0 + Z_{out})} \right) V_{out} \tag{1}$$

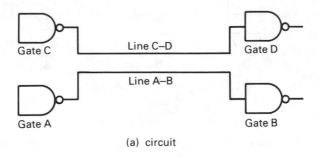

(a) circuit

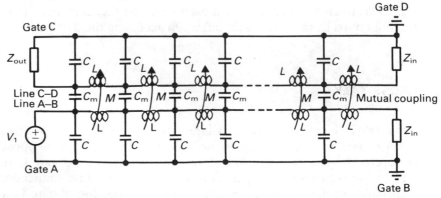

(b) Equivalent circuit

Figure 16.8   Cross-talk between signal lines

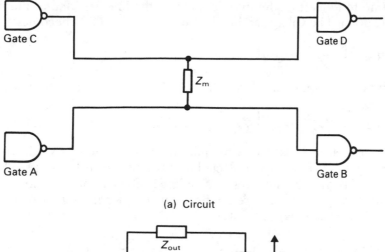

(a) Circuit

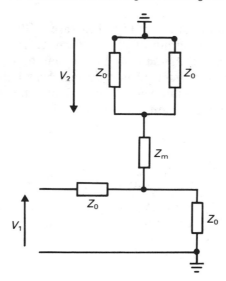

(b) Equivalent circuit for gate A driving line

(c) Line equivalent circuit (see text)

Figure 16.9   Cross-talk analysis; lumped impedance approach

Note that when the transient starts at A it is presented with an impedance Z_0 irrespective of the termination impedances.

Now referring to the transient signal equivalent circuit shown in Fig. 16.9(c), two characteristic impedances in parallel are shown for the C–D

line, one to the left of the middle point of the line and one to the right of the
middle point. The voltage at the middle point of line C–D becomes:

$$V_2 = \left(\frac{Z_0}{2(Z_0 + Z_m)}\right)V_1 \tag{2}$$

Combining the equations (1) and (2), we obtain:

$$V_2 = \left(\frac{Z_0}{2(Z_0 + Z_m)}\right)\left(\frac{Z_0}{(Z_0 + Z_{out})}\right)V_{out} \tag{3}$$

The voltage V_2 is that at the middle point of line C–D. The signal travels
towards gate C. Then it is reflected and travels towards gate D. The reflected
signal at C is given by the transmission line coefficient of reflection multiplied by
the forward signal. Therefore the final equation for the signal at gate D (before
any further reflections) is:

$$V_2' = \left(\frac{Z_0}{2(Z_0 + Z_m)}\right)\left(\frac{Z_0}{(Z_0 + Z_{out})}\right)\left(\frac{(Z_t - Z_0)}{(Z_t + Z_0)}\right)V_{out} \tag{4}$$

where Z_t is the output impedance of gate C. It is important to note that the above
equation is approximate; in practice the problem is much more complex.
However, it gives us a suitable equation to obtain a guide to the reflections that
may be encountered.

EXAMPLE
Suppose, all four gates in Fig. 16.8 are TTL gates. A falling 1-to-0
transition occurs on the output of gate A. Gate C has a static 0 output and an
output impedance of $50\,\Omega$. Gate A has an output impedance of $10\,\Omega$. The
connections are via two surface printed circuit tracks 1 mm wide running parallel
and 1 mm apart with a ground place 2 mm distant. The characteristic impedance
of the lines is $100\,\Omega$ and the mutual impedance is $200\,\Omega$. Determine the cross-
talk.

Using equation (3), we obtain the cross-talk as:

$$\frac{V_2}{V_{out}} = \left(\frac{100}{2(100 + 200)}\right)\left(\frac{100}{(100 + 10)}\right) = +0.15$$

i.e. cross talk of -15%. If the logic swing is 2 V, the cross-talk is 300 mV, in the
same direction as the initial transition. From equation (4), the cross-talk after
reflection at gate C is -5%. If the output impedance of gate C is $10\,\Omega$, the
reflection becomes worse at -12.4%.

16.4 NOISE AND DECOUPLING

We defined noise in Chap. 5 as unwanted electrical signals occurring in a
system. Noise becomes significant when it is imposed on logic signals to such
magnitude to affect the system. Some noise can be tolerated at the inputs of
gates as defined by the noise margins of the gates. Excessive noise must be

eliminated. Noise on logic signals within the system can come from various sources. The predominant source of noise in complex digital systems is caused by individual logic devices switching from one binary state to the other binary state, leading to voltage transients along power supply lines and noise on the device outputs. We have also seen the cross-talk effect described in section 16.3. External noise can be induced into the system by electrostatic or electromagnetic fields. The source may be itself an electronic device such as an SCR (silicon-controlled rectifier) or an electromechanical device such as a relay. Radiated noise can be reduced by shielding (enclosing the digital system with metal). The shielding material must be magnetic for electromagnetic shielding.

As regards to noise due switching of logic devices, three factors can be identified, namely:

(i) The d.c. supply current is different for each output logic level (e.g. an LSTTL 7400 part containing four NAND gates has a total supply current of 2.4 mA when all the outputs are at a 0 and a supply current of 0.8 mA when all the outputs are at a 1).

(ii) During the time that the output changes state, either from a 0 to a 1 or vice versa, the output line capacitance (and internal capacitances) must be charged or discharged. This results in a transient current demand to the supply.

(iii) Also during the time that the output changes state in logic circuits such as TTL, significant additional transient currents are generated if both output transistors at any time conduct simultaneously.

The current changes are depicted in Fig. 16.10. Both static changes and transient changes cause the supply voltage to vary and clearly any variation of the supply voltage will have an adverse effect on the operation of the gates. Supply variations are reduced by the use of smoothing or decoupling capacitors which are connected across the supply at various places within the system (C_1 and C_2 in Fig. 16.11).

An estimate of the values of the capacitors can be made for each of the effects separately. Firstly, consider (i) above. To take a simple example, consider a system with one LSTTL 7400 part with all the inputs joined together and a 1 MHz square-wave signal applied to the inputs. Let the specification call for a maximum change of 5% on the +5 V supply. Over the period that the outputs are at a 1, a current will be demanded from the supply, and when the outputs change to a 0, a different current will be demanded. The minimum value of the smoothing capacitor for a given maximum supply voltage change over the period of charging or discharging can be found from the equation:

$$I = C \, \mathrm{d}v/\mathrm{d}t$$

where I is the difference between the 0 and 1 level currents. Entering the values given, we get:

$$(2.4\,\mathrm{mA} - 0.8\,\mathrm{mA}) = C\,(0.25\,\mathrm{V})/(0.5\,\mu\mathrm{s})$$

or

$$C = (1.6 \times 10^{-3} \times 0.5 \times 10^{-6})/0.25 = 3.2 \times 10^{-9}\,\mathrm{F} = 3.2\,\mathrm{nF}$$

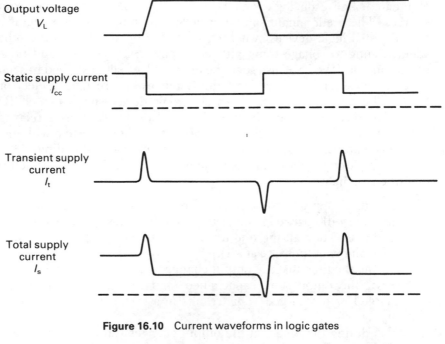

Figure 16.10   Current waveforms in logic gates

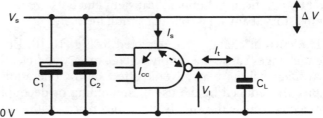

Figure 16.11   Smoothing capacitors

The exact maximum switching frequency might not be known in practice. Clearly a very large value of capacitor can be used assuming it will operate at the switching frequency. In typical systems comprising many gates, electrolytic capacitors with values in the range $50\,\mu F$ to $200\,\mu F$ are generally used on individual printed circuit boards.

Now consider (ii) and (iii) which generate transients only at the time of switching. To calculate a value of capacitor to control the transients, the various capacitances and inductances in the circuits need to be considered. We can identify the capacitance at the output of gates as a source of transient current when output logic transitions occur. We can also identify the inductances associated with the power supply lines which consume transient currents when changes in the power supply voltage occur. Inductances include the track inductance, internal inductance of the power connections of the devices, and the self-inductance of smoothing capacitors. All these inductances exist for (i) but can be neglected at lower frequencies. At very high frequencies, the inductance effect dominates. Also the resistances in the power circuits become significant.

Firstly though, let us perform a rather naive calculation for the transients due to discharging/charging load capacitors ignoring inductance and resistance. Suppose that the total load capacitance applied to the output of each of the four NAND gates is 50 pF which includes the track capacitance, input capacitance of logic devices attached to the outputs, and output self-capacitance. The output signal transition from a 0 to a 1 and from a 1 to a 0 follow nonlinear relationships, but let us assume linear transitions with slopes of 0.25 V/ns for a rising transition and 0.4 V/ns for a falling transition with a 50 pF load and a logic swing of 3.6 V. These are typical values for LSTTL.

Using $I_t = C_L \, dV_{out}/dt$, where I_t is the transient current, dV_{out} the output logic swing and dt the time that the transition occurs, we obtain the transient currents as:

Rising transition: $I_t = 4 \times 50 \times 10^{-12} \times 0.25 \times 10^9 = 50\,\text{mA}$
Falling transition: $I_t = 4 \times 50 \times 10^{-12} \times 0.4 \times 10^9 \ \ = 80\,\text{mA}$

These would be step functions of period dt. The rising transition occurs over 14.4 nsec (3.6/0.25) and the falling transition occurs over 9 nsec (3.6/0.4). We can obtain the value of the smoothing capacitor, C_S, from $C_S = I_t \, dt/dV_S$, where dV_S is the allowable supply voltage change. Thus:

Rising transition: $C_S = (50 \times 10^{-3} \times 14.4 \times 10^{-9})/0.25 \ = 2880\,\text{pF}$
Falling transition: $C_S = (80 \times 10^{-3} \times 9 \times 10^{-9})/0.25 \ \ \ = 2880\,\text{pF}$

In fact, the transient current and the time dt are not needed for the calculation of C_S as $C_S/C_L = dV_{out}/dV_S$. The 9 ns current pulse has an equivalent frequency in excess of 100 MHz (389 MHz using the formulae $f = 3.5/t$). The capacitor would need to operate at this frequency. This rules out electrolytic capacitors. High-frequency capacitors such as ceramic types must be used. These are not manufactured in very large values such as would be needed in systems employing many gates. Therefore, two types of capacitor are used, connected in parallel across the supply lines, at least one large value electrolytic capacitor and several smaller valued high-frequency capacitors distributed around the components.

The above calculation is not normally valid, especially for dynamic memory devices which have very high current transients. Let us perform a more realistic calculation by considering the effect of inductance. For this, we need to know the rate of change of the supply current, i.e. dI_S/dt. This is rarely given in the specification of logic devices, but suppose it is 20 mA/ns. Using the equation $V = L \, dI/dt$ the maximum allowable inductance with the values given would be:

$$L = 0.25/20 \times 10^6 = 12.5\,\text{nH}$$

To keep the inductance to 12.5 nH requires care in the circuit layout. For example, a normal ceramic 0.1 μF capacitor mounted very closely around each integrated circuit would typically have an inductance of around 5 nH to 6 nH, not including the self-inductance of the capacitance. The self-inductance of the capacitor is in the region of 3 nH to 4 nH. Dynamic memories have rather large values for dI_S/dt, perhaps $50\,\text{mA/ns}$. The total inductance in this case would need to be not more than $5\,\text{nH}$.

REFERENCES

1. Shepherd, J., A.H. Morton and L.F. Spence, *Higher Electrical Engineering*. London: Pitman, 1967.
2. *The TTL Data Book for Design Engineers* (2nd ed.)., Dallas: Texas Instruments, Inc., 1976.
3. Morris, R.L., and J.R. Miller, eds., *Designing with TTL Integrated Circuits*. Texas Instruments Electronics Series. New York: McGraw-Hill, 1971.

PROBLEMS

16.1 The output of a TTL NAND gate is connected to the input of a similar gate with a cable 3 m long. Estimate the time required for a 0-to-1 transition to settle to $0.2\,\text{V}$ of steady-state value, given the following.

Input characteristic of gates:

V_{in} (V)	I_{in} (mA)
5	+1
1.4	0
0.4	−1.6

Output characteristic of gates:

V_{out} (V)	I_{load} (mA)
5	+1
3.6	0
2.4	−10
0.4	+16
0.05	0

Characteristic impedance of cable $= 100\,\Omega$
Velocity of propagation in cable $= 2 \times 10^8\,\text{m/s}$.
Employ the graphical method of determining transmission line reflections, and piecewise linear models for the input and output characteristics.

16.2 The output of a TTL gate, A, is connected to the input of an NMOS device, B. A resistor, R, is connected from the input of device B to the supply (+5 V) to reduce transmission line reflections. Estimate the minimum value of R to give a maximum undershoot of −1 V on the interconnecting line at device B, for 1-to-0 logic transitions, given the following:

Gate A   1 level open-circuit output voltage = 3.5 V
            0 level open-circuit output voltage = 0.05 V
            0 level output impedance   = 30 Ω

Characteristic impedance of line = 150 Ω

The input current of device B can be ignored. Obtain a value for R assuming that the 1 level output impedance of device A is zero, and then repeat assuming that it is 750 Ω.

The resistor, R, is replaced by a pair of resistors, R_1 and R_2. R_1 is connected between the line and +5 V and R_2 is connected between the line and 0 V, at device B. Determine suitable values for R_1 and R_2 to give the same undershoot as above and a steady-state 1 voltage of 3.5 V on the line. Clearly indicate the steps taken to reach your solution. What is the principal advantage of using the pair of resistors?

16.3 (a)   Why is it common practice to insert a low-value resistor in series with memory driver gates on large memory boards?

(b)   A TTL logic gate is connected via a printed-circuit track to the input of an MOS memory device. The output impedance of the TTL gate is 25 Ω for both high and low logic levels and the input current of the MOS device is 10 μA. The low logic level is +0.5 V and the high logic level is + 3.5 V. The printed-circuit track has a characteristic impedance of 100 Ω. Estimate, by graphical means, the maximum overshoot and undershoot for fast logic transitions.

(c)   Estimate the minimum spacing of two parallel printed circuit tracks each arranged as above if the coupling between tracks is to be less than 10%. Take the mutual impedance between printed-circuit tracks to be proportional to the distance between tracks, and 100 Ω at 0.1 cm spacing.

16.4 The following relates to a single TTL inverter logic gate:

Logic low output voltage level	=	0.4 V
Logic high output voltage level	=	2.4 V
Rise time of output	=	7 ns
Fall time of output	=	5 ns
Propagation delay, low to high level	=	22 ns
Propagation delay, high to low level	=	15 ns
Input capacitance	=	15 pF
Logic low output supply current	=	5 mA
Logic high output supply current	=	2 mA
Supply voltage	=	+5 V

Three inverters are connected in cascade and driven by a 10 kHz square-wave logic signal. Sketch the supply current variations. Estimate suitable minimum decoupling capacitors if the supply voltage is not to vary by more than 5%. Neglect inductances. Make any other necessary assumptions.

Reliability

17.1 DEFINITIONS

In a system of electrical components, there is always a likelihood that over a period of time one or more components will suddenly fail to function. This will often cause the system itself to fail. In this chapter, we shall look at the likelihood that a failure will occur and possible designs to make the system resilient to failures such that the system will continue to function properly in the presence of one or more component failures. Firstly we need to define a number of terms.

17.1.1 Failure rate

Suppose a number of identical components are operated in a test. Over a period of time, components will fail at intervals. When a component fails, it is not replaced with a working component, i.e. it is a *non-replacement* test. We might obtain the decrease of working components shown in Fig. 17.1. (A continuous curve is shown: actually there will be step changes as a component fails.) At an instant in time, the slope of the curve is given by dN/dt, and there are dN failures in time dt. The parameter *failure rate*, λ, is associated with the components and can be defined as:

$$\lambda = -\frac{dN/N}{dt}$$

i.e. the fractional the rate of decrease of N, where N is the number of components still working.

An alternative test is the *replacement test*. In the replacement test, when a components fails, it is replaced with another component. This leads to slightly more failures during the test and a slightly higher value for failure rate. In the following, we will assume a non-replacement test.

Failure rate is not necessarily a constant; commonly it takes the form shown in Fig. 17.2. When a component is first operated, there is a greater likelihood that it will fail due to factors such as manufacturing defects, stress and internal temperature changes. Usually after perhaps 500 hours of operation, the failure rate settles down to a constant value. This is the normal operating period. At the end of the component's life, perhaps after a few years but depending upon the operating conditions, the failure rate begins to increase. This is the *wear-out* period. We can define an 'instantaneous' failure rate given by:

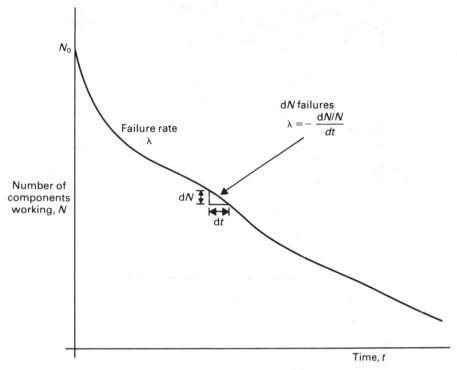

Figure 17.1 Instantaneous failure rate

$$\lambda(t) = -\frac{dN(t)/N(t)}{dt}$$

In many cases, we can assume that component failure rates under fixed conditions are constant. Constant failure rates are normally given in terms of %/1000 hr or failures/10^6 hr. For example, a constant failure rate of 5.6%/1000 hr can be written as $56/10^6$ hr.

Integrated circuits typically have failure rates in the region 1 to 1000/hr depending upon the complexity of the component, among other factors. For example, a 4-gate 74LS00 part has a failure rate of approximately $2/10^6$ hr while a 2200-gate Z-80 microprocessor has a failure rate of approximately $100/10^6$ hr (computed from reference [1]). Failure rates normally refer to the normal operating period.

For a constant failure rate component, we have:

$$\lambda dt = -\frac{dN(t)}{N(t)}$$

$$\int \lambda dt = -\int \left(\frac{1}{N(t)}\right) dN(t)$$

$$\lambda t = -\log N(t) + K$$
$$N(t) = K'e^{-\lambda t}$$

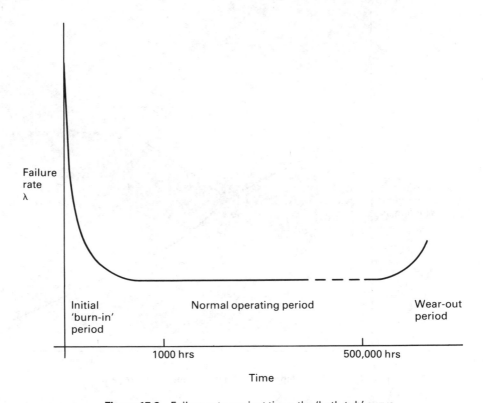

Figure 17.2   Failure rate against time; the 'bath-tub' curve

where K and K' are constants. At $t = 0$, $N = N_0$ (the initial number of components). Therefore $K' = N_0$ and

$$N(t) = N_0 e^{-\lambda t}$$

i.e. the rate of decrease of working components is an exponential function for a constant failure rate component, as shown in Fig. 17.3.

17.1.2 Reliability

The term *reliability* is defined as:

$$R = \frac{\text{number of components working at time } t}{\text{number of components working initially}}$$

Reliability has a value of unity at $t = 0$. For a constant failure rate component, we have:

$$R(t) = \frac{N(t)}{N_0} = e^{-\lambda t}$$

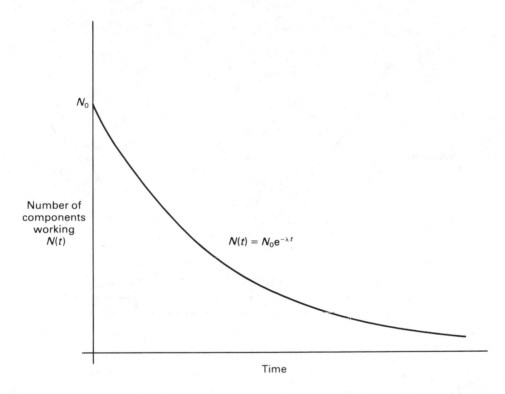

Figure 17.3 Decrease of working components against time for constant failure rate components

Hence reliability is also an exponential function for a constant failure rate component, as shown in Fig. 17.4. Reliability can be given as a ratio, say 0.999, or as a percentage, 99.9%.

For a constant failure rate system, after an operating time equal to $1/\lambda$, the reliability has reduced to 0.37 or 37%. After a time of $2/\lambda$, the reliability has reduced further to 0.135 or 13.5%. After a time $3/\lambda$, the reliability has reduced to 0.05 or 5%.

17.1.3 Mean time between failures

The term *mean time between failures*, MTBF, is the mean time between successive failures [2]. If a system is repaired, the system MTBF would include the repair time. The MTBF of a batch of components could be obtained by measuring the time that each component operates, and computing the mean operating time, i.e.

$$\text{MTBF} = \frac{\text{Summation of the component operating times}}{\text{Initial number of components}}$$

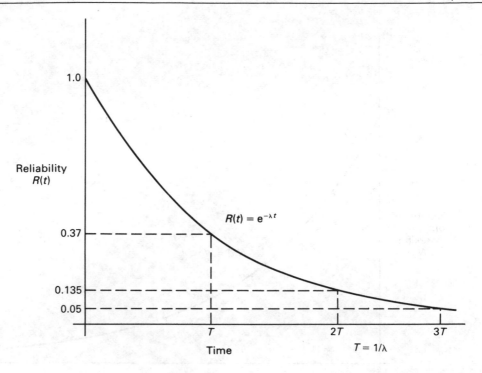

Figure 17.4   Reliability of a constant failure rate system

Ideally, we would like to perform the test until all the components have failed. Then all the operating times would be added together and the result divided by the original number of components, giving a mean value for the batch of componets. MTBF is a constant (whether or not the failure rates are constant).

In the general case, over a period of time from t to $t + dt$, $N(t)$ components are operating. The cumulative operating time over the period dt is given by $N(t)dt$. Integrating from $t = 0$ to $t = \infty$, we obtain the expression for the MTBF given by:

$$\text{MTBF} = \frac{\int_0^\infty N(t)\, dt}{N_0} = \int_0^\infty R(t)\, dt$$

The integration is performed to infinity to ensure that all of the components have failed.

For constant failure rate components, $N(t) = N_0 e^{-\lambda t}$ and MTBF is given by:

$$\text{MTBF} = \frac{\int_0^\infty N_0\, e^{-\lambda t} dt}{N_0} = \int_0^\infty e^{-\lambda t} dt$$

$$= 1/\lambda$$

i.e. the reciprocal of failure rate gives the mean time between failure but only for a constant failure rate system.

17.1.4 Non-constant failure rate

When the failure rate is not constant but a function of time, i.e.

$$\lambda(t) = -\frac{dN(t)/dt}{N(t)}$$

we get by multiplying by N_0/N_0:

$$\lambda(t) = -\left(\frac{dN(t)}{N_0}\right)\left(\frac{N_0}{N(t)}\right)\frac{1}{dt}$$

$$= -\frac{dR(t)/dt}{R(t)}$$

since $R(t) = N(t)/N_0$. Therefore:

$$\lambda(t)\,dt = -\frac{1}{R(t)}\,dR(t)$$

Integrating, we get:

$$\int \lambda(t)\,dt = -\int \frac{1}{R(t)}dR(t)$$

At $t = 0$, $R(t) = 1$. Therefore:

$$-\int_0^t \lambda(t)\,dt = \log R(t) - \log 1 = \log R(t)$$

$$R(t) = \exp\left(-\int_0^t \lambda(t)\,dt\right)$$

This expression can only be evaluated if the function $\lambda(t)$ is known. If it is constant, the expression reduces to that obtained before, i.e.

$$R(t) = \exp(-\lambda t)$$

Using the previous definition, MTBF is given by:

$$\text{MTBF} = \frac{\int_0^\infty N(t)\,dt}{N_0}$$

$$= \int_0^\infty \exp\left(-\int_0^t \lambda(t)\,dt\right) dt$$

which will be a constant but can only be evaluated if we know the function $\lambda(t)$. (With a constant failure rate, we get the previous value, i.e. $\text{MTBF} = 1/\lambda$.)

17.2 SYSTEM RELIABILITY

The terms we have introduced in section 17.1 regarding components under a test can be applied to the components in a functional system and for the system.

Let us consider the reliability of a system composed of several components. Firstly we define the terms *probability of working* and *probability of failure*.

17.2.1 Probability of working and probability of failure

The probability of a system (or component) working, P, is the same as reliability (see definition of reliability). The probability of a system (or component) failure, Q, is given by:

$$Q = 1 - P$$

For example, if the probability of working is 0.9 (90%), the probability of failure is 0.1 (10%). The reliability of a constant failure rate system after an operating time equal to the MTBF is 0.37 (see Fig. 17.4), or expressed alternatively, the probability of a system working at this time is 37%. In the following, we shall often use probability terms to obtain probability of working expressions, though of course reliability terms can be substituted.

17.2.2 Series configuration

A series configuration is one in which the complete system will fail if any one component in the system fails. Most computer systems are of this form. A system with a series configuration can be illustrated diagramatically as one in which the components are connected in series electrically, as shown in Fig. 17.5. The probability of the system working must be the product of the probabilities of working of the individual components, i.e.

Probability of system working, $P_s, = P_1 \times P_2 \times P_3 \times \cdots \times P_n$

where P_n is the probability of the nth component working. The reliability of the complete system is given by the product of the reliabilities of the individual components, i.e.

Reliability of system, $R_s, = R_1 \times R_2 \times R_3 \times \cdots \times R_n$

where R_n is the reliability of the nth component. Replacing the reliability with the constant failure rate exponential form, we get:

$$\exp(-\lambda_s t) = \exp(-\lambda_1 t) \times \exp(-\lambda_2 t) \times \cdots \times \exp(-\lambda_n t)$$
$$= \exp[-(\lambda_1 + \lambda_2 + \cdots + \lambda_n)t]$$

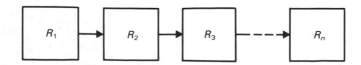

Figure 17.5 Components in a series configuration

i.e. the failure rate of the system, λ_s, is given by the summation of the individual failure rates. Therefore if the component failure rates are constant, the system failure rate must also be constant.

For a system of n identical components, we have:

$$P_s = (P)^n$$

where P is the probability of an individual component working. The probability of system failure, Q_s, is given by:

$$Q_s = 1 - P_s = 1 - (P)^n = 1 - (1 - Q)^n$$

where P is the probability of each component working and Q is the probability of each component failure.

EXAMPLE

If the series system is composed of 100 components each with a reliability or probability of working of 99%, the reliability of the system is:

Reliability of system $= 0.99^{100} = 0.366$

or expressed another way, if the components have a 99% chance of working, the system has a 36.6% chance of working. With 200 components, the reliability falls to 0.134 (13.4%). This illustrates that components need to have a very high reliability to give high system reliability.

17.2.3 Parallel configuration

A parallel configuration is one in which the system fails only if all the components in the system have failed, as opposed to a series configuration in which only one component need fail for the system to fail. Clearly a parallel configuration will lead to a greater reliability than a series configuration and is the basis of many fault-tolerant systems (section 17.4).

A system with a parallel configuration can be illustrated diagrammatically as a system of components connected in parallel as shown in Fig. 17.6. The probability of a system failure is given by the product of the individual probabilities of failure:

Probability of system failure, $Q_s, = Q_1 \times Q_2 \times Q_3 \times \cdots \times Q_n$

where Q_n is the probability of failure of the nth component. (This equation may be compared to a series configuration in which the system works only if all the components are working.)

The probability of the system working can be found by substituting $Q_s = 1 - P_s$ into the above relationship, i.e.

$$1 - P_s = (1 - P_1)(1 - P_2)(1 - P_3) \cdots (1 - P_n)$$

Substituting the component failure rates as before, we find that the system failure rate is generally not a constant, even if the component failure rates are constant.

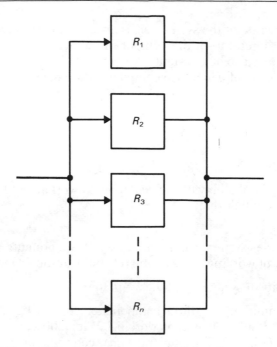

Figure 17.6   Components in a parallel configuration

For n identical components, we have:

$$Q_s = (Q)^n = (1 - P)^n$$

or

$$P_s = 1 - Q_s = 1 - (1 - P)^n$$

EXAMPLE

If a parallel system is composed of 100 components each with a reliability of 99% as in the series system example, the reliability of the system is:

$$R_s = 1 - (1-0.99)^{100} = 1 - 10^{-200}$$

i.e. the system has a $99.99 \cdots 99\%$ chance of working. It is unlikely that a 100-component parallel system would be feasible. However, even with 3 components configurated in parallel, we obtain:

$$R_s = 1 - 10^{-6}$$

or a 99.9999% chance of working.

17.2.4 Reliability assessment

Many systems fall into the series category and then the overall failure rate is given by the summation of the failure rates of the individual components. As the overall system has a constant failure rate, the MTBF is given by the reciprocal of the system failure rate. The probability of working (reliability) can also be calculated from the constant failure rate exponential equation $R(t) = e^{-\lambda t}$, if the operating time is known. In a system of many different components operating under different electrical and perhaps different environmental conditions, we should take the different reliabilities under different conditions into account. The general approach is to incorporate *weighting factors* which modify the basic failure rate according to the conditions that the components experience. Typical conditions are operating power, temperature and mechanical stress. Each component failure rate is multiplied by the appropriate weighting factor and the results summed to obtain the overall system failure rate.

A comprehensive reference giving the failure rates of all types of electrical components, comprehensive weighting factors and procedures is given in *Reliability Prediction of Electronic Equipment*, MIL-HDBK-217B US Department of Defense, [1]. Two reliability assessment treatments are identified. One is called the *parts count* method which gives a general idea of the system reliability during the system design phase. The other is called the *parts stress analysis* method which is a thorough treatment done when the design is finished and all the operating conditions are known. Firstly we outline the parts count method.

(a) Parts count method

In this method, each failure rate is multiplied by two weighting factors, a quality factor and a learning factor, leading to the system failure rate:

$$\lambda_s = \sum_{i=1}^{n} N_i (\lambda_G \pi_Q \pi_L)$$

where:

λ_s = total system failure rate (failures/10^6 hr)
λ_G = generic failure rate of the ith component (failures/10^6)
n = number of different components categories
N_i = number of components in the ith category
π_Q = quality factor of the ith component
π_L = learning factor of the ith component (for microelectronic devices only)

This failure rate applies if the whole system is operating in one environment, as would be usual. Failure rates are given for different environments and the appropriate failure rates chosen accordingly. Nine different physical environments are listed in reference [1],: ground benign (nearly zero stress), ground fixed, ground mobile, naval sheltered, naval unsheltered, airborne inhabited areas, airborne uninhabited areas, space flight and missile launch.

The quality factor refers to the manufacturing and testing methods employed for the component. More stringent testing will lead to a lower factor and a lower failure rate. Quality factors are used in both the parts count method and the parts stress method. There is a factor of 300 between the highest testing procedure (most stringent military specification) and the lowest (normal commercial testing with epoxy or similar packaging).

The learning factor can have a value of 1 or 10. The value of 10 is applied if the component is new and has been placed into initial production or where there have been major changes in design or production or where there has been an 'extended interruption in production or a change in line personnel (radical expansion)'.

Failure rates are given for types of components, not particular components. Bipolar digital devices are separated from others including MOS devices, digital or linear. Within each group, a range of internal gate numbers are categorized together at each environmental condition and the same generic failure rate listed. For example, a bipolar digital device with 1 to 20 gates has the same failure rate (0.029 for fixed ground conditions, 0.21 for missile launch), 21 to 50 gates the same failure rate, 51 to 100 gates the same failure rate, 101 to 500 gates the same failure rate, etc. A similar table is produced for MOS devices. Read-only memories are categorized according to the number of bits. Random access memory is quoted as having 3.5 times the failure rate of read-only memory.

Table 17.1 list the generic failure rates for bipolar and MOS devices operating at ground-fixed environment (G_F). This environment is defined as 'conditions less than ideal to include installation in permanent racks with adequate cooling air, maintenance by military personnel and possible installation in unheated buildings' [1]. Separate tables are provided for discrete components. Table 17.2 lists some common components, again under a ground-fixed environment.

Table 17.3 shows an example of the computation for digital system (having a series configuration). The result, 567.5044 failures/10^6, would normally be

Table 17.1   Generic failure rate, λ_G, of bipolar and MOS devices [1]. G_F environment (ground fixed)

Circuit complexity		TTL	Bipolar beam lead, ECL, Linear, MOS
	1 – 20 gates	0.029	0.048
	21 – 50 gates	0.062	0.19
	51 – 100 gates	0.094	0.31
	101 – 500 gates	0.22	0.82
	501 – 1000 gates	0.34	1.4
	1001 – 2000 gates	0.78	3.1
	2001 – 3000 gates	2.1	8.4
	3001 – 4000 gates	5.7	23.0
	4001 – 5000 gates	16.0	62.0
ROM*	≤ 320 bits	0.022	0.87
	321 – 576 bits	0.033	0.13
	577 – 1120 bits	0.052	0.20
	1121 – 2240 bits	0.078	0.30
	2241 – 5000 bits	0.12	0.46
	5001 – 11000 bits	0.18	0.70
	11001 – 17000 bits	0.28	1.1
Linear	≤ 32 transistors		0.052
	33 – 100 transistors		0.11

* RAM failure rate = 3·5 × ROM failure rate
π_Q = 75 for commercial part hermetically sealed
π_Q = 150 for commercial part packaged in organic material
   (eg. epoxy).

Table 17.2 Selection of component generic failure rates [1] G_F (ground fixed)

Component	Generic failure rate (failures/10^6 hr)
Resistors	
Composition, style RCR	0.002
Film, style RL	0.075
Film power, style RD	0.96
Capacitors	
Paper/plastic, style CHR/CPV/ CQR	0.0006
Ceramic, style CKR	0.022
Tantalum solid, style CSR	0.026
Aluminum dry electrolyte, style CE	0.41
Transistors	
Si NPN	0.18
Si PNP	0.29
Diodes	
Si, general purpose	0.12
Zener and avalanche	0.16
Connectors	
Circular, rack and panel, Printed wiring board	0.45
Switches	
Toggle	0.57
PC wiring boards	
Two-sided	0.0024
Multi-layer	0.30
PC wiring board connections	
Solder, reflow lap to PC boards	0.00012
Solder, wave to PC boards	0.00044
Other hand solder	0.0039
Crimp	0.0073

rounded to, say, 570 failures/10^6. The MTBF is given by $1/570 \times 10^6 = 1750$ hr. This rather low MTBF could be substantially improved by using component screening procedures (which would reduce π_Q from 75 to 45 for MIL-STD-883, method 5004, class C, or to 2.5 if class B. The highest screen procedure MIL-M-38510 class A produces $\pi_Q = 0.5$).

(b) Parts stress method

In parts stress analysis, several weighting factors are incorporated into the calculation to accommodate the operating conditions. Two types of conditions are identified: failure over a period of time due to mechanisms accelerated by temperature or electrical bias, and failure due to mechanical causes (including thermal expansion). These are summed together into one equation. The equation depends on the type of component. Monolithic MOS and bipolar digital devices have a similar general equation:

$$\lambda_P = \pi_L \pi_Q (C_1 \pi_T + C_2 \pi_E) \pi_P$$

Table 17.3   Example of parts count method

Component	N_i	λ_G	π_Q	π_L	$N_i(\lambda_G \pi_Q \pi_l)$ (failures/10^6 hr)
Resistors	6	0.002	1	1	0.012
Capacitors	10	0.022	1	1	0.22
TTL 1–20 gates	2	0.029	75	1	4.35
TTL 21–50 gates	5	0.062	75	1	23.25
MOS 1001–2000 gates	2	3.1	75	1	465.0
MOS 16K RAM	1	0.98	75	1	73.5
PC board	1	0.0024	1	1	0.0024
PC connections	300	0.0039	1	1	1.17
				Total	567.5044

where:

λ_P = device failure rate (failures/10^6)
π_L = device learning factor
π_Q = device quality factor
π_T = temperature acceleration factor (technology dependent)
π_E = environment factor
C_1 = circuit complexity factor (exponential function of number of gates)
C_2 = circuit complexity factor
π_P = pin factor (1 to 1.3 depending on the number of pins on package and device)

The above equation is used in subgroups, bipolar and MOS digital SSI/MSI and bipolar and MOS LSI and microprocessor. Bipolar and MOS memories are treated separately because of the high 'gate to pin' ratio. MOS includes all types including NMOS, PMOS and CMOS with normal integrated circuit processes.

Components within each type are classified more finely than in the parts count method. Digital devices are classified according to the number of internal gates (1, 2, 4, 6, 8, 10, 12, etc.) and the number of gates in a particular device, for example a 74LS00 (4 gates), Z-80 (2200 gates). Figure 17.7(a) and (b) give the failure rates for bipolar SSI/MSI and MOS LSI calculated from the data provided in the parts stress method of MIL-HDBK-217B.

17.3 RELIABILITY OF COMPLEX SYSTEMS

Systems may have a configuration that is neither series nor parallel. If they can be divided into parallel sections and series sections, the reliability of each of these sections can be calculated separately and the results combined as appropriate. However, if this reduction cannot be performed or there are additional aspects such as multiple failure modes, alternative methods need to be employed. We shall describe two methods that are suitable for all configurations, one using Bayes's probability theorem (section 17.3.1) and one using Boolean truth tables (section 17.3.2). Multiple failure mode problems are discussed in section 17.3.3 and solved using Bayes's theorem.

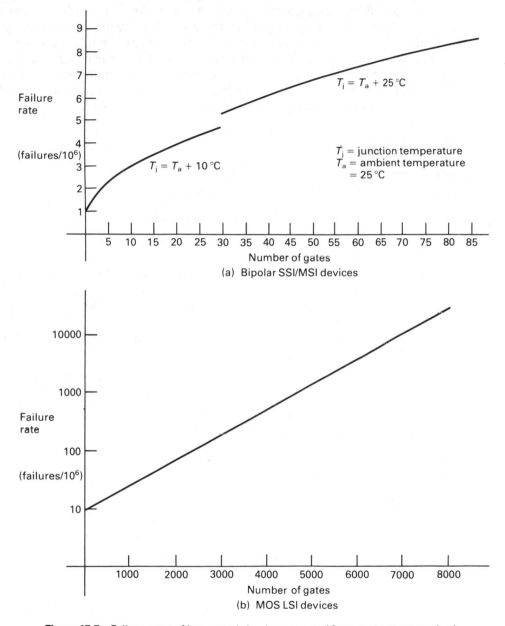

Figure 17.7 Failure rates of integrated circuits computed from parts stress method

17.3.1 Using Bayes's probability theorem

To explain Bayes's theorem, consider a pack of playing cards. The probability of drawing a card of the club suit is $13/52$ ($1/4$), as 13 of 52 cards are of the club suit. This is the *marginal* (or *simple*) *probability* of an event occurring.

The probability of drawing a card which is both of the club suit and a court-card (either jack, queen or king) is 3/52 as there are three cards in the court group, jack of clubs, queen of clubs and king of clubs. This probability is known as the *joint probability* as it depends upon the joint event of drawing a club and a court-card. If it is known that a club has been drawn, the probability that it is also one of the court cards is 3/13. This probability is known as the *conditional probability* and is related to marginal and joint probability in our example by:

$$3/13 = \frac{3/52}{13/52}$$

or more generally:

$$\text{Conditional probability} = \frac{\text{joint probability}}{\text{marginal probability}}$$

This relationship is known as Bayes's probability theorem [2].

Also, the summation of all the possible joint probabilities is equal to the marginal probability. For example, the (marginal) probability of drawing a court-card of any suit is given by the summation of the joint probability of drawing a court-card and club (3/52), the joint probability of drawing a court-card and spade (3/52), the joint probability of drawing a court-card and diamond (3/52) and the joint probability of drawing a court-card and heart (3/52), i.e. $3/52 + 3/52 + 3/52 + 3/52 = 12/52$. Generally:

$$P_a = P_{a1} + P_{a2} + P_{a3} + \cdots + P_{an} \qquad (1)$$

where

P_a = marginal probability that event a occurs

and

P_{an} = joint probability that both event a occurs and event n occurs

All n events must be mutually exclusive and form a complete list.

Replacing each joint probability by the product of marginal probability and conditional probability (Bayes's theorem) provides the equation:

$$P_a = P_{a/1}P_1 + P_{a/2}P_2 + P_{a/3}P_3 + \cdots + P_{a/n}P_n \qquad (2)$$

where

$P_{a/n}$ = conditional probability that a occurs given that event n has occured

and

P_n = marginal probability that event n occurs

We can use this expression to determine the probability of a system working. Suppose a system consists of two or more units. One unit is called A. Two mutually exclusive events are identified, one of which must occur, namely a system with A working and the system with A not working. We can write:

Probability of system working = (probability of system working assuming A works)×(probability of A working) + (probability of system working assuming A not working) × (probability of A not to working)   (3)

Let us now apply equation (3) to various system configurations, starting with a system having two components A and B.

(a) Two-component series configuration

Suppose A and B are in a series configuration. We shall arbitrarily choose components A for our expression. The various probabilities need to be determined. The probability that the system works if A works depends upon B, i.e. the probability that B works. The probability that the system works if A does not work is zero because the system cannot work is A does not work. Therefore the probability of the system working is given by:

$$P_s = P_A P_B + 0$$

where

P_A = probability of A working
P_B = probability of B working

This result is the same as previously, i.e. the probability of system working or reliability is given by the product of the individual component working probabilities or reliabilities.

(b) Two-component parallel configuration

Suppose A and B are in a parallel configuration. From (3), we get:

$$\text{Probability of system working} = 1 \times P_A + P_B \times (1 - P_A)$$
$$= P_A + P_B - P_A P_B$$

This result is equivalent to that obtained previously.

(c) More complex configurations

Figure 17.8 shows a system configuration in which the system can work if some of the components are working. In particular, the system works if:

A and C are working; or
A and D are working; or
A and E are working; or
B and E are working.

We shall apply equation (3) with A again chosen as working or not working. When A is working, we have the parallel combination of C, D and E as shown in Fig. 17.9(a) and the probability of this working is given by:

$$P = 1 - (1 - P_C)(1 - P_D)(1 - P_E)$$

as a simple parallel combination. It does not matter whether B is working and so B does not need to be considered. When A is not working, the system reduces to

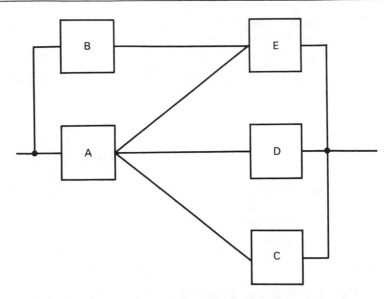

Figure 17.8   System which does not decompose into simple series or parallel configurations

a series combination of B and E as shown in Fig. 17.9(b), which has the probability of working of:

$$P = P_B P_E$$

Substituting these results into (3), we get:

$$P_s = (1 - (1 - P_C)(1 - P_D)(1 - P_E))(P_A) + P_B P_E (1 - P_A)$$

EXAMPLE
   If $P_A = 0.95$, $P_B = 0.90$, $P_C = 0.85$, $P_D = 0.80$ and $P_E = 0.75$, $P_s = 0.976625$

17.3.2 Boolean truth table method and probability maps

In the Boolean truth table method, a truth table is formed which lists all the possible combinations of components working or not working in a system and whether the complete system works in each case, determined by examination of the system configuration. A component working is indicated by a Boolean 1 and a component not working by a Boolean 0.

To take an example, consider the previous problem shown in Fig. 17.8. There are five components, A, B, C, D and E. Hence, there are 32 combinations of components working or not working, as shown in the A-B-C-D-E columns of Table 17.4. The next column indicates whether the particular combination leads to a working system or a system failure. For example, the condition of A working ($A = 1$), B working ($B = 1$), C not working ($C = 0$), D working ($D = 1$) and E not working ($E = 0$) leads to a working system because A and D are working. The probability of this particular event is given by:

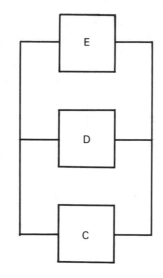

(a) System if A works

(b) System if A does not work

Figure 17.9   Reduction of system using Bayes's theorem

$$P_A P_B (1 - P_C) P_D (1 - P_E)$$

Given the actual probabilities, the system probability of the event occurring can be calculated. In our example, $P_A = 0.95$, $P_B = 0.90$, $P_C = 0.85$, $P_D = 0.80$ and $P_E = 0.75$ and the probability for $A = 1$, $B = 1$, $C = 0$, $D = 1$, and $E = 0$ is $(0.95) \times (0.90) \times (1 - 0.85) \times (0.80) \times (1 - 0.75) = 0.02565$. The other system working probabilities can be calculated similarly. All the probabilities are given in the final column of Table 17.4. The probability that the system will work is given by the summation of the individual probabilities given in the last column. With the values here, the summation is 0.976625 as before.

We can write the Boolean expression for P_s in terms of A, B, C, D and E:

$$P_s = \bar{A}\bar{B}C\bar{D}E + \bar{A}\bar{B}CDE + \bar{A}B\bar{C}\bar{D}E + \bar{A}B\bar{C}DE + \bar{A}BC\bar{D}E + \bar{A}BCDE + A\bar{B}\bar{C}D\bar{E} + A\bar{B}\bar{C}DE + A\bar{B}C\bar{D}E + A\bar{B}C\bar{D}E + A\bar{B}CD\bar{E} + A\bar{B}CDE + AB\bar{C}\bar{D}E + AB\bar{C}D\bar{E} + AB\bar{C}DE + ABC\bar{D}E + ABCD\bar{E} + ABCDE$$

where

      A = component A working

and

      $\bar{A}$ = component A not working

Table 17.4   Probability table

A	B	C	D	E	System	Probability
0	0	0	0	0	Fails	
0	0	0	0	1	Fails	
0	0	0	1	0	Fails	
0	0	0	1	1	Fails	
0	0	1	0	0	Fails	
0	0	1	0	1	Fails	
0	0	1	1	0	Fails	
0	0	1	1	1	Fails	
0	1	0	0	0	Fails	
0	1	0	0	1	Works	0.0010125
0	1	0	1	0	Fails	
0	1	0	1	1	Works	0.00405
0	1	1	0	0	Fails	
0	1	1	0	1	Works	0.0057375
0	1	1	1	0	Fails	
0	1	1	1	1	Works	0.02295
1	0	0	0	0	Fails	
1	0	0	0	1	Works	0.0021375
1	0	0	1	0	Works	0.00285
1	0	0	1	1	Works	0.00855
1	0	1	0	0	Works	0.0040375
1	0	1	0	1	Works	0.0121125
1	0	1	1	0	Works	0.01615
1	0	1	1	1	Works	0.04845
1	1	0	0	0	Fails	
1	1	0	0	1	Works	0.0192375
1	1	0	1	0	Works	0.02565
1	1	0	1	1	Works	0.07695
1	1	1	0	0	Works	0.0363375
1	1	1	0	1	Works	0.109012
1	1	1	1	0	Works	0.14535
1	1	1	1	1	Works	0.43605
					Total:	0.976625

This expression can be simplified algebraically using the equality $A + \bar{A} = 1$ (i.e. probability of working + probability of failure = 1), in the same way as simplifying Boolean expressions using the identical Boolean equality. However, care must be taken not to use Boolean equalities which are not valid for probability expressions. In particular, the Boolean equality $A + A = A$ which allows us in Boolean algebra to use a term repeatedly in simplifying expressions, is not allowed in simplifying probability expressions.

An alternative process to algebraic simplification uses the equivalent of a Karnaugh map, called a *probability map*. The probability map is labeled as a Karnaugh map with adjacent squares representing terms which have one variable different (variable true in one term and false in the other term). The probability function is mapped onto the probability map using 1's to indicate a working system and 0's to indicate a non-working system. The probability map for our problem is shown in Fig. 17.10. Note that each term describes an exclusive product of component probabilities. Groups of 1's are formed as in a Karnaugh map except overlapping groups are not allowed. There may be more than one selection of groups which will cover the 1's and these will give equivalent solutions. One solution is:

$$P_s = AD + \bar{A}CE + A\bar{D}E + \bar{A}B\bar{C}E$$

Substituting the probability values, we get the same result as previously (0.976625).

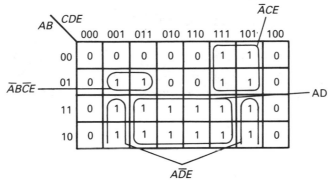

Figure 17.10 Probability map

17.3.3 Multiple modes of failure

So far we have considered a component which either works or fails completely. Now we will develop the technique further to cover components which have more than one type of failure, in particular components which have a mode of failure not leading inextricably to a system failure. A simple example is a circuit consisting of two semiconductor diodes D_1 and D_2 connected in series. A diode may work, fail producing a short-circuit connection, or fail producing an open-circuit connection. (Of course it is possible to have an intermediate failure.) We need to define what constitutes a working system. Let us say in this case that the system works if it has a rectifying action, i.e. has electrical conduction in one current direction but not in the other direction, and any voltage drop across the circuit is irrelevant. If one diode fails with a short-circuit, the system will still behave in this manner, while if one diode fails with an open-circuit, the system fails.

Equation (2) in section 17.3.1 (derived from Bayes's theorem) can be used to calculate the overall probability of working as follows:

Probability of system working =
(probability of system working if D_1 works)(probability of D_1 working)
+
(probability of system working if D_1 short-circuit)(probability of D_1 short-circuit)
+
(probability of system working if D_1 open-circuit)(probability of D_1 open-circuit)

Letting:

P = probability of diode working
$Q_{s/c}$ = probability of diode short circuit
$Q_{o/c}$ = probability of diode open-circuit

and assuming both diodes are identical, we obtain:

Probability of system working, P_s, $= (P + Q_{s/c})(P) + (P)(Q_{s/c}) + 0$
$$= P^2 + 2PQ_{s/c}$$

Note $P = 1 - Q = 1 - (Q_{o/c} + Q_{s/c})$. We could deduce P_s from considering all combinations which produce a working system, i.e. with both diodes working (P^2), plus two combinations of one diode working and one diode short-circuit $(2PQ_{s/c})$.

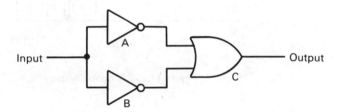

Figure 17.11   Logic circuit; gates have two modes of failure, with permanent 1 and with permanent 0 output

Taking another example more closely related to digital system design, consider the logic circuit shown in Fig. 17.11. Suppose each gate has two modes of failure, failure with a permanent 1 output and failure with a permanent 0 output. The failure are independent of the input conditions. The circuit is assumed to be working if the system output = 1 when the system input = 1, and the system output = 0 when the system input = 0. Selecting gate A, we get:

Probability of system working =
(probability of system working if A works)(probability of A working)

+

(probability of system working if A output permanent 1)(probability of A
                                 output permanent 1)

+

(probability of system working if A output permanent 0)(probability of A
                                 output permanent 0)

Letting

P_A = probability of A working
P_B = probability of B working
Q_{A0} = probability of A output permanent 0
Q_{B0} = probability of B output permanent 0

we get:

$$\text{Probability of system working} = (P_{\text{B}} + Q_{\text{B0}})P_{\text{C}}P_{\text{A}} + 0 + P_{\text{B}}P_{\text{C}}Q_{\text{A0}}$$

Generally, we will expect the probability of a system working to be higher if the system can continue to operate with particular failures. Such arrangements form the basis of a form a *fault-tolerant system*.

17.4 DESIGN OF RELIABLE SYSTEMS

In this section we shall examine some possible ways of improving the reliability of a system. The reliability of a system can be increased by adding component parts to the system which though redundant for normal operation lead to a parallel or semi-parallel system configuration. Reliable systems can also be designed by incorporating error checking and correcting circuits into the system so that when an error occurs, the error is corrected and the system continues to operate. Firstly, though, we consider adding redundant parts to a system.

17.4.1 System, gate and component redundancy

We can duplicate parts at:

(i)   System level (extra systems)
(ii) Gate level (extra gates)
(iii) Component level (extra capacitors, resistors, transistors, etc.)

One arrangement of system redundancy is to use three systems together with a *voter* circuit as shown in Fig. 17.12. Only one output from each system is shown. (For multiple outputs, a separate voter would be necessary for each output.) The voter chooses the outputs which are the same. If all three systems are working, all the outputs will be the same. If only two of the three systems are working, the voter chooses the two identical outputs. If more than one system is not working, the system fails. It is assumed that there is a negligible probability of two faulty systems producing the same ouput. Firstly, with the voter working, there are four conditions for the system to work:

(i)   All three systems working
(ii) System 1 and 2 working and system 3 not working
(iii) System 1 and 3 working and system 2 not working
(iv) System 1 and 2 working and system 3 not working

Therefore the probability of the system working is given by the probability of all three systems working plus the probabilities of the three combinations of two working systems and one failing system, i.e.:

$$\begin{aligned}
\text{Probability of system working} &= P^3 + 3P^2Q \\
&= P^3 + 3P^2(1 - P) \\
&= 3P^2 - 2P^3
\end{aligned}$$

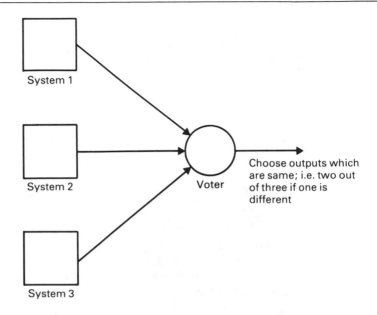

Figure 17.12   Triplicated system with a voter

or in terms of reliability and failure rate:

System reliability $= 3R^2 - 2R^3 = 3e^{-2\lambda t} - 2e^{-3\lambda t}$

This expression can be compared with the reliability of a single system, $R = e^{-\lambda t}$, as shown in Fig. 17.13. We find that indeed the reliability of the triplicated system is higher than the single system, but only for a period. The triplicated system reliability function crosses over the single reliability function at a time, t_0. This time can be found by equating the two reliabilities:

$e^{-\lambda t} = 3e^{-2\lambda t} - 2e^{3 - \lambda t}$

or $e^{-\lambda t} = 0.5$ or $t_0 = 0.7/\lambda$. Before $t_0 = 0.7/\lambda$, the triplicated system has a higher reliability than the single system but after this time, the single system has a higher reliability. Therefore the triplicated system can be used to increase the overall reliability during an operating period less than $0.7/\lambda$ or $0.7 \times$ (one system MTBF). The MTBF of the triplicated system (not a constant failure rate system) is found by integrating $R(t)$ i.e.:

$$\text{MTBF}_{\text{triplicated system}} = \int_0^\infty (3e^{-2\lambda t} - 2e^{-3\lambda t})\, dt = 5/(6\lambda)$$

which is slightly less than the MTBF of a single system $(1/\lambda)$.

We have not considered the reliability of the voter. The voter can be included into the probability equation as follows:

Probability of triplicated system working $= (3P^2 - 2P^3)P_v$

where P_v is the probability of the voter working. Hence the value for the reliability decreases if the effect of the voter is included. The probability of

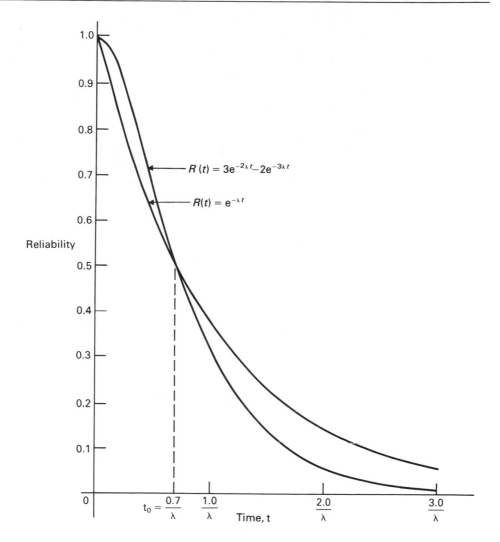

Figure 17.13   Reliability of single and triplicated systems

failure can of course be obtained by substituting $Q = 1 - P$ into the above equations.

An alternative method is to derive probability of failure equations. The system will fail if:

(i) All three systems fail
(ii) Any two systems fail (with one working)

There are three combinations of two systems failing with one system working. Therefore:

Probability of system failure, Q_s = (probability of all three systems failing + 3(probability of two failing)(probability of one working)

$$= Q^3 + 3Q^2P = 3Q^2 - 2Q^3$$

Including the voter, we get:

Q_s = (probability of triplicated system failing)(probability of voter working)
  + (probability of voter failing)
$$= (3Q^2 - 2Q^3)(1 - Q_v) + Q_v$$

The triplicated technique would normally be applied to (computer) systems rather than at the gate or component level. Then the voter would be a much simpler system than the triplicated systems and of much higher reliability. In such case, it may have a negligible effect on the overall reliability. If the voter has a significant effect, one could take the extreme measure of three voters and a super-voter taking two out of three voter outputs. The triplicated system accepts the presence of one error without causing an overall system failure. To handle two errors, five systems and a voter which selects three out of five outputs would be necessary.

It is possible to connect components or gates in parallel to increase the reliability of the system. A direct application of the parallel configuration is shown in Fig. 17.14(a) and (b). In (a), n components are connected in series and these are connected in parallel. Each series arm has a probability of working of P^n. Therefore the probability of the complete system working is given by:

$$P_s = P^n + P^n - P^nP^n = 2P^n - P^{2n}$$

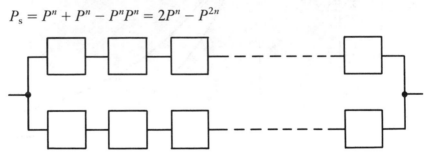

(a) Two series configurations in parallel

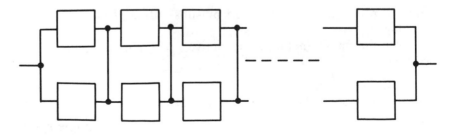

(b) Parallel pairs in series

Figure 17.14   Series–parallel configurations

Alternatively, the probability of a system failure can be derived, i.e.:

$$Q_s = (1 - (1 - Q)^n)^2 = n^2 Q^2 \qquad \text{as } Q \text{ approaches zero}$$

In Fig. 17.14(b), pairs of components are connected in parallel and these are then connected in series. The probability of each pair working is given by $2P - P^2$ and the probability of the system working is given by:

$$P_s = (2P - P^2)^n$$

The probability of failure is given by:

$$Q_s = (1 - (1 - Q^2)^n) = nQ^2 \qquad \text{as Q approaches zero}$$

From the two failure expressions, we can see that configuration (b) has a higher reliability than configuration (a) (an 'unreliability' of nQ^2 as opposed to $n^2 Q^2$). This assumes that the components have only one mode of failure.

An example of an implementation of series–parallel configurations at the component level would be four series–parallel connected diodes. It can be shown that configuration (a) produces a higher reliability than configuration (b) if the probability of a short-circuit is higher than the probability of an open-circuit. Conversely, if the probability of an open-circuit is higher than the probability of a short-circuit, configuration (b) produces a higher reliability (Problem 17.8).

Gates can have three possible modes of failure, failure with a permanent 1 output, failure with a permanent 0 output, and failure with an intermediate output level. To increase gate level reliability, gates can be connected in series–parallel configurations utilizing the fact that a permanent 0 on the input of an OR gate will not inhibit the OR gate, and a permanent 1 on the input of AND gate will not inhibit the AND gate. However, it is arguable whether fault-tolerant design at this level is worthwhile. The reader is referred to [3] for further information on fault-tolerant design and the association topic of design for fault testing.

17.4.2 System incorporating error detection and correction

An alternative approach to the design of reliable systems is to provide a means of detecting faults (errors) due to hardware malfunction, and correct the faults immediately they occur. A simple, widely used method of error detection is the parity system as mentioned in Chap. 1. To recapitulate, in the parity system an additional bit is appended to each binary word being transmitted between systems. This bit is arranged to be a 1 or a 0, whichever is necessary to make the number of 1's in the word, including the appended bit, even (for even parity). If a single-bit error has occurred, the number of 1's in the word will become odd which can be detected by logic. The appended bit is known as the parity bit and is often appended to words transmitted between peripherals and the system. The parity system is one example of introducing unused patterns into the coding of information. Whenever one of the unused patterns occurs, an error has been introduced.

Let us consider the general case of a binary word consisting of p bits. If some patterns are not used to represent valid information, and they occur, we know an error has occurred. The greater the number of unused patterns, the greater the ability to detect errors and, as we will see, the greater the ability to correct errors that do occur. If every combination of the p bits (i.e. all 2^p combinations) is used to represent valid information, there is no possibility of detecting errors by examining the patterns.

To take this idea further, consider a number of *code words* representing information. Of the possible binary patterns used for the code words, some will represent valid information while some will be invalid. A single-bit error in a correct word results in one bit changing from a 0 to a 1 or vice versa. Two bits in error will result in two bits changing. We arrange that correct code words are separated from each other by incorrect code words, as shown in Fig. 17.15. Here the patterns 0000 and 0111 are two correct code words while 0001 and 0011 are two of the incorrect code words between the correct code words. The incorrect code word 0001 differs from the first correct code word, 0000, by one digit and indicates a single-bit error. The next incorrect code word, 0011, differs from 0000 by two bits and indicates two errors from the correct code word, 0000, or one error from the second correct code word, 0111.

If in the above, all correct code words are separated by two incorrect code words, we can detect up to two errors as these would result in distinguishable incorrect codes. Three errors would result in a correct code word and thus could not be detected. If we assume only a single-bit error has occurred in our example, the correct code would be the nearest one to the incorrect code word, and hence could be deduced. For example, if the code word 0011 has occurred, we would know that not only has an error occurred, but also that the correct code word would be 0111, the nearest correct code word. This could be chosen to replace the incorrect code word. This is therefore a method of detecting errors and correcting errors exists based on the ability to recognize incorrect code words. The parity system has one incorrect code word between correct code words and hence cannot be used to correct errors, only to detect one error.

We define the 'distance' between two correct code words as the *Hamming distance, d*. The Hamming distance is the minimum number of digits that are different in two code words in a set of code words. With no incorrect code words, the Hamming distance is 1 and no error detection or correction is

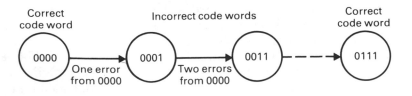

Figure 17.15   Code words

possible. The code words in Fig. 17.15 have a Hamming distance of 3. The following conditions apply:

(i)   *Detection of errors*. The necessary and sufficient condition to detect K errors or fewer is that the Hamming distance between two code words is $K + 1$.

(ii) *Correction of errors*. The necessary and sufficient condition to be able to correct K errors or fewer is that the Hamming distance between two correct codes is not less than $2K + 1$.

For the condition to correct errors, consider Fig. 17.16. A number of incorrect codes are sited between two correct codes. Let there be $2K$ incorrect codes. There are K incorrect codes closer to one correct code and K incorrect codes closer to the other correct code. K errors or fewer occurring from, say, the left-hand correct code word would result in one of the left-hand incorrect code words. This error can be corrected to the left-hand correct code word. Similarly, K errors or fewer from the right-hand code word would result in possible correction to the right-hand code word. However, more than K errors occurring in a code word could not be corrected. The overall Hamming distance between correct codes is $2K + 1$ as shown.

We could devise a coding scheme without any further information, by specifying codes with the appropriate Hamming distance for the desired detection and correction capability. Implementation of error detection and correction could be based around a read-only memory. For example, an 8-bit code word has 256 combinations. Using a 256×1-bit read-only memory, the incoming code word can address the memory and the contents indicate whether the code word is valid or invalid. For invalid code words, an additional mechanism is necessary. One way is to increase the number of bits stored in the memory to hold the nearest valid code word which can then be read out. For simplicity, even correct code words could be stored, and in all cases the contents of the memory is read out.

Hamming [4] developed a coding system which produces a correction

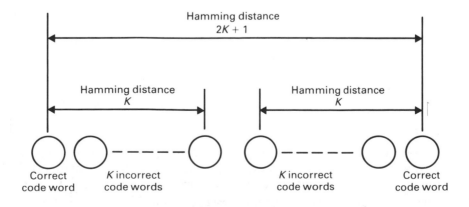

Figure 17.16   Condition to correct K errors

mechanism based on a simple calculation. We shall describe the method by example. Consider a 4-bit data word with digits D_1, D_2, D_3 and D_4. Three check digits, C_1, C_2 and C_3 are inserted between the data digits in the following positions:

Check and data digits: $D_4, D_3, D_2, C_3, D_1, C_2, C_1$
Bit number: $B_7, B_6, B_5, B_4, B_3, B_2, B_1$

leading to a seven-digit code word, B_1 to B_7. The check digits are computed as follows:

C_3 is computed to give $B_7B_6B_5B_4$ as having even parity $(C_3 = B_7 \oplus B_6 \oplus B_5 \oplus B_4)$
C_2 is computed to give $B_7B_6B_3B_2$ as having even parity $(C_2 = B_7 \oplus B_6 \oplus B_3 \oplus B_2)$
C_1 is computed to give $B_7B_5B_3B_1$ as having even parity $(C_1 = B_7 \oplus B_5 \oplus B_3 \oplus B_1)$

The even-parity system is calculated on groups of bits, one bit of which is a check digit. Hence C_1 will check whether there is one bit in error in the set $B_7B_5B_3B_1$. C_2 will check whether there is one bit in error in the set $B_7B_6B_3B_2$ and C_3 will check whether there is one bit in error in the set $B_7B_6B_5B_4$. Listing the patterns of $C_3C_2C_1$ for single-bit errors on $B_1, B_2, B_3, B_4, B_5, B_6$ or B_7:

Bit in error	C_3	C_2	C_1
No error	0	0	0
B_1	0	0	1
B_2	0	1	0
B_3	0	1	1
B_4	1	0	0
B_5	1	0	1
B_6	1	1	0
B_7	1	1	1

we see that the pattern obtained, if not 000, indicates an error and also identifies the position of the bit.

If $D_4D_3D_2D_1 = 1100$, the check digits are computed as $C_3 = 0$, $C_2 = 0$, $C_1 = 1$ and the complete code word is 1100001. Suppose an error has occurred in position six (B_6). Since this can only mean that the sixth bit changes from one binary state to another, B_6 must become a 0, and the code word becomes 1000001. To detect and correct the error, the parity computation is repeated, returning a 0 if there is even parity and a 1 if there is odd parity, ie.:

$B_7 \oplus B_6 \oplus B_5 \oplus B_4 = 1$
$B_7 \oplus B_6 \oplus B_3 \oplus B_2 = 1$
$B_7 \oplus B_5 \oplus B_3 \oplus B_1 = 0$ (least significant bit)

(The computation can be viewed as performing the arithmetic summation of the digits, returning only the least significant bit of the summation.) The binary number obtained with the least significant bit as shown identifies the position that the error has occurred, in this case, position 110 or position 6. Therefore B_6 can be corrected by changing the digit from a 0 back to a 1.

The Hamming scheme can be applied to any number of data digits. The check digits are in binary power positions 1, 2, 4, 8, 16, 32, etc., as required. The data digits are inserted between the check digits. The B bits in the check digit computation can be found by listing binary numbers in an ascending order from zero upwards and allocating the first check computation (C_1) to the least significant column, the next check digit computation (C_2) to the next least significant column, the next check digit computation (C_3) to the next column and so on. Whenever a 1 appears in a column, the corresponding binary number identifies the B digit to be included in the check digit computation allocated to the column.

The overhead of check digits becomes less significant as more data digits are encoded. For example, 8-bit data needs 4 check digits (i.e. a 50% increase), a 16-bit word needs 5 check digits (31.25% increase) while a 64-bit word needs 7 check digits (10.9375% increase). One application of the Hamming code is to increase the reliability of a semiconductor memory system. Consider a 1024K $\times$ 16-bit (1 M $\times$ 16 bit) memory system using 256K $\times$ 1-bit devices. Sixty-four devices are needed for a system without error detection/correction. The probability of working (reliability) of the system, assuming the system fails when one device fails, is given by:

Probability of system working, $P_s, = P_m{}^{64}$

where P_m is the probability of a memory device working. (Only the memory devices are considered.) The MTBF is given by:

$$\text{MTBF}_s = \int_0^\infty \exp(-64\lambda_m t)\mathrm{d}t = 0.0156/\lambda_m$$

where λ_m is the failure rate of each memory device [5].

If we add five Hamming check digits and the associated detection and correction logic, the memory would need to be 1024K $\times$ 21 bits (16 data digits plus 5 check digits). The number of devices is now given by 21 $\times$ 4 (i.e. 84). This memory system would continue to operate in the presence of one memory device totally faulty out of each group of 21 memory devices. (It would be possible to have up to four faulty memory devices each associated with different words and hence each fault could be corrected when the words are read.) The probability of working is given by:

Probability of system working, P_{hs}, = [(Probability of all 21 devices working) + 21(probability of 20 devices working and probability of one device faulty)]^4

as there are 21 combinations of 20 devices working and one device faulty. Hence the probability of working becomes:

$$P_{hs} = [P_m{}^{21} + 21P_m{}^{20}(1-P_m)]^4$$

and the MTBF is:

$$\text{MTBF}_{hs} = \int_0^\infty \{\exp(-21\lambda_m{}' + 21[\exp(-20\lambda_m{}')][1 - \exp(-\lambda_m{}')]\}^4\,\mathrm{d}t$$
$$= 0.0393/\lambda_m$$

or a 252% improvement in the MTBF over the system without correction. The calculation does not include the interface logic and clearly the extra detection/ correction logic will reduce the MTBF to some extent.

REFERENCES

1. *Reliability Prediction of Electronic Equipment*, MIL-HDBK-217B. US Department of Defense, 1974.
2. Smith, D.J., *Reliability Engineering*. London: Pitman, 1972.
3. Lala, P.K., *Fault Tolerant and Fault Testable Hardware Design*. Englewood Cliffs, N.J.,: Prentice-Hall, Inc., 1985.
4. Hamming, R.W., 'Error-detecting and Error-correcting Codes', *Bell Syst. Tech. J.*, 29 (1950), 147–60.
5. Lala, P.K., 'Error Correction in Semiconductor Memory Systems', *Electronic Engineering*, 51, no. 617 (Jan. 1979), 49–53.

PROBLEMS

17.1 A system consists of 500 components in a series configuration. The failure rate of each component is 0.03%/1000 hr. What is the system reliability over a period of 200 hours? What is the maximum component failure rate necessary if the system reliability is to be 0.99? In each case, calculate the system MTBF.

17.2 Prove that the reliability of a constant failure rate system after an initial operating period equal to the MTBF is approximately 37%.

17.3 A microprocessor system consists of the following units:

Unit	Number	Failure rate
Processor	1	λ_P
Main memory unit	3	λ_{MM}
Disk controller	1	λ_{DC}
Disk drive	4	λ_{DD}
Video terminal	1	λ_{VT}

each with a constant failure rate. The system configuration is shown in Fig. 17.17. For the system to operate, the processor, terminal and disk controller must function together with two of the memory units and three of the disk drives. Obtain an expression for the reliability of the system and the system MTBF.

17.4 Derive expressions for the reliability of the circuit shown in Fig. 17.18, given that each gate has two modes of failure, one with a permanent 0 output and one with a permanent 1 output. The failure rates are constant.

17.5 Apply Bayes's theorem to determine the reliability of each of the logic circuits shown in Fig. 17.19, given that the probability of an individual gate failure with a permanent 0 output is 0.1% and the probability of an individual gate failure with a permanent 1 output is 0.2%. These probabilities apply for a mission time

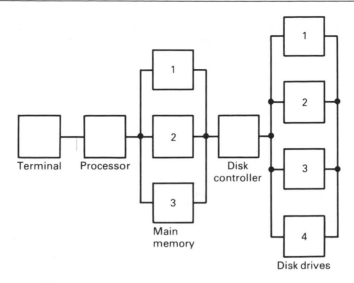

Figure 17.17   System configuration for Problem 17.3

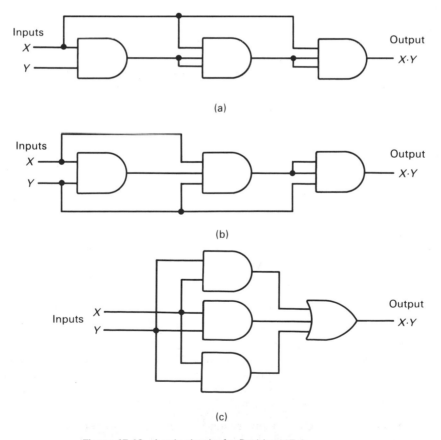

(a)

(b)

(c)

Figure 17.18   Logic circuits for Problem 17.4

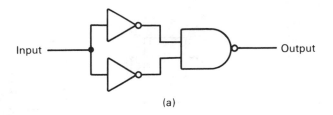

(a)

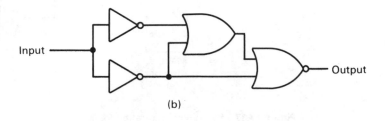

(b)

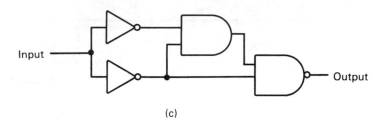

(c)

Figure 17.19   Logic circuits for Problem 17.5

(operating time) of 1000 hours. Determine the MTBF of the circuit shown in Fig. 17.19(a). Assume that the failure rates of the gates are constant. The circuits are defined as working if the output is the same as the input for both 0 and 1 input values.

17.6 Figure 17.20 shows a logic system consisting of four identical open-collector TTL gates and a pull-up resistor, R. Each gate has two modes of failure:

(i)   With the output short-circuit to $0\,V$
(ii)   With the output open-circuit

The corresponding failure probabilities are $Q_{s/c}$ and $Q_{o/c}$. Derive an expression for the reliability of the system in terms of $Q_{s/c}$ and $Q_{s/c}$. The failure rate of the resistor may be ignored.

17.7 Derive an expression for the overall reliability of five identical single-output subsystems with outputs connected to a voter. The overall system works if two or more outputs of the subsystems are the same. (It is assumed that the associated subsystems must be working.)

17.8 Determine the conditions required to cause a system of diodes connected in the configuration of Fig. 17.14(a) to be more reliable than diodes connected on

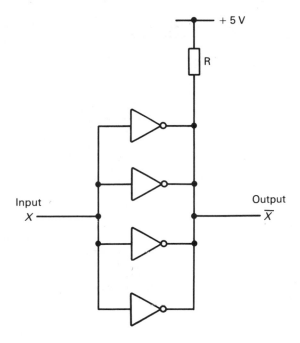

Figure 17.20   Logic circuit for Problem 17.6

configuration of Fig. 17.14(b) and vice versa, given that the diodes have two modes of failure, short-circuit failure and open-circuit failure, and there are four diodes.

17.9 Four message symbols are encoded as follows:

$$S_1 = 01101$$
$$S_2 = 10001$$
$$S_3 = 01110$$
$$S_4 = 11011$$

How many errors can be detected and how many errors can be corrected with this code? Devise a code for the four messages which allows the detection of two errors and the correction of one error using the minimum number of bits. (Do not use the Hamming code.)

17.10 Devise a Hamming code consisting of data digits and check digits to encode the 5-bit data word 10101. Show how one error can be detected and corrected.

Index